The Community Development Reader

The aim of this anthology on community development in the USA is to provide accurate accounts of the challenges and struggles of people to influence their shared landscapes in ways that enable them, not just to survive, but to flourish in the face of the vagaries and threats of the larger world.

The collection strives to be both critical and practice oriented so that clear-eyed analysis will continue to promote change and innovation in the field. The practice-oriented elements provide a record of important quasi-successful efforts to solve local problems such as the chronic shortage of affordable housing for moderate and low-income households, the creation of new institutions, and the promotion of inclusive civic communities through novel strategies for community organizing.

The result is a comprehensive reader for core courses in virtually every planning and policy program in the United States. Community development is also often covered in urban politics, social work and counseling programs, and service learning programs in the social sciences. No reader on the subject currently exists.

James DeFilippis is an Assistant Professor in the Edward J. Bloustein School of Planning and Public Policy, Rutgers, The State University of New Jersey. He received his PhD in Geography from Rutgers University in 2000, and his BA in Political Science and Geography from the University of Vermont in 1993. He is the author of *Unmaking Goliath: Community Control in the Face of Global Capital* (Routledge, 2004), which was named the "Best Book in Urban Politics, 2004" by the American Political Science Association. He has also published many articles and reports on housing, community development, urban politics, and local economic development.

Susan Saegert is Director of the Center for Human Environments (CHE) and Professor of Environmental Psychology at the CUNY Graduate Center, where she was also the first director of the Center for the Study of Women and Society. She received her PhD in Social Psychology from the University of Michigan in 1973 and her B.A. with honors in government from the University of Texas in 1968. Dr. Saegert has published five books including *Social Capital in Poor Communities* with Phil Thompson and Mark Warren (Russell Sage, 2001), and *From Abandonment to Hope: Community Households in Harlem*, with Jackie Leavitt (Columbia University Press, 1990). She has also published over fifty articles and book chapters on environmental psychology, women and the environment, crowding, environmental stress, and housing and health, as well as social capital.

The Community Development Reader

James DeFilippis and Susan Saegert

EDITORS

Routledge
Taylor & Francis Group

NEW YORK AND LONDON

First published 2008
by Routledge
270 Madison Ave, New York, NY 10016

Simultaneously published in the UK
by Routledge
2 Park Square, Milton Park, Abingdon, Oxon OX14 4RN

Routledge is an imprint of the Taylor & Francis Group, an informa business

Typeset in Sabon by RefineCatch Limited, Bungay, Suffolk
Printed and bound in the United States of America on acid-free paper by
Edwards Brothers, Inc., Lillington, NC

Library of Congress Cataloging in Publication Data
A catalog record has been requested for this book

ISBN10: 0–415–95428–2 (hbk)
ISBN10: 0–415–95429–0 (pbk)
ISBN10: 0–203–93556–X (ebk)

ISBN13: 978–0–415–95428–0 (hbk)
ISBN13: 978–0–415–95429–7 (pbk)
ISBN13: 978–0–203–93556–9 (ebk)

CONTENTS

PART IV. THEORETICAL CONCEPTIONS AND DEBATES

LIST OF ILLUSTRATIONS

FIGURES

TABLES

ACKNOWLEDGMENTS

Like any academic endeavor, this book has benefited from the contributions of many people besides the editors. First we want to thank the authors who wrote the various chapters for their legacy of scholarship on community and community development. The chapters included here mostly have been drastically shortened to fit the books purpose of being a broad overview of the field. The editing in many cases was so extensive that we strongly recommend that the interested reader consult the original work for the full argument, as well as citations of sources and references. Because of the substantial editing, we worked with the authors to assure their agreement on our fidelity to their intent. This task was made much easier by the authors being so responsive and collegial. In some particularly excellent cases, the authors even took the time to edit down their own chapters for us. Second, we should thank Matthew Furleiter, who worked with us as an intern during much of the time the book was being prepared, doing a ton of editing, reading, copyright work, and other odd jobs. Jared Becker at the Center for Human Environments also provided support of all kinds in making sure that the loose ends were tied up and last minute emergencies gotten through. Third, several people took the time to look over various stages of the book—from the initial table of contents, to sections,

chapters, and other contributions. In particular Bob Lake, Kathe Newman, Randy Stoecker, and Bob Fisher, as well as our friends and colleagues at the Aspen Institute Roundtable for Community Change, gave thoughtful and productively critical comments about the book, and it is certainly better because of their contributions. The anonymous reviewers also gave us both useful encouragement and direction.

This book has emerged not just from our academic interests and relationships, but primarily from what we have learned from so many practitioners in the field of community development and from residents striving to improve their communities. To no small degree, the extent to which this book is useful to practitioners has come from the fact that we have been fortunate enough to work with so many thoughtful and dedicated people in the field. There are too many to name, but our gratitude is immense.

Finally, our families have been incredibly supportive of us while we have been putting this enormous volume together. We want to thank them especially. In particular, our daughters, Alexa Madeline DeFilippis and Laura Saegert Winkel make us incredibly proud. This book is dedicated to them. May they always live in communities that enable them to continue to grow, develop, and prosper.

CHAPTER 1

Communities Develop

The question is how?

James DeFilippis and Susan Saegert

INTRODUCTION

Over the course of its 40-year modern history, community development has moved from a small-scale endeavor by a limited number of organizations fighting seemingly Quixotic struggles to improve the conditions and quality of life in a few poor urban neighborhoods to a mainstream set of practices and institutions. In doing so, community development has become a significant component of urban political economies in the United States. In many neighborhoods and cities, community development organizations are increasingly assuming the roles of local governments, and the organizations involved construct affordable housing, offer access to credit to low-income people, provide education and other social services, and more generally try to build the community's capacity to gain resources, achieve goals, and participate effectively in the American political economy.

Rather than trying to define community development, elaborate on the practices that constitute it, or recount its long history, this brief introductory chapter will, instead, revert back to first principles and ask the prior question of why development is important in and for American communities. To do this, our argument will proceed in two steps, which are framed as questions. First, what role do communities play—both in the larger political economy and in the daily lives of people? Second, how can development improve and reinforce communities that lack the power and resources to be places of support and opportunity?

Communities in this Reader refer to places where people live and work, though not necessarily doing both in the same place. They are the people, places, and institutions we encounter in everyday life that provide opportunities and support for our activities, as well as barriers and constraints. In this sense, communities are places of interdependence, even if that interdependence can be limited and not always beneficial to everyone involved.

A peculiar thing about communities, as we are using the term, and their role in the contemporary world is that, quite simply, they shouldn't exist. Social theorists like Tönnies, Simmel, Weber, Marx, Park, and Wirth, all argued that capitalist urbanization would inevitably disrupt the smaller-scale, inter-dependent social relations that had long been fundamental units of people's lives. Some lamented the demise of communities (notably Tönnies with his framework of contrasting *Gemeinschaft und Gesellschaft*, Tönnies, 1957 [1887]); others celebrated it (notably Marx, who argued that capitalist urbanization had rescued "the population from the idiocy of rural life"—Marx and Engels, 1967 [1848]); while still others simply wanted to understand how capitalist urbanism had created new forms of social interaction which undermined community (Simmel, 1950 [1903]; Wirth, 1938). But all were in agreement that smaller-scale communities (assumed to be rural, since the urban, by their definitions, did not really include communities—at least not as durable social formations) had ceased to be important realms in capitalism. And as larger-scale forms of economic organization brought more and more people to cities, the density of people, the complexity of the division of labor in society, and the variety of social interactions, would combine with the lack of economic necessity of smaller-scale units to inevitably undermine community as an important realm in people's lives and the larger world. One of the most important results of this intellectual tradition is that it has left us in a position of struggling to envision the realm of community playing a progressive—that is, forward-looking and forward-thinking—role in social change. In short, how can a social realm that is understood to be dying and exists as a vestige of the past, be a central part in the creation of the future?

This European tradition of community as an historical "given", eroded by modern capitalism, contrasts with the American pragmatists' view of community as an emergent set of relationships holding the potential for growth and change (Bernstein, 1998). In this second framework, community arises from the reciprocal relations among people, including those with unlike interests and ways of life. In this formulation, community is the matrix within which new, more democratic and inclusive forms of society can emerge. The borders of the pragmatist concept of community are not fixed, nor necessarily spatially demarcated, but they do involve a marriage of first-hand experience of the world with a collective process of communication and disputation about the meaning and implications of experience, about even what counts as experience. Dewey most strongly equated the growth of community with the gradual, always imperfect progress toward a more democratic society (cf. Dewey, 1916, 1954 [1927]). However, George Herbert Mead more fully worked out the dynamic relationship between the emergence of individual selves and the production of community (Mead, 1934). Both these ideas found practical application in Jane Addams' work at Hull House (Bridge, 2004). This second tradition provides the grounds for the idea of community as a space for contesting the social costs of capitalism to working-class and marginalized people.

Of course, neither the predictions of the demise of community, nor the hope of its democratic potential have been borne out. It is certainly true that the realm of the community has been irrecoverably altered by capitalist urbanization. And the spreading and deepening of capitalist social relations across the world, and into the most intimate parts of people's lives, have changed how and why communities matter. But communities continue to play a vital role in both capitalism as a globalized, but historically specific, social system, and in the localized daily lives of people in urban spaces. In short, communities do matter. Perhaps the clearest evidence of this (albeit at the risk of making the argument somewhat circular) is that people continue to act as though they matter. Efforts to improve, transform and stabilize communities are a staple of urban politics in the United States. As Tilly (1974, p. 212) put it:

> even in big cities people continue to act collectively at times on the basis of common territory: the people of a neighborhood resist urban renewal, white homeowners band together to resist black newcomers, disputes over the operation of schools bring geographical groupings clearly into view . . . their very existence identifies the need for a better understanding of the conditions under which collective action on a territorial basis occurs.

The first question for us here, therefore, is how do communities matter, which will shed some light on why people continue to act as though they do (and make it clear that such community-based action is not simply misdirected or misplaced).

WHY COMMUNITIES MATTER

While social theorists have clearly been wrong in predicting the demise of communities within capitalism, they were right in their understanding that the realm of community can only be properly understood through a discussion of its place and role in the larger political economy. Thus our discussion begins with capitalism and the world economy. Place-based communities are necessary loci for the functioning and reproduction of global capitalism, just as they have been for earlier historical forms of political economy. Yet as the early sociologists understood, these communities increasingly do not themselves control or contain the forces of either production or reproduction. Communities are therefore in the contradictory positions of being vital for the maintenance of the larger political economy, but significantly constrained in what they can achieve in terms of shaping or transforming that economy. We will briefly explore the roots and implications of this contradiction.

Communities are the realm in which social reproduction occurs. That is, communities are the sites for our housing, education, health care, daily convenience shopping, and the other activities that sustain us physically, emotionally, socially and psychologically. Labor is a peculiar commodity in capitalism in that, unlike other commodities, it needs to replenish itself when it is not being used, and is needed to produce more labor to be purchased in the economy in the future. A worker simply cannot continue to work without having time for sleeping, eating, and maintaining his or her health. And the long-term functioning of any social system (including capitalism) requires, at the very minimum, the reproduction of the population through rearing of children. Communities thus play the vital role of reproducing the labor power that is needed for capitalism to survive. And they do so through structures and institutions that are very often based on commodity relations— that is, we reproduce ourselves through a set of transactions that are usually, and increasingly, based on the market. Domestic property (housing) is, in the American form of capitalism, most often understood as a commodity to be bought and sold. The provision of our daily bread, through neighborhood supermarkets, grocery stores and bodegas, is unambiguously a set of commodity relations. And the practices of child-care provision are increasingly commodified, as households— rich, middle class, and poor—are becoming more likely to purchase their child care provision.[1] Communities are the realm in which current workers maintain their health and well-being, and future workers are born, bred, and educated. And they do so in ways that, often invisibly and intangibly,

re-inscribe the market as the primary arbiter of social relations.

These communities may not be the coherently, contiguously organized places of the modernist planner (Beauregard, 1991). But even in their postmodern fragmented and mutating form, they are commonly traversed spaces where people meet face to face, sometimes coordinate their actions and purposes, and, on occasion, act collectively to change the way these spaces and relations enable or constrain collective purposes. Community in this more emergent and mobile form fulfills a range of human desires from shelter and nurturance, through safety at home and in one's daily rounds, to historically rooted, politically and ecologically defined space in which individuals, households, and groups contest and cooperate with each other to make life possible.

How a community is situated in the larger capitalist political economy plays an enormous role in enabling or constraining the abilities of individuals and households to realize their goals and aspirations. How a community is situated in the global economy, in turn, is largely dependent upon institutions and a set of relationships that exist well beyond the community itself. Banks, and their mortgage-lending practices, industrial corporations and their decisions to locate a plant in (or, more commonly in the United States, away from) a metropolitan area, and towns in other countries with soon-to-be emigrants to the United States are all very real examples of how communities are shaped by a host of economic relations that extend well beyond any one community. Therefore, rightly understood, it is a difficult and ambiguous question the extent to which problems *in a spatially defined community* are *community problems*—given that so much of what produces communities are relations and decisions that exist well beyond any single community. And thus, this is the contradiction of the centrality and marginality of the community in capitalism.

But communities are not simply important because of their contradictory role in capitalism. Place-based communities are still important because people are finite creatures who have to live in real and limited times and spaces, and communities of face then ground our experience even as they do not fully cause or limit them. Even as people strive to find work, homes, investments, mates, schools for their children from menus of opportunity on the internet, social networks that may span continents, and institutional connections that may move them around the globe, every day they are some place. They are buying their groceries from a green market, or a supermarket, or a bodega; their children attend a well-equipped private school they pay a lot for, an excellent, mediocre or poor public school, a parochial school of a certain quality and denomination, all based a great deal on the nature of their place-based community. And despite all the rhetoric of hyper-mobility and globalization in the last 20 years, most people are relatively place-based. As Doreen Massey (1994, p. 163) put it, "Much of life for people, even in the heart of the First World, still consists of waiting in a bus-shelter with your shopping for a bus that never comes."

This rooting of people in places has significant impacts on people's personal development and growth, as well as their inter-personal social networks and relationships. People who share a space together build a common set of experiences, that, when accumulated over time and in different parts of life (common schools; places of worship; parks, etc.) form much of the basis of people's support networks in their daily lives. People in communities come to rely on each other for a variety of forms of support, from informal bartering of goods and services such as swapping child-care responsibilities to providing intangible emotional support when households are in times of stress and difficulty. This is particularly true in communities where households are not financially able to treat such services as commodities to be bought and sold, because they simply don't have enough money to do so.

As we already indicated, people's daily lives are, in communities, mediated through shared institutions in the political economy. A community's sharing of, for instance, a common position in a metropolitan area's real estate market (since, for instance, either housing abandonment or gentrification are community-level issues) forces people to try to work together to face these issues. Similarly, when a government disrupts a community, through either siting an unwanted land use or promoting a large development that will displace people, it is a threat to the lives and interests of many people in that community—and transcends any one person or household. People, in short, can and do form *communities*, by virtue of facing common sets of issues in their daily lives. This is particularly true when either the market or the state creates a situation in which those daily lives are under some form of threat. In communities, people experience intimately not only a surprisingly robust left-over *Gemeinschaft* but also form new ties as they share similar experiences with the structures and institutions of the larger political economy. Capitalist urbanization, in short, may have disrupted the older ties of social solidarity found in pre-capitalist villages and rural areas, but by virtue of its creation of spaces of common experiences, it has enabled new social ties to be formed.

Place-based communities anchor the way everyday life is planned, executed, and interrupted. Lives lived in communities now are not patterned by the coherent unity Tönnies attributed to community, nor by its supposed opposite of unmoored individualism. Communities are places where people encounter fragmentation, difference, challenge, and affirmation, cooperation, and support. Nothing in this introductory discussion, or the book itself, should be read as suggesting that communities are homogenous realms of people with completely shared interests or perspectives. But, having said that, communities are certainly important realms in the shaping of people's political and ideological understandings of the world, and tend to generate substantial "neighborhood effects" (Agnew, 1987) on political ideologies and understandings.

WHAT COMMUNITY DEVELOPMENT SHOULD DO

The nature of place-based communities as sites driven by capitalism and required for survival lead to a particular set of strengths and weaknesses in the endeavor of community development. Community development occurs when the conditions of surviving and thriving in a place are not being supplied by capital. Thus community development emerges in the context of the current limitations of the capitalist political economy to fulfill the needs and desires of the community.

This is not a strategic decision made by people who start their struggle against the limits and constraints of their position in capitalist society on the basis of analysis. Instead, it is an effort people make to increase their options when only limited human, social and economic capital are at hand. Some people do indeed martial the resources necessary to flee such places, which makes the struggles of those who remain always precarious. But many stay because of lack of options, commitment to their local social networks and ways of life. They have an interest in making the community provide better life chances in their own lifetimes and in those of future generations. Much of the work of community development then has been to find the tools, the strategies, the institutional arrangements that maximize what is a pretty weak resource base and find ways to gain access to the far greater resources, opportunities and power that lie outside the geographic community.

The chapters have been selected to depict both the embattled communities foreseen by the German sociologists and the ameliorative, expansive, democratic communities imagined by Dewey and Jane Addams. The history and future of community development lie in the contested terrain between the two. This battle for this terrain consists in efforts to do the following:

1   provide for the everyday needs of adults and children;
2   create institutions that more fairly and democratically allocate goods and resources;
3   cultivate relationships among people that promote human and cultural development, effective citizenship, and political will.

The aim of this Reader on community development is to present both the challenges and struggles of people within communities to influence the shared landscapes in ways that enable not just surviving, but flourishing— and shelter people from the vagaries and threats of the larger world.

Drawing on the European notion of community as an inherited social formation that reproduces hierarchy, division of labor, and ideology, many of the chapters dwell on the limits, divisions, and contradictions of place-based community development. The struggles of community organizations for greater equity and inclusion are direct efforts to overcome these contradictions. The American pragmatist ideal includes a democratic community as a goal to be attained, as well as a notion of community. This notion of community as subject to growth and change in both its composition and as the grounds for individual identities implicitly underlies the ongoing efforts of community developers to find new institutional forms, and to promote new forms of association that will overcome the limits of existing communities, both those that are sociologically and geographically defined.

STRUCTURE OF THE BOOK

Thus the collection strives to be both critical and practice-oriented. The critical components of the book come from our beliefs that clear-eyed analysis of what is being and has been done is vital for the field of community development if it is to continue to grow and affect positive changes in American cities. The practice-oriented components are not narrowly technical but instead provide a record of important, somewhat successful efforts to solve local problems such as the shortage of affordable housing for low and moderate income households, to develop new institutions to serve local needs such as Community Development Financial Institutions, and to promote the development of democratic, inclusive civic communities through different approaches to community organizing.

The book is divided into four parts. Part I

is devoted to an overview of the history and challenges of community development efforts. Part II describes the institutional and programmatic forms community development has taken and how they work. Some of the chapters in Part II are focused on a particular organizational form (such as the chapters on community development financial institutions [CDFIs], religious institutions, and philanthropies), while other chapters are devoted to particular issues in community development practice (such as the chapters on economic development, rural community development, and community-based social service delivery). Part III pulls together both theoretical and empirical work and is devoted to understanding what community is, what it provides, how it can be, and is being, built, and how community can be mobilized (or organized) to achieve collective goals. Finally, Part IV is devoted to a set of unresolved issues and debates with the field of community development, and asks such basic questions as: how should we understand housing in American communities?; how do the forces of oppression and differences in identity operate?; and what are the limits to community development efforts in the contemporary American political economy? The book ends with a concluding chapter that revisits some of the key themes, while pointing towards some emerging, and unresolved issues that will shape the field in this first part of the twenty-first century.

NOTE

1. As more low-income women have left welfare, there has been a dramatic increase in the amount of low-income children in publicly subsidized child care in American cities, in which child care is provided by workers who are paid by the government.

REFERENCES

Agnew, John (1987) *Place and Politics: The Geographical Mediation of State and Society*. Boston: Allen and Unwin.

Beauregard, R.A. (1991) "Without a Net: Planning and the Postmodern Abyss," *Journal of Planning Education and Research*, 10(3): 189–194.

Bernstein, R.J. (1998) "Community in the Pragmatic Tradition," in Morris Dickstein (ed.) *The Revival of Pragmatism: New Essays in Social Thought, Law and Culture*, Durham, NC: Duke University Press.

Bridge, Gary (2004) *Reason in the City of Difference*. London: Routledge.

Dewey, John (1916) *Democracy and Education: An Introduction to the Philosophy of Education*. New York: McMillan and Company.

Dewey, John ([1927] 1954) *The Public and Its Problems*. Athens, OH: University of Ohio Press.

Marx, Karl and Engels, Friedrich (1967 [1848]) *The Communist Manifesto*. New York: Penguin Books.

Massey, Doreen (1994) *Space, Place, and Gender*. Minneapolis, MN: University of Minnesota Press.

Mead, George Herbert (1934) *Mind, Self, and Society*. Chicago: University of Chicago Press.

Simmel, Georg ([1903] 1950) "Metropolis and Mental Life." In *The Sociology of Georg Simmel*. Trans. Kurt Wolff. New York: Free Press, pp. 409–424.

Tilly, Charles (1974) "Do Communities Act?" in M.P. Effrat (ed.) *The Community: Approaches and Applications*. New York: The Free Press.

Tönnies, Ferdinand ([1887] 1957) *Community and Society (Gemeinschaft und Gesellschaft)*. Trans. and ed. by Charles Loomis. East Lansing, MI: Michigan State University Press.

Wirth, Louis (1938) "Urbanism as a Way of Life," *The American Journal of Sociology*, 44(1): 1–24.

PART I

History and Future of Community Development

CHAPTER 2

Swimming against the Tide

A brief history of federal policy in poor communities [1]

Alice O'Connor

Community development is a time-honored tradition in America's response to poverty, but its meaning remains notoriously hard to pin down. The term has come to encompass a large number of different place-targeted interventions that have never quite added up to a coherent, comprehensive strategy. Nor have efforts to establish a federal community development policy been of much help. Instead, the historical evolution of policy has been disjointed and episodic, starting from ideas that first emerged in private, local reform efforts during the Progressive Era, moving through an extended period of federal experimentation from the New Deal to the Great Society, and devolving to an emphasis on local, public–private initiative beginning in the 1980s. The result has been a sizable collection of short-lived programs, that seem continually to replicate, rather than learn from, what has been tried in the past. Federal community development policy is notorious for reinventing old strategies while failing to address the structural conditions underlying community decline.

And yet, the push for place-based policy continues, as it has for the better part of the past sixty years. No doubt this has something to do with the geographic basis of political representation: naturally, members of Congress will support programs to stem decline and depopulation back home. In the wake of ghetto uprisings since the 1960s, federal aid for community development has also become a political quick fix, a palliative for communities on the verge of revolt. Equally important in keeping the idea alive has been a loosely organized grouping of grassroots activists, neighborhood groups, community-based providers, national "intermediary" institutions, and philanthropic foundations, a kind of community development movement that has made a business of improving poor places as a way of helping the poor. Geographically dispersed and internally conflicted though it may be, this movement has been largely responsible for keeping the idea of community development alive. It has had a significant effect on the shape of federal initiatives in poor communities and, despite recent decades of worsening local conditions and government retrenchment, it shows little sign of going away.

HISTORICAL PATTERNS IN FEDERAL POLICY: CONTINUITY AMIDST CHANGE

At first glance it may seem there is little to learn from a history of policies with origins in the New Deal political order. After all, policymakers are operating in a much circumscribed environment, now that the era of big government is over. And poor communities are struggling against much steeper odds in a globalized economy that values mobility and flexibility more than place. But the plight of poor communities does have instructive historical continuities. Like the abandoned farm communities and industrial slums of an earlier era, the depressed rural manufacturing towns and jobless inner-city ghettoes on the postindustrial landscape represent the products of economic restructuring and industrial relocation, of racial and class segregation, and of policy decisions that have encouraged these trends. The historical record also points to recurrent patterns within community development policy, which help explain its limitations in combating the underlying causes of decline.

First, government works at cross-purposes in its treatment of poor places. Small-scale interventions are intended to revive depressed communities while large-scale public policies undermine their very ability to survive. Nowhere are these policy contradictions more clear-cut and familiar than in the case of central cities, which were targeted for limited amounts of assistance and renewal beginning in the late 1940s even as more substantial federal subsidies for home mortgages, commercial development, and highway building were drawing industry, middle-class residents, and much needed tax revenues out to the suburban fringe. Rural farm communities faced a similar plight during the Depression and post-World War II years, when federal aid for local readjustment paled in comparison with support for the large-scale mechanization, commercialization, and industrialization that transformed the agricultural economy.

More recent community-based interventions have also been undercut by economic policy, which has favored flexible, deregulated labor markets and left communities with little recourse against wage deterioration and industrial flight. Public policy was similarly instrumental in the intensification of racial segregation in residential life by encouraging redlining practices in mortgage lending agencies, maintaining segregationist norms in public housing projects and by uneven commitment to the enforcement of federal antidiscrimination laws. Thus, having encouraged the trends that impoverish communities in the first place, the federal government steps in with modest and inadequate interventions to deal with the consequences —job loss, poverty, crumbling infrastructure, neighborhood institutional decline, racial and economic polarization—and then wonders why community development so often "fails." In its attempts to reverse the effects of community economic and political decline, federal policy has been working against itself.

A second pattern is that while the historical record is replete with examples of place-based strategies, they have always occupied a marginal position in the nation's antipoverty arsenal. In part this is because investing in declining communities runs counter to the dominant conventions of social policy analysis, which since at least the 1960s have been based on economic concepts and norms. Place-based policies are inefficient, even quixotic, according to conventional economic wisdom, in comparison with policies emphasizing macroeconomic growth, human capital, and individual mobility. Community investment also goes against the individualized model of human behavior underlying policy analysis, which presumes that people are principally motivated by rational self-interest in making life decisions. For those stuck in places with little hope of revival, the more rational choice is out-migration, according to economic calculation. Thus policy should promote "people to jobs," not "jobs to people" strategies. The analytic framework further denigrates community development for its inability to define and achieve clear-cut quantifiable goals and outcomes. After all, "building local capacity," "mending the social fabric," "cultivating indigenous leaders," and, most of all, "encouraging community empowerment" are amorphous objectives and difficult to measure. Nor does community development come out well in traditional cost-benefit analysis. Among other things, it takes time and experimentation, and its benefits are largely indirect.

Opposition to place-based programs is not simply analytic, however; it is grounded in politics and ideology as well. Community development meets continual resistance from those reluctant to interfere with the "natural" course of economic growth. It has also generated animosity among local politicians when it threatens to upset the local power base. And the debate over investing in place versus people has become artificially polarized in the politics of fiscal austerity since the 1970s. In a system structured principally to meet the needs of families and individuals, place-based programs have routinely lost out.

A third pattern in the movement advocating federal community development policy has been its reliance on unlikely or tenuous political alliances for support. In 1949, advocates of public housing reluctantly lined up with downtown real estate developers to help pass urban renewal legislation, an alliance that proved disastrous for poor and minority neighborhood residents. Several years later, policy analysts in the Budget Bureau joined forces with a group of activists, philanthropists, and social scientists to make "community action" the centerpiece of the War on Poverty, only to discover that they had widely varying definitions of action and, especially, of "maximum feasible participation" in mind. Community development corporations took the idea from anticolonialist, anticapitalist ghetto activists and remolded it into a form of "corrective capitalism" with government and foundation support. When forged at the local level, these types of alliances have been praised as expressions of community-based consensus. At the national level, however, they reflect a basic political reality: the most likely constituency for community development policy—the resident base—is mobile, unorganized and, especially as the two major parties compete to capture the suburban vote, diminishing in political power at the national level. Building national coalitions for change, then, has been a continual process of compromise with interests outside the community, often at the expense of the residents that community development seeks to assist.

A fourth pattern is that precisely because they cut across so many different policy domains, community development policies have suffered more than most from administrative fragmentation and bureaucratic rivalry. Even when administered by a designated community development agency, federal initiatives have drawn most of their funding from scattered sources, ranging from the Department of Housing and Urban Development to the Department of Defense, each with its own bureaucratic culture and priorities, and each eager to protect its turf.

This administrative fragmentation, to some extent a characteristic of the federal welfare state, also mirrors divisions within the community development movement. Integrated services, planning and economic devel-

opment, infrastructure rehabilitation, and political organizing might in theory complement one another, but in reform circles they have historically been promoted as alternative if not competing strategies. Urban and rural development networks have also operated along separate intellectual and bureaucratic tracks, a division that has been heightened by the increasingly urban bias in antipoverty thinking throughout the postwar years.

A fifth pattern is that the American government is both federalist and associationalist in its way of meeting community needs. It relies on a complicated and shifting mix of national and local, public and private, legislated and voluntaristic activity to carry out its objectives. This method is often justified in practical terms, in acknowledgment that no single blueprint can possibly respond to the widely varying needs of American communities and in the hope of tapping into the rich voluntary tradition for which the United States is famed. But it also reflects ideological convictions about the proper role of the state in social provision: government power should be limited, private and market mechanisms are more efficient and always preferable to public mechanisms, and local government is more democratic and responsive to popular preference and needs. The role of the state, in the associational ideal, is not to provide directly but to work in what Presidents Hoover, Carter and Clinton have celebrated as partnerships with businesses, volunteer groups, neighborhood associations, nonprofit organizations, and local governments to achieve the common good.

The reality, however, has been an interdependency and blurring of the lines between public and private, and a complicated system of public, private, local, state, and federal funding arrangements for communities in need. These arrangements in turn demand savvy grantsmanship—the entrepreneurial capacity to work the system—and flexibility. They also, in deferring to private sector provision and local practice, leave objectives such as equity, redistribution, and racial integration largely unaddressed.

A sixth pattern is that in its treatment of poor communities federal policy has operated within the two-tiered system of provision that marks U.S. social policy. In this system poor communities, like poor individuals, are assisted through means-tested programs, while their wealthier counterparts are subsidized through essentially invisible, federalized, non-means-tested subsidies such as highway funds, state universities, home mortgage assistance, and tax preferences. Poor communities are targeted as places for public assistance—public housing, public works, public income provision—while the middle class is serviced by nominally private but heavily subsidized means. Thus the retreat from the public in all walks of life has been doubly dangerous for poor communities. It has brought not only a loss in funds but the stigma of having been designated as "public" spaces in a society that equates "private" with quality and class.

Finally, despite its race-neutral stance, community development policy has continually been confounded by the problem of race. Minorities were routinely excluded from the local planning committees established in early federal redevelopment legislation, and their neighborhoods were the first to be bulldozed as a result. The programs of the 1960s were subsequently caught up in the politics of racial backlash. Race is deeply embedded in the structural transformations that beset urban and rural communities as well. Poverty and unemployment are more concentrated in minority than in white neighborhoods, and poor minorities are more likely to live in high-poverty areas than are poor whites. Yet race is rarely explicitly acknowledged in community development policy, and then only when it can no longer be avoided: within the confines of racial uprising and violence in the late 1960s and again in 1992.

One lesson from historical experience, then, is that community development policy has been undermined by recurring patterns in the structure of policy. Internal contradictions, marginalization, weak political coalitions, fragmentation, associationalism, second-tier status, and institutionalized racial inequality have kept community development policy swimming against the tide. As a closer look at the historical record will show, these patterns are not the product of immutable ideological or structural forces but of the political processes through which policy choices have been negotiated and made. Many can be traced to the very beginnings of the community development movement in the decades before place-based policy had become a part of the federal welfare state.

Progressive Roots

Although officially initiated in the 1930s, federal assistance to poor communities drew from principles and theories that had their beginnings in Progressive Era social science and reform. And from this period emerged the guiding assumptions and principles of place-based reform, many of which have been revised and repackaged in succeeding generations of community initiative.

One principle is that social interventions should be comprehensive, and address the entire array of problems facing poor people rather than focusing narrowly on poverty as an income problem requiring cash relief. The model for this approach in the late nineteenth and early twentieth centuries was the neighborhood settlement house, where low-income immigrant families could find services, job references, educational and cultural uplift programs and, most important, all the moral and social benefits thought to derive from interaction with middle-class "neighbors" or volunteers. Comprehensiveness also informed efforts to improve physical conditions in poor neighborhoods through clearing slums, building model tenements, and creating playgrounds and parks. Although they were more narrowly construed than the settlement house movement, these early housing and neighborhood improvement reforms started from the same basic premise: poverty was not an isolated individual pathology but an all-encompassing social condition which led to delinquency, crime, vice, family disintegration, and other forms of social disorganization that characterized urban industrial slums. Fixing the environment was a way of breaking the vicious cycle of urban poverty and physical decay. It would also, not coincidentally, help to protect and preserve the social peace.

For some Progressive reformers, efforts to

improve neighborhood conditions were part of a broader agenda that included wage and regulatory reform. For the most part, however, settlement workers and tenement house reformers were more narrowly interested in physical and social rehabilitation, which they believed to hold the key to assimilating urban migrants into the economic, social, and cultural mainstream. The reformers acknowledged that immigrant neighborhoods served a vital function as a steady source of low-wage labor in the urban economy and were a kind of staging ground from which urban newcomers would advance into the American way of life. This assimilationist framework anticipated the social scientific concepts associated with the Chicago School of urban sociology and eventually became absorbed into the canons of policy thought. It was also based on assumptions about the nature of neighborhood change: that it is part of organic or natural economic growth occurring outside the realm of political choice, that it is part of a similarly organic ethnic succession as immigrants assimilate into the mainstream, and that social disorganization, isolation, and community competence are expressions of group adaptation, or lack thereof, to the economic and social demands of urban life.

This perspective had important implications for reform: the objective should not be to change individuals or even cultural practices so much as to establish effective social systems of integration so that immigrants would have access to the opportunities and cosmopolitan influences of the urban mainstream.

A second major principle with Progressive Era roots is that community interventions should be planned in collaborations between experts and citizens. Searching for a middle way between laissez-faire capitalism and state socialism, planners used a combination of technical expertise and citizen consultation in efforts to regulate or control urbanization and economic change. Such efforts were first manifest in the "comprehensive city planning" movement of the 1910s and 1920s. The architects, intellectuals, philanthropists, and engineers who pioneered the movement developed physical blueprints for the total

urban environment that were meant to strike a balance between the demands of commercial, industrial, and residential well-being. Thinking of themselves as stewards for the interests of the community as a whole, the planners routinely looked to advisory boards of leading citizens (heavily chosen from business elites) to approve or help promote their blueprints, but rarely for advice on the plans themselves. In later years federal community development efforts would attempt to build on this model for local participatory planning, with equally limited representation of community residents.

A third principle that has informed community intervention since the Progressive Era is citizen or resident participation. By far the most troublesome and controversial concept in the history of community-based reform, participation has been interpreted in sometimes dramatically different ways. For settlement house workers and planners, resident participation was a way of improving and educating the poor while discouraging dependency by engaging them in local self-help activities. This idea of involvement later came under fire, however, from critics who charged that it treated local residents as passive and incapable, and used participation as a tool for co-opting them into conforming to the reformist vision of change.

The idea of local participation tapped into a more radical vein when expressed as a movement for indigenous control and self-determination. In the Chicago Area Project, a community-based anti-delinquency initiative that grew directly out of the research of the Chicago School, organizers employed workers from troubled neighborhoods as a direct challenge to social work professionals and outside expertise more generally. The project was governed by a neighborhood council, exclusively composed of local residents, who took control of setting the agenda and mapping the strategy for community change, calling on experts when the community determined it was warranted. In this concept of indigenous participation, soon to be embodied in Saul Alinsky's Back of the Yards Neighborhood Council, the natural and by implication more legitimate form of leadership came from within. This model of resident autonomy was also incorporated in the movement for worker-run housing in the 1930s, which reached its peak with the creation of the Labor Housing Conference, a national advisory organization with a substantial grassroots network.

These two models of participation, the one emphasizing mere involvement and the other self-determination and control, would remain a continuing source of controversy and confusion in the federal interventions to come.

The core principles of community development policy first emerged, then, during the Progressive Era, a time of economic restructuring and demographic transformation equal in scale to our own. Just as important for the community development movement is to see how these principles have endured, despite the many unresolved tensions and, especially in retrospect, evident limitations within Progressive Era community reform. The tensions between private provision and public intervention, grassroots planning and outside expertise, resident participation and indigenous control continued to cause contention, even polarization, within the movement throughout subsequent decades of reform. More troubling are the limitations within the Progressive vision, which also endured in the later community development movement. First is its nearly exclusive focus on environmental improvements to the neglect of the underlying problems of poverty, low wages, poor labor market conditions, and lack of political power. Second, it almost completely avoided the problems of racial exclusion and interethnic conflict, even as the first large-scale migration of blacks from the rural South was transforming the cities that gave shape to the concepts and strategies of place-based reform. Housing reformers and settlement house workers confined their efforts to the white immigrant population. Meanwhile, the presumably race-neutral instruments of Progressive reform, such as zoning and participatory planning, were systematically used to reinforce local segregationist norms. Community development, at least in the sense of what gained quasi-official recognition from foundations and policymakers, remained a largely segregated enterprise until the 1950s and 1960s, a reflection not only of the segregated spaces within which communities were forming, but also of the segregated world of reform.

FOUNDATIONS OF FEDERAL POLICY: THE NEW DEAL AND BEYOND

The Roosevelt administration's New Deal made a massive investment in shoring up distressed communities with direct job creation, public works, and infrastructure building, while also recognizing the plight of displaced rural communities with land distribution and planned resettlement. At the same time, the New Deal also laid the foundations for an indirect form of community development in two of its most far-reaching measures: the mortgage insurance system that would later help underwrite the postwar suburban housing boom and the investment in regional economic modernization that would transform the political economy of the South. By the end of the New Deal these hidden forms of federal community investment were on the verge of major expansion, while most of the direct job creation, public works, and resettlement policies had either fallen to opposition or been allowed to die. In their stead was the combination of public housing assistance, cash grants and services, and localized planning that would constitute the foundation for federal aid to poor or declining communities for the next four decades.

Perhaps the most significant New Deal measure in terms of future community policy was not specifically place-oriented at all. The Social Security Act of 1935 established the basic approach to social welfare provision that would regulate the federal approach to communities as well: individualized and income-oriented. This strategy implicitly rejected the environmentalist efforts of the community reform tradition. Despite a network of social work professionals in New Deal agencies, services were relegated to a relatively minor position in the Social Security Act. From the start, then, the federal welfare state created a fragmented administrative structure for providing cash and services and set up hurdles that future reformers would perpetually try to overcome.

In its reluctance to interfere with private markets, the Social Security Act also set the pattern for federal aid to communities. The Roosevelt administration was eager to work within and undergird the private enterprise system and, above all, to get the federal government out of the business of job creation and direct relief. Perhaps most important, the Social Security Act set the pattern for the two-tiered structure of federal social provision: on the top tier, a federalized, contributory, non-means-tested social insurance program for protection against income loss in old age and unemployment; on the bottom a localized, means-tested system of public assistance for poor women and children. Poverty, whether addressed at the individual or community level, would hereafter be treated separately from the problems of old age and unemployment.

A second New Deal measure, the Housing Act of 1937, created the basis for public housing, a mainstay of federal assistance to poor communities for decades to come. It also established a complicated political infrastructure for housing programs, based on an uneasy mixture of private profit and public purpose that reflected the administration's hope of achieving several not always compatible goals at once. One, shared by most New Deal programs, was to put the unemployed to work. Federal housing programs were also used for slum clearance, which made them appealing to urban developers but generated criticism from advocates for the poor. Federal construction projects administered by the Public Works Administration managed to serve both goals directly, creating thousands of government jobs on construction sites located in cleared-out slum areas.

With the Housing Act of 1937 the administration moved from direct government provision toward a more decentralized system of market subsidy and local control. It also incorporated another major goal: stimulating the private construction industry. Under the terms of the legislation, local housing authorities were created to issue bonds, purchase land designated for slum clearance, and contract with private builders to construct public housing. Thus they provided the public with affordable housing, the

unions with jobs, and the construction market with a subsidy from the federal government. Local real estate developers soon found that they, too, could get in on the benefits of public housing. They recognized that federal funds for slum clearance offered a rich public subsidy for potentially valuable downtown real estate that could be developed for more profitable purposes. Thus, by the end of the 1930s public housing was tied into a broad-based constituency that included labor, urban interests, and reform groups as well as private builders and developers. Meanwhile, by tying public housing almost exclusively to the goal of slum clearance and leaving locational decisions up to local initiative, the act essentially guaranteed that public housing would remain concentrated in central cities.

The overarching goal of New Deal housing policy, however, was to promote home ownership among working- and middle-class Americans, a goal it achieved largely at the expense of poor and minority city dwellers and the neighborhoods they inhabited. In 1933 the Roosevelt administration created the Home Ownership Loan Corporation (HOLC) to protect homeowners from the threats of foreclosure and high interest rates. In 1934 home ownership got a bigger federal boost when President Roosevelt signed legislation creating the Federal Housing Administration (FHA). By insuring long-term loans made by private lenders, the programs stabilized the home mortgage insurance market, made mortgages and home improvement loans more accessible to the middle and working classes, and provided a permanent stimulus for the private housing market. The benefits of these policies did not extend to slum dwellers, however, or to families with incomes too low to meet even subsidized mortgage requirements. Blacks and other minorities were also systematically excluded through officially sanctioned redlining, neighborhood covenants, and other forms of discrimination.

The New Deal established the foundations for federal aid to declining communities, but its legacy was decidedly mixed. For the next several decades politicians concerned about community deterioration could look to federal housing and planning programs for local rebuilding and development. New Deal policy also forged the political alliances that would help keep those programs alive. Perhaps most important the New Deal linked its efforts at local economic revival to the creation of stable jobs at decent wages. At the same time, New Deal policies laid the basis for a growing political, economic, and racial divide between middle-class and low-income communities. The insurance policies created by the Social Security Act provided economic security for millions. Mortgage subsidies put home ownership within popular reach. Their benefits were substantial but largely hidden, and they enjoyed a legitimacy that publicly subsidized welfare programs could never hope to achieve: social security because its benefits were partly financed by individual contributions; mortgage assistance because its benefits were mediated through the private market.

These benefits were simply unavailable to millions of marginally employed workers, tenant farmers, and minorities, who instead relied on visible, public, and regularly contested sources of federal support.

FROM SLUMLESS CITIES TO AREA REDEVELOPMENT: AID TO COMMUNITIES IN POSTWAR PROSPERITY

During the postwar decades the federal government made two massive investments in community development. Both relied on expansion of the hidden forms of federal subsidy initiated during the New Deal. One was the growth of suburbs, with the help of highway funds, business tax incentives, and home ownership subsidies now extended to returning war veterans as well as other groups. The other was the continued investment in defense and related industry that transformed once underdeveloped regional economies, particularly in the South. By the late 1950s the American suburb was the symbol of prosperity, while budding high-technology centers promised the triumph of American know-how during the cold war.

There were serious problems beneath the veneer of prosperity, however. Beginning in the 1950s, analysts raised fears that the distressed areas in America's older cities and rural communities were becoming permanent "pockets of poverty." Working within the New Deal policy framework, the federal response to these communities revolved around housing, local redevelopment, and subsidies for private industry, without significantly redirecting market forces. This response was reflected in two programs: urban renewal and area redevelopment, whose limitations contributed to the upsurge in community-based activism and reform in the 1960s.

Urban renewal came about in response to what journalists, academic urbanologists, and planners were beginning to refer to as a "crisis of metropolitanization" in the 1940s and 1950s. The combination of industrial decentralization, property blight, middle-class out-migration, and minority-group in-migration was changing the face of postwar cities, they warned, while newly incorporated suburbs were reaping the benefits of metropolitan growth. Municipal governments were powerless in this situation because they lacked the capacity to annex or to tax beyond their limited jurisdictions. One answer was to expand federal assistance for slum clearance, housing construction, and redevelopment in blighted inner cities. Urban renewal, as the policy established by the Housing Act of 1949 came to be known, promised to clear out the slums and revive the downtown economy by attracting new businesses and middle-class residents back to the urban core. Urban rebuilders also aggressively sought out federal subsidies for highway building, thinking to make the city friendlier to the age of the automobile along the way.

The strategy behind urban renewal emerged out of negotiations among public housing advocates, private builders, big-city mayors, and real estate developers who had been active in debates over the 1937 Federal Housing Act. Crucial to its operation was eminent domain, the power to amass land tracts for slum clearance, which the courts had determined was reserved for localities. Since 1937, eminent domain had been exercised by local housing authorities, which would buy or reclaim land and then contract with private developers to construct public housing. Following the Housing Act of 1949 it was exercised by local redevelopment authorities for purposes that went well beyond housing. In the debates leading up to passage of the act, developers lobbied for and won generous federal subsidies (two-thirds of the costs) of local land acquisition, and also demanded the flexibility to use reclaimed land for nonresidential purposes—all in the name of reviving the ailing downtown economy for the greater good of the community. Although skeptical of the motivation of developers, the public housing advocates were willing to go along with the arrangement as the price they had to pay for getting a public housing bill passed. They came to regret this decision, or at least their own failure to get enough in return. The 1949 legislation specified that a designated proportion of cleared land be used for residential purposes and that the bill include provisions for relocating displaced residents to "decent, safe and sanitary housing." In subsequent amendments the balance between housing construction and redevelopment was steadily shifted to the latter as Congress loosened the requirement that cleared land be used for housing construction. Evaluation studies also confirmed that requirements to help the displaced relocate were barely enforced.

By the late 1950s, public housing advocates had come to see the program as little more than a generous public buyout of land for private real estate interests. Among black urban residents, it became widely known as "negro removal." Highway building projects brought similar results, consistently displacing or breaking up low-income neighborhoods and encouraging rather than stemming the middle-class migration to the suburbs. After a decade, one conclusion was hardly contested: urban renewal was a boon for private developers and for the mayors who brought in the federal funds, and an unmitigated disaster for the poor.

While urban renewal focused on the blight brought about by decentralization and physical decay, the Area Redevelopment Act (ARA) of 1961 addressed joblessness in communities left behind by economic moderniza-tion and structural change. From the perspective of structural unemployment, depressed communities were suffering from a surplus labor problem, which, because it derived from macroeconomic shifts, demanded a coordinated national response. Furthermore, in the absence of federal resources and planning, state redevelopment agencies were simply competing with one another to lure existing businesses with the promise of tax breaks and cheap labor. The idea behind ARA, then, was to subsidize new job opportunities in declining communities. Watered down from five years of congressional negotiation, the final bill allocated only $375 million for four years, spread its resources to more than 1,000 urban and rural communities, and offered no leverage for regulating wage scales and benefits.

Once off the ground the Area Redevelopment Administration was subject to nearly continuous ridicule and attack as a Democratic party pork barrel. It also came under fire for some highly visible mistakes, such as funding enterprises that were nonunion, racially segregated, or simply not likely to survive. Having produced what by its own admission were limited results, the program was shut down in 1965 and replaced by the Economic Development Administration, which shifted the focus of policy to rural infrastructural development and regional planning. In at least one respect, the ARA did represent a significant step in the federal approach to community development. Alone among federal programs, it focused on economic change and structural unemployment as the sources of community decline and recognized the plight of labor surplus areas that, without a national development strategy, were forced to compete against one another to attract industry and jobs.

Urban renewal and area redevelopment had few defenders and many critics by the time their results were apparent. For some, they offered classic examples of what went wrong when government tried to interfere with the workings of a perfectly adequate free market system and the basic fallacy of trying to save doomed communities when migration was the better response. For others, they revealed the flaws in what amounted to a trickle-down strategy for helping the poor. Still others could see them principally as failures of planning: too much bricks and mortar and too few services, too little coordination across the various agencies involved, or too little representation for the poor. Underlying all these critiques were questions about the assumptions embedded in the New Deal policy framework: that slum conditions were the cause rather than the consequence of poverty, that private profit could be made to work for public ends, and that communities, left to their own devices, would voluntarily create plans that would represent the interests of the poor. For all their internal flaws, however, the real problem for post-war programs to aid declining communities was that they were undercut by the more powerful trends public policy was doing so much to encourage. With the federally paved march to the suburbs at full tilt and programs of rural modernization well under way, central cities and rural towns were continuously losing population, revenues, and the hope of survival.

COMMUNITY ACTION, MODEL CITIES, AND THE SPECIAL IMPACT PROGRAM

Federal aid to communities entered a new phase in the mid-1960s, turning from the bricks-and-mortar focus of urban renewal to the "human face" presented by the problems of urban economic decline and from upholding the segregated norms of local residential patterns to a more forthright integrationist agenda. Supporting these policy shifts was an upsurge in liberal activism at the national level, which reached a height in the declaration of the War on Poverty by President Lyndon Johnson in 1964. Organized citizen activism was also on the rise, much of it inspired by the gains and innovative strategies of the civil rights movement throughout the 1950s and 1960s. Later in the decade, liberal policies also became caught up in the social turmoil of antiwar protest and racial unrest, symbolized nowhere more powerfully than in the use of federal troops to quell violence in the nation's ghettos. The popular imagery of poor places had taken on a new, more urban and minority face by the late 1960s.

It was thus in a context of federal reform, citizen action, social protest, and heightening racial tension that the Johnson administration launched a rapid succession of federal programs and demonstration projects with the goal of comprehensive community renewal. These programs, including Community Action, Model Cities, the Special Impact Program, and an array of neighborhood-based service programs, attempted to push federal community policy beyond the New Deal framework by using federal power to alter existing political, economic, and racial arrangements in poor communities.

A centerpiece of the War on Poverty, the Community Action Program (CAP), was created during an intensive period of planning leading up to the Economic Opportunity Act of 1964, but the thought and action that gave it shape had been emerging at the local level for several years. Three local-level developments—relating to urban renewal, foundation-funded reform, and the civil rights movement—were of particular importance.

Urban renewal left a paradoxical legacy for liberal policymakers, for even as it bulldozed and undermined poor neighborhoods it strengthened local capacity for the planning and grantsmanship cities would need to survive. In its own response to the postwar "crisis of metropolitanization," the Ford Foundation had invested in an ambitious program to build up local urban expertise, including grants to universities for urban extension services and training programs. The fruits of this confluence of philanthropic interest and official demand were apparent in cities such as New Haven, Boston, Detroit, and Pittsburgh. Having successfully raised foundation and federal money for renewal in the 1950s, these cities were among the first in line for community action grants. The experience of urban renewal was also important in convincing liberal planners, social scientists, and federal housing bureaucrats that the problem of urban poverty went beyond housing to include the services, opportunity structures, and political representation available to the poor. Local organizing around renewal was by no means confined to official circles, however. Opposition among low-income residents to local redevelopment plans was crucial in laying the groundwork for more expansive local activism in the later 1960s. When planning for community action, liberal officials and local activists could agree on at least one major point: if community development were to work for the poor, the local status quo would have to be shaken up.

The new Community Action Agencies were required to ensure the "maximum feasible participation" of the poor. They could also, much to the dismay of local politicians, be organized outside official government channels. Ultimately, the hope was to stimulate more permanent reform of the local bureaucracy while engaging the poor in their own rehabilitation. Acting in concert with the spurt of economic growth and employment economists anticipated from the tax cut of 1964, CAP was to break down what planners thought of as barriers to prosperity for America's poor.

CAP was initiated in a burst of activity and enthusiasm that was almost as quickly halted by the political controversy it caused. Suddenly denied direct access to the federal funding pipeline, urban mayors, whose loyalty was crucial to the Democratic Party, threatened to revolt, earning CAP the enmity of Lyndon Johnson. Infighting among local organizations for control of antipoverty funds hurt the cause even further, and the meaning of "maximum feasible participation" remained subject to debate. CAP then suffered devastating blows in the summer of 1965 when the Conference of Mayors threatened to pass a resolution against it and congressional opponents claimed that the program was responsible for the racial uprising in the Los Angeles neighborhood known as Watts. Dissatisfaction also welled up from communities. Despite its innovations in services and service delivery, CAP could not deliver one badly needed ingredient for development: jobs for the residents of the low-income neighborhoods it served. The Johnson White House continually rejected proposals for a targeted job creation program for ghettos on the grounds that it was unnecessary and, as spending for the Vietnam War escalated, too expensive. Instead, seeking to stem its political losses and prevent further "long hot summers" like that in 1965, federal policymakers responded with two additional programs: Model Cities and the Special Impact Program, which were aimed principally at communities with concentrations of poor minorities.

On one level Model Cities was an attempt to make up for the failures of federal antipoverty initiatives: it combined services with bricks-and-mortar programs while giving control of local planning to city officials, thus avoiding the political liabilities of CAP. But Model Cities was also part of a longstanding movement involving urban legislators, liberal philanthropists, social scientists, and labor officials to establish a national urban policy. Despite several legislative setbacks, this movement achieved a major breakthrough with the creation of the Department of Housing and Urban Development (HUD) in 1965.

Emerging from the administrative task force appointed to create a blueprint for the new agency, Model Cities brought together many of the ideas that had been operating in the foundation experiments of the 1950s and early 1960s. The plan called for massive slum clearance to make way for the most up-to-date design and technology in construction. It also envisioned a more integrated healthy environment in the inner city, with a full array of public and private services for a mixed-income base of residents. But the Demonstration Cities and Metropolitan Development Act was passed in 1966 with a more circumscribed mission. More narrowly targeted on poor inner-city neighborhoods, it relied on the familiar mechanisms of local planning and federal agency coordination for a comprehensive attack on physical, social, and economic problems. The legislation called for the creation of local demonstration agencies under direct supervision of the mayor's office and made them eligible for existing federal human service, job training, housing, and infrastructure-building programs on a priority basis. The demonstration cities were also eligible for grants and technical assistance to generate redevelopment plans in poor neighborhoods. Participation by the poor was strongly encouraged but not directly supervised by federal authorities. Nor was there any designated agency with authority to enforce cooperation and coordination among agencies at the top. In a repeat of previous experience, even this limited plan was watered down in the legislative process.

While the administration task force was working behind closed doors to grapple with the physical and social revitalization of poor urban neighborhoods, Senators Robert F. Kennedy and Jacob Javits were conducting highly publicized hearings on America's looming urban crisis, a term that had become virtually synonymous with the ghetto and the fear of racial violence it provoked. Pitched as an inquiry into the full range of urban needs, the hearings were designed to draw attention to what the administration seemed to de-emphasize in its own service-oriented programs: the absence of jobs in the inner cities. The hearings also helped lay the political groundwork for an initiative that had started with Kennedy's visit to Brooklyn's Bedford-Stuyvesant neighborhood in late 1965: amending the Economic Opportunity Act to create the Special Impact Program.

In its statement of objectives SIP resembled a streamlined version of the ARA. Its basic idea was to revitalize poor communities, primarily through economic development but with an intensive component of services and training as well. SIP was more specific about its geographic target, however: neighborhoods characterized by high concentrations of poverty and tendencies toward dependency, chronic unemployment, and rising community tensions. And unlike the ARA, which funneled its loans and grants through separate bureaucratic channels, SIP proposed to put development funds in the hands of the communities themselves. It provided block grants to community-based organizations, which would in turn design, finance, and administer their own comprehensive development strategies.

SIP modeled its local activities on community development corporations (CDCs), organizations whose origins in the movement for black economic self-determination distinguished them from the more traditional small business orientation of the ARA. Such corporations had been cropping up in black urban neighborhoods for several years, and in the early 1960s some of the most prominent were linked to indigenous efforts to establish an alternative to white capitalist control. Under government and foundation auspices, CDCs were deradicalized and professionalized, and they developed a keener eye for the bottom line. It was in this form that the CDC movement expanded and diversified in the 1970s and became the central institution for local development. Setting aside $25 million for the first year, legislators expected that communities would work in partnership with the private sector to raise additional capital, create new neighborhood jobs, and invest in homegrown enterprises. The profits, in contrast to ARA's trickle-down approach, would then be invested directly in community improvement.

SIP's community development strategy got off to a rocky start. As the first community organization to receive funds under SIP, the Bedford-Stuyvesant Restoration Corporation provoked criticism and controversy when it established a parallel structure of corporations that dramatically, if unwittingly, replicated the very inequities the program was established to redress. One was run by blacks, community based, and designated to run the "inside" operations. The other was made up of prominent white business executives who signed on to generate private investment and deal with the "outside" financial world. The SIP program also met resistance from the anti-poverty bureaucrats in the Johnson administration, who had invested most of their efforts in encouraging individual mobility and dispersal rather than local investment and development. Even CAP, for all its focus on strengthening local institutions, was primarily concerned with helping individuals and families to move up and out.

SIP program administrators encountered additional pressure from the OEO's research branch, which was dominated by economists with a taste for quantifiable program results and wary of the program's multiple, vaguely specified long-range goals. When judged according to traditional measures—the number of people lifted out of poverty—the program's impact appeared limited, or at best unclear. Nor could SIP-funded CDCs claim to have created a substantial number of new jobs. After a decade of federal and foundation funding, it was also apparent that CDC for-profit enterprises were not able to survive without reliance on outside, largely government, funding. Indeed, they had and would continue to enjoy most of their success in housing construction and real estate management, for which they, like commercial developers, relied heavily on government support. Thus the CDC movement was particularly vulnerable to government retrenchment during the 1970s and 1980s.

Despite the program's many setbacks and shifts, the ideas embraced in SIP did manage to produce important results. Within two years it had invested in thirteen urban and rural CDCs, some of which are still operating. More generally, by pursuing neighborhood-based development as its central objective, SIP recognized the loss of local job opportunities that the next two decades of industrial dispersal would only make worse.

By 1967 the Johnson administration had amassed an array of policies aimed at poor communities: more, better, and integrated services; physical and human renewal; local economic development; community organizing; and empowerment. These policies in turn provided support for local activism and institution building, creating jobs and political opportunities for thousands of neighborhood residents and leaving community health centers, neighborhood service organizations, law centers, community development corporations, Head Start centers, and local action agencies in their wake. The initiatives also gave rise to a new network of nonprofit providers and intermediary organizations committed to community-based antipoverty intervention that would sustain the community development movement in decades to come. Expanding the scope of President Kennedy's antidiscrimination executive order, the Fair Housing Act of 1968 added another significant dimension to the federal capacity to combat place-based poverty.

For all their promise and ambition, however, the Great Society programs remained just that—programs, not a coherent community policy. They were too limited in scope and funding to alter the political inequities or combat the structural economic shifts that continued to segregate poor places as the "other America." Nor did policymakers overcome a basic ambivalence over whether their aim was to build up communities or help people leave them. The conflict between those two strategies would only become more sharply defined as local conditions deteriorated in the 1970s and 1980s.

THE ROOTS OF RETREAT: COMMUNITY POLICY IN THE 1970S

The 1970s brought dramatic changes in the economic and political context for community development policy. Unemployment and inflation rose sharply, while growth, productivity, and real wages stagnated. Reviewing the prospects for urban revitalization at the end of the decade, President Carter's Commission on a National Agenda for the Eighties was bleak. The transformation to postindustrialism was "inevitable" and "ineluctable," its report began, "necessitating simultaneous painful growth and shrinkage, disinvestment and reinvestment, in communities throughout the nation." Developing a national policy for community revitalization was "ill-advised," the report concluded, because it would conflict with the overarching goal of national economic competitiveness. The prospects for national policy were further diminished by the politics of racial backlash, working-class resentment, and sentiment against big government, which moved the political center steadily to the right and undermined the New Deal urban-labor-civil rights coalition that had supported community development in the past. Equally important, changes introduced under the banner of Richard Nixon's New Federalism profoundly altered the infrastructure of policy, in effect abrogating the special ties between the federal government and poor communities that had been forged in earlier eras. The result of these changes was a renewed emphasis on localism, fiscal austerity, and neighborhood ethnic solidarity in community development policy. This emphasis was meant to broaden community policy's appeal to the white working class, but it also marked the beginning of a steady decline of federal government involvement.

Underlying these efforts was a distinctive philosophy of social provision, known as the New Federalism, that sought to give states greater power and responsibility and to lighten federal restrictions in determining how public funding would be spent. It also envisioned a more efficient federal bureaucracy, reorganized to eliminate government waste. But Nixon's reforms were also based on a more clearly partisan agenda through which he aimed to forge a new electoral majority based on white working-class resentment of the black welfare poor and free the federal bureaucracy of its New Deal influences by bringing it under more direct presidential control. Unveiling his New Federalist agenda in the summer of 1969, Nixon promised to get rid of "entrenched programs" from the past and replace them with a system based on "fairness" for the "forgotten poor" and working classes.

During the next two years the administration introduced measures to achieve the New Federalist agenda, with far-reaching consequences for community development policy. The OEO was the first target for reorganization, which was aimed at curtailing its community action division and eventually led to the elimination of the agency itself. Nixon's plans for decentralization proved even more consequential for existing community-based programs. They introduced a new, less redistributive and centrally regulated way of providing federal aid to localities. Revenue sharing, enacted in 1972, provided funds to states and localities automatically rather than through categorical grants. In this way Nixon sought to reduce the federal role in determining how funds would be allocated and to end the New Deal tradition of establishing direct links to poor communities to offset their political weakness in state and federal legislative bodies. The administration's adoption of block grants, which came to fruition in the creation of Community Development Block Grants (CDBG) in 1974, gave localities still broader discretion in allocating funds and brought the flagship programs of the War on Poverty to an end. By the mid-1970s, Model Cities, CAP, and SIP were slated to be replaced by block grants. The Housing and Community Development Act of 1974 similarly revolutionized federal housing provision, shifting the emphasis away from new construction and toward rent subsidies, thus reducing the extent to which public housing could be linked to creating labor union jobs.

Following the changes introduced during the Nixon and Ford administrations, actual spending levels for community development, while remaining less than 1 percent of federal expenditures, rose fairly steadily for the rest of the decade. These expenditures were spread over a much larger number of communities and used for a broader range of purposes, however. Revenue sharing and block grants also brought a significant change in the overall distribution of funds, both within and between different kinds of communities, increasing funding in the suburbs and away from central cities and rural areas, providing more services and benefits to middle-class recipients, and moving a greater proportion of funds away from traditional Democratic strongholds in the Northeast and Midwest and toward the South and West. Meanwhile, the political relationship between federal government and poor communities deteriorated rapidly, symbolized nowhere more clearly than in the looming fiscal collapse of several major cities at mid-decade, while Washington stood by.

Assuming the presidency after eight years of Republican control, Jimmy Carter initially raised expectations of renewed federal attention to the special plight of poor communities. Responding to pressures from urban and civil rights leaders, he announced in 1977 that his administration would develop a comprehensive urban initiative that would restore Washington's commitment to the health of American communities. The intense period of planning that followed involved nearly every domestic agency and dozens of community development experts who advocated such innovations as the creation of a national community development bank. Caught up in an increasingly polarized debate over people-versus place-based programs, the planning group created an unwieldy collection of small job-creation, tax incentive, housing, social services, anticrime, and even public arts programs that looked to observers like more of the same. All of this was to be coordinated by an Interagency Coordination Council, but its powers and responsibilities remained unspecified. And, at Carter's insistence, the programs would involve a minimum of new spending.

Carter's comprehensive reform never got off the ground in Congress, but the administration did take incremental steps to restore some of the redistributive aspects of federal policy. In 1977 it changed the revenue-sharing formula to target needy communities. That same year Carter also acted to make up for the losses experienced by older industrial cities by initiating the Urban Development Action Grant (UDAG) program. This program, like urban renewal, offered federal matching grants that could be used for commercial, industrial, or residential development in central cities in hopes of creating jobs for neighborhood residents and reviving downtown economies. But it was never established whether the jobs created by UDAG-funded redevelopment actually went to neighborhood residents, and most of the funding was used for commercial redevelopment. Despite these initiatives, Carter did not attempt to alter, and indeed embraced, the fundamental structural changes that had been ushered in by Nixon: a new era of decentralization and diminished federal responsibility was at hand. In the wake of his failed urban initiative, domestic policy drifted farther away from place-based reform.

For all the setbacks and reversals in national policy, the legacy of the 1970s was not necessarily one of defeat for the community development movement. The increased emphasis on local initiative pushed community-based organizations to strengthen institutional capacity, while the vacuum created by federal withdrawal from housing construction opened up a market niche for CDCs. Community activists used the momentum of the 1960s to launch a new phase of organizer training and national network building that could be applied to a diverse range of community-based consumer,

environmental, and antipoverty concerns. Taking advantage of the emergence of attention to public interest issues among legislators and in the courts, these groups realized a major victory with the passage of the Home Mortgage Disclosure Act of 1975 and the Community Reinvestment Act of 1977. This legislation provided for public scrutiny of lending records and recognized the obligation of banks to lend in communities where they do business. Promoted as a weapon against discrimination and redlining, it also gave community groups a powerful tool in their own negotiations with local lending institutions. Although the successes of local organizations did not necessarily make up for the losses in federal support, they proved increasingly important in the decade ahead.

THE END OF THE NEW DEAL ERA?

In the 1980s the Reagan and Bush administrations greatly reduced the already diminished federal presence in poor communities. Playing on anti-government sentiment and fiscal fear, Republicans eliminated revenue sharing, UDAGs, and most other remaining development programs, cut Community Development Block Grants in half, and left a much diminished welfare and services sector as the only source of direct federal assistance to poor communities. The resources and mandate for enforcing housing discrimination law all but disappeared. The Reagan revolution also introduced a much more radical framework of decentralization and privatization than the president's predecessors had envisioned—in fact, it threatened to dismantle the federal policy infrastructure for community building altogether. Judging from the reductions in place-targeted federal funding, the revolution was a success. But the expansion in the number and size of high-poverty neighborhoods during the decade tells a different story.

Two initiatives emerged from federal retrenchment, both premised on the belief that the absence of government was the key to community revitalization. The first, enterprise zones, promised to introduce free market principles and restore entrepreneurial activity to low-income communities through a combination of government deregulation and generous tax breaks for businesses. Reagan's proposals were consistent with the supply-side philosophy embraced in his economic policies: allowing entrepreneurs to keep more of their profits, the reasoning went, would stimulate new investment and eventually trickle down to community residents. In keeping with their anti-interventionist premises, the proposals also rejected the components of local planning and supplemental government assistance that had characterized programs such as area redevelopment. Despite repeated legislative attempts, however, the enterprise zone idea was never adopted as national policy. But it was adopted in a number of states during the 1980s, where the designated zones were assisted by substantial government investment and planning and came to resemble earlier development policies more closely.

The other major initiative to emerge from the free market framework was a proposal to privatize and promote residential ownership in public housing, this time in the name of individual empowerment in low-income communities. Like the proposal for enterprise zones, this proposal never got off the ground, due partly to the fallout from political scandals in the Reagan administration's Department of Housing and Urban Development.

The administration was unable to eliminate or privatize all the social welfare programs it targeted for attack. But the Reagan revolution did succeed where it mattered most—redirecting federal fiscal and economic policies—and the impact on low-income communities was devastating. In addition to the withdrawal of federal aid, the communities suffered from the increased income inequality, capital flight, labor setbacks, and crippling budgetary deficits that resulted from Reagan-era policies. Hit hard by recessions at either end of the 1980s, poor communities were politically marginalized as well. And the very idea of community development policy, premised as it was on collective well-being and supportive government policies, was challenged by a harsh, individualistic

ideology positing that no intervention would work. Ironically, for the first time since the 1930s, federal policy in poor communities was actually in harmony with the direction of social and economic policy writ large.

Reagan-era changes did not devastate the community development movement, however, and in at least one sense they could be turned into a source of strength. Pushed to do more with less, CDCs moved aggressively to become more efficient operators and to tap into local and private sources of development support. Foundations created new intermediaries to provide support for existing and emerging community-based organizations, particularly in housing and economic development. The movement for comprehensive, integrated service delivery gathered momentum as a new generation of multiservice and systems reform initiatives got under way. And community organizers, galvanized by growing inequality and federal cutbacks, created training intermediaries and focused on strengthening national networks. Impressive as these achievements were, local initiatives were heavily absorbed in making up for lost ground and could only imagine what could have been achieved in a more supportive policy environment.

REVISING THE PAST: CLINTON'S COMMUNITY POLICY

Promising "a new way of doing business for the federal government," in 1993 the Clinton administration launched an initiative to revive declining communities. In December 1994 the administration designated eleven empowerment zones [EZ], each eligible for grants and tax breaks of up to $100 million, and 95 enterprise communities [EC] eligible for smaller grants and business incentives. In most places the initiatives were just getting under way as of the late 1990s.

The EZ/EC is different from past efforts, according to administration officials, in its rejection of old ways of thinking about the problems in urban communities. The program proposes to move beyond a focus on countercyclical grant-in-aid programs to an emphasis on enabling cities to compete in the global economy. It also seeks to invest in people and places, recognizing the old dichotomy as false. EZ/EC marks another innovation in its metropolitan framework for economic development. And unlike past efforts, it is "designed to foster locally initiated, bottom-up strategies that connect the public, business, and neighborhood sectors in community-building partnerships for change."

In fact, as both its title and the rhetoric accompanying it suggest, the Empowerment Zone/Enterprise Community initiative contains much that is familiar to veterans of the community development movement. Like enterprise zones, it relies heavily on tax incentives to promote private sector investment—only this time the tax breaks are tied to hiring residents of the zone rather than realizing capital gains. Like Model Cities it draws on existing housing, education, job training, and service programs for most of the funds that will be given to the designated areas. Reviving a strategy employed by the New Deal-era National Resources Planning Board in response to funding limitations, it designates two tiers of recipient communities, presumably as a way of sharing the wealth. Community planning boards also figure prominently in the EZ/EC legislation, which combines the experience of CAP and Model Cities to require evidence of participation from all sectors in the community, including government and the poor. Federal coordination is another feature of the program, this time supervised by an interagency Community Empowerment Board headed by Vice President Al Gore. And operating within a Nixonian New Federalist framework, it offers waivers from categorical program requirements and channels all federal grants through the states. It even borrows a note from organizer Saul Alinsky in its rhetorical appeal to the consensus ideal. Most striking from historical perspective is EZ/EC's endorsement of "four fundamental principles" that restate the essential themes that have defined community development from the start: economic opportunity in private sector jobs and training; sustainable community development characterized by a comprehensive coordinated approach;

community-based partnerships that engage representatives from all parts of the community; and "strategic vision for change" based on cooperative planning and community consultation.

Clearly, the EZ/EC plan rested on the hope that this time the federal government will be able to overcome interagency conflict, weak investment incentives, competition among local political interests, and racial inequity that have plagued community development policy in the past. In this hope it is banking on the expertise of the people who have been working in low-income communities for decades and on the willingness of industries to locate and hire in areas they have traditionally stayed away from. Unfortunately, EZ/EC also repeats other patterns that have left many wondering whether it, like its predecessors, is promising much more than it can possibly deliver. Even supporters agree that the funding is inadequate given the size of the task. Its associationalist tenor leaves critics skeptical about how much investment or job creation can be expected from the private sector and the extent to which community residents will be able to expect corporate responsibility. Like past federal demonstrations, it begs the question of what happens to the thousands of communities not chosen for support, and what happens to the EZ/EC sites once initial funding runs out. It also smacks of symbolic politics at a time when poor urban and rural communities command little more than rhetorical attention on the national agenda. Most of all the plan represents a very modest investment in community revitalization, especially in the face of an overarching policy agenda that encourages footloose capital, low labor costs, reduced social spending, and persistent wage inequality, and that brings about "the end of welfare as we know it" with little thought for the policy's effect on communities.

CREATING A NEW POLICY ENVIRONMENT

The historical record offers important insights about the intellectual origins, political frustrations, and recurring patterns of federal policy, but the challenges it poses to the community development movement are even more immediate and direct.

The first is to make a case for investing in communities as part of an antipoverty policy that focuses on income inequality, job opportunities, and racial exclusion as well. Such a policy would strengthen the position of residents with better wages and training while taking steps to stem the geographic dispersal of industry and jobs. It would enforce antidiscrimination regulations to stimulate lending in poor neighborhoods and ensure access to housing and jobs. And it would challenge the myth that mobility and community development are either/or choices. Most of all it would begin with the recognition that targeted community development—no matter how comprehensive, well planned, or inclusive—cannot reduce poverty all by itself. This is not to suggest that community development is futile without these larger changes, but with them it stands a much greater chance of success.

The second challenge for community development is to reassert the importance of the federal government's participation. This is no easy task in light of historical experience or the current political climate. It begins from an understanding that past failures do not prove that revitalization is impossible; few programs enjoyed the funding, time, or sustained political commitment necessary to make community development work. Indeed, the federal commitment to middle-class and affluent communities has been much more substantial and comprehensive, including housing, infrastructure, and tax incentives among its forms of support. It is also unrealistic to expect a revival in poor communities without both federal resources and direct public provision. Two decades of federal withdrawal sent neighborhood poverty soaring. And past efforts to stimulate private market development have not trickled down.

The third challenge is to reconstitute and strengthen the political coalition behind community development policy. This will take collaboration with labor, civil rights, and other traditional allies, but it can begin by addressing the barriers to mobilization within the community development movement itself. Particularly important is to examine how funding practices affect political mobilization by tightening the tensions between outside providers and communities and discouraging the kinds of activities that can help community-based organizations become more effective politically. Foundations are rarely willing to provide the long-term undesignated funding that organizations need to build capacity and institutional stability. Nor do they generally fund local organizing, advocacy, or coalition building among community organizations. Foundations also tend to compete with one another in developing their programs, leaving community-based organizations to steer among the divergent objectives, expectations, and even timetables of outside providers to meet their own organizational needs. The result is tension and mistrust, reflecting not only disparities in power and resources but a struggle for control over community-based initiatives that is built into the funding practices themselves. As an initial step toward more effective political mobilization, then, foundations need to be willing to examine and alter these practices and organize themselves into a more coherent and persistent voice for changes in policy.

The fourth challenge is to acknowledge not only how race has contributed to the problems in poor communities, but to explore how it may be part of the solution. A race-conscious strategy would identify how race continues to shape the policy decisions affecting political representation, housing location, transportation, social services, and access to jobs. It would move beyond the simplistic black–white dichotomy to investigate how racial barriers operate across ethnic, class, and gender lines. And it would make an explicit commitment to ending institutionalized as well as individual acts of racial exclusion.

Perhaps the most important and overarching challenge from history is to reverse the policy contradictions that keep community development swimming against the tide. Meeting this challenge requires focusing not only on community interventions but creating the economic and political conditions within which community development can actually work.

NOTE

1. For a fuller historical account with citations of sources, see the much longer original chapter:

O'Connor, Alice. (1999.) "Swimming Against the Tide: A Brief History of Federal Policy in Poor Communities," in Ronald Ferguson and William Dickens, *Urban Problems and Community Development*. Washington, DC: Brookings Institute.

CHAPTER 3

Community Control and Development

The long view

James DeFilippis

INTRODUCTION

The histories of community control and development are varied and disparate, and it is the rather ambitious goal of this chapter to bring these histories together. The chapter begins in the 1960s and discusses the emergence of the current community development movement. It then presents the trajectory of this movement away from its organizing roots and towards greater degrees of institutionalization and professionalization. This professionalization has seen the goal of community control, and the radical politics that sometimes informed that goal, get lost in the process, and we conclude by discussing the implications of this.

While there is a longer history to community control efforts that goes back to the early 19th century, community control reemerged as a broad set of movements in the mid-1960s. Broadly speaking, there were two different strands to this movement that are important for us here, the black power movement and the direct democracy movement. Together they yielded many institutional innovations and changes, but for the purposes of this book the most important institution to emerge was the "community development corporation" (CDC), which is the principal institutional vehicle for community development in the United States. But before we discuss the social movement roots out of which community development as a programmatic idea, and the CDC as its vehicle, emerged, we need to discuss the context of American politics that both fostered these movements and severely undercut their ability to effect systematic change.

FROM CAAs TO MODEL CITIES AND BEYOND

The Federal government enacted the Economic Opportunity Act in 1964 and with it, began the well known period of "The War On Poverty." This Act created, among many other things, a new vehicle for community-based organizing, planning and activism, the "community action agency" (CAA). The heart of the CAA initiative was community empowerment and activism, and the underlying philosophy of the Community Action Program (CAP) was the "maximum feasible participation" of community members.

It is unclear, at best, if within three years the CAAs were able to generate substantial community-level mobilization efforts. Nonetheless, by 1967 "they were sufficiently threatening or persuasive to precipitate a [change in] national urban policy" (Fainstein, 1987, p. 328). This shift in policy had two particular components. First, the CAAs were to be reoriented towards economic development activities, and away from the political organizing goals of their initial inception. The legislative form this shift in priorities took was that of the passage of the Special Impact Program (SIP) amendment to the OEO. The SIP legislation targeted local groups for specifically economic development projects, and this program was supplemented by the Federal Community Self-Determination Act in 1969, which drove the creation of many Community Development Corporations. Driven by federal support, it was after SIP, and the 1969 Self-Determination Act, that CDCs started to grow.

The second component of the shift in federal policies was the enactment of the Model Cities Program, which was designed to place the control over anti-poverty/neighborhood development policies back into the hands of city governments—and explicitly away from communities. As Halpern puts it: "Model Cities was to be community development decoupled from community action, or more specifically from community action's presumed tendency to engender conflict and disaffection" (Halpern, 1995, p. 118). This shift indicated the extent of how threatened many city governments were by the CAP. By funding CAAs directly, the CAP was enabling community organizations to bypass city governments and connect directly to the national scale.

These shifts in federal policies had profound implications for the practice of community organizing at the time. Groups had to choose between becoming more professionalized development organizations or maintain their political identity. But maintaining their political identity would mean the loss of the government funding they had come to rely on. Either way, the potential for community organizing and social change was significantly undercut. As Kotler observed, "The government wanted enterprise rather than political action in the neighborhood; it would move the people out of the meeting hall and put them behind cash registers" (Kotler, 1971, p. 7).

To some extent, therefore, 1960s federal neighborhood policy represented a very narrow window through which connections between community-level political organizing and community-based economic development and social service provision could be merged. But that window closed rather quickly and, in doing so, helped to solidify the divisions between organizing and development, which have come to be a dominant feature in urban politics in the last 30 years.

BLACK POWER AND BLACK CAPITALISM

One of the most powerful forces in driving issues of community control in the 1960s was the "black power" movement, which emerged from the larger civil rights movement. A significant strand of black power was the drive for "community control" (Carmichael and Hamilton, 1967), and this had two distinct components. First, it dealt specifically with issues of government decentralization and black participation and control: particularly education and policing. Second, it addressed the control over economic relations between blacks and whites. It is the latter of these two which helped drive the creation of CDCs.

There was not a clear, unifying underlying rationale of the economic component of the community control movement, and instead there was a variety of programs, goals and ideals. This, of course, echoed the longstanding debates by black leaders about how to structure, organize and promote black economic development. The 1960s version of this argument included calls for: direct community ownership by CDCs; co-operative ownership; and individually-owned firms. Despite the debates about what form black ownership should take, some of its most visible proponents were decidedly ambivalent about it.

This ambivalence quickly led to the assertion of the central role of black entrepreneurialism and capitalism in the realization of power within the black community. Thus black capitalism became, through its promotion by OEO policies, the Nixon administration, and the lack of clarity by leaders in black communities, the dominant form of black economic "community" control by the end of the 1960s. Community control thereby became black capitalism, and advocates for both explicitly and implicitly conflated these two goals. The radical potential of demands for black economic power thus became co-opted into simply a debate about how best to reproduce capitalist practices in black urban neighborhoods. The road of collective *community* control and empowerment was not taken (Shipp, 1996). A substantial political opportunity was lost.

DIRECT DEMOCRACY AND NEIGHBORHOOD GOVERNMENT

While the community control argument was being presented by black power activists and theorists, a nominally comparable but substantively different argument was being presented by those advocating neighborhood control and governance. These activists and writers were advocating government decentralization as a means to politically empowering the citizens of urban areas. This movement was a 1960s incarnation of the Jeffersonian-liberal tradition of small-scale participatory government. As Jane Jacobs wrote, "The governments of large modern cities are not only incomprehensibly complex today, but also their direct effects on citizen's lives are now so ubiquitous that they cannot help but fail when their functions are centrally organized. Many functions must be decentralized and brought under direct, continuing control of local communities" (quoted in Repo, 1977, p. 48).

Perhaps the strongest supporter of the neighborhood democracy movement was Kotler, the Executive Director of the National Association of Neighborhoods. He advocated for, "the radical politics of local control" (Kotler, 1969), as a rejection of both the centralized welfare policies of the New Deal/Great Society variety, and the central role of class in leftist politics. Both of these should be replaced, he argued, by an embrace of the Ancient Greek view of humans as almost inherently political beings mixed with a 20th-century perspective on the declining ability of humans to act as such. He stated, "True radicalism issues from a practical view of man's political nature, rather than a theoretical view of the state. Its object is to shape the state to fit the present purpose of popular struggle—local rule—not to reshape man to fit a theoretical state. For the left to engage in a politics of liberty requires that it free itself of the modern heritage of revolution and address the principles of local control" (Kotler, 1969, p. 96). Thus, like the black community control movement, not only did the neighborhood government movement fail to address issues of capital and class relations, it embraced the capitalist

political economy. This was, in short, a movement for localized democracy as an end in itself, not a movement to use the framework of local democracy for changes in the larger-scale, *or even local*, political economy.

OPPORTUNITIES LOST

The possibilities of connecting these separate movements, struggling for local control, albeit in different forms, were always fairly slim. In many ways they were fighting for different goals with different constituencies. But at the same time, they were conscious political efforts to create institutions in which local-scale actors had greater control over their lives. They also shared a rhetorical belief in "community" participation and control, and it was this goal that brought these activists together, on paper at least in the form of books written at the time (see, Benello and Roussopoulos, 1971).

At the same time, their understandings of capital and class were extremely limited and neither directly confronted capital or even adequately theorized capitalism. In this way, the movements failed to appreciate the inherent importance of capital and class relations in the American political economy. As Katznelson (1981) argued, this failure to understand class led to movements sliding into the prefigured "trenches" of American urban politics in which *class* is dealt with at work, and *community* is dealt with at home— and both are dealt with inadequately. This set the community and neighborhood control efforts up to either disappear or become institutionally co-opted. And this is largely what happened in the 1970s and 1980s.

NEO-ALINSKYISM AND THE NEIGHBORHOOD MOVEMENTS OF THE 1970s

Local politics in the 1970s is best understood as having evolved from the 1960s, particularly from the direct democracy strand of organizing, and they were dominated by what has been called "the neighborhood movement" (*Social Policy*, 1979). In truth, this was less a movement than a diverse set of localized responses to particular issues that largely stemmed from people's attempts to protect their neighborhoods from threats and encroachments from without. Accordingly, the politics of the organizations in this "movement" varied tremendously, largely in relation to the character of the threat from without and the perceived sources of that threat.

The 1970s also saw the emergence of a set of populist organizations that were large in scale and relatively unencumbered by an ideologically defined set of goals. The principal figure behind this movement was Saul Alinsky who had emerged nationally as a prominent critic of some of the explicitly socialist and race-based organizing efforts of the 1960s. Instead, he and his organization, the Industrial Areas Foundation (IAF), argued for a brand of organizing that assumed that the only long-term goal should be the mobilization of people to take power for themselves. Along with the IAF, there was the emergence of national groups such as the Association of Community Organizations for Reform Now (ACORN) and statewide groups such as Massachusetts Fair Share.

These groups were run by largely white, primarily middle-class staffs and organizers, and the model of organizing was basically the same in every locality: organizers from the national organization would meet with local people to discuss with them what their concerns were, and then work to mobilize larger numbers of people in those localities to address these concerns. The national organizer, therefore, brings no agenda to the locality but instead allows the issues, and the solutions, to be defined by those within the locality. The recipe, therefore, was for a situation in which the local IAF organizations, lacking any coherent ideological framework, became about neighborhoods "getting what they could." This left them poorly positioned to deal with larger social forces, processes and changes.

This is not to say that politically progressive organizing did not occur in the 1970s, for that would be unfair and an oversimplification of community politics at the time.

First, while the neo-Alinsky organizers were self-avowedly "non-ideological," their goals of increased participation in, and the democratization of, urban politics were certainly laudable. They also recognized that there are inherent conflicts in society, and understood that power is only appropriated through struggle. Second, there were important community-based efforts to prevent the displacement of low-income residents by the continued construction of roads through inner-city neighborhoods, and by the last remnants of the Urban Renewal program's demolition. Third, substantial political and legal victories were won by those who struggled against the practice of financial institution redlining. The efforts of these organizers yielded the Federal Home Mortgage Loan Disclosure Act (1975) and the Community Reinvestment Act (1977).

CDCs: PROFESSIONALIZATION AND A NEW GENERATION

But these disputes bring us back to CDCs. While the neighborhood movement was emerging in the 1970s, the older CDCs were facing uneven outcomes, as some grew while others failed. They shared a common experience, however, in which community control of the economy declined in importance and profit-making became the dominant goal. This was partly driven by the difficult realities of the markets these groups were operating within. But was also a function of the changing priorities of the OEO which was still the dominant source of funding for these "1st generation" CDCs. The OEO increasingly pushing profit-making above all other goals. The Nixon administration terminated the OEO, however, and CDC funding was significantly cut. The first generation CDCs were therefore left to deal with this loss of funding and they did so by becoming increasingly individualist and entrepreneurial in their orientation and goals.

Evaluations at the time indicate the extent to which community control had become less important relative to the goal of economic development. Kelly (1977) found that only 35% of CDC board members considered,

"Providing opportunities for community-controlled ownership of businesses and property," to be *one of their three highest priorities* (Kelly, 1977, p. 25). And she plainly states: "the community economic development movement in no way opposes or contradicts the American tradition of individual entrepreneurship" (Kelly, 1977, p. 21).

A "second generation" of CDCs was created in the late 1970s and the early 1980s, as neighborhood protest organizations became CDCs. In becoming CDCs, they transformed themselves from being confrontational in their dealings with city governments, banks, etc., to co-operative in those relationships as they became more immersed in the structures they were originally protesting against.

Shelterforce magazine observed that there tended to be a three-step process to the transformation of oppositional community organizations to CDCs in the late 1970s and early 1980s. First, the groups emerge out of opposition to something (redlining, displacement, etc.). Second, the groups become somewhat more proactive, and begin direct political lobbying of city halls to enact their agendas. Third, the groups realize the limits of public money, and begin working to fulfill their agenda themselves (Fulton, 1987). Importantly, this was not a process of political co-optation, but instead one of professionalization. These groups were not created to fundamentally transform the structures that govern the urbanization process. They emerged out of localized problems and conflicts and it was not ideologically inconsistent to deal with local scale problems as a developer rather than an adversarial activist. These transformations were not, therefore, normative—they were merely programmatic.

NON-PROFITS FOR HIRE: THE 1980s AND 1990s

The period of the 1980s and 1990s marked the coming of age for community development, as the number of CDCs grew rapidly, along with a heightened public awareness of them—and an increased set of burdens and expectations was placed upon them. This growth of activity has been evident both in the number of CDCs and in their average size. While only about 150 first generation CDCs were created in the late 1960s and early 1970s (and many failed within a few years), by the early 1980s another 500 to 750 second generation CDCs had been created (Pierce and Steinbach, 1987). The number of CDCs nationwide, therefore, essentially grew at modest, but significant, rate through end of the 1960s and the 1970s, and beginning in the late 1970s and early 1980s began to grow much more rapidly. This growth has continued to the present (see Introduction, this volume).

The growth of CDCs has been accompanied by changes in their structures, goals, and relationships with the public and private for-profit sectors. First, CDCs grew in spite of, and partially in reaction to, the shrinking desire of the public sector to provide goods of collective consumption—particularly affordable housing. Shrinking public resources left CDCs directly facing the impacts of these cutbacks. Local governments exacerbated this loss of federal money by increasingly withdrawing from the provision of social services and housing in the 1980s. CDCs thus filled the vacuum left by the state—both at the local and federal levels. And CDCs were not limited to just affordable housing, as they branched out into the areas of social service provision, education, etc.

The second transformation emerges from the first. Because of the decline in public sector support, funding for CDCs and CDC activities went from a "one stop shopping" towards more "creative" forms of financing, often referred to as "patchwork" financing (Vidal, 1996). CDCs increasingly found themselves putting together the funding for projects from a variety of sources, such as private investments made to receive a Low-Income Housing Tax Credit (after 1986), financial institution loans made to satisfy CRA requirements, grants from foundations, etc. This patchwork financing has furthered the process of professionalization in community development, because the financial management capacities it requires greatly exceed those of the prior, single-source financing.

Such expertise has often come from the national intermediaries that were constructed in the late 1970s and early 1980s. In the space of four years, 1978–1981, the Neighborhood Reinvestment Corporation (NRC); The Local Initiatives Support Corporation (LISC); The Fannie Mae Foundation; and The Enterprise Foundation, were all created. Together they finance, provide technical assistance for, and generally shape the structure of the community development industry.

Together, this growing network of CDCs, foundations, and other not-for-profit organizations, have created a situation in which, in many poor neighborhoods, CDCs have functionally become "the Shadow State" (Wolch, 1990). They provide the goods and services that formerly virtually defined municipal governments. This role was embraced by the state, as it willingly walked away from the provision of these services, and looked to the community-based sector to fill in the holes it has left behind.

Most of whatever remained of the radical politics that were part of CDCs' histories, was lost, as they became increasingly part of the urban political machinery and political organizing receded further from their goals and mission. The Ford Foundation's definitive guide to community development in the 1980s put it: "with rare exceptions, the 1960s are now as much history for them (CDCs) as for the rest of American society. One can't very well hurl his body into the path of an oncoming bulldozer when he (or she) is the developer" (Peirce and Steinbach, 1987, p. 8).

"NEO-LIBERAL COMMUNITARIANISM": COMMUNITY DEVELOPMENT TODAY

The community development industry in the 1990s and 2000s has progressed along much the same lines that had been established in the earlier periods. In the last decade the field has been dominated by various programmatic initiatives or trends focused on how to best go about "doing" community development. This has included discussions of "community-based assets," "consensus organizing," "social capital construction," and "community building," among others. Rather than discuss these initiatives individually, it is more useful to explain the perspectives and objectives that they all share.

First, they are unambiguously market-based in their larger goals and programmatic details. This has probably been made most explicit by Michael Porter through his Initiative for a Competitive Inner City, who has argued that, "a sustainable economic base can be created in inner cities only as it has been elsewhere: through private, for-profit initiatives, and investments based on economic self-interest and genuine competitive advantage" (Porter, 1997, p. 12). But Porter is far from alone in making these arguments, and the dominant understanding at this point is that for CDCs to be successful, not only must they adopt an explicitly entrepreneurial set of goals and practices, but they must also work with the corporate sector.

The second shared attribute is a promotion of non-confrontational forms of engagement and organizing. Community development is now a collaborative process, and the more conflictual ideals of black power, and neo-Alinsky organizing have been rejected. Michael Eichler, the president of the "Consensus Organizing Institute," described, "the essential attribute of consensus organizing: instead of taking power from those who have it, consensus organizers build relationships in which power is shared for mutual benefit . . . Cooperation, rather than confrontation became the modus operandi for solving a neighborhood problem" (Eichler, 1998). Within the current understanding of cooperation, there is almost contempt for past organizing efforts, and Grogan and Proscio state, "The community organizing and planning of that period (the 1960s) was soon squandered on divisive or extremist political tactics, including the in-your-face style of protest that Tom Wolfe famously dubbed, 'mau-mauing' " (Grogan and Proscio, 2000, p. 66). Low-income inner-city residents are now understood to have a shared set of interests with the larger society they exist within, and organizing and development should be structured accordingly. Unequal power relations are completely ignored in this framework.

While it might seem a bit paradoxical, given the neo-liberal market orientation described above, the current period in community development is also characterized by a powerful re-assertion of the idea of *community*, and a particular version of *communitarianism*. This communitarian framework is one which posits a belief that there are shared interests among individuals in a community, and thus community development should be about creating the social relationships which allow those mutual goals to be realized. This thus mirrors the consensus organizing, in that the assumption is of shared interests—the difference is one assumes it for relations between people in the community and the rest of the world and the other for relations between people within a community. There are two principal figures in this understanding of community. The first is John McKnight, who has argued for a framework of community development centered around "community-based assets" (Kretzmann and McKnight, 1993; McKnight, 1995). The second is Robert Putnam, whose work on social capital (Putnam, 2000) has become axiomatic in community development theory and practice. Both argue that relations within communities tend to be largely "win-win" relations, and both take that framework one step farther to assume that *individual* gains and interests in the community are synonymous with *collective*, or community, gains and interests. Both also assume that communities are functions of, and defined by, the attributes and relationships of people within them. Thus not only does this particular form of communitarianism fit with consensus or non-confrontational organizing, but it also fits with the neo-liberal, market-based perspectives and policies that govern community development activity.

Together these three perspectives, which dominate the theory and practice of community development, can best be described as a form of *neo-liberal communitarianism*. This neo-liberal communitarianism has, at its core, a belief that society is conflict-free, and it gets this from both halves of its theoretical framework. It also represents the fruition of the de-politicization of community development that came with its split from community organizing in the late 1960s. This de-politicization also needs to be understood as both a product, and producer, of their support from the public sector. The political logic of CDCs in American politics has therefore come full circle. The federal government, which initiated the movement for community development by sponsoring often radical political organizations working towards community control and empowerment, now supports CDCs exactly because they are no longer connected to any political movement. And the goals of CDCs have also come full circle. Initially conceived as vehicles that would use the market as a means to the end of community control and development, they have now become vehicles for the market, in which the goal of community control is not even an issue.

SNAPSHOTS FROM THE FIELD OF CONTEMPORARY COMMUNITY DEVELOPMENT

There are significant problems that come with the dominant framework of neo-liberal communitarianism. But rather than address those problems here, I will leave that to other contributors to this volume (see, in particular, Chapter 36 by Stoecker, and Chapter 37 by Fraser *et al.*). Instead, I will simply highlight two "moments" that occurred at the end of the 1990s as indicative of what community development has become and where it is going.

The first is an extended memo in *The Neighborworks Journal* (the journal of the NRC) by the senior vice-president of the Fannie Mae Foundation. In it he issued a call for "A New Paradigm for Community Reinvestment." The new paradigm called for greater collaboration between community developers and outside investors and businesses. It included a promotion of the idea of place-marketing in which community development projects could take on names such "The Woodlands," "Celebration" and

"Redwood Shores." He even stated, "some of these places could be treated as *urban blank slates*, where the development takes on an image the investors choose" (Carr, 1999, p. 21, emphasis added). In this new paradigm, the first role for government is to "assist private firms to *extract value from community assets*" (Carr, 1999, p. 22, emphasis added).

Finally, that summer I was at a meeting at the Urban Justice Center in New York planning a march from Washington, DC, to New York City as part of the now international Economic Human Rights Campaign. In the course of the discussion one of the issues that arose was contacting other local organizations who might be sympathetic to the march in order to solicit their support. One of the people in the room suggested that we should contact the Association of Neighborhood and Housing Development (ANHD). ANHD is the principal trade association for CDCs in New York City. The response from the roomful of 30 local community and political organizers to the mention of its name was a unanimous, "Who?"

REFERENCES

Benello, C.G. and D. Roussopoulos (eds.). 1971. *The Case for Participatory Democracy: Some Prospects for a Radical Society*. New York: Grossman Publishers.

Berndt, H.E. 1977. *New Rulers in the Ghetto: The Community Development Corporation and Urban Poverty*. Westport, CT: Greenwood Press.

Carmichael, S. and C.V. Hamilton. 1967. *Black Power*. New York: Vintage.

Carr, James. 1999. Community, Capital and Markets: A New Paradigm for Community Reinvestment. *The Neighborworks Journal*, Summer: 20–23.

Eichler, Michael. 1998. Look to the Future, Learn from the Past. *Shelterforce*. September/October.

Fainstein, S. 1987. Local Mobilization and Economic Discontent. In M.P. Smith and J. Feagin (eds.) *The Capitalist City*. Cambridge, MA: Blackwell.

Fulton, W. 1987. Off the Barricades, Into the Boardrooms. *Planning*. August: 11–15.

Grogan, Paul and Tony Proscio. 2000. *Comeback Cities*. New York: Westview Press.

Halpern, R. 1995. *Reuilding the Inner City: A History of Neighborhood Initiatives to Address Poverty in the United States*. New York: Columbia University Press.

Katznelson, Ira. 1981. *City Trenches: Urban Politics and the Patterning of Class in the United States*. Chicago, IL: University of Chicago Press.

Kelly, R.M. 1977. *Community Control of Economic Development*. New York: Praeger.

Kotler, M. 1969. *Neighborhood Government: The Local Foundations of Political Life*. Indianapolis, IN: Bobbs-Merrill Company.

Kotler, M. 1971. The Politics of Community Economic Development. *Law and Contemporary Problems*. 36: 3–12.

Kretzmann, J. and J. McKnight. 1993. *Building Communities from the Inside Out: A Path Toward Finding and Mobilizing a Community's Assets*. Chicago: ACTA Publications.

McKnight, John. 1995. *The Careless Society: Community and Its Counterfeits*. New York: Basic Books.

Pierce, N. and C. Steinbach. 1987. *Corrective Capitalism: The Rise of America's Community Development Corporations*. New York: Ford Foundation.

Porter, Michael. 1997. New Strategies for Inner-City Economic Development. *Economic Development Quarterly*. 11(1): 11–27.

Putnam, Robert. 2000. *Bowling Alone*. New York: Simon and Schuster.

Repo, Marjaleena. 1977. The Fallacy of "Community Control," in John Cowley, Adah Kaye, Marjorie Mayo and Mike Thompson (eds.) *Community or Class Struggle?* London: Stage 1.

Shipp, Sigmund. 1996. The Road Not Taken: Alternative Strategies for Black Economic Development in the United States. *Journal of Economic Issues*, 30(1): 79–95.

Social Policy. 1979. Organizing Neighborhoods: Special Issue. September/October.

Vidal, A. 1996. CDCs as Agents of Neighborhood Change: The State of the Art. In D. Keating, *et al.* (eds.). *Revitalizing Urban Neighborhoods*. Lawrence, KS: University of Kansas Press.

Wolch, J. 1990. *The Shadow State: Government and Voluntary Sector in Transition*. New York: The Foundation Center.

CHAPTER 4

Community Building

New (and old) lessons about the politics of problem-solving in America's cities

Xavier de Souza Briggs

INTRODUCTION

"Community building" is the popular label for a variety of efforts to organize and strengthen social connections and build common values that promote collective goals—literally, to build *more* community (an interim goal) as a way of achieving some set of desired tangible outcomes: safer neighborhoods, healthier children and families, preserved cultural traditions, economic growth, and more (Briggs 2003a; DeFilippis and Saegert, in this volume). In this brief chapter, I examine the emergence, meanings, and tensions of community building as a strain of contemporary social reform, with a focus on what I see as its dual agenda—changing political dynamics (empowerment) and changing social outcomes (in the global parlance, "development" or social progress). I will also identify some of the civic skills and institutional capacity that that dual agenda demands but often lacks.

While the term community building has traveled a bit across borders, it is especially popular in the U.S. and often includes at least an implicit critique of more traditional, expert-dominated, "top-down" approaches to meeting human services, health, education, housing, and other needs in cities, suburbs, and rural communities. In particular, community building became, in the 1990s, a way of distinguishing creative action, primarily at the local level, to better engage the citizen-clients affected by service delivery in key decisions and in the delivery itself and to create lasting connections (community) with a "capacity" value lasting beyond the immediate program or project. But community

builders face important dilemmas and barriers, some of which reflect age-old lessons about getting things done in changing democratic societies, most of all those wherein decision-making power and capacity to implement are decentralized and fragmented. For these reasons, I begin with a look at when and why community building emerged.

THE EMERGENCE OF COMMUNITY BUILDING

Studies of politics typically focus on conflict and power, for example, which interest groups shape the public agenda, how lawmakers and chief executives bargain over policy, and who wins particular decisions. Yet the shape of politics is also about norms that indicate *who* can act legitimately on matters of shared concern and *how* they should act, usually reflected in the roles that institutions, both public and private, are expected and allowed to play. Over the first half of the twentieth century, for example, systematic attempts to raise living standards or change social outcomes in the wealthy industrial nations—what James Scott (1998) has artfully termed "schemes to improve the human condition"—came to be dominated by relatively centralized government planning and bureaucratic delivery mechanisms. The development of professional fields such as city planning, public health, strategic management, and policy analysis (or "decision analysis") accompanied a rapid expansion in the scope and sophistication of government-fundedandgovernment-delivered services (Friedmann 1987).

In America, social movements produced some of this shift, but so did activists and investigative journalists who were not formally linked to larger movements. They exposed disparities—in the brutally competitive and unhealthy modern industrial city—and argued for bold reforms. The original hope, most evident in the work of social reformers in Europe and North America in the early decades of the twentieth century, was that by shifting action on social problems from *charity* to *public policy*, government could achieve both scale and efficiency in social welfare, leaving business to be the engine of growth.

But by the 1960s, and with some signs of alarm long before, the cracks in this design were all too clear: Some government programs were driven by values that reflected the priorities of particular interest groups (such as investors and financial institutions or empire-building public officials) or social groups (such as a dominant racial group) and not a broad societal consensus, let alone what observers worldwide refer to as a "pro-poor" or inclusionary agenda; centrally planned programs often came to reflect a bureaucratic focus on *proceduralism* (following official rules) rather than a commitment to *results* for clients; such "top-down" programs also lacked vital information or "local knowledge" (Scott 1998), where professionals failed to consult, or to do so in meaningful ways, with the communities they served (Arnstein 1969); as a corollary, big, rule-driven bureaucracies were generally not the best incubators of innovation; perverse incentives, though sometimes installed in the name of social equity, thwarted markets and private initiative rather than triggering or building on them; a focus on government as the exclusive guarantor of social welfare can inappropriately relieve business and the civic sector of responsibility and latitude; and, on the most basic level (that of getting results), by failing to win the trust and cooperation of the other, nongovernmental sectors of society, top-down public programs often failed to bring the needed actions to bear on problems that require "coproduction," i.e. the capable and coordinated action of more than one player or sector (Briggs 2003c). The vital importance of coproduction has become especially apparent in fields such as community health, since successful initiatives so often depend on the active support of community opinion leaders, support networks, and of course clients (patients) themselves (Winkler 1999), but the same imperative applies in public safety, education, economic development, and other domains as well, which require local flexibility and the blending of many kinds of knowledge and tangible resources.

The social movements that fed modern community development in America reacted, in part, to the shortcomings of public planning and policymaking outlined above, not merely to a lack of resources or to the seriousness of social problems themselves (Fainstein and Hirst 1995; Halpern 1995). A generation later, in the late 1980s and early 1990s, with government downsizing, economic inequality widening, and the role of business and nonprofits expanding in many realms, a new wave of criticism and reflection evolved—once again emphasizing political influence (the issue of who shapes policy), to be sure, but also targeted at the fragmented and incomplete approaches to *implementing* social interventions (the issue of who acts on target problems and how). The tendency of many social initiatives to focus on need and pathology, rather than building on strengths and assets, has helped to shape the latest chapter of critique and reform hopes (Kretzmann and McKnight 1993), and so has the aim of building more indigenous "community capacity" (Chaskin *et al.* 2001), including useful social connections or "social capital" (Briggs 1997, 2004; Briggs and Mueller 1997; Hyman, in this volume; Putnam 1993, 2000; Rohe 2004; Vidal 2004; Warren, Saegert and Thompson 2001; Woolcock and Narayan 2000). Community building arose in this specific context, therefore, but must also be understood as a contemporary variation on older criticisms of policy and politics, as outlined above. Like older variants of social reform, moreover, community building faces some important dilemmas.

DILEMMAS AND LESSONS

When community building emerged in common usage in the 1990s, it was defined by the National Community Building Network and other key institutions as an *alternative* to well-established but often disappointing approaches toward the same ends—safer streets, children ready to learn in school, healthier families, a cleaner environment, and more. Advocates of community building held that stakeholders should be engaged in decisions that matter and often in improving delivery itself. Formal social programs and more informal civic "initiatives" would benefit from insider knowledge not held by experts, and greater citizen trust would improve implementation as well as outcomes. A respect for local places and the assets in target communities would encourage appropriate respect and a pragmatic building on strength, in place of the perpetually needs-driven logic that made the beneficiaries of social problem-solving into problem-holding clients who needed "fixing" (Stone 1995; Walsh 1997).

But after a decade or more, it seems clear that these hopes have met with serious institutional barriers and posed more dilemmas than advocates may have realized. Three key dilemmas, which have already shaped reactions by public and private funders and others to these arguments, and which will help define the future of the community building ideal, are about *efficiency* (the scale and coordination of problem-solving efforts), *power* (who decides what, how the deciding gets done), and *performance and accountability* (how success and failure are defined and measured, who is held responsible for what).

First, in developing more bottom-up, custom-crafted efforts, today's community builders have struggled to achieve the scale and level of coordination that large, modern bureaucracies were invented to enable. Some of the scale problem is a function of insufficient monetary and other resources, but it is also about the labor intensiveness of working out new, more user- or customer-friendly solutions to persistent, large-scale problems, such as school failure, illiteracy, urban pollu-

tion, and more. Skills and leadership ability are one major issue here: If one cannot clone the "walk-on-water" school principal or human services manager from one small-scale intervention to the next, then what?

A second dilemma is about *power and participation*, more specially about finding appropriate levels and forms of participation by citizen clients and other stakeholders in the governance and delivery of social programs, i.e., engagement that: does not lead to process paralysis (where progress is stalled), allows more than the show of participation (where decisions have already been made), and promotes transparency and accountability (rather than a new "tyranny from below," by manipulators). That is, community building efforts struggle with the tensions inherent in developing and using power legitimately—tensions familiar and pervasive in democratic societies, such as the U.S. and key emerging democracies in the developing world, wherein civic action must often span multiple sectors and levels of authority (Briggs 2003b; Cooke and Kothari 2001; Fung 2004; Kadushin *et al.* 2005; Stone 2001).

Robert Chaskin (2005) has argued, for example, that local community building initiatives frequently struggle with a tension between "democracy" and "bureaucracy," a contrast that echoes the argument above that community building reflects an often unexamined dual agenda—empowering on one hand and reliably producing results (ideally, on time and on budget) on the other. Sometimes, these agendas reinforce each other, but sometimes they conflict. For this reason, as a strain of social reform, community building calls for more durable and varied forms of "civic capacity" (Stone 2001) across multiple levels of local decision-making, from that of informal community groups and community-based nonprofit boards to citywide philanthropies, business-civic groups, local government, and more.

Third and finally, as to how *performance and accountability* are defined and tracked, community building targets intermediate outcomes of connectedness, trust, and other features of social life that can be challenging to measure, as well as social outcomes that are often difficult to change significantly— e.g., a citywide high school graduation rate, employment rates among disadvantaged youth, etc. Front-line practitioners, as well as funders, evaluators, political authorities, and others debate how quickly community building efforts should be expected to produce the end outcomes (social "products") versus the intermediate achievements (presumably better processes and community capacity; Chaskin *et al.* 2001). And complex processes of chain and effect often make the tracking of these efforts, not to mention the task of attributing their effects, difficult indeed (Connell, Kubisch, and Schorr 1995).

SUMMARY AND PROSPECTS

Despite all these challenges, community building is more than a fad or reform buzzword. It reflects our fascination with community and our need to make it a more central, vital force in a rapidly changing world. It also reflects deep misgivings about expert-led "solutions" to social problems that produced neither satisfactory outcomes (tangible results) nor collective capacity to respond to our shared problems in ways that reflect democratic values. But to advance the community building agenda, advocates for change will need to acknowledge the dual agenda and the ways in which the parts compete and introduce classic tensions. Civic skills such as negotiation and dispute resolution, intermediary organizations that act to limit fragmentation and build bridges of trust, and institutional recipes that allow for some shared decision-making as well as coordination, enforcement of standards, and other keys to effectively producing results on social problems—these are some of the essentials. They are important frontiers for practice as well as research and training.

References

Arnstein, Sherry. "A Ladder of Citizen Participation." *Journal of the American Institute of Planners* 35(1969): 216–224.

Briggs, Xavier de Souza. "Social Capital and the Cities: Advice to Change Agents." *National Civic Review* 86(1997): 111–117.

Briggs, Xavier de Souza. "Community Building." In *Encyclopedia of Community: From the Village to the Virtual World*, edited by Karen Christensen and David Levinson. Thousand Oaks, CA: Sage Publications, 2003a.

Briggs, Xavier de Souza. *Planning Together: How (and How Not) to Engage Stakeholders in Charting a Course.* The Community Problem-Solving Project @ MIT. [World Wide Web page www.community-problem-solving.net]. Cambridge, MA: Massachusetts Institute of Technology, 2003b.

Briggs, Xavier de Souza. *Perfect Fit or Shotgun Marriage?: The Power and Pitfalls in Partnerships.* The Community Problem-Solving Project @ MIT. [World Wide Web page www.community-problem-solving.net]. Cambridge, MA: Massachusetts Institute of Technology, 2003c.

Briggs, Xavier de Souza. "Social Capital: Easy Beauty or Meaningful Resource?" *Journal of the American Planning Association* 70(2004): 151–158.

Briggs, Xavier de Souza and Elizabeth Mueller with Mercer Sullivan. *From Neighborhood to Community: Evidence on the Social Effects of Community Development.* New York: Community Development Research Center, 1997.

Chaskin, Robert J. "Democracy and Bureaucracy in a Community Planning Process." *Journal of Planning Education and Research* 24(2005): 408–419.

Chaskin, Robert J., Prudence Brown, Sudhir Venkatesh and Avis Vidal. *Building Community Capacity.* New York: Aldine de Gruyter, 2001.

Connell, James, Anne Kubisch, and Lisbeth Schorr. *New Approaches to Evaluating Community Initiatives: Concepts, Methods, and Contexts.* New York: The Aspen Institute, 1995.

Cooke, Bill and Uma Kothari, eds. *Participation: The New Tyranny.* London: Zed, 2001.

Fainstein, Susan S. and Clifford Hirst. "Urban Social Movements." In *Theories of Urban Politics*, edited by D. Judge, G. Stoker, and H. Wolman. Thousand Oaks, CA: Sage, 1995.

Friedmann, John. *Planning in the Public Domain: From Knowledge to Action.* Princeton, NJ: Princeton University Press, 1987.

Fung, Archon. *Empowered Participation.* Princeton, NJ: Princeton University Press, 2004.

Halpern, Robert. *Rebuilding the Inner City: The History of Neighborhood Initiatives to Address Poverty in the United States.* New York: Columbia University Press, 1995.

Kadushin, Charles, Mathew Lindholm, Dan Ryan, Archie Brodsky, and Leonard Saxe. "Why Is it so Difficult to Form Effective Community Coalitions?" *City & Community* 4(2005): 255–275.

Kingsley, G. Thomas and James O. Gibson. *Community building: Coming of Age.* Washington, DC: The Urban Institute, 1997.

Kretzmann, Jody and John McKnight. *Building Communities from the Inside Out: A Path Toward Finding and Mobilizing Community Assets.* Evanston, IL: Institute for Policy Research, Northwestern University, 1993.

Putnam, Robert. *Making Democracy Work: Civic Traditions in Modern Italy*. Princeton, NJ: Princeton University Press, 1993.

Putnam, Robert. *Bowling Alone: The Collapse and Revival of American Community*. New York: Simon & Schuster, 2000.

Rohe, William. "Building Social Capital through Community Development." *Journal of the American Planning Association* 70(2004): 158–164.

Scott, James. *Seeing Like a State: Why Certain Schemes to Improve the Human Condition Have Failed*. New Haven, CT: Yale University Press, 1998.

Stone, Clarence. "Civic Capacity and Urban Education." *Urban Affairs Review* 36(2001): 595–619.

Stone, Rebecca. *Core Issues in Comprehensive Community Initiatives*. Chicago: Chapin Hall Center for Children at the University of Chicago, 1995.

Vidal, Avis. "Building Social Capital to Promote Community Equity." *Journal of the American Planning Association* 70(2004): 164–168.

Walsh, Joan. *Stories of Renewal: Community Building in America*. New York: The Rockefeller Foundation, 1997.

Warren, Mark, Susan Saegert, and J. Phillip Thompson. "The Role of Social Capital in Combating Poverty." In *Social Capital and Poor Communities*, edited by S. Saegert, J.P. Thompson, and M. Warren. New York: Russell Sage, 2001.

Winkler, Meredith, ed. *Community Organizing and Community Building for Health*. New Brunswick, NJ: Rutgers University Press, 1999.

Woolcock, Michael and Deepa Narayan. "Social Capital: Its Significance for Development Theory, Research, and Policy." *World Bank Research Observer* 15(2000): 225–249.

PART II

Community Development Institutions and Practice

CHAPTER 5

Introduction to Part II

James DeFilippis and Susan Saegert

This section of the book covers the breadth of the institutions and practices of community development in the United States. The chapters share several characteristics that we think are important for this book. First, there are no case studies here. All the chapters are discussions of general organizational forms or kinds of community development practice. This was a conscious choice, because the aim of this section is to present the broad universe of community development. Case studies can be useful, in terms of appreciating the complexity and messiness of practice. But they can also be limiting, in terms of their ability to generate generalizable knowledge—and it was this form of knowledge that we are valuing for this section of the book.

Second, none of the chapters are celebratory. That is, none of them celebrate community development, and the kinds of organizations they are discussing. Some purposefully foreground the questions of difficulties in the field, while others include discussions of the problems involved in community development in their general descriptions and analyses of the field. But none of the articles are written in promotion of community development. Too often literature in this field is written by those interested in singing its praises. But we find this troubling for two reasons. The first is that fully understanding community development means being able to appreciate the difficulties and contradictions in the field. Glossing over difficulties only renders difficulties more troublesome when they arise. The second is that the best way to "promote" community development is to present it in such a way

as to have its potential and limits most clearly understood. Community development efforts do not benefit from having the expectations of them raised by those who celebrate them—in fact, the opposite is more likely true, as they suffer from being unable to meet expectations that are unrealistically high.

Part II begins with two chapters on community development corporations (CDCs) which are the most important organizational form taken by community development efforts. CDCs, as shown in Chapter 3, have grown dramatically in their numbers, size and activities since the early 1980s. These CDCs are justifiably best known for their production of affordable housing. But CDCs do more than just construct housing, and instead engage in a range of activities from small business development, to workforce training, to social service provision. This range is thoroughly described by Glickman and Sevron in Chapter 6. But the growth of CDCs has not occurred without a whole set of problems and difficulties. CDCs can, and sometimes do, fail. The question of what can be learned from these experiences is taken up by Rohe, Bratt, and Biswas in Chapter 7, so the problems can be avoided or mitigated elsewhere and in future practice. Given the importance of housing to communities, and community development work, the book devotes an extended chapter (by Chapter 8 Stone) to the different forms in which social or not-for-profit ownership of housing can, and does, occur in the United States.

From there, Part II shifts gears to focus on issues of finance capital in community development. In general, there are two different, but related, ways in which finance capital can be brought into efforts for community development. The first is through direct ownership by community development financial institutions (CDFIs). CDFIs take several different forms, from large banks to very small micro-enterprise lenders, and these are discussed in Chapter 9 by Benjamin, Rubin, and Zielenbach. The second is through utilizing the Community Reinvestment Act (CRA) to get for-profit banks to invest in community development. The CRA, its uses, and the politics behind it, are the subjects covered in Chapter 10 by Squires. The issue of finance capital in community development logically brings up the issues and practices involved in community economic development (CED). CED has become increasingly important in the past 20 years, and the various types of practices, and the assumptions that inform them, are the topic of Chapter 11 by Wiewel, Teitz, and Giloth.

The next two chapters (Chapters 12 and 13) foreground issues of service provision in community development. As the public sector has increasingly contracted out the provision of services to people in American cities, the role of community-based not-for-profits has correspondingly increased. The first of these two chapters, by Levanthal, Brooks-Gunn, and Kamerman, focuses on social service provision to families and children, and the importance of *community* in the outcomes that come from their provision and consumption. The second, by Cordero-Guzmán and Quiroz-Becerra, addresses the practices of immigrant community-based organizations. As immigrants transform American cities, and are often in neighborhoods in which community development is needed and/or occurring, it is increasingly important that discussions and analyses of community development understand the particular needs and interests of immigrants.

The cluster of chapters that follow (Chapters 14–17) highlight a set of different institutional actors or partners in community development efforts. The first, by Foley, McCarthy, and Chaves, addresses the often vital role of religious institutions in community development. Faith-based institutions have long played a central role in American civic life—particularly at the local level—and this is certainly true today. This is followed by a discussion of the roles of local governments in community development in Chapter 15 by Rich, Giles and Stern. Emphasis is placed here on the relationships between local governments and community organizations, and the extent to which those relations are collaborative and productive (and the extent to which they are not). Finally, the roles of foundations are analyzed by Brown, Chaskin, Hamilton, and Richman in Chapter 16, as they ask the vital question of how foundations can be more productive and supportive in their work with community development organizations.

Despite the urban focus of the book, and much of the community development field more generally, we would be remiss if we did not include a chapter that explicitly foregrounds the particular concerns, issues, and practices of community development in rural areas. Collins and Merrett's Chapter 17 presents the perspective of community development in rural contexts. It argues for both recognizing the importance of rural communities and understanding how the issues involved in development are different in rural communities than they are in urban ones.

The organization of the chapters into discrete groups is not meant to imply that community-based efforts can be so neatly divided. In practice, different organizational forms come together—for instance: immigrant CBOs often build housing; and larger organizations have been known to contain both a CDC and CDFI. In fact, in many places, where the community development field is firmly entrenched, there can emerge a "community development industry system" (Frisch and Servon, 2006; Yin, 1998), in which there is a whole inter-locking network or web of organizations, intermediaries, churches and government agencies involved in community development. Thus the pieces of the field, represented as chapters here, need to be understood as inter-connected rather than distinct, in both analysis and practice.

REFERENCES

Frisch, M. and L. Servon (2006) "CDCs and the Changing Context for Urban Community Development: A Review of the Field and the Environment," *Community Development: Journal of the Community Development Society* 37(4): 88–107.

Yin, J. (1998) "The Community Development Industry System: A Case Study of Politics and Institutions in Cleveland, 1967–1997," *Journal of Urban Affairs* 20(2): 137–157.

CHAPTER 6

More than Bricks and Sticks

Five components of community development corporation capacity

Norman J. Glickman and Lisa J. Servon

INTRODUCTION

The extent to which CDCs perform their tasks successfully is known as *capacity*. Although CDCs and funders stress the importance of capacity, it remains imprecisely defined. The ambiguity results in confusion over what CDCs "do" and how they do it. Capacity must be delineated more specifically before the term can be useful to CDCs, funders, policy makers, and the general public.

CDCs wrestle with systemic, structural problems in the economies of cities. Quite clearly, most long-term economic trends are beyond the control of neighborhood groups. This makes their jobs especially daunting. Intermediaries have been created as vehicles to help CDCs deal with this array of problems. Several funders have established community development partnerships (CDPs) and collaboratives—intermediaries that operate at the local level. These CDPs bring together the human and financial resources of community-based organizations, national and local foundations, for-profit corporations, and governments to help rebuild low-income neighborhoods. In this chapter, we look at the activities CDCs and CDPs undertake to build the capacity of CDCs. We present a framework that operationalizes notions of capacity into five components. We believe that this more concrete way of thinking about capacity will be particularly useful to practitioners, funders, and policy makers.

DEFINING CAPACITY

The literature on capacity is uneven. The term is often defined narrowly, usually in terms of housing production and economic development. For example, many practitioners hold that a CDC that builds 100 units of housing a year has more capacity than one that builds 20. However, this definition oversimplifies a complex concept and process; the result is an understatement of the capacity of CDCs. New research highlights how capacity extends beyond housing production. An overemphasis on production distracts from the image of community building as a social, not merely a physical, process (Rubin, 1994). In order to be useful, capacity must be defined both more broadly, to take account of the wide array of CDC activities, and more specifically, to include the details of CDCs' work to rebuild poor communities. There is no simple or unified definition of capacity, and we believe working toward one would be an exercise in futility. We have therefore divided the definition of capacity into five major components: resource, organizational, network, programmatic, and political. Examining the separate elements makes the concept as a whole more manageable.

The following sections treat the components of capacity separately in order to illustrate what CDCs need and what strategies they implement in order to build capacity. We recognize, however, that this is overly simple: changes that affect one com-

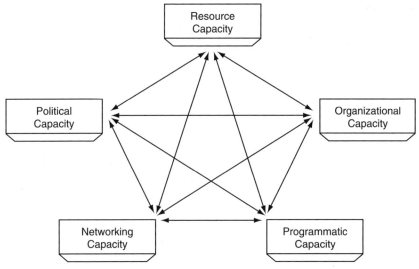

Figure 6.1 Interaction among capacity components

ponent of capacity directly reverberate to the other components. For example, a funder's decision to stop supporting a CDC affects its resource capacity directly, but it also may indirectly diminish the CDC's programmatic and organizational capacity. Figure 6.1 illustrates these interaction effects as a pentagon of forces at work. The specific ways in which changes in one component of capacity affect the other components vary from one CDC to another, depending on the particular context in which each operates.

One other critical aspect of capacity cuts across all five components—flexibility. Flexibility has two sides: responsiveness and resiliency. Responsiveness refers to a CDC's ability to change focus and direction in response to shifts in the environment in which it works. Resilience refers to a CDC's ability to rebound from setbacks and continue the pursuit of its mission even when the environment in which it works is uncooperative. A resilient CDC has staying power.

RESOURCE CAPACITY

The ability to increase, manage, and sustain funding is central to a CDC's ability to build capacity: it is often the foundation for capacity building in the other components we have identified. Resource capacity includes raising funds, managing them, and deploying them appropriately. Table 6.1 documents these aspects of resource capacity and shows how each relates to the needs and strategies of CDCs.

Long-term Operating Support
Healthy CDCs require a sufficiently stable funding environment to initiate operations and expand them over time. Vidal (1992, 12) found that "the single most important constraint on the growth of CDC activity is the need for additional capital," with one of the three most necessary types of capital being general operating support. There are several strategies that CDCs and partnerships pursue to help raise funds in this area.

One is obtaining multiyear operating support for the CDCs' work. Multiyear support enables CDCs to formulate and implement long-term planning (McGrath 1995; Vidal 1992). Ford- and LISC-sponsored operating support programs (OSPs) are good examples of this. OSPs typically commit to three or more years of technical and financial assistance for CDCs, filling a critical gap in CDC support. Long-term support also frees the CDCs to plan and execute programs without having to worry about meeting monthly payrolls and constantly chasing other funds.

Funding agencies, public and private, often designate the use of funds toward the program side, leaving a much smaller pool of

Table 6.1 Resource capacity

Capacity-building needs	Capacity-building strategies	Effects on CDCs	Potential limits and problems
Long-term operating support	Devote major effort to securing flexible, multiyear support	Capacities in all areas of activity increased	
	Allocate fund-raising efforts between support for operating costs and program costs		
Resources for stabilization and expansion	Attract and maintain multiple funders	Funding diversified	Possible dilution of CDC mission; CDC could grow too quickly
	Attract multiyear support	Enhanced ability to leverage additional funds	Patchwork financing difficult to manage
	Allocate sufficient staff hours to researching and pursuing new funding sources	New funding sources identified, solicited, and possibly attracted	
Development capital	Obtain funds from public sector		Funding declining in real terms
	Raise funds through low-income housing tax credits		Technically difficult procedure
	Obtain funds from national foundations	Tap pool of nonprofit funds	
	Charge development and other fees	Able to plow funds back into other programs and reinvest in additional housing	Funds not available until projects are complete
	Develop mixed-income/mixed-use projects to generate fees		Simultaneous challenge to keep rents low and need for fee income; Convincing public finance entities/lenders to allow nonprofits to charge development fees comparable to those charged by market developers
Access to funders	Train development staff in grant-writing techniques	Up-to-date knowledge may increase possibility to build resources	
	Advocate to funders regarding the importance of long-run operating support for CDCs	Long-run sustainability established; additional funding/support received	This is often a political exercise as well as a resource capacity issue
	Create and participate in networking opportunities, conferences, social events, etc.	CDCs better able to solicit funding from more sources	
	Obtain joint funding with other CDCs to collaborate on projects	Economies of scale achieved	Poor performance by one partner may adversely affect other partners
	Initiate and participate in matching grant programs		
	Establish arrangements for sharing space, labor, and technical assistance	Provide CDCs with access to expertise, funding, labor, and information	
Balanced portfolio risk	Diversify project types to reduce dependence on single categories of housing production	CDCs less vulnerable to market forces that may adversely affect their portfolios	CDCs tied to low-income communities, making locational diversification difficult to achieve

funds for operating needs. Successful CDCs put sufficient effort into securing these scarcer resources.

Resources for Stabilization and Expansion

As CDCs grow, they require resources for the stabilization and expansion of their activities. This requires broadening and deepening their funding base. The funding environment for CDCs can be erratic, and successful CDCs cannot afford to rely heavily on one or two funders without agreements of long-term support. Reliance on multiple funders can also lessen the effect of changes in the funding environment and increase a CDC's autonomy (Vidal 1992, 56). At the same time, however, multiple backers may also place conflicting demands on CDCs, and patchwork fundraising can be complex and tedious. Inconsistent and multiple reporting requirements by different sources also mean time-draining work for CDCs. In addition, CDCs that pursue support from multiple sources run the risk of spreading themselves too thin. Finally, embryonic CDCs sometimes accept more funds than they can manage; CDCs that grow too quickly may be unable to support that growth over the long term.

Development Capital

Money for projects typically comes from several sources, including the federal government (e.g. CDBG, HOME), intermediaries (for predevelopment), some CDPs, and some state and local programs. For affordable rental housing, CDCs engage in the technically difficult process of structuring low-income housing tax credits (LIHTC), which requires lawyers and financial experts. CDCs often receive development and management fees for their projects and services to help pay for their up-front costs in development projects and for the ongoing management. CDCs also negotiate conventional and special financing arrangements with financial institutions for construction and permanent mortgages.

It is generally more difficult for CDCs to obtain capital for economic development than for housing. CDBG funds are more limited, but other federal grants from the Office of Community Services (OCS) or intermediaries may provide predevelopment funding.

Access to Funders

One way for CDCs to obtain resources is to train development staff in effective grant-writing techniques. In addition, partnerships and CDCs may initiate matching grant programs with other funders. Matching grant programs can greatly expand a CDC's funding base. Also, some partnerships encourage the CDCs they work with to collaborate on projects. Collaboration has become increasingly necessary as funding decreases and resources are spread thin. Linking up with other CDCs both expands what community groups can accomplish and broadens the range of funders to which a CDC has access. However, turf issues remain thorny and a poor performance by one partner can adversely affect other partners.

CDCs have the most difficulty getting unrestricted risk capital that allows them to act quickly on development opportunities. Some CDCs have positive fund balances, and have been able to fund initial investment in new projects without needing to apply to external sources for risk financing. The majority of CDCs, however, are too lean to support a cushion.

Balanced Portfolio Risk

CDCs try to balance their portfolio risk by diversifying by project and type to reduce dependence on a single market. However, CDCs are limited geographically in their ability to diversify because of the neighborhoods they target.

Interaction Among the Components

Resource capacity is clearly connected to the other components in critical ways. Sufficient resources, for example, enable a CDC to build organizational capacity by hiring staff with necessary skills, compensating them appropriately and continuing to train them. Resource capacity also abets programmatic capacity by giving CDCs the freedom to run programs that meet community members' needs. Finally, a CDC with resources can command political power.

ORGANIZATIONAL CAPACITY

Organizational capacity comprises the depth, skills, and experience of board and staff members (Table 6.2). Without the ability to coordinate and work through problems strategically, CDCs work inefficiently, while increased organizational capacity allows a CDC to get more from its resources. Scarce resources and extensive needs mandate that CDCs strive continuously to perform at maximum efficiency. Ongoing skill development is therefore essential. Because funding is increasingly based on performance, good organization is critical.

Effective Executive Director

Leadership by the executive director is central to organizational capacity (Kelly 1977; McGrath 1995). CDC leadership requires vision and a blend of interdisciplinary skills that include entrepreneurship, talent in negotiations, and aptitudes for communication, development, finance, public relations, and management. Executive ability at the top of the organization is crucial to success and succession of leadership is difficult. Because of low salaries and benefits, CDCs are extremely vulnerable to sudden losses of key people, but continuity of leadership is closely linked to a CDC's goal attainment. To bolster this leadership and maximize the organization's efficiency, CDCs try to create clearly defined objectives and to divide responsibility among the board, executive director, and staff.

Competent and Stable Staff

In addition to a competent executive director, the rest of the staff must be of appropriate size, talent, and structure. To build a competent organization requires staff training and, sometimes, the employment of outside consultants. However, CDCs face large barriers to gaining access to adequate training, including lack of funds and time for it.

Long hours, low pay, and inadequate fringe benefits contribute to a high burnout and turnover among CDC staff. The effort to continually recruit, orient, and train new people takes away from a CDC's ability to meet its goals and maintain a stable organization. CDCs try to compensate employees with competitive salaries, benefits, and pensions, but small budgets make it difficult for many CDCs to hire and retain staff (Vidal 1992). A lack of appropriately skilled applicants may also hinder CDCs. Many CDCs, therefore, hire consultants for specialized functions in lieu of permanent staff. Although this gives CDCs more flexibility, outsiders seldom have the knowledge of the community or the organization that permanent employees have.

Effective Fiscal Management

While sound fiscal management is important in any kind of organization, it is particularly important for nonprofit organizations that often run on shoestring budgets (Nye and Glickman 1996). In order to deploy their dollars most effectively, CDCs allocate sufficient staff hours to accounting and budget management. Emergent CDCs may fill this need with non-specialists and part-time consultants. CDCs and CDPs increasingly recognize the value of management information systems (MIS) and are building capacity in this area.

Board Development and Leadership

Leadership is important on a CDC's board, as the board carries the CDC's long-range vision for the neighborhood and provides the continuity for the organization. Board members are chosen for a variety of reasons: They are recognized community leaders and live in the neighborhood; they have specialized talents (architects, lawyers, bankers, etc.); or they have good contacts with funders and businesses. An effective board helps create a clear vision of the CDC's future, aids the CDC's strategic planning, and participates in determining how the nonprofit is managed. There is sometimes tension, however, between board members and CDC staff. Staffers may feel that board members interfere with their duties to run the organization on a day-to-day basis, or board members may feel that they are being ignored by staff and are not given room to play their fiduciary roles.

Table 6.2 Organizational capacity

Capacity-building needs	Capacity-building strategies	Effects on CDCs	Potential limits and problems
Effective executive director (ED)	Hire person with range of skills necessary to lead internally and advocate on behalf of organization externally		
	Ensure that ED maintains good relations with board, community, and political figures		
Competent and stable staff	Ensure that ED hires competent staff to support all aspects of the organization	Managed growth	
	Train key employees		
	Employ technical consultants when necessary		Technicians may lack a personal history in community work
	Compensate (salaries, benefits, and pensions) employees commensurate with skills, experience, and commitment to CDC	Employee turnover lowered	Higher salaries are perceived as contrary to the mission of serving very low income people
Effective fiscal management	Allocate staff hours to accounting, budget management, and fiscal planning		
	Train relevant staff using up-to-date fiscal management skills		
	Employ management information systems and train CDCs to use them	Increased efficiency and effectiveness	
Board development and leadership	Select board with diverse talents and connections		
	Recruit board members with expertise and external contacts	Increased resources and skills	
	Create vision with clearly articulated objectives	Shared vision obtained	
Managed growth	Review organizational performance regularly		
	Assess operational needs, sometimes change programs		
Project management	Monitor time and cost efficiencies of construction		
	Use management information systems to control costs and ensure quality and affordability of projects		
	Contract out to professional property managers		
	Plan strategically	Reflexive thinking encouraged	
Evaluation	Build evaluation into funding requests		
	Participate in funder's evaluation design	Ensure that data gathered are appropriate	

Managed Growth

Strategic planning encourages CDCs to think reflectively and plan for the long term. The role of local partnerships in this process is often critical because CDCs rarely have the time or resources to set aside for strategic planning, and so CDPs often build it into their relationships with CDCs. Partnerships also use the goals set by the strategic plans to judge the progress of CDCs.

The uncertain funding environment coupled with the changing nature of community needs makes managing growth a difficult task for CDCs. Embryonic CDCs face a steep learning curve with respect to organizational capacity. Emerging CDCs are better able to manage growth and create a structure that allows for more specialization of staff, and this stage may involve shifting to a more hierarchical structure, a difficult step for organizations built on a consensual foundation. Mature CDCs find ways to introduce change and allow for reflection on their work.

Project Management

Effective project management is another important aspect of organizational capacity. To manage projects effectively, CDCs must try to continuously monitor time and cost efficiencies of construction. By keeping track of these elements, a CDC tries to control costs to ensure the quality and affordability of its projects. CDCs sometimes contract out to professional property managers when appropriate and when funding permits. Most CDCs, especially newer organizations, usually have to make do with in-house expertise because they cannot afford consultants.

Evaluation

In order to plan for the future, CDCs draw on the knowledge of what they have—and have not—done well in the past. CDCs therefore try to build evaluation into their funding requests. To avoid conflicts, CDCs and partnerships need to work together in evaluation design. Evaluations designed solely by the funder may fail to capture CDCs' accomplishments, and miss not easily measured outcomes. There is also a widespread feeling in the field, though rarely discussed in print, that CDCs often exaggerate their successes in evaluations that have consequences for their funding.

Interaction Among the Components

Increasing organizational capacity helps CDCs build capacity among the other components as well. It enables CDCs to devote sufficient time to fund-raising, which pays off in the form of increased resource capacity. Also, a CDC that is managed and staffed well will be better able to programmatically offer the services that the community requires. Finally, a CDC with sufficient organizational capacity will help build political capacity because it will likely be better connected to the local political system, and more effectively create linkages with other organizations.

PROGRAMMATIC CAPACITY

CDCs engage in a wide variety of programs, including building and managing housing, economic development, family services, crime fighting, and job training. The typical CDC is active in three program areas: (1) housing; (2) either commercial real estate development or business enterprise development; and (3) one noneconomic development program area, typically some type of social service or advocacy work. Capacity building in these diverse fields requires great organizational dexterity, and successful CDCs take on new programs only after extensive strategic planning and careful deliberation.

Types of programmatic capacity building differ for CDCs at different stages of development. For instance, embryonic CDCs usually focus on a single activity—often housing—so as not to become stretched too thin too quickly. Often the initial activity is tied closely to the availability of funds—a link that continues throughout the life of the CDC. New CDCs try to obtain training in all areas of their chosen activity and begin to network with other organizations and institutions that can help them become established. Emerging CDCs often begin to expand to new program areas as new needs arise—and as funding becomes available.

Mature CDCs try to recognize and attend to new community needs. The first part of this section focuses on skills related to specific program areas: housing, commercial development, economic development, and organizing. The second part deals with aspects of programmatic capacity that apply to all CDCs regardless of their programmatic agenda (Table 6.3).

Skills Related to Housing
Housing continues to be the dominant focus of CDCs. In order to build housing efficiently, most CDCs work to develop skills and engage in training, in such diverse areas as predevelopment planning, site selection and feasibility analysis, market analysis, housing finance, marketing, construction management, permitting and zoning, property management, and government program regulations—in addition to training construction workers. As CDCs acquire larger portfolios of housing, they seek training in asset management for the long-term needs of their projects.

Skills Related to Commercial Development
Commercial development consists of building and rehabilitating structures for nonresidential use. Many of the skills required for building and managing housing are transferable to commercial development, making it a logical step for CDCs wishing to expand. However, commercial development entails substantially greater risks. Close attention to market analysis and feasibility, and businesses' needs for facilities, is critical. On the positive side, most of the activities associated with commercial real estate development "have relatively low start-up costs and are reasonably inexpensive ways to provide visible benefits to residents" (Vidal 1992, 71). CDCs also engage in commercial development because it indirectly helps to fulfill economic development goals, such as providing jobs, needed goods and services, and luring resources into target neighborhoods.

Skills Related to Economic Development
CDCs, whose missions include economic development, connect their constituents to the local and regional economies. They do this in several ways. First, CDCs help match people with jobs by providing them with, or referring them to, appropriate training programs. Second, CDCs make linkages to local businesses and negotiate employment agreements to ensure that residents will have access to jobs in the community and regionally. Third, community organizations educate constituents about the forces driving unemployment and low wages, which can give residents the motivation they need to organize and fight those forces.

CDCs also foster the creation, stabilization, and expansion of small businesses within the community (Bendick and Eagan 1991) by providing training and technical assistance for business development. This strategy has the potential for job creation and for keeping money circulating in target communities (Servon 1998). To this end, some CDCs have begun to experiment with microenterprise and alternative financial institutions. Although these strategies operate on a much smaller scale than traditional economic development strategies, they provide participants with critical skills ranging from economic literacy to effective time management (Servon 1997).

Skills Related to Organizing
Many CDCs carry out community organizing, and organizing is a natural adjunct to CDCs' primary activities because it builds support for them. Organizing, however, requires its own set of skills and resources. Some CDCs become affiliated with local organizers, such as the Industrial Areas Foundation; others hire an organizer to do this work in their community. One potential downside to community organizing, however, is that CDCs may have difficulty balancing the multiple interests that surface as a result. For example, organized tenants may demand better housing conditions than the CDC is able to afford with the available housing funding. In addition, CDPs sometimes hesitate to dedicate resources to it because of concern that organizing is too "political" and the results are difficult to measure. Finally, organizing can alienate potential partners in city hall and elsewhere. On the other hand, effective organizing can

Table 6.3 Programmatic capacity

Type of capacity	Capacity-building needs	Capacity-building strategies	Effects on CDCs	Potential limits and problems
Skills related to specific program areas	Skills related to housing	Provide training and technical assistance in all skill areas	Increased production skills	
		Do predevelopment planning	Better understanding of the production process; costs kept down	
		Do site selection, market and feasibility analysis		
		Gain better understanding of housing finance, marketing, and program regulation		
		Strengthen property management skills		
	Skills related to commercial development	Develop same construction and management skills for housing	Fulfill other community needs	
		Develop retail or office properties		
	Skills related to economic development	Provide training and technical assistance for entrepreneurial and business development		
		Participate in public and private economic development projects	Private funds leveraged; expertise from for-profit firms gained	
		Conduct employment training and or referrals	Increased skills of community residents; higher wages in neighborhood	
		Promote education of residents to reduce unemployment and increase wages		
		Encourage development of community-based financial institutions and greater responsiveness of private banks		
		Target job and employment programs that keep money in the community		
		Engage in or promote microlending activities and other investment in small, local businesses	Neighborhood economy strengthened	
	Skills related to organizing	Learn different methods of organizing		
		Become affiliated with a local organizer or hire a professional organizer to do this work		Funding is difficult to obtain
Skills that apply to all CDCs	Responsiveness to changing community concerns	Continually reassess community needs and incorporate into CDC mission		
		Hire staff with knowledge of, and a strong commitment to, the community		
		Hire residents	Ensures critical connections to the community	

garner respect for community organizations from those same powerful forces.

Responsiveness to Changing Community Concerns

Successful CDCs continually reassess whether their resources and activities are appropriately focused on current community needs. As these needs grow and change, CDCs try to incorporate them into the CDC mission and phase out those activities that are no longer a priority. A changing program mix generally signifies responsiveness, but some CDCs claim that funders pressure them to shift to new activities that, although they may be currently "hot" or trendy, may not be best for the community. Wide-ranging community participation in strategic planning can help ensure that a CDC continues to serve its constituents in a way that responds to changes in the community without compromising the stability of the organization. Effective CDCs hire staff with knowledge of and a strong commitment to the community. Hiring residents is a particularly good way to ensure that critical connections to the community are maintained.

Mutually Supportive Programs

Successful CDCs also tend to structure and operate their programs in ways that make them mutually supportive. A CDC that already engages in building housing, for instance, is more likely to expand into a related area, such as housing management or housing advocacy, than to enter into a completely new area, such as business development. Because all CDCs work in an environment of limited resources, it is critically important that they recognize and capitalize on ways that they can make existing resources and skills do double duty.

Interaction Among the Components

Programmatic capacity helps build resource capacity because a CDC that delivers successful programs will attract funders more easily. Programmatic capacity and organizational capacity are also tightly linked—one is hardly possible without the other. Programmatic capacity is connected to political capacity in that a CDC that is managing successful programs is in a strong position to command attention from political actors and to obtain participation from community residents.

NETWORKING CAPACITY

The ability to build networks with other organizations is an important aspect of capacity building among CDCs. CDPs often play important roles in helping CDCs to create these networks—partnerships, by definition, are linking mechanisms. Keyes *et al.* (1996) argue that "capacity is shaped not just by the competency of each individual nonprofit group, but by the strength of the nonprofit's institutional network" (Keyes *et al.* 1996, 203). Networking serves a number of purposes: it connects institutions (CDCs to private firms, nonprofits, etc.); it also helps bring individuals closer to each other and to institutions both inside and outside the community. These networks involve financial, political, and economic relationships and help community organizations achieve their goals more quickly and efficiently. The elements of this dimension of capacity are: building stronger relationships with other organizations, moving organizations' agendas forward, creating mutually supportive programs, and increasing political leverage (Table 6.4).

Relationships with Other Organizations and Institutions

CDCs often work most effectively by developing networks and partnerships with others to bring new stakeholders to the neighborhood. CDCs develop coalitions, thus brokering relationships with other institutions, and decision-makers from the private and philanthropic sectors. Also, when a CDC recognizes a new need in its community, it can fill this need by partnering with another organization rather than filling it itself. Relationships of this kind boost CDC efficiency by allowing them to specialize. Partnerships also serve as intermediaries between CDCs and various "downtown" actors—especially local governments and corporations. Central here is the education of

Table 6.4 Networking capacity

Capacity-building needs	Capacity-building strategies	Effects on CDCs	Potential limits and problems
Strong relationships with other organizations and institutions	Broker relationships between CDCs that complement each other	Makes them more efficient by allowing specialization	Opportunity cost in time spent outside CDC's specific mission
	Partner with other CDCs to fulfill unmet community needs		
	Pressure other organizations to make activities complement CDCs and agenda		
	Support/work in coalitions	Relationships with other relevant actors built	
	Partner with public and private groups to carry out housing, real estate development, and economic development projects	CDCs gain expertise and partners learn about the community	
Promotion of CDCs' agendas externally	Broker relationships among CDCs that complement each other		
	Partner with other CDCs to fulfill community needs		
	Pressure other organizations to make activities complement CDCs' efforts		
Access to non-financial resources	Create and participate in networking opportunities, conferences, and social events	CDCs showcase their accomplishments and connect with each other to share information	
	Disseminate regular updates of CDC activity to existing and potential funders	Improved relations between CDCs and funders; Increased awareness among parties	
	Create links to other CDCs, job training, and other service providers in area		
Mutually supportive programs	Choose new program areas that draw upon existing skills		
	Establish partnerships with other programs to extend CDCs' reach		

people and organizations outside the CDC community about the abilities and importance of CDCs. Finally, there are networking opportunities such as conferences and community and cultural events. These events allow CDCs to promote their accomplishments, and connect with each other and share valuable information about funding sources.

Promotion of CDCs' Agendas

CDCs try to bring external actors into community development activities. They educate banks, local governments, and employers about neighborhood concerns, and provide powerful stakeholders with a better understanding of the community development process. CDCs also look for opportunities to partner with public and private groups to carry out housing, real estate, and economic development projects.

Access to Non-financial Resources

The parts of CDC agendas that require non-financial resources can also be supported by networking. To this end, CDCs create links to networks of other CDCs, job-training programs, workforce development specialists, and other service providers in the area (Harrison and Weiss 1998). Neighboring CDCs can establish arrangements for sharing space, labor, and technical assistance and for cooperating on program activity. These relationships provide CDCs with access to expertise and information. We are cautious about drawing firm conclusions regarding the relationship between the number of partnerships and CDC capacity—we do not believe that more partnerships necessarily translate into greater capacity. CDCs must be strategic about the specific organizations with which they partner and about the kinds of arrangements into which they enter.

Interaction Among the Components

Networking helps embed CDCs in the life of the city and region in which they operate. It can help with resource capacity building by putting community organizations in front of funders. Network capacity also builds programmatic capacity, because it enables CDCs to do more and to extend their reach beyond what they could do on their own. Network capacity is the external analog to organizational capacity; it defines the ways the organization can do business as it faces outward to the rest of its community. Finally, it affects the political capacity of the CDC through the creation of relationships with political actors at all levels.

POLITICAL CAPACITY

Although political capacity manifests itself in many ways—community participation, political leverage, educated constituents, and conflict management—this component of capacity primarily refers to two elements (Table 6.5): CDC's influence with government officials at all levels; and CDC's legitimacy within the community it serves. Both types of political capacity help a CDC build other types of capacity.

Building political capacity is not easy. In many ways, it is the trickiest kind of capacity building that CDCs negotiate. Although CDCs, by and large, agree that political capacity is important, some collaboratives are uneasy about trying to build the political capacity of CDCs. Although the CDCs need their local governments' help for tax abatement, letters of support, and so forth, funders tend to shy away from supporting direct political action because it seems too much like lobbying to them.

Community Participation

Without a strong and active constituent base, CDCs face difficulty arguing their cause outside the community. Newer CDCs must gain trust and a common vision for change in their communities, and maintaining these remains an important task throughout the life of the CDC. Mature CDCs, with their greater experience and visibility, position themselves as political players to support their efforts. To maximize community participation, CDCs try to hold community meetings at convenient times and places, and often provide transportation and child care. CDCs also engage in community planning exercises, share development plans, and seek out community residents for CDC committees and

Table 6.5 Political capacity

Capacity-building needs	Capacity-building strategies	Effects on CDCs	Potential limits and problems
Community participation	Hold community meetings at convenient times, places		
	Include community representatives in setting agenda		
	Encourage community organizing and support		Conflict among multiple interests
	Ensure that board and staff are representative of the community	Community needs effectively addressed	Process may become bogged down because of factionalism
	Encourage community input in CDC activities	CDC perceived as part of community	
	Employ an internal democratic structure	CDCs become more accountable to the community	
	Establish clear lines of accountability between CDC and community	CDC respected and trusted within community	
Political leverage	Advocate with, and educate public and private officials about, community needs	Increased citywide visibility	Some funders neither approve of nor fund advocacy; run risk of violating 503(k)3 rules
	Broker relationships between local public officials and community	CDC legitimacy increased	Change in political administration may hurt CDC
	Undertake outreach to downtown business and other community groups		
	Facilitate voting in community elections	Community development policy influenced	
		Possible backlash from government if change in administrations	
	Create opportunities for constituents to take on positions of responsibility citywide		
	Train staff in negotiation/conflict resolution	Arbitration skills developed	
Educated constituents and partners	Disseminate information on government policy, activities, and economic forces that affect residents	Residents made more aware of issues that affect them	
	Develop leadership within the community		
	Make information about CDCs' activities readily available to community	Increased awareness of activities and strategies of CDC	
	Educate banks, local governments, and local employers about their customers and potential employees	Greater understanding of community on the part of critical actors	
	Partner with public and private groups to carry out housing, real estate development, and economic development projects	CDCs gain expertise and partners learn about the community	
Conflict management	Heighten sensitivity to the multiple interests of the community, businesses, and governments		
	Mediate conflicting interests from within and without community		
	Maintain strong and regular communication with all stakeholders		

neighborhood events. Many community organizations involve key community leaders in their decision-making and agenda-setting processes. Sharing real power with community members increases participation because the larger community is more likely to believe that its interests are being represented. Organizing also builds participation because it turns community members into stakeholders.

Community representation in CDCs is an important aspect of participation. Without it, government officials, funders, and the community at large may be skeptical of the CDC's ability to be effective or to speak for the neighborhood. To obtain community representation, a CDC can try to ensure that its board and staff reflect the makeup of the community (Gittell, Gross, and Newman 1994), and can train active residents for positions of increasing responsibility. Successful CDCs provide education, training, support, and confidence building for leaders within the community.

The CDC's internal structure should be democratic to maintain an adequate level of accountability to the community. An elected board and an involved membership create clear lines of communication between the organization and the neighborhood. However, tension sometimes develops as CDC staffs clash with community activists. CDCs therefore worry about the costs of being "too" democratic—that is, there is a trade-off between maintaining an open process and the need to make a decision and get something done.

Political Leverage

In order to increase their political leverage, many CDCs work on building relationships with, and educating, local officials. CDCs often seek to increase public services to low-income neighborhoods. Cities where local government involvement in community economic development is substantial show higher levels of CDC activity than other cities (Vidal 1992, 14). However, organizations that become too connected to one political administration may fall quickly out of favor when that administration changes. They also run the risk of being co-opted by the administration. An additional problem is that patronage from local elected officials can insulate CDCs from pressures to manage themselves efficiently (Ferguson and Stoutland 1996).

Educated Constituents and Partners

A CDC is enhanced by educated constituents who vote, and articulate and argue for their own needs. CDCs therefore disseminate information on government policy, government activities, and economic forces that affect residents. Educating community members in this way helps them feel more in control of the forces that influence their lives and encourages them to participate politically to effect change. Training community members also helps increase CDCs' political legitimacy.

Conflict Management

Awakening participants' political consciousness can give rise to political schisms. Disagreements with other community actors—over issues such as race and ethnicity, or owner versus renter—can be a drain on time and resources. CDCs must balance the demands of an array of widely divergent actors. CDCs therefore try to understand and communicate with the multiple stakeholders and interests of the community, businesses, and local government. Partnerships can help CDCs manage conflicting interests by acting as a mediating party, and providing training for CDCs in conflict resolution.

Interaction Among the Components

Political capacity builds and is built by the other four components of capacity. A CDC that has political clout is better able to command other kinds of resources. Conversely, organizational capacity and programmatic capacity enable a CDC to obtain greater political attention. And to the extent that political capacity equals legitimacy and participation, organizational and programmatic capacity are enhanced as a result. Probably more than any of the other categories, increases in political capacity are dependent on the success of CDCs in creating networks with other community development players.

CONCLUSION

CDCs selectively use the strategies identified with each component to move their community-building activities forward. No CDC employs all the strategies discussed in this article. But many are trying to work on all five components simultaneously, to the extent possible. Partnerships help them to extend their reach and balance their efforts across the five components; they also try to persuade them to work on areas that have been neglected. In the end, CDCs build capacity by increasing their ability to do the following:

1. Think through strategic plans to help themselves.
2. Raise funds to build and manage housing and economic development projects.
3. Demonstrate effective leadership and vision.
4. Better organize themselves internally by hiring, training, and retaining the best staff possible.
5. Organize members of the community to participate in activities that improve their neighborhood.
6. Develop networks of CDCs and other service providers.

Tensions in the capacity-building process exist because the power relationships between CDCs and funders are uneven. CDCs do not always like the prospect of changing programmatic course when funders' interests change, for example. There has been some tension over the directions that some funders are taking—work force development, regional job strategies, and so on—which some CDCs feel do not build on the capacity that they have developed over time. Other CDCs question whether becoming more comprehensive is necessarily a good thing; some prefer to further develop their capacity in "bricks and sticks."

At the same time, funders argue that some CDCs are inefficient and unwilling to make necessary changes in their operations. CDCs are different from other kinds of nonprofits in that they must maintain their ties to their neighborhoods. This elevates the importance of the capacity relating to the training of local citizens and the participation of residents. A key question remains: Can neighborhood organizations become more financially and technically efficient and retain their ties to the people they represent?

It is also important to better understand the potential comparative "weightings" of the different types of capacity. The categories presented here are of different levels of importance to community organizations. In addition, it is useful to understand the trade-offs between different kinds of capacity. All efforts involve the cost in lost opportunity of not pursuing some other kind of capacity. We also need more accurate assessments of the role of collaboratives in their communities, and of the CDCs' contributions to neighborhoods. These assessments, in turn, will provide more useful evaluation tools and concepts and lead to better strategic planning by these groups. We expect that CDCs will be able to use the results of this investigation in their ongoing work.

REFERENCES

Bendick, Marc, Jr., and Mary Lou Eagan. 1991. *Business Development in the Inner City: Enterprise with Community Links*. New York: Community Development Research Center, New School for Social Research.

Ferguson, Ronald F., and Sara E. Stoutland. 1996. Community Development, Change, and Sustainability in Community Support Systems. Paper presented at the Conference of the National Community Development Policy Analysis Network, November.

Gittell, Marilyn, Jim Gross, and Kathe Newman. 1994. *Race and Gender in Neighborhood Development Organizations*. New York: City University of New York, Howard Samuels State Management and Policy Center.

Harrison, Bennett, and Marcus Weiss. 1998. *Workforce Development Networks: Community-Based Organizations and Regional Alliances*. New York: Sage.

Kelly, Rita Mae. 1977. *Community Control of Economic Development: The Boards of Community Development Corporations*. New York: Praeger.

Keyes, Langley C., Rachel Bratt, Alex Schwartz, and Avis Vidal. 1996. Networking and Nonprofits: Opportunities and Challenges in an Era of Federal Devolution. *Housing Policy Debate* 7(2): 201–29.

McGrath, Laura. 1995. *Building Organizations to Develop Better Communities: An Evaluation of Technical Assistance Provided to John Heinz Neighborhood Development Program Grantees*. Washington, DC: Community Information Exchange.

Nye, Nancy, and Norman J. Glickman. 1996. *Expanding Local Capacity through Community Development Partnerships*. Report prepared for the Ford Foundation. New Brunswick, NJ: Center for Urban Policy Research.

Rubin, Herbert J. 1994. There Aren't Going to Be Any Bakeries Here If There Is No Money to Afford Jellyrolls: The Organic Theory of Community Based Development. *Social Problems* 41(3): 401–21.

Servon, Lisa J. 1997. Microenterprise Programs in U.S. Inner Cities: Economic Development or Social Welfare? *Economic Development Quarterly* 2(May): 166–80.

Servon, Lisa J. 1998. Credit and Social Capital: The Community Development Potential of U.S. Microenterprise Programs. *Housing Policy Debate* 9(1): 115–49.

Vidal, Avis. 1992. *Rebuilding Communities: A National Study of Urban Community Development Corporations*. New York: Community Development Research Center, New School for Social Research.

CHAPTER 7

Learning from Adversity

The CDC school of hard knocks

William M. Rohe, Rachel G. Bratt, and Protip Biswas

When East Side Community Investments, Inc. experienced financial crisis and ultimately failed, it was a wake up call to all who care about community development corporations and the work that they do. East Side had been one of the biggest and most productive CDCs in the country.

Previous studies of CDCs focused on their rapid growth and success across the country. However, the time has come to take a close look at the failures and to learn from them. East Side Community Investments was not unique. Our research into CDC failure led us to examine more closely four other organizations that failed or were forced to downsize, and to draw lessons from their experiences so that other CDCs could avoid their fate.

MILWAUKEE: COMMUNITY DEVELOPMENT CORPORATION OF WISCONSIN (CDCW)

In the late 1980s Milwaukee's leaders in both the public and private sectors saw a need for a large developer of affordable housing. CDCW was created in 1989 to develop small- to medium-sized apartment complexes in the predominantly African-American Northside area. Northside has the highest poverty rate in the city and many older housing units in need of repair. Facing political pressure from the city, its major funder, CDCW also took on properties from other CDCs that had gone out of business. Many of these properties needed repair and had problem tenants and low occupancy rates. CDCW staff spent considerable time turning these developments around.

By 1997 CDCW had developed 21 separate housing projects with a total of 722 units, and was the property manager for its own and other developers' rental complexes. The organization had a staff of 25 and an annual operating budget of more than $1 million.

But financial problems also began to surface in 1997. For some time CDCW had been losing money on its property management operation because of soft demand for housing in the Northside area, inadequate tenant screening and personnel problems. Unable to compete effectively with the higher salaries and better working conditions offered by private management companies, CDCW was having trouble keeping competent management staff. The financial losses did not create an immediate crisis because the organization was able to cover the deficit with funds generated from its multifamily development work.

In 1998 CDCW's development activities were also affected by changes in city policies. CDCW was staffed to rehabilitate multifamily developments using the Low-Income Housing Tax Credit (LIHTC) program, but the city decided to focus its resources instead on the purchase, rehabilitation and resale of single-family homes. The city allowed neighborhood organizations to determine how Community Development Block Grant funds would be spent in their areas, and these groups drastically reduced the funding for affordable housing. CDCW was unable to keep up with the rehabilitation of single-family units and had trouble selling units once they were rehabilitated. This combination of problems severely reduced CDCW's operating income and the red ink began to spread.

CDCW belatedly sought assistance, but was unable to secure funding. City officials felt that the organization was too far in debt and was unlikely to overcome its problems. CDCW asked its lenders to restructure their loans, but without city support the lenders were unwilling to do so. In March 1999 CDCW filed for bankruptcy and closed its doors.

MINNEAPOLIS: WHITTIER HOUSING CORPORATION (WHC)

The Whittier Housing Corporation was an offshoot of the Whittier Alliance, which was created in 1978 to revitalize Minneapolis's Whittier neighborhood. For the next 12 years the alliance pursued its mission by sponsoring a variety of neighborhood improvement activities, including buying and rehabilitating multifamily housing developments.

In 1990 the Whittier Alliance was chosen to participate in the Neighborhood Revitalization Program, which provides $20 million a year for neighborhood development and improvement projects in Minneapolis. The Alliance developed a plan that provided additional affordable rental housing and social services for the area's lower-income residents. But homeowners and private apartment owners got wind of the plan, orchestrated a takeover of the Alliance and developed a plan that did not include rental housing. The new board had little interest in continuing to own and manage the multifamily properties the Alliance had developed during the 1980s, so WHC was established as a separate organization and the properties—seven leasehold cooperatives with 16 buildings and 158 units—were transferred to it.

Many of these buildings needed further renovation. WHC sought assistance from the Interagency Stabilization Group (ISG), a consortium of the city's major funders of CDCs. But the ISG would not provide funding without seeing a stabilization plan; when WHC complied, the plan was judged inadequate. Eventually, the ISG provided some support, but it was not enough for extensive rehabilitation. WHC staff also had difficulty finding effective property manage-

ment companies and the buildings continued to decline. At its height WHC had a staff of three—a director, a co-op organizer and a secretary—and contracted with private asset and property managers. In 2000, after a final attempt to secure additional equity investments from the National Equity Fund, WHC went out of business.

SOUTH DALLAS: OAK CLIFF DEVELOPMENT CORPORATION (OCDC)

OCDC was formed in 1987 by the housing outreach program of a local Lutheran church in response to an overwhelming demand for affordable housing in the South Dallas area. Since its inception OCDC has focused on developing homeownership projects for low- and middle-income families with support from the region's financial and philanthropic institutions. In 1993 OCDC was made administrator for the Dallas in-fill housing program, which enabled the organization to focus on new construction of single-family homes. With adequate administration fees for the expanded services provided by the contract, OCDC hired additional staff. At its peak, OCDC had over eight full-time staff members.

But even as OCDC flourished, several experienced staff members moved on to better positions, leading to project delays. The organization also had to contend with vocal community opposition—accompanied by unfavorable media and political attention—to its Independence Park Project, a planned development of 112 new homes. The most significant factor leading to the organization's downsizing, however, was the loss of the in-fill housing contract and the subsequent reduction of OCDC's operating budget.

The city elected not to renew OCDC's in-fill housing program contract when it expired. Caught unprepared, OCDC unsuccessfully appealed the decision. During this time holding costs and legal fees drained the organization's reserves. Housing production suffered greatly, cutting into OCDC's income from developer fees. OCDC also was unsuccessful in finding alternate sources of operating support, and was forced to reduce its staff to an executive director and one part-time employee, greatly diminishing its production capacity.

PHILADELPHIA: ADVOCATE COMMUNITY DEVELOPMENT CORPORATION (ACDC)

ACDC was founded in 1968 and was among Philadelphia's first CDCs. The organization, which completed its first housing project in 1971, also developed an area master plan that led to positive changes in public policy, including more financial resources for target neighborhoods. ACDC also undertook several larger housing projects and led a successful effort to designate the Diamond Street area the city's first historic district. By 1998 ACDC had completed 365 houses.

Throughout these years, the organization received widespread recognition for its work and was well supported by funders. Much of the organization's success is attributed to the charismatic leadership of its founder, who served as president of the Board of Trustees until 1996. She was also de facto executive director; for most of her tenure ACDC did not have an executive director. During these years, the number of permanent staff members was kept to four or five. The organization relied on consultants and contract employees to supplement its staff.

ACDC began facing challenges when its founder developed health problems and was unable to devote the same time and energy to day-to-day activities. Staff members could not handle the complexities of development projects. After the founder resigned, the board found it difficult to provide leadership, especially after several other members resigned. Communications with funders suffered and ACDC lost much of its operating support, which led to staff layoffs. Several development projects stalled and became community eyesores.

The search for a new executive director was not easy for ACDC. The first two choices did not work out, and the third's tenure was cut short by illness. Development of new projects decreased, along with developer fees.

Without adequate operating support the ACDC was forced to downsize its staff. Existing plans went unfinished, and for several years virtually no new projects were started.

DRAWING LESSONS

These four examples lead us to several suggestions for avoiding downsizing and failure.

1. Develop and periodically revise strategic plans. Changes in local housing markets and city policies were two major problems faced by the downsized and failed CDCs. Strategic planning can help anticipate and respond to these changes. In Milwaukee the weakening demand for housing in CDCW's target area was at least partially responsible for the unexpected turnover and vacancy rates in the organization's rental housing portfolio. Similarly, a soft rental market in the Whittier neighborhood in Minneapolis did not allow for rent increases that were needed to cover rising maintenance and repair costs. CDCs need to read the market and position themselves to remain competitive.

Unanticipated changes in city policies also played an important role in the failures of CDCW and WHC and in the downsizing of OCDC in South Dallas. Strategic planning that assesses the political environment may help organizations anticipate, influence and effectively respond to changes. CDCs need to be involved in formulating, reviewing and commenting on city policies that may affect them.

Strategic planning is neither cheap nor easy and many CDCs will need financial support and technical assistance to implement this critical exercise.

2. Diversify activities, geographic areas served, clientele and sources of funding. CDCs must tread a thin line between diversification and specialization; a strategic plan should address how much it should do of either. Specialization requires a narrower range of staff expertise, which is deepened with each new project, but also makes an organization vulnerable to changes in funding priorities and community desires. Diversification makes an organization less vulnerable to those changes but may lead to

performance problems caused by a lack of staff expertise or financial resources.

CDCs that failed or were downsized tended to have narrowly focused missions in terms of activities, geographic areas served, clientele served and funding sources. For example, OCDC specialized in in-fill housing and WHC specialized in multifamily development. They had little to fall back on when local support for these activities evaporated.

Also, CDCs that targeted small and/or homogeneous geographic areas were vulnerable to changes in market conditions in those areas. The units owned and managed by both CDCW and WHC were concentrated in neighborhoods where the demand for housing decreased significantly. Rents could not be raised to meet higher operating costs and financial problems ensued. A larger, more diverse target area allows a CDC to diversify the location of its properties and reduces the organization's vulnerability to market weakness.

Housing very low-income households typically requires deeper subsidies that are difficult to come by these days, and CDCs that focus exclusively on these households may increase their financial vulnerability. In Minneapolis all of WHC's housing developments served very low-income households that could not afford the rent increases necessary for proper building maintenance. A portfolio that includes housing for moderate-income households may provide enough revenues to cross-subsidize developments for very low-income households and generate more community support.

CDCs that mostly rely on one funding source seem to be particularly vulnerable. Abrupt changes in the policies of city agencies, foundations, or other principal funders can leave CDCs with little time to find replacement funds. The CDCs in Milwaukee, Minneapolis and Dallas were all heavily dependent on single sources of funding which left them in serious financial crises when that funding was interrupted. Diverse funding sources also provide CDCs more autonomy and some protection from the dictates of funders who want CDCs to adopt certain agendas or programs at the expense of local concerns.

The decision to diversify should be approached cautiously and should involve both residents and the local CDC support community. It is also likely that diversification is not possible or desirable for very small CDCs that are just beginning to gain expertise in a given area. Becoming proficient in delivering or carrying out the group's core set of activities is important for all young CDCs. There also may be risks associated with increased diversification that are not evident in our case studies; if not done carefully, and with sufficient resources, it may lead to poor performance and loss of funder or community support.

3. Work hard to earn and maintain the support of residents. A lack of community support for various CDC activities was an important factor in the failure or downsizing of three of the organizations studied. In Minneapolis vociferous community opposition to the Whittier Alliance's focus on rental housing for very low-income households led to the "takeover" of the Alliance and the creation of WHC. Similarly, OCDC's plan in Dallas for a new 122-unit subdivision of affordable homes generated considerable community resistance and contributed to the loss of city funding.

Board members and staff need to build support for CDC activities by opening up a dialogue with community residents, involving them in the review of proposed activities and inviting them to join committees. The board should periodically convene general meetings with the larger community and hold social events in those areas where projects are being developed. CDCs also must ensure that the properties they own or manage are well-run and maintained.

4. Pay more attention to training and retention of board members and staff. Project development problems were implicated in all four case studies, including inaccurate financial projections leading to cost overruns, overly optimistic underwriting assumptions, inadequate cost control and accounting systems and poor quality construction. Property management problems also consistently appeared among the four CDCs, including inadequate procedures to screen and evict tenants, inadequate property maintenance

and lack of social support services for tenants. Passive boards were another factor in organizational decline.

These problems may have been avoided if staff and board members had periodic training to provide strategic leadership and set policy guidelines for staff. We need to better understand why many staff and board members are not taking advantage of national initiatives to increase CDC capacity, and ensure that they receive the training they need. In particular, what may be needed is access to tailor-made on-site consulting help. Outside experts, who could be sent to a CDC to work with the board or staff on a range of issues, or who could help sort through issues with funders, may be the most important type of assistance that is needed.

Many organizations found it difficult to retain experienced staff because city agencies and private sector companies pay substantially higher salaries. Organizations need to offer better staff salaries and benefits to increase retention, and must plan for leadership transitions. Of course, public agencies and local and national nonprofit intermediaries can ensure competitive salaries and generally support CDCs by instituting programs that provide funds to cover core operating expenses. This support can be contingent on standards of productivity and professional competence.

5. Maintain frequent and open communication with support community and respond quickly to problems as they develop. Communication problems played an important role in all four case studies: between executive directors and their boards, between executive directors and funders and between executive directors and city officials or politicians. When CDCs are undertaking potentially controversial projects, they would be wise to inform and involve local political leaders early in the process. This is particularly true of CDCs that rely heavily on support from local government.

Identifying and acknowledging problems as they arise is also important. CDCW management did not ask for help in addressing property management problems until the organization was in deep financial trouble. Similarly, several of those interviewed in Minneapolis felt that WHC's problems should have been dealt with sooner and more decisively. Funders also should have stepped in sooner, either to provide the necessary support or to find other organizations to take over the units.

The cases presented here signal some important warnings. Strategic planning that assesses the opportunities and threats in the local political and economic environment, and that assesses the organization's mission in light of changes, should be a standard practice among CDCs. Staff training and retention also helps create effective and financially sound organizations. Ongoing communication with both the residents of the service area and funders is also critical to maintaining political and financial support. Finally, if CDCs do get into trouble, it is important that they identify the problems quickly and reach out to their local CDC support communities for assistance. For their part, communities need to respond positively by helping CDCs work through problems so they can continue providing vital services to their communities.

CHAPTER 8

Social Housing

Michael E. Stone

Community development has emerged as a field in part because of the demonstrable inability of the mainstream, for-profit housing sector to provide decent, truly affordable housing for low-income people. To redress this inability, a large and increasing share of housing must be treated as a social resource rather than as a commodity yielding private windfalls. Since, all housing contains both social and individual rights and interests, differing only in the nature and extent of their social characteristics, it is thus appropriate and useful to conceptualize a continuum of housing ownership forms. As discussed in this chapter, "social ownership" encompasses that portion of the spectrum where the over-riding social interest is to ensure security of tenure and permanent affordability.

Social ownership of housing and land may be traced back to neolithic villages and Native American cultures. Within the capitalist era, various alternatives to the commodification of material life were put forth during the 19th century, and many European countries have accepted the notions of social ownership earlier and have gone much further toward their realization than has the United States (see Harloe 1995; Stone 2003). Even in the United States, significant strands of non-speculative and social ownership have emerged, despite the ideological domination and political force of the purveyors of unfettered private ownership. They amount to a little over 4 million housing units, about 4 percent of all housing in this country. Their accomplishments and potential provide encouragement and hope, while their limitations and contradictions provide lessons on the dilemmas of partial and piecemeal reform.

The chapter begins with a definition of social ownership. The bulk of the chapter then examines the nature and scope of existing models of social ownership, grouped into two major categories: socially owned rental housing, consisting of public housing, non-profit rental housing and mutual housing associations; and nonspeculative home-ownership, consisting of limited-equity cooperatives, ownership with community land trusts and some resale-restricted individual ownership. The models are evaluated in terms of differences in the degree of social control. The chapter concludes with identification of various routes through which the amount of social housing can be increased.

THE CONCEPT OF SOCIAL OWNERSHIP

Housing is defined here as socially-*owned* if it meets all of the following criteria:

- it is not owned and operated for profit;
- it cannot be sold for speculative gain; and
- it provides security of tenure for residents.

Social ownership embraces the notion that housing should be permanently removed from the possibility of resale in the speculative private market. This means that once the original cost of producing or acquiring the housing is paid off, the only costs would be for operations and any additions, alterations and capital improvements. Even if nothing else were to change, the substantial expansion of such a "social sector" of housing would, over time, mean a sizable reduction in the housing costs for a growing proportion of the population. It would also mean slowing and eventually reducing the growth of mortgage debt as the mortgages on existing housing are paid off once and for all.

There are many different forms that "social housing" can take, including:

- ownership by public agencies, such as local and regional housing authorities;
- ownership by private nonprofit organizations; and
- ownership by residents themselves, individually or collectively, with resale restrictions that permit, at most, a "limited-equity" return on investment.

The unifying concept is not the particular type of entity owning the housing but the existence of enforceable provisions preventing the housing from being sold in the speculative private market. Indeed, for housing to be fully social, these provisions should apply "permanently," "forever," or "in perpetuity."

SOCIAL RENTAL HOUSING

Public Housing

Public housing is by far the most extensive and most maligned form of social ownership in this country. As of 2001, local housing authorities owned 2 million housing units (U.S. Census Bureau and HUD 2002: Table 1A-7), about 2 percent of all housing: 1.3 million of these under the federal program (U.S. Department of Housing and Urban Development 2000)—a reduction of about 100,000 from the early 1990s (Dolbeare 1991)—the remaining 700,000 under various state and local programs. In addition, the Department of Defense owns and operates about 400,000 family housing units, the "other public housing program" (Hartman and Drayer 1990; Twiss and Martin 1999). Given the focus of this book is on community development, only a few points will be made about public housing. First, the real estate industry from the outset attacked public housing ideologically and constrained

it operationally through restrictions on design, location and management as well as funding, making virtually inevitable the well-publicized problems with some public housing (Bratt 1986). Second, despite these problems and the too-successful attempts to discredit the concept of public housing (and social enterprise generally), more complete and balanced examinations reveal that for the most part public housing has had a remarkable record of success in providing physically decent, nonspeculative, mortgage-free and cost-effective housing to poor people (Bratt 1986, 1989).

Third, public housing remains a vital resource despite its checkered history and reputation (Fuerst 2000). Many housing authorities have more people on their waiting lists than are currently living in their developments. Some have closed their waiting lists because the wait is as long as 20 years. Fourth, while giving priority for public housing to the most needy households is quite appropriate in a society where low-cost housing is scarce and housing is not a right, the deepening concentration of the poorest households in public housing added fuel to attacks on the very idea of public housing, blaming public ownership and management (and/or the residents themselves) for the poverty of the residents.

Fifth, in some cities, large public housing developments are situated in areas where, in recent decades, urban redevelopment and gentrification have raised land values, making the sites ostensibly too valuable for poor people. Thus, since the 1980s, there have been increasingly strong forces working to reduce the amount of public housing, through density reduction in existing projects, wholesale demolition, sale to private developers and conversion to mixed-income (including market-rate) housing. The prevailing public housing policy of the 1990s and into the new millennium—known as HOPE VI—largely embodies the principles of public housing replacement, with substantial displacement and loss of units even where local housing authorities retain ownership (Pitcoff 1999; Vale 1999; Keating 2000; National Housing Law Project et al., 2002).

While prevailing current sentiment gives

little encouragement, public housing is an essential ingredient in addressing the housing crisis, in part because it is unequivocally outside the speculative market and also because it includes an established, operational infrastructure for producing, financing and managing housing, including the power of eminent domain.

Nonprofit Rental Housing

Unfortunately, there are few precise figures on how many housing units are under ownership by private nonprofits, due to the ambiguity of definitions, overlap of categories and lack of any entity (public or private) that has been given or assumed responsibility for compiling and disseminating such information. Nonetheless, I estimate that as of the early 21st century, there are about 1.3 to 1.7 million rental units in nonprofit ownership. This consists of about 1.1 to 1.3 million subsidized rental units, plus roughly 200,000 to 400,000 other rental units in nonprofit ownership that have received no government subsidies or possibly just capital assistance from nonfederal public or private sources.[1] This is a significant number, but it is just slightly over one-half the number of units owned by local public housing authorities, and about 1½ percent of all housing units in the United States.

In the late 19th century, moral righteousness and enlightened self-interest on the part of some capitalists stimulated a modest move toward "philanthropic housing." Nonprofit projects were developed in a number of cities in the early part of the 20th century, totaling several thousand units (Abrams 1946: 170ff). By eliminating development and rental profits, the housing was slightly less expensive initially than speculative new housing. But with construction costs to be paid off from rents, the units were still more expensive than the tenements occupied by poor and working-class people, so the residents were mostly of middle-income. Had these developments remained out of the speculative market, by today, they might be debt-free social housing and hence much less expensive than speculatively owned apartments of the same vintage or newer. However, most were eventually sold. As Charles Abrams aptly put it (1946: 175), "Philanthropy could no more solve the problem of housing than it could solve the problem of poverty."

In the modern era, private nonprofit housing has evolved and expanded through several phases, in which the lessons of this historical experiment have been learned gradually and unevenly but sufficiently to hold the promise of an increasingly important role in the growth of the social sector of housing.

The most clearly identifiable and longest-lived component of modern nonprofit ownership consists of federally financed and subsidized Section 202 housing for the elderly and handicapped, a program created in 1959 as the first of a series of subsidized housing production programs for private development and ownership. Unlike all subsequent programs, though, 202 has from the outset been restricted to development and ownership by nonprofit (and public) entities. The result has been the emergence over the past four decades of a set of organizations specializing in such housing, although some regional and community-based nonprofits have included 202s among their broader housing repertoire.

Section 202 housing was financed through below-market direct federal loans until changed to capital grant financing by the Housing Act of 1990. Projects built since 1974 also receive Section 8 rental subsidies. In addition, an owner may not sell the housing into the speculative market, at least during the 40-year term of federal financing and regulation. And even in the rare instances of foreclosure, Section 202 projects have been transferred to other nonprofit owners. These features, together with the capital grant financing and supportive services provided by the 1990 Housing Act, make the 202 program a premier model of privately owned nonspeculative housing. As of the late 1990s, there were about 200,000 units of Section 202 housing (HUD 2000).

Unfortunately, there does not exist a well-established model of nonelderly housing that embodies all of the attractive features of 202 housing. During the 1960s and early 1970s, socially motivated nonprofit developers did produce nearly 200,000 housing units under the FHA Section 221(d)(3) and 236 interest-reduction programs that had been created primarily for profit-making developers. (Nonprofit production comprised over a one-fourth of the total under these programs—[Clay 1987: 9].) However, many ended up defaulting on their mortgages (as did many profit-motivated owners). The housing was taken over or resold by HUD, in some cases to speculative owners, so this experience does not offer the encouragement provided by the Section 202 program. Also, apart from weaknesses in the federal programs themselves, nonprofit owners had to contend with inadequate resources, lack of experience, an unsympathetic HUD and the challenges of trying to serve and empower some of the neediest populations and communities (Bratt, 1989: 185–191). Nonetheless, approximately three-fourths of these units remain in some form of nonprofit ownership.[2]

Beginning in the late 1960s, another type of nonprofit housing model was emerging, one that has proven much more successful at producing and operating housing under the government subsidy programs. However, in order to be successful, these housing providers have had to buy into many of the rules of profit-making development and stretched the meaning of nonprofit ownership. Community development corporations, regional housing development corporations and "intermediaries" providing technical assistance have been set up, with staffs that attempt to combine training and experience in business and finance with social concern. While these entities are themselves nonprofit corporations, and their housing commitment almost always is to permanent nonspeculative ownership, in order to benefit from the financial incentives provided through the Internal Revenue Code (notably the Low Income Housing Tax Credit), they have to enter into partnerships with profit-motivated investors.

When a nonprofit organization needs to market its housing plans to potential investors and also meet the underwriting criteria of mortgage lenders to obtain financing, the needs of prospective residents may at times have to be compromised. Once the housing is occupied, in order to maintain investor confidence in the development and the organization, the housing may need to be managed quite conservatively in terms of tenants' rights and rent levels. Even though these tensions may be mitigated with deep, income-determined subsidies, a nonprofit owner can face disturbing role conflicts between its obligations to the residents and the investors. Furthermore, because the tax benefits are of finite duration (typically 15 to 20 years, depending upon the type of tax benefit), down the road the investors will want to bail out when they no longer have any financial incentives. Unless the deal has been structured so that they can fully recover their initial investments as well as their profits from the tax shelters, the investors will expect to be bought out at this point—necessitating sale of the housing to owners who might turn it into market-rate housing, unless financing is available for the nonprofit or the residents themselves to buy out the investors.

In sum, the current prevailing model of nonprofit development and ownership might more properly be understood to be "quasi-nonprofit" or even "compromised nonprofit" ownership. Only if social financing replaces dependence on profit-motivated investors can the growing number of these community-based and regional nonprofit housing providers have a viable alternative to partnerships with profit-motivated investors and thus be able to achieve true social ownership.

Mutual Housing Associations

There is one other, more fully social model of nonprofit ownership—the mutual housing association (MHA)—that began in Europe over a century ago but has only emerged in the United States over the past two decades (Goetze 1987; Bratt 1990). One version, the federated MHA, consists of a group of resident-controlled limited-equity co-ops (see below) or nonprofit developments (Krinsky and Hovde 1996: 10). The other version, referred to as an integrated MHA, has been promoted since the late 1970s by the Neighborhood Reinvestment Corporation (NRC) and differs from other models of social ownership in several significant respects.

First, the NRC mutual housing approach has deliberately eschewed outside profit-seeking investors in order to avoid role conflict and possible pressure to sell the housing when the tax shelters run out. Second, NRC MHAs try to finance nearly all acquisition and development costs through upfront capital grants, although often they have had to use some debt due to limited availability of grant resources. Third, residents are expected to make a modest initial capital contribution (often waived for low-income people), which is recoverable with interest upon moving out but cannot otherwise grow and is not a marketable property interest; the goal is for residents to put up 5 percent of the total cost, with capital grants covering the rest. Fourth, a portion of each resident's monthly charges is supposed to go into a fund that will provide part of the capital grants for additional units, although generally only middle- to high-income residents pay high enough monthly charges to contribute to the capital fund. Fifth, the membership of each NRC mutual housing association consists of residents, prospective residents and local public and community officials. A majority of the governing board consists of residents and prospective residents, so the housing is largely owned and controlled collectively by residents. Sixth, organizational development is emphasized as much as the physical development of the housing, with residents required to participate and expected to take care of minor maintenance of their units, even though professional management is an integral part of the model. Finally, residents have lifetime security of tenure, as long as they meet their financial and other membership obligations and do not violate the rights of others. They may designate a family or household member as the successor to their unit but may not sublet; this ensures that every resident is an association member who is expected to participate in the organization.

Because of the experimental nature of this mutual housing model and because it has attempted to operate outside prevailing government programs and financing mechanisms, it has grown slowly and remains limited in scale despite early interest and enthusiasm. As of late 2002, there were only eleven NRC mutual housing associations that together owned about 8,300 occupied units (NeighborWorks Network 2003). Nonetheless, an encouraging analysis found that mutual housing associations would be more cost-effective to the federal government than nearly any other approach in assisting very-low-income households on a long-term basis (Bratt 1990). Thus, despite its extremely small scale so far, there are compelling economic as well as social advantages to the mutual housing model. It is an emerging approach that comes quite close to realizing many of the goals set out here for true social housing.

RESIDENT SECURITY, POWER AND CONTROL IN SOCIALLY OWNED RENTAL HOUSING

People who reside in housing owned by public agencies, nonprofit organizations and integrated mutual housing associations are legally tenants. Some people regard this as a fundamental weakness of these forms of ownership, as residents ostensibly have no opportunity to realize any of the psychological, social and economic benefits of homeownership. It is important, though, to challenge the notion of a sharp binary polarity between rental and ownership.

Even in the private housing market, neither tenancy nor homeownership is a unitary concept. An alternative form of tenure under social ownership, in combination with no debt costs, can yield resident benefits that are competitive with conventional homeownership. Of greater subtlety and more immediate relevance, though, concepts of residential property have been undergoing considerable evolution so that the diverse forms of ownership, as well as their combinations and modifications in practice, have produced virtually a continuum on the dimensions of security of tenure, resident control and economic benefits.

For example, even in private rental housing the history of tenant organizing, legislation and litigation reveals that there are significant objective differences among tenancy-at-will, lease tenancy, tenancy with formal resident organization and collective bargaining, and tenancy with statutory and regulatory controls on conditions, evictions and rents.

Within existing subsidized rental housing, the history of public housing certainly demonstrates how low-income residents can be disenfranchised, abused and degraded almost as much by public as by private landlords. Yet in public housing organizing and advocacy led to legislative and administrative redefinition of the scope of residents' power and rights and the meaning of public ownership, even if some of these rights have been undermined since the late 1980s. Public owners have enforceable legal, constitutional and financial obligations to residents greater than can be imposed on private owners. Thus, resident ownership is not necessarily the only or best route to greater power, security and control.

For tenants in private nonprofit housing and mutual housing associations, the legal leverage and claims on public resources are, of course, less than for public housing residents.. However, the organizational circumstances are usually quite different as well. Certainly, some of the socially oriented nonprofits that developed subsidized housing in the 1960s and 1970s lacked the financial capacity and organizational ability to sustain their social commitment to their tenants.

In contrast with many of the early nonprofits, some community development corporations and all mutual housing associations have explicitly involved residents in decision-making and, in some cases, management and operation of the housing as an integral part of the philosophy of the organizations. In such situations, there is not only objective resident power and security of tenure but also a considerable sense of "ownership" in the psychological sense even if in formal legal terms the residents are tenants. In addition, while residents do not build up any wealth through their housing, resident-savers can on average do as well financially as conventional owners depending upon the financing and cost structure of the housing.

Furthermore, residents of participatory nonprofit rental housing can in principle have as much autonomy to fix up and change their units as do residents of physically equivalent limited-equity co-ops or condominiums. Finally, what must be weighed against some formal differences in legal status between participatory social rental and nonspeculative homeownership are differences in financial risk. In the contemporary situation of ownership by a community development corporation, mutual housing association or regional nonprofit housing corporation, the ownership entity transcends not only the individual unit but also the particular building or development and usually is connected to an infrastructure of intermediaries that have provided financial and technical assistance. This means that the residents, most of whom are low-income people, do not have to carry fully by themselves the cost burdens of unanticipated housing problems or changes in their own economic circumstances or of their fellow residents, in contrast with individual private ownership.

Along most dimensions, being a tenant in socially owned rental housing is not necessarily inferior to being a nonspeculative homeowner—or speculative owner. It may have real advantages and attractions not only for those of low or moderate income but for many with higher income as well.

NONSPECULATIVE HOMEOWNERSHIP

Limited-Equity Cooperatives

As of 2003, there were approximately 1.2 million housing units under cooperative ownership in the United States. About 425,000 of these are limited-equity or zero-equity co-ops, of which over one-half are in New York. The remaining 765,000 are market-rate cooperatives (National Association of Housing Cooperatives 2003). The latter group includes 550,000 conversions from rental housing, mostly in New York City, similar to condo conversions in other parts of the country. The other 215,000 market-rate co-ops are mostly middle-income developments that originally had resale restrictions but in most cases now permit members to sell their shares at the market price.

During the 19th century, programs for cooperative ownership of workplaces and residences were integral parts of the utopian and revolutionary critiques of capitalism in the United States as well as in Europe. However, the earliest U.S. co-ops (in New York between 1876 and 1885) did not embody this radical vision but were instead a form of homeownership for high-income urbanites, presaging modern luxury co-ops and condos (Siegler and Levy 1987: 14).

It was not until the 20th century that the first nonspeculative, socially oriented co-op housing was developed. Most of these were in New York City and under union auspices. In the early part of the century, several workers' housing cooperatives were developed (Abrams 1946: 181; Siegler and Levy 1987: 14), but most did not last. In the late 1920s, New York State passed a limited-dividend housing law that, among other things, facilitated co-ops for moderate- to middle-income people (Siegler and Levy 1987: 14). One of the first was the Workers Cooperative Colony in the Bronx developed by the Amalgamated Clothing Workers. With the first units completed in 1928, it grew eventually to 1,400 units and still remains a co-op. However, despite state tax exemptions, the co-ops developed by labor groups in New York were affordable only to higher-paid workers. During the 1930s, depression conditions led to increased national interest in co-ops, but postwar era ideological and economic conditions shunted co-ops to the margin of housing policy (Leavitt 1995).

While these early housing cooperatives were structured to assure continued affordability to members of the affinity group, there is nothing intrinsically nonspeculative about cooperative ownership. In any co-op, the housing is owned by a corporation made up of "cooperators," with each share in the corporation corresponding to either a particular dwelling unit or a proportion of the square footage of the entire building. Unless explicitly defined otherwise, a share is a marketable commodity that may be sold for whatever the owner can get. In addition, unless the co-op agreement requires the owner of shares to be a resident of the unit, an owner may sublet the unit and charge whatever the market will bear.

Within this framework, the distinctly limited-equity form of co-op emerged as a housing strategy for helping to maintain long-term affordability and resident control for people of moderate if not low income. In a limited-equity co-op, the share price is set by formula, not by the market, in order to restrict or eliminate any speculative gain. The co-op corporation retains a first-option right to purchase a departing member's share at the formula price. In addition, occupancy and share ownership are generally coterminous—apart perhaps from approved temporary subletting—in order to prevent "landlordism" and to ensure that residents are people who have a legal and financial stake in the housing.

Interestingly, the growth of interest in the limited-equity co-op model over the past two decades does not simply hark back to the early co-ops. It also rests upon a substantial but little known historical foundation of several hundred thousand co-op units developed in the three decades prior to 1980. The great majority of these were unsubsidized, middle-income cooperatives, with federal or state government mortgage insurance or financing. In addition, an entire infrastructure evolved to undertake development and provide technical assistance, services and training for co-op housing (Siegler and Levy 1987: 16–19; National Association of Housing Cooperatives 1990). Indeed, after World War II, some progressive housers advocated a large-scale co-op program as part of urban redevelopment, to complement public housing for households who could not qualify for the latter and as a model for eventual conversion of public housing to resident control (Abrams 1946: 179–187). However, as indicated above, from the mid-1950s until the mid-1960s, interest in co-ops by middle-income households waned in the face of "anti-collectivist" ideology and the suburban triumph.

In the late 1960s and the 1970s, several factors led to renewed interest in nonspeculative housing cooperatives, within a rather different political and economic context. The emphasis on community control and resident empowerment in the federal antipoverty program contributed to the eligibility of co-ops for federal housing subsidies. About

60,000 co-op units were created under the HUD Section 221 and 236 programs between the mid-1960s and mid-1970s (National Association of Housing Cooperatives 1990). Also, the emergence of the modern women's movement rekindled interest in co-ops—integrally connected with supportive services, as in the 19th-century feminist notions—as a residential model especially well suited to the needs of single women (young and elderly) and women as single parents (Hayden 1984; Novac and Wekerle 1995).

In addition, wholesale disinvestment and abandonment of vast amounts of housing in major cities across the country led to some spontaneous, grassroots building takeovers of unoccupied buildings and resident operation of occupied buildings. Especially in New York City, where effective title of many thousands of buildings passed to the city, the movement demanded not only rehabilitation but also title to the buildings as limited-equity co-ops (Leavitt and Saegert 1990). However, since the late 1970s, the limited-equity co-op movement has been impelled rather less by the housing needs of the very poor than by declining opportunities for conventional (or even condominium) home-ownership among moderate- to middle-income people. Over this period, about 150,000 additional limited-equity co-op units have been developed, with more than one-half of these being in New York City (National Association of Housing Cooperatives 2003).

Ironically, the ideal of resident control in a limited-equity co-op includes the risk that the residents may at some point reorganize as a market co-op. Because cooperatives are legally autonomous corporations, this possibility is real and has been occurring. Only if the co-op incorporation documents preclude such dissolution, or if there is an entity that has some legal leverage and a broader public interest, can this risk be avoided. Where there is public involvement—through, say, mortgage insurance, publicly donated land or public grants, loans or subsidies—then contractual requirements or deed restrictions can protect the limited-equity requirement indefinitely. The strongest legal protection of permanency, though, is through owner-ship of the land by a government agency or broadly based community land trust (described in the next section). Under such an arrangement, the co-op corporation owns the structures but leases the land, with the ground lease stipulating retention of the co-op's limited-equity character.

Nonspeculative co-op units have been created through both new construction and building conversions. Most have involved multifamily structures, but some, such as the Route 2 Co-op in Los Angeles, include one-family houses. While income mixes vary, including some low-income and some higher-income people, the middle range prevails. Although some public programs and public funds in the form of land, loans and grants have often assisted, financing has generally come from quasi-public mortgage lenders (such as state housing finance agencies and the National Cooperative Bank) that offer terms slightly below market. Each co-op has tended to be unique, not only in the circumstances that led to its creation but also in the resident mix, the financing sources and terms, and the limited-equity formula (Heskin and Leavitt 1995). While this uniqueness reflects an encouraging creativity and resourcefulness, it also makes more difficult policies that could facilitate more rapid expansion of the model.

Ownership with Community Land Trusts

While the origins of most of the other models of nonspeculative ownership are primarily urban, the community land trust (CLT) has rural roots. These traditions include Native American concepts as well as several 19th-century movements, most notably utopian socialist experiments in common ownership; Henry George's notions of land as the principal locus of unearned wealth and social exploitation; and aristocratic support for nongovernmental nature preserves and parks.

Yet, despite its roots, the land trust movement that began in the 1960s and has been growing at an accelerating rate since the late 1970s does not seek to restore a vanished past or opt out of modern society. It operates within, while seeking to transform, contemporary real estate law. It is concerned with the active productive uses of land, including but not limited to residential use, in opposition to speculative holding and use of land. It is, in this sense, concerned with issues of responsible and active land use and planning, rather than preservation per se and resistance to development. And it seeks to use land tenure as the organizing locus for the expansion and realization of democratic decision-making (Institute for Community Economics 1982; Davis 1984; Krinsky and Hovde 1996).

The model vests title to the land itself in a nonprofit community organization—the land trust—to be held in nonspeculative ownership in perpetuity. Individuals are granted the right to use the land for their own benefit and with considerable individual autonomy. The formal legal link between the trust that owns the land and the people or organizations who use it is the ground lease, which grants lifetime or 99-year tenure (inheritable and renewable), subject to certain conditions. Thus, as it relates to housing, the form of ownership of the buildings may be anywhere on the ownership spectrum depending upon the terms of the ground lease under which the housing owners are allowed to use the land. In principle, the house owner could be a landlord renting the dwelling for whatever the market rent might be or a homeowner free to sell the house at the market price (exclusive of land). In practice, the land trust movement has been committed primarily to "permanently affordable homeownership" (Davis and Demetrowitz 2003), using the ground lease terms to enhance affordability, security of tenure, resident ownership and nonspeculative transfer of houses in perpetuity. The actual form and conditions of ownership of the dwellings depend on the local context and individual circumstances.

Community land trusts acquire land by donation if possible, but often by purchase. Therefore, their immediate impact on the cost of housing depends upon their ability to obtain land at less than market prices, gain access to below-market financing for land acquisition that may include development as well and subsidize residents through resources the CLT receives as a charitable organization. Over the long term, housing costs are reduced primarily by preventing resale of the land and controlling the price at which the residential structures may be resold. As with other forms of nonspeculative ownership, deep affordability remains constrained by continued dependence on debt financing and by residents' incomes.

The ways in which the community land trust approach distinguishes itself are, first, the dual ownership structure, which explicitly accepts individual property rights while establishing and protecting social or community rights. On the one side, the private ownership of one's dwelling, opportunity to accumulate some wealth through home-ownership and unrestricted right to pass the home to one's heirs enhance the appeal of the model by building on deeply rooted ideological traditions. On the other side, broad-based land trusteeship is intended to provide a legal and social framework for maintaining nonspeculative ownership forever. The goal is to strengthen established—though weaker—traditions of community, in ways that skirt popular skepticism about government. The second distinctive feature is the broader community development and land reform agenda, which, it is argued, can facilitate economic development and community empowerment and hence begin to address the income side of the affordability issue and aspects of the quality of life beyond just housing itself (Institute for Community Economics 1982: Chapter 2; Davis 1984: 219–222; White and Matthei 1987: 47–64; Krinsky and Hovde 1996).

However, just as each of the other social housing models faces certain fairly distinctive constraints, so does the CLT approach. First, because a CLT allows a leaseholder to own the buildings on the land, imposing a limited-equity and first-option resale restriction on building owners may lead to legal challenges as "restraints on alienation" (Davis 1984: 223), although apparently this concern has been overcome (Institute for Community Economics 2001).

Second, because the supply of land that can be acquired through donation or below-market purchase will always be small, and the ability of CLTs to purchase substantial amounts of private land at market prices will always be limited, only a broader and more radical land reform agenda will enable the CLT movement to alter significantly the effects of land speculation on housing costs.

Given the grandness of the vision, the recent emergence of the model and the lack of public programs and resources specifically for land acquisition, it is not surprising that the land trust movement is still modest in scale. Between the late 1960s and the mid-1980s, the number of community land trusts grew slowly, with some losses along the way; in 1985, there were fewer than 20. Since 1985, though, the growth has been substantial, reaching almost 50 in 1991 and 133 in operation or development by 2001 (Institute for Community Economics 2002). This upsurge has emerged directly out of the housing affordability crisis, as land trusts increasingly have been created in cities and towns, with "forever" housing as their primary focus. Although CLTs have been established in all parts of the United States, about one-half are in New England, which has experienced some of the most severe affordability problems and where grassroots organizing—both rural and urban—has long been a way of life.

In the entire country, there were only about 6,000 housing units on CLT-owned land as of the end of 2001 (Institute for Community Economics 2002). Nonspeculative housing under the CLT model is thus comparable in scale to mutual housing associations and orders of magnitude less than public, nonprofit rental and limited-equity co-op housing. Nonetheless, again analogous to mutual housing associations, the land trust emphasis on organizational development, participation and personal growth, along with the creation of permanently affordable homeownership housing, will undoubtedly make the model increasingly popular.

Resale-Restricted Individual Ownership

Since the 1980s, the principal response to declining opportunities for conventional homeownership has not, in fact, been promotion of social ownership programs but those public (and some private) programs to assist first-time homebuyers with mortgage financing at interest rates somewhat below market, "soft" second mortgages (i.e., deferred repayment), reduced or waived closing costs and proposals for tax-exempt or tax-deferred saving for downpayments. In addition, many localities have provided publicly owned land at little or no cost and offered below-market construction financing and even some partial capital grants to stimulate construction of below-market housing for homeownership. Because the participating homebuyer is able to obtain a house with below-market financing, possibly at a below-market price, most programs impose some resale restrictions in order to lessen the potential for owners to reap windfalls when they sell in the speculative market.

In most instances, however, the provisions are so weak that the housing may not be characterized as nonspeculative even for the initial owner, and generally the housing is fully in the speculative market with the second and subsequent owners. The weakest restrictions permit the owner to sell freely in the speculative market but then repay the subsidies out of the sales proceeds. While this supposedly enables the funds to be recycled to other buyers, repayment typically is interest-free (and inflation-free), and often the amount that must be repaid declines with time, so eventually no recapture occurs. Another approach places limits on the price for which the house may be sold, usually allowing an annual increment above the original purchase price equal to the overall rate of inflation or some fixed rate, such as 5 percent. The public agency then has a first option to purchase at this price or may require sale at this price to another qualified buyer. While this might appear to prevent speculative windfalls, it does not, because of the financial leverage involved in low downpayment residential purchases, even assuming modest market appreciation.

Although rarely done in practice, there is no reason why the formula for resale-restricted individual ownership could not be a limited-equity formula comparable to those used in limited-equity co-ops. Under such circumstances, it would be possible to achieve nonspeculative individual ownership. There are, however, some legal and practical problems with the enforcement of most resale restrictions, whether mild or strong. Recapture provisions pose the least difficulty because they are easily secured through property liens, which pose no legal or enforcement difficulties, since the owner would not be able to sell without discharging the lien. Price, equity and first-option limitations are more problematical because they generally involve deed covenants, which in most states are legally limited in duration and enforceability. The best approach is thus to allow the buyer to own the house but not the land—to have the land owned by a land trust or public agency.

Some might wonder why a low-income family should be forced to accept a resale restriction, and especially a permanent limited-equity restriction, in order to achieve homeownership. Why shouldn't such households be permitted to accumulate whatever wealth the real estate market provides, just as higher-income households have been able to achieve? Are not resale restrictions a form of discrimination, against low-income homebuyers in general and homebuyers of color in particular, as the latter have for so long been denied homeownership through discriminatory sales and lending practices?

Certainly, any household who wishes to have unrestricted homeownership should be able to do so through conventional purchase and financing terms, without discrimination—but also without public or community financial assistance. If, however, a household receives downpayment grants, below-market loans and possibly deferred payment loans, that household is in effect entering into shared ownership with the community—the community thus legitimately having certain rights to the property. What does the homebuyer get from such an arrangement? First, access to homeownership, with the associated status and security of tenure that presumably would not otherwise be affordable. Second, exclusive use and control of the living space—for instance, it is not necessary to share the space with the community "co-owner" nor be constrained by a landlord. Third, potential income tax

benefits from the deductibility of mortgage interest and property taxes. Fourth, no rent payments on the community's share of the property. Fifth, the opportunity to build wealth on the homebuyer's share of the property. What does the homebuyer *not* get? The right to sell the community's share and thereby appropriate for private gain the wealth that rightly belongs to the community. Nonspeculative homeownership, with permanent limited-equity resale restrictions, is thus not only not discriminatory but is more than fair to those who participate in it.

INCREASING THE AMOUNT OF SOCIALLY OWNED HOUSING

How could the amount of social housing in our nation be expanded? There are a variety of routes, including:

- production of new housing, by nonprofit or public developers, or by for-profit developers for transfer upon completion to social ownership;
- preservation of existing subsidized rental housing, with transfer from for-profit owners to social owners;
- conversion of private rental housing, where owners are irresponsible or are otherwise willing to sell, through the use of receivership, eminent domain and tenant buy-out rights and assistance (see Stone 1993: 228–231, 248–249);
- foreclosure protection and equity conversion as an option for low-income and elderly homeowners in return for their agreeing to current or future transfer to social ownership (see Stone 1993: 226–228, 238–239; Stone 2002);
- permanent limited-equity resale restrictions with subsidized first-time homebuyer programs (see Stone 2002).

Historically, most of the social housing in the United States has been provided through publicly subsidized new construction and substantial rehabilitation, even though this is the most capital-intensive, costly, time-consuming and complex of the available routes. Recently, however, considerable attention has been focused on strategies to preserve subsidized housing that was built by private developers in the 1960s and 1970s and convert it to true social ownership (see Chapter 7). However, to date, relatively little effort has gone into the other routes, which are surely the most cost-effective ways of achieving substantial increases in stock of social housing.

CONCLUSION

The notion that housing can be situated outside the speculative market has a long and established albeit constrained and little-recognized history in the United States. Various forms of nonspeculative ownership exist in practice, and real estate law continues to evolve to encompass new ideas and new economic and political realities. Each form of ownership has its trade-offs, its partisans and its critics. They differ in the degree to which they are truly and permanently nonspeculative and should be evaluated along these dimensions. Nonetheless, the various forms of socially owned rental and nonspeculative homeownership have a number of common components that distinguish them from both conventional rental and speculative homeownership and point toward true resident-controlled social ownership. The notion that housing should not and need not be a speculative commodity clearly is growing in legitimacy. As a practical matter, meaningful community development will require that social housing not only become more acceptable in concept but will be greatly expanded in quantity and become the attractive alternative to conventional homeownership.

REFERENCES

Abrams, Charles. 1946. *The future of housing*. New York: Harper and Brothers.

Achtenberg, Emily Paradise. 1989. Subsidized housing at risk: The social costs of private ownership. In *Housing issues of the 1990s*, eds. Sara Rosenberry and Chester Hartman, 227–267. New York: Praeger.

Bratt, Rachel G. 1986. Public housing: The controversy and the contribution. In *Critical perspectives on housing*, eds. Rachel Bratt, Chester Hartman and Ann Meyerson, 335–361. Philadelphia: Temple University Press.

Bratt, Rachel G. 1989. *Rebuilding a low-income housing policy*. Philadelphia: Temple University Press.

Bratt, Rachel G. 1990. *Neighborhood reinvestment corporation-sponsored mutual housing associations: Experiences in Baltimore and New York*. Washington, DC: Neighborhood Reinvestment Corporation.

Clay, Phillip L. 1987. *At risk of loss: The endangered future of low-income rental housing resources*. Washington, DC: Neighborhood Reinvestment Corporation, May.

Davis, John Emmeus. 1984. Reallocating equity: A land trust model of land reform. In *Land reform, American style*, eds. Charles C. Geisler and Frank J. Popper, 209–232. Totowa, NJ: Rowman and Allanheld.

Davis, John Emmeus, and Amy Demetrowitz. 2003. *Permanently affordable homeownership. Does the community land trust deliver on its promises? A performance evaluation of the CLT model using resale data from the Burlington community land trust*. Burlington, VT: Burlington Community Land Trust.

Dolbeare, Cushing N. 1991. Unpublished tables prepared for Low Income Housing Information Service.

Fuerst, James S. 2000. Public housing in Europe: Lessons from abroad. *Journal of Housing and Community Development*, January/February, 25–30.

Goetze, Rolf. 1987. *The Mutual Housing Association: An American demonstration of a proven European concept*. Washington, DC: Neighborhood Reinvestment Corporation.

Harloe, Michael. 1995. *The people's home? Social rented housing in Europe and America*. Oxford: Blackwell.

Hartman, Chester, and Robin Drayer. 1990. Military-family housing: The other public housing program. *Housing and Society*, 17: 67–78.

Hayden, Dolores. 1984. *Redesigning the American Dream: The future of housing, work and family life*. New York: Norton.

Heskin, Allan, and Jacqueline Leavitt, eds. 1995. *The hidden history of housing cooperatives*. Davis: Center for Cooperatives, University of California.

Housing Partnership Network. 2002. *Corporate report 2001–2002*. Boston: The Housing Partnership Network.

Institute for Community Economics (ICE). 1982. *The community land trust handbook*. Emmaus, PA: Rodale Press.

Institute for Community Economics (ICE). 2001. *The community land trust legal manual*. Springfield, MA: ICE.

Institute for Community Economics (ICE). 2002. *Community land trust (CLT) activity in the United States*. Springfield, MA: ICE.

Keating, Larry. 2000. Redeveloping public housing: Relearning urban renewal's immutable lessons. *Journal of the American Planning Association*, 66: 384–397.

Krinsky, John, and Sarah Hovde. 1996. *Balancing acts: The experience of mutual housing associations and community land trusts in urban neighborhoods*. New York: Community Service Society of New York.

Leavitt, Jacqueline. 1995. The interrelated history of

cooperatives and public housing from the thirties to the fifties. In *The hidden history of housing cooperatives*, eds. Allan Heskin and Jacqueline Leavitt, 79–104. Davis: Center for Cooperatives, University of California.

Leavitt, Jacqueline, and Susan Saegert. 1990. *From abandonment to hope: Community households in Harlem.* New York: Columbia University Press.

National Association of Housing Cooperatives (NAHC). 1990. Summary of housing cooperative units in the United States. Alexandria, VA: NAHC, March.

National Association of Housing Cooperatives (NAHC). 2003. Summary of housing cooperative units in the United States. Washington, DC: NAHC, January.

National Congress for Community Economic Development. 2000. November 14. http://www.ncced.org

National Housing Law Project, Poverty & Race Research Action Council, Sherwood Research Associates, Everywhere and Now Public Housing Residents Organizing Nationally Together. 2002. *False HOPE: A critical assessment of the HOPE VI public housing redevelopment program.* Oakland, CA: National Housing Law Project.

National Low Income Housing Preservation Commission. 1988. *Preventing the disappearance of low income housing.* Report of the Commission. Washington, DC: The Commission.

NeighborWorks Network. 2003. Mutual housing associations: Output by type of units. http://www.new.org/network/strategies/mutual/ mha_new.html

Novac, Sylvia, and Gerda Wekerle. 1995. Women, community, and housing policy. In *The hidden history of housing cooperatives*, eds. Allan Heskin and Jacqueline Leavitt, 281–293. Davis: Center for Cooperatives, University of California.

Pitcoff, Winton. 1999. New hope for public housing. *Shelterforce*, March/April, 18–21, 28.

Siegler, Richard, and Herbert J. Levy. 1987. Brief history of cooperative housing. *1986 Cooperative Housing Journal.* Washington, DC: National Association of Housing Cooperatives, 12, 14–19.

Stone, Michael E. 1993. *Shelter poverty: New ideas on housing affordability.* Philadelphia: Temple University Press.

Stone, Michael E. 2002. *The ECHO program: Equity Conversion and Homeownership Opportunity*, May. www.cpcs.umb.edu/users/mstone/Stone-ECHO_Program_May02.pdf

Stone, Michael E. 2003. *Social housing in the UK and US: Evolution, issues and prospects.* London: British Foreign and Commonwealth Office, Atlantic Fellowships in Public Policy. http://www.cpcs.umb.edu/users/mstone/Stone-UK_Soc_Housing_Oct03.pdf

Twiss, Pamela, and James A. Martin. 1999. Conventional and military housing for families. *Social Science Review*, 7: 240–260.

U.S. Census Bureau and U.S. Department of Housing and Urban Development (HUD). 2002. *Current housing reports. American housing survey for the United States in 2001.* Report H150/01. Washington, DC: GPO, October.

U.S. Department of Housing and Urban Development (HUD). 2000. A picture of subsidized households. Summary of the United States. July 11. www.huduser.org/datasets/assthsg/statedata98/us.html

U.S. General Accounting Office. 1986. *Rental housing: Potential reduction in the privately owned and federally assisted inventory.* Washington, DC: GPO, June.

Vale, Lawrence J. 1999. The future of planned poverty: Redeveloping America's most distressed public housing projects. *Netherlands Journal of Housing and the Built Environment*, 14: 13–31.

White, Kirby, and Charles Matthei. 1987. Community land trusts. In *Beyond the market and the state*, eds. Severyn T. Bruyn and James Meehan, 41–64. Philadelphia: Temple University Press.

NOTES

1. First, as indicated in the text, there were about 200,000 occupied 202 units in 1998 (U.S. Department of Housing and Urban Development 2000).

   Second, under the Section 221(d)(3) BMIR, Section 236 and Rent Supplement programs, 192,000 units were originally under nonprofit ownership (Clay 1987: 9). However, due to financial difficulties in both for-profit and nonprofit developments, HUD took over about one-fourth of all the units. While there are differing figures on how many remain in direct nonprofit ownership, how many are still held by HUD and how many have been resold to nonprofits (Clay 1987: 9; U.S. General Accounting Office 1986: 23; Achtenberg 1989: 228–229), I estimate conservatively that at least 150,000 units originally produced under the programs are still owned by nonprofits.

   Third, about 180,000 units owned by nonprofits were developed under various early unsubsidized FHA mortgage-insurance programs but subsequently received Section 8 subsidies, or, in a very few cases, other subsidies (U.S. General Accounting Office 1986: 23). No hard data are available on how many are still part of the subsidized nonprofit inventory, but I am assuming at least 150,000.

   Fourth, while there is virtually no official information on nonprofit ownership of units produced under the HUD Section 8 and HOME production programs, the best estimates come from studies of community-based developers. A 1998 census of such developers revealed that they have produced about 550,000 below-market units (National Congress for Community Economic Development 2000). Given the history of these organizations, most of these units have been rental housing. However, to some extent they have been producing units for homeownership. Without hard data, there is no way of knowing how many of the 550,000 CDC units are in the latter category, but it is probably less than 100,000. So, I am conservatively including 450,000 CDC units in the total of nonprofit rentals.

   Fifth, the latter group of organizations does

not include city-wide and regional nonprofits that do not fit the "community-based" definition. Such regional nonprofits have produced or preserved over 300,000 below market rental units (Housing Partnership Network 2002). It is likely that some of the at-risk subsidized housing such entities have preserved from going to market-rate rents includes some of the older nonprofit housing in the third category above. So to be conservative, I have assumed their net addition to the total below market "social" rental housing stock to be 250,000 units.

Combining the estimates for the five groups yields an aggregate estimate of 1,200,000 subsidized units in nonprofit ownership. Allowing for a margin of error of 100,000 units yields the text estimate of 1.1 to 1.3 million units.

Not included in this total are nonprofit rental units without subsidies developed under the various early federal mortgage-insurance programs.

No estimates are available for the number of units in this category. Also not explicitly included in the estimate are Farmers Home Administration Section 515 subsidized rental units. There are about 300,000 units under this program (National Low Income Housing Preservation Commission 1988: 17). It is not known how many are under nonprofit ownership, but it is possible that some if not most of these are included in the categories above. Note, finally, that the text estimate does not include nonprofit housing produced or acquired without federal involvement, either under state or local programs or with no government assistance at all. Again, no estimates are available for this category. It is thus likely that the actual total figure for nonprofit rental units is somewhat higher.

2. This is a very rough estimate based on anecdotal evidence, since no systematic accounting is available.

CHAPTER 9

Community Development Financial Institutions

Expanding access to capital in under-served markets

Lehn Benjamin, Julia Sass Rubin, and Sean Zielenbach

Affordable credit, basic financial services, and investment capital are critical to community health. Individuals need mortgages to purchase and maintain their homes. Developers require financing to build and rehabilitate commercial properties, community facilities, and affordable housing. Businesses need capital in order to grow. Community residents and local institutions require safe, affordable financial accounts where they can keep and build their assets. Unfortunately, low-income communities and individuals have limited access to financial services, affordable credit, and investment capital. The lack of such financing has hampered efforts to improve conditions in these areas.

This chapter looks at one response to this problem: the community development financial institution (CDFI). CDFIs work to improve economic conditions for low-income individuals and communities. They provide a range of financial products and services that often are not available from more mainstream lenders and financiers. CDFIs augment their financing with counseling and educational services that increase their borrowers' economic capacities and potential. There currently are 748 certified CDFIs throughout the country, ranging in asset size from $5,000 to more than $1 billion (www.cdfifund.gov; CDFI Data Project, 2003). Institutional forms vary, from federally regulated banks and credit unions to unregulated, nonprofit and/or for-profit loan funds and venture capital funds.

Today's CDFIs have a number of predecessors. The first minority-owned banks targeting low-income areas were established in the late 1880s (DuBois, 1907). The 1930s and 1940s saw the emergence of credit unions, many of which were designed to serve African Americans who did not have access to credit (Isbister, 1991). Several of the community development corporations (CDCs) that were first created in the late 1960s and early 1970s provided financing for small businesses as part of their broader economic revitalization efforts (Halpern, 1995; Perry, 1987). The 1980s saw the emergence of nonprofit loan funds that worked to promote affordable housing and small business development. Many of these organizations—including the Local Initiatives Support Corporation, the Enterprise Foundation, Boston Community Loan Fund, and the Delaware Valley Reinvestment Fund —focused primarily on helping CDCs obtain the financing and technical skills necessary to carry out their projects (Walker, 1993).

The coalescence of these various initiatives into a recognized development finance industry occurred in the early 1990s, facilitated by two federal initiatives actively supported by the Clinton administration. The first involved increased enforcement of the federal Community Reinvestment Act (CRA). Enacted in 1977, the CRA mandates that banks address the credit needs of their entire service area and prohibits them from discriminating against any portion of their markets. Clinton-supported revisions in 1995 judged banks more on their actual lending and investment performance than on their marketing and outreach efforts in low-income and minority communities, which contributed to greater lending in these areas (see Belsky, Schill, & Yezer, 2001).

The second, related initiative involved the

establishment of the Community Development Financial Institutions (CDFI) Fund in 1994. First championed by candidate Clinton and based in large part on his experiences with the Chicago-based South Shore Bank, the Fund sought to increase the availability of affordable capital in historically underserved markets. It has fostered the development of community development banks, credit unions, loan funds, and venture capital funds. The Fund certifies organizations as CDFIs, ensuring that they meet a certain set of institutional criteria. It also provides capital to CDFIs both directly and indirectly through regulated banks and thrifts. Since its inception, the Fund has provided a total of more than $775 million in direct funding to over 300 CDFIs and has facilitated approximately $1 billion in CDFI-related investments from banks through its Bank Enterprise Award program. The Fund's efforts have significantly expanded the development finance industry, as the number of certified CDFIs more than doubled from 1996 to 2006. (A list of certified CDFIs can be found at www.cdfifund.gov.)

This chapter provides an overview of CDFIs in the context of development finance. It explores issues regarding the assessment of CDFIs' impact and looks at some of the challenges CDFIs face going forward.

BASIC FINANCIAL SERVICE PROVISION

Checking and savings accounts are the most basic financial assets that most households own. When housed in insured depository institutions, these kinds of accounts provide a safe place to keep money, create opportunities to build wealth, and often serve as prerequisites for obtaining credit. Households without such accounts face a number of financial disadvantages, including having to use currency exchanges to cash checks and struggling to establish the credit history necessary to purchase a home. Low-income households without transaction accounts are 43% less likely to have positive net financial assets, 13% less likely to own a home, and 8% less likely to own a vehicle

than those with such accounts (Carney & Gale, 2001). With 8.7% of U.S. families having no checking or savings accounts with an insured financial institution, the need for affordable, accessible financial services is clear (Bucks, Kennickell, & Moore, 2006).

Community development credit unions and community development banks provide basic financial services at little or no cost to their members or customers. They offer basic savings and checking accounts with no monthly fees and very small ($10 or less) minimum balance requirements. CDCUs and CD banks also offer certificates of deposit (CDs) that can be purchased for as little as $100, and special savings vehicles such as Individual Development Accounts (Sherraden, 1991). Virtually all CDCUs and CD banks spend considerable time helping their members and customers improve their credit ratings—principally by reducing debt and repairing credit histories—with the goal of increasing their asset-building capacities. CDCUs and CD banks are the only CDFIs to make consumer loans to households for critical purposes such as purchasing an automobile, paying for health care, and investing in education.

CD banks and credit unions also work to combat "fringe banking" in low-income communities. "Fringe bankers" include payday lenders, currency exchanges, checkcashing outlets, pawnshops, and rent-to-own stores—each of which typically charges high transaction and/or loan fees. Users of fringe bankers often pay two or more times as much in interest and fees as they would if they had an account at a regulated institution (Mullen, Bush, & Weinstein 1997; Stegman 1999; Caskey 2001).

CD banks and credit unions provide an accessible alternative to fringe bankers. Most CD banks and credit unions are located in low-income areas and/or serve predominantly low-income individuals. Their numbers have increased significantly over the last decade. As of 2003, there were 54 CDFI Fundcertified CD banks with almost $8 billion in assets and at least 265 CD credit unions with $4 billion in assets (CDFI Data Project 2003).

HOUSING FINANCE

Community development and development finance efforts have historically focused most on the creation and/or rehabilitation of housing. The home is the primary asset for most Americans, and homeownership is a time-tested way of building individual and family wealth. Homeownership also serves as a linchpin of broader neighborhood development strategies, as it tends to contribute to more stable residential areas and can spark additional investment (Rohe & Stewart, 1996).

Single-Family Financing

The stability of a residential area depends on the availability of affordable mortgage financing. For many years a number of banks redlined poorer and minority neighborhoods, and even now, banks struggle to manage the risks associated with lending in these areas. Mortgage default rates in low-income census tracts are generally 15% higher than in moderate-income ones and 31% higher than in middle-income ones (Capone, 2001). Low-income borrowers are also more likely to default than are moderate- or middle-income borrowers (Van Order & Zorn, 2001).

The vast majority of borrowers in these areas do not default, however, and advocates for these communities have helped create alternative financing institutions to meet local capital needs. CDFIs such as the South Shore Bank, the Santa Cruz Community Credit Union, the Colorado Assisted Housing Corporation, and many organizations within the Neighborhood Reinvestment Corporation's NeighborWorks network developed partly in response to unmet mortgage needs. The NeighborWorks members alone have provided mortgage financing to over 60,000 low-income families in the past 10 years.

The growing emergence and activity of CDFI lenders have coincided with substantially increased lending in lower-income markets on the part of conventional financial institutions (Bostic & Robinson 2004). Heightened CRA enforcement, along with greater understanding of the profit potential within lower-income markets, has led conventional lenders to develop "sub-prime" products that better address the needs of borrowers making as little as 50% of the area median income. For example, borrowers can now make down payments of 3% or less of the home's purchase price. In certain areas (Boston, for example), banks have offered subordinated second mortgages in conjunction with conventional firsts so as to reduce further the amount of up-front equity a borrower must provide (Campen & Callahan, 2001). Such loans may also carry more flexible terms than conventional mortgages and generally have higher interest rates to compensate for higher risks of borrower default.

The increased availability of capital in these markets has led CDFIs to adapt and expand their financing products. While some CDFIs offer first mortgages, the institutions generally are more supplementary lenders. Most of the home purchase lending on the part of NeighborWorks members, for example, involves "soft" second (or even third) mortgages. These loans, which are subordinate to first mortgages held by more conventional financial institutions, typically cover up to 30% of the purchase price and carry significantly below-market interest rates. CDFIs also offer down payment, closing cost, and home repair/maintenance loans. Taken together, these products help make homeownership more affordable for lower-income borrowers, ensure the homes' livability, mitigate default risk for conventional lenders, and preclude the physical decline of neighborhoods.

Prospective CDFI borrowers often must attend homeownership training before being able to obtain a loan. Such education may involve a series of group sessions over multiple weeks (the typical NeighborWorks model) and/or one-on-one meetings with a CDFI staff member. The goal is to enable the prospective borrower to address prior credit issues and meet the CDFI's (and/or a conventional lender's) underwriting standards. Many CDFIs also offer post-purchase counseling to help buyers make their payments and identify and avoid predatory re-financing or other deceptive lending practices.

Multi-Family Financing

Just as CDFIs serve as intermediaries between low-income households and conventional financial markets, they often serve as a conduit between nonprofit housing developers and mainstream capital providers. Some of the larger community development loan funds—including LISC, the Enterprise Foundation, and the Low Income Investment Fund—have historically concentrated significant resources on building the financial and organizational capacity of CDCs and similar affordable housing organizations. They have helped the organizations develop sound financial and accounting practices, identify contractors, address asset management issues, and generally become more business-like in their orientation to real estate development. They have also worked to involve conventional lenders in projects, usually by providing up-front, higher-risk financing to help the projects get underway. LISC, for example, was a pioneer in the creation of "pre-development" loans: low- or no-interest debt with balloon repayments of principal to cover various land acquisition, architectural, environmental, legal, and other up-front costs associated with preparing a site for development. CDFIs have often provided CDC developers with construction loans to build or rehabilitate the planned housing units. As conventional lenders grew comfortable enough with projects to provide permanent mortgage financing, the CDFIs' loans have generally taken subordinate positions.

Developments require a significant amount of subsidy for lower-income individuals to be able to afford the units. In addition to helping developers identify and obtain various grant monies, CDFIs such as LISC and Enterprise successfully pushed for the creation of the Low Income Housing Tax Credit (LIHTC). Since its implementation in 1986, the LIHTC has enabled taxable investors to take a credit against their federal income tax for investing monies in low-income housing developments. The resulting equity has substantially reduced project financing costs and has contributed to the creation of thousands of additional housing units for lower-income families (Cummings & DiPasquale, 1999; DiPasquale & Cummings, 1992; McClure, 2000).

COMMUNITY FACILITY FINANCING

Many nonprofits struggle to obtain financing for important neighborhood projects such as childcare centers, health clinics, and charter schools. Nonprofit organizations' reliance on grant funds as their primary source of revenue, along with the inherent uncertainty of philanthropic and public support amid shifting economic and political winds, often makes conventional lenders hesitant to finance these projects. CDFIs offer various pre-development, construction, and working capital financing to enable these projects to go forward. Many of the loans are structured with balloon repayments of principal, so they can easily be replaced by conventional financing in the future. Community facility financing remains a relatively small percentage of the CDFI industry's overall portfolio but has grown substantially in the past few years.

SMALL BUSINESS FINANCING

A healthy, growing business sector provides critical goods, services, and employment opportunities to local residents. Without access to external capital, companies must use their own earned income to finance their growth and investments, limiting how quickly they can expand. Equity capital is particularly crucial for young companies, which lack the cash flows necessary for debt repayment.

Minority, female, and low-income entrepreneurs, as well as small businesses located in distressed communities, frequently struggle to obtain necessary financing. Higher transaction costs associated with making small loans; higher default risks inherent in lending to smaller, less well capitalized companies; and residual racial, ethnic, or gender discrimination have combined to limit debt capital available to these companies. Venture capitalists, the primary source of conventional equity capital, are reluctant to invest in companies unless they are very rapidly growing, have the potential for quick, highly lucrative exits, are located in a handful of states and major markets, and need at least two million dollars or more.

Debt

CDFIs work with small businesses with the potential to generate benefits for low-income people and/or communities. Among the typical criteria are the creation of jobs that require minimal skills and hold opportunities for advancement, commitments to livable wages and employee benefits, and environmentally friendly practices. In most cases, the businesses are unable to meet their capital needs from more traditional sources. This is especially true for micro-enterprises, companies that usually have 5 or fewer employees and annual revenues of $250,000 or less. (For more information on micro-enterprises, see Edgcomb, Klein, & Clark 1996; Clark *et al.* 1999; and Servon 1999.)

CDFI financing generally goes toward facility purchase, expansion, and modernization; working capital; and equipment purchase. Loans typically carry 3- to 5-year terms and market or below-market rates. They may be structured as lines of credit or may convert to equity or otherwise contain warrants, royalties, or other features that enable the CDFI to share in the business's success. Unlike conventional lenders, CDFIs often provide small business loans for as little as $1,000. CDFIs lend both independently and in conjunction with conventional lenders. In some cases, CDFIs may guarantee a portion of banks' loans in order to help borrowers build relationships with conventional financial institutions.

Equity

Community development venture capital (CDVC) funds provide equity to businesses in exchange for a portion of ownership in the form of preferred or common stock in the companies. Such investments serve as patient capital, giving young firms the funds they need but not requiring immediate repayment. Unlike traditional equity providers, which

look for the promise of significant economic growth before investing in a firm, CDVCs often invest in companies that have only moderate growth but significant job creation potential. Most CDVC funds target manufacturers, which typically offer higher wages and better benefits than service sector jobs and can employ individuals with lower education and skill levels (Mayer, 1998; Phillips-Fein, 1998). CDVCs also tend to be more willing to invest in companies located in rural and low-income areas (Rubin, 2001).

CDVCs must exit their investments in order to make a profit and free up capital for new investments. Most CDVC exits occur when the portfolio company is acquired by another business or when the company's owner or management buys out the CDVC's share. In general, CDFI equity investors tend to hold their investments much longer than traditional venture capitalists. That tendency reflects both the greater difficulty of exiting the types of companies in which CDVCs invest and the unwillingness of CDVC managers to force exits that would hurt the companies' longer-term prospects (Rubin 2001).

CDFIs that finance businesses typically provide intensive technical assistance to their borrowers and portfolio companies. For example, CDFIs help emerging companies with writing business plans, developing marketing strategies, and establishing financial management systems. They do so through their own staff members as well as through outside experts brought in to increase the companies' knowledge, sophistication, and market readiness.

ASSESSING CDFIs' IMPACT

Like all entities engaged in community development, CDFIs struggle to identify appropriate indicators for measuring the impact of their activities. CDFIs generally have described their impacts in terms of specific, quantifiable measures such as jobs created, housing units refurbished, mortgages provided, and day care facilities developed. These impacts are assumed to lead to broader, longer-term improvements in their targeted markets. Unfortunately, definitions of impact, along with the indicators and measurement used, vary widely.

Attributing causality is also problematic. For example, most affordable housing developments have a number of different funding sources. While a CDFI's involvement may have been critical to the deal's viability, each of the other capital providers could easily argue that its monies were equally essential. There also are many factors external to the CDFI that help determine if a project or business succeeds. Consider the case of a CDFI making a business loan for the purchase of a new piece of equipment. Over time the business grows and hires additional workers. Part of that growth likely stems from the enhanced productivity resulting from the new equipment, and part results from the growing market for the business's goods and strategic actions taken by the company's management and workforce. Is the CDFI, therefore, responsible for creating the new jobs? The CDFI's financing and related technical assistance likely contributed to the improved health of the company, but is unlikely to have been the sole relevant factor. Furthermore, determining the relationship between the CDFI's activities and the growth of the company's workforce becomes increasingly difficult over time.

How, therefore, should we assess CDFIs' impact? One way would be to think in terms of direct and indirect effects of a CDFI's activities. Direct effects are those that result immediately and specifically from a CDFI's financing or technical assistance (a business purchases a new piece of equipment with a CDFI's loan dollars, a family purchases a home thanks to a CDFI mortgage, etc.). Indirect effects are those that materialize later as a result of factors including, but not solely related to the CDFI's activities (the new piece of equipment enables the business to expand into a new market, hire additional employees, and pay more taxes; the new homeowners help stabilize the surrounding community). Obviously, the impacts become increasingly diffused as we move further away from the original financial transaction, and measuring and attributing them accurately becomes more difficult.

We also need more realistic expectations of CDFI impacts. After all, CDFIs are relatively small financial institutions that provide related education and counseling activities. The impact of any CDFI is inevitably limited relative to broader economic and political forces. Affordable homeownership ultimately depends less on the structure of a CDFI's loan than on the strength of the local housing market and the effect of national interest rates. An expansion of the Earned Income Tax Credit is likely to have a much greater impact on reducing poverty in a given community than will the efforts of even the largest and most effective CDFI.

CDFI PROSPECTS

An ongoing question is the appropriate long-term role for CDFIs. Are they alternatives to conventional financial institutions, necessary intermediaries between such institutions and lower-income communities, or financial innovators that demonstrate the viability of such communities? CDFIs clearly cannot meet all of the financial service needs of lower-income communities by themselves. At the same time, most conventional financial institutions currently are not (and likely never will be) providing some of the products and services that CDFIs offer. From a policy perspective, is it better to support further expansion of CDFI capacity or to enable and encourage conventional financial institutions to take over the CDFIs' financing activities? Additionally, little attention has been paid to the important role that CDFIs play in advocating for lower-income communities, helping to shape policies that affect their financial health.

While CDFIs appear to have helped expand access to affordable credit and investment capital in many previously underserved communities, sustaining and building upon these gains is hardly guaranteed. To date, CDFIs have relied on subsidized capital to make most of their activities possible. It is no accident that the most dramatic increases in financial service provision in lower-income markets occurred in the 1990s, a time of widespread economic prosperity, strong political support for domestic development finance, and consistent enforcement of the CRA. These factors enabled CDFIs to receive significant financial support from banks, foundations, and the federal CDFI Fund. Conditions have changed dramatically since 2000. The economy has weakened, foundation enthusiasm for CDFIs has waned, there has been little if any support for community development and reinvestment from the Bush Administration, and funding from all levels of government has been limited by severe budget shortfalls.

CDFIs have recognized the need for innovation in order to survive the current political and economic environment. Individual CDFIs have merged and formed partnerships to cut costs. Many CDFIs have identified and focused on their most lucrative and socially meaningful activities, while outsourcing loan processing and back office operations to cut expenses. Other CDFIs have diversified their base of borrowers and their mix of products. There also has been an industry-wide effort to find ways to attract and use market-rate capital and to free up existing capital by selling CDFI-originated loans on the secondary market. Regardless of the role that CDFIs ultimately play, their experiences to date have demonstrated both the financial needs and the market opportunities of lower-income communities.

REFERENCES

Belsky, E. S., Schill, M., and Yezer, A. (2001). The effect of the Community Reinvestment Act on bank and thrift home purchase mortgage lending. *Proceedings*, (May), 271–300.

Bostic, R. with B. Robinson (2004). Community banking and mortgage credit availability: The impact of CRA agreements. *Journal of Banking and Finance*, pp. 3069–3095.

Bucks, B. K., Kennickell, A. B., and Moore, K. B. (2006). Recent changes in US Family Finances: evidence from the 2001 and 2004 Survey of Consumer Finances. *Federal Reserve Bulletin* 92, pp. A1–A38.

Campen, J. T., and Callahan, T. M. (2001, April). Boston's soft-second program: Reaching low income and minority homebuyers in a changing financial services environment. Paper presented at Federal Reserve System's conference on Changing Financial Markets & Community Development, Washington, DC.

Capone, C. A. (2001). Research into mortgage default and affordable housing: A primer. LISC: The Center for Home Ownership. Available: http://www.liscnet.org/resources/2002/05/affordable_793.shtml? Affordable Housing [January 2004].

Carney, S., and Gale, W. (2001). Asset accumulation in low-income households. In T. M. Shapiro & E. Wolff, (Eds.), *Assets for the Poor: The Benefits of Spreading Asset Ownership*. New York: Russell Sage Foundation.

Caskey, J. P. (2001). *Check Cashing and Savings Programs for Low-income Households: An Action Plan for Credit Unions*. Madison, WI: Filene Research Institute, Center for Credit Union Research.

CDFI Data Project. (2003). Community development financial institutions: Providing capital, building community, creating impact. Available: http://www.cfed.org/enterprise_development/CDFIData/ [January 2004].

Clark, P., Kays, A., Zandniapour, L., Soto, E., and Doyle, K. (1999). *Microenterprise and the Poor: Findings from the Self-employment Learning Project Five Year Study of Microentrepreneurs*. Washington, DC: The Aspen Institute.

Cummings, J. L., and DiPasquale, D. (1999). The low-income housing tax credit: An analysis of the first ten years. *Housing Policy Debate*, 10(2), 251–307.

DiPasquale, D., and Cummings, J. L. (1992). Financing multifamily rental housing: The changing role of lenders and investors. *Housing Policy Debate*, 3(1), 77–116.

Du Bois, W. E. B. (Ed.). (1907). Economic co-operation among Negro Americans. Available: http://docsouth.unc.edu/church/dubois07/menu.html [February 2004]. Atlanta: Atlanta University Press.

Edgcomb, E., Klein, J., & Clark, P. (1996). *The Practice of Microenterprise in the U.S.* Washington, DC: Self-Employment Learning Project of Aspen Institute.

Halpern, R. (1995). *Rebuilding the Inner City: A History of Neighborhood Initiatives to Address Poverty in the United States*. New York: Columbia University Press.

Isbister, J. (1991). *Thin Cats: The Community Development Credit Union Movement in the United States*. Davis, CA: University of California, Center for Cooperatives.

Kennickell, A. B., Starr-McCluer, M., & Surette, B. J. (2000). Recent changes in U.S. family finances: Results from the 1998 survey of consumer finances. *Federal Reserve Bulletin*, 86, 1–29.

Mayer, N. (1998). *Saving and Creating Good Jobs*. Washington, DC: Center for Community Change.

McClure, K. (2000). The low-income housing tax credit as an aid to housing finance: How well has it worked? *Housing Policy Debate*, 11(1), 91–114.

Mullen, E., Bush, M., & Weinstein, S. (1997, March). Currency exchanges add to poverty surcharge for low-income residents. Woodstock Institute. Reinvestment Alert 10. Available: *http://woodstockinst.org/document/alert10.pdf* [January 2004].

Perry, S. E. (1987). *Communities on the Way: Rebuilding Local Economies in the United States and Canada*. Albany, NY: State University of New York Press.

Phillips-Fein, K. (1998). The still-industrial city: Why

cities shouldn't just let manufacturing go. *The American Prospect*, (September–October), 28–37.

Rohe, W. M., & Stewart, L. S. (1996). Home ownership and neighborhood stability. *Housing Policy Debate*, 7(1), 37–81.

Rubin, J. S. (2001). Community development venture capital: a double-bottom line approach to poverty alleviation. *Proceedings of the Changing Financing Markets and Community Development, Second Federal Reserve System Community Affairs Research Conference*, 121–154. Washington, DC: Federal Reserve System.

Servon, L. J. (1999). *Bootstrap Capital: Microenterprise and the American Poor*. Washington, DC: Brookings Institution Press.

Sherraden, M. (1991). *Assets and the Poor: A New American Welfare Policy*. New York: M. E. Sharpe.

Stegman, M. A. (1999). *Savings for the Poor: The Hidden Benefits of Electronic Banking*. Washington, DC: Brookings Institution Press.

Van Order, R., & Zorn, P. (2001). Performance of low-income and minority mortgages. Available: http://www.jchs.harvard.edu/publications/homeownership/liho01–10.pdf [January 2004]. Washington, DC: The Brookings Institution.

Walker, C. (1993). Nonprofit housing development: Status, trends and prospects. *Housing Policy Debate*, 4(3), 369–413.

CHAPTER 10

No Progress Without Protest

Gregory D. Squires

Twenty-five years after the passage of CRA legislation, it's important to recall the vital role that advocacy and organizing played—and continue to play—in the struggle to increase access to capital.

After decades of overt redlining and racially discriminatory lending practices, financial institutions are once again returning to the nation's cities. As Paul S. Grogan and Tony Proscio observed "Not only have community-based organizations found it vastly easier to line up financing and equity investments for their projects, but millions of individual borrowers and home buyers have found credit where for decades there had been only rejections."

Between 1993 and 2000 the share of single-family home purchase mortgage loans going to low- and moderate-income borrowers increased from 19 percent to 29 percent. According to the National Community Reinvestment Coalition, the share of loans going to black households increased from 3.8 percent to 6.6 percent, while the Hispanic share increased from 4.0 percent to 6.9 percent.

Homeownership rates are at all-time high levels. In the first quarter of 2001 the national homeownership rate rose to 67.4 percent. The Joint Center for Housing Studies found that African American homeownership climbed to 47.6 percent and the Hispanic homeownership rate reached 46.3 percent. In central cities the homeownership rate reached a record high of 51.2 percent in 2000, according to the U.S. Department of Housing and Urban Development. All of these figures were the highest in the nation's history. Though much remains to be done, clearly there has been progress in recent years.

Noting the greater availability of credit in urban and minority markets, some prominent observers attribute such change to the maturing of 1960s style protesters who grew up and now pursue "progress over protest." Lost in what is in fact a premature declaration of victory is the vital role that advocacy and organizing efforts have played and continue to play in ongoing struggles to increase access to capital in distressed neighborhoods.

ADVOCACY AND ACCOMPLISHMENT

Community development is big business today. Billions of dollars are spent by a range of investors, development organizations and consumers. In observing that community development has emerged as an industry, Lawrence B. Lindsey, former economic policy advisor to President George W. Bush, patronizingly concedes that "The protest banner can still be held reverently in our box of mementos, along with the love beads [and] peace signs." From his perspective, effective proponents of urban communities act differently today; now they are "business people." According to Lindsey the evolution is very simple, "It is called growing up."

In their widely acclaimed book *Comeback Cities*, Grogan and Proscio ridicule those with a "preference for confrontation over visible results." As Lindsey would no doubt agree, they applaud the sixties and seventies activists who, they claim, "exhausted by the antagonisms and fruitless turmoil, were more than ready to turn their newfound community-organizing talents to some practical redevelopment projects." Interestingly, they attribute much of the recent success in urban revitalization to the Community Reinvestment Act (CRA), the federal law that emerged from the Alinsky-style radicalism they dismiss. To this day its effectiveness is grounded in large part in the power neighborhood groups have acquired through a range of advocacy and organizing efforts that Grogan and Proscio also scorn.

Community development is clearly changing. Many lenders see investment opportunities in neighborhoods they would not have considered just a few years ago. Financial institutions and community development groups are sitting down as partners and "doing deals." In many cases it is the protest organizations that, as a result of their advocacy, were able to bring the lenders to the negotiating table leading to the partnerships. Financial intermediaries like the Local Initiatives Support Corporation and quasi-governmental organizations like the Neighborhood Reinvestment Corporation and Fannie Mae are providing capital. Community development finance institutions have been created to contribute to these efforts. Government agencies have used the proverbial stick as well as the carrot, passing laws like CRA and filing lawsuits to prod reinvestment. No doubt some lenders have simply responded to the signals of the marketplace and found profitable loans and investments in areas they had not previously considered. There are many facets to community reinvestment today.

But those who juxtapose organizing and advocacy efforts against accomplishments and results distort history and current social reality. Community reinvestment is also an emerging social movement. Like other social movements that sought to alter systems of unequal power and privilege (the two most vivid examples of which are the labor movement and civil rights movement), struggle and conflict are intrinsic to community reinvestment efforts. Advocacy and accomplishment are pieces of the same mosaic. And this does not apply just to historical developments. Heated debates over the Financial Services Modernization Act and its implementing regulations indicate that conflicting interests persist. If advocacy and organizing are passé, so is progress in community reinvestment.

STRENGTHENING CRA

Advocacy and organizing are primarily means to various ends. If the basic objective is to increase access to capital on equitable terms to all segments of metropolitan areas, the question remains as to what new policies and practices will realize these ends.

The Community Reinvestment Modernization Act of 2001 (HR 865) introduced by Rep. Tom Barrett (D-WI) and Luis Gutierrez (D-IL) broadens application of CRA beyond federally chartered depository institutions, increases data disclosure requirements and strengthens oversight responsibilities of appropriate authorities.

The proposed legislation was inspired by two trends. First, the continuing disparities in wealth, homeownership and access to financial services between economically distressed, predominantly nonwhite central cities and more prosperous, disproportionately white, outlying urban and suburban communities. Second, the continuing consolidation within and among financial services industries that was reinforced by the Financial Services Modernization Act permitting banks, insurers and securities firms to enter into each other's businesses in ways that had previously been prohibited by federal law.

To address these trends, the bill would enhance access to financial services for citizens of all economic circumstances and in all geographic areas; enhance the ability of financial institutions to meet the credit needs of all communities; and ensure that community reinvestment keeps pace with affiliations that are occurring in the financial services marketplace.

The sponsors of the bill did not expect it to become law in the near future, and indeed it did not receive serious consideration in Congress. Most of the provisions would not be considered politically feasible today. But the political center does change. And it does so in response to advocacy and organizing efforts that generate a constituency for policies that, while perhaps not in favor at the moment, become policy in the future.

NO PERMANENT VICTORIES

Three or four years prior to its passage, most of the civil rights legislation of the 1960s would have been considered unrealistic. The same could be said about the sweeping welfare reform legislation passed in the Clinton Administration. It took the martyrdom of Martin Luther King Jr. to secure passage of the Fair Housing Act in 1968. It took a Democratic president, advocating what had long been a conservative Republican policy, to get welfare reform. But in both instances there had been years of scholarly research, intellectual debate, conflict and struggle. And there had also been years of advocacy and organizing—on all sides—from the neighborhood level to state houses to the Congress and White House.

The community reinvestment and fair lending victories that have been achieved—in part through the use of tools like the Fair Housing Act, the Home Mortgage Disclosure Act and CRA—reflect a similar history. "Community organizing has been the driving force of the reinvestment movement from the beginning," according to two of the movement's pioneers, Calvin Bradford and Gale Cincotta. "At any given point, a legislator, an agency official or some government agency can play an important part in an issue or policy; but over the long haul, community reinvestment remains a movement determined by people power."

Local neighborhood organizations, working with supportive members of the media, the academic community and some elected officials and representatives of financial institutions themselves (sometimes brought kicking and screaming to the bargaining table) have used a variety of tools to change the way lenders do business in the nation's cities. And the Community Reinvestment Modernization Act would likely not have been produced if it were not for the advocacy efforts of the National Community Reinvestment Coalition, ACORN, the National Training and Information Center and community organizations around the country.

Saul Alinsky argued that there are no permanent friends or permanent enemies. And there are few, if any, permanent victories. Progress has been made in fair lending and community reinvestment, but that progress is threatened, as the rise of predatory lending in recent years demonstrates. Homeownership may be at record levels today, but low-income and minority neighborhoods remain underserved. Future goals for community reinvestment and fair lending seem reasonably clear, as do the tactics and strategies for achieving them. Sustaining the type of efforts responsible for past victories and required for future ones remains the challenge of the day.

RESOURCES

"Mortgage Lending in Boston: Interpreting HMDA Data," by Alicia H. Munnell, Lynn E. Browne, James McEneaney and Geoffrey M.B. Tootell. *American Economic Review*, 1996, 86 (1): 25–53.

"The Legacy, the Promise, and the Unfinished Agenda," by Calvin Bradford and Gale Cincotta. *From Redlining to Reinvestment: Community Responses to Urban Disinvestment*, Gregory D. Squires, ed. Temple University Press, 1992.

The 25th Anniversary of the Community Reinvestment Act: Access to Capital in an Evolving Financial Services System. Joint Center for Housing Studies, 2002.

The Color of Credit: What is Known About Discrimination in Mortgage Lending, by Stephen Ross and John Yinger. The MIT Press, 2002.

All Other Things Being Equal: A Paired Testing Study of Mortgage Lending Institutions, by Margery Turner, Fred Freiberg, Erin Godfrey, Carla Herbig, Diane K. Levy and Robin R. Smith. www.huduser.org.

Discrimination in Metropolitan Housing Markets: National Results from Phase I HDS 2000, by Margery Turner, Stephen L. Ross, George C. Galster and John Yinger. The Urban Institute, 2002.

Unequal Burden: Income and Racial Disparities in Subprime Lending in America, U.S. Department of Housing and Urban Development, 2000.

Comeback Cities, by Paul Grogan and Tony Proscio. Westview Press, 2000.

CHAPTER 11

The Economic Development of Neighborhoods and Localities

Wim Wiewel, Michael Teitz, and Robert Giloth

INTRODUCTION

The practice of neighborhood-based economic development arises out of decades of community organizing and antipoverty efforts. Housing rehabilitation and construction are the main activities of most Community Development Corporations (CDCs) and other neighborhood groups, but they also engage in economic development, which includes assisting business creation and retention, developing commercial and industrial space, and job training programs.

Yet despite these many years of experience, we still lack a comprehensive theory of community economic development. A good theory of neighborhood economic development needs to include an accurate and complete economic perspective, which explains both internal dynamics and linkages between neighborhoods and the larger economy. Second, such a theory must be based on a realistic understanding of sociopolitical conditions to gain clarity for action: what the basis for intervention at the neighborhood level can be, and how, when and where interventions can be effective. But because such a theory does not currently exist, this chapter begins with practice, to discover elements of implied theory in the actual work of neighborhood economic development practitioners. This review of strategies and their relative success will help in the exploration of an integrated theory of neighborhood economic development.

NEIGHBORHOOD ECONOMIC DEVELOPMENT PRACTICE

This section discusses eight forms of neighborhood economic development practice. After a brief definition, we analyze each by exploring its theoretical basis in regard to (a) the economic basis of the practice in terms of the neighborhood economy and its linkage to the larger economy, and (b) the assumptions in regard to the normative basis for action and the sociopolitical conditions that make success possible. Table 11.1 summarizes this section.

Business retention involves neighborhood organizations promoting the stabilization of existing businesses and industrial districts (Center for Urban Economic Development, 1987). These businesses are frequently bypassed by market trends and by public actors because of their location, size, sector, or profit level. Neighborhood business retention identifies business problems, organizes business leaders, provides technical assistance and loan packaging, organizes collective services (e.g., security or employment referral), launches industrial real estate projects (e.g., industrial parks or incubators), and advocates for public policies (e.g., industrial protection, land use controls, or specialized loan programs) beneficial to specific industrial locations, economic sectors, and firm sizes (Giloth and Betancur, 1988).

Commercial revitalization involves neighborhood organizations promoting the

Table 11.1 Forms of neighborhood economic development

Neighborhood economic development strategies	Economic assumption		Sociopolitical assumptions	Conditions for effectiveness
	Neighborhood	Region	Levers for intervention	
Business retention	Business–neighborhood jobs link; Appropriate scale	Neighborhood business part of regional economy	Plant closing	Business characteristics; State of economic development organization
Commercial revitalization	Commercial areas linked to neighborhood income	Regional hierarchy of commercial places; Competition	Commercial strip decline; Effects on residential neighborhood	Modest incomes; Slow pace of change
Business ventures	Lack of entrepreneurs; Lack of neighborhood $$; Undervaluation of neighborhood	Disinvestment/barriers; Potential marketplace	Neighborhood income leaks; Plant shutdowns; Lack of entrepreneurs	Exceptional markets, people, & organizations
Entrepreneurship	Underuse of neighborhood human resources	Barriers Marketplace	Life skills of residents; Lack of alternatives; Welfare reform	Ongoing support system; Self-reliance
Neighborhood capital accumulation	Neighborhoods have underused/disinvested resources	Disinvestment by larger institutions	Lack of neighborhood organization & financial resources	Level of investment; Leadership; Scale & nature
Education and training	Underused human resources	Regional economic assets	Consensus on need for educational reform & competitive work force; Impact on poor	Private sector role; Broader involvement of public/private
Labor-based development	Neighborhood as workplace & residence; Economic clustering	Growing regional sectors	Plant shutdowns	Existing industry-neighborhood links; Sectoral clustering
Community organizing/planning	Unequal power & resources; Strength in numbers and organizations	Targets for change	Inequitable resource distribution	Legal guidelines; Strength of coalitions; Support of public sector

economic growth of commercial districts by sponsoring marketing campaigns, special service (i.e., taxing) districts, commercial strip management (as at shopping centers), business attraction and retention services, and targeted real estate development. Neighborhood business organizations undertake this work because it represents a common interest that no single business can accomplish.

Business ventures. Neighborhood organizations initiate or facilitate new business ventures because neighborhood locations lack indigenous entrepreneurs and are unattractive to market-driven actors. The assumption underlying this strategy is that local businesses hire locally and spend locally, hence strengthening neighborhood economies. Common ventures include construction companies, cooperatives, property management firms, and recycling businesses.

Entrepreneurialism is a variant of the business venture strategy that assumes that homegrown entrepreneurs will enhance neighborhood ownership, employment, and development. It therefore trains and nurtures entrepreneurs, attempting to tap human resources that have been underused (McKnight and Kretzmann, 1990).

Neighborhood capital accumulation involves neighborhood ownership and control over land, businesses, investment, and financial capital because neighborhood resources and opportunities are being drained, disinvested, or neglected (Gunn and Gunn, 1991). Frequently this strategy requires establishing new institutions, such as community development corporations (CDCs), land trusts, community development credit unions, or development loan funds that invest resources in neighborhood development ventures.

Education, training, and placement as a strategy invests in the human capital of neighborhoods and attempts to connect people with jobs. This strategy addresses the mismatch in regard to skills and geography of neighborhood residents and the labor market. Its initiatives provide basic skills, employment training, transportation, job readiness, antidiscrimination efforts, job linkages, and ongoing on-the-job supports.

Labor-based development begins by identifying the employment skills of neighborhood residents, particularly the unemployed and recently displaced workers; it then seeks industries that require similar occupational skills. Industries that meet this criterion and are growing in the region are then analyzed in terms of their location, employment, capital, and business assistance needs. Finally, a plan is developed to address how these industries can be attracted to specific industrial districts and sites and linked with the existing labor force (Ranney and Betancur, 1992).

Community organizing/planning alters the power relationships that constrain the flow of resources and opportunities to neighborhoods. Community organizing/planning mobilizes the power of numbers-residents, businesses, and institutions-to advocate, demand, negotiate, and plan. Frequently, neighborhoods band together in citywide coalitions to maximize their strength and to address systemic biases in the decision-making processes and actual allocations of public and private resources. Typical targets for such organizing/planning are city hall, banks, federal dollars (e.g., CDBG), and big development projects (Giloth, 1988).

LINKAGE TO THE NEIGHBORHOOD AND REGIONAL ECONOMY

What are the theoretical notions reflected in these neighborhood development strategies? First, what does each strategy assume about the neighborhood economy and its linkage to the larger economy?

Business Retention

Business retention assumes that there is a beneficial relationship (or a potential one) between neighborhood industries, residents, and retail businesses because of proximity. It combines this social benefit orientation with a recognition of the importance of market-based factors of industrial location, such as infrastructure, transportation, access to markets and suppliers, and labor force.

Neighborhoods may also be the most appropriate organizational level at which to gather information, bring together businesses for cooperative purposes, and implement service programs. When organized at the citywide level, such activities are frequently dominated by downtown interests, the largest firms or sectors, or promising high-growth sectors. Consequently, neighborhood industrial councils resemble mini-growth coalitions and comprise landowning firms, banks, utilities, and realtors that promote specific industrial districts.

Neighborhood industries are connected to regional markets, are affected by inter-industry and corporate relationships, experience locational and agglomeration advantages or disadvantages, and are the target of competition for economic development between regions. Consequently, if regions lose competitive advantage or experience disinvestment, neighborhood locations within these regions will falter as well. Hence regional economic development policies (and national policies with regional implications) affect the viability of neighborhood business locations.

Commercial Revitalization

Neighborhoods are part of a market-based hierarchy of commercial places defined by types of goods, family income, and transportation access. The neighborhood shopping district is home to a mix of convenience and trade goods sold by businesses that depend upon the consumer incomes of neighborhood residents. When consumer preferences are not met in neighborhoods, neighborhood income leaks to other shopping districts. Changes in neighborhood income and demographic characteristics, modes of transportation, consumer preferences, retail efficiencies, and the emergence of shopping malls have disrupted neighborhood shopping districts over the past 20 years. Consequently, neighborhood commercial groups also function like mini-growth coalitions, marketing the viability of specific neighborhood commercial areas.

Neighborhood shopping districts are part of regional hierarchies of commercial areas that are constantly evolving-particularly in response to the decline of city populations and the growth of suburbia. As a result neighborhood shopping districts compete with other city and suburban retailing centers.

Development of Business Ventures

This as a strategy is grounded in the lack of neighborhood entrepreneurs, leaks of neighborhood income, and the undervaluing of neighborhood market opportunities due to racial prejudice.

The insufficient rates of return for neighborhood businesses result from low neighborhood income, high operating costs, and higher thresholds of profit required by larger businesses. This perspective even questions whether a market-defined rate of return is an appropriate measure for business investment in neighborhoods given the theorized social benefits that accrue in neighborhoods from business development but that are not counted on the private balance sheet (e.g., employment effects on crime, social welfare, family life).

Lack of business development and ownership in neighborhoods means that income is drained elsewhere. Moreover, outside institutions—for example, banks—may undermine the neighborhood business environment by creating a scarcity of capital. Alternatively, business ventures that capitalize on neighborhood locational attributes (e.g., amenities, history, culture) may become regional attractions.

Entrepreneurship

This shares the basic assumptions of the business venture strategy but is also concerned with underused human resources. That underuse occurs because of diminished opportunities and the lack of sociocultural supports needed to encourage entrepreneurs.

While the larger region may be a competitor for a neighborhood, especially for its commercial businesses, it also serves as a potential marketplace for newly inspired or organized entrepreneurs.

Neighborhood Capital Accumulation

Even poor neighborhoods have financial, human, and organizational resources that can provide a foundation for neighborhood development (Gunn and Gunn, 1991). Unfortunately, these resources are drained from neighborhoods by absentee ownership, lack of local businesses, and institutional disinvestment. That drain of resources from neighborhoods is often related to race and class.

The neighborhood drain of resources occurs because of gaps in neighborhood economies and because of structured forms of disinvestment (i.e., redlining or deindustrialization) that are directed by regional and national institutions. As a development strategy, neighborhood-based financial institutions have been able to attract social investments from the region.

Employment, Training, and Placement
Many inner-city neighborhoods are defined, in labor market terms, as redundant, surplus, or marginalized. The roots of this pattern lie in the functioning of the labor market in conjunction with the historic legacy of racism. Lack of trained and job-ready workers has prompted business communities in many areas to advocate educational reform. Their impetus is the negative impact of the lack' of highly trained, technical 'workers on the competitive position of the region and their own businesses. Teitz (1989) posited a neighborhood's labor force as its key economic asset and in fact its only developable one. One problem with such a strategy, however, is that it may simply let successfully trained individuals leave the neighborhood.

Labor-based Development
This seeks to reestablish the neighborhood as workplace and residential space. That strategy may work best with a cluster of neighborhoods, or a subsection of the city, because of the workplace/residence separation and the need to have a critical mass of specific skills to attract specific industry. Sectors and firms growing or attracted to the region are the target for the labor-based strategy, in particular, manufacturing sectors that contain smaller firms and are labor intensive.

Community Organizing/Planning
Low- and moderate-income neighborhoods have unequal political power in relation to major private interests and public sector bureaucracies. Neighborhoods are viewed as secondary in relation to land-based interests that promote downtown and big development projects as the engines for city growth. Community organizing builds upon the neighborhood strength of numbers of people and organizations. It focuses on citywide/regional patterns of power and resource distribution, attempting to increase the recognition of neighborhoods and the responsiveness of regional institutions to neighborhood concerns.

SOCIOPOLITICAL CONDITIONS AND THE BASIS FOR ACTION AND SUCCESS

Organizations continue to use these strategies because they rest on plausible theoretical notions about the economy. How well they work in particular situations depends on how well they fit particular economic conditions. Sound economics is not enough, however. Strategies must resonate with values and they must be appropriate to the social and political situation. What are the assumptions of these strategies regarding the basis for action and the conditions for success?

Business Retention
Threats of firms closing or moving may precipitate the involvement of neighborhood organizations. Usually the possibility of losing a neighborhood anchor, or having residents laid off, is a powerful motivator.

Variables related to the scale, diversity, ownership, sectoral clustering, and location of industries on a regional and neighborhood basis affect whether cooperative strategies among neighborhood industries are feasible. The level of economic development organization within the neighborhood and its city also affects whether neighborhood business retention is a viable strategy (Ranney, 1988).

Commercial Revitalization
Declining sales, strip deterioration, and changing demographic characteristics have encouraged neighborhood retailers to join together to redefine the focus, management, and marketing strategies for their commercial areas. The negative effects of declining commercial areas on nearby residential

neighborhoods have also spurred community action. Successful commercial revitalization requires modest income levels and a controllable pace of neighborhood change. It also works when there are few nearby competitors—suburban or city shopping malls, for example.

Business Venture
Business venture opportunities result from an analysis of neighborhood income leaks, export opportunities, business shutdowns, and sheltered neighborhood markets. Their pursuit is often motivated by the perceived absence of any viable alternatives. They have proven difficult except when there are exceptional markets, human resources, and organizational capacity. Neighborhood organizations frequently do not have the entrepreneurial experience, drive, and resources to make fledgling businesses thrive; their ventures face all the rigors that confront start-up businesses in addition to the challenges of operating in neighborhoods or markets that private entrepreneurs ignore (Wiewel and Giloth, 1988).

Entrepreneurship
Most people have life experiences and skills that are translatable into business opportunities, even when business is defined as a micro business or self-employment. Here, too, the absence of other viable alternatives is an important motivation and so is the American image of the "self-made man." A public sector motivation is the concern for enabling welfare recipients to get off welfare; with few jobs available, and a lack of child care and basic skills, part-time self-employment is a viable alternative.

Most small businesses fail—an outcome that probably also applies to firms initiated by entrepreneurial and micro-business programs as well. These efforts, however, despite the failures, may enable people to become more self-reliant and to learn from failure. In this regard, the most successful programs are those that provide ongoing supports for entrepreneurs; neighborhood organizations have been able to organize such support models (Center for Urban Economic Development, 1987).

Neighborhood Capital Accumulation
Lack of financial resources for investment in viable neighborhood ventures often precipitates interest in establishing alternative financial or development organizations. That issue is often highlighted by Community Reinvestment Act (CRA) analyses that show lack of credit flows to neighborhoods by mainstream financial institutions.

There has been a proliferation of neighborhood-oriented financial institutions; very often, however, these institutions operate in larger environments than just single neighborhoods. At the neighborhood level, capital accumulation has been aided by community development corporations, through their development and ownership of housing and other real estate.

Employment, Training, and Placement
The employment needs of the business community and the deplorable state of public education in U.S. cities have created the policy space for the overhauling of educational bureaucracies, experimentation with popular education at the school, family, and neighborhood levels, and innovative job training, placement, and support programs. The differential impact on minority and poor communities has also provided a touchstone for community outcry.

These initiatives are complicated; their success for any neighborhood depends upon the strength of the contacts with the private sector, the stability of the job base, and the support for basic skills, job readiness, as well as ongoing support. In a broader sense, overhauling the education and welfare systems that inhibit quality employment and lifelong learning is a long-term strategy that reaches beyond individual neighborhoods.

Labor-based Development
A catalyst for this strategy is a plant shutdown or a series of shutdowns that affect sectoral clusterings of firms (e.g., steel, fabrication) that result in massive displacement of workers with accumulated skills. Retraining is one option to get them back in the labor force; the labor-based approach designs development strategies based upon their existing job skills.

This strategy attracts higher wage jobs to neighborhoods by offering an array of inducements, including labor force training and business support services. It is most effective where there are industrial districts that already employ neighborhood people and have locational and infrastructure attributes attractive to a broad range of firms.

Community Organizing/Planning

The ongoing motivation for community organizing is the inequitable distribution of resources to neighborhoods and the social and economic impacts related to that distribution. Handles for community organizing, given these inequities, include public budgeting, the use and abuse of public incentives, planning, and approvals by private developers for large public/private projects that yield questionable benefits for neighborhoods. Legislation such as the Community Reinvestment Act provides a more predictable path for raising these resource issues.

Community organizing/planning depends upon legislative or administrative guidelines (e.g., the CRA), the breadth and depth of community coalitions, the supportiveness of public institutions, the profitability of private development, and the localized nature of proposed solutions. Organizing has been less successful when it has challenged private decision making and ownership or has advocated broad redistributional programs. Occasionally, community organizing has spilled over into political campaigns that, when successful, have made bureaucracies more supportive of neighborhood economic development (Clavel and Wiewel, 1991).

WHAT DOES A THEORY OF NEIGHBORHOOD ECONOMIC DEVELOPMENT NEED?

The first section of this chapter identified two substantive requirements for community economic development theory. First, the theory should concern itself with the neighborhood economy and its linkages. Second, the theory must also be sociopolitical because the activity with which it is concerned is rooted in a particular form of social institution and its practitioners act explicitly within a political framework.

The actual experience of practitioners suggests three additional, more abstract requirements for a theory. First, the theory must be instrumental, that is, it should provide guidance for action rather than simply a positive explanation of how things behave. Second, it should also be normative that is, it must embody a set of objectives and arguments for realization. This assertion is closely related to the idea of instrumentality in the sense that an instrumental theory demands some goal. It is also consistent with the entire history of community economic development, which has been driven by the desire for change and improvement in the conditions under which people live. Third, a neighborhood economic development theory requires a positive understanding of the contextual world in which the action that it deals with will be played out. This term describes the kind of understanding of relationships and interactions necessary for effective action.

PROBLEMS AND POTENTIALS IN COMMUNITY ECONOMIC DEVELOPMENT THEORY

How well does current community economic development theory stand up to these criteria and how might it be improved? On the whole, it does not do well. While practice has generated an array of approaches and, to some extent, techniques, there is little in the way of an integrated theoretical framework that can give those elements coherence.

Although the variety of approaches suggests that this field is dominated by instrumental thinking, virtually none of the approaches contains the essential elements of instrumentality, namely, guidance as to when and how they may be more or less effective and predictive power about their impacts. The theoretical and substantive content of most books being written about economic development is thin. Careful assessment of the effectiveness of the practice elements laid out above has not been done. Not much is known about where they do and do not work or how they interact with each other. For instance, does providing job training cause an exodus of skilled people from the neighborhood rather than improvement in conditions? Good theory is essential as a guide to practice, both to build the arguments for innovation and to provide support to continue when innovations fail.

What about the normative content of current theory? Is that not an area of great strength? At one level, this is certainly the case. Practitioners are committed to community goals in the face of enormous obstacles and pressures, often to their own personal disadvantage. Yet, there are also problems of normative scope.

The nature of the field itself gives rise to serious conflicts in objectives among its proponents, probably far more so than in conventional economic development. Although practitioners are aware of such conflicts and live with them every day, virtually no theoretical attention has been paid to their nature and to their resolution. Where solidarity is conceived of as a supreme virtue, recognition and acceptance of the reality of conflicting objectives are difficult to attain. But when serious attention is paid to objectives and building consensus, as in the case of community organizing, the effort may be so great and the compromises so deep that the original economic objectives are lost in the political mobilization.

The third abstract characteristic of a community economic development theory—namely, an appropriate positive understanding of the contextual environment in which actions will be taken—presents a mixed picture. Certainly, economic development practitioners are all too aware of the constraints of the larger economy under which they work. Yet, it is also the case that community groups often do not understand or accept the reality of those constraints. In part, this is a tribute to their determination to achieve change in the face of what are formidable, indeed, impossible, obstacles.

Does this mean that community groups should know more about supply and demand? In some instances, yes; the history of worker takeovers demonstrates quite clearly the cost of illusions about business

viability, and it is encouraging that more recent efforts are recognizing this most explicitly. But in a larger sense, conventional economic theory is not the only way in which to understand development. There is too much legitimate questioning and debate for that. The questions raised by conventional theory about the way in which markets work in a capitalist economy cannot, however, be ignored, no matter what injustice and distributional inequity may exist in their operation.

Similar problems exist in relation to the substantive content of community economic development theory. Clearly, a theoretical basis for this field must be both economic and sociopolitical in nature. Current practice revolves around activities that are economic in nature, but they are not integrated into an economic theory of community development that has much real content. In part, this is due to the history and evolution of the field, which has emerged from political struggles and attempts to preserve communities in the face of change and enhance their well-being in the face of exploitation, discrimination, and prejudice. A broadly accepted theory of community economic development is a long way off, and practice reflects this.

Are there some substantive elements that might contribute to a theory of development and practice? One important consideration flows from the experiences of the few instances where community economic development has been brought to the forefront of policy. These experiences suggest that the central role of community economic development action is to employ political means to achieve broadly redistributive goals through economic growth focused on particular populations and communities. The essential purpose is communitarian, but the method is to employ market mechanisms, reinforced, by political efforts to generate the necessary resources for investment and to establish rules that are consistent with the larger market environment, yet supportive of community goals. There are, then, three necessary requirements to be satisfied by the process, and they must be mutually consistent for it to work.

First, the gains to communities should

arise primarily from the enhancement of the productivity and creation of assets of community populations rather than solely through redistributive transfers. This implies that the realities of the market must be understood, recognized, and dealt with. Second, the objectives of community development are established at the local level, but they have to be realizable and consistent.

Third, the use of political power in, relation to community economic development is primarily to facilitate the process of productivity enhancement and asset creation. The distinction here is between the politics of economic development in the community realm and the politics of other social goals, such as effective participation. It is, to some extent, an artificial distinction in practice, especially because the various elements of community development are intended to be mutually reinforcing, but from the perspective of economic development, it emphasizes the political willingness to come to terms with the market. This agenda is modest in comparison with the conceptions of sweeping social change that have historically informed some forms of community development. Nonetheless, it can form a viable basis for integrating actions for economic development.

A second consideration that might be brought to a theoretical structure focuses on what community economic development means and what the community itself brings to the process. It is important, and overdue, to sort out what it is in development that enhances the community and what it is that flows to the individual, the family, and the household or other smaller social units. This inevitably again raises the definitional problem of community. Do neighborhoods and communities in fact have collective or organic qualities for purposes of goal setting? The origins and character of community development suggest so, but this requires caution about the form and meaning of collective or aggregate goals. From a developmental point of view, it leads to the issue of the relationship between the potential state that a community might realistically achieve and what it brings to the development process.

What does the community provide for the development process? While it is a common part of conventional practice to carry out some sort of resource assessment, there is little theoretical basis to assign meaning and significance to those resources for economic development. What exactly does constitute community or neighborhood resources? This is an issue that is worth much more theoretical exploration, especially with respect to those aspects of community that do not inhere in any particular individual or specific piece of property. For example, if a community is attractive for investment by virtue of its collective character or location, who should realize the gain and who should bear the cost? It is equally important, however, to ask what those collective resources actually are, how they affect development, and what will happen to them if development does occur.

One of the exciting aspects of community economic development is that it is being created largely through practice. Unlike traditional economic theory, where academic theoreticians are usually far removed from the entrepreneurs and firms that make decisions, in community economic development those who practice are frequently also those who think, speak, and occasionally write about it. Obviously, under these circumstances theory often takes a back seat, and not as much theoretical work is being produced as one might wish. But what there is, is close to the field, and likely to be tested in practice. Given the newness of the field, it is reasonable to expect that continued growth and development in the years and decades ahead

REFERENCES

Center for Urban Economic Development (1987). *Community Economic Development Strategies: A Manual for Local Action.* Chicago: Center for Urbain Economic Development, University of Illinois at Chicago.

Clavel, Pierre and Wiewel, Wim (eds.), *Harold Washington and the Neighborhoods.* (pp. 238–269). New Brunswick, NJ: Rutgers University Press.

Giloth, Robert (1988). "Community Economic Development: Strategies and Practices of the 1980s." *Economic Development Quarterly* 2(4): 343–350.

Giloth, Robert (1991). "Making Policy with Communities: Research and Development in the

Department of Economic Development." In Pierre Clavel and Wim Wiewel (eds.), *Harold Washington and the Neighborhoods* (pp. 100–120). New Brunswick, NJ: Rutgers University Press.

Giloth, Robert and John Betancur (1988). "Where Downtown Meets Neighborhood: Industrial Displacement in Chicago, 1978–1987." *Journal of the American Planning Association* 54(3): 279–290.

Gunn, Christopher and Hazel Dayton Gunn (1991). *Reclaiming Capital: Democratic Initiatives and Community Development*. Ithaca, NY: Cornell University Press.

McKnight, John and Jody Kretzmann (1990). *Mapping Community Capacity*. Evanston, IL: Center for Urban Affairs and Policy Research, Northwestern University.

Ranney, David (1988). "Plant Closings and Corporate Disinvestment." *Journal of Planning Literature* 3(1): 22–35.

Ranney, David and John Betancur (1992). "Labor Force Based Development: A Community Oriented Approach to Targeting Job Training and Industrial Development." *Economic Development Quarterly* 6(3): 286–296.

Teitz, Michael (1989). "Neighborhood Economics: Local Communities and Regional Markets." *Economic Development Quarterly* 3(2): 111–122.

Wiewel, Wim, Bridget Brown, and Marya Morris (1989). "The Linkage Between Regional and Neighborhood Development." *Economic Development Quarterly* 3(2): 94–110.

Wiewel, Wim and Robert Giloth (1988). "Should Your Group Start a Business Venture?" In Mary O'Connell (ed.), *The Neighborhood Tool Box* (pp. 22–23). Chicago: Center for Neighborhood Technology.

CHAPTER 12

Communities as Place, Face, and Space

Provision of services to poor, urban children and their families[1]

Tama Leventhal, Jeanne Brooks-Gunn, and Sheila B. Kamerman

We would like to thank the Foundation for Child Development and the U.S. Department of Housing and Urban Development for their support of neighborhood programs and the Aspen Institute Roundtable on Comprehensive Community Initiatives for Children and Families, the Russell Sage Foundation, and the Social Science Research Council for their support of neighborhood research. We also would like to acknowledge the National Institute of Child Health and Human Development Research Network on Child and Family Well-being. In addition, we would like to thank Mercer Sullivan for his helpful comments on the original chapter. The authors are particularly grateful to the Big Cities seminar participants at Columbia University for their stimulating discussion.

INTRODUCTION

Research on neighborhoods undertaken in the 1980's and 1990's was partially a response to the worsening conditions in poor neighborhoods in America's cities beginning in the 1970s (Wilson 1987; Wilson 1997). Scholars from a variety of disciplines began to document the detrimental impacts of neighborhood poverty on child and family well-being. Much of this work, as exemplified in the publication of *Neighborhood Poverty: Context and Consequences of Children* (Brooks-Gunn, Duncan, and Aber 1997a; Brooks-Gunn, Duncan, and Aber 1997b), used demographic information on neighborhoods from the US Decennial Census in conjunction with data on individual children and families. Policy attention increasingly focused on the alarmingly high number of children living in urban neighborhoods marked by high concentrations of poverty (in excess of 30 percent; Kahn and Kamerman 1996; O'Hare and Mather 2003).

How do communities, especially those with high concentrations of poor people, actually provide services and strengthen families' efforts to provide food, love, shelter, health care, safe streets, and learning experiences for their children? This chapter focuses on the ways in which neighborhood research can be used to inform the design of services for low-income, urban families with children (and indirectly, in reforming or altering the systems in which services are embedded), and to evaluate the outcomes of service initiatives. We make a distinction between four general approaches to delivering services to children in cities: (1) categorical programs; (2) family and community support services; (3) community development corporations (CDCs); and (4) comprehensive community initiatives (CCIs). Services are generally delivered through categorical programs, which consist of federally mandated programs, such as Woman, Infants, and Children (WIC), Head Start, and Temporary Assistance for Needy Families (TANF). A number of programs, such as the State Children's Health Insurance Program (S-CHIP), are funded under block grants to states giving more local autonomy to these programs. The second strategy concentrates on integrating services for children and families in a community-based setting as well as fostering ties among community residents through the provision of family and community support services. The third approach, CDCs, focuses on housing, job creation, and civic infrastructure. The fourth strategy, CCIs, integrates the first three approaches to service delivery by providing coordinated and integrated services in a neighborhood-based setting and incorporating housing and community development.

Accordingly, this chapter addresses three issues: (1) how to conceptualize the relationships among children, families and neighborhoods; (2) how social science has enhanced our understanding of urban children's lives, particularly as related to service provision; and (3) how the provision of services to poor, urban children varies as a function of the definition of community employed and informs the design of urban services for children.

CHILDREN IN FAMILIES
IN COMMUNITIES

This section addresses how neighborhoods affect children directly as well as how neighborhoods may indirectly influence children by affecting their families—especially parents.

Neighborhood Effects on Children

Prior to the publication of *Neighborhood Poverty* in 1997, relatively few studies had considered how neighborhood structural conditions might affect children's development (Brooks-Gunn, Duncan, and Aber 1997a; Brooks-Gunn, Duncan, and Aber 1997b). What followed was an expanded body of neighborhood research. Neighborhood income or socioeconomic status (SES)—a combination of social and economic indicators—has been the most commonly investigated neighborhood structural dimension. Researchers often separate measures of neighborhood SES into high-SES/affluence (e.g., income, percent professionals, and percent college-educated) and low-SES/poverty (e.g., percent poor, percent female-headed households, percent on public assistance, and percent unemployed) because the presence of poor and affluent neighbors may have differential associations with child and adolescent outcomes. Other structural

characteristics frequently examined include racial/ethnic mix (e.g., percent Black, percent Latino, and percent foreign-born) and residential instability (e.g., percent moved in last 5 years, percent households in current home less than 10 years, and percent renters).

We conducted several large-scale reviews of the neighborhood research which found that for preschool and school-age children, neighborhood affluence (compared to middle-income) was positively associated with their verbal ability, IQ scores, and school achievement (Leventhal and Brooks-Gunn 2000). Neighborhood low-income (compared to middle-income), on the other hand, was associated with children's mental health problems. For adolescents, high-income/SES neighbors were also associated with school achievement and educational attainment, particularly for male youth. Neighborhood low-income was adversely associated with adolescents' mental health, criminal and delinquent behavior, and sexual and fertility outcomes.

The studies reviewed identified specific structural dimensions that were associated with particular classes of outcomes, but do not address the mechanisms through which neighborhood effects are transmitted to children and youth. We proposed several theoretical models, highlighting different underlying processes, to explain potential pathways of neighborhood influences (Leventhal and Brooks-Gunn 2000). The first model, *institutional resources*, posits that neighborhood influences operate by means of the quality, quantity, and diversity of community resources—learning, recreational, social, educational, health, and employment. The second model, *relationships and ties*, highlights families as a potential mechanism of neighborhood effects including parental attributes (e.g., mental and physical health, coping skills, and efficacy), social networks, and behavior (e.g., supervision/monitoring, warmth, and harshness) as well as home environment characteristics (e.g., learning and physical environments, family routines, and violence). The last model, *norms and collective efficacy*, hypothesizes that neighborhood influences are accounted for by the extent of community formal and informal institutions present to monitor residents' behavior, particularly peer groups, and physical threats in the neighborhood, notably violence and availability of illegal and harmful substances. The models are intended to be complementary rather than conflicting, with the utility of each model for explaining neighborhood effects on child well-being depending, in part, on the outcome studied, and, in part, on the age group examined.

Neighborhood Effects on Families

As indicated by the *relationships and ties model*, the effects of neighborhood-level conditions on children may operate indirectly through parental behavior and family functioning. Some data support this premise: Over and above sociodemographic factors, neighborhood characteristics are associated with both maternal characteristics, such as depression, as well as with parenting behaviors, such as warmth and harshness. Several studies explicitly examining indirect neighborhood effects via the home environment report that quality of the home environment accounted for associations among neighborhood SES and children's academic achievement, verbal abilities, and behavior problem scores.

Given that neighborhood characteristics affect parental well-being, parenting and the home environment, focusing on the intersection of families and neighborhoods appears to be central for the provision of services to urban children. Perhaps one of the most important facts is that parents are advocates or brokers for their children's receipt of community resources. Parents must interact with community-level agencies and institutions to garner resources for their children. For example, parents select preschools and schools for their children, obtain health services for their children (especially for children with disabilities or risk conditions), and create extra-curricular activities for their children. Few studies, however, provide information on the process by which parents in poor communities obtain, create, and structure opportunities for their children despite scarce institutional resources.

In the same vein, federal policy initiatives for children also must be viewed in the context of children in families in communities. Many programs intended to serve (primarily low income) children, such as immunization campaigns and Early Periodic Diagnostic and Screening Test (EPDST), encounter surprisingly low levels of participation, especially among poor families or those residing in poor neighborhoods (albeit varied levels of outreach). Parental involvement appears to be a missing component to the design and implementation of these services. Alternatively, the success of Head Start is often attributed to its efforts to engage parents as well as local community members in the program. Thus, federal and community programs are important neighborhood resources for families, but their efficacy depends largely on the family and the community.

PROVISION OF SERVICES AND DEFINITIONS OF COMMUNITY

Defining or operationalizing the notion of community (as is common practice in neighborhood-based research) is not a high priority for designers of community-based services (Sullivan 1996). Predicaments may arise if alternative definitions of community are used by family and community support services, CDCs, CCIs, and categorical programs (and with categorical programs not doing it the same way either—e.g., health districts, police precincts, school districts, etc.). Drawing upon the work of Kubisch (1996) and Sullivan (1996), we have identified three different approaches to defining communities: (1) communities as "place"; (2) communities as "face"; and (3) communities as "space". Defining communities as "place" is common in much of social science research, where communities are conceived of as neighborhoods (geographical locales) and bureaucratically-defined catchments. Viewing communities as "face" emphasizes the psychological associations that residents have within their community; in other words, the community is comprised of relationships and social supports. The last definition, communities as "space", views communities as physical and built environments for living, working, and political organizing. Clearly, these different definitions of community have implications for service delivery. This section will illustrate how the provision of services to poor, urban children and their families varies as a function of the definition of community employed.

Communities as Place

Viewing communities as "place"—neighborhoods or geographical or bureaucratic locales—suggests that communities are manageable units around which to organize and deliver services (Kubisch 1996). Employing a place-based definition of community has two main implications for the provision of services to urban children. The more moderate and ubiquitous approach is categorical programs, and the more ambitious strategy is system reform.

Categorical Programs

While categorical programs (e.g., WIC, Head Start, Healthy Start, and Medicaid) are federally mandated, they are delivered at the community-level (according to bureaucratic units). Not all communities have the same number, intensity, quality, or availability of services (physical and mental health, social, recreational, child care, educational, job training). Poor, urban communities typically lack available and high quality services. Thus, a critical issue that most researchers and policy makers have failed to address adequately is how to determine what programs and services are available in the community (the US Decennial Census does not measure availability of services), and whether or not available services are effective.

Service Reform

Although categorical programs utilize geographical definitions of community, not all categorical programs define community the same way. Consequently, service reform has become a popular, place-based initiative. Place-based definitions may be more flexible than the bureaucratic systems (i.e., categorical programs) in that they represent more precisely the local community. For example, the New Futures initiative funded by the

Annie E. Casey Foundation in five cities seeks to restructure the way communities organize, finance, and deliver educational, health, and other services to at-risk youth.

Schorr with Both (1991) attributed the success of system reform programs to their (1) flexibility, comprehensiveness, and responsiveness; (2) child-orientations as well as family- and community-orientation; (3) high-quality staff; (4) efforts to reach the most at-risk populations and target services accordingly; (5) superior management; and (6) theoretical approach rooted in client-orientation and long-term prevention models. Clearly, these characteristics stand in contradistinction to current ways that most bureaucratic institutions and systems deliver services. In particular, categorical funding, standardized program operations, equity in distribution of services, and short-term goals pervade the contemporary culture of human services (Schorr and Both 1991). This discrepancy continues to fuel the service reform movement.

In general, the criticisms of categorical programs as well as system reform are relevant *regardless of the age group being served*. Which elements of successful programs are central to serving children has not yet been identified. Clearly, service reform programs need to target families, not individuals, because even within families, individuals are served by different programs (children themselves also receive services from different programs; Ooms 1996). Thus, viewing communities as places permits modest service reforms that make current categorical services more user friendly and less bureaucratic, but does not encompass a more coordinated and integrated approach to service delivery as discussed in the next section.

Communities as Face

In defining communities as "face", relationships between individuals constitute community. Hence, community in many ways comprises psychological associations more than geographic units. The *community* is perceived of as a system of supports (Kubisch 1996), and this definition, in terms of policies and programs, translates into the integration of services provided to children and families as well as communities, representing a more holistic approach than service reform. Typically, programs consist of community-based multiservice organizations that promote the well-being of children and families (i.e., family and community support services). Establishing these programs usually requires system reform—interagency coordination, creation of an umbrella agency, or some combination of both (Kagan and Pritchard 1996). Several relationships are highlighted by this approach: (1) relationships within families; (2) relationships between families and service providers; (3) relationships among service providers; and (4) relationships among members of the community.

Relationships within Families

Families are the smallest psychological unit that constitutes community. Parents are typically seen as the provider and overseer of children's linkages with services. This perspective depicts a rather dyadic, unidirectional view of families. However, relationships within families are bi-directional (i.e., children influence parent's behaviors) and triadic or higher (i.e., fathers as well as adult kin are part of the family system). Closer appraisal of family functioning by services providers is merited. Supports available within the family may play a large role in linking children with services in the community.

Relationships between Families and Service Providers

Relationships also put a face on families and service providers. Specifically, Ooms (1996) has argued that despite references to children and families, service programs tend to emphasize individuals within the family rather than focusing on family functioning and relational systems. Consequently, a primary means of facilitating services to poor, urban children is for service providers to recognize their embeddedness with family and community systems. Such a notion points to the need to coordinate and integrate community-based services for families—the goal of the family support movement.

Although the service integration model has received widespread support, the related initiatives have primarily been instituted at only the state and local levels. This approach, however, may be overrated in some respects. Programs typically act as entry points to services and do not necessarily deliver services directly to children and families. This fact places increased importance upon the relationship among service providers.

Relationships among Service Providers

The whole notion of service integration is based in part on the premise of putting a face on service providers. In essence, the aim is to build a community among service providers. Again, this goal requires restructuring the context of social services as well as increasing the flexibility of categorical funding (Schorr and Both 1991). Several other barriers that need to be addressed include relations between federal and local authorities as well as locus of leadership, technical obstacles (such as creating uniform data systems), and discrepant regulations across systems (Kagan and Pritchard 1996). For example, in one community initiative, children in the custody of child protective services were placed with neighborhood families rather than with foster care homes in the suburbs. Thus, the ultimate strength of building relationships between service providers is predicated on maintaining the face of families who receive the respective services.

Relationships within Communities

Community relationships frequently are placed under the umbrella of family support. Often an implicit (rather than explicit) goal of integrated service programs is to build social connections among community residents. Although building social networks is not a primary target of CDCs (which are discussed later), it may be a secondary outcome of these community-based programs. A study of three CDCs found that residing in the CDCs affected community social relations (Briggs, Mueller, and Sullivan 1997). Residents of the CDCs were more likely to greet or exchange words with their neighbors than were non-CDC residents. These findings suggest that intimate connections within neighborhoods may be less likely in poor neighborhoods than in more middle-income neighborhoods. Thus, supportive relations within the community context may be less in close relationships and more in weak or informal ties and such connections probably reduce feelings of isolation. Programs attempting to build community ties note that they grow incrementally and are often hard-won.

Communities as Space

Defining communities as "space" identifies communities as physical and built places for activity—living, working, and political organizing. The primary target of CDCs and initiatives such as the Empowerment Zone and Enterprise Communities has been housing and economic development (Briggs, Mueller, and Sullivan 1997). The former activity entails the creation and management of affordable housing and the latter activity involves both job training and job creation. Organizational governance is another component, but since this aspect of CDCs has more distal effects on children, it is not discussed here. Little research, however, exists on the effect of CDCs on residents, and virtually nothing on their impact on families and children.

This fact reiterates the point that although community development initiatives influence children, they are not typically child-oriented. For example, both housing and economic development only indirectly affect children by potentially improving families' economic circumstances. Affordable housing may free up income for other family needs. Economic development vis-à-vis maternal employment also may have positive effects on children despite continued low income. Given the salience of familial factors in predicting child outcomes over and above neighborhood factors (Leventhal and Brooks-Gunn 2000), the ability of CDCs and other community development initiatives to enhance familial outcomes is likely to have serious benefits for children.

In the previous section, we discussed the fact that many CDCs often have an effect on community building, which appears to influence children as well. CDCs also may influence children's and families' lives by improving the safety of neighborhoods. While programs to improve neighborhood safety are not necessarily considered to belong to the domain of spatial definitions of community, CDCs often regard reducing neighborhood danger and in turn enhancing safety as *instrumental* to improving housing, economic development, and community building. Moreover, safety may be one of the most important benefits of CDCs for children.

The Integration of Place, Face, and Space

The final strategy for delivering services to poor, urban children and their families—CCIs—takes the most holistic approach by viewing communities as the integration of "place", "face", and "space". Specifically, CCIs are comprehensive, community-based multiservice organizations that define communities as geographic places around which to organize services ("place"), foundations for social support networks ("face"), and areas of residence, commerce, and civic activity ("space"). Theoretically, such an approach enables poor, urban communities (and the families and children who reside in them) to develop the capacity to address a range of problems they confront (Brown and Richman 1997). For example, the Center for Family Life in Brooklyn, New York (funded by the Annie E. Casey Foundation as one of four child services programs) is designed to be a preventative, collaborative, comprehensive, flexible, and family-focused community-based initiative. The Center runs job training and placement programs, operates advocacy workshops, and offers an emergency food program. In addition, the Center administers school-based programs for children, youth, and families in three community schools. A range of services are provided free of charge including counseling and therapy; neighborhood-based foster care programs; school-age child care and after-school programs; summer programs for children and youth; recreational activities for children, youth, and families; youth employment programs, and parent workshops. As in the example provided, components of these programs that focus on children include education and family support services and provision of extra-curricular activities. Other features of CCIs that are less child-focused entail housing, commercial revitalization, small business development, and community organization.

As evident from CCIs, definitions of community may vary by the age of the residents. For example, children may be more geographically-bounded or place-based than adults. With several exceptions, children in most cases go to neighborhood schools, play on nearby playgrounds, and have friends who live close by. Adults, in contrast, have more far-flung networks (i.e., face-based perceptions of community). In urban communities, few individuals live in neighborhoods around places of work as in the old working-class neighborhoods (i.e., less space-based communities). This discrepancy between children's and adult's geographic boundedness suggests that CCIs have a more critical role to play for children and families with children (as opposed to individuals or families, in general).

If social organizations or place-based institutions are the most salient community for children, then bootstrapping on existing social connections (school, playground, neighborhood, health clinic) may be the most effect route to serving poor, urban children and their families (Sullivan 1996). Since schools are one of the only institutions that see virtually all children, many comprehensive programs have targeted the school as the center of the community. Increasingly, schools have taken on other missions, such as social and health services, in addition to education. It is essential to examine whether or not we can expect schools to provide a range of services and whether or not in doing so, we jeopardize the quality of education provided.

CONCLUSION

We have considered four general types of service delivery models for poor, urban children and families that vary as a function of the definition of community employed. The mechanisms for providing services to poor, urban children and families covered were categorical programs, family and community support services, CDCs, and CCIs. Of the approaches discussed, family and community support services (integrated services) are the most explicitly child-focused.

Most income transfer programs provide money (or food stamps) to parents, and do not directly serve children. Programs typically focus on mothers going to work and not on children's needs (i.e., if the mother reaches her welfare time limit, then cash benefits are terminated). Even food stamps are given to parents (with the exception of the school lunch programs, which provide food to children directly), and, in a sense WIC, which supplies milk, cereal, etc. The earned income tax credit and minimum wage are aimed at giving families (parents) more disposable income. Child-oriented services for mothers moving off of welfare include a few parenting classes and referrals to local child-care agencies. In addition, mothers making the transition from welfare to work are given vouchers (i.e., cash subsidies) to obtain child care. Thus, the lack of a child-centered approach among categorical programs may impede service delivery to poor children. Parental involvement appears to be a missing link in the design of these programs.

Changes in the allocation of some federal funds to the states and the fact that states do not have to match funds for specific programs in the way that they have been required to do, have altered the way in which some services are delivered to children and families. At the minimum, these changes have affected the level of dollars allocated to programs, such as TANF. What seems apparent is that for poor and near-poor urban communities, child- and family-oriented services have been reduced. What remains less clear is how these cuts affect families and consequently, the communities in which these families reside.

Block grants (used for programs such as TANF) give states and local governments greater flexibility to administer these programs. In theory, this approach allows states and local communities to tailor programs to meet the needs of their population. Critics, however, argue that block grants give states too much latitude and could jeopardize the well-being of children and families if funds are not used to provide family support and child services and are shifted to other types of programs. One potential advantage of block grants is that it could foster system reform and increased coordination across service delivery systems, since states will have greater flexibility to run programs.

Community development initiatives have as their primary goal housing development, economic rejuvenation (creation of jobs) as well as job training. Several community-based strategies incorporate a social dimension; although, this aim is still not necessarily a child-centered approach. Thus, community initiatives need to look at families more explicitly. Some recent CCIs are attempting to examine children and families more concretely. However, it is still important to acknowledge that, frequently, child-oriented programs are embedded in the service of adult-oriented programs.

The Carnegie Corporation (1994) report, *Starting Points*, first brought attention to the declining status of young children in the United States. One of the final recommendations was to mobilize communities to support children and their families. Federal, state, and local action as discussed in this chapter were called for to meet the needs of children and families. To date, however, little systematic effort has been initiated at the community-level on behalf of children. Despite shifting resources to the community level, children are usually not a primary target of these funds. Thus, we still have a long way to go in meeting the report's call to action.

NOTE

1. More extended text and references are available in the original chapter from which the current chapter was adapted (with permission): Leventhal, T., Brooks-Gunn, J., and Kamerman, S. (1997). Communities as place, face, and space: Provision of services to young children and their families. In J. Brooks-Gunn, G. Duncan, and J. L. Aber (eds.), (1997) *Neighborhood Poverty: Policy Implica-* *tions in Studying Neighborhoods* (Vol. 2) (pp. 182–205). New York: Russell Sage Foundation Press.

REFERENCES

Briggs, Xavier de Souza, E. Mueller, and M.L. Sullivan. 1997. *From Neighborhood to Community: Evidence on the Social Effects of Community Development.* Community Development Research Center, Graduate School of Management and Urban Policy, New School for Social Research, New York.

Brooks-Gunn, J., G. J. Duncan, and J. Lawrence Aber. 1997a. *Neighborhood Poverty*: Vol. 2. *Policy implications in studying neighborhoods*. New York: Russell Sage Foundation.

Brooks-Gunn, Jeanne, Greg J. Duncan, and J. Lawrence Aber. 1997b. *Neighborhood Poverty*: Vol. 1. *Context and consequences for children*. New York: Russell Sage Foundation.

Brown, Prudence and Harold A. Richman. 1997. "Neighborhood effects and state and local policy." Pp. 164–181 in *Neighborhood Poverty*: Vol. 2. *Policy implications in studying neighborhoods*, edited by J. Brooks-Gunn, G. J. Duncan, and J. L. Aber. New York: Russell Sage Foundation.

Kagan, Sharon Lynn and E. Pritchard. 1996. "Linking services for children and families: Past legacies, future possibilities." Pp. 378–393 in *Children, Families, and Government: Preparing for the twenty-first century*, edited by E. F. Zigler, S. L. Kagan, and N. W. Hall. New York: Cambridge University Press.

Kahn, A. J. and S. B. Kamerman. 1996. *Children and their Families in Big Cities: Strategies for service reform*. New York: Cross-National Studies Program, Columbia University School of Social Work.

Kubisch, Anne C. 1996. "On the term community: An informal contribution." Pp. 256–260 in *Children and their Families in Big Cities: Strategies for service reform*, edited by A. J. Kahn and S. B. Kamerman. New York: Cross-National Studies Program, Columbia University School of Social Work.

Leventhal, Tama and Jeanne Brooks-Gunn. 2000. "The neighborhoods they live in: Effects of neighborhood residence upon child and adolescent outcomes." *Psychological Bulletin* 126: 309–337.

O'Hare, William and Mark Mather. 2003, October. *The Growing Number of Kids in Severely Distressed Neighborhoods: Evidence from the 2000 Census.* Baltimore, MD: The Annie E. Casey Foundation and the Population Reference Bureau.

Ooms, Theodora. 1996. "Where is the family in comprehensive community initiatives for children and families?" Family Impact Seminar, Washington, DC.

Schorr, L. B. and D. Both. 1991. "Attributes of effective services for young children: A brief survey of current knowledge and its implications for program and policy development." Pp. 23–45 in *Effective Services for Young Children*, edited by L. B. Schorr, D. Both, and C. Copple. Washington, DC: National Academy Press.

Sullivan, Mercer L. 1996. "Local knowledge and local participation: Lessons from community studies for community initiatives." Paper prepared for Roundtable on Comprehensive Community Initiatives for Children and Families. Washington, DC: Aspen Institute.

Wilson, William Julius. 1987. *The Truly Disadvantaged: The inner city, the underclass, and public policy.* Chicago: University of Chicago Press.

Wilson, William Julius. 1997. *When Work Disappears.* New York: Alfred J. Knopf.

CHAPTER 13

Community-Based Organizations and Migration in New York City

Héctor R. Cordero-Guzmán and Victoria Quiroz-Becerra

In recent years there has been increasing inter-est on the part of social scientists in the study of immigrant groups, organizations and ser-vice providers. In this chapter, I address two specific theoretical and empirical gaps in the literature on immigration and organizations. First, I discuss factors related to the devel-opment of immigrant organizations and pre-sent the main characteristics of immigrant groups, organizations and service providers in New York City. Second, I examine the functions that these organizations have in four areas of the migration process: the development, management and mainten-ance of networks; the provision of social ser-vices to immigrant children and families; the articulation of needs and the development and management of community resources; and the maintenance of ties and connec-tions to the countries and communities of origin.

THE LITERATURE ON IMMIGRANT GROUPS AND ORGANIZATIONS

New York has always been an important center for migration (Cordero-Guzmán *et al.* 2001). The volume of recent migration and the diversity of national origins have resulted in the formation of many new organizations and have presented challenges and opportun-ities to established immigrant organizations and service providers.

Some researchers have emphasized the importance of immigrant networks to the adaptation and incorporation of immigrants and to the development and maintenance of immigrant communities. Massey and his collaborators (1987) recognize the role of voluntary associations when they write: "Thus far we have considered various social relationships that make up immigrant net-works, but no less important are certain institutional mechanisms that facilitate the formation and maintenance of social ties. A variety of voluntary associations established by immigrants in the United States promote regular interpersonal contact, greatly facili-tating the process of adaptation and mutual assistance" (1987: 145).

Other researchers have focused directly on the role of community-based organizations (or CBOs) in various aspects of the immigra-tion process and some key themes begin to emerge. Lissak (1989) analyzes the history of social services to immigrants, the early development of settlement houses, and the involvement of the Chicago School in that process. Jenkins (1981 and 1988) addresses the role of ethnicity in social service provi-sion and how social work practice had to adapt to changing and diverse populations. Basch (1987) looks at voluntary associations among the Vicentians and Grenadians and finds that these groups provided direct assistance to immigrants. Kasinitz (1992: 111–23) discusses the role of community organizations in political representation and incorporation among Caribbean and West Indian populations. In an important paper, Hagan and González Baker (1993) document the influence of CBOs in shaping policy during the implementation of the Immigration Reform and Control Act (IRCA) after it was signed into law in 1986. They argue that CBOs performed a central role in the legalization process and in the actual shaping and implementation of the policy at the local level: "The community group role evolved from the INS [US Immigration and Naturalization Service] vision of paperwork assistant into an activist role on behalf of applicants. Indeed, the local INS itself changed in the wake of community group influence, becoming more receptive to community concerns and more accountable to community interests" (1993: 521). Their research documents how the "task force" created by the local CBOs produced publicity materials, appeared in the media, contacted officials, and ultimately sued and won in order to clarify and establish regulations affecting immigrants applying for legalization.

While several researchers have examined the role of CBOs in various aspects of the migration process, we do not have a more complete picture of who these groups are, what kinds of programs and services they provide, where they are located, who they serve, and what kinds of resources they have. This chapter seeks to add to our knowledge by placing immigrant organizations and service providers, as a group, at the center of immigration, organizations, community development, and non-profit research.

TYPES OF IMMIGRANT ORGANIZATIONS

An immigrant organization is an organization formed by individuals who are members of a particular ethnic or national origin group, for the purpose of providing social services primarily to immigrants from the same ethnic or national group. Immigrant organizations differ from other social-service providers in that they explicitly incorporate cultural components, and a consciousness of ethnic or national-origin identity, into their mission, practices, services, and programs. Some organizations, originally formed to provide services to particular groups, or to the general population, have evolved over time and tried to adapt to the needs of the new national-origin groups that have come into the region. As new immigrant communities are established and grow, their

families and children receive services from existing social-service agencies, which may or may not be run by members of their own ethnic or national-origin groups. But, over time, immigrant communities face both internal community pressures and external pressures for representation that lead them to begin to form "their own" organizations.

There are three broad types of groups that form the immigrant social service delivery system:

- First, there are immigrant groups, associations and clubs. These groups are usually concerned with promoting social and economic ties, connections and activities between immigrants from particular countries or regions. They also have close economic, social and political contact to their areas of origin, are mostly organized around community events, and have a relatively small social service base. These types of groups include the Hometown Associations (HTA) that proliferate in many immigrant communities and are often small, have a tight leadership, and are mostly focused on home community issues (Orozco 2000). These groups, however, form the basis from which more formalized organizations emerge.

- Second, there are immigrant organizations. These groups have been formally incorporated as non-profit organizations. They have a service portfolio, a direct social-service base with clients, paid professionalized staff, offices open to the public with regular service hours, and some sources of donations and funding. These organizations are usually involved in a broad range of social services to immigrants from a particular country (or region) and are central to the social service delivery system for particular ethnic groups and in many ethnic or immigrant neighborhoods.

- Third, there are the service providers with a large metropolitan-level social-service base. These organizations provide social services to clients from a variety of countries and also provide services to non-immigrant clients (often from racial and ethnic minority groups). These organizations are older, larger, often with multicultural staff, and many have offices or projects in several neighborhoods.

THE FORMATION OF IMMIGRANT ORGANIZATIONS

Why, when, and how are immigrant organizations formed? Several factors are related to the formation of immigrant organizations. *First*, organizations are usually formed in immigrant communities that are relatively large and growing. *Second*, as the immigrant population settles and their various needs develop, the groups begin to articulate a distinct sense of their social-service needs. This usually has two components: first, the group develops a sense of what services it particularly needs (needs assessment); and second, it develops a sense of what it needs differently or the types of services that must be provided in a way that is consistent and sensitive to the cultural and social practices of the group. If a group does not have an unmet demand for services or the service can be readily obtained from other existing providers the incentives to start new organizations are clearly lowered.

A *third* element related to the formation of immigrant organizations is the existence of a social-service professional and human-resource base from the immigrant community that works to start, guide, direct, manage, and administer the new organizations. In several instances the founders of organizations worked in the senior staff of metropolitan-level service providers or in service organizations from related groups; eventually these persons left the entities to start organizations that they see as more directly positioned to serve and strengthen "their communities". Human resources are key to organizational survival and development and many of the staff who work in immigrant organizations are educated in some of the leading policy and management schools in the city and have developed experiences in both their communities and in more mainstream institutions and organizations.

A *fourth* element is connections to the metropolitan social service delivery system. In New York, the state funds community-based social services largely through a network of non-profit providers. This means that someone from the community has to have the capacity to understand the grants and contracts application process and all of the intricacies of program development, design, management, reporting, and evaluation. Some human resource capacity and connections to the metropolitan social-service delivery system are key assets that need to be present within the immigrant community in order for its associations to develop into more sustainable organizations.

The *fifth* element is organizational resources and capacity. Members of immigrant communities who come with experience in the formation and management of organizations, sometimes acquired in the country of origin, are more likely to form and sustain organizations. In the case of social service providers, particularly from low-income immigrant communities where "internal" resources may be more difficult to obtain, factors related to connections and networks with external resources are essential in securing the flow of funds that are needed to manage and maintain a non-profit organization.

While there are other reasons why organizations are started, we found these five factors to be present in most of the stories we heard related to the context and reasons why national origin groups form their organizations.

THE CHARACTERISTICS OF IMMIGRANT GROUPS, ORGANIZATIONS AND SERVICE PROVIDERS

In order to get a better sense of the main characteristics of the sector, we asked organizations about some of their main attributes. In this section we present some of the main characteristics of immigrant organizations and service providers in New York City[1] (Table 13.1).

Table 13.1 Main characteristics of immigrant groups and organizations in New York City

	Year organization started (n = 82)	Annual budget $US (n = 74)	FT staff (n = 81)	PT staff (n = 60)	Percent bilingual staff (n = 83)	No. of clients (n = 80)	Percent immigrant clients (n = 79)	Percent undocumented (n = 33)
Mean	1970	7.5m	113	54	70	13,582	64	29
Median	1976	1.0m	17	2	80	3,500	65	20
Minimum	1893	$7,300	0	0	0	75	10	0
Maximum	1995	120m	2,000	1,000	100	250,000	100	95

Source: New York City Survey of Immigrant Groups and Organizations (2000)

Year Started and Location

Since the 1950s there have been two historical markers of American immigration that have also been periods where a large number of immigrant organizations have been formed. The first period is during the late 1960s and early 1970s, following the civil rights movement and changes in the racial, ethnic or national composition of immigration flows to the United States with increasing numbers coming from Asian, Latin American and Caribbean countries. A second period of organizational growth occurred during the late 1980s following the Immigration Reform and Control Act (IRCA) of 1986 which saw an acceleration of mass immigration to New York.

In terms of location, 45 percent of the organizations were located in Manhattan, 24 percent in Brooklyn, 20 percent in Queens, 6 percent in the Bronx and 5 percent in Staten Island. Manhattan is therefore overrepresented if we compare the location of the organizations to the location of immigrants in New York City (since Manhattan only houses about 18 percent of immigrants). This is likely due to its central location for metropolitan level organizations, accessibility for clients from the five boroughs and the availability of office space.

Staff Size and Characteristics

In terms of full-time (FT) staff, the average number of employees is 113 and the median is 17. Around a quarter of the organizations have fewer than five FT employees and another 25 percent have between six and 16; the largest 25 percent of the agencies have more than 50 employees.

The information on the percentage of the staff who are bilingual indicates that these organizations are a significant linguistic resource and asset. In more than 80 percent of the organizations over 40 percent of the staff is bilingual. In 37 percent of the agencies all the staff are bilingual. In terms of the languages spoken by staff, 70 percent of the agencies reported that some of their staff spoke Spanish. The other most common languages were, in order, Korean, Chinese, Haitian Creole and Russian. Clearly, one of the central defining features of immigrant organizations is the presence of a significant proportion of staff who can speak several languages.

Budgets

The average annual budget for the organizations was $7.5 million while the median was $1 million. Measures of central tendency provide some information but the dispersion in the data is quite interesting. The bottom 10 percent of the agencies had a budget of less than $80,000. Another 39 percent had budgets between $120,000 and $800,000. The bottom quartile of the distribution is below $250,000. At the top of the distribution, 25 percent of the organizations had budgets higher than $4 million. The top five agencies have budgets of $25, $28, $35, $72 and $120 million.

Sources of Funding

The most common sources of funding for immigrant organizations are: government contracts and sub-contracts (56 percent), community fundraisers and individual donations (18 percent), foundation grants (15 percent), corporate contributions (5 percent), funds from the church, and, in rare instances, fees for services.

Looking more closely at the sources of funding, it is clear that a significant amount of agency budgets come from government. More than half of the agencies received over 65 percent of their budgets from government sources. Grassroots funding is the second most important source of funding for these groups. At the lower end of the distribution, 30 percent of the groups do not generate any grassroots funding and another 40 percent of groups receive between 1 and 20 percent of their budget from grassroots fundraising. For the top 25 percent of the agencies, 10 percent receive between 25 percent and 40 percent of their funding from grassroots, and the other top 15 percent of organizations receive more than 50 percent of their income from grassroots activities (with one organization reporting that all income came from grassroots funding).

Another source is organized philanthropies or foundations, but half of the agencies received less than 8 percent of their budgets from foundations. Only 10 percent of the organizations had more than 35 percent of their budget coming from foundations. Similarly, immigrant organizations receive a small share of their budgets from corporations. Around a half of the groups do not receive any contributions from corporations and another third received less than 17 percent of their budget from corporations. Two organizations received 20 percent of their budget from corporations, three received 25 percent and one received 45 percent.

Number and Type of Clients

The organizations served an average of 13,582 clients annually, and the median was 3,500. The smallest agency served 75 clients while the largest (by far) indicated that they served 250,000 persons.

The organizations' clients were, on average, 64 percent immigrant (or foreign born), and the median was 65 percent. The bottom quartile had fewer than 30 percent immigrant clients. One in seven of the agencies indicated that 100 percent of their clients were immigrants. The organizations also stated that, on average, 29 percent of their clients were undocumented (the median was 20 percent).[2]

THE FUNCTIONS OF IMMIGRANT GROUPS, ORGANIZATIONS AND SERVICE PROVIDERS

Figure 13.1 sets out the various roles and functions of immigrant organizations and suggests that they are centrally involved in all four key parts of the migration process. Let us take each in turn.

Assistance with the Immigration Process

The first role that immigrant CBOs play is to assist families in the immigration process by providing advice and legal help for individuals who want to change their immigration status or sponsor relatives to come to the United States. These services include (in parenthesis is the percentage of organizations indicating they provide that particular service): (a) citizenship services (76.5 percent) which involve providing the citizenship classes and support services necessary for the naturalization exam; (b) legal services (59 percent) involves the preparation of all of the legal paperwork involved in the immigration and naturalization process, together with legal advice and counsel, certified fingerprinting, adjustment of status petitions, alien relative petitions, visa extensions and advanced parole, work authorization, affidavits of support, diversity lottery visas, replacement of green cards, etc; and (c) interpretation and translation services (72 percent) which involves translation and interpretation of documents and other materials between English and other languages. These services are central to the migration process but many organizations also provide shelter and other forms of initial support, access to community networks and information that are essential to newly-arrived immigrants.

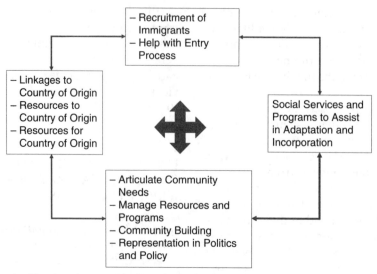

Figure 13.1 The role of immigrant community-based organizations in the migration process

Adaptation and Incorporation of Immigrants

The second role of immigrant organizations is to provide services related to the adaptation and incorporation of immigrants into the new society. Unlike immigration services, most of these services can be dispensed both to immigrant and non-immigrant populations, but there are specific needs and challenges associated with providing services to the former. These include such matters as language, differences in knowledge about social services, cultural sensitivity, awareness of the most appropriate method to deliver services, and recognition of groups' particular needs (Jenkins 1988; Padilla 1997).

General social services (80 percent) involve a wide array of economic, social and health services designed to improve the socioeconomic status of the population. Specific social services include twelve tasks. Benefits counseling (79 percent), business counseling (28 percent), educational services (89 percent), employment and training (or workforce development) services (66 percent), family counseling and case management services (63 percent), food or nutrition services (53 percent), general health services (54 percent), general legal services (34 percent), housing services (60 percent), mental health services (54 percent), substance abuse treatment (36 percent), and transportation assistance (46 percent).

Another set of services provided by community-based organizations involves programs for individuals undergoing special circumstances. These include: crime victims (40 percent); the disabled (50 percent); domestic violence victims (59 percent); HIV/AIDS (53 percent).

A third group of services provided by immigrant organizations involves programs for particular sub-groups of the population. Included in this category are: children's services (63 percent), day-care services (35 percent), Gay and lesbian issues (36 percent), senior-citizen services (62.5 percent), women's services (58 percent), and youth services (78 percent).

While most of these services treat discrete needs, many are designed to help immigrants maneuver through existing bureaucracies and programs. In that sense they help immigrants incorporate into the New York social-service infrastructure, and into the city's social fabric more generally. This should not be seen as a unidirectional process of "Americanization" but rather as a complex process of adapting to a new environment while simultaneously retaining elements of practice and action that emanate from the rules, practices and cultures of the countries of origin. Organizations help immigrants adapt while at the same time, often very deliberately, they help to maintain specific cultures and traditions. The importance of Americanization for immigrant socio-economic incorporation has always been contested and immigrant aid societies have had to balance awareness and respect of the particular cultural practices of their groups with the need for immigrants to adapt to their new, often more complex, social environment.

The tension between integration and the maintenance of customs and ties is present in most groups and has existed throughout the history of immigrant organizations. Archdeacon (1983: 184), for example, argues that "for the social activists who moved into immigrant neighborhoods and established settlement houses, the term [Americanization] meant giving the newcomers the wherewithal to survive in a modern industrial society. They tried to teach those who came to their settlement houses English, American social customs, and, when necessary, the rudiments of household management, health care, and sanitation. The best of those reformers, including the renowned Jane Addams of Chicago, performed their work without purposefully assaulting the immigrants' native cultures." One of the main challenges for immigrant CBOs, then, is to manage both the processes of adaptation and incorporation while at the same time recognizing and maintaining particular cultural practices.

Representation for the Immigrant Community

Another key function of immigrant organizations can be described as providing representation to the immigrant community. This process has several components that include:

- articulating the needs of the community to metropolitan-level policy makers;
- serving as an advocate and network for their ethnic groups;
- activities that can be categorized as "community building";
- providing representation in politics; and
- representing the community in policy making, management and implementation.

Many CBOs are actively engaged in organizing immigrants in their communities as a way to influence service delivery and inform members of the group about service needs in their communities. Community relations, organizing and advocacy (88 percent) involves advocating on behalf of the community and its members, or their ethnic/national-origin group, organizing residents and group members around issues of relevance and importance to the community, and advocating to elected officials, government bureaucrats and others on particular challenges and needs of the community

Organizations also provide a form of what can be called "social capital" or "community building" in terms of a set of resources, knowledge, services and information and are central to the reconstitution, formation and management of immigrant social, political and economic networks. CBOs are often engaged in activities which are not individual- or family-centered but involve the development of networks between residents and other organizations in the community with the purpose of building the physical, cultural, and human resources of the community. For instance: cultural heritage programs (70 percent), community economic development (72 percent), conflict resolution (52 percent), and labor rights and laws (33 percent).

Immigrant organizations also represent the needs and concerns of their particular group(s) in media discussions on immigration, ethnicity and social-service provision to immigrant populations. According to Hagan and González-Baker (1993), public education and information, and the policy making associated with that, are central roles in many organizations as they seek to inform policy debates on matters related to the socio-economic adaptation and incorporation of the group at the local and national level.

Lastly, immigrant CBOs are engaged in a complex relationship with elected officials. Such relationships range from one of complete dependence, to an attitude of cooperation and common benefit, and even to mutual disdain, contempt and neglect. However, as documented by Marwell (2003), immigrant CBOs are actively engaged in building "political" constituencies and, in many instances, senior staff among the organizations in our study both actively ran for and in some cases won elected office.

The "representation" aspect of immigrant CBOs raises some questions and poses several challenges to the field. First is the question of what Salamon (2002) calls "the legitimacy challenge", or determining exactly what the relationship is and should be between the organizations and the grassroots community. Second, immigrant CBOs, like all non-profits, face human resource, management, and other resource challenges that impact on the quality of their programs. Third, organizations face pressure to accommodate to Requests for Proposals (RFP) that may or may not fit an assessment of their specific community needs and priorities. The pressure to respond to funding imperatives versus community needs certainly affects the functioning, credibility and legitimacy of organizations. A fourth challenge, related to the complexity of managing the relationship between CBOs and elected officials (or party machines), is the potential for patronage politics and, in the worst cases, corruption. Fifth, immigrant organizations, particularly those that receive government funding, are in a contradictory relationship *vis-à-vis* the state in that they may advocate for particular programs and positions but at the same time as they receive significant state resources for their programs they are the *de facto* state representatives and agencies in their communities (Cordero-Guzmán and Navarro 2000). From the perspective of clients, they are receiving state-entitled services through the CBO, and therefore sometimes the line between "the CBO" and "the state" is blurred in practice.

Linking Immigrant Communities to their Countries of Origin

The fourth role of immigrant organizations is to serve as a liaison between ethnic/national communities and their countries of origin. Managing this relationship has three main components. First, facilitating and encouraging the flow of economic resources, remittances and other investments to the country of origin. Many organizations have particular linkages to the main sending regions in the countries of origin and often sponsor not only movement of resources but delegations and visits to and from the countries of origin. Some networks reaching to the country of origin are central in providing linkages between elected officials, government bureaucrats and political parties in the sending and receiving areas.

Second, organizations are involved in facilitating and managing the flow of news and information and in the preparation of cultural, religious or patriotic activities of importance to the country of origin. And third, many organizations are engaged in activities designed to increase the level of information, public awareness, and political advocacy in the United States and attempt in many ways to influence US policy toward the country of origin. There are some challenges involved in managing the relationship to the country of origin mainly that while the immigrant community seeks to have active involvement and role in politics and policy in the country of origin this often meets resistance from political party leaders in the countries of origin who would rather limit the involvement of these organizations (and communities) to raising funds and resources, and to advocating in the United States on behalf of home country government policies and interest (Graham 2001).

CONCLUSION: CBOS AND MIGRATION PROCESSES

Immigrant groups, organizations and service providers fulfill several important social functions, fill key service gaps in their communities and are involved in all stages of the immigration and adaptation process. They are involved in the recruitment of immigrants, as people find out about possibilities of bringing relatives; they help others obtain visas; and they are involved in the actual entry and settlement process. Through their various services, CBOs play a central role in the orientation of immigrants, their reconstruction of social ties, and their adaptation and incorporation process. Immigrant organizations also play a central role in all aspects of community formation and development, including building community pride and identity, representation in politics (through personnel, connections and various kinds of support), in policy discussion, formulation and implementation, in managing the relationship with elected officials, and in managing the flow of metropolitan (federal, state and city) and private or donation resources to the local communities through various grants, loans and other forms of funding for programs and activities. Lastly, these groups are part of the linkages to and from the country of origin. They provide resources and information, including materials, human resources and funds for projects and activities, and are a resource to the countries of origin in the United States. All of these activities open up contacts, opportunities, information, exchanges, networks, development possibilities, and, ultimately perhaps, more migration.

The more than 300 community-based organizations that make up the backbone of the immigrant service delivery system in New York City, and that are replicated in cities and towns throughout the United States and other migrant destinations, are a vital part of the fabric of their communities and of a diverse civil society. Immigrant organizations are at the centre of programs that assist in the social, economic and political incorporation of immigrants and in efforts to maintain contacts, investments and linkages with the countries and regions of origin. Understanding the role and functions of immigrant associations, their connections to metropolitan and national policy-makers, and their linkages to their communities is central to theoretical debates, research, and understanding practice in the fields of organizations, community development, race and ethnicity, and migration studies.

NOTES

1. The data that follow come from information provided by immigrant organizations in New York City between September 1999 and August 2000.
2. Many organizations did not answer this question, which is understandable in the light of changes in the laws which allow organizations to service undocumented clients in some government-funded programs (child health) but not others (food stamps). Some church groups refuse to receive government funds in order to free themselves from any restrictions on providing services to the undocumented. Many other agencies feel that restrictions on serving the undocumented run counter to their mission of serving everyone in need regardless of immigration status and they try, often with great difficulty, to find private funds to service that population.

REFERENCES

Archdeacon, T. (1983) *Becoming American: An Ethnic History*. New York: Free Press.

Basch, L. (1987) "The Vicentians and Grenadians: the role of voluntary associations in immigrant adaptation to New York City", in Foner, N. (ed.) *New Immigrants in New York*. New York: Columbia University Press, 159–94.

Cordero-Guzmán, H. and Navarro, J.G. (2000) "Managing cuts in the 'safety net': what do immigrant groups, organizations, and service providers say about the impacts of recent changes in immigration and welfare laws?" *Migration World*, 28(4): 20–6.

Cordero-Guzmán, H., Smith, R. and Grosfoguel, R. (eds) (2001) *Migration, Transnationalization and Race in a Changing New York*. Philadelphia: Temple University Press.

Graham, P. (2001) "Political incorporation and re-incorporation: simultaneity in the Dominican migrant experience", in Cordero-Guzmán, H., Smith, R. and Grosfoguel, R. (eds) *Migration, Transnationalization and Race in a Changing New York*. Philadelphia: Temple University Press, 87–108.

Hagan, J. and González Baker, S. (1993) "Implementing the US legalization program: the influence of immigrant communities and local agencies on immigration policy reform", *International Migration Review*, 27(3): 513–35.

Jenkins, S. (1981) *The Ethnic Dilemma in Social Services*. New York: The Free Press.

Jenkins, S. (ed.) (1988) *Ethnic Associations and the Welfare State: Services to Immigrants in Five Countries*. New York: Columbia University Press,

Kasinitz, P. (1992) *Caribbean New York: Black Immigrants and the Politics of Race*. Ithaca: Cornell University Press.

Lissak, S.R. (1989) *Pluralism and Progressives: Hull House and the New Immigrants, 1890–1919*. Chicago: University of Chicago Press.

Marwell, N.P. (2003) "Ethnic and post-ethnic politics in New York City: the Dominican second generation", in Kasinitz, P., Mollenkopf, J. and Waters, M. (eds) *The Second Generation in Metropolitan New York: Ethnographic Insights*. New York: Russell Sage, 227–56.

Massey, D.S., Alarcón, R. Durand, J. and González, H. (1987) *Return to Aztlán: The Social Process of International Migration from Western Mexico*. Berkeley: University of California Press.

Orozco, M. (2000) *Latino Hometown Associations as Agents of Development in Latin America*. Washington, DC: Inter-American Dialogue.

Padilla, Y. (1997) "Social services to Mexican American populations in the United States", in Cardenas, G. and Ugalde, A. (eds) *Health and Social Services among International Labor Migrants*. Austin: University of Texas Press, 9–27.

Salamon, L.M. (2002) *The State of Non-Profit America*. Washington, DC: Brookings Institution Press.

CHAPTER 14

Social Capital, Religious Institutions, and Poor Communities

Michael W. Foley, John D. McCarthy, and Mark Chaves

Religious institutions play a significant, if little understood, role in poor communities in the United States. Among the institutions of civil society, churches are often the last to leave deteriorating neighborhoods and dwindling communities and the first to return. Religiously based social service efforts carry an important part of the burden of providing for the needs of poor communities. Congregations and local denominational bodies frequently build broad community coalitions on behalf of policy change and to strengthen both private and public social services for the poor. Congregation-based community-organizing programs have been among the most successful efforts to mobilize residents of poor neighborhoods for political action on behalf of local needs. What some call "para-church" organizations—religious-based outreach and community action groups like Habitat for Humanity, Bread for the World, and Teen Challenge—devote themselves to addressing the needs of individuals and groups in poor communities in diverse and sometimes controversial ways. To what degree these diverse religious-based organizations have proven effective agents for generating and mobilizing social capital within and for poor communities remains an open question.

The role of religion in social life continues to be viewed with great ambivalence by many social scientists. Strongly held expectations that modern life would erode the importance of religious belief through secularization have been resistant to the accumulated evidence of its ongoing centrality to the lives of most Americans (Casanova 1994). Recent manifestations of religiously inspired

collective action have been met with great consternation, especially concerning the role of evangelical Christians. In contrast, other scholars have positively evaluated the disruptive potential of religiously inspired collective action, stressing its potential for empowering disadvantaged groups, such as the U.S. civil rights and peace movements, the Solidarity movement in Poland, and the anti-apartheid movement in South Africa. Such analyses agree that intense solidarity can be generated within religious groups. They disagree, however, in their valuation of the uses that are made of that solidarity. We remain alert to this dilemma of religious solidarity in what follows. And we are particularly concerned with how religious groups, at the same time, create bridges to diverse groups beyond their own boundaries.

RELIGION AND POVERTY IN THE UNITED STATES

The United States is a religiously active nation where the vast majority of citizens profess a belief in God and identify with an organized religion. Rates of religious involvement are quite high compared with other nations: somewhere between 25 and 40 percent of adults regularly attend worship services. Religiously active citizens give substantial amounts of money and time to their churches, a proportion of which supports the activities of denominational bodies.

Many religious groups take various forms of action that either are explicitly aimed at combating poverty in poor communities or indirectly may affect it. First, religious groups may provide resources to poor individuals and poor community institutions from their own stock or through linkages with governmental and nongovernmental sources. Second, religious groups may proselytize in poor communities in an effort to absorb poor individuals and families into religious groups already endowed with social capital. Third, they may attempt to empower poor communities by employing their own social capital in ways that benefit not only their own members but also individuals and families who are not members. In practice, of course, the programs of many religious organizations combine some part of each of the three elements.

SOCIAL CAPITAL IN THE ACTIVITIES OF RELIGIOUS INSTITUTIONS

Individual human capital (education, training, language ability, and so on) is independently important to individual success, but the social networks in which individuals are embedded have an important impact on the degree to which such potential is realized. Thus, the social capital argument insists that we will see higher yields from the same human capital in communities that have more social capital. And those effects are commonly supposed to redound to the good of the community as a whole to one degree or another. Any institution that creates and builds on social networks builds social capital, and to the degree that such an institution also links the group to others in the same community and beyond the community, it has a multiplier effect, at once creating and making available resources to a widening array of actors.

Both the kinds of resources available to individuals and groups and the character of this availability are important from the social capital perspective. Social ties may give individuals access to dead-end jobs or opportunities for criminal gain and encourage the formation of antisocial groups like gangs. Dense but closed social networks may effectively isolate individuals and groups or polarize communities.

Mapping the Religious Terrain

Congregations and other religious institutions, simply by virtue of being social organizations, embody social capital. Although congregations are the most numerous of religious institutions, there are also a great many religiously inspired organizations that bring together large numbers of individual congregations, provide services to congregations, or carry on activities alongside congregations at both the local and national levels. The landscape includes everything from a welter of religious professional and trade organizations to specialized national-level education and advocacy groups, to local interfaith coalitions.

We can distinguish four categories of organizations that might provide significant social capital for poor communities:

1. *Denominations and other large-scale associations of congregations that provide representation and support for congregations:* At the local level, these may be represented as dioceses or other local judicatory bodies, federations of congregations of the same religious tradition, or councils of churches; some, but not all, provide direct financial assistance to congregations, support religious schools and training centers, and engage in or support communitywide advocacy and social service activities.

2. *Local coalitions of religious bodies designed to carry out community service and local advocacy across denominational lines:* These are sometimes congregation-based, generally through the voluntary participation of local clergypeople with special interests in interfaith dialogue or community service; in other cases, they rest on local representatives of national-level structures, such as denominations, federations, and councils of churches.

3. *Community development and social service organizations, both denominationally based and freestanding, that provide specialized social services or community development activities at the local level, with or without direct*

connection to congregations: These range from such denominationally supported entities as Catholic Charities USA to freestanding organizations like Habitat for Humanity, to congregation-based organizing efforts.

4. Congregations, or groups of believers who meet together on a regular basis at a fixed place or places for worship and other activities: Congregations typically claim a regular membership that may or may not be formally registered, as well as occasional or even regular participants who are not formally counted as members.

CONGREGATIONS AS SOURCES OF SOCIAL CAPITAL

Congregations build both human and social capitol, providing access to resources in a wide variety of ways. Of all religious institutions, they are the most intimately involved in the life of their community, though the degree and character of that involvement varies considerably. We distinguish characteristics of the social structures that congregations generate and in which they are enmeshed from the resources available to poor communities through religious bodies and their activities.

At key points in our discussion, we draw on new data from the National Congregations Study (NCS) that allow us to profile the comparative social capital position of two sorts of congregations: those heavily composed of low-income participants, and congregations located in communities with heavy concentrations of low-income people (Chaves, 1998).[1]

Social Capital as Structured Access to Resources

Extended Social Networks
Congregations provide both adults and youth with extended social networks that offer informal support, an environment of trust and acceptance (reinforcing such networks), and access to educational and job opportunities. A study by Christopher Ellison

and Linda George (1994) based on three thousand household interviews, for instance, demonstrates that church attendees "enjoy larger, denser, and more satisfying social net-works, and greater access to social support than do their unchurched counterparts." These effects were relatively modest in size, but robust across both income and denomination, suggesting that the enhancing social network consequences of religious involvement do not appear to be greater in conservative Protestant congregations, which are well known for their high rates of internal social solidarity, nor are they weaker in poorer, typically smaller congregations.

In general, we have very little systematic evidence about the structure of social networks within congregations, the processes that produce them, the variation in the structure of social ties that link congregations to wider social networks, or the social and demographic features of congregations (for example, racial-ethnic and class composition) that might shape those structures. We would expect that congregations that enjoy more mixed membership, whether racially or socioeconomically, would provide greater social capital to their poorer members.

Results from the National Congregations Study survey point to somewhat surprising conclusions in this regard. The pattern of results indicates that the vast majority of members of congregations located in even the poorest neighborhoods are not themselves poor. Fully 82 percent of the households in congregations located in census tracts with 40 percent or more of the residents below the poverty line earn more than $25,000 per year. And 83 percent of the households in tracts with 30 percent of the residents below the poverty line do as well. These results suggest that churches in very poor communities remain socioeconomically heterogeneous, with all the advantages in terms of greater and more diverse social capital that status entails. The results also suggest that most churchgoers in poor communities participate in relatively stable congregations.

Broader Social Linkages

Congregations are rarely isolated social organizations. More commonly, they enjoy relations with other community institutions and congregations, larger religious bodies, and specialized, parallel religious organizations or private and public institutions. Interfaith coalitions specialize in such linkages, as do many of the specialized para-church organizations.

The National Congregations Study data can give us some insights into the extent and kind of linkages that congregations in poor neighborhoods provide. Like their counterparts elsewhere, roughly half the congregants in these neighborhoods belong to congregations that maintain linkages with sources of outside consultant aid, and most belong to a national denomination, dispelling the image of the predominance of disconnected, storefront churches in neighborhoods like these. When we turn to poor congregations per se, however, the picture changes. In contrast to our findings for congregations in poor neighborhoods, those that are heavily composed of low-income participants (which may or may not be located in poor neighborhoods) appear to be less well endowed with social capital and less able, accordingly, to reach out to their communities. Poor congregations are smaller than more affluent congregations. They are less likely to be linked to their community through use of their facilities, less likely to belong to a national denomination, and less likely to draw on outside assistance in managing their affairs.

These findings are suggestive. Nevertheless, we know very little about the character of such ties across religious groups, their importance for local congregations, particularly in poor communities, and their significance for religious-based social capital generation in and for poor communities. Such questions await further research.

Resources and Outcomes

Social capital provides access to resources—financial, human, cultural, and social. The following discussion focuses on those resources enjoyed or provided by congregations that are most relevant to addressing poverty, including resources that might contribute to building, expanding, or sharing social capital.

Information Flows

Congregations provide conduits of information on community problems, available resources (for both individual and community advancement), and the state of the world. They may also provide language classes or job training, early childhood education, and regular schooling.

One specialized form of information flow has to do with referrals of individuals to social service agencies. Local congregations often enter into cooperative arrangements with other organizations, such as denominational offices, affiliated social service agencies, and sometimes government agencies, or they may maintain lists of suitable contacts for individuals requiring social services. Such ties, which are prime examples of "bridging social capital," also provide church officials and members with information, training, contacts, and occasionally funding to further their own social service delivery efforts.

Free Spaces

Congregations often provide "free space" for social and political organizations within their community. A number of studies have indicated that the use of congregations' facilities by other religious groups, social service agencies, and community and political organizations of many sorts is widespread. Church halls and meeting rooms host everything from crafts fairs to Alcoholics Anonymous chapters, to candidates' forums for local and national elections, sometimes as a part of congregation-sponsored activities, sometimes for a fee, sometimes gratis. Some congregations open their doors to candidates, allowing them to speak at regularly scheduled services; others avoid any hint of political involvement. Still others accommodate campaigners for special issues of public concern, such as abortion, gay rights, or school prayer, while eschewing direct involvement with electoral politics. Congregations and their denominations range from liberal to ultraconservative in their political preferences. The more important question, however, from the point of view of providing such "bridging" opportunities, has to do with their willingness to host outsiders or actively support broader civic events within the purview of their work. NCS data show that most congregants belong to congregations that make their facilities available to outsiders (67 percent). Congregations in poor neighborhoods are as likely to do so as others, but poor congregations are much less likely to provide such a service to the community.

Socialization, Community Service, and Political Participation

Many religious organizations specialize in the education, indoctrination, and training of young people, through religious schools, catechetical instruction, Bible study, workshops, and summer camps. NCS data show that 22 percent of congregants in poor neighborhoods attend churches that maintain a school, while 18 percent of those in poor congregations have one. Ninety percent of the membership of poor congregations and 95 percent of those who attend churches in poor neighborhoods have a religious education program in their congregation. Although the content of such efforts is often controversial from the point of view of secular institutions and values, it may include significant components of secular education and training, leadership development, and community service orientation. Church-run schools, for example, often not only provide essential academic preparation but also incorporate notions of community service into the curriculum (Youniss, McLellan, and Yates 1997).

James Coleman's own notion of social capital was shaped by his analysis of the impact of Catholic schooling on students from poor communities. Coleman and others have argued that such schools provide superior social capital for their students, owing to the combination of distinctive values, close supervision by teachers, and greater parental involvement than is true of public schools (Coleman and Hoffer 1987): In such a setting, values of community service and civic engagement are reinforced on a daily basis through interaction with committed adults and other students undergoing the same experience.

Congregations also provide volunteer opportunities and occasionally political information to their members. NCS data show that 59 percent of those involved in congregations in poor neighborhoods (and an equal percentage in other neighborhoods) belong to churches that sponsor organized efforts to encourage volunteering; 22 percent (as opposed to 11 percent elsewhere) are exposed to organized efforts to discuss politics; and 21 percent (versus 11 percent in more affluent neighborhoods) are part of efforts to lobby public officials. By contrast, just 9 percent of the membership of poor congregations belong to churches that have organized efforts to discuss politics, 48 percent are exposed to volunteering programs, and 11 percent belong to churches that lobby public officials. In each category, poorer congregations are at or below the means for more affluent congregations.

Thus, congregations—particularly those in poor neighborhoods—can be important arenas for building and nurturing community leadership as well as serving as platforms for civic participation and collective mobilization. Recent research on civic participation in the United States backs up these claims. In *Voice and Equality* (1995), Sidney Verba, Kay Lehman Schlozman, and Henry Brady have shown that membership in a local congregation provides citizens with opportunities to develop civic skills through involvement in the everyday activities of their church. The authors also show that a large proportion of political activity follows from personal contacts and direct solicitation, and that, while the workplace and other voluntary organizations are important loci of such activities, churches play the biggest role in that regard. They argue that religious participation is especially important for poor and minority citizens since they are as likely to be church members as their better-off counterparts but substantially less likely to learn civic skills through higher education, on the job, or in other voluntary associational settings. We also know that weekly church attenders volunteer more (Greeley, 1997).

Authority and Legitimacy

Congregations and their religious and lay leaders often enjoy a prima facie legitimacy that allows them to carry out activities and engage the moral energies of citizens where others might face a more uphill battle. At the same time, of course, the identification of a religious body with a cause or project may diminish its appeal for some citizens and groups.

In practice, the presumed authority and legitimacy conferred on religious bodies by their members enhance the ability of pastors, religious publishers, and denominational spokespeople to transmit their version of the received truth for a given religious tradition. The shared understandings that result contribute to the solidarity experienced among members of a tradition; a solidarity that in the best of cases transcends racial, ethnic, linguistic, or national boundaries. Messages about the state of the world, the role of believers in the community, and appropriate forms of behavior can also partake of this legitimacy (though with varying degrees of persuasive power), at times lending strength to religious and community organizations, but in other instances weakening their ability to build bridges and sustain action.

Clergy are highly likely to speak out on social issues, and many church members receive encouragement in church to engage in political action as well as volunteer work of many kinds. The findings of the *Voice and Equality* study found that clergy often discuss political issues from the pulpit. NCS data confirm these findings, showing that political discussion and even lobbying activities are common in a significant percentage of congregations, and still more common among congregations in poor neighborhoods.

The southern civil rights movement illustrated how congregations could be mobilized to become the building blocks of both local and national efforts aimed at achieving justice for oppressed people, providing early and determinative leadership to the movement. Mark Chaves and Lynn Higgens (1992), in an analysis of a national survey of congregations, show that congregations made up of mostly African Americans remain quite a bit more likely to participate in civil rights and

social justice efforts than all-white congregations, and that they are substantially more likely to engage in community development activities. Although many community development activities among African Americans are the work of individual churches, coalitions of local congregations devoted to empowering poor communities are the main vehicle in congregation-based organizing. Leaders of such coalitions can build on the social networks provided at the congregational and denominational levels to mobilize people and resources for community action.

DENOMINATIONS, INTERFAITH COALITIONS, AND SPECIALIZED SERVICE ORGANIZATIONS

Congregations are the most numerous of religious organizations and the closest to their communities in many respects. But congregations generally originated in the efforts of supra- or extracongregational organizations to meet local needs. These are rich sources of social capital for local religious groups and their communities. Though our knowledge is limited, we explore in this section what we do know about the ways in which these sources of social capital affect poor communities.

Supracongregational Organizations

Denominations and associations of nondenominational congregations such as the American Council of Christian Churches often focus their energies at the national level, in public education and advocacy on behalf of religious interests. Many such associations have little direct control over the activities of local congregations, and the divisions between local pastors and national organizations on such issues as "charitable choice" are often significant. Nevertheless, most such organizations provide educational resources to local congregations; their national and regional meetings enable local religious leaders to acquire a wider circle of contacts; and some associations provide significant levels of financial and other support to poorer local congregations. They thus represent an important layer of social capital for both pastors and their congregations.

The nationally sponsored educational and advocacy campaigns of these associations of congregations, moreover, can have a significant impact at the local level in encouraging or discouraging certain types of political activities on the part of congregation members, highlighting some aspects of the "social gospel" at the expense of others, and encouraging community service of one type or another within congregations, as well as providing information about national policy issues. Any evaluation of the impact of these activities on communities, however, has to take into consideration the large degree of "slack" between positions advocated at the national level and those acceptable to local pastors and their constituents.

More important perhaps from a social capital perspective, national associations of congregations provide local religious leaders with ties that can be crucial to mobilizing resources for local initiatives and the maintenance or strengthening of local congregations. Such resources, moreover, can include training (building human capital) and financial support.

Any evaluation of the impact of the ties and opportunities represented by associational membership must take into account the considerable variability between and within religious traditions. Catholic dioceses have varied considerably in their willingness to subsidize urban schools and parishes from the center or through sister parish arrangements with affluent suburban parishes, or to shut them down in response to white outmigration. Declining personnel has led many denominations, including the Catholic Church, to decide more often to move with the membership rather than try to serve (and attract) a new black or immigrant membership in the old neighborhoods. Many denominations simply lack the organizational structure required to tax richer congregations in support of poorer ones. Some, however, manage to supplement their own resources through "cooperative ministry" with other denominations. Evidence from the NCS is mixed in this regard. Poorer

congregations are much less likely than others to receive consultant help, and less likely to be affiliated with a denomination. On the other hand, roughly half of both poor congregations and those located in poor neighborhoods belong to one or another local association.

Interfaith Coalitions

Especially among poorer congregations without strong denominational or other national-level ties, resource scarcity and social isolation may be overcome by participation in local interfaith coalitions, united ministries, and other associations of congregations. Most communities of any size appear to have at least one such body. Many coalitions house local chapters of larger movements with a social agenda, such as Church Women United, CROP, or Habitat for Humanity. A small minority of such coalitions focus exclusively on religious concerns and interfaith dialogue. Though some appear to lean to the more conservative side of the political spectrum on social issues, most can be categorized as distinctly liberal. In their ability to link congregations and para-church organizations in programs and projects of benefit to the larger community, they are an important instance of social capital mobilized for both congregations and communities.

From the point of view of the sorts of social capital available to poor communities, in fact, interfaith coalitions appear to provide one of the most important vehicles through which local religious bodies and affiliated organizations attempt to address problems of poverty, social isolation, and personal and family distress in poor communities. Such organizations play a number of roles: they serve as collective advocates on such issues as gun control and local spending for community problems; they provide social services of all kinds, in many cases recruiting volunteers from local churches and the larger community; they engage in community education on social issues, through workshops, training programs, work in the schools, and publicity; and they provide "free spaces" and resources for other, specialized organizations devoted to volunteerism in service to the community, community development, or social service delivery.

CONGREGATION-BASED ORGANIZING AND POOR COMMUNITIES

The congregation-based organizational template was developed by Industrial Areas Foundation (IAF) leaders after the death of the organization's longtime leader, the notorious community organizer Saul Alinsky. We are most knowledgeable about the groups that make up the IAF network, and hence about the details of the IAF model, since so much effort has been devoted to describing it. In addition, there are several other networks of local groups that mirror the IAF model, including the Gamaliel Foundation, based in Chicago; the Pacific Institute for Community Organization (PICO), based in Oakland, California; and Direct Action and Research Training (DART), based in Florida.

The CBO Formula for Organization Building

The several congregation-based organizing (CBO) networks enter communities in a similar fashion, looking for ecumenical support from a number of congregational leaders before they commit an organizer to a community. The support includes enough financial resources, from dues assessed from member congregations, to hire a lead organizer and provide the rudiments of an umbrella organization linking the participating congregations. An organizing committee is formed, and the lead organizer meets with pastors and lay leaders from participating congregations, typically in *"one-on-ones"*— *short* meetings aimed at sizing up their leadership potential and creating bonds with them. In this way, a cadre of leaders is formed out of the congregations to take part in leadership training. These leaders, in turn, carry on one-on-ones aimed at identifying additional leaders who can also receive leadership training. Thus, the premise of the organizing strategy is to build on the preexisting relationships between congregational members. It is driven by the desire to identify and train local leaders in relational skills and to have them build ever-widening circles of relationships. Eventually, leaders work to build relationships with outside allies, community leaders, power brokers, and ordinary citizens outside of their own group.

How CBOs Create Social Capital in Poor Communities

The question that needs to be asked is whether the CBO adds social capital value to poor communities beyond that which we have previously argued already exists as a result of the special characteristics of religious congregations. We believe that it does in a variety of ways.

Each of several CBO networks concentrates significant resources on what they call leadership development. Beyond the ongoing systematic training in one-on-ones already described, each network fields longer-term training sessions for leaders that include elements of what used to be called civic education, led by experienced trainers and shaped by systematic curricula. These training sessions range from the Standard IAF ten-day sessions to weekend retreats. If the widespread efforts of CBOs are at all successful in motivating and encouraging their local leaders through such training to build denser social relations, they have, by definition, added to the stock of community social capital. A key to relational organizing is the ongoing development of new relationships between leaders and ever-expanding circles of community members (see Speer & Hughey, Chapter 24, this volume).

CBOs also work to create linkages among organizations. Their organizational template explicitly links numerous congregations together into a coherent structure, and as a result, the pastors and members of each congregation are tied to one another. One consequence of the thickening of ties across congregations is access to one another's organizational networks. In each of the networks there is a steady flow of information between communities as a result of these ties.

Moreover, several of the CBO networks have created statewide organizations more tightly linking all of their affiliates as a basis for statewide mobilization.

Congregation-based organizations aim to build organizations to empower poor communities. By building on congregations, they inevitably build class-heterogeneous groups, first, because most congregations in poor communities include many families who are not poor, and second, because many CBOs include among their affiliate congregations some that are more middle-class. Finally, relational organizing induces leaders to develop social ties broadly and offers training in accomplishing this goal. As a result, the social capital built through the CBO strategy is highly likely to build socially heterogeneous social capital.

CONCLUSION

The various forms of social capital and social resources enumerated here collectively contribute significantly to community well-being in poor communities, particularly through the ability of congregations to mobilize their members around local needs. The networks, social solidarity, and broader linkages enjoyed by many religious institutions can provide the basis for community building, community organizing and political action, and individual advancement. They provide access to resources such as education, community service, and leadership opportunities; information about social service agencies, community organizations, and political events; leadership, foot soldiers, and "free space" for social and political initiatives; and formal and informal social services of all kinds.

The varied resources embedded in religious congregations have not escaped the notice of social service providers and planners. Community health program professionals have for some time capitalized on the legitimacy of church educational programs in designing church-based health education programs and community health outreach efforts, particularly among African American churches.

These same social networks and reserves of legitimacy explain the ability of local congregations to mobilize citizens, whether directly, through religiously sponsored social and political activities, or indirectly through the skills and leadership training that they provide and through activities that use the physical plant and resources of congregations for social and political action on behalf of the community. And social service agencies of all sorts depend on the support and volunteer labor of congregations or their members in virtually every community in the United States.

Religious participation is less affected by socioeconomic position than almost any other form of social behavior, so that church membership is relatively stable across the economic spectrum. To the degree that churches provide training in civic skills, opportunities and motivation for participation in civic affairs and politics, and networks for upward mobility, they are among the great equalizers in American society. The evidence presented here, however, points strongly to significant differences on almost all measures of social capital between poor congregations (those whose membership is predominantly poor people) and congregations in poor neighborhoods, where we find many multi-class congregations. The latter are richer in social capital and in the resources that make social capital especially important in poor communities. They are also more likely to have strong linkages to the larger society and to be more deeply involved in community affairs and political life than either congregations in more affluent neighborhoods or those made up mostly of poor members.

The social capital that religious congregations represent, however, is not without its limitations. Sometimes the relative homogeneity of congregations and the close interpersonal ties among members may lead to isolation. More frequently perhaps, religiously defined social boundaries limit the participation of the broader community in programs and constrain the sort of work congregations undertake. Religious bodies can also be potent vehicles for the perpetuation of inequalities, through some of the same mechanisms by which they train members in citizenship and provide leadership to the larger community. Most of the more hierarchical institutions, and even many of the more egalitarian ones, restrict the degree to which women may play leadership roles, though the degree and extent to which this is true have shifted back and forth over time.

The important role that many religious organizations can and do play in poor communities, however, should prompt greater attention among social scientists and policymakers alike to the ways in which such social capital is developed and deployed by institutions. Even poor congregations may be rich in social *capital*, but congregations of all sorts are apt to be relatively poor in precisely those resources necessary to address the problems of joblessness, poverty, crime, ill health, and low levels of educational achievement in poor communities. Any lasting impact, however, will depend on the larger environment, including first of all governments with the resources and the will to reverse long-term ends toward wage deflation and shrinking government services.

NOTE

1. A fuller account of the findings from this study can be found in the 2001 longer version of this chapter, "Social Capital, Religious Institutions, and Poor Communities," by Foley, Edwards and Chaves in *Social Capital and Poor Communities* edited by Saegert, Thompson and Warren and published by the Russell Sage Foundation.

REFERENCES

Casanova, J. 1994. *Public religions in the modern world*. Chicago: University of Chicago Press.

Chaves, M. 1998. *National congregations study: Data file and codebook*. Tucson: Department of Sociology, University of Arizona, Tucson.

Chaves, M. and L. Higgens. 1992. Comparing the community involvement of black and white congregations. *Journal for the Scientific Study of Religion* 31: 425–40.

Coleman, J. and T. Hoffer. 1987. *Public and private high schools: The impact of communities*. New York: Basic Books.

Ellison, C.G. and L.K. George. 1994. Religious involvement, social ties, and social support in a southeastern community. *Journal for the Scientific Study of Religion* 33: 46–61.

Greeley, A. 1997. Coleman revisited: Religious structures as sources of social capital. *American Behavioral Scientist* 40: 587–94.

Verba, S., K.L. Schlozman, and H.E. Brady. 1995. *Voice and equality: Civic voluntarism in American Politics*. Cambridge MA: Harvard University Press.

Youniss, J., J.A. McLellan, and M. Yates. 1997. What we know about engendering civic identity. *American Behavioral Scientist* 40: 620–31.

CHAPTER 15

Collaborating to Reduce Poverty

Views from city halls and community-based organizations

Michael Rich, Michael Giles, and Emily Stern

INTRODUCTION

The past few years have witnessed an unprecedented growth in collaborative efforts between city halls and community based organizations (CBOs) to reduce poverty and/or revitalize neighborhoods. These initiatives are characterized by a new language (e.g., collaboration, empowerment, community building) and a new sense of optimism that the intractable problems of poverty and neighborhood decline can be overcome.

This new, collaborative approach to poverty reduction and neighborhood revitalization in many U.S. cities is due in part to three intersecting streams of activity: (1) comprehensive community initiatives launched by national and local foundations, local governments, and, in some instances, residents themselves (Kingsley, McNeely, and Gibson 1997; Stone 1996); (2) efforts to broaden and expand the work of community development corporations to also include human services, community-based strategic planning, and neighborhood mobilization (Briggs and Mueller 1997; Walker and Weinheimer 1998); and (3) new federal government initiatives such as empowerment zones and enterprise communities, Healthy Start, Operation Weed and Seed, and school-to-work programs, which emphasize partnerships, collaborations, and community building.

The purpose of this chapter is to gain a better understanding of the ways in which community organizations and city governments are working together to reduce poverty and revitalize neighborhoods, the factors that either contribute to or inhibit effective collaborations, and the strategies communities are using to foster more effective collaborations. The evidence comes from surveys conducted in summer 1998. The city government survey was sent to all local governments of cities with a 1990 population of 50,000 or greater. The CBO survey instrument was sent to the executive directors of a random sample of nonprofit organizations in cities with populations of 50,000 or greater.

THE STATE OF CITY–CBO RELATIONS

A primary purpose of the survey was to assess the variety of ways in which city governments and CBOs are working together to reduce poverty and revitalize neighborhoods and to assess the factors that facilitate or hinder the effectiveness of that interaction. We asked respondents to characterize the "typical" city government–CBO relationship around poverty reduction and/or neighborhood revitalization issues in their city. Possible responses ranged from "do not work together on these issues," to "take collective action and share power in dealing with these issues." In the discussions that follow, we treat responses in the survey's last two categories (Table 15.1) as indicating the presence of "collaborative" city–CBO relationships.

The responses reveal a mixed picture regarding the state of relations between city governments and CBOs. Although relatively few of the respondents characterized the typical city–CBO relationship in the highest category ("take collective action and share

Table 15.1 Assessment of typical city–CBO relationship by type of respondent

	Total %	City %	CBO %
Do not work together on these issues	3	4	3
Work on separate activities with limited interaction	7	0	11
Work together on an irregular or ad hoc basis on these issues	33	23	38
Work together regularly and consistently on these issues	49	64	43
Take collective action and share power in dealing with these issues	7	9	6
Total percentage	100	100	100
N	324	101	223

power"), almost half (49%) indicated that city governments and CBOs typically work together regularly and consistently on poverty and neighborhood revitalization issues. A substantial minority (43%) of the respondents assessed city–CBO relationships as irregular, ad hoc, or more limited.

City officials generally offered a more positive impression of city–CBO interactions than their CBO counterparts. A substantial majority of city respondents (73%) characterized typical city–CBO relationships in the two most positive categories. In contrast, only 49% of the CBO respondents characterized typical city–CBO relations in their community in collaborative terms.

The state of city–CBO relationships may be a reflection of city characteristics. Larger cities with their greater administrative hierarchy may find it more difficult to adopt power-sharing arrangements with community organizations. Likewise, cities with larger poverty populations may have a more difficult environment in which to work. Having a greater number of communities in need of revitalization may make it more difficult for city governments to meet the expectations of community-based organizations for programmatic coordination and power sharing. In the simplest terms, such cities have more CBOs vying for the attention of city government.

The patterns reported in Table 15.2 are consistent with these expectations. Respondents from larger cities, cities with nonwhite populations above the national median, and cities with poverty populations above the national median are less likely to view city–CBO relationships positively. However, these

Table 15.2 Percentage collaborative responses by city demographics

	N	% Collaborative*
Population		
50,000 to 99,999	101	62
100,000 to 249,999	95	57
250,000+	128	51
% nonwhite		
Below national median	117	62
Above national median	207	53
% below poverty		
Below national median	79	62
Above national median	245	54

Note: * Differences in percentage collaborative among categories are not statistically significant at .05.

differences are not of sufficient magnitude to attain statistical significance.

COLLABORATION BY PROGRAM AREA

The overall assessments of city–CBO relations may obscure variation across specific issue areas. To address this possibility, respondents were asked to indicate the typical level of city–CBO interaction in a variety of program areas. The percentage of respondents characterizing city–CBO relationships in the issue area as collaborative are reported in Table 15.3. Only city and CBO respondents who reported their organizations were working in a program area are included in this analysis.

City officials are again more positive than their CBO counterparts in the characterization of the state of collaboration across program areas. On average, across the 14

Table 15.3 Percentage reporting collaborative responses by program area and type of respondent

Program Area	% of respondents working in area		% Collaborative	
	City	CBO	City	CBO
Affordable housing	100	89	73	48
Public safety	100	68	75	45
Homeless assistance	100	86	68	43
Senior services	97	62	62	31
Neighborhood improvements	100	74	62	33
Youth development	97	68	59	22
Economic development	99	73	55	26
Community organizing/advocacy	97	88	54	26
Family support	94	81	43	27
Employment and training	95	73	40	20
Health care	85	67	36	27
Child care	91	67	43	19
Transportation	91	66	36	24
Adult education	88	67	24	17
Average			52	29

Notes: a. The denominator of the percentage, total respondents in the category, varied between 88 and 104 for city respondents and 136 and 229 for CBO respondents.
b. All city–CBO differences in percentage collaborative respondents are significant at least at .05 except health care and adult education.

program areas, 52% of the city respondents but only 29% of the CBO respondents characterize city–CBO relations as collaborative. For both city and CBO respondents, these assessments are considerably lower than in Table 15.1, where the focus was on the state of the "typical" city–CBO interaction. The pattern of assessment across the various program areas is strongly correlated $(r = .84)$. In other words, city and CBO respondents tend to rate the same program areas as high or low in collaboration.

The patterns of collaboration across substantive policy areas tend to map closely the activities of city governments and CBOs. Evidence of higher levels of collaboration seems to be greatest in those program areas where city governments and CBOs have some degree of responsibility—either directly or indirectly (e.g., affordable housing, homeless assistance, public safety). On the other hand, the data suggest lower levels of collaboration in program areas where city governments and/or CBOs have not traditionally played a prominent role in service delivery or

have been major recipients of federal aid programs (e.g., adult education, transportation, health care, child care, family support).

COLLABORATION BY PROGRAM PHASE

City–CBO relations may vary not only across program areas but also by when collaboration occurs. For example, some collaborative relationships may only be exploratory or advisory in nature and confined solely to the formative phases of a program, such as identifying key stakeholders, assessing community needs, and developing a vision to guide the program. Other forms of collaborative relationships between city government and CBOs may extend deeper into the life cycle of public programs and involve joint/shared participation in funding, implementation, and/or evaluation. Table 15.4 reports the proportions of respondents characterizing city–CBO relations in the two

Table 15.4 Percentage reporting collaborative relationships by program phase and type of respondent

Program phase	Type of respondent	
	City	CBO
Identifying community needs	69	35
Developing project/program concept	51	28
Developing plan/budget	38	20
Inclusion of key stakeholders	61	28
Identifying/securing funding	50	31
Initial project/program implementation	47	24
Ongoing project/program management	39	22
Monitoring and evaluation	39	26
Average	49	27

Notes. a. The denominator of the percentage, total respondents in the category, varied between 104 and 105 for city respondents and 224 and 228 for CBO respondents.
b. All city–CBO differences are significant at least at .05.

most collaborative terms for eight phases of program development.

The extent of perceived collaboration varies considerably across the phases of initiatives. Collaboration is judged to be highest in the early phases of a project such as identifying community needs, developing the project concept, and including key stakeholders. The exception to this pattern is "developing the project plan and budget," which had relatively low levels of perceived collaboration. Assessments of collaboration were lower for the ongoing aspects of a typical initiative such as implementation, project management, and evaluation. Once more, city respondents were more likely than CBO respondents to characterize city–CBO relations as collaborative. City and CBO respondents' assessments of the degree of collaboration by program phases also were strongly correlated ($r = .85$). Thus, city and CBO officials tended to agree on which phases are characterized by more collaboration and which by less.

As a follow-up, both sets of respondents were asked to indicate the phase of an initiative that was most essential to achieving effective collaboration. Although they differ somewhat in rank order, the top four choices for both city and CBO respondents were the same: identifying community needs (49% city, 47% CBO), inclusion of key stake-holders (42% city, 28% CBO), developing project/program concept (28% city, 26% CBO), and identifying and securing funding (20% city, 39% CBO). Thus, not only do both city and CBO respondents perceive greater collaboration in the earlier phases of an initiative than in the later but both sets of respondents also view the earlier phases as more crucial to successful collaboration.

BENEFITS AND BARRIERS TO COLLABORATION

Why should city governments and CBOs work together to reduce poverty and revitalize neighborhoods? Proponents of collaboration frequently point out that "collaboration changes the way we work" and note such positive attributes as building consensus, promoting diversity and inclusiveness, taking a strategic as opposed to a programmatic approach to problem solving, and emphasizing long-term as opposed to short-term accomplishments (Gray 1989).

We asked city government and CBO officials to indicate what types of benefits were typically achieved in their communities as a result of their current collaborations (Table 15.5). City respondents were much more positive than CBO respondents in their assessment of the benefits of current collabor-

Table 15.5 Percentage of respondents identifying a benefit of collaboration by type of respondent

Benefit	Type of respondent	
	City	CBO
City gains better understanding of community needs	95	75
Partners gain better understanding of each other's capacity	93	67
Activities are better aligned with community priorities	92	67
Strengthens other partnerships within the community	91	65
Activities are more effective at achieving goals	87	63
Activities are more comprehensive	78	65
Creates an atmosphere of mutual trust	85	57
Creates a forum to address competing views and priorities	89	52
Involves residents in planning and implementation	91	60
Builds appreciation for efforts of city hall and CBOs	83	56
Fosters connections with other groups	88	61
Large-scale activities can be undertaken	66	63
CBOs gain access to city's technical resources	90	50
Larger pool of funding is available	68	52
Promotes leadership development	79	49
Fosters connections across city departments	83	43
Responsibility and accountability are shared	74	42
Creates a forum to address racial and class biases	65	38
Average	83	57

Notes: a. The denominator of the percentage, total respondents in the category, varied between 101 and 105 for city respondents and 215 and 221 for CBO respondents.
b. All city–CBO differences are significant at least at .05, except larger-scale activities can be undertaken.

ations. The percentage of respondents reporting that a specific benefit had been achieved averaged 83% for city respondents, compared with 57% for their CBO counterparts.

Once again, the assessments of whether various benefits were achieved were significantly correlated ($r = .56$). Even so, there is considerable difference of opinion between city and CBO respondents on a few benefits. Nine out of 10 city respondents believe that their current collaborations provide CBOs access to city technical resources, but only 50% of CBO respondents see that benefit accruing from current collaborations. A discrepancy of similar magnitude occurs with regard to the benefits of "fosters connections across city departments" and "creates a forum to address competing views and priorities."

A follow-up question asked respondents to identify the three most important benefits

of collaboration. Four of the five most frequently cited benefits were the same for city and CBO respondents: "activities are better aligned with community priorities" (city 46%, CBO 33%), "larger pool of funding is available" (city 26%, CBO 42%), "activities are more comprehensive" (city 23%, CBO 17%), and "activities are more effective at achieving goals" (city 24%, CBO 20%). City respondents included "involves residents in planning and implementation" (city 27%, CBO 13%) among their top five benefits, whereas CBOs included "city gains better understanding of community needs" (city 19%, CBO 24%). By and large, the benefits of city–CBO collaborations identified by respondents as most important are also perceived as accruing from current collaborations by more than 80% of city and 60% of CBO respondents (Table 15.5). The one major exception is "larger pool of funding is available," which two-thirds of city respondents but a bare majority of CBO respondents perceive as flowing from current city–CBO collaborations.

There is far less agreement between the two groups concerning the greatest barriers to effective collaboration. Apart from identifying inadequate city funding and lack of trust as important barriers to effective city–CBO collaboration, there is little else that city and CBO respondents agree on with regard to important barriers. CBO respondents point to city government and the local political environment as the primary obstacles to effective collaboration to reduce poverty and revitalize communities. For CBO respondents, an overly bureaucratic city government that does not want to release control is the major obstacle to effective collaboration. The city respondents, on the other hand, see CBOs with limited resources, poor administration, and parochial interests as the major stumbling block. A lack of mutual trust and poor communication reflect and reinforce these views of one another.

STRATEGIES FOR EFFECTIVE COLLABORATION

As the preceding discussion of barriers makes clear, effective collaboration between city governments and community-based organizations does not occur spontaneously—it requires concerted effort and commitment on the part of both partners. The survey asked city and CBO respondents to identify some of the strategies they have used in their collaborations and to indicate how valuable certain strategies could be in making their collaboration more effective.

Using city government funding or incentives for community-based activities was the most frequently employed collaboration strategy and one of the strategies perceived to be most valuable (Table 15.6). Nevertheless, the city and CBO responses reflect different perceptions of how often city funding and incentives are used. Of city officials, 82% said their local government makes funding or incentives available for collaborative community-based activities, whereas only

63% of CBO respondents reported that they initiate these types of activities using city government funding or incentives. Various approaches to open channels of communication between partners are frequently employed and perceived as valuable.

Perhaps the most interesting finding in this area involves the adoption of a comprehensive and strategic approach to poverty reduction, an approach that many advocates of collaborative problem solving have encouraged. For example, the empowerment zone/ enterprise community initiative based its designation of zone communities in part on the quality of the community-based strategic plan developed by multiple stakeholders (e.g., government, community, private sector, etc.). Fifty-six percent of the city and slightly less than half of the CBO respondents indicated that they have actually employed a comprehensive and strategic approach to poverty reduction and/or neighborhood revitalization. However, approximately 70% of both groups view this strategy as very valuable in creating successful collaborations.

DISCUSSION

Collaboration has become a watchword in city–CBO relationships. Academic observers, private foundations, national policy organizations, and federal government programs have increasingly advocated and provided incentives to foster collaborative interactions between city governments and community-based organizations. The present study has reported the results of a survey on the current status of city–CBO relationships and prospects for increased collaboration in the future. The findings are mixed.

The barriers to collaboration identified in the survey response are substantial and deeply embedded. City respondents see the major hindrances to collaboration arising from characteristics/traits of the CBOs, and CBO respondents see the major barriers arising from shortcomings of city administrators. Moreover, the identified barriers reflect characteristics that serve the particular organizations well while working against

Table 15.6 Strategies used to bring about more effective collaborations and their perceived value by type of respondent

Strategies	City		CBO	
	% Employing strategy	% Responding "Very valuable"	% Employing strategy	% Responding "Very valuable"
Initiating community-based activities using city government funding/ incentives	82	79	63*	57*
Using advocacy efforts to raise public awareness of issues and needs	49	41	60	56*
Developing a forum for increased communication between city government and CBOs	66	64	51*	58*
Creating a CBO consortium or network to work with city government	61	55	58	52
Sharing/exchanging ideas on best practices for successful partnerships	44	58	51	52
Adopting a comprehensive and strategic approach to poverty reduction or community revitalization involving multiple partners and program areas	56	72	48	70
Initiating targeted outreach to private sector partners with city and CBOs	56	54	39*	52
Creating a spin-off organization to implement joint projects	33	27	30	26
Bringing in a third-party intermediary to help develop collaboration	30	18	27	29*
Number of respondents	104		219	

Notes: a. Because respondents only rated the value of strategies that they employed, the number of respondents potentially varies across the strategies. For this set of respondents, the actual number was never more than one or two less than that shown in the table.
* City–CBO difference significant at least at .05.

collaboration. For example, the failure of CBOs to see the citywide picture that city respondents see as a barrier to collaboration reflects the very nature of CBOs, their linkage to the local community. Likewise, city government's bureaucratic decision structures and assertion of control that CBO officials see as barriers to collaboration are responses by city governments and officials to real organizational needs for structuring authority and maintaining accountability. Poor communications and lack of trust, which are identified as barriers by both sets of respondents, in part reflect the difficulties of bridging this organizational divide. Developing trust is exceptionally difficult when it requires relaxing or deviating from strategies and approaches that have served organizations well in the past.

The positive finding of the survey is that despite these apparently fundamental barriers, a large amount of city–CBO collaboration is occurring. The percentage of respondents reporting collaborative city CBO relationships varies across program areas and by the type of respondent, but on balance the results indicate that a large percentage of cities and CBOs are working together regularly. In addition, the respondents see these collaborations as yielding substantial benefits—city governments have a better understanding of community issues and are able to design and implement programs that better fit community needs. These are benefits anticipated by proponents of collaboration. It would seem that the efforts and incentives to promote collaboration between cities and CBOs have enjoyed notable success.

Although the survey reveals substantial evidence of city governments and CBOs working together regularly, and both sets of respondents responded favorably to questions about city–CBO "collaborations," the identified relationships seem best characterized as a "thin" version of collaboration. Scholars define *collaboration* to require but not be limited to working together on a regular and consistent basis. Academic definitions and associated discussions of collaboration typically include a power-sharing relationship between partners. For example, Gray (1989, 5) defined collaboration as "a process through which parties who see different aspects of a problem can constructively explore their differences and search for solutions that go beyond their own limited vision of what is possible."

The results of this survey indicate that city governments and CBOs are working together, and a larger number are working together on a regular and consistent basis. However, relatively few of the respondents—either in response to questions regarding "typical" city–CBO interactions or to questions focused on city–CBO interactions in specific program areas—describe those relations in terms of cities and CBOs sharing power. Moreover, when the focus turns to city–CBO interactions at the various phases of initiatives, the most positive assessments appear to be in the early formative stages of initiatives. This is consistent with respondents' perceptions of the benefits of collaborating. The responses to these questions cluster around better awareness of community needs and shaping of program initiatives to reflect community priorities. Both sets of respondents see greater city–CBO collaboration early in the initiative process, and both tend to see the benefits of collaboration in those phases. Involvement in implementation, ongoing project management, and joint accountability for outcomes (e.g., monitoring/evaluation) are not only less likely to occur, but city and even CBO respondents see these issues as less central to city–CBO relations.

Although the fact that a large percentage of cities are working regularly and consistently with CBOs to engage the communities in needs assessments, and initial project design is a very positive finding, this thin version of collaboration may not produce the beneficial outcomes suggested by some proponents of collaboration. For example, as Chrislip and Larson (1994, 13) noted, when collaboration is successful, the benefits often affect the entire community:

> When collaboration succeeds, new networks and norms for civic engagement are established and the primary focus of work shifts from parochial interests to the broader concerns of the community. Collaboration ... not only achieves results in addressing ... substantive issues ... it also builds "civic community."

The fundamental reordering of city–CBO relations anticipated in such descriptions of collaboration is unlikely to proceed from the thin version of collaboration apparently at work in the minds of most city officials and CBO directors. Of course, the adoption and spread of the thin version of collaboration may be a necessary step to the fuller version envisioned by scholars of organizational dynamics. The emphasis that both city and CBO respondents place on communication and trust as important to facilitating collaboration is underscored by the overwhelming agreement by both sets of respondents that a comprehensive and strategic approach to poverty reduction and community revitalization is an effective strategy. Many of the private and public initiatives emphasizing collaboration have included comprehensive, strategic planning as a funding prerequisite. This approach brings public, private, and community stakeholders into a neutral setting and strives to obtain consensus concerning problems, strategies for addressing problems, allocation of responsibilities, and monitoring. In sum, this approach flattens the city hierarchy by bringing responsible decision makers directly to the table and offers the potential of minimizing the obstacles of control and "turf" embedded in lower levels of city administration. It also places CBO officials in a decision-making realm where the larger picture of citywide needs comes into focus. The facilitated nature of this process offers the potential for real communication across the city–CBO divide.

In short, comprehensive strategic planning has evolved as a process to address most of the barriers to collaboration identified by city and CBO respondents. Their responses to the survey indicate their recognition of that fact.

Strategic planning, however, is not a panacea. As a strategy for advancing collaboration, it has two major challenges. The first involves challenges to its internal success. The participants have to include the major stakeholders, persons with authority (not simple representatives) must be at the table, the various parties must see the process as potentially important and commit to it, and the facilitation must go well. Even if a planning process is successful, the shared understandings, trust, and commitments made by the participants must be exported to the larger community. Implementation in the face of embedded hierarchies and parochial community views is the second challenge to successful strategic planning.

In closing, the results of the National League of Cities survey indicate that collaborative approaches to persistent poverty and neighborhood revitalization are no longer confined to a handful of cities but have become fairly widespread across cities of all sizes and conditions. Future research is needed to understand more fully the dynamics and determinants of these relationships in individual cities. Although national surveys can aid in identifying the scope and frequency of city–CBO partnerships, case studies and comparative

REFERENCES

Briggs, X. D., and E. J. Mueller, with M. L. Sullivan. 1997. *From neighborhood to community: Evidence of the social effects of community development.* New York: New School for Social Research, Community Development Research Center.

Chrislip, D. D., and C. E. Larson. 1994. *Collaborative leadership: How citizens and civic leaders can make a difference.* San Francisco: Jossey-Bass.

Gray, B. 1989. *Collaborating: Finding common ground for multiparty problems.* San Francisco: Jossey-Bass.

Kingsley, G. T., J. B. McNeely, and J. O. Gibson. 1997. *Community building: Coming of age.* Washington, DC: Urban Institute.

Stone, R., ed. 1996. *Core issues in comprehensive community-building initiatives.* Chicago: University of Chicago, Chapin Hall for Children.

Walker, C., and M. Weinheimer. 1998. *Community development in the 1990s.* Washington, DC: Urban Institute.

CHAPTER 16

Toward Greater Effectiveness in Community Change

Challenges and responses for philanthropy[1]

Prudence Brown, Robert Chaskin, Ralph Hamilton, and Harold Richman

INTRODUCTION

Foundations of all types seek to improve low-income communities and the circumstances and opportunities of the people who live in them. Their efforts have produced promising results: houses have been built, organizations strengthened, residents mobilized, collaboration enhanced, services delivered, employment increased, and so forth. But funders acknowledge that their support has yielded less for communities in the short term than they and their community partners initially hoped and that the work is more complex and longer-term than initially anticipated.

This chapter aims to shape a discussion about philanthropy and community change that builds on the lessons that funders have learned, clarifies the challenges they have identified, and describes some promising approaches they are taking to address these challenges. It is the product of ongoing research on philanthropy and community change at the Chapin Hall Center for Children, including a series of 45 interviews conducted in 2001–2002 with a diverse group of current and former foundation executives and staff; representatives from community-change organizations and intermediaries; evaluators, researchers, and technical assistance providers; and close observers of foundation efforts.[2]

Our respondents suggest that foundations can become more effective by further refining how they *think* about community change, how they *do* community-change work, and how they *learn* from their efforts. Specifically, they underscore the need to address:

- the clarity and realism in foundation's goals, expectations, ideas, and strategies;
- the alignment between the goals and strategies, and foundations' means and modes of practice;
- the sufficiency and effectiveness of current methods to inform, assess, and revise foundation thinking and practice.

Addressing these issues is a "doable" task, one in which some foundations are already deeply engaged.

The analysis that follows has important limitations. Treating *thinking, doing* and *learning* sequentially, as we do below, could make community change efforts seem linear and simple, when, in fact, they are quite the opposite: complex, highly iterative and requiring constant adjustments in thinking and doing in response to learning about conditions and opportunities on the ground. Although the struggle to keep the three activities connected and aligned in practice is constant, we separate them in order to clarify and highlight aspects of each. Further, our focus on philanthropy should not suggest that foundations are lone and sufficient agents working to promote community change. Indeed, foundations are only one of the many players that include community organizations, service providers, private business, and public, political and civic actors (see, e.g., Ferguson and Stoutland 1999; Kubisch *et al.* 2002; Chaskin 2003). We concentrate on the role of foundations, however, in order to better understand their particular role in the ecology of community change. Finally, the chapter's tone and structure—which begins with concerns before moving on to potential solutions—may appear to overemphasize the importance of challenges while minimizing the progress being made. Over the last ten years funders *have* made progress on these issues. We present the challenges upfront both because that is what we heard in interviews with the people closest to foundations' community change work and because we believe this approach can help stimulate productive debate and help to articulate a potential philanthropic agenda.

FOUNDATION THINKING

How foundations *think* about community change shapes their goals, expectations, strategies, and investments. Unclear or incomplete thinking can get in the way of foundations' effectiveness in promoting community change.

Communities are notoriously complex. They can be conceptualized and operationalized in many different ways, and are perceived and used differently by different people, in ways that are often connected to age, race, class, length of residence, the state of local resources, and the nature of social organization within particular communities (e.g., Wellman and Wortley 1990; Lee, Campbell, and Miller 1991; Furstenberg 1993). How to define them, and what they provide as a basis for social action is by no means straightforward (Chaskin 1997; Sampson 1999). To make this more complicated, the precise goals of foundation-supported community-change efforts are sometimes unclear, indicating a confusion about whether they are intended to improve the lives of people in poverty or eliminate poverty, build community capacity, reform public systems, connect individuals to economic opportunity, promote social capital or democratic participation, address structural racism and inequity, or all of these things. This lack of clarity is often coupled with a tendency to inflate expectations—to overestimate how much difference foundations' ideas, skills and money are likely to make. To make matters worse, grantees frequently collude with this misjudgment because they want the foundation to become a champion—and significant funder—of their work.

A common dynamic between foundation boards and staff also contributes to a lack of realism. While board members are often excited by the idea of "getting at root problems," they can also be impatient with complex, long-term solutions; they look for clear "causal stories" and relatively simple solutions (see Stone 1989). In these circumstances, staff may ignore the field's experience and over-promise what can be achieved. For example, the timeframe of most grants is usually shorter than the time actually needed to make substantial change in a community; many foundations continue to work within three- to five-year timeframes although both experience and research have demonstrated that measurable community-level change usually takes longer, and that there are likely fundamental limitations to what action at the neighborhood level alone can accomplish (e.g., Halpern 1995; Jargowsky 1997).

Bringing greater clarity and realism to foundations' goals, expectations, and ideas for community change would strengthen the intellectual underpinnings for community-focused philanthropic investment. It would also provide a more effective basis for ongoing learning and improvement. Many foundations have started to use theory of change and logic models to shape their community change efforts. Further work is needed to develop these theories, apply them systematically and ground them in evidence of prior success. Unclear goals and expectations make it hard to articulate the assumptions about cause and effect that are the key to a viable theory (and, consequently, to good decisionmaking). Often, even when assumptions are specified, the logic that guides them and the interim measures of progress that make them testable are not clear. The theory of change used in one foundation effort, for instance, tied an increase in civic capacity to poverty alleviation. Yet neither foundation staff nor the community participants were able to explain in any detail the steps by which the intangible asset of civic capacity would be transformed into the tangible asset of increased income. Increased civic capacity and poverty alleviation can both be valid goals, but clarity about the meaning of each and about the relationship between them (if any) needs to be thought through and mapped out if the foundation's expectations, investment, and outcomes are to align. Certainly "coherence" can be overdone, but the lack of sound and articulated theory leaves little basis for shaping consistent action or for interpreting the results.

Most funders recognize the importance of grounding their strategies in a realistic understanding of a community's capacity. Although strategy and existing capacity need to go hand in hand, a realistic community "reading" is hard to get and requires more time than many foundations are prepared to invest. As a result, some funders enter community work with inadequate knowledge about neighborhood conditions, capacities, and trajectories. This lack of understanding can slow, impede, or even derail their strategies, and sometimes make the neighborhood less receptive to other change initiatives. For example, misreading the neighborhood's politics or appointing local leadership without an appreciation of these politics can create unproductive internal conflict among neighborhood groups, passive resistance to participation and change, or a cynical sense of "here we go again" with all parties trying to get something from the funder for themselves but lacking commitment to a collaborative change effort (Chaskin 2003).

Similarly, more attention needs to be paid to the political and macrostructural influences that shape community circumstances (e.g., Logan and Molotch 1987; Wilson 1987; Massey and Denton 1993). Grounding strategies in a more rigorous assessment of the external dynamics and structural constraints that affect communities would also improve the chances that foundations' community-change activities produce their intended results. Private market forces, public policies and funding streams, embedded structures of racial preference and discrimination, and other external factors do not invalidate the value or potential of community-level work. But an incomplete appreciation for external dynamics, constraints and opportunities in foundation strategy-making can lead to inadequate resources (if the flow of public and private dollars is not addressed) or to misdirected resources (if the dollars are invested on less strategic ventures).

An additional challenge for foundations is to become clearer internally about their core beliefs about community change, more aware of the requirements and risks inherent in the choices they make, and more consistent in aligning the two. Such alignment speaks to a central paradox at the heart of philanthropic thinking and practice: foundations' quest for greater impact is not usually accompanied by an increased tolerance for conflict or risk. On one hand, real community change is inherently risky, political and fractious because it affects the distribution of power and resources. Although substantial change can sometimes be achieved without turmoil, that is not often the case. On the other hand, foundations are wary of stimulating such conflict even as they seek to achieve ambitious ends. Some may avoid certain approaches that are deemed "too political" or that lead to more fundamental questions about the power structure. Alignment between thinking and doing, between community-change goals and foundation capacity requires continuing attention.

Implications for Action

More effective *thinking* about community change may entail several kinds of actions including:

- *Using more rigorous, diligent processes to assess communities.* This includes using demographic and administrative data to select investment targets, taking extra time to analyze community capacities and dynamics (history, culture, needs, strengths, and leadership), and situating a community in a broader context.

- *Aligning goals with realistic expectations.* This requires a greater commitment to clarity and realism, both about what might be achieved in a community and about a foundation's preparedness to play the necessary roles; a more critical analysis of ideas and assumptions; and a willingness to treat progress as developmental.

- *Clarifying thinking about conflict and risk.* Change can be messy, especially when it occurs in the politically charged environments of communities. Foundations need to acknowledge this, specify their level of tolerance for them, and design their strategies according.
- *Using a more disciplined, systematic process for strategy development.* This includes better theories of change and better ways of using the theories—processes that make goals explicit, specify actions and outcome expectations, identify key change agents, recognize internal and external barriers, and address issues of intervention quality, dosage, extent, and timing.

FOUNDATION DOING

How foundations act on their thinking and the degree to which their actions align with their goals, expectations, and strategies for community change, is the second important dimension of foundation-sponsored community change. As used here, *doing* refers to an array of implementation topics, such as how foundations' relationships with communities are constructed and executed, the way foundations support the development of "community capacity", and the roles foundations play in community change. "Foundation Doing" also includes the way that foundations organize themselves internally as well as the external means they employ, such as operating through intermediary organizations, lead agencies, or collaborative bodies.

Many foundations' relationships with communities are driven by a new interest in shared commitment, contribution, and action on both sides of the grantmaking table. Nonetheless, the rules, expectations, and boundaries of relationships between community-change funders and grantees are often unclear and rarely specified at the front end. The vagueness of terms can help the parties establish a positive tone early on. Not surprisingly, each side interprets what is said (and not said) according to its own interests and experience. But apparent agreement can mask real differences in perspective that can have high costs in the long term.

Apparent agreement can also cloak a deep misunderstanding about the nature of the relationship. One oft-repeated scenario is that the relationship begins auspiciously but the community's progress is slower than expected. Within two or three years, the foundation's internal dynamics shift as its board becomes impatient, new executive leaders and program staff with different priorities come in, or new and different ideas grab the foundation's attention and displace old enthusiasms. Consequently, foundation staff feel internal pressure to justify the investment by showing that the project has produced measurable outcomes. The program officer begins making non-negotiable demands on community grantees, despite previous assurances of support and patience. This is the point where major tensions and conflict often come into play.

Because feedback and accountability mechanisms are not usually built into the funder-community relationship—such as a regular venue where concerns can be raised, a set of pre-agreed operating standards that will guide all parties, or some kind of performance measures for the relationship itself—the inconsistency (perceived or actual) between initial assurances and the demands for measurable progress and accountability two or three years along is not checked and becomes a pattern. The less powerful partner—the community—has little recourse, community trust declines and resentment grows. Ultimately, these unresolved issues fester and become impediments to the foundation's effectiveness in the community.

Many funders are seeking a better way to work with communities, and they acknowledge that they are still learning what these "partnerships" entail. Some suggest that foundations' donor guidelines, organizational cultures, board and management expectations, reporting requirements, and legal constraints do not fit easily with the processes and attitudes required to build mutual, trust-based partnerships. But without institutional structures and accountability mechanisms to support and guide the new behaviors, foundations' interest in partnering with communities often gets ahead of their ability to act on that vision consistently or over the long term.

Foundations have increasingly invested in building community "capacity," in recognition that the most pervasive and sustainable change stems from a community's ability to envision, develop, and lead its own solutions (Chaskin *et al.* 2001). Efforts to develop local leaders, provide technical assistance on specific topics, build local supports for change, and connect community members to resources within and outside their neighborhoods have all helped to increase community capacity. But these efforts are still too often the exception rather than the rule, and even where they exist they are often incomplete and not yet well-integrated into community-change efforts. Funders are still learning the exact scope, sequence, amount, and types of capacity development that communities need and want, and the best techniques for bringing this about. One result is that foundation practice sometimes places too much emphasis on building the capacity of one or a few organizations as a proxy for community infrastructure while giving too little attention to building the broader infrastructure itself—the whole range of individuals, organizations, and associations in a community that have the ability, commitment, and resources to address community-level problems.

Foundations have opportunities to influence community change in many ways that reach beyond the traditional role of grant-maker (Hamilton *et al.* 2004; Sojourner *et al.* 2004). They can facilitate relationships between the powerful and the disenfranchised, foster excitement around creative ideas, disseminate useful information, and advocate for difficult but necessary policy changes. They possess organizational resources—skills, relationships, access, capacities, and financial clout—that could be used to promote community change. Although some foundations are testing out these new roles, others point to an internal culture, structure, management style, and set of procedures that tend to be overly bureaucratized and compartmentalized and appear ill-suited to promoting the kind of flexible, integrated, and hands-on involvement that

seems to benefit community-change efforts. As a result, most foundations continue to tread a more familiar path and, in doing so, miss an opportunity to leverage their influence, credibility, networks and institutional resources on behalf of community change.

Implications for Action

More effective philanthropic practice will require greater specificity and shared understanding about the terms for funder-community relationships, better alignment of grantmaking activities with the goal of building long-term community capacity, and more innovative use of foundations' institutional resources to support community change. It will also require some foundations to address their own internal ambivalence about mutual relationships with communities or at least become clearer and more consistent about the kind of relationship they are willing to have.

Further improvement will come from acknowledging, legitimizing, and openly discussing the tensions in community-foundation relationships, including issues around power, race and class. This may include:

- *Adopting an operating style aligned with community change goals and strategies.* Foundation representatives need to consider a range of potential working styles, select a style that matches foundation goals and strategies, understand the institutional capacities needed to implement the style, and secure support from the board.
- *Negotiating terms for community engagement.* Foundations and their community partners need to specify explicit roles, expectations, rules for engagement and decision making, relationship boundaries, accountability measures, and processes for monitoring and improving their partnership.
- *Building community capacity.* Foundation representatives need to understand what community capacity is and how it is produced. Effective support for community capacity also means assuring long-term core operating funds for an

array of key community institutions, efforts, and networks.

- *Expanding foundation potential as a non-monetary resource for the community.* Externally, foundations can use their credibility and leverage to help communities make strategic connections to influential players in the private, public, and philanthropic sectors. Foundations can also further leverage their financial power through direct investment, loan guarantees, access to favorable credit terms, and program-related investments.

FOUNDATION LEARNING

How foundations learn about community change—that is, the way they assess, interpret, revise, share and apply their knowledge—is the third and final focus of this chapter. As used here, foundation learning refers both to the *content* of their knowledge about philanthropy and community change, and to the *processes* through which such knowledge is shared and applied within and beyond the field. In this sense, foundation learning is the feedback mechanism between foundation *thinking* and *doing*, or the field's system for the "production, distribution, and application" of knowledge (Hamilton *et al.* 2005).

Over the years, philanthropy has recognized the need for good information to inform practice and policymaking. Foundations' investments in research and evaluation and in the distillation of practical lessons have established an important baseline of information and tools. As funders expand their efforts at community change, they also need to expand efforts to collect, analyze, organize, apply, and share knowledge.

Some foundations have made significant investments in research and evaluation that have borne fruit. That said, the extent and nature of philanthropies' usable knowledge about critical ideas and issues in community change—such as synergy, social capital, community capacity, empowerment, community asset development, or resident involvement—are still limited and often dis-

connected from users' needs. Respondents cite a lack of commitment to building systematic knowledge about community change and insufficient attention to tacit knowledge from the field. In addition, the knowledge development about community change supported by foundations tends to be narrowly defined in the context of program evaluation (largely driven by concerns about accountability) with an investment in evaluation serving as a kind of proxy for a system of learning instead of as a critical component of that system. And, because many evaluations focus primarily on tracking compliance with foundations' grant terms, many assessments fail to address critical issues for strategy development and practice.

Too much useful knowledge is still unavailable to foundations and community practitioners, often due to the fact that existing knowledge is rarely extracted from individuals and foundation files and then made available. But the lack of access to potentially useful information is also caused by foundations treating some reports and evaluations as proprietary. In fact, only a few foundations currently make a commitment to sharing all their evaluation materials. Further, many of the learning materials that do exist do not get at the crucial operational issues funders and others want to hear about. Sometimes these documents' usefulness is limited by a funder or evaluator's level of candor. Other times, a report fails to address the issues that users consider most significant, or the information is presented in a format tailored for program officers but not for community practitioners or others. As a consequence, many funders, community practitioners and researchers call for a richer, more complete and more useful range of knowledge products. These products would include more periodic, time-sensitive and interim information, as well as more refined and applicable long-term findings.

Committing to learning about community change is only half the battle for foundations, however. How will they systematically and routinely interpret lessons and incorporate them into practice? How will they create safe, productive opportunities for staff reflection and debate? How can learning within one foundation contribute to the knowledge of foundations, practitioners, policymakers, and social scientists in general? And how can a foundation's learning methods spawn ongoing knowledge development? These questions point to the need for a more intentional system of learning about philanthropic investment in community change. Lacking an effective system, lessons about community change do not serve as the basis for cumulative knowledge or lead to changes in practice. People and institutions tend to repeat known processes without making necessary innovations.

Implications for Action

Over the long term, more effective foundation thinking and practice will require a different stance toward knowledge and learning and an array of new mechanisms to help generate, collect, distribute, and internalize the knowledge. More than a decade ago a group of foundations created the Aspen Institute's Roundtable on Comprehensive Community Initiatives as one such intentional learning vehicle. More recently, a number of foundations have been taking steps to re-orient their organizations' internal and external stance toward knowledge generation, sharing, and application. These range from establishing learning goals for staff, to sharing information publicly, to expanding the use of the internet for reporting, to creating new venues for foundation peer exchange. The challenge for the field is to bring together these pieces of an evolving approach to foundation learning into a more complete and effective whole. A new kind of foundation accountability for learning will also be needed. Two types of actions are especially important:

- *Fostering learning that supports community change.* Funders need to treat learning as a core objective of philanthropic work. This requires developing an intentional but loosely structured learning "system"—a collection of principles, commitments, and linkages that can be implemented by foundations and others. An effective system would emphasize a commitment to inquiry and to openly sharing knowledge, a recognition that knowledge has multiple sources and is collected through multiple means, and a dedication to collecting and shaping knowledge according to users' needs—both within and beyond foundations.

- *Promoting learning within individual foundations.* Raising the profile of learning in foundations requires changes in individual foundation's organizational culture and behavior, new board practices, new reward systems for foundation staff, and new administrative practices and support structures. Grants may need to include support for learning—separate from and in addition to money for evaluation. Reporting requirements might be changed so they more directly contribute to learning. Foundations also could establish high-level staff positions for people who manage organizational learning, knowledge development, and knowledge dissemination to communities, as some have already done.

CONCLUSION

The philanthropic sector is at an important crossroads with respect to community-change efforts. Many funders are impatient with the *status quo* and eager to achieve more complete, lasting results—and they have an increasingly rich and useful base of ideas and experience on which to build. That combination of factors may be what is needed to push the field forward. The challenges that foundations face are not reasons to avoid the work with communities but opportunities to improve it.

NOTES

1. This chapter is adapted from Brown *et al.* (2003). See also Brown and Fiester (2007).
2. See Brown *et al.* (2003) for a complete list of interviewees and their affiliations.

REFERENCES

Brown, Prudence, Robert J. Chaskin, Ralph Hamilton and Harold Richman. *Toward Greater Effectiveness in Community Change: Challenges and Responses for Philanthropy.* Chicago: The Chapin Hall Center for Children, 2003. www.chapinhall.org

Brown, Prudence and Leila Fiester. *Hard Lessons about Philanthropy and Community Change from the Neighborhood Improvement Initiative.* Chicago: The Chapin Hall Center for Children, 2007. www.chapinhall.org

Chaskin, Robert J. "Perspectives on Neighborhood and Community: A Review of the Literature." *Social Service Review* 71 (1997): 521–547.

Chaskin, Robert J. "Fostering Neighborhood Democracy: Legitimacy and Accountability within Loosely Coupled Systems." *Nonprofit and Voluntary Sector Quarterly* 32 (2003): 161–189.

Chaskin, Robert J., Prudence Brown, Sudhir Venkatesh and Avis Vidal. *Building Community Capacity.* New York: Aldine de Gruyter, 2001.

Ferguson, Ronald F. and Sara E. Stoutland. "Reconceiving the Community Development System." In *Urban Problems and Community Development*, edited by R.F. Ferguson and W.T. Dickens. Washington, D.C.: Brookings, 1999.

Furstenberg, Frank. "How Families Manage Risk and Opportunity in Dangerous Neighborhoods." In *Sociology and the Public Agenda*, edited by W.J. Wilson. Newbury Park, California: Sage Publications, 1993.

Halpern, Robert. *Rebuilding the Inner City.* New York: Columbia University Press, 1995.

Hamilton, Ralph, Prudence Brown, Robert J. Chaskin, Leila Feister, Harold Richman, Aaron Sojourner and Joshua Weber. *Learning for Community Change: Core Components of Foundations that Learn.* Chicago: Chapin Hall Center for Children, 2005. www.chapinhall.org

Hamilton, Ralph, Julia Parzen and Prudence Brown. *Community Change Makers: The Leadership Roles of Community Foundations.* Chicago: Chapin Hall Center for Children, 2004. www.chapinhall.org

Jargowsky, Paul A. *Poverty and Place: Ghettos, Barrios, and the American City.* New York: Russell Sage Foundation, 1997.

Kubisch, Anne C., Patricia Auspos, Prudence Brown, Robert Chaskin, Karen Fullbright-Anderson, and Ralph Hamilton. *Voices from the Field*, Vol. II: *Reflections on Comprehensive Community Change.* Washington, D.C.: The Aspen Institute, 2002.

Lee, Barrett A., Karen E. Campbell, and Oscar Miller. "Racial Differences in Urban Neighboring." *Sociological Forum* 6 (1991): 525–550.

Logan, J. and H. Molotch. *Urban Fortunes: The Political Economy of Place.* Los Angeles, CA: University of California Press, 1987.

Massey, D. and N. Denton. *American Apartheid: Segregation and the Making of the Underclass.* Cambridge, MA: Harvard University Press, 1993.

Sampson, Robert J. "What Community Supplies." In *Urban Problems and Community Development*, edited by R.F. Ferguson and W.T. Dickens. Washington, D.C.: Brookings, 1999.

Sojourner, Aaron, Prudence Brown, Robert J. Chaskin, Ralph Hamilton, Leila Fiester and Harold Richman. *Moving Forward While Staying in Place: Embedded Funders and Community Change.* Chicago: Chapin Hall Center for Children, 2004. www.chapinhall.org

Stone, Deborah. "Causal Stories and the Formation of Policy Agendas." *Political Science Quarterly* 104 (1989): 281–300.

Wellman, Barry and Scot Wortley. "Different Strokes from Different Folks: Community Ties and Social Support." *American Journal of Sociology* 96 (1990): 558–588.

Wilson, W. J. *The Truly Disadvantaged: The Inner City, the Underclass and Public Policy.* Chicago: University of Chicago Press, 1987.

CHAPTER 17

The Place of Rural Community Development in Urban Society

Christopher D. Merrett and Timothy Collins

INTRODUCTION

This chapter makes two arguments. First, we suggest that community development occurs differently in rural versus urban communities. Second, we argue there is an urban bias in community development theory, which causes policy makers to overlook issues affecting rural places—especially environmental issues. To make these arguments, section one defines the term "rural." Section two explores how the idea of "rural" intersects with "community" to suggest that urban community development theory may not always apply in rural places.

I. DEFINING RURAL

The term "rural" defies easy definition, but this section attempts to do so in two ways. First we explore how rural communities have been portrayed in two contrasting ways: as agrarian idylls and as backward social problems to be solved. Second, we place rural communities in a broader geographical context to explore why the term still matters.

Rural Idyll or Rural Problem

For many people, rural places represent an aesthetic ideal. Early European explorers perceived the "New World" as an untouched land with unlimited resources (Marx 2000). This Arcadian view of small towns and rural regions persists today with the continued popularity of *Andy Griffith Show* reruns and advertisements showing SUVs exploring pristine wilderness landscapes (Sack 1997).

Rural areas are viewed as utopian places of abundance and harmony for all.[1]

Thomas Jefferson idealized rural life when he identified yeoman farmers as the foundation of American democracy. Agriculture was good work; each farmer would till about the same amount of land with relative economic and political equality. President Theodore Roosevelt (1909, 6) echoed this sentiment in the *Report of the Country Life Commission*, when he described farming as "one of the most dignified, desirable, and sought-after ways of earning a living." The rural idyll is a resilient symbol despite the hardscrabble reality of farming or mining as portrayed in John Steinbeck's *Grapes of Wrath* or in John Sayles' movie *Matewan*.

When rural places are not described idyllically, they are stigmatized as outmoded. In the 19th century, Europeans migrated to American cities in search of jobs. As cities grew, agricultural production could not keep up with rising demand for food. Rural policies focused on increasing agricultural productivity not on improving rural communities. Better roads, land grant universities, consolidated schools teaching agricultural science and home economics, and rural electrification were intended to increase commodity supplies, while reducing transportation time from rural farms to urban markets (Cronon 1992). Thus, rural places represented a problem for capitalism. Modernization was the solution.

Modernization was propelled by advances in mechanization and technology. Firms such as John Deere and International Harvester developed new farming technologies, hastening the onset of market-oriented agriculture, especially after the Civil War. Mechanization lowered the demand for labor, allowing fewer farmers to cultivate more land. Technology adoption by many individuals seems rational, based on the likelihood of increased efficiency and profits (Cochrane 1993). But widespread substitution of capital for labor propelled out-migration to cities. As a result, agriculture continued to dominate the visible rural landscape, but the number of farms declined from 6.4 million to 2.1 million between 1920 and 2004 (Ghelfi and McGranahan 2004). Of 2,052 nonmetropolitan counties in 2003, only 440 were farming-dependent, down from about 2,000 in 1950—mostly in the Great Plains stretching from Texas to the Dakotas.[2]

In addition to the declining number of farms, a bimodal distribution of farm size has occurred with the largest 10 percent of farms accounting for 70 percent of agricultural production. The corollary is that many farms are too small to support a household. Hence, over half of all farmers work off-farm, with many working full-time jobs to secure health and retirement benefits.

Geography of Rural Regions

Some researchers downplay "rural" as a social scientific category (e.g. Goodall *et al.* 1998). For example, the US Census defines as urban any population cluster of at least 50,000 inhabitants. Rural is then defined as anything that is not urban. Census definitions now recognize "micropolitan statistical areas," with at least one urban cluster with a population between 10,000 and 50,000 (Parker 2005). The classification recognizes that smaller cities surrounded by rural areas face different problems than larger metropolitan areas. Counties that are not metropolitan or micropolitan are called noncore. These counties represent rural as residual or peripheral because they are not defined by what they are, but rather what they are not.

Despite being maligned as a social category, empirical evidence shows rural places and processes still matter demographically and economically (Table 17.1). Rural regions have 17 percent of the American population,

but cover 75 percent of the land area. Rural areas have older, slower growing populations. But rural areas are changing nonetheless. For example, the Hispanic population growth rate is higher in rural areas. Rural regions have higher poverty and unemployment rates because of lower levels of educational attainment and wages.

These differences are due in part to the dispersed distribution of people across the rural landscape. As far back as von Thünen in the early 19th century, transportation costs have been used to measure the impact of distance on human behavior. Rural regions suffer from diseconomies of scale because low population density increases per-unit costs of providing goods and services, including telephone, education, electricity, water, sewerage, public transit, and broadband internet.

One positive consequence of this development lag is that some rural communities were able to recruit manufacturing investment from the industrial cities of the Northeast and Midwest. When urban wages and production costs began to rise, many firms left places such as Detroit or Chicago and relocated to small towns where unions were weak and wages were low. However, rural American workers can no longer compete on the basis of low wages. Mexican or Chinese laborers will work for even less. And because of a consistent decline in farm-related employment, rural communities struggle to identify their next competitive advantage.

II. COMMUNITY DEVELOPMENT THEORY AND PRACTICE

Community Development in Theory

This section contends that community development theory has an urban bias because it evolved to solve urban problems. Until the industrial revolution, most people lived in agrarian societies. The intertwined growth of industry and cities in 19th-century Europe prompted scholars to explore rural–urban differences. In 1887, Ferdinand Tönnies distinguished between two types of societies. *Gemeinschaft* referred to pre-modern agrarian societies where personal relationships, face-to-face interactions, and attachment to place defined the community. These community relationships have been described as "fields of care" (Tuan 1974) and "economies of affection" (Hyden 1983). Modernizing forces including agricultural mechanization and capitalist market penetration eroded social bonds of pre-capitalist communities. In its place emerged *Gesellschaft*—urban modernity defined by contractual rather than personal relationships (Bonner 1998). This dichotomy defines poles of a rural–urban continuum. Tönnies and later Lewis Mumford concluded rural people were dehumanized when drawn into urban society (Gerlach and Hamilton 2004). Others such as Max Weber optimistically described modernization as the transition from "traditional" or "sacred" rural communities to "rational" or "secular" urban societies (Woods 2005, 9). Progress is assumed to follow a trajectory from traditional rural places (R) to modern urban spaces (U$_1$) (Fig. 17.1).

Viewing rural communities as problems to solve, coupled with linear notions of progress, means modernization is a zero-sum process: as modernization advances, social restrictions in place-defined communities weaken. In 18th-century communities, most people labored under repressive social hierarchies and local fiefdoms enforced by royal dictates and religious dogma. Revolutionary ideas we now associate with Thomas Jefferson and Adam Smith sparked liberal change in the 18th century. Both argued individuals are rational actors with innate political and economic rights. The truly progressive element was that these were (at least theoretically) universal freedoms—which applied to people regardless of place.

But the spread of universal values came at a cost. As capitalism and democracy diffused through Europe and beyond, writers raised concerns about the impact of modernization, industrialization and urbanization on workers, families and communities. Karl Marx famously railed against capitalism, but other critics of modernity include the Romantic-era poet William Blake, who described the urban factories of the Industrial Revolution as "dark, satanic mills." Charles Dickens' *Tale of Two Cities* and Charlie Chaplin's

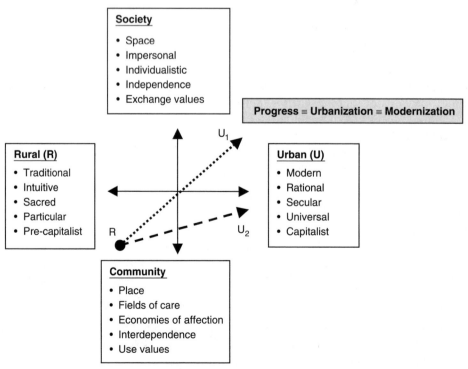

Figure 17.1 Progress and the rural–urban continuum

movie *Modern Times* both describe ennui and social dislocation caused by industrialization and urbanization.

The problem was that rural communities defined by deeply rooted social relations and a subsistence economy were not productive sites for capitalism. Nor were they particularly hospitable to democracy. Modernization thrust subsistence communities into a cash economy where products were sold into capitalist markets. The most competitive producers survived, while other community members moved away or became laborers. Communities originally defined by personal relationships were increasingly defined by wage relations and trade connections to regional, national, and global markets. This represented progress to some, but Tönnies and others saw something had been lost. Closely-knit communities had intrinsic social if not monetary value.

Community development theory emerged to resolve the urban problem that while modernization brings prosperity and universal values, it also erodes close social relationships and attachment to place. Community development theory—and practice—attempts to strike a balance between promoting universal, modern values such as economic individualism and political egalitarianism, while retaining the sense of place people have to their local communities. Instead of modernization tracing an inevitable path from place to space (R to U_1), it might move along an alternative trajectory (R to U_2) from traditional to modern *places* within capitalist spaces (Fig. 17.1). The challenge, however, is to explain why *quantitative* population differences create *qualitative* distinctions in how communities work. This can be done by asserting a rural perspective into our discussion of community development theory.

The problem of rural community development theory is that researchers and practitioners often neglect how rural communities can be qualitatively different from urban ones (Lawrence 1997, but see Amato 1993 and Castle 1998). This occurs because community development theory developed to address urban problems. But rural communities differ from urban ones in many

ways. For example, small rural communities may stifle diverse viewpoints and lifestyles. The rural idyll of homespun friendliness has a dark, exclusionary side that tends to emphasize conformity. Minority populations such as Gays, Blacks, women, or those with different religions can be ostracized for expressing views opposed to local norms (Fellows 1996; Loewen 2005). Urban centers such as San Francisco's Castro neighborhood can become refuges where alternative viewpoints and practices are accepted.

Class divisions and power structures also evolved differently in rural places (Murdoch 1995). Small-scale capitalists such as farmers rely on migrant or family labor. Extractive industries such as mining and forestry are characterized by exploitative labor relations, low wages, and remote locales. It is difficult for unions to organize and challenge the rural status quo. Strategies used to mobilize urban communities must be modified to address different social processes of rural places.

It is also possible that rural residents define their relationship with the natural environment differently than urban residents. For a trivial, but maybe meaningful example, consider the nicknames of rural high school sports teams such as the Farmington Farmers and the Hoopeston Cornjerkers in Illinois, the Hematites of Ishpeming, Michigan and the Biglerville Canners in the apple orchards of Pennsylvania. These nicknames denote rural communities closely connected to their surrounding natural environment and economic base.

Connections between people, nature, and economics suggest a starting point for a theory of rural community development that is not derivative of urban theories. Wilkinson (1991, 7), drawing on Pierre Bourdieu, approaches the community as a field of social interactions:

What is needed is a conception of community that recognizes its complexity. The community is an arena of both turbulence and cohesion, of order and disarray, of self-seeking and community-oriented interaction; and it manifests its dualities simultaneously. It should be studied for what it is and on its own grounds—not as an ideal type of an old form of social life, but as a dynamic and changing field of interacting forces.

The interactionist perspective is not concerned with whether power structures are elitist or pluralist. Instead, it focuses on different arenas of community decision-making to determine degrees of elitism or pluralism and their impacts on decision making. This approach also recognizes the dynamic nature of decision-making. Understanding shifting patterns of alliances and power is crucial for community development researchers and practitioners.

Mehrhoff (1999, 37), in the tradition of Leopold (1986), adds another level of complexity to the idea of community by considering the importance of the natural environment. He notes that global pressures, linked with a lack of awareness of and respect for the local ecology, challenge community survival. He concludes, "Community prosperity in the long term must rest on healthy natural systems. In fact, a community's natural environment can become the logical starting point for undertaking a fundamental reordering of a community's identity and future vision."

The environmental/sustainability perspective adds a new dimension to community development research and theory, which has typically only emphasized socioeconomic factors (e.g. Logan and Molotch 1987). In fact, rural community development theory can be differentiated from urban-focused theory by emphasizing sustainable interactions between nature and human society. According to Ikerd (1990), a community is sustainable if its processes are: (1) environmentally conserving; (2) community supporting; and (3) economically profitable. Sustainability is a paradigm that builds on earlier notions of conservation, and it challenges Adam Smith's economic tenet of rational individualism. These ideas underpin a theory of sustainable rural community development that links natural, built, financial, political, social, and cultural capital to build community capacity with goals of a healthy ecosystem, vibrant regional economy, and healthy, happy communities (Emery and Flora 2006). The point is that rural community development theory

becomes distinct from urban theory when it expressly addresses place-based environmental and natural resource issues.

Community Development in Practice

Rural community development practitioners must recognize the urban origins of community development theory and then adjust existing theories or develop new ones for rural places. Writers discuss the "urbanization of injustice" (Merrifield and Swyngedouw 1997), the "urbanization of poverty" (Davis 2004) and even the "urbanization of neoliberalism" (Brenner and Theodore 2002) as if these processes are somehow disproportionately urban. US Census data (Table 17.1) show rural poverty rates have always been above urban areas. The same case can be applied to wages. By virtue of location, rural areas also experience injustice and neoliberalism. The 1980s farm crisis was merely the rural manifestation of the crisis of Fordism (Cloke and Goodwin 1992).

Consider more specific examples. Many economic developers exhort local governments to compete for new businesses (Eisinger 1987). However, rural communities are disadvantaged when competing against urban areas because of distance and declining populations, tax bases, and physical infrastructure. Rural places face limits when offering incentives, educational, or recreational amenities to recruit firms and jobs.

So-called "trickle-down theory" is another biased idea. The trickle of economic benefits starts mainly in cities and may not even reach rural places. In fact, cities attract wealth. Rural realities disprove the axiom that "a rising tide lifts all ships." During the 1990s, the United States experienced unprecedented economic and population growth. Yet many rural places experienced demographic and economic decline. In response to emerging "rural ghettos," some experts proposed "small town triage" to focus scarce public resources only on places with a chance of recovery (Daniels and Lapping 1987; Davidson 1996). Planners suggested moving people from fading communities to cities, letting the landscape revert

Table 17.1 A socioeconomic comparison of urban versus rural counties, 2000

Category	Metro	Nonmetro	Total
Social and Geographic Characteristics			
• Population	232,579,940	48,841,966	281,421,906
• Proportion of US Population (%)	82.9	17.1	100
• Population Rate of Change, 2003 (%)	3.4	1.2	3.3
• Population Density (persons / mi²)	259.3	18.5	79.6
• Elderly Population (% over 65 years of age)	11.9	15.0	12.4
• Black Population (%)	8.4	12.8	12.1
• Hispanic Population (%)	14.1	5.4	12.6
• Hispanic Population Change (%)	57.5	63.8	57.9
Earnings and Income			
• Poverty (% below the poverty line, 1999)	11.9	14.8	12.4
• Median Family Income (1999 dollars)	51,300	35,900	47,800
• Earnings per Job, 2002 ($)	43,051.62	27,966.32	40,757.94
• Unemployment Rate (% in 2003)	6.3	7.0	6.1
• Median Home Value ($)	120,933	78,841	108,300
Educational Attainment			
• % aged 25 or more with a high school diploma	81.3	76.7	80.4
• % aged 25 or more completing college	32.8	20.8	30.7
Geography			
• Total US Land Area (square miles)	897,095	2,640,344	3,537,438
• % of Total US Land Area	25.4	74.6	100
• Counties (number)	1,090	2,052	3,142

Source: Parker (2005) and US Census (2000).

to a prairie or "buffalo commons" (Popper and Popper 1987).

These fatalistic views ignore rural communities that successfully participate in the global economy by pursuing place-based or endogenous economic development strategies (Lyons 2002; Ray 1999). We describe five different community and economic development strategies below that share a common concern for entrepreneurship and sustainability's triple bottom line: economics, equity, and the environment.

Community Supported Agriculture (CSA)
Rural economic growth is found in places that have re-imagined their relationship to the land. CSA exemplifies this approach. It simultaneously creates a sense of community, while generating profits for small-scale farms operating in environmentally-sustainable ways. A CSA is a consumer cooperative where a farmer sells subscriptions or shares to several dozen households. The farmer takes this money and buys seeds and other inputs to start the growing season. As crops ripen, subscribers can

expect a weekly basket of vegetables, fruits, herbs, cut flowers and other items. The farmer and subscribers both share the agricultural bounty and risks. This is a growing social and environmental movement in America with nearly 2,000 CSAs representing over 150,000 people.

Agritourism
Agritourism, like ecotourism, lets entrepreneurs parley environmental knowledge into profits. Farmers can offer educational experiences to urban tourists who are willing to pay to learn about agriculture and country life. Activities include barn tours, hayrides, u-pick gardens, orchards, hiking, horseback riding, and mountain biking. To teach students where their meals come from, some farmers have planted "pizza farms," a circular plot divided into wedges. Each wedge is planted with an ingredient used to make pizza. One wedge might have herbs; another might have wheat. Yet others might have tomatoes or a grazing dairy cow as the source of cheese. Each wedge is divided by a pathway so tourists can get close to each

ingredient. In Massachusetts, the Hyland Orchard and Brewery combines a brewpub with a petting zoo so parents and children can have fun. Agritourism, like CSAs, reconnects people to rural places and the environment.

Producer Cooperatives

Rural communities have long relied on low wages to recruit manufacturers from urban areas. However, this advantage is disappearing. To reduce the risk of capital flight, communities can own the manufacturing facilities they host. Farmers lead this strategy. Instead of shipping raw commodities such as soybeans elsewhere for processing, farmers are forming so-called new generation cooperatives (NGCs) to process locally-grown commodities in the community. This increases on-farm profits, generates local jobs, and increases the local tax base, while taking advantage of the rural competitive advantage in crop production. NGCs also lessen the risk of capital flight because farmers and other community investors own the processing facilities (Merrett and Walzer 2001).

Community Foundations

Capital flight is a problem when factories leave town. But a more insidious form of capital flight also diminishes prospects for rural communities. Retired farmers are sometimes able to pass the operation on to their children. However, many farmers sell their land to their neighbors and move into town. Proceeds from the farm sale can be very large. While the farmer is alive, the wealth remains in the rural community. However, when the farmer dies, much of the wealth is bequeathed to children who have moved to the city.

Community foundations are a strategy to capture some of this wealth before it is transferred to the city. Community foundations are non-profit-tax exempt entities administered on behalf of a local community. Retirees can designate the community foundation to receive part of their estate as a way to help support future hometown development. States such as Nebraska give tax breaks to those who donate to community foundations. The community foundation's assets generate interest income that can be used to establish a revolving loan fund to promote local entrepreneurship, or improve local schools or other community infrastructure.

Renewable Energy

Rising fuel prices are prompting policy debates about alternative energy sources. Rural regions have a competitive advantage in producing renewable energy, including ethanol, biodiesel, and wind power. Ethanol can be produced from corn, wheat, potatoes, switch grass, sugarcane, sugar beets, and other plants. Biodiesel can be produced from oilseeds such as soybeans, canola and sunflower. Increasing use of biofuels can benefit farmers and rural communities, especially if they form NGCs to produce biofuels locally.

Wind energy represents another economic opportunity for rural residents. Wind farms can be built at a range of scales depending on community receptivity. Each wind turbine requires about a quarter acre of land. Farmers hosting turbines can receive several thousand dollars a year in revenues from each unit. This is far more lucrative than growing crops on the same quarter acre. Wind turbines also generate local tax revenues.

Wind turbines also have the potential to stave off school consolidations. Rural schools struggle to balance their budgets in the face of rising energy costs and shrinking tax revenues. Schools in Iowa and Illinois have built wind turbines to reduce their energy costs and generate revenues to balance their budgets. This is a true community development strategy because a school is the foundation for rural communities. That was true at the beginning of the 20th century and it is true at the beginning of the 21st century.[3]

III. CONCLUSIONS

This chapter began by suggesting rural communities develop differently than urban ones. We then argued that the urban bias in community development theory has undermined efforts to improve rural communities. Our starting point was to show how rural communities were perceived as a social problem to be fixed through industrialization and urbanization. In their haste to modernize the countryside, 19th-century policymakers ignored the erosion of social relations that anchored rural communities in place. Social scientists have been trying to recapture the fleeting ideal of community ever since.

Writers have recently theorized that places persist to the extent that they are embedded within networks of social relations based on trust (Granovetter 1985; Putnam 2000). The question is how do we put this theory into action? We suggested rural communities can be strengthened by focusing on economically profitable, community-supporting, and environmentally friendly development strategies. This approach also provides lessons for urban community development.

At the beginning of the 20th century, policy makers attempted to modernize rural places by bringing elements of the city to the countryside. At the beginning of the 21st century, we suggest a sense of community can be achieved in an urban setting by bringing elements of the countryside to the city. Examples of successful urban community development strategies that draw on this notion include community gardens, CSA, the creation of green spaces, and farmers markets. In fact, the entire Smart Growth movement is tinged with the notion that we need to live in small-scale communities where we can nurture a sense of place. The words of Raymond Williams (1973, 296) still resonate: "there is almost an inverse proportion ... between the relative importance of the rural economy and the cultural importance of rural ideas."

NOTES

1. This idealized view, though, ignores indigenous Americans who already lived here in great numbers—and that the land had to be taken, often through violent means (Denevan 1992).
2. Farming-dependent counties are those where at least 15 percent of earnings or jobs are directly linked to the farm economy (Parker 2005).
3. There is some community resistance to wind turbines from people who find them to be unsightly, noisy, or hazardous to birds. Others find wind turbines to be an attractive addition to the landscape, more so than cell phone towers or grain silos. Research sponsored by the National Fish and Wildlife Federation finds that more birds are killed by feral and household cats than by any other source (Winters and Wallace 2003).

REFERENCES

Amato, P. 1993. Urban-rural differences in helping friends and family members. *Social Psychology Quarterly.* 56: 249–62.

Bonner, K. 1998. Reflexivity, sociology and the rural-urban distinction in Marx, Tönnies and Weber. *The Canadian Review of Sociology and Anthropology.* 35 (2): 165–190.

Brenner, N. and N. Theodore. 2002. Cities and the geographies of "actually existing neoliberalism." *Antipode.* 34(3): 349–379.

Castle, E. 1998. A conceptual framework for the study of rural places. *American Journal of Agricultural Economics.* 80 (August): 621–631.

Cloke, P. and M. Goodwin. 1992. Conceptualizing countryside change: From post-Fordism to rural structured coherence. *Transactions of the IBG.* NS (17): 321–336.

Cochrane, W. 1993. *The Development of American Agriculture: A Historical Analysis, 2nd Edition.* Minneapolis, MN: University of Minnesota Press.

Cronon, W. 1992. *Nature's Metropolis: Chicago and the Great West.* New York: W.W. Norton.

Daniels, T. and M. Lapping. 1987. Small town triage: A rural settlement policy for the American Midwest. *Journal of Rural Studies.* 3(3): 273–280.

Davidson, O. 1996. *Broken Heartland: The Rise of America's Rural Ghetto.* Iowa City, IA: University of Iowa Press.

Davis, M. 2004. Planet of slums. *New Left Review.* 26 (March–April): 5–34.

Denevan, W. 1992. The pristine myth: The landscape of the Americas in 1492. *Annals of the Association of American Geographers* 82: 345–368.

Eisinger, P. 1987. *The Rise of the Entrepreneurial State.* Madison, WI: University of Wisconsin Press.

Emery, M. and C. Flora. 2006. Spiraling-up: Mapping community transformation with community capitals framework. *Journal of the Community Development Society,* 37(1): 19–35.

Fellows, W. 1996. *Farm Boys: Lives of Gay Men from the Rural Midwest.* Madison, WI: University of Wisconsin Press.

Gerlach, N. and S. Hamilton. 2004. Preserving self in the city of the imagination: Georg Simmel and *Dark City. Canadian Review of American Studies.* 34(2): 115–134.

Ghelfi, L. and D. McGranahan. 2004. One in five rural counties depends on farming. *Amber Waves.* 2(3): 11.

Goodall, C., K. Kafadar and J. Tukey. 1998. Computing and using rural versus urban measures in statistical applications. *The American Statistician.* 54(2): 101–111.

Granovetter, M. 1985. Economic action and social structure: The problem of embeddedness. *American Journal of Sociology.* 91(3): 481–510.

Hyden, G. 1983. *No Shortcuts to Progress: African Development Management in Perspective*. London: Heinemann.

Ikerd, J. 1990. Agriculture's search for sustainability and profitability. *Journal of Soil and Water Conservation*. 45(1): 18–23.

Lawrence, M. 1997. Heartlands or neglected geographies? Liminality, power, and the hyperreal rural. *Journal of Rural Studies*. 13(1): 1–17.

Leopold, A. 1986. *A Sand County Almanac*. New York: Ballantine Books.

Loewen, J. 2005. *Sundown Towns: A Hidden Dimension of American Racism*. New York: New Press.

Logan, J. and H. Molotch. 1987. *Urban Fortunes: The Political Economy of Place*. Los Angeles, CA: University of California Press.

Lyons, T. 2002. Building social capital for rural enterprise development in the United States. *Journal of Developmental Entrepreneurship*. 7(2): 193–216.

Marx, L. 2000. *The Machine in the Garden: Technology and the Pastoral Ideal in America*. New York: Oxford University Press.

Mehrhoff, W. 1999. *Community Design: A Team Approach to Dynamic Community Systems*. Thousand Oaks, CA: Sage.

Merrett, C. and N. Walzer, eds. 2001. *A Cooperative Approach to Local Economic Development*. Westport, CT: Quorum Books.

Merrifield, A. and E. Swyngedouw, eds. 1997. *The Urbanization of Injustice*. New York: New York University Press.

Murdoch, J. 1995. Middle-class territory? Some remarks on the use of class analysis in rural studies. *Environment and Planning A*. 27: 1213–1230.

Parker, T. 2005. Measuring rurality: 2004 county typology codes. *Economic Research Service Briefing Rooms*. Online: http://www.ers.usda.gov/briefing/rurality/typology.

Popper, F. and D. Popper. 1987. The Great Plains: From dust to dust. *Planning*. 53(12): 12–18.

Putnam, R. 2000. *Bowling Alone: The Collapse and Revival of American Community*. New York: Simon and Schuster.

Ray, C. 1999. Endogenous development in an era of reflexive modernity. *Journal of Rural Studies*. 15(3): 257–267.

Roosevelt, T. 1909. *Report of the Country Life Commission*. Senate Document 705. Washington, DC. Available online: http://chla.library.cornell.edu.

Sack, K. 1997. Mount Airy Journal; Reality plays a bit part on Mayberry Days. *New York Times*. September 29. Online: http://query.nytimes.com/gst/fullpage.html?sec=travel&res.

Tuan, Y. 1974. Space and place: Humanistic perspective. *Progress in Human Geography*. 6: 233–46.

U.S. Census. 2000. American Factfinder. http://factfinder.census.gov/.

Wilkinson, K. 1991. *The Community in Rural America*. New York: Greenwood Press.

Williams, R. 1973. *The Country and the City*. New York: Oxford University Press.

Winters, L. and G. Wallace. 2003. *Impacts of Feral and Free-Ranging Cats on Bird Species of Conservation Concern*. The Plains, VA: American Bird Conservancy.

Woods, M. 2005. *Rural Geography: Processes, Responses and Experiences in Rural Restructuring*. London: Sage Publications.

Understanding, Building, and Organizing Community

CHAPTER 18

Introduction to Part III

James DeFilippis and Susan Saegert

Community development efforts depend on the idea that communities exist. However, as discussed in the introduction to this book, sociologists have long proposed the disappearance of community. In contrast, the second perspective, attributed to John Dewey, portrays community as not given but as emergent. Neither position allows a theorist or practitioner of community development to take the entity that they seek to develop as a given. Robert Sampson's Chapter 19 introduces this section, lays out the state of the debate about community within sociology, and defines community as place-based and still a significant unit of social organization. He identifies several key functions of place-based communities and the conditions that support high levels of achievement of these functions. The chapter ends with cautions concerning the potential capacity of communities to provide collective goods and the requirement of support from higher levels of political and economic organization. Richard Sennett's chapter follows. In Chapter 20, Sennett questions the reality of community, presenting it instead as an ideology that can be mobilized for specific, in his view mostly repressive ends. Harold DeRienzo in Chapter 21 views community as distinct from the physical neighborhood, and as having a contingent reality. For him community can be emergent, but it is not a given. DeRienzo describes current economic, social, and political forces in the United States that tend to undermine the existence of community. He then addresses forms of community organizing and evaluates their potential for creating community in the current context. His Chapter provides a transition to the other chapters in this section on community organizing and community building.

The idea of community as emergent animates most theories of community organizing and community building. However, the two schools of thought differ in what it is that emerges. Within the community organizing tradition, communities are divided between the "haves" and the "have nots". For the "have nots", communities do not provide the collective goods identified by Sampson, or do so only at a minimal level, while the "haves" are positioned to achieve their collective and individual interests by virtue of their greater power. Community organizing seeks to mobilize the interests of the "have nots" and organize them into effective units of collective action so as to change the balance of power in the community. In contrast, community builders approach locales as potential communities that lack the social ties and identification of shared interests required for these locales to function as communities. Community builders start by building relationships among local residents and organizations and developing settings within which mutual interests and opportunities for cooperation in achieving them can emerge. Community builders assume that functioning communities do not have one single fault line of privilege versus disadvantage that divides them. Rather, people and organizations are presumed to have multiple and shifting interests and capacities. The task of community building is to provide opportunities to build relationships that can lead to effective collective actions and satisfying relationships. As the chapters in this section illustrate, the line between these two perspectives increasingly blurs. However, the starting point for efforts in the two traditions almost always differs.

Community organizers begin with oppositional strategies and tactics that heighten conflict between the "haves" and "have nots." For those who accept this division as a given, strategies for community building are seen not as genuine efforts to build communities that do not exist but as efforts by the "haves" to reduce unrest among the "have nots" or at best to provide a slightly higher level of access to resources without challenging the underlying division. Robert Fisher's Chapter 22 lays out the history of these two traditions in the United States along these lines. He calls community building the "social work" approach and identifies its origins in the settlement house movement. He identifies two oppositional approaches that include: (1) the political activist tradition with roots in as varied efforts as ward boss organizing, the Communist Party, the labor movement, and Saul Alinsky's form of local organizing, as well as with African American and gay rights organizing; and (2) the primarily middle-class neighborhood maintenance approach identified most often as the "not in my backyard" tradition.

Community organizers posit opposing and already existing and identifiable interests for both the "haves" and "have nots." The initial work of organizing must be done to support local "have nots" in recognizing their interests. Problems of building relationships are acknowledged and addressed. However, identifying collective goals and identity among "the have nots" is presented as largely a matter of process. Alliances with "haves" are strategically cultivated and usually issue-based and temporary. The best-known national exponents of community organizing choose to work with already existing identifiable collectives, thus side stepping in theory, if not always in practice, the need for building social relationships and local organizations from scratch. The Industrial Areas Foundation (IAF) and PICO choose as their starting point faith-based congregations. Much of the work described by community builders thus is assumed to have been done at some level by these

religious institutions.[1] The chapters by Mark Warren on the Texas IAF (Chapter 23) and by Paul Speer and Joe Hughey on PICO (Chapter 24) provide comprehensive analyses of the goals and methods of this school of community organizing. Warren includes race and religious denomination as bases of solidarity that can both divide and unite groups across boundaries. Both chapters include a strong emphasis on the development of relationships and collective interests, thus illustrating the increasing tendency for the community organizing tradition to adopt some of the analyses and methods associated with community building. Warren, in fact, reinterprets the idea of relationship building in the "emergent community" tradition, and, like Dewey, sees it as fundamental to a viable democracy.

Bill Traynor begins the chapters on the community building approach. In Chapter 25, he first defines the idea and traces it to foundation-led efforts to expand and improve the workings of Community Development Corporations. In contrast to the class analysis that underlies the practice of community organizing, community development derives from a pluralist notion of democracy and seeks to rebuild a functioning public sphere. Traynor offers a sober analysis of the internal contradictions and difficulties CDCs faced in attempting to integrate community building into their development-oriented organizations. He also critiques community organizing practices as relying on "levels of commitment, loyalty, time, and belligerence that have never been for everyone and increasingly stand out as in-organic to the experience of most people" (p. 219). In contrast, he proposes that community building is best understood as having roots in a market-based model, rather than a model of political conflict. Levels of commitment and goals can vary across individuals and across time. His focus is on establishing peer-to-peer relationships rather than on binding individuals to an existing group. The crux of his argument is that community building can better be understood as a popular economic mobilization rather than as a vanguard political movement. He then lays out a framework for this form of organizing which he calls network organizing.

James Hyman also analyzes the challenges of community building. While Traynor focus on understanding forms of organization and how to create them, Hyman looks at the incentives and disincentives from an individual's point of view that influence engagement in the public sphere. In Chapter 26, he describes the pivotal role theories of social capital have had in thinking about community building but clarifies the distinction between networks rich in social capital and actual civic engagement.

Xavier de Souza Briggs drills down one more level to look at the enactment of civic processes meant to engage citizens in the public sphere. This close-up look at how individuals actually interact reveals the class, race, gender, and role divisions within communities that make the development of inclusive, productive civic engagement very difficult. Thus his chapter brings us back to an acceptance of the structural differences in interest and group identification that characterize society. However, rather than treating these divisions as givens, he views them as variable codes and scripts potentially subject to cross-group understanding and transformation. In Chapter 27, he concludes that

> we should collect and share principles for reading communication codes and power relations, especially in multicultural settings, and for responding in ways that promote mutual learning. Such competence is critical for doing democracy "up close" in a world of diverse publics and complex public problems.
>
> (p. 239)

The two final chapters in this part compare different ideologically based organizing practices. In Chapter 29, David Greenberg looks at how different ideological bases and group identities prove crucial to the success or failure of organizing efforts, not because they are ideologically correct but because of the way they work in the particular local historical and organizational context. Thus the position of a group on issues of conflict and race are crucial. But the choice made will be

likely to succeed not because of some inherent property of the position, but because it is congruent or incongruent with the political opportunities that emerge in specific contexts. He argues that organizing efforts that are very congruent with the inter-organizational context stand greater chances of achieving goals, but are less likely to restructure basic power dynamics of a locale.

Susan Stall and Randy Stoecker take a different comparative tactic in Chapter 28. They present what they see as two opposing models for organizing: the Alinsky model and the woman-centered model. They then compare the models in terms of their assumptions about human nature, power and politics, leadership development, and the organizing process. Different understanding of the relationship of public and private spheres underlie many of the divergent positions of the two models. They conclude that both models have strengths and weaknesses. Therefore combined models are likely to prove more effective. Specifically, they commend including the building of primary relational bonds around social reproduction as a good way to broaden the social change agenda. At the same time, they conclude that the public sphere remains an arena in which conflict is necessary. Therefore, power-oriented public sphere organizing remains a prerequisite for success.

The final two chapters continue to reflect a basic tension in community organizing and community building between justifications in terms of ideological and value correctness versus a focus on context as a determinant of efficacy. The first approach is less concerned with what will work than with what should be done. The second approach views ideological positions as significant for success and related to how radical the changes achieved maybe. But it remains agnostic on the issue of the correctness of particular ideological and strategic approaches.

NOTE

1. ACORN (Association of Community Organizations for Reform Now) begins with an analysis that assumes both the reality of class groupings and the identifiable, opposing goals of different classes. They target organizing toward the poorest

and most disenfranchised segments of the working class. While there are several useful lengthy accounts of how ACORN works we were unable to find a succinct yet comprehensive chapter to include in this collection. For those who wish to understand the ACORN approach more fully, we recommend Delgado, 1985.

REFERENCE

Delgado, Gary. 1985. *Organizing the Movement: The Roots and Growth of ACORN*. Philadelphia: Temple University Press.

CHAPTER 19

What Community Supplies

Robert J. Sampson

Community seems to be the modern elixir for much of what ails American society. Indeed, as we reflect on the wrenching social changes that have shaped our recent past, calls for a return to community values are everywhere. From politicians to private foundations to real estate developers to criminal justice officials to communitarians, the appeal of community is ubiquitous.

Consider just a few examples of the efforts to mobilize action under the rubric of community. Among private foundations many programs have settled on community as a conceptual umbrella to coordinate new initiatives. Meanwhile the growing community development corporation (CDC) movement has long singled out community as a meaningful unit of social intervention to improve the lives of the poor. In the criminal justice system the move to community-based strategies has included increased community policing, community-based prosecution policies, and community corrections. Even real estate developers are beginning to take heed of modern discontent with urban sprawl and suburban anonymity. They are proffering new visions of living arrangements that promote neighborliness, local interaction, and common physical space with architectural integrity, all in an attempt to restore some semblance of community. And in intellectual discussions, the rise of communitarianism as a serious movement is centered on community responsibility and civic engagement as the structure supporting social justice and the good society.

Whatever the source, there has emerged a widespread idea that something has been lost in American society and that a return to community is in order. The loss is expressed most frequently in terms of the decline of civic life and the deterioration of local neighborhoods.

But if community has come to mean everything good, as a concept it loses its analytical bite and therefore means nothing. What exactly do we mean by community? Does the term refer to geographic locales, such as neighborhoods? Or to common membership in some association or group? Does it mean shared values and deep commitments, and if so to what? What in fact does community supply that makes it so in demand? Not only are the answers unclear, the current appropriation of community rhetoric elides any references to the dark side of communal life. One might ask, what do we stand to lose by a return to community—what does community deny? Perhaps more important, does the current drumbeat of allusions to community values bespeak a mythical past, raising the paradox of returning to nowhere?

The thesis of this chapter is that community does matter, albeit not in the simple way that current yearning suggests. Communities are an important arena for realizing common values and maintaining effective social controls. As such, they provide important public goods, or what many have termed "social capital," that bear on patterns of social organization and human well-being. There is hope in this conception, for it reveals ways to harness social change to reflect the nature of transformed (not lost) communities. Especially in low-income, socially disadvantaged neighborhoods, dimensions of social capital may work to buffer the forces of sociodemographic changes that have battered the idea of community. But the concept is not an unqualified good, and thus one must also come to grips with such potential adverse consequences as local corruption and the social exclusion of outsiders.

To tackle these matters, this chapter begins by reviewing some of the defining themes of community and neighborhood, placing present concerns within the framework of intellectual history. Although not apparent from recent debates, there is a long history of research and theory on urbanism and community in the United States.

I next highlight the social dimensions by which communities in the United States are stratified ecologically. Neighborhoods vary a great deal in terms of racial isolation and the concentration of socioeconomic resources, and social dislocations such as crime and poor health come bundled in geographical space.

I then turn to the heart of the topic: what community supplies and how structural forces in the larger society shape the internal dynamics of communities. Specifically, I explicate a theory of community social organization and the public-good aspects of social capital such as informal social control mechanisms, network ties to extra-local power, mutual trust, capacity for efficacious action, and organizational resources that communities can in theory provide. Just as important, I delineate what research has revealed about the ways structural forces (for example, inequality and stability) promote or inhibit these public goods.

COMMUNITY: LOST, FOUND, AND LIBERATED

The "loss of community" is by no means a new concern. The basis of the classic urban paradigm in sociology is related to the massive social changes of the late nineteenth and early twentieth centuries. Concern over the presumed decline of traditional forms of personal association in small towns and neighborhoods under the advance of urbanization and industrialization was widely expressed by early sociologists such as Tönnies, Durkheim, Simmel, and Weber. Wirth (1938)

later expanded these concerns by positing that size, density, heterogeneity, and anonymity were socially disintegrative features that characterized rapidly changing cities. He contended that these defining elements constrained social relations to be impersonal and superficial and that this estrangement undermined family life and the intimate bonds of local community.

Wellman (1979) summarizes this classical tradition in urban sociology under the label "Community Lost," invoking the idea that the social ties of modern-urbanites have become impersonal, transitory, and segmented, hastening the eclipse of community and feeding the process of social disorganization. Community Lost is thus a salient theme that has a venerable history in twentieth-century America.

Research, however, suggests that Wirth's thesis is naive and the pronouncement of the loss of community premature. Ethnographic research in the 1950s and 1960s discovered thriving urban communities and ethnic enclaves where kinship and friendship flourished. Especially in poor urban neighborhoods, the evidence of dense social networks and local identification remained strong (see Gans, 1962; Jacobs, 1961; and Stack, 1974).

Even quantitative studies began to challenge the hegemony of Community Lost. In an important 1975 survey replication in a Rochester, New York, neighborhood of a study conducted there in 1950, Hunter (1975) found a decrease in the use of shopping, entertainment, and other facilities but no change in informal neighboring and local interaction. Indeed, the local sense of community had increased, leading him to conclude that "the hypothesized consequences of an ecological and functional increase in scale have not resulted in a social and cultural-symbolic loss of community." Summarizing these findings, ethnographic and quantitative alike, Wellman (1979) declared a mid-century era of "Community Saved."

As suburbanization and technological change have increased in the past two decades, scholarship has begun to reach a compromise in the Community Lost and Community Saved arguments. The research of theorists on social networks has shown that, contrary to the assumptions of a decline in primary relations and to the Community Saved image of dense parochial ties, modern urbanites have created non-spatial communities—viable social relations dispersed in space (Tilly, 1973). Modern urban dwellers, for example, might not know (or want to know) their neighbors on an intimate basis, but they are likely to have interpersonal networks spread throughout the city, state, and even country. Wellman refers to this expanded concept of community as "Community Liberated," or what might be thought of as community beyond propinquity. This does not mean local relations are unimportant, but only that they are no longer controlling for many areas of social life.

Fischer (1982) has presented a similar vision of what urbanism has wrought and what it means to think of communities as liberated. Clarity is accomplished by emphasizing the distinction between the public and private spheres of social life. In the urban world of strangers a person typically has the capacity to know people categorically, to place them by appearance (age, ethnicity, lifestyle) in one of many urban subcultures. But this is a situational not a psychological style, and it says nothing about attitudes and action in the private sphere. City dwellers have not lost the capacity for deep, long-lasting relationships; rather they have gained the capacity for surface, fleeting relationships that are restricted. Consequently, urbanism's effects are specified: estrangement occurs in the public sphere—less helpfulness, more conflict—but not in the private sphere—personal relationships and psychological well-being.

It is unfortunate that the present nostalgia for community has emerged almost oblivious to a research cycle of Community Lost, Saved, and Liberated. The evidence supports the argument for Community Liberated, showing that community has been transformed rather than lost. I use this framework to understand what community supplies in mass society. The evidence is now clear that urban dwellers rely less than they have in the past on local neighborhoods for psychological support, cultural and religious nourishment, and economic needs and transactions. They can shop, work, go to church, and make friends throughout geographical space and, increasingly, cyber space. This alone suggests that interventions in the local community are unlikely to succeed if they attempt to penetrate the private world of personal relations.

I contend that we do not need communities so much to satisfy our private and personal needs, which are best met elsewhere, nor even to meet our sustenance needs, which for better or worse appear to be irretrievably dispersed in space. Rather, local community remains essential as a site for the realization of common values in support of social goods, including public safety, norms of civility and mutual trust, efficacious voluntary associations, and collective socialization of the young.

The local community remains important for another reason—economic resources and social-structural differentiation in general are very much spatially shaped in the United States. Income, education, housing stock—the bedrock of physical and human capital—are distributed unevenly across geographical space, often in conjunction with ascribed characteristics such as racial composition. The continuing and in some cases increasing significance of such ecological differentiation is fundamental to our understanding of community.

Before addressing ecological differentiation, however, I must first digress to consider the operational definitions of community and neighborhood in modern society. The complexity of the phenomenon is staggering; Hillery (1984) reviews close to one hundred definitions of neighborhoods. The traditional definition of a neighborhood, as used by Park, Burgess, and other members of the early Chicago School, refers to an ecological subsection of a larger community, a collection of both people and institutions occupying a spatially defined area that is conditioned by a set of ecological, cultural, and political forces. In an almost utopian way, Park defined neighborhood as "a locality with sentiments, traditions, and a history of its own" (Park, 1916, p. 95). He also claimed that the neighborhood was the basis of social and political organization, albeit not in a formal sense.

Park's definition overstates the cultural

and political distinctiveness of residential enclaves, but there are aspects of it worth preserving. Most important is the recognition first that neighborhoods are an ecological unit and second that they are nested within successively larger communities. There is no one neighborhood, but many neighborhoods that vary in size and complexity depending on the social phenomenon of interest and the ecological structure of the larger community. This idea of embeddedness is why Choldin (1984) argues for the term *subcommunity*, emphasizing that the local neighborhood is integrally linked to, and dependent on, a larger whole. For these reasons, one can think of residential neighborhoods as what Suttles (1972, p. 59) calls a "mosaic of overlapping boundaries" or what Reiss (1996) calls an "imbricated structure."

ECOLOGICAL DIFFERENTIATION AND COMMUNITY STRATIFICATION

A wealth of research has studied the ecological differentiation of American cities. Research traditions rooted in "social area analysis" and "factorial ecology" have established structural characteristics that vary among neighborhoods, chiefly along the dimensions of socioeconomic stratification (poverty, occupational attainment), family structure, residential stability (home ownership, tenure), race or ethnicity, and urbanization (density).

This research has demonstrated that many social indicators coalesce in physical space. Current research is attempting to investigate how macro forces lead to the clustering of social and economic factors in urban areas. The best-known result is Wilson's (1987) theory of "concentration effects" that arise from living in a neighborhood that is overwhelmingly impoverished. Wilson argues that the social transformation of inner-city areas in recent decades has resulted in an increased concentration of the most disadvantaged segments of the urban black population, especially poor, female-headed families with children. At the national level in 1990, fully 25 percent of poor blacks lived in concentrated poverty neighborhoods compared with only 3 percent of poor whites (Jargowsky, 1997, p. 41). The consequences of these distributions are profound because they mean that relationships between race and individual outcomes are systematically confounded with important differences in community contexts.

The concentration of poverty and joblessness has been fueled by macroeconomic changes related to the deindustrialization of central cities where low-income minorities are disproportionately located. These changes include a shift from goods-producing to service-producing industries, the increasing polarization of the labor market into low-wage and high-wage workers, and the relocation of manufacturing away from the inner cities. The related exodus of middle- and upper-income black families from the inner city has also, according to Wilson, removed an important social buffer that could potentially deflect the full impact of prolonged joblessness and industrial transformation. Wilson (1996) argues that income mixing within communities was more characteristic of ghetto neighborhoods in the 1940s and 1950s and that inequality among communities today has become more pronounced as a result of the increasing spatial separation of middle- and upper-income blacks from lower-income blacks.

Focusing on racial segregation, Massey and Denton (1993) describe how, in a segregated environment, economic shocks that push more people into the ranks of low-income earners not only bring about an increase in the poverty rate for the group as a whole but also cause an increase in the geographic concentration of poverty. This geographic intensification occurs because the additional poverty created by macroeconomic conditions is spread unevenly over a metropolitan area. The greater the segregation, "the smaller the number of neighborhoods absorbing the shock, and the more severe the resulting concentration of poverty" (Massey, 1990, p. 337). At the other end of the income distribution, the growing geographic concentration of (predominantly white) affluence suggests a society increasingly bifurcated by wealth. Although for different reasons, both Wilson and Massey contend that race-linked social change is a structural force that is reflected in local environments.

The recognition of the spatial clustering of social problems actually has a long history. In the 1920s Shaw and McKay (1969) discovered that the same Chicago neighborhoods characterized by poverty, residential instability, and high rates of crime and delinquency were also plagued by high rates of infant mortality, low birth weight, tuberculosis, physical abuse, and other factors detrimental to child development. This general empirical finding has emerged repeatedly. Clearly, there is a connection between the healthy development of children and community structure.

In short, research on ecological differentiation has established some facts. First, there is considerable race-linked economic inequality among neighborhoods and communities, evidenced by the clustering of indicators of both advantaged and disadvantaged socioeconomic status and racial isolation. Second, social problems come bundled at the neighborhood level, including but not limited to crime, social disorder, and poor child health. Third, the ecological concentration of poverty, racial isolation, and social dislocations appears to have increased significantly along with the concentration of affluence, especially during the 1980s and 1990s.

Despite increased urbanization and a complex imbricated structure, neighborhoods and residential subcommunities remain persistent in American society. As any real estate agent or homeowner will attest, location does matter. It remains for a theory of community to specify the social mechanisms by which structural dimensions of community, especially the concentration of urban poverty, racial segregation, and residential stability, matter. It is to this issue I now turn.

THEORY OF COMMUNITY SOCIAL ORGANIZATION

At the most general level, community social organization may be thought of as the ability of a community structure to realize the common values of its residents and maintain effective social controls. Social control should not be equated with repression or forced conformity. Rather, it refers to the capacity of a social unit to regulate itself according to desired principles, to realize collective, as opposed to forced, goals. This conception is similar to Tilly's (1973) definition of collective action: the application of a community's pooled resources to common ends. There seems to be a consensus among Americans on the virtues of neighborhoods characterized by economic sufficiency, good schools, adequate housing, and a clean, healthy environment. The capacity to achieve such common goals is linked to informal relationships established for other purposes and more formal efforts to achieve social regulation through institutional means (see Kornhauser, 1978, p. 24).

The present framework of social control does not rest on homogeneity, whether cultural or socio-demographic. Diverse populations can and do agree on wanting safe streets. And social conflicts can and do rend communities along the lines of economic resources, race, political empowerment, and the role of criminal justice agents in defining and controlling drug use, gangs, panhandling, and police misconduct. Conflict usually coalesces around the distribution of resources and power, not the content of core values. As Selznick (1992, pp. 367, 369) has written, "communities are characterized by structural differentiation as well as by shared consciousness." The goal of community is thus unity in diversity, or the reconciliation of partial and general perspectives on the common good.

This sociological conception of social control addresses the longstanding criticism that theories of community social organization deemphasize social conflict. Recognizing that collective efforts to achieve common goals are variable and coexist with conflict, I thus use the term "differential social organization." In other words, I accept that communities lack homogeneity as I define them and focus on the variable forms of organization, formal and informal. Furthermore, my definition embraces geography rather than solidarity or identity as the major criterion identifying a community. Following Tilly (1973, p. 212), I "choose to make territoriality define communities and to leave the extent of solidarity problematic." When formulated in this way, the dimensions of community social organization are analytically separable not only from racial segregation, concentrated poverty, instability, and other exogenous sources of variation but from the social goods that may result.

Networks, Social Capital, and Collective Efficacy

The social-control way of thinking about community is grounded in what Kasarda and Janowitz (1974, p. 329) call the "systemic" model, in which the local community is viewed as a complex system of friendship and kinship networks, and of formal and informal associational ties rooted in family life, on-going socialization processes, and local institutions. Important systemic dimensions of community social organization are the prevalence, interdependence, and overlapping nature of social networks, local participation in formal and voluntary organizations, and the span of collective attention that the community directs toward local problems.

Thus conceived, the systemic model of social capital borrows insights gleaned from the social network paradigm in sociology. As a theoretical project, network analysis rejects the attempt to explain social process in terms of individual cognition or categorical attributes such as poverty or ethnicity. What counts more are the *social relations among persons* and the *structural connections among positions*. Applied to the local community, network analysis investigates the constraining and enabling dimensions of patterned relationships among social actors in an ecological system. The important point to take from this view is that community composition, the aggregation of individual characteristics, matters primarily as it bears on network structure.

The systemic or network analysis of social control is theoretically compatible with more recent formulations of what has been termed *social capital*. Coleman (1988, p. 98) defines social capital by its functions: it is created when the structure of relations among persons facilitates action, "making possible the achievement of certain ends that in its absence would not be possible." Social capital is a social good embodied in the relations among persons and positions. In other words, social capital is lodged not in individuals but in the structure of social organization. Putnam (1993, p. 36) has defined social capital in a similar fashion as "features of social organization, such as networks, norms, and trust, that facilitate coordination and cooperation for mutual benefit."

It follows that communities high in social capital are better able to realize common values and maintain effective social controls. Consider the case of childrearing, which is analyzed typically from the perspective of families. Neighborhoods characterized by extensive obligations, expectations, and interlocking social networks connecting adults are best able to facilitate the informal social control of children. Such close local networks provide the child with social capital of a collective nature, as reflected in the idea that "it takes a whole village to raise a child."

Social networks alone, however, are not sufficient to understand local communities. After all, networks are, differentially invoked; and in fact dense, tight-knit networks may actually impede social organization if they are isolated or weakly linked to collective expectations for action.

Private ties notwithstanding, then, it is the linkage of mutual trust and the willingness to intervene for the common good that defines the neighborhood context of what Sampson et al. (1997) term *collective efficacy*. Just as individuals vary in their capacity for effective action, so too do neighborhoods vary in their capacity to achieve common goals. It follows that the collective efficacy of residents is a critical feature of urban neighborhoods, regardless of the demographic composition of the population.

Institutions and Public Control

The present integration of a social capital and systemic network model of community social organization should not be read as ignoring institutions or the political environment of which local communities are a part. The institutional component of the systemic model is the neighborhood organizations and their linkages with other organizations, within and outside the community. Neighborhood organizations are the structural embodiment of community solidarity. For example, Kornhauser (1978, p. 79) argues that when the horizontal links among institutions in a community are weak, the capacity to defend local interests is weakened. Moreover, institutional strength is not necessarily isomorphic with neighborhood cohesion. Many communities exhibit intense private ties among friends and kin yet still lack the institutional capacity to achieve social control.

Vertical integration is potentially even more important. Bursik and Grasmick (1993) emphasize the importance of *public* control, defined as the capacity of local community organizations to obtain police and fire services, block grants and other extralocal resources that help sustain neighborhood social stability and local control.

LINKING STRUCTURAL DIFFERENTIATION AND SOCIAL ORGANIZATION

The preceding discussion underscores the reality that community social capital does not emerge from a vacuum. It is embedded in structural contexts and a political economy of place. Structural differentiation and extralocal political economy shape the dimensions of neighborhood social organization

Research shows that local friendship ties and the density of acquaintanceship vary widely across communities and that these variations are positively related to residential stability in a community. Stability is typically measured by average length of residence and the prevalence of homeownership. Community stability is independently associated with collective attachment to community and rates of participation in social and leisure activities. Furthermore, community residential stability has significant contextual effects

on an individual's local friendships and participation in local social activities even after accounting for factors such as age, social class, and life cycle (Sampson, 1988). Consistent with the predictions of the systemic model, these findings suggest that residential stability promotes a variety of social networks and local associations, thereby increasing the social capital of local communities.

Neighborhood variations in informal social control and institutional vitality are also systematically linked to patterns of resource deprivation and racial segregation, especially the concentration of poverty, joblessness, and family disruption. Wilson (1996) has described the corroding effects on neighborhood social organization of concentrated joblessness and the social isolation of the urban poor. He argues that in areas of economic distress where men are marginalized from the labor market and often family life as well, the incentives for participation in the social aspects of community life are reduced.

Similarly, Brooks-Gunn *et al.* (1993) reported that for many child and adolescent outcomes such as low IQ, dropping out of high school, problem behaviors, and out-of-wedlock births, the *absence* of affluent neighbors was more important than the *presence* of low-income neighbors. In particular, high economic status proved to be more important than the poverty status, racial composition, or the family structure of neighborhoods. Aber (1992) found that neighborhood socioeconomic status and joblessness interacted to predict adolescent outcomes: it was in conditions of high jobless rates that the absence of affluent neighbors served to depress academic achievement scores.

Studies have explored the mechanisms of community social organization more directly, especially how they are shaped by ecological differentiation. Elliott *et al.* (1996) examined survey data from neighborhoods in Chicago and Denver, which revealed that a measure of informal control was significantly related to adolescent outcomes in both places—positively to school achievement and conventional friendships, for instance, and negatively to delinquency. A similar finding was reported in Sampson's (1997) analysis of a community survey in Chicago designed to measure the willingness of neighbors to intervene in skipping school, spray-painting graffiti, and like public acts of deviance by children. Variations in the informal social control of children across eighty neighborhoods were positively related to residential stability and negatively related to concentrated poverty. In fact, informal social control accounted for more than half of the relationship between residential stability and lower rates of delinquency.

Although limited, the cumulative results of recent research support the idea that neighborhoods characterized by mistrust, sparse acquaintanceship networks among residents, attenuated social control of public spaces, and a weak institutional base coupled with little participation in local voluntary associations face an increased risk of crime, social disorder, and troublesome youth behavior. Perhaps more important, these dimensions of community social capital or collective efficacy are systematically structured (although not determined) by differences in wealth, jobs, family status, and residential tenure. Once again, however, one must be careful not to view structural patterns as arising solely from processes indigenous to neighborhoods. To understand neighborhood variations and ultimately to design community interventions, one must also take into account urban political economy.

Political Economy

Empirical research on the political economy of American cities has shown that structural differentiation is shaped directly and indirectly by the spatial decisions of public officials and businesses. The decline and destabilization of many central-city neighborhoods, for instance, has been facilitated not only by individual preferences as manifested in voluntary migration patterns, but government decisions on public housing, incentives for suburban growth in the form of tax breaks for developers and private mortgage assistance, highway construction and urban renewal, economic disinvestment in central cities, and zoning restrictions on land use.

Consider public housing and the legacy of urban renewal. Bursik (1989) has shown that the construction of new public housing projects in Chicago in the 1970s was associated with increased rates of population turnover, which predicted increases in crime independent of the area's population composition. Skogan (1990) has noted that urban renewal and forced migration contributed to the wholesale uprooting of many urban communities, and especially that freeway networks driven through the center of many cities in the 1960s destroyed viable, low-income neighborhoods. Across the nation, fully 20 percent of all central-city housing units occupied by blacks were lost in the 1960s because of urban redevelopment. This displacement does not even include that brought about by evictions, rent increases, and other routine market forces.

Equally disturbing, Wilson (1987) documents the often disastrous consequences of municipal decisions to concentrate minorities and the poor in public housing. Opposition from organized community groups to building public housing in their neighborhoods, de facto federal policy to tolerate extensive segregation against blacks in urban housing markets, and the decision by local governments to neglect code enforcement and the rehabilitation of existing residential units have all contributed to segregated housing projects that have become ghettos for many poor minority members.

The responsibilities of private development and business do not emerge unscathed, either. The idea of cities as growth machines (Logan and Molotch, 1987) reflects the marriage of private markets and enthusiastic governments to pursue aggressive development, often at the expense of previously stable communities with strong patterns of local social organization. Tax breaks for suburban development and federally supported housing mortgages have been especially prominent in the hollowing out of many urban centers. Historically, real estate agents have aided racial segregation and neighborhood instability by acting as panic peddlers in an effort to induce or accelerate the pace of neighborhood change. Joining them have been banks that redlined mortgage applications and promoted economic disinvestment in the inner city.

Zoning, a seemingly innocuous administrative practice, has undermined the social aspects of traditional urban life. By design, zoning is intended to create separate geographical spaces, and it has done so by cutting up neighborhoods into artificial segments, which disrupts patterns of social interaction and human activities. Indeed, the eerie lack of people walking and interacting on the streets of many suburban developments attests to zoning's dehumanization of the environment.

Whether through the purposeful segregation of low-income public housing, highway construction, urban renewal, government subsidized development by the private sector, zoning, redlining, blockbusting, or something so simple yet powerfully symbolic as gated communities with no sidewalks, it is no longer possible to think of neighborhoods as natural areas created by the aggregation of individual preferences alone. Clearly, government, business, and the political economy matter to an understanding of what communities can and cannot supply.

CONCLUSION

Urbanization and modernity notwithstanding, local communities and residential neighborhoods remain a prominent feature of American society. In this chapter I have proposed a community-level framework to explain why. I have explored the meaning, sources, and consequences of what communities supply from the perspective of a theory of social capital and collective efficacy.

It is appropriate to close, however, with some words of caution on the limits of community. Achieving common goals in an increasingly diverse society is no easy task and has proven a problem for communitarian thinking in an age of individual rights. In the pursuit of informal social control and collective goods, there is always the danger that freedoms will be restricted unnecessarily, that people will face unwanted and even unjust scrutiny. For example, surveillance of "suspicious" persons in socially controlled communities can easily become translated into the wholesale interrogation of racial minorities (see Skogan, 1990). Suppose further that a community comes together with high social capital and cohesion to block the residential entry of a racial group. Put more bluntly, what if racism is a shared value among residents of certain neighborhoods? Such exclusion happens too often, prompting Suttles (1972) to warn of the dark side of "defended neighborhoods."

Consider also the historical connection between official corruption and local solidarity. Whyte (1943, p. 126) was one of the first to document the ironic consequences of dense, multiple relationships in cohesive communities for law enforcement. "The policeman who takes a strictly legalistic view of his duties cuts himself off from the personal relations necessary to enable him to serve as a mediator of disputes in his area." By contrast, "the policeman who develops close ties with local people is unable to act against them with the vigor prescribed by the law." It follows that police corruption is an ever present danger under conditions of high social capital even as it aids in dispute resolution and informal social control because of interlocking social ties. It was the nature of such corruption that originally led to decentralized policing and an emergency-based patrol response in which officers were randomly assigned across neighborhoods. The nationwide move to embrace community policing has perhaps not recognized the risks inherent in the community side of the equation.

Obviously, Americans would not do well to think of racism, norms of social exclusion, and instruments of corruption as desirable forms of social capital, and we must balance community with a normative conception of social justice. It is for this reason that I have focused on widely expressed desires regarding community—especially social order and public safety. My strategy relies on a vision of urban America based on shared values for a safe and healthy environment, not on policies that divide by race and class. Nonetheless, pursuit of community goals must proceed cautiously and with respect for individual rights, diversity, and limits on state power. Fortunately, legal justice and community are not the antinomy common wisdom suggests. Constitutional law has long been concerned with balancing individual rights against the need to promote the health and safety of communities. The very idea of police power suggests the tension, long recognized by the Supreme Court, between individual rights and the pursuit of social order. Bringing law and social justice back into discussions of community development is a welcome and necessary move in the attempt to unite diversity in the name of community.

Finally, I caution against falling into the trap of local determinism. Part of the appeal of community is the image of local residents working collectively to solve their own problems. A defining part of American tradition (nostalgia?) is to hold individuals as well as communities responsible for their own fate. Like Saul Alinsky, I too have embraced the American ideal of residents joining forces to build community and maintain social order. This is not the only or even the most important story, however. As I have been at pains to emphasize, what happens within neighborhoods is in large part shaped by extra-local social forces and the political economy. In addition to encouraging communities to mobilize via self-help strategies of informal social control, it is incumbent on government to mount aggressive strategies to address the social and ecological changes that have battered inner-city communities. The specific nature of such efforts is beyond the scope of this chapter, but that should not detract from the importance of restorative moves at the political and macro-social level. Recognizing that community social action matters, in other words, does not absolve society of the responsibility for seeking equality of opportunities at the neighborhood as well as the individual level.

REFERENCES

Aber, Lawrence. 1992. "Adolescent Pathways Project." Paper prepared for the Committee for Research on the Urban Underclass, Social Science Research Council, Russell Sage Foundation.

Brooks-Gunn, Jeanne, and others. 1993. "Do Neighborhoods Influence Child and Adolescent Behavior?" *American Journal of Sociology* 99: 353–95.

Bursik, Robert J. 1989. "Political Decision-Making and Ecological Models of Delinquency: Conflict and Consensus." In *Theoretical Integration in the Study of Deviance and Crime*, edited by Steven Messner, Marvin Krohn, and Allen Liska, pp. 105–17. Albany, NY: State University of New York at Albany Press.

Bursik, Robert and Harold Grasmick. 1993. *Neighborhoods and Crime: The Dimensions of Effective Community Control*. Lexington, MA: Lexington Books.

Choldin, H. M. 1984. "Subcommunities, neighborhoods, and suburbs in ecological perspective." In *Sociological Human Ecology: Contemporary Issues and Applications*, edited by M. Micklin and H. M. Choldin, pp. 237–76. Boulder, Colorado: Westview Press.

Coleman, James S. 1988. "Social Capital in the Creation of Human Capital." *American Journal of Sociology* 94: S95–S120.

Elliott, Delbert, and others. 1996. "The Effects of Neighborhood Disadvantage on Adolescent Development." *Journal of Research in Crime and Delinquency*. 33: 389–426.

Fischer, Claude. 1982. *To Dwell among Friends: Personal Networks in Town and City*. Chicago: University of Chicago Press.

Gans, Herbert. 1962. *The Urban Villagers*. New York: Free Press.

Hillery, G. A. 1984. "Definitions of Community: Areas of Agreement." *Rural Sociology* 20: 111–23.

Hunter, Albert. 1975. "The Loss of Community: An Empirical Test through Replication." *American Sociological Review* 40: 537–53.

Jacobs, Jane. 1961. *The Death and Life of Great American Cities*. New York: Random House.

Jargowsky, Paul. 1997. *Poverty and Place: Ghettos, Barrios, and the American City*. New York: Russell Sage Foundation.

Kasarda, John, and Morris Janowitz. 1974. "Community Attachment in Mass Society." *American Sociological Review* 39: 328–39.

Kornhauser, Ruth. 1978. *Social Sources of Delinquency*. Chicago: University of Chicago Press.

Logan, John, and Harvey Molotch. 1987. *Urban Fortunes: The Political Economy of Place*. Berkley, CA: University of California Press.

Massey, Douglas S. 1990. "American Apartheid: Segregation and the Making of the Underclass." *American Journal of Sociology* 96: 338–39.

Massey, Douglas S., and Nancy Denton. 1993. *American Apartheid: Segregation and the Making of the Underclass*. Cambridge, MA: Harvard University Press.

Park, Robert. 1916. "The City: Suggestions for the Investigations of Human Behavior in the Urban Environment." *American Journal of Sociology* 20: 577–612.

Putnam, Robert. 1993. "The Prosperous Community: Social Capital and Community Life." *American Prospect* (Spring): 35–42.

Reiss, Albert J. Jr. 1996. Personal communication.

Sampson, Robert J. 1988. "Community Attachment in

Mass Society: A Multilevel Systemic Model" *American Sociological Review* 53: 766–69.

Sampson, Robert J. 1997. "Collective Regulation of Adolescent Misbehavior: Validation Results from Eighty Chicago Neighborhoods." *Journal of Adolescent Research* 12: 227–44.

Sampson, Robert J., Stephen Raudenbush, and Felton Earls. 1997. "Neighborhoods and Violent Crime: A Multilevel Study of Collective Efficacy." *Science* 277: 918–24.

Selznick, Philip. 1992. *The Moral Commonwealth: Social Theory and the Promise of Community*. Berkeley, CA: University of California Press.

Shaw, Clifford, and Henry McKay. ([1942] 1969) *Juvenile Delinquency and Urban Areas*. 2nd edn. Chicago: University of Chicago Press.

Skogan, Wesley. 1990. *Disorder and Decline: Crime and the Spiral of Decay in American Neighborhoods*. Berkeley, CA: University of California Press.

Stack, Carol. 1974. *All Our Kin: Strategies for Survival in a Black Community*. New York: Harper and Row.

Suttles, Gerald. 1972. *The Social Construction of Communities*. Chicago: University of Chicago Press.

Tilly, Charles. 1973. "Do Communities Act?" *Sociological Inquiry* 43: 209–40.

Wellman, Barry. 1979. "The Community Question: The Intimate Networks of East Yorkers." *American Journal of Sociology* 84: 1201–31.

Whyte, William F. 1943. *Street Corner Society: The Social Structure of an Italian Slum*. Chicago: University of Chicago Press.

Wilson, William Julius. 1987. *The Truly Disadvantaged: The Inner City, the Underclass, and Public Policy*. Chicago: University of Chicago Press.

Wilson, William Julius. 1996. *When Work Disappears: The World of the New Urban Poor*. New York: Alfred Knopf.

Wirth, Louis. 1938. "Urbanism as a Way of Life." *American Journal of Sociology*. 44: 1–24.

CHAPTER 20

The Myth of a Purified Community

Richard Sennett

A NEW PURITAN ETHIC

"Community" is a deceptive social term. People speak of a "community" of interest—for instance, men who do the same kind of labor or depend on each other to make money. There are also "communities of direction," like churches or ethnic groups whose members feel emotional ties to one another. Yet, even in everyday language, the idea of a community is not interchangeable with the idea of a social group; a community is a particular kind of social group in which men believe they share something together. The feeling of community is fraternal, it involves something more than the recognition that men need each other materially. The bond of community is one of sensing common identity, a pleasure in recognizing "us" and "who we are."

The emotions involved in this feeling of solidarity are complex, and writers on society understand little about them. At the opening of this century, the German social thinker Ferdinand Tönnies tried to sketch out the differences between a community life, in which people felt emotional ties with each other as full human beings, and group life, in which men felt their ties in terms of emotionally neutral, specialized tasks they performed together. The generation Tönnies taught tended to view this split between community and group as opposite poles of social experience. In the great flowering of sociology at the University of Chicago in the decades following the First World War, writers such as Robert Park, Louis Wirth, and Robert Redfield began to cast the differences between the two as the differences between village and city. While in village life men felt they belonged together and shared with each other in the full range of human activity, in the city, said these writers, men came to feel a part of each other's lives by virtue of functional tasks performed in common; the tasks were themselves so specialized that men's feeling of relatedness was split into innumerable fragments. In the city, complex emotional interactions between men would only get in the way of doing the specialized tasks.

The trouble with this idea of two poles—village-community versus city-group—is that it has proved itself too neat and simple to account for the varieties of community solidarity. For what modern researchers have uncovered, particularly in affluent city and suburban areas, is that men frame for themselves a belief in emotional cohesion and shared values with each other that has little to do with their actual social experiences together. The specific contents of this belief is the new puritan ethic.

Social researchers have become convinced that the feeling of common identity in community life, the projection of threads uniting a group of people, could occur *in advance* of any communal experience between the people involved. This striking idea is that the need to project a common character of community life often comes to be at war with the actual way men act with each other. People project an image of "who we are," as a collective personality, on a wholly different plane from, and in advance of, the character of what they share.

One striking portrayal of such a community was made by Vidich and Bensman, who studied a small town in New York State.

They found that community participation and decision making in the town were shared by only a small number of people; they found such social forces as class, ethnic background, and age to play decisive roles in cutting off contacts between people in the community. And yet, the people of this small town voiced a strong, almost desperate, belief in themselves as a unified group with warm and sustained contacts between all the members of the town community. The actual contacts were mainly centered on discussing the varying fortunes of town members; but these people believed themselves engaged with each other in a much wider, more important way, and they reacted with hostility when challenged by the researchers on the degree of their cohesion. This feeling of solidarity the Polish sociologist Florian Znaniecki calls a community cemented by an act of will rather than by acts of experience.

This same projection of community solidarity, opposed to community experience, struck me forcibly in looking into the chain of events leading to the ouster of a prosperous black family from a wealthy suburb outside a midwestern city. In this suburb the rate of divorce was about four times the national average, the rate of juvenile crime began to approach the worst sections of the city to which it was attached, the incidence of hospitalization from emotional collapse was frequent. Yet the people of the community united in a great show of force to drive the black family from its home three days after it had moved in because the residents said, among other things, that "we are a community of solid families" and "This is a happy, relaxed place, and the character of the community has to be kept together." The importance of this incident isn't simply that the residents of the suburb lied, but why they lied in this particular way.

Some writers have argued that "insecurity" as such is at the root of this need for an image of community, of "us." But putting the matter in this way brings up the issue of individual growth: the purifying of identity may be forged in a life as a means of evading experiences that can be threatening, dislocating, or painful. Is there a connection between this community by an act of will, this identity

of a coherent "us," and the tools generated in adolescents by which individuals acquire a purified "me," resistant to new experience?

The connection exists, I believe. The images of communal solidarity are forged in order that men can avoid dealing with each other. The mechanisms of repression Vidich and Bensman found were myths that kept men from having to interact and understand each other as they really were. The small town in upstate New York and the suburb where "bad" black families were excluded feared conflict because conflict involved confrontation between men, friends as well as enemies, and that was an uncontrollable and therefore threatening social event. By an act of will, a lie if you like, the myth of community solidarity gave these people the chance to be cowards and hide from one another.

HOW THE MYTH OF COMMUNITY PURITY IS FORMED

The feeling of a common identity is a counterfeit of experience. People talk about their understanding of each other and of the common ties that bind them, but the images are not true to their actual relations. But the lie they have formed as their common image is a usable falsehood—a myth—for the group. Its use is that it makes a coherent image of the community as a whole: people draw a picture of who they are that binds them all together as one being, with a definite set of desires, dislikes, and goals. The image of the community is purified of all that might convey a feeling of difference, let alone conflict, in who "we" are. In this way the myth of community solidarity is a purification ritual.

Involved here is a collapsing of the experiential frame, a condensing of all the messy experiences in social life, in order to create a vision of unified community identity. It is exactly this detour around social contact and experience in the making of a coherent common identity that reveals the marks of adolescence on the community process.

Adolescence has been described as a stage of life in which the individual finally attains his full range of human powers, but is empty of adult-like experience to guide him in using those powers. This imbalance in the time scales of growth is particularly acute in the realm of ethical and social choices. Young people have the power to be free, to choose their future careers, to explore themselves outside the boundaries of family and school, to have full and diverse erotic relations; but they sense no history of freedom under these terms in their own lives. Some adolescents do have the strength to hold themselves back, and let a diversity of painful, confused, and contradictory new experiences enter their lives, before they take the active steps that will confirm them in an identity. But most young people are denied the strength to endure ambiguity of this kind, and exercise their new powers to form *conscious* meanings and value relations to themselves about experiences they are yet to have. In this way, the experiential frame is controlled in advance; its impact on the reality a youth perceives is muffled because unexpected or painful new experiences are rejected as unreal. They don't fit into the schemes of coherent order the young person is now able to articulate consciously to himself.

It is the same projection—a picture of "us" as a coherent being in advance of actual social relations—that links the feeling of communal solidarity to the patterns of avoidance learned in adolescence. Certain tools of avoidance used by a human being to deal with crises in his own growth patterns are subsequently transferred to the way he understands himself as a social being. This transfer of a skill learned in adolescence is how the myth of a purified community comes into being.

The illusion retained by adolescents caught by the desire for purified identity is that they chose a coherent and secure routine with knowledge and experience of all the alternatives to security. There is no reason why people, having learned such a technique of avoidance in their individual lives, could not learn as adults to share it together. Communally painful experiences, unknown social situations full of possible surprise and challenge can be avoided by the common consent of a community to believe they already know the meaning of these experiences and have drawn the lessons from them together.

It is a truism among students of small groups that people feel most uneasy and most challenged by perceiving the "otherness" of the people around them. Finding the differences between oneself and the world outside oneself seems to be much more difficult to bear than finding the points of similarity. The fear of "otherness," of that which one does not know, is exactly of a piece with what men fear about *themselves* and their own powers when those powers ripen in adolescence. From adolescence people take a power for mythmaking into their adult community lives to blunt the conscious perception of "otherness."

A community is not simply a social group or an unrelated collection of individuals living in the same place. It is a group in which people belong to each other, share something in common. What is distinctive about this mythic sharing in communities is that people feel they belong to each other, and share together, because they are the *same*.

The narrowness of this feeling can best be seen by contrasting it to the sharing and sense of belonging in a strong love. As Denis de Rougemont has so wisely remarked, the sharing that occurs in deep relations of intimacy grows out of loving the distinctiveness, the uniqueness of the other person, not in the merging of selves into one homogenized being. But in the purification of a coherent community image, fear rather than love of men's "otherness" prevails. Out of this fear is bred the counterfeit of experience. The "we" feeling, which expresses a desire to be similar, is a way for men to avoid the necessity of looking deeper into each other; instead, men imagine that they know all about each other, and their knowledge becomes a vision of how they must be the same.

In this way the "we" feeling can grow up among people whose lives strike the outsider as so disparate in actuality, who seem in fact to share very little with each other and matter very little in each other's lives. The counterfeit sense of community is not bred, I believe, out of peculiarities in local or even American conditions. Rather it is bred out of the way human beings learn at a certain point in their own growth how to lie to themselves, in order to avoid new experiences that might force them to endure the pain of perceiving the unexpected, the new, the "otherness" around them. Through this peculiar learning process "belonging" to one another becomes a shared sense of what we think we ought to be like, as one social being, in order not to be hurt.

But resolving the fear of "otherness" through this myth of solidarity affects the ways the community, as an entity in itself, will operate over the course of time.

THE SOCIAL STRUCTURE OF THE MYTH

The myth of solidarity in community life speaks to a more complex human problem than social conformity. Usually discussions of conformity to mass values and mores have treated the human beings involved as being, at their very worst, passive creatures manipulated by an impersonal system. Thus is there supposed conformity without pleasure, mindless obedience to the norms. This is much too flattering a picture of the human impulses at work.

When the desire for communal sameness is understood as the exercise of powers developed in everyday life rather than as the fruit of some abstract creature called "the system" or "mass culture," it is inescapable that the people involved in this desire for coherence *actively* seek their own slavery and self-repression. They would be insulted if the issue were stated so boldly, of course; yet it is their acts, their impulses that create the communal forms. The social images do not materialize out of thin air; they are made by men, because men have learned in their individual lives, at one stage of development, the very tools of avoiding pain later to be shared together in a repressive, coherent, community myth.

When the French writer Alexis de Tocqueville came to America a century and a half ago, he was struck by the grip this repressive myth had on American community life. The Americans he observed needed to be assured by each other that they were the same—that is, *equal in condition*. Tocqueville believed they felt this need because they felt insecure about their own dignity as men; the act of drawing together, in confirming to each other their sameness and their coherence in a common image, warded off the apprehension of threatened dignity. The issues so far explored could be expressed in Tocqueville's terms, as a way men counterfeit a feeling of dignity through an image of equality. There is born in adolescence, and subsequently reified in community life, a means of reassuring oneself that the process of learning about life has occurred even as the substance of learning is avoided. The result is a feeling of dignity in the image of sameness, of equality of condition, as Tocqueville put it, that men forge for themselves.

There are three marked social consequences of this myth of dignity through communal solidarity.

The first is the loss of actual participation in community life, the loss of situations of confrontation and exploration between individual groups of men. Tocqueville believed this occurred because the individuals of the community convinced themselves that since the community was in hands much like their own, no matter who ruled, the community was in good hands. If each man was dignified, then all were dignified and could be trusted. Thus men could return to their real concerns, Tocqueville said, which were the petty, routine, isolated pleasures of everyday life. Solidarity in name and isolation in fact were, Tocqueville said, cause and effect.

But the psychological ideas of this essay put the matter in a different way. Innate to the process of forming a coherent image of community is the desire to avoid actual participation. Feeling common bonds without common experience occurs in the first place because men are afraid of participation, afraid of the dangers and the challenges of it. Therefore, withdrawing from participation is not simply a possibility under these conditions, as Tocqueville believed; it is the driving power that produces the urge of men to feel socially alike, to share a myth of common identity.

Thus, in the wealthy suburb whose residents were suddenly faced with the possibility of having to deal with a real situation—the introduction of a prosperous black family in their midst—the racial prejudice was a product of something in the lives of the suburbanites themselves, something that had little to do with their feelings about blacks. The racial prejudice was a cover for their fear of having to be social beings, to deal with each other in order to cope. In order to defend against this social participation, and all its pain, they had to proclaim a lie about who they were.

The incident suggests a second consequence of the feeling of coherence in a community: the repression of deviants. Again, Tocqueville saw the brute repression of deviants as a necessity if men were to keep convincing themselves of their collective sameness. The "poets of society," the men who challenged the norms, would have to be silenced so that sameness could be maintained. But when the "we" feeling is understood as a myth bred in the life cycle, the repression of community practices is more than just a means to an end; in fact, it is exactly the same process of repression that the majority, the "we," exercise against themselves. We do not expel this black family from our neighborhood in order to make the neighborhood a nicer place, although that is what we tell ourselves. What we are afraid of is that something "other" will come to matter to us, and then we might be hurt by our own exploration of "otherness."

So the expressions of common identity and the repression of deviations are both aspects of men's fear of power within themselves. To permit the freedom of deviation would be to care about the unknown, the other, in social contacts. The myths of community are self-destructive in that they take a strength developed on the eve of adulthood and use it to repress other human strengths, like curiosity and the desire to explore.

But as Kai Erikson has pointed out, total repression of deviants would rob society of a means of defining itself; there must be room for "them" for "us" to exist as well. But the myth of a common "us" is an act of repression, not simply because it excludes outsiders

or deviants from a particular community, but because of what it requires of those who are the elect, the included ones. The elect must give up complex or conflicting loyalties, and they *want* to do this, want to become slaves to each other, in order to avoid the strengths in themselves that would make them explorers beyond comfortable limits.

The third consequence of this desire for an image of coherent, shared community life lies in its relation to violence.

The myth of community solidarity disposes men, I believe, to escalate discord with other communities or with outsiders too powerful to be excluded to the level of violent confrontation. Essentially, communities whose people feel related to each other by virtue of their sameness are polarized. When issues within or without the community arise that cannot be settled by routine processes, it seems that the whole fabric of the myth is in jeopardy because of an intractable issue or event that cannot be assimilated. This occurs because the basis of community order is community sameness; problems that can't fit the mold challenge the feeling of being together because of being alike. In situations like these, everyone's dignity is threatened, and people can't ignore it. They feel that the very survival of the community is at stake, and in a sense, they are right. Having so little tolerance for disorder in their own lives, and having shut themselves off so that they have little experience of disorder as well, the eruption of social tension becomes a situation in which the ultimate methods of aggression, violent force and reprisal, seem to become not only justified, but life-preserving. It is a terrible paradox that the escalation of discord into violence comes to be, in these communities, the means by which "law and order" should be maintained.

In this way some communities, through such tools as the police, respond totally out of proportion to the provocations they receive. I am thinking here about the reactions in most American suburbs after the chain of riots from 1964 to 1968. These riots unlike most insurrectionary outbreaks, did not burst the boundaries of the black ghettos; they never involved mass shootings or mobs storming government centers; rather they focused on the seizure of small articles of property, food, or liquor. However, the reaction in the white suburbs was that "we" were threatened, that blacks were spilling out of the ghettos, that actual civil war and personal attack were imminent. Gun sales in the suburbs rose sharply, grandmothers began to learn how to shoot to kill, liberals suddenly began to understand the "logic" of the separatist movement, the police were unleashed in the cities in a wave of violent reprisals and mindless destructiveness. The overwhelming feeling of "us" being mortally threatened, so incommensurate, so out of touch with the actual tragedy of self-destruction, is the puzzle of these civil disorders. This kind of reaction, this inability to deal with disorder without raising it to the scale of mortal combat, is inevitable when men shape their common lives so that their only sense of relatedness is the sense in which they feel themselves to be the same. It is because men are uneasy and intolerant with ambiguity and discord in their own lives that they do not know how to deal with painful disorder in a social setting, and instead escalate disorder to the level of life or death struggle.

And finally, the economic environment of abundance in a community strengthens each of these consequences of the urge toward community coherence.

THE ROLE OF ABUNDANCE IN THE MYTH

One recurrent image in the language of society is the great, teeming chaos of cities. Its fascination and its terror come from the diversity within the city's borders; the garment district of New York, for example, spills into a district of offices which spills into a district of social-work agencies which spills into a district of elegant townhouses which spills finally into the great shopping areas around Fourteenth Street. Anyone walking through this diversity in lower midtown feels an enormous vibrancy in the overlap of so many different kinds of life. This diversity was created in the history of New York because none of these areas of activity had enough power to control its own limits as

a community. None of them was rich and centralized enough to wall itself off, and so each suffered the intrusion of others by necessity.

As Jane Jacobs has observed, this penetration of diverse modes of labor and life into each other has been a characteristic feature of the neighborhoods of great American cities, but a characteristic that is in the process of dying off. The reason it is dying lies, I believe, in the role abundance plays in forming communities of self-conscious solidarity.

Material abundance in a community provides the power for enforcing a myth of coherent community life. It does so in two ways. The first, and obvious one, is that a community with adequate monetary resources can materially control its boundaries and internal composition. The old neighborhoods in cities were complex precisely because no one group had the economic resources to shield itself; the brownstone dwellers did not have the money to live one family to a house, and so shield the housing unit from influences outside the circle of one family; residential life in turn could not be shielded from commerce, much as people might have wanted to get away from the noisy bars and shops on the first floors of city buildings. People simply hadn't the resources to move out. An economy of scarcity in cities has, at least historically, defied myths of coherence in community affairs; people haven't had the cash to realize their own desires.

Now, with large sectors of the urban population achieving modest wealth for themselves, those desires for coherence, for structured exclusion and internal sameness, can be played out. Whole urban regions can be divided geographically by class, race, ethnicity; "unsightly" activities like stores and entertainment can be hidden from home life, so that community identity through a broad simplification of human activities is achieved.

But abundance plays a subtler and perhaps more dangerous role in shaping the desire for a common identity. For in communities that are poor, or in times of scarcity, sharing between individuals and families is *a necessary* element of survival. The sharing of appliances, or even of basic necessities as food, has often been remarked on by visitors to the black ghettos of American cities; historically, however, the same communal sharing, which brings people together and necessitates direct social contacts between them, has been a feature of many diverse city neighborhoods; services, skills, and possessions that could be shared provided a focus for concrete communal activities.

It is the hallmark of abundance that the need for such sharing disappears. Each family has its own vacuum cleaner, its own set of pots and pans, its own transport, etc. Thus the necessity for social interaction, the necessity to share, is no longer a driving force in communities of abundance; men can withdraw into their self-contained, self-sustaining homes. This means that the feeling of community, of being related and bound together in some way, is cut off from a region that in the past furnished communal experiences. When much less *must* be shared, there is a much smaller fund of experiences on which

individuals can draw to assay the character of each other: In framing a sense of communal bonds, men are inclined much more easily to envisage how they are the same rather than what they actually do in their relations with each other.

Abundance, in other words, increases the power to create isolation in communal contacts at the same time that it opens up an avenue by which men can easily conceive of their social relatedness in terms of their similarity rather than their need for each other.

These are the dimensions of the myth of communal solidarity. It appears as something possible, even probable, in men's lives, as a result of experiences in adolescence. But the myth is more than just a logical social possibility of psychic growth. It is a real force in modern social life, and it has a special relationship to the development of cities during this century. The gradual dominance of this myth is the hidden story behind the community patterns that have been evolving in cities during the last seventy years.

CHAPTER 21

Community Organizing for Power and Democracy

Lessons learned from a life in the trenches

Harold DeRienzo

It is difficult, if not ultimately self-defeating, to undertake a community organizing effort without some understanding or appreciation of the economic, social, and political environment within which such an effort will operate, along with some anticipation of how our work fits (or not) within that context.

But in the process of deciding on the kind of community organizing effort to undertake and how such an effort will be received and what chances such an effort has for success, it also necessary to test our own assumptions about, and to be clear as to how we ourselves define, community. After all, if we do not start from a grounded premise, and we undertake to do "community organizing" nonetheless, then we are presuming, probably to our own frustration and to the detriment of those on whose behalf we purport to be working, that community exists and that it is possible to use that reality for the development of, or to further, some collective human benefit. On the other hand, if we are actually intent upon "organizing community," then we need to know what we are attempting to organize and what are the internal and external supports and constraints we have to work within. But either way, knowing (or at least having a sense of) what we are trying to organize or knowing the state of community within which we are attempting to organize should be a critical first step before we get started. And, I also believe that the prevailing practice of not paying better attention to the importance of the goals we choose, of being sloppy with terminology, and thereby being sloppy in the programs we develop, ultimately creates frustration on all sides and in

the end does an injustice and disservice to the very people we purport to be helping.

Before defining community, however, it helps to define a contrasted perspective of "neighborhood," especially since the terms "neighborhood" and "community" are so often used interchangeably.

To my way of thinking, a neighborhood is little more than a "housing services cluster" where residents live in close enough proximity to provide the underlying economic bases to support an array of necessary and/or desired services. I say "and/or" desired services because a low income neighborhood may be able to do little more than support a bodega on every corner, given the fact that there is a high density of population but with each household barely able to afford necessities.

In a neighborhood, each household is an independent economic entity, with the source of economic capacity derived, for the most part, from without the confines of the given area. So the characteristics of a neighborhood are:

1. Atomization. Each household exists as a self-contained social unit, a collective consumption unit (for goods, media, information and politics) and, economically speaking, an individual labor-bargaining unit in the regional, national and global economy.

2. External Economic Dependency. The means needed to maintain lifestyles are primarily obtained from outside of the neighborhood.

3. Service Infrastructure. The individual neighborhood components (houses, with

little substantive relevance to who resides within them) are connected by an infrastructure comprised of utility and transportation networks, shopping and other service hubs, education and other supportive services.

In contrast to this rather "stripped down" concept of neighborhood elaborated on above, the concept of "community" is much more powerful, but just as difficult to achieve and maintain in reality as is the power. In fact, community and power (in the traditional sense) are interrelated and functionally interdependent, as explained below.

For "community" to exist, I believe there need to be three necessary and integrally related components:

1. *Commonality*. Something—geographical circumstances, children, beliefs, needs, issues, (private) troubles that are recognized as (public) issues, or whatever—something that any group of people may hold in common must exist for there to be a basis for community. But although commonality is a necessary *component*, this first component of community is often seen as the only necessary basis for a community organizing effort—the beginning and the end of most practitioners' quests in search of the bases for their work. But without a more expansive perspective, most such efforts almost always will fail once the external supports for the effort are removed.

2. *Interdependence*. This is a difficult concept to appreciate, especially for those who fund comprehensive community initiatives, community-building, and ambitious community organizing efforts. What interdependence presumes is that a necessary component of community is economic. E.g. Max Weber (1968) defining an urban community as: "predominance of trade-commercial relations." Wendell Berry (1993) defining community as the "locally understood interdependence of local people, local culture and local economy." In my experience, since the funders and the outside prot-

agonists (you know, the ones with all the answers) start with the premise that the world is as it is because of some natural law or natural order of things, the goal then becomes to teach people how to survive and thrive within this world that, after all, works so well for them. But let any one of them lose their household incomes and find themselves without the benefit of family or inherited wealth and they will learn soon enough that the "community" that they believe they live in, is not a community at all, just a local residential service cluster that sustains them only to the extent that it is supported by them through their outside economic endeavors. "Community," without some economic capacity that defines the relations between and among its members and advances the quality of life of those within that "community," is not a community at all, just an aggregation of people within some set of shared circumstances.

3. *Collective Capacity*. This third necessary component of community follows from the first two components—commonality and interdependence. For a community to be a community there must be an internal capacity to accomplish goals that are commonly resolved to be necessary or desirable. For the most part, in established communities, the vehicles for accomplishing the commonly held agenda of its members are called institutions. And I would maintain that it is possible to gauge the relative health of any community by determining the extent to which its institutions are controlled by the residents or by outside resources. But implicit to understanding community, and it fits well within the conventional definition of power as a covenant among people, is that collective capacity only results from each individual having something to offer to the collective "pot" from which common good can be achieved. Ask yourself the question: with no access to the primary sources of wealth (natural resources, information, technology, means of production, and the like) and with most

people possessing or trending towards negative wealth, what opportunity is there for entering into such contracts and, by so doing, creating the bases for exercising power?

Having defined community, I would maintain that most of the community-building efforts that I have been exposed to or participated in would fall under two categories or models: (1) the "Static Enhancement" Model, and (2) the "Transformative" Model.

The Static Enhancement model accepts the prevailing social, economic, political order as a given, and then seeks to infuse resources into the local organizing efforts to "enhance" the capacities of local residents to adjust to and thrive within the given circumstances—the recognized and accepted status quo. But this premise is totally misplaced in that reality is not fixed and is not predetermined. To quote from Isaiah Berlin (1991), "... ends are not ... objective values, discoverable within man or within the transcendent realm ... Ends are not discovered at all, but made, not found but created." In other words, "reality" is not some immutable existence or some force incapable of being influenced and to simply be reckoned with. "Reality" is being made, transformed, continually. The real question for all of us is whether we will be subjects of that transformation (continually acting upon that reality) or objects (totally at the mercy of whatever is reality at any given time, to borrow a concept from Paulo Freire). This brings us to the next model.

The Transformative Model accepts that reality is being made and remade continually and also accepts that people working together actually can be a part of making history, not merely observing it. This leads to a need to appreciate the economic and political context within which we organize and to have an appreciation of the concept of power.

When I was young, I believed that living in a democracy, people had political power and that political expression and political preference expressed through political processes (mostly voting) would define our social structures, our economic system and our insti-

tutional framework. But that was naive. Politics, social structures, predominant culture and institutional arrangements—all of which comprise the arrangements for sharing power within our society—are necessarily defined by the needs of the predominant economy. The needs of that economy—concentrated access to resources, information, technology and wealth; a mobile and disciplined work force; encouragement towards individual and household consumption; the tolerance for the "family" as the most expansive acceptable social unit; government that is limited in its regulatory intrusion, and so on—is anathema to the very concept and (as I believe we are seeing now) the very reality of community. This cannot be ignored if we are truly serious about community organizing. And if we are not that serious, then let's be honest and declare community an anachronism and go on to project some alternative set of humane social arrangements that will ensure that we do not become slaves to the very private, consumptive lives we have accepted and cling to with abandon.

Due to this dominant and preemptive social trend towards individual consumption, there is increasing individual isolation, political disenfranchisement and economic marginality in our society. If we are going to organize in order to improve lives and transform any aspect of current power sharing arrangements, these dynamics that both destroy and prevent community must at least be recognized and drawn into our considerations and our work.

This brings us to the concept of power, a concept that goes hand-in-hand with the concept of community. Hannah Arendt (1963) distinguishes between strength (our individual attributes held in isolation against all others) and power, which she defines in terms of a mutual covenant binding people together into what amounts to a power structure, and embodied within community. Power, like community, lasts for as long as people remain working together and disappears as soon as they disperse. But more important, due to the structure and continual processes of community (expressed through the three attributes of commonality, interdependence, and collective capacity), power remains always latent and accessible because community exists. But like power, community is a fragile circumstance. Once people disperse (into isolation) and give up commonly held circumstances, refrain from mutually supportive activities, and allow the means for collective capacity to erode, community dies and takes the capacity for exercising power along with it. And, just for the record, community is not and cannot be sustained by organizing. Community is only sustained by the infrastructure of relations and networks and processes that make up that community. Similar to being able to gauge the absence of community by the total control of local institutions by outside forces, the recognized need for constant organizing is also an indication of the absence of community. In a sense, a call for constant organizing is an attempt to compensate for a lack of power due to the absence of community.

Given the circumstances outlined above, current community organizing efforts, I believe, can be characterized in three ways:

1. *Organizing for Domestication.* These efforts are generated most times by outsiders who believe that they have the answers and that by teaching people how to think, how to dress, how to act, what values to bring to any circumstance, and so on, that these people will be saved. Unfortunately, too many of my colleagues are perfectly happy with this form of organizing. They treat people as objects to be manipulated, many times for their own selfish ends (control, power, money, self-aggrandizement, or whatever).

2. *Organizing Around Issues—Issue-Specific Mobilization.* This form of organizing is very important in that these efforts often are undertaken to stop a major regressive action that would hurt large segments of the population. But important as these efforts are, they must be recognized for what they are—efforts organized and undertaken to minimize the hurt and not to change any of the underlying dynamics that politically empowered the proposed actions to begin with. These are necessarily stop-gap activities that use the threat of disruption and the possible risk of creating the public perception of social wrong to prevent or minimize harm.

3. *Transformative/Developmental Organizing.* This form of organizing has as its goal the long-term, structural transformation of power-sharing arrangements. How is such a thing accomplished? First, it is necessary to recognize the challenges that any community organizing effort is confronted with. Secondly, it is necessary to strike at the heart of the problem by seeking to change the destructive dynamics of individual isolation, economic marginality and the resulting political disenfranchisement. There is no specific work plan. But most approaches that seek to directly attack those symptoms of a dying community and seek to change the destructive dynamics that destroy and prevent community represent a good start. A few examples follow:

   1. Public Space: It amazes me how willingly we are giving up public space in favor of private isolation, individual consumptive gratification and total self-reliance. The first order of business for any totalitarian regime is to destroy public space and replace it with fear, distrust, loathing, individual insecurity and suspicion. [Think of the potential for this in the wake of 9/11.] But in our society, we seem to be voluntarily giving up public space in favor of some consumption-dominated nirvana. [An East Berliner after the fall of the Berlin wall reportedly lauded the wonders of western-style democracy that he characterized as "canned beer and no responsibility."] Any community effort must seek to restore the use of public space.

   2. Institutional Accountability and Control: The organization I work for sponsors a citywide mutual housing association called CATCH, a citywide group that redevelops abandoned and distressed properties, trains residents and turns control of the corporations over to

residents. Our local affiliate, the Central Harlem MHA, is the only community development corporation in Harlem that is resident-controlled. The struggle has been difficult and the challenges ahead are many, but the potential is that when local residents effectively control the resources of nearly 600 units of housing and all of the internal demand (repair jobs, supplies, contracting services, etc.) that goes along with it, this will begin to facilitate the necessary attributes of community and make a small beginning in tearing away the destructive anti-community dynamics of isolation, economic marginality and political disenfranchisement.

3. Political Involvement: On its own, political involvement is a useless exercise, but in tandem with other community building activities, can make a difference. I believe, consciously or unconsciously, that one reason that ACORN joined with unions to form the Working Families Party in New York was based on a frustration with having to maintain membership by continually organizing one mobilization campaign after another. It remains to be seen if this direct political involvement will make a difference (i.e. long-term use of public resources to maximize local economic participation and maximize economic and social benefits), but it is a worthwhile effort.

The underlying goal of any legitimate community effort need not be very dramatic. The goal of any community organizing effort should be to concurrently promote human values and to reverse the destructive dynamics that isolate people, marginalize them economically and disenfranchise them politically. Whatever evolves from such efforts may or may not fit our conventional definition of community, but will necessarily constitute the humane and sustainable attributes we all seem to long for in pushing our rhetoric about values of community.

REFERENCES

Arendt, Hannah. 1963. *On revolution*. New York: Viking Press.

Berlin, Isaiah. 1991. *The crooked timber of humanity: chapters in the history of ideas*. Edited by Henry Hardy. New York: Knopf.

Berry, Wendell. 1993. *Sex, economy, freedom and community*. New York: Pantheon Books.

Weber, Max. 1968 [1958]. *The city*, translated and edited by Don Martindale and Gertrud Neuwirth. New York: Free Press.

CHAPTER 22

Neighborhood Organizing

The importance of historical context

Robert Fisher

INTRODUCTION

Neighborhood organizing has a history as old as the neighborhood concept itself. It is certainly not a product simply of sixties dissent. Community-based resistances—around geographic communities such as a neighborhood or communities of cultural identity such as the black or women's community—have become the *dominant* form of social action since the 1960s, replacing more class and labor-based organizing (see, for instance, Epstein, 1990; Fisher and Kling, 1993). This ever-increasing significance helps explain the widespread contemporary interest in community-based organizing and the importance of this book. But it tends to obscure the rich and fundamental history prior to the 1960s that undergirds current neighborhood-based activity and it narrows the debates about neighborhood organizing to contemporary limits. To illustrate the point, this chapter begins with a discussion of the varied types of neighborhood organizing that have persisted since the late nineteenth century and the lessons to be learned from them. It follows with a discussion of neighborhood organizing since the 1980s, demonstrating how the political economy of the larger historical context heavily impacts the nature and potential of neighborhood organizing.

TYPES OF NEIGHBORHOOD ORGANIZING

Since the 1880s, there have been three main types of neighborhood organizing (see Table 22.1). The social work approach is best characterized by the social settlement movement, which began in the United States in 1886, and by contemporary social service delivery at the neighborhood level, such as neighborhood centers or health clinics. The political activist approach is best reflected in the work of oppositional efforts which see power as the fundamental issue. These date back to the ward-based political machines of the nineteenth century, but as social efforts are best reflected in the efforts of the Communist Party in the 1930s, the efforts of Saul Alinsky and followers since the late 1930s, New Left neighborhood organizing in the 1960s, and a host of current neighborhood based grouping since then, perhaps most notably in African-American and gay male communities. The neighborhood maintenance approach also originated in the late 19th century, when more middle-class residents sought to defend their neighborhood against change and perceived threats. The ongoing history since the 1920s of neighborhood protective associations, whose primary concern is maintaining or improving property values, is the classic example (for a fuller discussion of these, see, Fisher, 1994).

LESSONS FROM THE PAST

Simply stated, there have been a number of key lessons from the past of neighborhood organizing that should inform the study of contemporary efforts.

1) Neighborhood organizing has a long and important history. As Table 22.1 and examples above illustrate, neighborhood organizing is not simply a product of the past

Table 22.1 History of neighborhood organizing: three dominant approaches

	Social work	Political activist	Neighborhood maintenance
Concept of community	social organism	political unit power base	neighborhood residence
Problem condition	social disorganization social conflict	powerlessness exploitation neighborhood destruction	threats to property values or neighborhood homogeneity insufficient services
Organized group	working and lower class	working and lower class	upper and middle class
Role of organizer	professional social worker enabler and advocate coordinator and planner	political activist mobilizer educator	elected spokesperson civic leader interest-group broker
Role of neighborhood residents	partners with professional recipients of benefits	fellow activists indigenous leaders mass support	dues-paying members
Strategy	consensual gradualist work with power structure	conflict mediation challenge power structure	consensual peer pressure political lobbying legal action
Goals	group formation social integration service delivery	obtain, maintain, or restructure power develop alternative institutions	improve property value maintain neighborhood deliver services
Examples	social settlements community centers Cincinnati Social Unit Plan Community Chests United Community Defense Services Community Action Program United Way	unemployed councils tenant organizations Alinsky programs Student Non-Violent Coordinating Committee (SNCC) Students for a Democratic Society (SDS) Association of Community Organizations for Reform Now	neighborhood preservation associations neighborhood civic clubs property owners' associations

generation, nor is it a transitory phenomenon. It is a means of democratic participation, a means of extra-political activity, a way to build community, obtain resources, and achieve collective goals. Neighborhood organization has been an integral, on-going, and significant basis of civil life in the United States for more than a century. Whereas people continually choose in astounding numbers not to participate in the electoral process, underscoring both the inability of politicians to galvanize the electorate and the alienation of citizens from the political process, this is not true for participation in neighborhood organizations. Of course more people vote than work in citizen action efforts, due to voting's relative effortlessness and institutional support. But Americans have always turned readily to organizations at the grassroots level to build community, meet individual and collective needs, and participate in public life. This is as true today as it was one hundred years ago.

2) Neighborhood organizing cuts across the political spectrum. While all neighborhood organizing is a public activity, bringing people together to discuss and determine their collective welfare, it is not inherently reactionary, conservative, liberal, or radical. Nor is it inherently inclusive and democratic, or parochial and authoritarian. It is above all a political method, an approach used by varied segments of the population to achieve specific goals, serve certain interests, and advance clear or ill-defined political perspectives. Organizations can be creative efforts open to innovation and supportive of progressive struggles as well as defensive responses to external pressures. The form an organization takes depends on a number of

factors, especially the ideology and goals of its leadership, constituency organized, and local context.

3) Neighborhood organizing efforts develop in a larger context that transcends local borders and determines the dominant form of neighborhood organizing in any era. Conditions at the local level directly spawn and nurture neighborhood organizing projects. The organizers, residents, local conditions, and many other factors at the grassroots level combine to forge consistently unique neighborhood organizing experiences. But while neighborhood organizing projects do have a significant origin, nature, and existence of their own at the local level, they are also the products of national and even international political and economic developments. To no small degree, the larger political-economic context determines the general tenor, goals and strategies, even the likelihood of success, of local efforts.

Examples abound. It was the liberal reform political economy of the Progressive Era, the period from approximately 1900 through 1917, that responded positively to the social settlement idea and that legitimated the first era of neighborhood organizing. While other types of neighborhood organizing existed in this period, it was the social work approach, best exemplified in the social settlements and the Cincinnati Social Unit Plan, which dominated the era.

In the depression era of the 1930s the social work approach had much less salience and support. As capitalism collapsed, as one reform solution after another failed to halt the economic depression, the political activist type of neighborhood organizing, most notably the radical efforts of the Communist Party in many cities and the urban populist work of Saul Alinsky in the Back of the Yards neighborhood in Chicago, personified grassroots activity. The hotly debated and precarious political economy of the era legitimated citizen action and political ferment at the grassroots level.

In the post-World War II era the conservative cold war economy stifled the political activist approach of the depression era and nurtured the neighborhood maintenance type of neighborhood organizing. Of course, homeowners' and property associations had been strong in the United States since the 1920s. The business of protecting property values was especially important in the United States, where homes were economic investments and where the lack of government protection and support for maintaining communities put the onus of neighborhood maintenance and development on property owners. The conservative eras of the 1920s and 1950s, however, tied this necessity for neighborhood associations to a reactionary politics. Segregationist goals became quite typical of neighborhood associations, interconnecting the protection of property values with a politics of neighborhood exclusion.

Of course the relationship between the national political economy and neighborhood organizing is not a one-way street where the dominant form of neighborhood organizing is *determined* by the national political economy of an era.[1] The historical process is much more complex, more of a dialectical interaction between the national political economy and grassroots resistances and initiatives. In the 1960s and the first part of the 1970s, when the political activist type of neighborhood organizing came to dominate again, the national political economy both produced the change and was the product of it. It was the grassroots resistance of the southern civil rights movement, the student New Left, and the rebellion in black urban slums that pushed the national political economy left, that expanded the political discourse to legitimate grassroots resistance, that demanded the passage of social policy to address the needs of the poor and people of color. The shift in political economy at the national level, expanded with LBJ's Great Society and War on Poverty programs, developed in response to these challenges. These legitimated further the political activist approach, so much so that a heyday of political activist neighborhood organizing continued well into and through the 1970s, causing some commentators to herald a "backyard revolution" in the making. It is this interpenetration between the national political economy and community organizing that comes across so vividly in the history of neighborhood efforts.

NEIGHBORHOOD ORGANIZING IN THE 1980s AND 1990s: CONTEXTUALIZING PRACTICE

The importance of the national, even global, political economy in shaping the nature of neighborhood organizing was especially evident in the 1980s and 1990s, in the increasing importance of CDCs and the widespread adoption by most neighborhood organizations of more moderate strategies.

In the 1980s, as we know all too well, the United States made a clear turn to rightwing politics at the national level. The twelve years of Reagan/Bush policy from 1981–1993 promoted a neoconservative agenda grounded in rightwing programs, policies, and political discourse. Responding to the heightened demands of an emerging global economy and the challenged status of U.S. corporations in it, neoconservatives sought to cut social costs. They went after labor unions, government programs, and claimant movements; they shifted even the limited political dialog about human needs completely to corporate needs; they delegitimized the public sector and public life and pushed people into increasingly private spheres and private conceptions of the good life.

In the neoconservative 1980s, the impact of national context on local organizing was enormous. While a wide variety of efforts continued, promoting democratic resistance and left insurgency, it was the neoconservative political economy that largely determined the direction of most community organizing during the decade, pushing them into community economic development and moderate strategies.

Community Economic Development

In general during the 1980s concern with broader social issues and social action receded. In the economic crisis of the past few decades, economic survival became the paramount issue for most individuals, organizations, businesses, and cities. As economic support for social services and solving social problems declined due to opposition at the federal level and shrinking tax bases at the local, and as political discourse in the nation revolved around free market solutions to *all* problems, neighborhood organizing efforts moved into the business of economic development (Peirce and Steinbach, 1990).

This trend is nowhere more evident than in the rapid growth and spread of community development corporations (CDCs) in the last 25 years. CDCs first sprang up in the 1960s, when they were tied to the civil rights and anti-poverty movements of the period, and were funded by a few foundations and Great Society programs. There were only about a 100 organizations in this first wave, but among them were such well-funded, significant efforts such as The Woodlawn Organization and the Bedford-Stuyvesant Restoration Corporation. For its multitude of important projects the Bed-Stuy CDC received about $4 million in federal support annually.

The second wave of community development organizations came in the 1970s, when the number of development projects increased tenfold. These were smaller efforts that began in opposition to urban renewal, redlining, factory closings, or the lack of tenant rights. For those involved in community economic development, most funds came from foundations, primarily The Ford Foundation, and federal sources, such as the Community Services Administration and the Office of Neighborhood Development. The idea of community economic development caught on in the Carter Administration, and by the late 1970s, CDCs, with all their virtues and drawbacks, were central components of the limited but significant, federally-assisted neighborhood development movement.

Beginning around 1980, however, CDCs found government support drastically cut. The new, third wave of CDCs that developed in the privatization campaigns of the Reagan years were forced into becoming much more businesslike than their predecessors. They had to exhibit "business talent and development skills once thought to be the exclusive province of the for-profit sector," as one report put it (Peirce and Steinbach, 1987, p. 30). The Community Services Administration and the Office of Neighborhood Development were dismantled. Other sources of federal funds were dramatically cut back. The bottom line for CDCs, as with seemingly everything else in the decade, was economic success. The primary goal, as Benjamin Marquez argued in an astute analysis of CDCs role, was to "correct the market's failure to provide jobs and services to the community." Added to this, for the CDCs in minority neighborhoods, was to help build a non-white middle class by developing highly specific and measurable development projects in which neighborhood people could work for their own economic betterment (Marquez, 1993). The new CDCs became less like community organizations and more like small businesses and investment projects, evaluated on their economic success. Most avoided political controversy, were dominated by professionals with a technical orientation, had narrow memberships bases, and rejected social action activity.

While market demands forced most CDCs to become so oriented to economic success that they were not able to sustain their work for community empowerment, they did not always give up on these goals by choice. They were forced into it. The absence of public support, newly rigid interpretations of IRS restrictions on political activity of nonprofit groups, the necessity of seeking funds from and joining in partnerships with private sector leaders, and the orientation of the CDC approach to economic investment and development decisions, all pushed CDCs away from politics and an analysis of power. "This lack of fiscal and political support," Marquez concluded, "has forced CDCs to accommodate themselves to rather than redirect the course of the free market."

Economic development has become a central issue for progressive organizing efforts that formerly spurned or discounted the strategy. Many older, prominent community organizing efforts now do community economic development, from ACORN to NPA (National People's Action) and IAF (Industrial Areas Foundation). To their credit, these political activist projects see community economic development as part of a much larger program of community work that also includes organizing, empowerment, advocacy, and social action. Still, community

economic development has become virtually synonymous with neighborhood organizing, as if organizing and empowerment were rooted in economic development issues, as if neighborhood struggles were always the same as community economic development, as if working in partnership with local banks and putting in "sweat equity" were the answers to urban poverty and housing shortages.

It has not quite worked out that way. "If the primary success story of the last 25 years has been the development of a legitimate, skilled nonprofit development sector with the proven capacity to create and preserve housing, jobs and businesses," Bill Traynor of the Community Training and Assistance Center in Boston summed up the problem, "the major failure has been the proliferation and dominance of a narrowly focused—technical—production related model of community development which is estranged from strong neighborhood control or direction and which does not impact the range of issues which affect poor neighborhoods" (Traynor, 1993, p. 4).

Moderate Strategies

Most activists promoting community economic development would probably defend their consensual approach as appropriate for the Reagan-Bush-Clinton years. To have a chance at community development, efforts must be in tune with capitalist economic development and have a working relationship with the powers that be in the public and private sector. Given the shift in the national political economy, organizers think they must now be more community economic development minded.

Neo-Alinsky organizer Shel Trapp saw a natural progression in his work. First, organizations defend the neighborhood; then they take an "offensive" stance. "That's when you start to link development with organizing," he argued (quoted in Katz, 1990, p. 49). Robert Rivera, an IAF organizer, put it similarly: "There are two types of organizing. One that is *for*, the other is *against*. Now you have to be *for* something. It's a different style of organizing" (Rivera, 1991).

But at play in the 1980s was more than a "life cycle" of organizing. Community economic development and building community partnerships with local economic and political elites became the dominant form of neighborhood organizing because of the demands and constraints of organizing in a neoconservative political economy. Organizers were willing to rewrite history (good organizing has always been *for* things) in an effort to distance themselves from the radicalism of the past, maintain current support, and legitimate their efforts in a context hostile to social action.

The changes that took place in community development corporations are emblematic of the way organizing responded to the conservative context of the '80s and '90s, but moderate strategies during that period were by no means limited to CDCs. Most neopopulist, political activist neighborhood organizing efforts during the 1980s and early 1990s adopted more moderate strategies, and a more moderated version of oppositional politics. Battle lines shifted. "To a surprising extent, claimed Newman and Williams, "the grass roots no longer 'fight the power.' They fight for a share of the power. Sometimes they win a sizable share . . . . [Sometimes they] team up with the established elite that they once derided and that once spurned them." (Newman and Williams, 1990, p. 12) Even National People's Action (NPA), criticized by some organizers as too confrontational, opposed being "out in the streets making symbolic statements, when you can be in the boardroom negotiating specific agreements that win for neighborhoods" (Trapp, 1992, p. 2).

Consider the evolution of the Industrial Areas Foundation, the direct descendant of Alinsky organizing, in these decades. IAF had organizing projects in New York, New Jersey, Maryland, Tennessee, Arizona, California, and Texas, but it was strongest in Texas. Throughout the state, in San Antonio, Houston, El Paso, Austin, Fort Worth, and in the Rio Grande Valley, IAF organizers and active members struggled for utility reform, improved public education, government accountability, healthcare for the indigent, and basic public services, including water

and sewers for the "colonias" (see Warren, Chapter 23, this volume). Most visibly they organized "get out the vote" efforts to promote bond packages to help IAF neighborhoods, held "accountability sessions" to keep politicians publicly in line with IAF objectives, encouraged voter registration, and worked to improve schools by halting the drop-out rate, stopping drug use and violence, and getting parents more involved. More quietly, in the day in and day out practice of community organizing they served as "schools of public life," empowering neighborhood residents by giving them "an opportunity to do something about things that [they] have been frustrated all their lives."[2]

IAF organizations do all this remarkably well, as many commentators have noted. Peter Applebome (1988) in the *New York Times* proposed that the IAF Network is "in ways large and small . . . changing politics in Texas." And Mary Beth Rogers, Chief of Staff to former Texas Governor Ann Richards, concluded in her study of Texas IAF that these "are virtually the *only* organizations in America that are enticing working poor people to participate in politics." (Rogers, 1990, p. 2).

While still following much of the Alinsky style of organizing, in the 1980s and 1990s IAF made some significant changes in their organizing method to meet the needs of new constituents and adapt to the demands of the conservative context. The major change in IAF organizing was a shift from a radical politics to a strategy of moderation. Where CDCs look for consensus, IAF groups focus on the importance of "standing for the whole."

Of course, many in power still see IAF as a radical protest group, and even during Alinsky's lifetime some IAF projects, such as The Woodlawn Organization, shifted from "conflict to coexistence." In the 1980s, however, this developed into an organizing credo. Now, IAF sought to organize "community sustainers" and "core moderates," especially women in mainline religious congregations and civic organizations. They wanted the civic volunteers who already work tirelessly for the PTA or church group—the folks, IAF said, who already protect the community and stand for the whole.

The strategy of moderation pushed IAF organizers to distance themselves from radicals and social movements. Whereas Alinsky took pride in being a radical, in the current IAF radicals are seen as alienated outsiders. "IAF now almost makes a fetish of its commitment to moderates," noted organizer trainer Mike Miller (Miller, 1992). He asked, "Will the next book be *Reveille for Moderates?*"

Standing for the whole seeks to legitimize grassroots organizing in the eyes of both the powerless and the powerful, both of whom IAF assumes, as do CDC proponents, to be fundamentally moderate in outlook. It seeks to create a working relationship between those with and without power in order to promote the interests of its members. In the 1980s confronting government officials became—according to IAF—less and less productive. Even when local government officials were sympathetic with the issues, they felt they did not have the resources to address them. So "standing for the whole" included developing working relationships with business and government leaders in order to further the goals of both IAF constituents and the larger community.[3]

The strategy of moderation, the commitment to moderates, the grounding of IAF efforts in mainstream religious institutions, and a definition of power which emphasizes building relationships led, however, to a politics which limited the parameters of IAF's work, and excluded alliances with other movement activists and organizations, as Mike Miller and others persuasively argued. It encouraged IAF to work alone with its constituency and mainstream allies, and to avoid confronting the harsh realities of power that continue to oppress their constituents.

The moderate strategy, for all its short-term gains, is fraught with traps. Most important, the emphasis on moderation and negotiation and a more interest group style of politics can change the role of the organizer. Standing for the whole moved some in IAF away from the Alinsky idea of the organizer being in the background, working his or her way out of a job, focusing on primarily developing community residents to lead the organization. The more IAF got involved in negotiating with government officials and corporate executives, the more some organizers came center stage to be the brokers and spokespersons for the organization. And the more the organizer became the broker, the more potential, as in all interest group organizing, to be both co-opted and, worse, ignored. Moderate strategy ultimately bargains away the tactic of radical protest. The American Medical Association and other powerful interest groups can afford to be moderate; the organizations of poor and working people must always fight for power.

NEIGHBORHOOD ORGANIZING TODAY

The responses of grassroots efforts to shifts in the national political economy always produce strategies that both replicate and challenge existing power relations. For all its obvious limitations, a focus on community economic development has built a broad base of real technical expertise and created innovative projects which in a limited way help meet the dire need for housing and in poor neighborhoods. The politics of moderation gives up on more radical change but it helps build the capacity for governance, gets advocates to the bargaining table, and wins modest victories.

Given the dramatic tensions and shifts occurring worldwide, both in the global economy and in national political struggles, we can expect in the near future to see the political economy encourage more of the same: continued proliferation and preference for grassroots efforts, continued focus on community economic development as global competition remains heated and as nation-states and corporate-elites persist in avoiding domestic social needs, and continued diverse strategies with most funding and support going to moderate approaches which are willing to work with business and government leaders.

Current events will likely continue to overwhelm such neighborhood efforts. It is much more difficult to be optimistic now about the prospects of neighborhood organizing than it was 20 or 25 years ago. It is no paradox neoconservatives call for neighborhood-based solutions and "empowerment" of citizens; they know well that these are less expensive strategies for problems that require costly national and global solutions *and* neighborhood-based initiatives. Without the existence of a social movement able to push the national political discourse left, win funding for social programs and redistributional policies, and struggle for state power, we can expect, at best, incremental change from the top and important but modest victories at the grassroots.

Whatever the context ahead, neighborhood organizing, even with its limits, will remain essential: as schools of democracy and progressive citizenship, as seeds of larger resistance efforts, as demonstrations of the persistence of public life in an increasingly private world, as the vehicles of struggle in which we win victories, develop skills, forge identity, and legitimate opposition, and as potential grassroots components of the next major social justice movement.

To play such roles, however, neighborhood organizing must both build on *and* go beyond the contemporary context. It must benefit from the new skills and strategies learned in the last 20 years *and* challenge the neoconservative political economy which heavily shapes organizing in the contemporary era. While the history of neighborhood organizing makes clear that national context is fundamental, it also instructs that conflict —ideological and direct action challenges— is essential to push the context, policies, and programs towards meeting basic human needs, implementing more democratic processes and promoting economic justice.

NOTES

1. There are other caveats to offer related to the typology of neighborhood organizing and the relationship between national and neighborhood efforts. For example, each type of neighborhood organizing is evident in all eras. It is not as though one ends and the other begins. For the past century there have been continuous efforts at building service delivery organization, radical opposition, and neighborhood protection associations. It is just that each period tends to produce a *dominant* form most appropriate to it. In addition, there is a good deal of overlapping of the types. Political activist organizations also deliver services. Service organizations also seek to maintain neighborhoods. Neighborhood maintenance often entails being very political and activist. Nevertheless, the essential points of this chapter remain: neighborhood organizing has a long history, this history reveals a highly varied politics, and the national political economy is critical to shaping a dominant form of neighborhood organizing in varied historical eras.

2. Ernesto Cortes quoted in Harry Boyte, *Commonwealth: A Return to Citizen Politics* (New York: Free Press, 1989), 191, endnote 21.

3. "Standing for the Whole," Industrial Areas Foundation statement, 1990; *Organizing for Texas Families and Congregations*, referenced in Pearl Ceasar, ed., "Texas IAF Network: Vision, Values, and Action," brochure published by Texas IAF Network, 1990, 13.

REFERENCES

Applebome, Peter. 1988. Changing Texas Politics at its Roots. *New York Times*, May 31.

Epstein, Barbara. 1990. Rethinking Social Movement Theory. *Socialist Review*, 90 (January–March): 35–66.

Fisher, Robert. 1994. *Let the People Decide*. New York: Twayne Publishers.

Fisher, Robert and Joseph Kling (eds.). 1993. *Mobilizing the Community: Local Politics in the Era ofthe Global City*, Newbury Park, CA: Sage.

Katz, Jeffrey. 1990. Neighborhood Politics: A Changing World. *Governing*.

Marquez, Benjamin. 1993. Mexican-American Community Development Corporations and the Limits of Directed Capitalism. *Economic Development Quarterly*. 7(3): 287–295.

Miller, Mike. 1992. Saul Alinsky and the Democratic Spirit. *Christianity and Crisis*. 52 (May 25). copy sent to author, no page numbers.

Newman, M. W. and Lillian Williams. 1990. People Power: Chicago's Real Clout. *Chicago Sun Times*, April 6, p 12.

Peirce, Neal and Carol Steinbach. 1987. *Corrective Capitalism: The Rise of America's Community Development Corporations*. New York: Ford Foundation.

Peirce, Neal and Carol Steinbach. 1990. *Enterprising Communities: Community-Based Development in America*. Washington, D.C.: Council for Community-Based Development.

Rivera, Robert. 1991. Lecture at the University of Houston. April 18.

Rogers, Mary Beth. 1990. *Cold Anger: A Story of Faith and Power Politics*. Denton: North Texas State University Press.

Trapp, Shel. 1992. Dynamics of Organizing. *Disclosure* (March–April).

Traynor, Bill. 1993. Community Development and Community Organizing. *Shelterforce*. (March/April).

CHAPTER 23

A Theology of Organizing

From Alinsky to the modern IAF

Mark Warren

On a winter's day in 1975 George Ozuna's grandmother asked him to accompany her shopping in downtown San Antonio.[1] The high school senior got his shoes and began the long walk from the Hispanic south side of town to Joske's Department Store, the largest retail establishment in the city. When the pair arrived, George immediately realized something was going on. Hundreds of Hispanic grandmothers, housewives and churchgoers had gathered outside the store. They entered en mass and began trying on clothes. And they didn't stop. They continued to try on clothes all day, grinding store operations to a halt. The protesters were all members of Catholic parishes active in Communities Organized for Public Service (COPS), a new organization fighting to improve conditions in San Antonio's impoverished and long neglected south and west side neighborhoods. While they disrupted business, COPS leaders and its organizer, Ernesto Cortes, Jr., met with the store's owner. They demanded that he use his influence on San Antonio's city council to pass COPS' $100 million budget proposal for infrastructural improvements and increased services to Mexican American neighborhoods.

The next day COPS supporters disrupted banking operations on a busy Friday afternoon at the central branch of Frost National Bank by continuously exchanging pennies for dollars and vice versa. Upstairs COPS leaders and organizer Cortes met with Tom Frost, Jr., one of the most influential men in San Antonio. The Joske Department Store manager had refused COPS' demand for assistance and now Frost, although polite, declined to call the mayor as well. Cortes, as the organizer, was supposed to let COPS leaders do the negotiating; but he watched them fold as Frost stalled.

As Cortes later recounted in a speech to farm workers, "My leaders freeze, and they don't do anything . . . I believe in the Iron Rule of organizing: never do anything for anybody that they can do for themselves. But they ain't doing for themselves! They're collapsing; they're folding. Our people are downstairs waiting with no instruction, no word and they don't know what to do. I decide I've got to do something, so I move my chair over to Mr. Frost, and he's got a blood vessel that's exposed, and I focus on it and I look at it. I just keep moving, he moves away, and I move closer with the chair. Then finally he says something, and I say, 'Mr. Frost, that's a bunch of balderdash. You're the most arrogant man I've ever met.' And he gets up. We have a priest there and Mr. Frost says, 'Father, you better teach your people some manners and some values.' And finally the priest says, 'Well, Mr. Frost, I don't know about that, but you know, you're apathetic and I think that's much worse.' "

Despite little initial success, COPS continued its protests and the tide began to turn. Prime time television crews started covering the actions, scaring away paying customers. Pressure mounted on business leaders. The head of the Chamber of Commerce came to negotiate with Cortes. But the organizer made him wait until COPS leaders could be rounded up to participate. COPS eventually won the city's commitment for $100 million worth of desperately needed improvements to its neighborhoods. For the first time, Mexican Americans had flexed their political muscle in San Antonio, and they gained new drainage projects, sidewalks, parks and libraries for their efforts.

Militant, direct action tactics geared towards winning put COPS squarely in the tradition started by Saul Alinsky and codified in his books *Rules for Radicals* and *Reveille for Radicals*. After his encounter with Cortes, the banker Tom Frost bought a case of these books and distributed them among the power elite of San Antonio so that they could better prepare to deal with COPS. COPS and the IAF are still known for these militant tactics. The casual observer who sees only these tactics, however, will miss the fundamental changes to Alinsky's way of organizing that Cortes began to make with his work in San Antonio. Twenty years after the tie-up at his bank, Frost, now an influential figure in Texas state politics as well, gave this author his last remaining copy of *Rules for Radicals*, claiming it was no longer relevant. According to Frost, "I told Ernie [Cortes] he's now working out of another book. And I asked him just what is that book? Ernie said he's still writing it."

Considered the "father of community organizing" Alinsky was the first to attempt to mobilize industrial workers and their families into direct action where they lived, as opposed to where they worked.[2] Although Alinsky's organizing projects scored impressive victories, most were short-lived or failed to maintain the progressive vision and participatory character upon which they were founded. Trained under the IAF in the early seventies, Cortes began organizing COPS using Alinsky's methods. Almost immediately, though, he began to revise Alinsky's approach. The modern IAF would come to base its local organizations in the institutions and values of faith communities. Its organizers would become a permanent feature of local affiliates using relational organizing to reach beyond pastors to foster the participation of lay leaders. And the IAF would come to link these leaders across racial lines, attempting to build broad-based organizations that would help ensure a commitment to the common good, rather than narrow group interests. While Alinsky took a rather utilitarian view of churches as repositories of

money and people to be mobilized, the modern IAF developed a close collaboration with people of faith, fusing religious traditions and power politics into a theology of organizing.

SAUL ALINSKY AND THE ORIGINS OF THE IAF

Saul Alinsky founded his first community organization, the Back of the Yards Neighborhood Council (BYNC), on Chicago's southwest side in 1939. Since that time, despite Alinsky's impressive achievements, and the significant legacy he left to American populist organizing, the local organizations he built largely failed to sustain themselves as participatory political institutions. By the early seventies, the IAF could count many individual successes, at least in the short run. But neither the local organizations it formed, nor the IAF itself, had found a way to establish long-lasting institutions that could sustain broad participation and an independent base of power for poor communities.

Upon Alinsky's death, Ed Chambers took over as director of the IAF, and began to make some significant changes to Alinsky's organizing approach. To stabilize the IAF's precarious financial situation, Chambers moved to extend contracts with community organizations after the initial two to three year start-up period. Chambers wanted to develop long-term relationships with local organizations, both to keep the flow of money into the IAF and also because he thought community organizations needed the kind of extended training that the IAF could provide. Chambers also systematized the training of organizers themselves and promoted the professionalization of the occupation by upgrading pay. While Alinsky liked to run a one-man show, Chambers set up a cabinet of senior organizers to provide collective supervision to the IAF's efforts.

Chambers put the IAF on a new road that held out the possibility of mutual interaction and collaboration between professional organizers on the one hand and community leaders from local organizations on the other. Although Chambers had the germ of these ideas in his head, the new model of organizing would be initiated in practice through the organizing work of Ernesto Cortes. Cortes began to organize Communities Organized for Public Service (COPS) in San Antonio. Through that effort, and in coordination with Chambers and IAF efforts in other parts of the country, Cortes began to write the new book on organizing to which the banker Tom Frost alluded.

COMMUNITIES ORGANIZED FOR PUBLIC SERVICE (COPS)

Ernesto Cortes, Jr. arrived back to his home town of San Antonio in 1973. His goal was to build an organization to give voice to poor and working Mexican Americans in San Antonio's forgotten west and south sides. Within a few short years he and a group of committed Catholic clergy and lay leaders had built a powerful organization that broke the Anglo elite's monopoly on political power in San Antonio. In the process, the modern IAF came to base its organizing work almost exclusively in religious congregations and to reach deeply into religious networks to build organizations based upon religious values as much as material interests. By doing so, the IAF began to build organizations meant to last and to maintain participation over time.

While Hispanics made up a majority of San Antonio's nearly one million residents by the early seventies, they were almost entirely excluded from political representation at city hall. The city displayed an old-fashioned colonial atmosphere, as the growing Hispanic community, reaching a majority of the city's population by 1970, remained a "sleeping giant" (Rogers, 1992). Cortes, however, thought the sleeping giant might be ready to wake up.

At first, Cortes followed Alinsky's methods and attempted to recruit to COPS a variety of neighborhood social organizations, including churches, PTAs and social clubs. About twenty-five Catholic parishes, however, soon emerged as the bedrock of COPS, while the other institutions proved too unstable or unsuited for the ensuing political conflict. The Catholic Church hier-

archy provided both funds and encouragement of pastoral support for COPS. As COPS became established, the largest part of its budget came from dues paid by member parishes, the funding principle followed by all IAF affiliates.

Support by the Archdiocese of San Antonio for COPS represented the culmination of several trends both in the larger Catholic Church and in the diocese of San Antonio. Vatican II heralded a greater openness in the church, encouraged lay participation, and pushed the church to address concerns for social justice and the plight of the poor. In many ways the diocese of San Antonio was ahead of these trends. In addition to the support of San Antonio's bishops, a movement of Hispanic clergy contributed to the development of COPS. Tapping the funds, legitimacy and institutional leaders from the Catholic Church conformed to traditional Alinsky methods. But in organizing COPS, Cortes began to make a profound innovation. He went beyond the priests and the usually male presidents of parish councils and began to reach more deeply into the networks of lay leaders that spread out from the church. He started with priests, got the names of potential supporters from them and moved through the community. He recruited leaders, now mostly women, from the ranks of parish councils, fund-raising committees, and church-goers who were active in PTAs and social clubs. These were people connected to parishes and rooted in the dense networks of extended families and friends that constituted San Antonio's Hispanic neighborhoods. Rather than activists committed to the cause, COPS leaders cared primarily about the needs of their families and the religion that bound them together.

Reflecting on the early years of COPS, Cortes explains that "we tried to bust the stereotypes . . . to see leaders not necessarily as someone who could speak or persuade a crowd. We wanted to see leaders as people who have networks, relationships with other people." These leaders were often women, and many of them were excited about the opportunities the new organization offered. Once Cortes found someone whom he thought had potential to be a COPS leader, he could be dogged in pursuit. He first met Beatrice Cortes (no relation) at a parents meeting about the closing of a neighborhood school. In 1981 Mrs. Cortes became COPS' fourth president.

In COPS the IAF began to develop a different strategy than Alinsky to recruit lay leaders, a strategy the IAF would come to call relational organizing. Rather than mobilize people around an issue, Cortes engaged people's value commitments to their community. He got community leaders to talk with each other about community needs first, before identifying an issue around which to act. Specific plans for action emerged out of conversations at the bottom, rather than issues identified by activists at the top. Relational organizing worked to bring community leaders together to find a common ground for action and to develop the capacity to act in the interests of the broader community. By reaching beyond institutional leaders, the IAF unleashed the deeper capacities of the communities within these churches. By continuing to recruit from these networks, the IAF generated a continual stream of new leaders to bring fresh energy and new ideas into local organizations.

To unleash the leadership capabilities of these women, however, the IAF needed to innovate again. The organization could not be led by a coalition of official representatives from member social institutions, as Alinsky's organizations had been run. Room had to be made for the leadership of the lay parishioners Cortes was recruiting, many of whom were women traditionally excluded from official church positions. As a result, COPS created a hybrid organizational form. Its members were institutions, that is, churches. But the organization was not a coalition, composed of institutional representatives. Its leadership was drawn more broadly from the membership of those institutions, and leaders operated together in a single organization. COPS' structure allowed member parishes and neighborhood leaders to take action for the needs of their own particular neighborhoods at the same time as the organization could also act with a single will, as something more than the sum of its parts.

COPS mobilized its strong church base to challenge the power monopoly of the Anglo elite. In these early battles for recognition, COPS acquired a reputation for pursuing militant and confrontational tactics. Because COPS leaders were embedded in social relationships, they could consistently provide large turn-outs of hundreds of Mexican Americans to these actions, something never accomplished before in San Antonio. The militant tactics proved successful, and COPS began to win important victories.

While mass mobilization provided one key source of COPS' power, the organization quickly began to see the importance of voter turn-out as well. In 1976 it allied with environmentalists to block the construction of a large shopping mall over the Edwards Aquifer, the city's only source of drinking water. By mobilizing their friends and neighbors, COPS leaders provided crucial votes to block the project and quickly became a force to reckon with on important public issues facing the city. With increased voting by Hispanics and sufficient support from Anglos and African Americans, Henry Cisneros won election in 1981 as the first Mexican American mayor of San Antonio since 1842 and the first Hispanic mayor of a large American city. Meanwhile, COPS expanded its role in determining city policy through its influence on the councilors elected from the five districts where it was concentrated.

During this period the IAF institutionalized what came to be known as "accountability sessions." As COPS mobilized supporters through its church base, candidates would face audiences of potential voters numbering in the hundreds, and sometimes thousands. After the meeting, COPS informed its supporters about the candidate's stand on the issues, thereby influencing the outcome of the election without a formal endorsement. If COPS had gained a public commitment from a successful candidate at an accountability night, the organization pressured the official to make good on that promise after the election. Once the IAF standardized this routine in COPS' electoral campaigns, it extended the format to all its large public actions in all its affiliates, whether the invited guest was a candidate for office, a current public official or a business leader.

City bonds came to represent another source of public funds for COPS' projects and, eventually, an important venue for building alliances. The state of Texas requires municipalities to hold elections for voters to approve the sale of city bonds. Bond elections became a way for COPS to build alliances with development oriented interests and city officials who wanted the city to fund capital projects. Since middle class voters in established neighborhoods often resist the tax implications of large bond campaigns, COPS could supply the inner city votes required to pass bond packages. In return, COPS got its share of these funds, as well as leverage for its other proposals.

The IAF's explicit emphasis on organization building helped COPS move from issue to issue. IAF organizers trained COPS leaders not to think primarily about the cause or the issue, but to consider whether that action would build the capacity of the organization. In this way, when an issue campaign was over, the organization could build upon the capacity generated in that campaign to begin to initiate another. There was yet another way that COPS' approach marked a clear change from at least some of Alinsky's projects and helped to sustain its participatory character. COPS did not administer the programs it campaigned for itself. COPS refused to accept any government money directly. Instead, COPS would allow public agencies to handle the administration, while its leaders carefully watched to make sure the programs went as planned. Rather than administration, COPS organizers and leaders remain focused on organizing.

COPS now had an organizing approach that proved powerful in gathering many kinds of resources for its neighborhoods. COPS combined careful research and planning by its leaders with large-scale mobilizations to public actions, and demonstrated its ability to turn out voters too when necessary to win its campaigns. By the organization's twentieth anniversary convention in 1994, COPS had channeled to its neighborhoods close to $1 billion from a wide variety of sources. Pragmatic and willing to compromise, COPS seldom made proposals beyond its political means, and consequently did not suffer many losses. But its most serious failures came when the organization, concerned that the needs of its constituents were being overlooked, attempted to oppose the plans of powerful developers—without proposing constructive projects of its own.

BRINGING VALUES AND INTERESTS TOGETHER

In 1976 Ernesto Cortes left San Antonio to begin an organizing project in the largely Mexican American community of East Los Angeles. He founded the United Neighborhoods Organization (UNO), which became a powerful community organization active in the IAF network to this day. In the past, under Alinsky's direction, the IAF would have left COPS leaders on their own to continue their efforts upon Cortes' departure. But this time, in keeping with the new emphasis placed by IAF director Ed Chambers on continuing a financial relationship between affiliates and the organizing staff, the IAF sent organizer Arnold Graf to San Antonio.

While continuing a contractual relationship between the IAF and its local organizations contributed to keeping the IAF itself financially viable, it had a much deeper significance. It placed local affiliates and IAF organizers in a long-term relationship, where each could be influenced by the other. IAF organizers would now be present to ensure that its local affiliates did not violate the network's broad principles. Continual influence by an organizer connected to the larger IAF network helped to broaden the outlook of local leaders and expand their capacity for action. Moreover, having organizers who were accountable to a larger authority, the IAF itself, for the development of new leaders, made it less likely that local affiliates could become dominated by a small group of entrenched officials, a problem that also plagued Alinsky's projects.

Through their long-term relationship with people of faith, IAF organizers became interested in religious traditions in a way that Alinsky never did. A self-interested motivation may have been sufficient for the kind of short-term campaigns that Alinsky's projects pursued. But the IAF wanted to build institutions that would last for the long term, not rise and fall around one issue. To sustain people's participation, something more than self-interest would be necessary.

The new women leaders of COPS, like Beatrice Cortes, demonstrated the viability of this new approach to organizing. The power and status that came with her election to its presidency may have given her extra drive. But leaders like Mrs. Cortes talked about their involvement in faith terms, as part of their religious responsibility to the community. Meanwhile, if religion helped motivate leaders to action, that political experience deepened and clarified religious commitment.

Contact with the priests in COPS and UNO reignited Ernesto Cortes' earlier interest in theology. Cortes was raised in the Catholic Church and had begun to study theology seriously in graduate school. There he read mostly Protestant theologians, like Reinhold Niebuhr, Paul Tillich, Karl Barth, Dietrich Bonhoefer and Harvey Cox. Cortes brought these theological concerns with him to IAF training in Chicago. But Ed Chambers was initially skeptical. An ex-seminarian himself, Chambers had been involved with the Catholic Worker movement in New York before allying with Alinsky. But he had adopted Alinsky's tough, secular brand of power politics. Nevertheless, now that he was at the helm of a weak IAF network, Chambers was open to considering Alinsky's limitations and trying new approaches. Chambers himself began to argue that political organizing should emerge from the intertwined values of family and religion (Rogers, 1992).

When Cortes moved to East Los Angeles to organize the United Neighborhoods Organization, he continued his effort to ground IAF organizing in religious traditions, and to confront the tensions that arose in combining practical politics with faith ideals. He found many religious traditions that spoke powerfully about the obligations of people of faith to intervene in public life. Cortes and UNO priests developed a workshop that drew upon the stories of Pentecost

and Sinai to strengthen lay leaders' commitment to the UNO effort. In the UNO context, these central events in people's religious traditions became symbols for the decision to draw from faith to take action to build a community. Over the course of the next twenty years, retelling stories from a largely Christian tradition and identifying potent symbols of community building became a central organizing tool for the IAF.

The ferment in Catholic social thought in the seventies motivated many priests and women from religious orders to get involved in the IAF. These women, including Sisters Christine Stephens, Maribeth Larkin, Pearl Caesar and others, became key organizers for the expanding Texas network. Catholic social thought emphasized that the root cause of evil lay in unjust economic and social institutions, and emphasized the responsibility of the church to work for social justice. Catholic teachings therefore provided a way to link religious responsibility with the self-interest of poor communities, precisely what IAF organizing came to be about (Chambers, 1978).

RELATIONAL ORGANIZING AND INSTITUTION BUILDING

IAF organizing in San Antonio built upon the strong social fabric of Hispanic Catholic communities and the viability of their parish institutions. But in East Los Angeles, the Hispanic communities were newer, more transient and more fragmented. Lay leaders in UNO did not have the kind of well-established and expansive social networks available to COPS leaders. The IAF could not simply mobilize existing networks, it had to build them as well. But this task was beyond the capacity of IAF organizers alone to accomplish. The IAF staff decided to try, for the first time, to train UNO leaders in relational organizing themselves. In other words, leaders learned how to conduct the individual, relationship-building meetings IAF organizers used to recruit leaders. UNO leaders began holding these meetings with each other, in order to deepen collective bonds, as well as with their fellow parishioners and neighbors, in order to forge broader support for the organization's efforts.

In addition to individual meetings, UNO leaders also began conducting house meetings, which then became a standard part of IAF organizing as well. Cesar Chavez had used house meetings to organize farm workers in California. The IAF realized such meetings could help bring disconnected community residents together to talk about common concerns and develop plans of action. House meetings and individual meetings became ways to strengthen community and undertake political action—and to link the two together for mutual benefit.

In the mid-seventies a group of Protestant ministers in Houston, impressed by the success of COPS, invited the IAF to organize in their city. The new Houston sponsoring committee convinced Cortes to return to Texas from East Los Angeles in 1978 to organize.

In the late seventies Houston was a boomtown. Business dominated the city from its founding, and Houston was still run by a small group of economic elites. Business was used to getting its way in a city that had no zoning laws, poorly funded public services and weak public institutions. But while much of Houston boomed in the seventies, a large part of its African American and rapidly growing Hispanic populations lived in poverty.

Organizing in Houston posed a different kind of challenge to the IAF than it had faced in San Antonio. There, COPS operated in a relatively compact geographic area containing a well-established Hispanic community with a common history. But Houston was a huge, sprawling city that lacked many clearly definable neighborhoods with shared histories. Houston's Hispanic community was much newer, dispersed around the city, and quite diverse, as it included many Central Americans as well as Mexican immigrants.

African Americans in Houston's fifth ward did form a historic community. But, unlike the parish priests on the Hispanic west and south sides of San Antonio who were largely uninvolved in politics prior to COPS, black ministers in the fifth ward were deeply intertwined with electoral politics. They regularly endorsed candidates, supplying the votes of their members in exchange for some resources to their community. Although these resources were perhaps rather meager, many ministers feared the loss of any desperately needed funds that might come if they disrupted electoral relationships by joining the nonpartisan IAF effort. The IAF had to convince these ministers to engage their faith traditions in a different kind of politics and in an untested organization. For many African American ministers, the IAF represented a gamble. Moreover, although many admired the IAF's achievements in COPS, they saw the organization as one committed primarily to Hispanics.

In Houston, though, the IAF effort did have one unusual source of strength in its efforts to build a base in the black community. Many African Americans had come to Houston from Louisiana and so were Catholics. With the strong backing of Houston's Bishop John Markovsky, the Houston IAF affiliate, The Metropolitan Organization (TMO) attracted several black Catholic churches along with Hispanic Catholics and Anglo Protestants. TMO made it a point to address concerns in the black community and began to have a number of small, but important victories in fighting high electric bills, improving public transportation and combating drugs in school. Eventually some black Protestant ministers saw the benefits of TMO to the black community and took the first steps towards involvement.

In Houston the IAF faced the problem that many of the individual religious institutions within TMO were weak. They had too few members, insufficient finances, and a small leadership base which often barely extended beyond the pastor and a few key church officials. Although the Texas economy boomed in the seventies, when the oil crisis hit in the early eighties, IAF organizing throughout the state had to confront the rapid deterioration of social institutions. For IAF organizing to succeed, it could not assume the existence of healthy base institutions. Although the IAF had always argued that political action would redound to the benefit of communities, it now had to pay closer attention to institution building within communities.

In response to these conditions, the IAF offered the services of its organizers for "parish development." The term reveals its Catholic roots, but was meant to apply to churches in all denominations. To accomplish these goals, IAF organizers used the network's relational organizing technique of conversation leading to action. Parish development processes helped to identify new leaders, build a consensus and forge collective leadership for the church.

Not all Catholics, however, accepted the IAF's challenge to engage the church in political action. The IAF effort in Houston nearly collapsed when a prominent group of wealthy and conservative Catholics opposed the church's involvement in TMO. Led by George Strake, later the chairman of the state Republican Party, the group tried to squash the IAF effort. Bishop Markovsky, however, held firm in his support and the effort continued.

At its height, TMO had sixty congregations representing about 75,000 families. Despite the gains made from parish development work, TMO struggled with Houston's sprawling size and weak neighborhoods. It simply could not achieve the kind of power and prominence that COPS had attained in San Antonio.

BUILDING BROAD-BASED ORGANIZATIONS

While the IAF experimented with multiracial and interfaith organizing in Houston, COPS was struggling to break out of the confines of the Hispanic west and south sides of San Antonio. In the late seventies the IAF began to look beyond the Hispanic west and south sides of San Antonio to build a base among African Americans concentrated on the city's east side. Conditions seemed ripe for organizing among African Americans. The predominantly black east side suffered from high levels of poverty and had, like the Hispanic west and south sides, been long neglected by the city government. Moreover, many black pastors were tremendously impressed by the accomplishments of COPS. In fact, they were jealous of growing Hispanic power. In their eyes, COPS was an organization that really worked to bring power to poor people of color, but it was all going to Mexican Americans.

Perhaps even more so than in Houston, however, African American Protestants in San Antonio were hesitant to become part of an IAF operation they saw as Hispanic and Catholic. African Americans constituted a relatively small share of the city's population, about 8 percent. Since COPS was so big and powerful, many black pastors feared they would be dominated by the Hispanic giant and that their concerns as African Americans would be ignored by the IAF. Many of these ministers hoped to build their own black church-based network instead. In order to give the black community more independence and autonomy within the IAF, the network decided to build a separate organization for San Antonio's African Americans, founding the East Side Alliance (ESA) in 1983. Although this tactic helped assuage the most immediate fears of African Americans that they would be dominated by the Hispanic COPS, the fundamental problem remained. In 1980, the IAF formed the Metropolitan Congregational Alliance (MCA) among mainly white, and to a lesser extent Hispanic, congregations on the north side. The IAF's theologically based organizing appealed to many clergy and lay leaders in these congregations, both Anglo as well as Hispanic, Protestant as well as Catholic. The religiously motivated MCA leaders, however, struggled to tap the self-interest of their relatively affluent congregants. To them, the IAF was for poor Hispanics.

Despite the obstacles each organization faced, MCA and ESA persisted and won victories on a number of issues. In the late eighties MCA and ESA merged into the Metro Alliance, making one stronger organization. Metro Alliance became a tri-racial organization, roughly one third each Anglo, Hispanic, and African American. Composed of Catholic, Methodist, Unitarian, Episcopalian, Lutheran and Baptist denominations throughout the east side and north side of San Antonio, Metro Alliance covered (albeit sparsely) the five city council districts outside of COPS areas. Without giving up its independence, the Metro Alliance gained the political muscle of COPS to make its efforts more successful.

The weaknesses of organizations formed separately by race and neighborhood in San Antonio, and the subsequent difficulties of uniting them, taught the Texas IAF an important lesson. From now on, the IAF would establish its Texas affiliates as what it called broad-based organizations. All organizations would now be metropolitan-wide and multiracial, as representative as the population as a whole.

CONCLUSION: A SYNERGY OF FAITH AND POLITICS

By the early eighties Cortes and the IAF had written a good part of that "new book" which revised Alinsky's model of organizing in a number of significant ways, allowing the IAF to build and sustain local organizations with broad participation in a growing number of cities across Texas. The new model served as the framework for the modern IAF's organizing efforts across the country and pushed community organizers in other networks to take faith, values and relational organizing seriously as well.

In San Antonio, Cortes began to reach beyond institutional leaders into the social fabric of the churches on the west and south sides of the city. He chose not to start with an issue around which to mobilize. Instead, he asked lay leaders to talk amongst themselves to identify their concerns and find a basis for cooperative action. By doing so, he unleashed the capacity of indigenous leaders, particularly women who were immersed in and often responsible for community life. These women cared about their families, their communities and their faith as much as about any particular issue. Where Alinsky emphasized self-interest, and saw his base religious institutions solely as repositories of hard resources like money and people, the IAF began to take faith traditions, and the relational strengths of women lay leaders, seriously.

IAF organizers began to talk about two kinds of power, unilateral and relational (Loomer, 1976). Unilateral power represents "power over" others, the kind of power Alinsky generated in his projects. But the new IAF sought to create relational power as well, that is, the "power to" act collectively together. While the faith/politics and values/interest combination proved powerful in founding and sustaining IAF organizations, it was not without its inherent tensions. Too strong an emphasis on faith and values led to idealism, and sometimes failures. Too much emphasis on interests and pragmatic politics, however, led to alliances with development interests that some found unappealing. Another kind of tension between faith and politics resulted in religious opposition to IAF organizing, as happened in Houston. Despite the tensions, the IAF was able to build a powerful synergy between faith and politics, and other community organizers around the country began to take notice. The Pacific Institute for Community Organizing (PICO), led by organizers trained in the Chicago Alinsky tradition, had built a number of organizations along the west coast that pursued issue-based and neighborhood organizing. Struggling with instability in their efforts and learning from the IAF experience, PICO adopted a faith-based organizing strategy in the eighties.

Through its organizing the IAF also began to establish an institutional structure to mitigate the kind of narrowness that plagued Alinsky's projects. A foundation of religious caring for the community gave IAF organizations stability, so that they could persist beyond one issue and build their capacity over time. Meanwhile, the IAF organizers, permanently attached to local organizations, served as a counterweight against domination by narrow groups of leaders. In addition, the IAF began to build organizations in Texas that reached beyond one constituency, whether by neighborhood or race. Broad-based organizations required leaders from any one community to broaden their perspectives as they attempted to cooperate with people from other traditions. By the nineties, the synergy of faith and politics that Ernie Cortes began to create in San Antonio in

1973 had thoroughly transformed Alinsky organizing.

NOTES

1. Sources for all accounts of events can be found in the full version of this chapter, Chapter 2 in *Dry Bones Rattling: Community Building to Revitalize America*. Princeton, NJ: Princeton University Press, 2001.
2. Discussion of Alinsky draws on S.D. Horwitz (1989) *Let Them Call Me Rebel*. New York: Alfred A. Knopf; F.P. Finks (1984) *The Radical Vision of Saul Alinsky*. New York: Paulist Press; R. Slayton, (1986) *Back of the Yards*. Chicago: University of Chicago Press; R.J. Bailey (1974) *Radicals in Urban Politics: The Alinsky Approach*. Chicago: University of Chicago; D.C. Reitzes and D.C. Reitzes (1987) *The Alinsky Legacy: Alive and Kicking*. Greenwich CT: JAI Press; N. Betten and M.J. Austin (1990) The conflict approach to community organizing in N. Betten and M.J. Austin (eds) *The Roots of Community Organizing, 1917–1939*. Philadelphia: Temple University Press; R. Risher (1984) *Let the People Decide: Neighborhood Organizing in America*. Boston: Twayne Publishers.

REFERENCES

Alinsky, Saul D. (1969) *Reveille for Radicals*. New York: Vintage.

Alinsky, Saul D. (1971) *Rules for Radicals*. New York: Random House.

Chambers, E. (1978) *Organizing for Family and Congregation*. Hyde Park, NY: Industrial Areas Foundation.

Loomer, B. (1976) Two conceptions of power. *Criterion* (Winter): 12–29.

Rogers, Mary Beth (1992) *Cold Anger: A Story of Faith and Power Politics*. Denton: University of North Texas State Press.

CHAPTER 24

Community Organizing

An ecological route to empowerment and power

Paul W. Speer and Joseph Hughey

In this chapter we describe the relationship between empowerment and power based on research in community organizing contexts. Specifically, we conceptualize empowerment as the manifestation of social power at individual, organizational, and community levels of analysis. Due to their explicit efforts at developing both individual empowerment and social power, we highlight the efforts of a national community organizing network.

A COMMUNITY ORGANIZING NETWORK

The examples of community organizing we describe are based on work of PICO, a national network of community organizations in cities across the United States. PICO was started in Oakland, CA, in 1972 as a neighborhood organization. (See Reitzes & Reitzes, 1987, for a history of PICO.) This network uses a pressure group approach and an institutional base drawing upon faith communities.

Community organizations that affiliate with this network use the PICO model of organizing and participate in its system of technical assistance. Affiliated organizations apply a set of organizing principles and practice a cycle of community organizing using congregations as their base. Technical assistance from PICO includes staff and leadership development composed of training conferences, on-site evaluations, leadership seminars for organization members, and staff monitoring and training. The PICO model is an organizing process; local activities of PICO organizations (i.e., organizing issues

and sustained campaigns) are generated locally.

In our research, we have observed the PICO organizing process and collected data qualitatively, through attending meetings, conducting in-depth interviews, observing leadership development training, reviewing documents, and participating in staff retreats. Beyond the PICO network, we participated in research with 14 separate community organizing efforts. These included other national organizing networks, organizing efforts targeting specific problems such as substance abuse prevention and crime prevention, community development corporations employing community organizing, neighborhood organizations, and independent grass-roots organizations. We chose to describe PICO because its methodology employs explicit organizing principles and a cycle of organizing through which both empowerment and social power are hypothesized to unfold. Our goal in this chapter is to reference the PICO network for descriptive rather than evaluative purposes. We believe these descriptions help demonstrate promising concepts for empowerment theory and for community development practice.

EMPOWERMENT, POWER, AND ORGANIZING

Power may be conceptualized as a multidimensional phenomenon. Of particular interest to community organizing are the instruments of social power. Three instruments of power are described by Gaventa

(1980) in his analysis of the oppressive use of power in Appalachian communities. The first instrument of power is manifested through superior bargaining resources that can be used to reward and punish various targets (Polsby, 1959). It is generally maintained that this dimension represents the popular and traditional understanding of power: those with the greatest resources, for example organized money or organized people (Alinsky, 1971), have the greatest power. The second instrument of power is the ability to construct barriers to participation or eliminate barriers to participation through setting agendas and defining issues (Bachrach & Baratz, 1962). By controlling the topics, timing of discussion, and range of discourse within a topic, those with relatively more power can effectively limit participation and inclusion of perspectives in public debate by the relatively powerless. The third instrument of power is a force that influences or shapes shared consciousness through myths, ideology, and control of information (Lukes, 1974), as in the notion that private enterprise is superior to governmental action.

Empowerment in community organizing may be conceptualized, then, as the ability of community organizations to reward or punish community targets, control what gets talked about in public debate, and shape how residents and public officials think about their community. From this standpoint, community organizations become empowered only when they have the capacity to exercise three instruments of social power. Before describing how these instruments are manifested at different levels of analysis, it is important to articulate empowerment principles and process utilized by this network of community organizations.

PRINCIPLES OF COMMUNITY ORGANIZING

Community organizing in the PICO network is guided by a set of organizing principles. Three principles are particularly important to the empowerment process practiced in this form of community organizing.

Empowerment Can Only Be Realized Through Organization

PICO views community functioning as the product of competing and complementary interactions by those with power—organizations—operating in their own self-interest. Thus, communities operate as a consequence of ever-changing sets of organizations who compete to enforce their self-interest and prevail with regard to various community issues. PICO organizations strive to become capable of competing adeptly in their communities on issues that fall within their organizational self-interests. This perspective draws on the organizing tradition of Alinsky (1971), who stated that social power comes in two forms: organized money or organized people. Similarly, Galbraith (1983), asserted that social power is accessed only through organization and that organizations hold power to the extent that members collectively pursue a common goal or purpose.

Social Power is Built on the Strength of Interpersonal Relationships

According to the PICO model, relationships based on shared values and emotional ties between individuals produce bonds that are more meaningful and sustainable than relationships based on rational or emotional reactions to community issues alone. This focus on relationship development is also supported in the literature (Alinsky, 1971; Pierce, 1984; Robinson & Hanna, 1994; Speer, Hughey, Gensheimer & Adams-Leavitt, 1995). In a case study of two pressure group community organizations, Speer et al. (1995) drew the distinction between relation-focused and issue-focused organizing. Although the two community organizations studied used a similar organizing process, one group emphasized issue development, and the other stressed relationship development. Members of the relation-focused group perceived their organization as more intimate and less controlling, reported more frequent interpersonal contact with community members, had greater levels of psychological empowerment, and demonstrated a greater degree of organizational power. Relation-focused organizing is particularly meaningful when considering the principle that empowerment comes only through organization. When people come together around an issue rather than relationships, the group is more likely to dissolve after the issue is addressed (Keddy, 2001). In contrast, relation-based organizing seeks to capitalize on the lasting power inherent in relationships (Robinson & Hanna, 1994).

Individual Empowerment Must Be Grounded in a Dialectic of Action and Reflection

Iterative cycles of action and reflection that unfold in the PICO network require individuals to act in community as part of an organization. Relationships among individuals built through action-reflection provide vehicles through which cognitive, emotional, and behavioral components of individual empowerment (Zimmerman, 2000) become manifest. Participation in a community organization provides experience that challenges individual cognitions of social power and provides a collective context through which emotional reaction to that power can be processed or reflected upon (Keddy, 2001). Moreover, organizational participation supplies a behavioral avenue through which an individual's cognitive insights and emotional responses can be acted upon. Elsewhere, Freire (1970) and Kieffer (1984) described this action-reflection process as "dynamic praxis." This principle comports with two concepts within empowerment theory: empowerment as an intrapsychic phenomenon and empowerment as a process cultivated by specific settings, that is, empowering organizations (Peterson & Zimmerman, 2004; Zimmerman, 2000).

THE CYCLE OF ORGANIZING

In the PICO network, these three principles of organizing anchor a cycle of organizing practice consisting of four interrelated phases: assessment, research, action, and reflection. (See Speer *et al.*, 1995, for a more complete description of this cycle of organizing.) Briefly stated, assessment is the process through which critical issues affecting a community are identified and defined by organizations. Assessment is conducted one-on-one; organizational members speak face-to-face with each other, usually in their homes, to gather information about community issues and to deepen relationships among community members. One-on-one conversations are intended to reconnect individuals and to facilitate dialogue and enhance relationships. The one-on-one process is the critical feature in the assessment phase and represents the manifestation of the principle that power flows through relationships. Issues identified through assessment focus the organization through the next three phases.

The research phase represents the mechanism through which participants examine causes and correlates of issues identified in the assessment phase. Information about the nature of the issue and its potential influences and solutions is gathered through organizational meetings with knowledgeable community entities. Key to the research process is uncovering the ways in which allocation of community resources affects a particular issue and how organizational entities or players exercise social power around an issue.

The action phase is a collective attempt to exercise social power developed through organization. Actions are public events that demonstrate organizational power. Organizations display social power by bringing together large numbers of disciplined community members along with media, public officials, and other organizations concerned with an issue. The action process entails both strategy development and organizational mobilization for collective action. Key to strategy development is examination of contradictions uncovered in the research process; typically, contradictions are apparent contrasts between the expressed values of powerful community entities and their actual practices, policies, or funding priorities. Following strategy development, members are mobilized to participate in collective actions directed toward specific community targets. The action phase culminates in meetings called "actions" that are held to display what is considered to be the social power of the community organization. The organization's power is directed toward a target in the community (e.g., city government, a financial institution) to extract a tangible and measurable shift in the flow of community resources.

Finally, in the reflection phase, members consider how their organizations evolved through the organizing cycle. Reflection entails exploration of the effectiveness of implemented strategies, discussion of lessons learned, identification of emerging leadership, consideration of how social power was demonstrated, and calculation of future directions for the organization.

Taken together, the three organizing principles, anchoring the four-phase cycle of organizing, form the basis through which this network of community organizations and the individuals that constitute them become empowered. Implications of this approach for community development practice are that: (1) empowerment is achieved only through organization; (2) organization is built on the strength of relationships among its members; and (3) relationships are developed as individuals act together and reflect on that action. Each of these principles becomes manifest through the cycle of assessment, research, action, and reflection. Although PICO holds that social power can only be developed at an organizational level of analysis, it understands that ultimately all collective effort is carried out by individuals.

THE MANIFESTATION OF SOCIAL POWER AT MULTIPLE LEVELS OF ANALYSIS

According to the PICO network, community organizations are empowered only when they have the capacity to exercise the instruments of social power. The process of developing social power and the outcomes associated with those efforts can be understood at individual, organizational, and community levels of analysis. Table 24.1 displays the conceptual representation of empowerment as discussed in this chapter and as we understand its application in the PICO network.

Empowerment at the Individual Level of Analysis

The manifestation of social power at an individual level of analysis is represented through the individual actions that contribute to developing an organization's social power (a process) and changes within individuals that result from working in an organization to develop social power (an outcome). As a process, individual empowerment is expressed through membership in an organization, relationship building with community members, and practice of an action-reflection dialectic through the organizing cycle. Empowerment outcomes at the individual level of analysis are products of cognitive, emotional, and behavioral changes in individuals resulting from the exercise of social power (Zimmerman, 2000).

Empowerment at the Organizational Level of Analysis

Based on the principle that power comes only through organization, the organizational level of analysis is the most critical for community organizations. Empowering organizations serve as contexts to develop individual empowerment whereas empowered organizations wield social power. PICO leverages this dynamic by stressing the reciprocal relationship between the empowering and empowered functions of organizations. Empowerment as an organizational-level process is enacted through multiple participatory niches for individuals, development of interorganizational relationships, and a sustained pattern of organizing actions.

Empowerment outcomes at the organizational level of analysis reflect the three instruments of power (Gaventa, 1980). First, the ability to reward and punish is accomplished through the numbers of participants an organization can mobilize. Second, social power is expressed through shaping topics

Table 24.1 Conceptualization of empowerment applied to the organizing domain

	Process	Outcome
Individual	Organizational membership Relationship building Action/reflection	Knowledge of power Emotional connectedness Organizational participation
Organizational	Participatory niches Inter-organizational relationships Organizational actions	Reward and punishment Define topics and extent of debate Shaping community ideologies
Community	Multisector development Institutional linkages Target community issues	Multiple empowered organizations Cross-sector collaborative efforts

Source: Model adapted from Zimmerman (2000).

for debate. One PICO organization shifted public dialogue from a focus on how best to use public resources for expansion of tourism to a focus on coordination of multiple community agencies and institutions address issues such as dangerous buildings and increased community policing. In the third dimension of power the organization seeks to reinterpret community activities and shape how communities collectively think about relevant issues. Often this is accomplished through other powerful entities within a community such as public or corporate officials and agencies that came to interpret issues from the perspective of the community organization. For example, another PICO organization explicitly attempted to change the perception of substance abuse from a law enforcement issue to a public health issue. After much effort, media stories reflecting this message began to appear. Subsequently, public health language emerged in quotes from the mayor and the chair of the city's task force on substance abuse.

Empowerment at the Community Level of Analysis

At the community level, the empowerment process is expressed through the following: multisector relational development, institutional linkages across sectors, and collective attention to common community issues. Empowerment outcomes at the community level of analysis are expressed in multiple empowered organizations within a community and collaboration across multiple sectors within a community.

AN ECOLOGICAL ANALYSIS OF COMMUNITY ORGANIZING

Four principles of ecology can be used to demonstrate individual empowerment and organizational power in community organizing (Kelly, 1987). We analyze examples of PICO organizing efforts using the ecological principles of interdependence, cycling of resources, adaptation, and succession.

Interdependence

Within community organizing, interdependence means that all persons and organizations within a community are connected and thus dependent on one another at individual, organizational, and community levels. Nevertheless, even within the religious congregations where PICO organizes, individuals are often out of relationship, and their network of relationships is thin. To rectify this and to build congregation-based organizations, interdependence at the individual level is bolstered through the one-on-one process. At the organizational level of analysis, interdependence is promoted through public research and action with other community organizations. Interdependence is demonstrated through power that is developed and expressed through organization-level relationships within which individuals are nested. To operate at the community level, individual congregations join forces with other organized congregations across a city or town to create the power necessary to move community-level issues. These federated organizations are fashioned out of the coinciding organizational interests of single congregations, thus interdependence.

In one example, 14 congregations developed a federated organization to pressure a city government, a parks commission, and a public school district to work together, rather than apart, to make the needs of inner-city youth their top priority. The 14 organizations decided to work through one cycle of assessment, research, action, and reflection. Working together to develop relationships and organizational power, about 40 leaders from the 14 single congregations gathered many times to assess their community efforts on youth issues, i.e., drug abuse, recreation, violence.

Through a research phase lasting over a year, the 14 congregations jointly conducted about 23 public research events designed to uncover the extent of available community resources and how they were controlled. Participants discovered that many swimming pools, gymnasiums, computer, and health facilities were withheld from children after school hours and during the summer months due to absence of a working relationship between the public schools, city government, and recreational institutions. From this phase, the federated congregations moved to the action phase. This phase was designed to stimulate interdependence among city, school, and recreation institutions where none had previously existed. Federated action events were organized by participants from each congregation. In one example, about 1,000 persons enacted a carefully scripted and disciplined event attended by public and private officials—the city's mayor, the school superintendent, various board members, the news media, leaders of civic and neighborhood groups, and contingents from each of the 14 congregations. The action consisted of testimony from adults and children who shared personal impacts resulting from the lack of resources for youth. Research conducted by organization members was also presented that documented resources controlled by separate institutions and the lack of functional relationships—

interdependence—among the institutions. The critical moment of the event was a call for specific, measurable steps to be taken by city government, the school district, and the parks commission. As a result, these three public entities agreed to sign a formal and public agreement to share resources. Sharing of resources, and thus the beginning of interdependence, began with appointment of high-ranking representatives from each institution to negotiate among themselves and with the congregations for eventual opening of school facilities for recreation and health care.

Cycling of Resources

A key element of organizing for power is changing the distribution or flow of resources within a community. Influencing this cycling of resources demonstrates the potency of an ecologically sensitive approach to empowerment and power. Cycling of resources comes into sharpest focus during the research and action phases in the cycle of organizing. In the research phase, participants attempt to identify community entities capable of altering undesirable community conditions. Participants attempt to discover what resources exist around an issue, what organization or institution controls resources capable of addressing a specific issue, and how resources such as money and property are transferred between organizations and institutions. Based on research phase findings, actions are organized to alter the distribution of resources.

For example, one congregation's organization uncovered a financial link between deteriorated housing owned by absentee landlords and a local social service agency. Research revealed payments from the agency to absentee landlords for housing newly resettled immigrants in exceptionally substandard housing. This flow of resources from the agency to absentee landlords supported poor living conditions for immigrants. In a research meeting, organization leaders asked the agency to use its financial leverage to force landlords into improvements of their deteriorated properties. The leaders were rebuffed. Next, the leaders dug deeper to uncover agency funding sources. Armed with this information, this one organization held an action event attended by about 500 community members. In the action, the organization made public the relationship between the agency and absentee landlords. The organization then presented information about the agency's funding sources and asked for a show of hands for those who would be willing to send letters to the agency's funders requesting termination of funding if the agency did not pressure its landlords to improve the properties. Specifically, the organization demanded specific properties in question be improved to comply with city building, fire, and health codes. The collective power of a hall full of raised hands in the presence of the media and many public and private officials produced the agency's capitulation on the spot. Using research and action based on understanding the cycling of resources, the organization's power was demonstrated through punishing the agency who funded these landlords and by shifting the debate from a focus on who funded the landlords to a focus on who funded the social service agency.

Adaptation

Kelly (1987) defined adaptation as "role changes the individual goes through to become a responsive member of the organization" (p. 14). Applied at the organization level, adaptation entails actions by organizations to fill available community niches or pry open new ones. PICO organizations create multiple and varied roles for individuals, behavioral niches, arranged in a horizontal fashion. As organizations move through the cycle of organizing, there is no fixed set of roles available for participants, e.g., president, secretary, or treasurer. The fixed number of available niches that elections typically entail limits development of individuals by locking them into a few relatively permanent roles, potentially constraining individual development. In contrast, the principle of adaptation recommends many roles including conducting one-on-one conversations with congregation and community members,

asking questions of public and private officials during meetings, arranging media coverage for the organization and its agenda, researching public records, contributing information to public records, leading public events, mobilizing organization members to attend an event, time-keeping for events, arranging venues for events, telephoning organization members, or arranging transportation. These roles are developed with the explicit intention of increasing the niche breadth of individual members and their organizations.

Another way to promote individual adaptation is rotation of roles among individuals. For example, one member may be exceptionally proficient at researching public records but shy about presenting information publicly. This individual might be encouraged by others to be a time keeper for a public meeting that would only necessitate him or her ringing a bell at a specified time to halt discussion. Later, during the reflection phase, the individual might examine the experience with the support of others, and he or she may be better prepared to step forward for a more visible public role.

At the organizational level, each local congregation seeks to expand its community habitat to become an active and powerful player in the community (Long, 1958). PICO organizations may move into an available niche that is avoided by other community organizations or institutions. For instance, organizations may pose questions to community institutions, say, a city government, that the institutions do not want asked or are unwilling to answer. One PICO organization publicly questioned the priority of expanding a city's convention center relative to developing a comprehensive approach to addressing the community's substance abuse problem. This shifted debate in the community, a demonstration of organizational power, but produced a negative reaction by other powerful players. Members of the community organization met with the highest public official in the county one week after publicly criticizing a proposed convention center expansion. This official told the group that he had recently met with the community's corporate elite and that this group was angered by such a public criticism. This official punctuated his message by pounding his fist on his desk and shouting, "Don't ever criticize this convention expansion again!" A member of the organization responded by pointing at this official and saying, "Don't tell us what to say!" Although the organization did not have the power to block the $100 million convention expansion (this was never an organizational aim), they were successful at occupying the role of publicly pressuring city, county, and corporate entities to increase money for substance-abuse treatment and prevention by $9 million, a niche other organizations avoided.

Succession

The principle of succession holds that environments change naturally over time; and while change benefits some populations, it is simultaneously detrimental to others. Furthermore, succession implies that resources discarded by some populations may be useful to others. Succession is manifested in community organizing in several ways. First, most communities involved in this network are poor, minority, urban communities. Over time issues confronting these communities are often the product of gradually deteriorating physical and social infrastructures that accompany the outflow of resources such as city services and people (e.g., Wallace, Fullilove, & Wallace, 1992). This succession benefits some but harms many of those who remain in a community. The remaining community residents, often viewed as discarded, represent the fundamental resources for organizing.

Organizationally, PICO works to take advantage of what Park (1936) called the "serial character" of succession through intentional rotation of roles among participants and organizations within federations to prevent entrenchment of individual leaders and organizations. Whereas rotation of roles has adaptive significance for individuals, succession implies that changes in roles within and between organizations can increase the vitality of the organization itself. When individuals or organizations stay in one role for a substantial period, their per-

spective on community functioning and organizational development can become calcified, leading to assuming a gatekeeper role which can discourage participation, thus limiting the extent to which the organization is capable of renewing itself.

At the community level, succession is manifested and can be leveraged by taking into account the shifting equilibrium in relationships over time between community organizations and their targets of actions. This aspect of succession is recognized in the notion that there are no permanent allies and no permanent enemies—a notion articulated by Alinsky (1971). This is an extension of Long's (1958) assertion that communities are the product of ever-changing sets of players who combine and recombine around issues within their organizational self-interest.

CONCLUSIONS

This chapter highlights issues useful to development of empowerment and power. We believe empowerment is a term that has been applied so broadly as to diminish its value and usefulness. To correct this, empowerment phenomena must be linked with social power. Often the phenomena described as empowerment are more closely related to self-efficacy, sense of achievement, personal adjustment, or similar constructs (Riger, 1993). As noted in definitions of empowerment (Peterson & Zimmerman, 2004; Swift & Levin, 1987), subjective feeling is an important aspect of empowerment; however, the dominance of conceiving empowerment in this light avoids linking it to power and social change. Within community organizing, power is posited as influencing communities not by intervening only at the individual level, but by influencing economic, social, educational, legal, and political systems, which, in turn, affect individuals. From the community organizing vantage point, the key implication for empowerment theory is that empowerment is an individual-level phenomenon whereas power is more appropriate for organization and community levels, drawing as it does on a better developed scholarly body of work (e.g., Lukes, 1974; Gaventa, 1980).

The second issue of importance to empowerment theory and community practice is the emphasis on a reciprocal or dialectical feature of the empowerment and power. For example, PICO's method stresses a dialectical process between individual development and organizational action. That is, interventions that attend to cultivating individual development in the context of exercising organizational power exemplify this empowerment and power, what New-brough (1992) termed "both psychology and community pursued at the same time" (p. 20). Similarly, Trickett (1994) argued that "it makes no sense to search for particular constellations of empowering qualities of people unless those qualities are linked to specific contexts in which they are effective in accomplishing specific empowerment goals" (p. 588).

Third, community development practice may be informed by the principles and cycle of organizing we highlighted. Activities that stress simultaneously building organization, cultivating relationships among members, and engaging in an action-reflection dialectic emerge as critical principles. Connecting community residents to share critical concerns (assessment), uncovering the allocation of community resources related to a community issue (research), mobilizing residents to act on contradictions between expressed values and actual practices (action), and consideration of lessons learned throughout the process (reflection) are specific steps for use in community development practice. Lastly, the methods we described develop individual empowerment and organizational power, and both are important to view ecologically. Ecological principles illuminate the relationship between empowerment and social power as well as the interplay between levels of analysis.

REFERENCES

Alinsky, Saul. *Rules for radicals*. New York: Random House, 1971.

Bachrach, Peter and Baratz, Morton S. "Two faces of power." *American Political Science Review* 56 (1962): 947–952.

Freire, Paulo. *Pedagogy for the oppressed*. New York: Herder and Herder, 1970.

Galbraith, John Kenneth. *The anatomy of power*. Boston, MA: Houghton Mifflin, 1983.

Gaventa, John. *Power and powerlessness: Quiescence and rebellion in an Appalachian Valley*. Urbana: University of Illinois Press, 1980.

Keddy, Jim. "Human dignity and grassroots leadership development." *Social Policy* 31 (2001): 48–55.

Kelly, James G. "An ecological paradigm: Defining mental Health Consultation as a preventive service." *Prevention in Human Services* 6 (1987): 1–35.

Kieffer, Charles H. "Citizen empowerment: A development perspective." *Prevention in Human Services* 3 (1984): 9–35.

Long, Norton E. "The local community as an ecology of games." *American Journal of Sociology* 64 (1958): 251–261.

Lukes, Steven. *Power: A radical view*. London: Macmillan, 1974.

Newbrough, John R. "Community psychology in the postmodern world." *Journal of Community Psychology* 20 (1992): 10–25.

Park, Robert Ezra. "Human ecology." *American Journal of Sociology* 17 (1936): 1–15.

Peterson, N. Andrew and Zimmerman, Marc A. "Beyond the individual: Toward a nomological network of organizational empowerment." *American Journal of Community Psychology* 34 (2004): 129–146.

Pierce, Gregory F. Augustine. *Activism that makes sense: Congregations and Community Organization*. Chicago, IL: ACTA Publications, 1984.

Polsby, Nelson W. "The sociology of community power: A reassessment." *Social Forces* 37 (1959): 232–236.

Rappaport, Julian. "Terms of empowerment/examples of prevention: Toward a theory for community psychology." *American Journal of Community Psychology* 15 (1987): 121–144.

Reitzes, Donald C. and Reitzes, Dietrich C. "The Alinsky legacy: Alive and kicking." In *Social movements, conflicts and change*, edited by L. Kriesberg. Greenwich, CT: JAI, 1987.

Riger, Stephanie. "What's wrong with empowerment." *American Journal of Community Psychology* 21 (1993): 279–292.

Robinson, Buddy and Hanna, Mark G. "Lessons for academics grassroots community organizing: A case study—the Industrial Areas Foundation." *Journal of Community Practice* 1 (1994): 63–94.

Speer, Paul. W., *et al.* "Organizing for power: A comparative case study." *Journal of Community Psychology* 23 (1995): 57–73.

Swift, Carolyn and Levin, Gloria. "Empowerment: An emerging mental health technology." *Journal of Primary Prevention* 8 (1987): 71–94.

Trickett, Edison J. "Human diversity and community psychology: Where ecology and empowerment meet." *American Journal of Community Psychology* 22 (1994): 583–592.

Wallace, Rodrick, *et al.* "Family systems and deurbanization: Implications for substance abuse." In

Substance abuse: A comprehensive textbook, edited by J. H. Lowinson, P. Ruiz, & R. B. Millman. Philadelphia, PA: Williams and Wilkins, 1992.

Zimmerman, Marc A. "Empowerment theory: Psycho-logical, organizational and community levels of analysis." In *Handbook of Community Psychology*, edited by J. Rappaport and E. Seidman. New York: Plenum Press, 2000.

CHAPTER 25

Community Building

Limitations and promise

Bill Traynor

Among the important shifts in the community development movement over the last decade has been the incorporation of "community building," practice, resulting in a more comprehensive approach to community renewal than has been practiced in the past and challenging community-based organizations such as CDCs to broaden their efforts and reconnect with residents. In the process these same organizations have been retooling and reexamining their relationship with, and role within, the communities they serve. Practitioners, funders, and policy experts in our field are exploring a broader approach to community redevelopment which includes an aggressive effort to redevelop the civic and social infrastructure alongside the physical infrastructure.

But this work has not proven easy to grasp or to practice well, and today it remains only sporadically resourced by foundations, in part because its impact is hard to measure. Moreover, most of the work that has been supported has been limited to encouraging CDCs and others to engage residents it *their* work—a supply-side strategy—popularized through the Comprehensive Community Initiative (CCI) era of the 90's. Rather than investing in building new community infrastructure so that residents can better connect with each other (an essential component of social capital development) the CCI era invested in large, well-established community-based organizations. Rather than investing in new thinking and practice, this era saw efforts to adapt traditional community organizing practice to a new setting. The result was "community organizing-lite," a largely undisciplined and under-resourced foray into community-building that raised more challenges than it was able to address.

Nonetheless, the lessons we have learned as a field during this time have been important ones, so while "community building" remains elusive as a movement per se, its potential as a field of practice continues to grow. This is critical as the conditions for community building, particularly in urban neighborhoods, continue to erode. A renewed commitment, coupled with new thinking and practice focused more on building a new demand environment in community is needed if this work is to have an impact.

WHAT EXACTLY IS COMMUNITY BUILDING?

Efforts to define the term "community building" have been a ritual part of nearly every conference on community building in the last decade. This ritual has illuminated different facets of our collective understanding, but has been unable to reveal a universally useful definition. Some of these definitions, posted on the National Community Building Network website are representative of the range of ideas embraced by "community building."

- "An ongoing process where members of a community share skills, talents, knowledge and experiences that strengthen or develop themselves and the community."
- "Continuous, self-renewing efforts by residents, community leaders and professionals engaged in collective action

aimed at problem solving and enrichment that results in improved lives and greater equity and produces new or strengthened institutions, organizations, relationships, and new standards and expectations for life in community."

- "Community building has come to refer to a variety of intentional efforts to (a) organize and strengthen social connections or (b) build common values that promote collective goals (or both)."

For the purposes of the community development field, it has been possible (and some may feel enough) to define community building in reference to a number of important shifts in the *practice* of community development, mostly in response to changing conditions that practitioners and supporters of community development were experiencing. Some of these conditions were external; wholesale demographic shifts driven by new waves of newcomer populations, the need to create more complex community development strategies for both hot market environments and chronically soft markets, and the shrinking of federal and state commitments to urban redevelopment to name a few. Other conditions were attributable to the development of the community development industry itself which had drifted for two decades toward a concentration on affordable housing production as the principal strategy for community renewal at the expense, some thought, of more comprehensive approaches. The "community building" response was varied but included:

- A shift toward more comprehensive approaches to community development that involve a wide range of non-bricks and mortar activities. Also, a perspective that recognizes the multiple linkages between housing and economic development and the wide range of efforts that the Local Initiatives Support Corporation (LISC) has referred to as "social development."
- A heavier emphasis on community organizing as a strategy for identifying and developing community leaders and shaping the kinds of local issues that affect the progress of the community renewal effort.
- A renewed emphasis on community planning, and the development of a community building plan, as a prerequisite to development activities.
- A more intensive effort to include and involve neighborhood residents in the organization, planning, and implementation of community renewal efforts. This stems from a recognition that when residents have a stake in making positive change, the change is likely to be more long-lasting.
- More emphasis on making sure there are clear lines of accountability between the CBO and the community that it represents.
- More interest in developing collaborative relationships among CBOs and achieving a continuum of support at the neighborhood level.

Community building seen in this way—as a set of activities complementing or enhancing an affordable housing or economic development agenda—has now been widely practiced by many CBOs over the past decade and with mixed success.

More recently, community building is emerging in a different light—being seen as an important (some would say essential) activity which stands on its own as a field of practice. Today, there is a growing recognition by practitioners that there is a fundamental condition that consistently undercuts all our efforts to rebuild struggling communities—chronic disengagement. In many communities, civic life—from the city council chambers to the block club meeting room—can be a hostile environment for the average person, ruled by cynicism and division, and dominated by entrenched habits of isolation and detachment. Exploring the sources of this disengagement could be a whole separate article. It is enough to say that *a community needs a functional civic infrastructure in order to shape and sustain physical and economic development of any kind*, whether implemented by non-profits, private developers or the public sector. This is particularly true of urban areas that have now experienced four or five decades of decline, combined with historic demographic shifts from "old timer" to newcomer populations. The degradation of the civic habits and institutions that supported public life in these places has been dramatic if not complete. Those habits and institutions have not been rebuilt to either accommodate these new populations or to address the mobility and diversity of city life in the 21st century.

The unique hallmark of community development is that—in the information age and the global economy—it remains steadfastly place-based. Place—we would maintain—is still important, especially for those who cannot afford to purchase another place when this one gets too run down. But our field is engineered to build the physical things place-based communities need—the new homes, community centers, small businesses, and increasingly to engage residents in those efforts. We have not been engineered—or resourced—to build the infrastructure of relationships and conditions needed to re-weave a strong community fabric in place; that is, connecting people to each other and removing the barriers to engagement in public life. The fact is that as powerful and effective as community building and community organizing efforts have been over past decades, we have never really embraced the possibility that our principal challenge now, may be nothing short of *creating newly functional civic environments* and finding a way to re-populate public life in our cities.

In this context, "community building" in its most ambitious form, is increasingly being seen as the process of creating a newly functioning public sphere that attracts and engages more than the miniscule fraction of residents whose voices are typically heard. Simply reforming the practice of CDCs and others to expand programming or engage residents in their work will not meet the real challenges of community building. Rather, the challenge of community building moving forward is to find ways to shape a new environment that holds a myriad of opportunities for people to step back into public life in a way that feels safe, fun and productive. This will require new thinking

and new practice and a willingness to work on both the supply side of the problem as well as the demand side.

SUPPLY SIDE COMMUNITY BUILDING: REFORMING THE DELIVERY SYSTEM

For the most part, community building emerged in the early 90's as a supply side strategy, fostered first by foundations and others frustrated with the pace of change represented by the "bricks and mortar" CDC approach. Their goal? To use the same delivery system that was created to deliver bricks and mortar to deliver "community building"—essentially to reform the supply-side institutions to be more engaged and responsive to residents.

Many of the earliest CDCs, born from community organizing and driven by a local constituency, routinely packaged efforts like youth development, community organizing, and adult education with their real estate development work. For many years, however, biases among funders of community efforts, and among community development practitioners themselves, toward a housing production agenda made sustaining these broad, activist approaches extremely difficult. Eventually, by the early 80's, the CDC movement became synonymous with affordable housing development. At best, the major funders of CDCs viewed community building work as ancillary to the principal real estate development work of the CDC. Alternatively, the few dollars available for community organizing flowed toward so-called "pure" organizing groups. Despite the paucity of interest and funding, a small minority of CDCs continued to mount broad efforts.

Attitudes shifted in the 90's and community building practices emerged into the mainstream of the CDC movement. Most major national foundations, and many regional and community foundations, sponsored their own versions of Comprehensive Community Building initiatives (CCIs), experiments in the fusion of community building practice and community development. Technical assistance organizations, consultants, and intermediary groups also got involved in this work in large numbers. In addition, a number of national alliances formed to support this work. Most notable of these was the National Community Building Network (NCBN), an alliance of funders of "locally driven urban initiatives" formed in 1993 to influence public policy and provide forums to discuss community building initiatives, and the Aspen Institute's Roundtable on Comprehensive Community Revitalization.

The "CCI era," driven by funding from powerful foundations such as Annie E. Casey, Ford, Rockefeller, Edna McConnell Clark and others, touched most of the major metropolitan areas of the country at one time or another in the decade of the 90s. Though these initiatives differed in many ways, the essential premise was the same: provide multi-year funding and technical support to existing CBOs to take on the challenge of comprehensive community change. And these initiatives saw some success in reforming CBOs to take on new work. A 25-year-old CDC in Boston retools to conduct a resident-driven planning process for the first time in 2 decades. A Denver organization expands its work to major efforts in community organizing and cultural development. A Washington, DC, development corporation fields a team of four community organizers to build resident leaders and shape a community agenda. A St. Paul economic development group begins a major youth leadership effort.

It may be fair to say that in the mid to late 90's funders and policy people were far more exuberant and clear about the potential for community building than the practitioners— the staff and leaders of the CBOs who were called on to carry out this work. The CCI era was decidedly "funder driven" and in fact many of the foundations which sponsored CCI's were shifting their practice as well, as Foundation staff were getting intensively involved in the operations of the initiative. For CBOs, this shift by funders to the CCI approach came after years of accumulating a real estate development portfolio, and at a time when organizations were embattled by budget cuts and worsening local conditions. Moreover, for the previous decade, CBO Executive Directors and Board Leaders had built their organizational capacity around a funding environment that really only valued a narrow real estate production-oriented agenda. The rules were changing and there were few organizations with the energy and capacity to take on the kind of organizational challenges which this work posed.

But with some early successes, an encouraging funder environment and a growing awareness of the need to change, many CBOs took on the challenge of significantly broadening the scope of their work. They participated in these efforts for a wide variety of reasons. Many saw it as a source of core operating support or "soft" program money that they could use as flexible revenue to fill gaps in staffing. Some CDCs, recognizing that the future would hold fewer housing resources, were searching for another important role to play in the community. Others, recognizing the limitations of real estate-based strategies, were trying to address the "human development" needs of their residents. Still others, who have gotten away from or never developed the ability to organize and mobilize their constituency, felt the need to develop more political clout in an age of dwindling resources.

RETOOLING THE CBO; LIMITS AND CHALLENGES

Through the CCI era, practitioners and funders alike learned a great deal about the challenges of transforming CBOs to take on a robust community building approach. It turns out that building and integrating the core capacities required by successful community building efforts is not as simple as adding another program or product. Rather, these changes often demand a fundamental redefinition of the organization and its relationship to the community it serves.

Because many of the groups participating in community building initiatives principally work in real estate development, they sometimes have a difficult time adapting to community building approaches. Their real estate work tends to be structured, disciplined, and outcome oriented. Yet, curiously, this same level of discipline and structure often does not extend to the newer work. First, community-based groups remain preoccupied with a real estate development agenda, which is still viewed as the bread and butter of the organization. Second, a strong bias remains, reflected in the labeling of real estate related work as "hard" and non-real estate related work as "soft." Soft work is viewed as work that is hard to define, can be accomplished in the margins, and that just about anyone can do. These efforts are often taken on with a lower level of expectations, a measure of ambivalence, and/or a lack of clarity by the organization's leadership.

More troubling for some CBOs, the CCI-sponsored community building program could be like a Trojan Horse, arriving as a promising source of flexible operating support but causing some unintended and unanticipated consequences for the organization, its board, and its executive director. Community building strategies focused on "building resident engagement" or "developing the residents' voice in decision-making," if they had any success, put pressure on the CBO to listen, be responsive, and open up its decision-making apparatus to new voices. At a fundamental level, new habits of sharing power and influence are called for and unless the CBO is prepared to change in this way, tensions inevitably result.

Unfortunately, many of these community building projects were ill-defined at the point of funding. Early efforts tended to be loosely organized with little quality control. Because the quality and outcomes of this work can be more difficult to measure than, for instance, housing production, it can be difficult to distinguish between excellence and mediocrity, between a group that is going through the motions and a group with real ambition. Developing strong enough body of best practice or industry standards for this work, from which to easily separate the high quality performers from the rest of the field, has thus far been elusive. CBOs and funders alike continue to grasp for ways to define excellence in practice and success.

THE EMERGENCE OF "COMMUNITY ORGANIZING-LITE"

Ultimately, the principal community building tool of the CCI era has been a weak derivative of the traditional Alinsky style of community organizing, sometimes referred to as "*community organizing-lite.*" Bonifide Alinsky-legacy organizers don't recognize this practice as "organizing" and are loathe to consider the "community builders" of the CCI era as "organizers" at all. And its true that depending on the circumstances, organizing-lite can veer wildly and easily into advocacy, social services, and civic engagement work or even more hard-to-define forms of "soft" community work. Suffice to say that because the practice was built as a "supply side" intervention—to connect existing groups to the community—the quality and the approaches that have been used are as different as the intentions of the host organizations.

In the CCI era, "community organizers" embedded in CDCs and other non "organizing-only" CBOs often complained of a lack of support and direction from their boards or staff supervisors. When new organizers were brought into the organization, they rarely had the support and guidance they need to succeed. In many cases there was no culture of organizing in the CBO, and the executive director was not oriented enough to the work to provide adequate support to the organizer. Sometimes, because of past history, key staff or board members were skeptical or fearful of community organizing. By and large the community organizing strategy was not sufficiently clear or well understood. Under these conditions, the organizer's work inevitably becomes more and more disjointed. The organizer becomes seen as a kind of utility outreach/event specialist whose job is to service the other "line staff" in the organization. This situation can be extremely frustrating for the organizer. It was not unusual, in many of the CCI's to see 2–3 "organizers" come and go in a year or two. Minimally, the new organizer is under-utilized and the community building effort suffers.

If the organizer is dynamic and successful, despite a lack of organizational support and direction, the situation can become even more hazardous. In some cases, organizers successfully built new constituencies (task forces, committees, etc.) among residents, only to then meet resistance as they attempted to integrate these new people into the organization. The new constituents inevitably challenge the existing leadership seeking a role in redefining the organization or shifting its programmatic emphasis. The friction that this dynamic causes between the CBO and emerging groups of resident leaders can ultimately be productive, but, if handled haphazardly, it could also be very damaging to the CBO and the community renewal effort.

The limitations of grafting community building onto a complex and fast moving community development agenda, and the ineffectuality of "community-organizing lite" thinking and practice both proved daunting and have led to questions about whether the impact has been worth the investment. In the CCI era, even the best organizer supported by the best CBO had trouble breaking through the levels of disinterest, distrust and disenfranchisement that they found in many urban neighborhoods. Ultimately, these community builders were practicing a set of approaches developed at another time, for another reason, on behalf of community institutions that, for the most part, were at least ambivalent about the role and purpose of community building.

BUILDING COMMUNITY IN PLACE: RETHINKING OUR VIEW AND PRACTICE

An effective approach requires a clear view of the problem, and our principal failure as community builders over the last decade is that we have not fully come to terms with the depth and breadth of the problem. Most community building efforts, even those that have recognized the importance of rebuilding civic infrastructure, have launched strategies that assume a level of civic functioning—however basic—that simply does not exist.

Even community organizing approaches, whose goal is to effect forms of "collective action" and representative democracy, depend on some functional level of community infrastructure that is hard to come by. That is not to say that there aren't highly motivated and functional community members at work, or that there aren't functional institutions at work at the community level. But a disconnected array of individuals and institutions—even if you can manage to periodically, and with great effort, marshal episodes of collective action and get "representative" voices on your board or task force—does not necessarily constitute a functional community.

COMMUNITY ORGANIZING IS NOT COMMUNITY BUILDING

A major lesson of the CCI Era is that community organizing, "lite" or not, is probably not the right tool for the job of rebuilding community. Community organizing—at least the Alinsky-legacy form that is the most widely practiced and upon which organizing-lite practice has been loosely based—is a specific, tactical and highly structured approach to power building and to confronting entrenched interests. It is fundamentally a *political form* which trades on ideological and didactic notions of connectivity, affiliation and belonging designed to recruit and mobilize a small subset of the population. It is a form that was shaped by the ideological warfare of political parties and the labor movement in the beginning of the last century and further shaped and molded by the cold war and then later on by the civil rights movement. Today, the modern version of the best of Alinsky-legacy organizing has rooted itself in faith-based institutions with "faith" serving as a proxy for weakened political and class-based ideology. Nonetheless, the paradigm of "belonging" in these groups—whether fueled by faith or political ideology—calls for levels of commitment, loyalty, time and belligerence that have never been for everyone and increasingly stand out as in-organic to the experience of most people.

This in-organic quality of Alinsky-legacy organizing is not, as some claim, due solely to the call to confrontation—which is admittedly a difficult leap for many people and an extraordinary leap for most CDCs. More troublesome for community building purposes, is that the processes and habits that we are left with, even in a barely derivative organizing-lite approach, are still highly structured and mostly tactical. The practice focuses on winnowing "leaders" from the pack, claiming those leaders as its own, engaging those leaders in fairly narrow and formal leadership roles, and encasing those leaders in rigid and ideological structures which are at least partly designed to give the institution legitimacy. Some elements of this, such as formal, semi-permanent leadership roles, rigid and hierarchical "committee" structures, and the perpetuation of leadership styles focused on "speaking for the group" or "leading the meeting" are today, simply habits of organization that are artifacts of a political organizing form.

The in-organic quality of community organizing puts it in alignment with a range of other community and political institutions whose "habits of organization" fail to resonate today. In fact, data shows that over the past few decades, people of all classes and races are fleeing structured, high affiliation-level organizations of all kinds in great numbers. In their place, demonstrated by recent internet-based *communities-of-connection* type movements, buttressed by a genuine information-technology revolution, is a new 21st century paradigm for belonging; one that has *market* rather than *political* roots. In this new market paradigm, ideology is replaced by value, and loyalty is trumped by choice. The "member" of the new millennium wants to be connected but not obliged; to be part of many, and owned by none, and to be surgical in his commitment of resources and time. Low-level affiliation (more akin to "club" membership than to vanguard membership), flexibility, provisionality and informality are the hallmarks of the new membership organization. In these groups, the evidence is not that people are getting involved less, but that they are getting involved in a different way.

A new form of organizing is needed which understands and capitalizes these changes in the nature of affiliation and which is explicitly designed to meet the challenges of building community infrastructure in place—still a critical environment for community for those who choose, or who are stuck in, struggling urban areas. In the community development world we are not building community in the ether—we are building it in specific places, presumably places where the presence of "community" is lacking and could be helpful if it were built. In today's urban areas, marked by density, diversity, persistent poverty, ambiguous economic prospects and public institutions (like schools) suffering from a paralyzing level of dysfunction, it could be argued that effective community building that leads to a robust community infrastructure is the *only* pre-condition that can possibly impact these conditions. It also happens that it is the only pre-condition that those who live and work in these areas can take an active role in changing. In a global economy where places are connected only indirectly to the sweet spots of economic growth, a highly functional, efficient and active civic environment may be the most important competitive economic advantage of the age for those who are most dependent on place for opportunity. This new community organizing approach has to aspire—not just to getting poor people represented in the supply side—or to yielding episodic moments of collective action, but to building a functional civic infrastructure that optimizes the aggregate contribution of all residents and stakeholders toward making that place work. In short, to building a "demand environment" for economic development and a functional civic sphere.

AN ALTERNATIVE APPROACH—BUILDING THE "DEMAND SIDE" OF COMMUNITY ENGAGEMENT

At the cellular level, place-based "community" starts with a single relationship of trust and mutual benefit that one resident or stakeholder shares with another. It is the aggregate of those relationships, along with the loose connections that bind a diversity of them together, that forms the *structural framework for community*. But, it is the cumulative capacities for collective decision-making, problem solving, mutual support, collective action, information sharing, and most importantly, the creation and exchange of value (time, goods, services)—which this infrastructure facilitates—that is ultimately "community."

The fact is, at the cellular level, there are far fewer peer-to-peer connections now than in the past. There are far fewer organically grown institutions that are helping these peer-to-peer connections form. And there are even fewer efforts explicitly designed to build the loose connections that help to weave those peer-to-peer connections into a productive community fabric. In short, the "demand-side" of community change and community development—the extent to which the aggregate actions and voices of people are driving change in community—has been severely fractured and decimated over the decades. Fewer voices, fewer different voices, sporadic action, and the inability to generate genuine representative samples of both, constitute a market failure in the classic sense. Where there is no demand there can be no reasonable gauge of value. Where there is no reasonable gauge of value, there can be no effective supply or efficiency in delivery. In this environment, attempts by foundations, intermediaries, many CBOs and many municipal governments to improve the quality of life for poor and struggling families are a veritable "shot in the dark." Colored by decades of failed attempts at reform, it is no wonder that cynicism and distrust among residents for these well-meaning institutional interventions continue to be pervasive.

To effectively attack the challenges of building genuine community, radically new thinking and practice are needed, starting with an acknowledgment that there is no short cut to reaping the aggregate benefits of community without an aggressive investment in building genuine community at the cellular level. At a minimum this means investing in opportunities and space for peer-to-peer

connections, allowing for new forms of community institutions to emerge based on more organic habits of connection and affiliation, and resourcing the information infrastructure—literally the roads and rails of opportunity today—that even the poorest residents need to get connected to civic and economic life. In short, this requires new efforts aimed at developing the "demand-side" of community, guided by a different paradigm of community and community building—one that sees community as a marketplace and community building as a market making strategy.

COMMUNITY BUILDING AS A POPULIST ECONOMIC MOVEMENT, NOT A POLITICAL MOVEMENT

Viewing community as a latent marketplace of potential relationships and opportunities, governed, as marketplaces will be, by the availability of value and choice is a helpful starting place to develop new thinking and practice. In this way, community building can be attacked as a process of *popular economic mobilization* rather than as a vanguard political movement. There are those, myself included, who see the formation of strong communities as a political act in an economic and political environment that would rather not hear from or respond to poor people, people of color and their communities. But for those who are doing the hard, day-to-day community building work of meeting neighbors, getting involved in schools, building block clubs, or organizing clean-ups, it is a more simple matter of trying to *maximize the value of place for themselves and their families*. Our concern should be helping to support residents in this process as well as helping remove the barriers to this pursuit.

But this will not be easy. In today's urban communities, this process—the process of "getting involved" is, for the most part, difficult, boring, nonproductive and often scary, especially for newcomer populations. An environment marked by these characteristics is the last place any of us would want to spend time, so it's not surprising that most people don't and won't. *Community building* needs to focus on changing this experience, by re-shaping the fundamental interface for thousands of people—in a given place—to meet other people, build relationships of value, participate in civic life, and pursue individual and family economic goals. Simply put, community building has to build *habits of engagement* to replace the deeply embedded *habits of detachment* that dominate place.

THE NETWORK ORGANIZING FORM; ADVANTAGES FOR COMMUNITY BUILDING

Community as a marketplace does not require thousands to act in consort through carefully orchestrated episodes of collective action—the community organizing lite approach—it only requires that the net aggregate, cumulative impact of their actions and decisions lead to a functional and accountable civic sphere—which includes opportunities to act collectively. But how to create an environment that actually encourages civic engagement? Some activists, like myself, who have been struggling with how to shape a strategy designed to shape a new place-based environment have turned to network theory for direction.

A network is best understood as *an environment of connectivity* rather than an organization in the traditional sense. At its best, it is an environment that is *value*-driven and self-generating, where control and decision-making are dispersed and where "being well connected" is the optimal state for any participant. Networks are established in order to create efficiency and optimum value for its participants—with only as much infrastructure as is needed to create effective connectivity. For instance, I would describe our network in Lawrence, Massachusetts, not as an organization, but as a *bundle of thinking, language, habits, value propositions, space and practice—all designed to comprise an environment that more effectively meets people where they are and offers myriad opportunities and levels of engagement*. The network form is attractive

for community-building precisely because it relies on and fosters a robust, active demand environment through the aggregate the pursuit of value and exercise of choice. It is also desirable for community building because its fundamental characteristics; low-level affiliation, value and choice driven, flexibility, informality, responsiveness, etc, are more organic to the experiences of most people and therefore more accessible as a form of belonging.

As community builders, we can't control all aspects of the civic environment or guarantee that we can enact a wholesale shift in habits. But we can be intentional about the kinds of environments that we are part of creating, and funders can do a better job of resourcing creative, new approaches focused on shaping the demand-side. The network form, adapted to the community-building task, provides clear clues for shaping a new form of organizing, and increasingly practitioners are recognizing some common characteristics of this form:

Fun First

First, the environment has to be welcoming, friendly and fun. Community building is not all business, it's not even mostly business. It is relationship building and the business flows from the strength and the patterns of relationships that are built. In this way, relationships are the *"roads and rails"* for progress and positive change at the community level. With this infrastructure much can happen, without it much will fail. Therefore community building does not start in meetings. It starts—typically—with eating and talking. Abundant opportunities for *people to people connections* have to be programmed into the life of the network.

Low-Level Affiliation

Unlike traditional organizing which formally or culturally challenges you to be all in or all out, the network seeks an explicitly "low level of affiliation" and assumes that this is but one of the many things you are choosing to be a part of. It is a layer of engagement that fully accommodates the members' other interests in life; family, church, work, block club, book club etc. This is a more organic life condition for most people and much more in sync with the kind of transactional affiliation that is the norm of most people in the information age. Instead of loyalty, ideology, or guilt, the network relies on value—through specific value propositions and new relationships—to attract members.

Form Follows Function

The forms of organization that dominate the network environment have to be informal, flexible and action-oriented. A network has to be vigilantly responsive and therefore has to be a "shape shifter" in order to move capacity to the places it is needed. The semi-permanent forms of traditional community building; standing committees, formal leadership positions etc., are not helpful in a network environment because they are not easily dismantled. In a network organizing environment, two important principles shape what form a certain activity should take—whether that is a sewing class, a city budget reform effort, or a program "committee." The first is *form follows function.*; a habit in the network where the group will always ask itself this question—"what form best suits this function?" The upshot of this habit is that, by and large, network members are organized in very informal, provisional and flexible groups where positional leadership titles are de-emphasized, leaders change often and the group is decidedly next-step focused. The other principle is *open architecture is best.* Again emphasizing informality and provisionality, the groups embrace the idea that people will come and go and therefore they work hard to keep the group perpetually accessible to new people. This is accomplished with simple facilitation techniques designed to hold onto the institutional memory of the group while making the work and the deliberations accessible to new voices.

The Connector as Leader

Leadership in the network environment is focused more on being a connector than a spokesperson or even a facilitator. In a network environment the connections are all. The more connected you are to other people, information and opportunity, the more value you can extract from the environment. So in this context there is no more valuable a role than helping others to form and find those connections. Increasingly, members are trained to be "weavers" and the "weaver" is an honored and acknowledge leadership role in the network environment.

Information Rich

Self-navigation, peer support/exchange and viral marketing are hallmarks of an effective network environment. For these things to happen, the environment must be "information rich." In fact, access to good, timely information is one of the primary value propositions of membership in the network. Building a network environment therefore requires early and significant investments in communications and information technology, and the reinforcement of member behavior focused on dissemination of information. Effective network members are not brokers of relationships or information, they are transmission nodes.

Interactive Spaces

Building place-based community using a network approach has the added characteristic of shaping new places and forums for "bumping-up" time. In a network, you want to create as many opportunities for people to bump up against other people as possible. This is advantageous to information sharing and relationship building. The problem is that opportunities that are too contrived or controlled will diminish the sense of choice that is so critical to all of us. We can however, try to re-design the spaces and interactions that already exist so that they are more conducive to peer-to-peer connections. Informal time can be programmed into meetings and events. Spaces can be re-designed to encourage intimacy and comfortability. Organizing activities that encourage residents to meet and interact on their stoops or in their homes is critical toward developing the doorstep-level connections that help people feel connected on the street and block. In many ways, the stoop, the sidewalk, the street, the alley, the next corner; this is the toughest frontier for community building in dense urban areas.

Diversity of People and Choices

The power of being connected in a network environment is directly related to how diverse its membership and its choices. The network organizer is intentional in starting and connecting a variety of activities—programs, issues, projects, that would attract a variety of people to the network and offer a range of choices for doing different things. They are also intentional about shaping many levels of engagement which meet the needs of a wider range of people, allowing for and encouraging members to get only as involved as they want to be at any given time. An important part of the choice environment is also the choice to create something that you think is important for the network to invest in. A healthy network environment is designed to support the development of a myriad of small, short-term activities that resonate with members.

Using Collective *and* Aggregate Power

A network environment takes advantage of two kinds of accountability and mobilization mechanisms in order to (a) decide what is valuable to the members, (b) establish values and norms, and (c) articulate demand and move to collective action. Most of our CBOs and community building work relies on the deliberation of small numbers of people in order to establish credibility and make decisions. The network allows for that to happen as well. But it allows for another dimension—the aggregate articulation of demand. Like a market environment, the network looks at the decisions (choices) that members are making in order to understand what is valuable and what is needed moving forward. Also, the network can act like a consumer collective and use its collective demand to shape the services that are available to struggling families. A network community building approach, investments in ways to "listen" to the network—effectively to see and hear what members are doing with their time and energy. An effective ability to track network activity is necessary to wielding aggregate power.

Network forms are only a part of a new wave of thinking about engagement and connectivity. In marketing, in national and state politics, in national and international movement building, the principles of network forms are taking hold and proving potent. These principles can be applied to place-based community building as well. In low income communities, as in the rest of the world, groups that offer an affiliation that is more transactional and more provisional, will earn engagement from a busy and discriminating public. Groups that build an infrastructure that provides a range of value that is responsive to rapid change—will be able to sustain engagement. And groups that demonstrate a genuine interest in, and infrastructure for, listening and responding to their members—will build powerful constituencies.

There is latent power and effectiveness in urban communities which can be unleashed by the potency of robust networks of relationships. New thinking and practice are needed which embrace, rather than fear or ignore the challenge of rebuilding civic life. While its true that, at the cellular level, relationships are built one by one, networks of relationships can grow exponentially if community builders and their allies stop worrying about defining "it" and get a lot busier building "it."

CHAPTER 26

Exploring Social Capital and Civic Engagement to Create a Framework for Community Building

James B. Hyman

INTRODUCTION

This chapter focuses on community building as the foundation for community-empowered change, with the key question being, how can this happen? How can communities effectively organize and assert themselves to affect positive results for their children, their families, and their neighborhoods? To address this question, we propose a framework that we believe will make community building more concrete and comprehensible as an approach to resident-driven community improvement. The framework is put forward in a "generic" form. The processes it outlines can be applied across a variety of community concerns, be they matters of safety, housing, policing, or traffic patterns.

The American Heritage Dictionary defines *citizenship* as the status of a citizen with its duties, rights, and privileges. This chapter is written to explore an emerging expression of those duties, rights, and privileges as applied in the new change strategies being pursued by increasing numbers of neighborhoods and communities in the United States. Responding to our decades-old history of narrowly designed, problem-focused, government-sponsored social interventions, communities are increasingly exploring improvement strategies that are more local, that are more comprehensive, and that encourage the involvement of community residents.

Community building is a term being used to describe this new approach. It is guided by two fundamental beliefs—that the community is the appropriate focus for revitalization efforts; and that enhancing the capacity of communities to engage and support residents is essential to success (Stone, 1996). Community building assumes that associations within a geographic area are important for community well-being; that bringing together a broad spectrum of stakeholders will provide a better understanding of problems; that sustainable solutions are based on knowing the facts, building on assets, and having a shared vision of improvement; and that an independent community-based capacity for analysis, planning, and convening is essential for success (Walsh, 1997).

As such, this new "field" of work is supported by the best traditions of democracy and citizenship. The challenge is figuring out how to exercise these beliefs. How does one enhance a community's ability to engage its residents and sustain their involvement in an effective community improvement effort?

Currently, the approach is to meet communities on their own terms. Initiative sponsors start where the communities are—identifying, and then building on, the assets and structures that are already there to build new and increased capacities for resident engagement, self-determination, and change. This approach respects the organic and unpredictable nature of community processes. However, to be successful in the long term, community building needs to establish a framework—a set of axioms, hypotheses, or principles that can provide a common language and guide its actual practice.

We present such a framework, drawing heavily on notions of social capital and civic engagement. More precisely, we argue that community building must begin by building relationships between community residents and that the social capital embedded in those relationships can be used to improve the welfare of both residents and the community. Subsequently, we will demonstrate how these relationships can be channeled for civic purposes and organized and sustained for community efficacy. The social capital construct is our starting point.

SOCIAL CAPITAL: WHAT IS IT? AND HOW IS IT CREATED?

Robert Putnam's 1995 article, "Bowling Alone," catapulted the concept of social capital into the mainstream of popular language, public discourse, and policy debate. The construct is enjoying immense popularity. It embodies many of the attributes normally associated with American democracy including trust and individual and group efficacy. It also has the benefit of political correctness and political expediency: The poor are not powerless to change their circumstances.

With all of this appeal, social capital is increasingly being used as an explanation for almost any positive outcome of individual socialization and socializing behavior. In fact, concern for its over-application led Alenjandro Portes to protest that, "the point is approaching at which social capital comes to be applied to so many events and in so many different contexts as to lose any distinct meaning" (Portes, 1998). It is therefore important that we clarify what we mean by the term.

Portes (1998) attributed the first systematic contemporary analysis of social capital to Pierre Bourdieu (1985), who defined the concept as "the aggregate of the actual or potential resources which are linked to possession of a durable network of more or less institutionalized relationships of mutual acquaintance and recognition." This definition suggests that social capital has two parts: the relationships that allow individuals access to resources possessed by others, and the amount and quality of the resources themselves.

James Coleman and Robert Putnam are perhaps the two best-known proponents of social capital in the United States. Coleman's work stated, "Social capital is created when relations among people change in ways that facilitate action" (Coleman, 1988). Putnam, by contrast, believed that "social capital refers to features of social organization such as networks, norms, and social trust that facilitate coordination and cooperation for mutual benefit" (Putnam, 1995).

From these interpretations we can infer several things. The first is that social capital is an asset representing a collection of resources. The second inference is that these resources are embedded in relationships, and the third element is that social capital is directed and purposeful. We will combine these insights into a unifying definition: *Social capital is an asset representing actionable resources that are contained in, and accessible through, a system of relationships.*

CIVIC ENGAGEMENT AS A PRECURSOR TO SOCIAL CAPITAL

In "Bowling Alone," Putnam explored the role of social capital through discussions of civic engagement in the United States. As examples of civic engagement, he cites voter turnout, reading the newspaper, participation in such public forums as PTAs, and in such private organizations as choral societies and bowling leagues. These examples suggest that, to qualify as civic engagement, behaviors neither have to involve others, be organized in any particular way, nor be directed at any particular action, goal, or outcome. They can proceed as independent and autonomous behaviors of individuals. Indeed, for Putnam, civic engagement may merely mean the kind of external activity that "gets people off the living room couch."

This formulation suggests that civic engagement is not itself a form of social capital. It requires that neither relationships nor intent to act be in evidence. For example, neither reading the paper nor voting presumes that social capital has been created. Indeed, Putnam's work suggested that social capital grows out of "networks" of this civic engagement—that engagement with others offers a forum for relationship building that facilitates access to social assets.

Civic engagement, then, is a precursor to social capital. We can think of it as analogous to static electricity—inert energy that has not yet been directed into current. Social capital, on the other hand, is created when this civic engagement is "excited" by some catalytic issue or event and directed toward a particular end or purpose.

Two assumptions are implicit here. The first is that, with regard to the well-being of communities, civic engagement is additive across individuals and has positive cumulative impacts. This simply suggests that the welfare of communities increases with increases in the numbers of civically engaged members. The second assumption is that a community's social capital should also be expected to increase with increases in civic engagement. That is, the more inert energy a community has, the easier it may be to harness and deploy. Simply put, social capital presumes and depends on individual civic engagement as a vehicle for building relationships, and, as it relates to individual and community welfare, the more the better.

COMMUNITY BUILDING AS THE NEW FOUNDATION FOR COMMUNITY CHANGE

The community-building paradigm that has emerged in recent decades assumes an ability to harness the relationships and social capital, which result from this civic engagement, into a coherent collective and deploy them through a focused strategy. However, these community-building dynamics do not occur on their own. They must be deliberately pursued. Indeed, the actual practice of community building focuses on enhancing the abilities of communities to function in these ways. Yet, because of the social, economic, political, and structural differences between and among communities, the question of how to build these capacities through deliberate intervention and investment has so far eluded any general formulation.

The community-building framework presented here offers a model for how communities can increase and sustain the engagement of residents in a community change process. In doing so, it attempts to address two major questions: How do the concerns of individual residents rise to become foci for community-wide concern and action? And, when they do, how can community resources be marshaled in a sustainable effort to address them? The simple answer is that the concerns of individual community members must somehow find their way into a "community conversation," so they can resonate with other community members in a way that can gain their support and provoke them to action. Second, to effect change, community members and their allies must come together to act in a collective effort. Starting and maintaining these conversations and organizing the community for action are major community-building challenges.

THE BEGINNINGS OF A FRAMEWORK

Our framework suggests that how this comes about is a very complex process. Indeed, as originally constructed, this framework may be too complex to have practical value to people in the field. To make it more comprehensible, we present the detailed framework in Figure 26.1, superimposing circles to represent five distinct clusters of activity that make up its major components.

As an overview, Figure 26.1 suggests a "closed system" wherein civic engagement is a function of the incentives, human capital, participation costs, and hierarchical needs that condition individual "appetites" and preferences for the kinds of "external involvements" that we believe Putnam intends by the term *civic engagement*.

The framework further suggests that this civic–external engagement can be converted (appropriated or intentionally organized) into social capital as a deliberate response to some catalyst. Civically engaged individuals may decide to come together in response to some issue, event, or need. Their success at coming together creates the social capital that is then directed toward some community action or activity in an effort to achieve an outcome. Finally, the outcome, in turn, feeds back into the considerations that condition

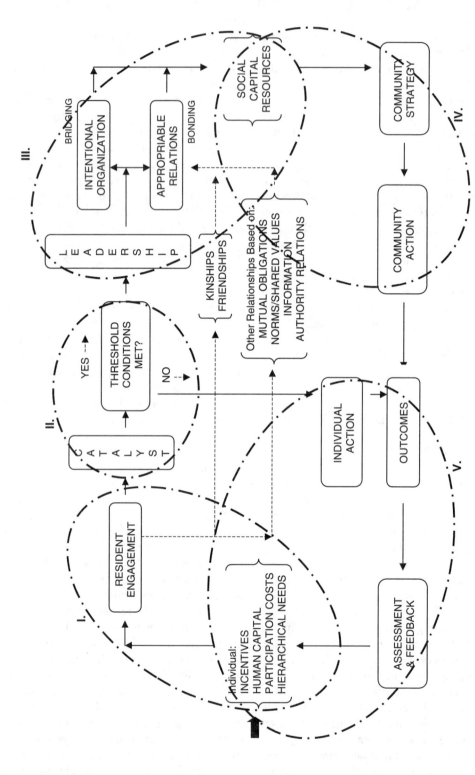

Figure 26.1 Collective efficacy framework assessment/investment clusters

individual appetites for further civic engagement.

As such, the framework is an iterative process. The cycle shown in Figure 26.1 can be repeated again and again while focusing on a different community issue each time. A neighborhood's concern for police conduct, gang activities, traffic patterns, or educational reform might each be a separate focus of this community-building process. In the real world, however, it is likely that several neighborhood issues might be pursued simultaneously and that this process may be occurring independently or in tandem in different parts of the same communities.

We also assume that this framework has cumulative effects on communities—that is, the strength of the community-building effort should increase with every successful iteration. Every positive story arising about residents' experiences and about successful actions should make it easier to organize and sustain community interest in subsequent community actions and activities. Examining Figure 26.1 cluster by cluster provides a more detailed understanding.

Cluster I: Resident Engagement

Rationale

Community residents have to become more engaged with each other in ways that will facilitate relationships and the exchange of information. Cluster I is about resident engagement. It attempts to understand what determines whether individuals become externally active in their communities. Figure 26.1 hypothesizes that individual preferences for civic engagement are influenced by a combination of the incentives, human capital, participation costs, and hierarchical needs facing residents as follows:

Incentives

There are at least two aspects of the incentives issue to consider—one is the expected benefit from engagement. For instance, much of what we choose to do reflects some calculation of an expected return—some net direct benefit that warrants our investment of time and effort. Alternatively, there may be intrinsic interests where we may do something because it is the right thing to do; or because the value we see is in the doing of it and not in a consequent return.

Human Capital

Preferences for resident engagement can also be influenced by one's personal makeup, particularly by issues of self-esteem, confidence, and perceptions that one has something of value to contribute.

Participation Costs

Two components of participation costs are worth noting. One relates to costs or "burden." Access to transportation, working hours, and childcare, as examples, can raise significant barriers to participation. The other component is the "opportunity cost" of alternative uses of leisure time. This component is difficult to parse because of difficulties inherent in assessing valuations of leisure activities. For example, one person may find the opportunity to watch a soap opera on TV just as compelling as another's opportunity to attend a public hearing.

Hierarchical Needs

Finally, there is the issue of the priority that people attach to civic involvement in the face of other needs. Residents who are more secure socially and financially may be better positioned to participate in community affairs than lower income residents who may be more preoccupied with issues of daily survival and family maintenance. Our framework hypothesizes then that these four considerations are among the determinants of individual preferences for civic engagement. There are likely other factors such as upbringing and parental histories and influences that contribute as well to these preferences. So, one of the first goals of community building should be to invest in strategies that will encourage more social interaction, engagement, and exchange in the neighborhood. Increases in engagement should create more opportunities for residents to form and strengthen relationships. Friendships, kinships, or acquaintances based on other functional relationships might each be enhanced by more frequent interaction.

Cluster II: Agenda Building

Rationale

Residents must find or create forums for sharing and prioritizing their concerns and their aspirations for the community. Cluster II focuses on the process by which matters important to individuals in the neighborhood become matters of concern for an entire community. Community sentiment is not an easy commodity to arouse. In fact, in our framework, we assume that, given a choice, most individuals, because of economies of time and effort, would prefer to resolve issues by themselves. Working in groups can be stressful because of its uncertainties, inefficiencies, and demands for compromise. Consequently, we presume that an individual's first response and preferred course of action, given any catalytic event or issue, is to "go it alone" and just "take care of it." In developing our framework, it is important to speculate about the conditions under which individuals would choose the less-preferred option of involving others in addressing their concerns.

We believe this choice requires that two sets of threshold conditions be met. The first threshold is reached when an individual feels he or she is unlikely to be successful acting alone. This will occur if the person believes

- That he or she lacks access—that the jurisdiction, or level of authority to which an appeal must be made, lies beyond his or her reach.
- That he or she lacks clout—that the gravity or complexity of the issue in question is too large to be effected by his or her actions or appeals alone.

If this threshold is reached, the individual may choose to abandon the cause altogether. Alternatively, he or she may decide to join with others in an effort to effect the desired change. But for this joining option to take place, a second set of conditions must also hold, in particular,

- The catalytic event in question must be deemed significant by some critical mass of other community residents who also see it as beyond their abilities to resolve on their own.
- Some person(s) or entity(ies) must come forward to assume the leadership that will provide a fulcrum for organizing and for channeling community energies and action.

Reaching this second threshold will put an individual's issues on the community agenda. So, a second major goal of community builders should be to foster ongoing opportunities for broad community conversations that will permit the airing and prioritizing of resident concerns into a community agenda for change.

Cluster III: Community Organizing

Rationale

Residents must organize around trusted and capable leadership, taking stock of their social capital and other assets. Leadership is the first component of our organizing Cluster precisely because community expression needs a center around which to revolve. Someone or something must "stand point" as a receptacle for community sentiments, a fulcrum for community energies, and an interpreter and transmitter of community will. An immediate concern for the success of community building, then, is whether there is an ample supply of competent and approachable leadership around which the community can organize.

James S. Coleman suggested that communities can organize themselves and their resources in one of two ways: through intentional organizing or through "appropriable social organization" (Coleman, 1988). *Appropriable* social organization refers to organizing efforts that rely on the neighborhood's ability to adapt or redirect relationships that may already exist. As such, it raises questions about whether relationships that are grounded in one set of issues or circumstances can be directed to other ends and purposes. So, for instance, a community leader who wants the city to support a summer youth employment program might attempt to enlist or "appropriate" the support of family and friends or the school PTA in that campaign.

Communities with a wealth of neighborhood groups, volunteer organizations, or community-based organizations are presumed to have a strong latent capacity for this form of organizing. By contrast, many of the communities of concern to community builders may not. In these lesser-endowed communities, the energy for community-driven change must be intentionally organized. These intentional efforts force us to consider what it takes to strengthen the level of organization in places where relationships are weak or do not exist. It is a deliberate effort to bolster relationships and build capacity for effective action. The distinction between these two forms of organizing then relates to the presence and to the strength of organizations and relationships in the community. In practice, we might expect most community-driven change efforts to involve some combination of both organizing types.

Cluster III highlights the resources that are available to a community once it is organized. These resources reflect the social capital contained in residents relationships as well as other community and organizational assets that can be marshaled and deployed on the community's behalf.

Cluster IV: Community Action

Residents must pool their assets into an action strategy and build bridges to other resources that will be needed for success. Community building is about enhancing local capacities to act on the issues and concerns that affect community welfare. In this light, one can think of all of the framework's other clusters as processes that support Cluster IV. Indeed, our framework suggests that resident engagement, agenda building, and organizing are indispensable components of community-empowered change. But ultimately, a community's success in improving the welfare of its resident families and children will depend on what it actually does and how well it does it. In Cluster IV we focus on issues of resources, planning, and the execution of strategies.

Resources

Community building action strategies require attention to both the people and the institutional resources that may be needed. There are two aspects to the people-resources question. One is the focus we highlighted earlier on engaging and organizing some critical mass of people to give momentum to a shared community change agenda. Another, however, is enlisting particular persons both within and outside the community for whom, by virtue of their positions, talent or expertise may be critical to success. Much of a community's agenda will likely focus on securing a needed service, activity, or facility of function. Institutional resources, particularly those of community-based organizations (CBOs), will be important because these institutions will act as vehicles for delivering these fought-for benefits. As such, the framework's focus on harnessing the social capital resources of residents should not preclude capacity-building efforts among local nonprofits and entities. Community builders may want to support local nonprofits in their financial, organizational, and systems development efforts. They might also seek to create more opportunities for residents to collaborate with CBOs as a means of establishing legitimacy and trust.

Planning and Execution

Perhaps the most central question in any local change effort is, "What can and will a community actually do?" Community actions can range from a one-time showing of sentiments and solidarity to more sustained efforts at lobbying, authoring legislative proposals, or launching political campaigns, or both, and more. The important point is that the action that is ultimately taken be driven by a strategy and guided by some kind of plan—preferably a plan characterized by clearly stated goals, a preferred set of outcomes, criteria for what constitutes success, and some mechanism for accountability.

The effective execution of a community strategy boils down to accountability and competence. Do people do what they are supposed to do, and do they do it well? If so, we can assume that we have maximized our potential for impact, given the resources and strategies that were deployed. But good execution will not, by itself, ensure success. Misaligned or ineffectual resources deployed through an ill-conceived plan will likely not produce positive results no matter how well the action is executed. So, investors in community-building efforts may wish to provide resources for planning and technical assistance to enhance the likelihood that action strategies will have desired impacts.

Cluster V: Communication and Message Development

Community builders will need to keep an open line of communications with residents and their community partners about all aspects of the change effort, but particularly as it relates to developing and communicating positive messages about progress and results. Communications are an integral part of any community-building effort. How an initiative describes itself, how it positions the issues, how it recruits participants, how it publicizes events, and how it disseminates results are all important to encouraging and maintaining resident energy and engagement. Skillful communication strategies can also help energize and engage funders, policymakers, and other important audiences whose cooperation may be needed for community efforts to succeed.

Indeed, communication is important at every stage of community building. At a very basic level, sharing information about what is going on is a fundamental responsibility of the leadership. But communication about methods, operations, and progress can also contribute to long-term learning and the accumulation of "best practices."

In Cluster V, however, the focus is specifically on communicating about outcomes. This narrower discussion is particularly important because of the pivotal connections between those outcomes, how they are received by residents, and the initiative's ability to maintain itself as a community-driven change effort. The focus here is on the potential for using communications strategies to nurture and sustain community-building momentum.

Indeed, sustainability is perhaps the most difficult challenge facing community-building initiatives—how to keep resident interest going so that they continue their engagement with the affairs of the neighborhood. Intuitively, we suspect that residents will continue being engaged as long as they can see some benefit both for themselves and for their neighborhoods. Being clear about these direct and neighborhood benefits, and communicating progress toward their attainment, is of critical importance to maintaining engagement. Our tendency, however, is often to neglect one in favor of the other.

Most of what we regard as outcomes from community-led movements consists of an issue-oriented scoreboard of wins and losses. From this perspective, the bottom line is whether—and how well—an action worked. Substantive results are critically important to resident-driven initiatives, and rightly so. After all, the principal driver of this new paradigm is the promise that community building will bring greater success in dealing with persistent social problems than did earlier approaches. Developing and communicating messages about the success of an event can help maintain residents' commitment and keep the momentum going.

But equally important to sustainability may be the extent to which community building provides real and valued rewards to the individual residents who participate. For example, it can be argued that a primary goal of community building should be enhancing the *human* capital of residents—increasing their skills, abilities, and confidence in dealing with the issues that affect their families and neighborhoods. Leadership training, for example, can be transformative in these regards. So, in addition to communicating "wins" on community issues, community-building initiatives should seek opportunities to tell stories about benefits to individual residents and to their personal development through participation.

The intent is to use communications strategies to sustain the community-building effort—to influence how residents assess their appetites for community engagement and encourage them to get involved. Achieving a broad recognition that members of the community have benefited personally and been successful in securing benefits for the neighborhood is the best marketing strategy for the initiative's continuation.

As such, our framework is indeed recursive—beginning with a concern for individual behaviors and the need to encourage individual residents to become engaged with their communities, and ending with strategies to affect those behaviors and offer further encouragement.

CONCLUSIONS

As an emerging expression of citizenship and American democracy, community building is becoming an increasingly popular approach to addressing social welfare in the United States. Intuition tells us that comprehensive, locally focused interventions, informed and guided by the people they are intended to serve, may indeed hold more promise than earlier approaches. But to prove itself as a replicable intervention strategy, community building needs to become more disciplined. It needs to clarify the principles and processes that constitute its practice. And it needs to document them as practiced in communities to evolve as a field of work and study. This chapter is offered as fodder for that goal.

REFERENCES

Bourdieu, P. (1985). The forms of capital. In J. G. Richardson (Ed.), *Handbook of theory and research for the sociology of education* (pp. 241–258). New York: Greenwood.

Coleman, J. S. (1988). Social capital in the creation of human capital. *American Journal of Sociology, 94,* S95–121.

Portes, A. (1998). Social capital: Its origins and applications in modern society. *Annual Review of Sociology, 24,* 1–24.

Putnam, R. D. (1995). Bowling alone: America's declining social capital. *Journal of Democracy, 6,* 65–78.

Stone, R. (1996). *Core issues in comprehensive community-building initiatives.* Chicago: Chapin Hall Center for Children.

Walsh, J. (1997). *Stories of renewal: Community building and the future of urban America.* New York: The Rockefeller Foundation.

CHAPTER 27

Doing Democracy Up-Close

Culture, power, and communication in community planning

Xavier de Souza Briggs

> The planner who approaches the cultural framework with technical expertise alone soon finds others' perceptions of his role quite narrow and his operating arena and impact highly circumscribed . . . On the other hand, focusing on process alone limits the planner to symbolic emotional support roles and unduly hampers his capacity for professional judgment.
>
> (Bolan, "Community Decision Behavior:
> The Culture of Planning" (1969, 308))

Decades have passed since Bolan insisted that planners be more than technicians or sources of "emotional support" in the communities in which they work, and the stakes are higher than ever. With ethnic diversity on the rise in traditional "settler states" such as the United States, Canada, and Australia, as well as in Europe, and with increased attention to diversity in many younger democracies in the developing world, professionals and others engaged in local planning and problem-solving (hereafter, "planners") face higher expectations that they behave in culturally competent ways and promote more inclusive decisionmaking (Sandercock 2000). This is perhaps most visible in the ways that planners communicate and handle power dynamics within and among groups. Yet despite relevant and even provocative contributions in planning theory and the social sciences over the past two decades, there has been remarkably little effort to examine culture and power in face-to-face communication, such as in the planning meetings on which so much local work hinges. More specifically, researchers have often treated these topics as abstractions for theorizing, not as concrete problems and opportunities for the planners involved (Forester 1985). Many practitioners, for their part, have either adopted "cookbook" recipes for handling groups and situations (generic rules for facilitating successful meetings or resolving disputes, for example) or have generated a rich craft knowledge from trial and error—but not necessarily in forms that are conscious, shareable, and open to debate.

I focus on face-to-face planning episodes and planners' choices within them, examining a brief ethnographic account of talk-based, face-to-face interactions or "speech occasions" (Austin 1961; Searle 1969). The accounts are derived from my field-notes as consultant to a large-scale, multi-neighborhood community planning and development initiative in a northeastern U.S. city. I emphasize that planners and other public service professionals should seek to understand and respond to the diverse communication codes and subtle power relations that shape face-to-face encounters, and I provide advice on how to do both (for details, see Briggs 1998). Such understanding and response—"knowing-in-practice," to use Schön's (1982) phrase—are especially crucial where planners aim to get results while meaningfully involving various "publics" or stakeholders in decisionmaking.

Those efforts require effective practices and constant learning, not just having the right values. Otherwise, many face-to-face interactions in a diverse society will struggle along at needlessly high levels of confusion, distrust, and even resentment. The risk and opportunities entailed in such interactions are especially significant when planners enter disadvantaged areas, as is the case with many community planning efforts. But the principles developed here apply to most face-to-face encounters and are part of a larger effort to free planning in democratic societies from communication "distortions" (Forester 1989), not to mention irrelevance.

WHY COMMUNITY PLANNING IS IMPORTANT AND HARD

Increased social diversity—in the U.S., it comes alongside growing economic inequality—has sharpened the focus on politics and public participation in local planning and decisionmaking in democratic societies. Friedmann (1987, 14), for example, argues that the pace of change and complexity of problems in the public arena call for "a renewal of politics, initially at the local scale of citizen encounters." Innes (1996) offers consensus building, and underscores the role of "communicative action" (Innes 1995), to redefine the ideal of effective planning. Influential voices outside the planning field likewise agree that strong democracy is threatened by the loss of activities and associations that engage people locally, face-to-face (Barber 1984; Fung 2004). Renewed efforts now aim quite often to build local social cohesion or "social capital" (Putnam 2000), empowerment and "community capacity" (Chaskin et al. 2001).

Democracy is a labor-intensive business, especially in diverse societies. But relatively little action-oriented research has considered how to make that business work at the micro level, face to face, through talk—with planning or policymaking as a part. For the most part, we have "how to" guides on public meetings and other media that are terse on points of power and culture. In general, rhetoric is rarely studied today, as it was 2,000

years ago, notes Brown (1983, 136), "to explain the relationships between the practice of language and the exercise of power."

This study thus addresses an important gap in research and reflective practice, using a major community planning initiative to highlight cross-cultural confusion, power relations, and other problems in face-to-face meetings and, to a lesser degree, the contexts that surround them. For my purposes here, "community planning" is synonymous with "neighborhood planning": efforts by which residents and others in a spatially defined area, often working in tandem with planning professionals, seek to develop a blueprint for their collective future—to protect what they have and secure improvements in their quality of life. In America, the roots of such planning efforts run deep, at least as far back as the reformist era of the late nineteenth and early twentieth century, when settlement houses began to appear in crowded industrial cities (Rohe and Gates 1985). Community planning is policy development on the micro level, often with deliberation at its heart, but it is also an effort by local stakeholders to write themselves a story. Baum (1997, 295), in a detailed study of two community planning processes in Baltimore, describes such planning as the effort to help move residents' conversations with themselves and with technical experts from "communities of memory" to future-oriented "communities of hope." At all stages, clear, trustworthy face-to-face communication among actors is crucial to getting significant and sustainable results.

There are several reasons for which community planning, after roughly two decades in obscurity, is once again attracting great interest nationwide. First, where such planning is participatory, it reflects a broad effort to shift public and private decisionmaking toward models that favor stakeholder involvement, from site-based management in business to models for "reinventing government" (Fung 2004; Osborne 1993). Second, community planning is increasingly prescribed as a trigger for efforts to revitalize low-income urban neighborhoods, and life in such neighborhoods came back on the screen politically in the 1990s.

But as Chaskin (2005) observes, many

community planning processes face powerful tensions between *democracy* (the ethos of associational action) and *bureaucracy* (the imperatives of programs, budgets, and expectations from funders and other external authorities). Grassroots activists, who founded community-based organizations to plan for and revitalize forgotten neighborhoods, now worry that some of these organizations have outgrown their constituencies (Gonzalez 1993). Mayors and planning departments worry, as before, that local visions will favor parochial interests over citywide priorities. And those who engage in community planning, whether as consultants, public officials, or citizen planners, worry, as always, that the fruit of their efforts may occupy little more than shelf space.

Whereas earlier research and commentary on community planning focused squarely on issues of culture, power, conflict, and the legitimacy of the planner's role (e.g., Peattie 1968; Rein 1969; Arnstein 1969; Bolan 1969; Ecklein and Lauffer 1972), most recent work celebrates programmatic best practices or stories of winning advocacy campaigns. With a few notable exceptions, this work is quite journalistic, thin on concepts to guide analysis or show why the "formulas" fail in some contexts. Descriptive accounts and professional primers, both old and new, mostly allude to the miscommunication, cross-cultural gaps, and subtle power relations that characterize public encounters. Fortunately, a large body of research in anthropology, communication, sociolinguistics, and sociology has addressed these issues in detail.

PREVIEW AND APPROACH

I examine a single planning episode, emphasizing how key aspects of community planning practice reflect the dynamics of "social performance": socially organized, politically subtle, culturally shaped, and talk-based public interactions or speech occasions in which participants play roles much like performers in a play (Goffman 1959). I focus on broad patterns of social performance common to a range of face-to-face citizen encounters in which planners and other public service professionals may find themselves, not the intricacies of group behavior generally, to which a vast and distinct literature is devoted. The speech occasion presented below was edited from fieldnotes I took as consultant to a large-scale planning process in five densely populated, high-poverty, predominantly African-American and Latino neighborhoods in a single city (I use pseudonyms for person and place names below). I am a mixed-race, male planner, and these ethnographic accounts—drawing on both participant observation and informal (naturalistic) interviewing—are, by nature, personalistic and subject to interpretive bias.

It's 8:30 PM on a mid-winter night in the Clydewood neighborhood, an overwhelmingly African-American and Latino area where almost half the population lives below the poverty line. The planning task force made up of residents and chaired by a local community development corporation (CDC) is meeting for the third time at a neighborhood youth center. The room is small for the 16 persons present, and long tables have been arranged in a "U" shape to face the front. Fred, the CDC executive director, chairs the meeting, welcoming participants, reminding residents of the larger objectives, and leading everyone in a prayer at the start, group hug at the close. Like most of the task force members, he is African-American and over 50. Two hired planning consultants are standing: Julio, a 30ish Hispanic planner, is facilitating, and Karen, a white Anglo (non-Hispanic) planner in her mid-40s, is recording comments on large sheets of butcher-block paper on the wall. The planners met with Fred before the meeting to go over meeting roles and review a tentative agenda. Julio and the residents are doing most of the talking. He asks general questions about social services in the area and probes on their responses; from time to time, he encourages residents to explore different topics and to modify the comments recorded. Midway through the meeting, the group is discussing the rehabilitation and conversion of an abandoned city-owned building for use as a youth center. Shari, one of only two teenagers present, is standing in one corner as she expresses strong concerns that the facility be designed with youth ["users" in the planning jargon] in mind. She is African-American, 17 years old.

"Y'all gotta listen to the young people; we don't never get anything made for us right! Don't never get asked . . ." Shari, who stands a slender but strong 6-foot-2, is pumping the air with her outstretched fingers and moving her head from side to side across her shoulders for emphasis. I make a mental note that her body is saying as much as her mouth. Julio asks her to be more specific about how the proposed youth facility should be designed: "Ok, so what do you want to see there? Enter it in your mind's eye—what does it look and feel like?" Based on earlier conversations and her comment a moment ago, I get the sense that this is a question Shari is seldom asked, and Shari seems caught off guard. She is still and silent as Julio probes further. I see that Karen is staring at Shari and quivering with (what looks like) fear. Later, when the meeting is wrapped up, I confer privately with Karen, who tells me how threatened she felt by Shari's behavior. Julio and I then talk to her about the verbal and nonverbal cues that different people use to communicate. Julio said that he "read" Shari as emphatic, impassioned but not at all threatening to the planners or process.

In this encounter, a technically able planner, due perhaps to her life stage, as well as her class and ethnic background, was unable to decode the speech of a community resident, a young woman who, among other contributions, played an important "bridging" role, connecting the local task force to youth in her neighborhood. Far from being threatening, Shari was, by local reputation, an ambitious and outspoken leader among her peers—well-liked by local leaders and by project staff because she cared deeply about the issues our planning effort emphasized. To Karen, though, Shari's emphatic outburst connoted threat. Because Shari was (literally) standing tall in a sit-down meeting, and because her body language underlined her strong feelings about the issues at hand, Karen was silent and visibly on edge for the remainder of the meeting.

Planning efforts struggle over situations like this one, wherein planners: (a) differ from other meeting participants in their sense of the proper bounds of the social performance and of the various aims of social actors in the situation; and (b) fail to reliably

decode the speech of their resident constituents, let alone *en*code their own speech for those constituents to understand (the latter being a feedback problem not evident in the narrative above but one with which Karen struggled in many other instances). These problems, different *conceptions* about what is to come in a meeting and *code confusion* once talk begins, can have devastating effects, alienating participants, threatening the trust needed to develop and act on plans collaboratively over time, and inhibiting valuable exchange and learning.

Speech occasions like the one presented above are "socially performed." People (social actors) assume roles in face-to-face interaction in order to manage the impressions of fellow actors (Goffman 1959). Moreover, social actors rely on verbal and nonverbal forms or "codes" that are familiar to them (Hymes 1974; Kochman 1981). Goffman's performance framework captures the broad parameters of the situation: Actors seek to manage the impression of other actors, not necessarily to manipulate but to maintain a normal, understandable exchange, in other words to "uphold the situation" (Goffman 1971, 23). Code concepts, on the other hand, reveal the substance of communication and confusion, as well as specific talk strategies within those parameters.

For example, the planners described above wanted to project objectivity and respect for resident views while steering discussion in ways that informed their work, and these planners may not have reached a tacit *or* explicit consensus on these situational, as opposed to technical, aims in advance, despite the pre-meeting. Based on later observation and informal interviews, the residents present brought a range of intentions: to project authority as the "old guard," to ensure that younger voices were not suppressed by these older figures, and so on. Staff added more unstated agendas. Conversations with Karen reflected scant awareness on her part of these multiple agendas and role performances, above and beyond the factual exchange assumed by rational theories of planning and policymaking, in which participation merely generates "input."

The raw material of the encounter

consisted largely of verbal and nonverbal communication organized along ethnic, class, institutional, and other dimensions. The following basic concepts will help us analyze this episode: *Scripts* are the conventions or expectations that different actors bring to a particular face-to-face encounter (community task force meeting, public hearing at city hall, etc.), and *codes* are the specific linguistic forms used to talk (Saville-Troike and Kleifgen 1986). The evidence is that Karen and Shari differed according to the scripts they brought to the meeting—their expectations as to appropriate behavior, what constitutes *emphasis* versus *threat*, and so on—as well as the codes they employed, both verbally and nonverbally. More specifically, Karen felt threatened by Shari's volume and emphatic tone, as well as her nonverbal signals: standing for emphasis, pumping the air with her hands, swaying her head from side-to-side as she looked at the planners—in other words, by a style of face-to-face rhetoric rooted in ethnicity and social class (Kochman 1981; Gumperz 1982). Karen's script also reflected an institutional logic: her tendency to focus on what Chaskin (2005) labels "bureaucracy" in community planning (budgetary and programmatic imperatives) rather than democracy (collective voice and action).

Typical of such confusion, neither Shari nor Karen were aware that there was a communication problem, nor that code confusion could change the outcomes of the meeting, as well as future relations among the actors involved (Hymes 1974; Wolfgang 1979). When planners and other actors in a social setting share life stage, ethnicity, class level, and other social traits, the chance for code confusion and mistaken intentions are much reduced: *codes and scripts will largely coincide in homogeneous settings*. But in the practice of community planning, so often conducted across these social borders, common communication conventions can hardly be assumed.

OPTIONS FOR ACTION

What to do? Discussions, whether public or private, about acceptable conventions (scripts), along with the range of forms (codes) to expect, would have helped Shari, Karen, and others to exchange information.[1] This is part of the "norming" that groups can do in advance of their work together (Hackman 1990). Forester (1989) has called explicitly for a focus on planning as mutual "sense making." But to norm and make sense together effectively, actors involved in a situation must be aware that scripts exist and have some sense of what their own scripts include.

In general, when verbal and nonverbal behavior are confusing and even threatening, ask insiders what they think such behavior means, and be ready for a range of answers. While I am not suggesting that planners become behavioral scientists, the field researcher's healthy concern for the range of cultural assumptions present in a setting like the one described, and a willingness to ask elementary questions, can go a long way (Lofland and Lofland 1995). Although one may trigger suspicion and defensiveness with probing inquiry, my experience is that most people understand the need to get second opinions about "what went on" (to debrief an encounter) and, further, that people appreciate being counted enough to offer their insights. A few relatively neutral probes that might have been helpful for Karen, with or without her colleagues' input after the meeting, include the following:

> What did Shari mean when she said "young people never get asked"?
> Shari, what did you mean when you said . . .? Say more about . . .
> Do other young people feel strongly about that?
> I don't know about that [issue/sentiment]. What's that all about?

Although social performances and code clashes can be terribly confusing, we nevertheless tend to actively *fit* meanings to them, to make sense of them, rightly or wrongly, based on prior experiences (Garfinkel 1967). If code and other performance problems are therefore common but fairly invisible to the key actors involved, all sides of the encounter may become angry, not just uncomfortable, because actors tend to read intentions into what has "gone wrong" in the interaction (Erickson 1979, 122). These stand-offs are, at worst, highly paternalistic and parochial on the part of outsiders with authority ("these community people don't know what they want, their ideas aren't helpful, and they don't see the bigger picture," or "we could never get that past the board!") and resentful in the view of residents ("those racist 'experts' are at it again, they don't know what I know and don't care to learn it"). Such inferences may confirm the worst fears and preconceptions each side of the interaction has about the other.

Where *decoding* is concerned, because social meanings are subject to various filters, it is critical, as suggested above, to ask various actors—young and old, richer and poorer, newcomers and long-termers, from various ethnic groups—what means what and what actors intend. As for *encoding* effectively, planners who are able to "code switch" to make themselves understood in particular settings bring undeniable advantages to these encounters. This practice, also known as "style switching," was first documented by researchers among African-Americans (Mitchell-Kernan 1972), but is practiced by members of various groups who navigate across boundaries of communication. Moreover, "going street"—an informal way to describe switching from standard American English to a particular group's dialect—was described in literature long before social scientists deemed the phenomenon important enough to study. It is a survival skill for people who must function in two or more social worlds or "speech communities" (Gumperz 1968), each with its preferred patterns of communication. As I have elaborated elsewhere (Briggs 1998), power dynamics, and notable power imbalances, are often at play in these encounters as well.

These concepts focus attention on the understandable differences that human actors bring to these settings and away from simplistic analyses that hold confusion and anger to be—always and everywhere—signs of conscious prejudice or the will to dominate.

DISCUSSION AND IMPLICATIONS

I could have subtitled this chapter "trouble at community meetings." Planners, especially those working in neighborhoods or other field settings, are often called upon to be more than informed technicians, to assume a variety of public roles that support effective communication and shared decisionmaking processes. But knowing what you don't know is important, and the largely unrecognized dynamics I have examined here are also important, for reasons of legitimacy as well as effectiveness. Our still insufficient attention to the links among communication, culture, and power, reinforces the belief that, like the stereotypical technicians of old, planners and policy professionals work top-down and write technical reports, diagnosing social problems and removing pathology "over there," with little consideration to local knowledge, values, or culture (Gans 1968; Scott 1998; Tauxe 1995). We cannot simply ignore the performance aspects of face-to-face interactions or prescribe formulaic responses to the challenges examined here. Nor should we simply retreat to value statements about how important it is to engage the public in decisions that matter. Rather, we should collect and share principles for reading communication codes and power relations, especially in multicultural settings, and for responding in ways that promote mutual learning. Such competence is critical for doing democracy "up close" in a world of diverse publics and complex public problems.

NOTE

1. In other sessions, we, the consultant team, shared with participants some of our conventions for communicating and listening during the meeting and asked about their expectations. We also debriefed amongst ourselves after each meeting and shared the tasks of checking our interpretations of events with other actors involved. Time and role, of course, constrained us in all of these efforts.

REFERENCES

Arnstein, Sherry R. "A Ladder of Citizen Participation." *Journal of the American Institute of Planners* 35 (1969): 216–224.

Austin, John. *How to Do Things with Words*. London: Oxford, 1961.

Barber, Benjamin. *Strong Democracy: Participatory Politics for a New Age*. Berkeley: University of California Press, 1984.

Baum, Howell S. *The Organization of Hope: Communities Planning Themselves*. Albany, NY: State University of New York Press, 1997.

Bolan, Richard S. "Community Decision Behavior: The Culture of Planning." *Journal of the American Institute of Planners* 35 (1969): 301–310.

Briggs, Xavier de Souza. "Doing Democracy Up Close: Culture, Power, and Communication in Community Building." *Journal of Planning Education and Research* 18 (1998): 1–13.

Brown, Richard H. "Theories of Rhetoric and Rhetorics of Theory: Toward a Political Phenomenology of Social Truth." *Social Research* 50 (1983): 126–157.

Chaskin, Robert J. "Democracy and Bureaucracy in a Community Planning Process." *Journal of Planning Education and Research* 24 (2005): 408–419.

Chaskin, Robert J., Prudence Brown, Sudhir Venkatesh, and Avis Vidal. *Building Community Capacity*. New York: Aldine de Gruyter, 2001.

Ecklein, Joan L. and Armand A. Lauffer, editors. *Community Organizers and Social Planners*. New York: John Wiley and Sons, 1972.

Erickson, Frederick. "Talking Down: Some Cultural Sources of Miscommunication in Interracial Interviews." In *Nonverbal Behavior: Applications and Cultural Implications*, ed. A. Wolfgang. New York: Academic, 1979.

Forester, John, editor. *Critical Theory and Public Life*. Cambridge, MA: MIT Press, 1985.

Forester, John. *Planning in the Face of Power*. Berkeley, CA: University of California Press, 1989.

Friedmann, John. *Planning in the Public Domain: From Knowledge to Action*. Princeton, NJ: Princeton University Press, 1987.

Fung, Archon. *Empowered Participation*. Princeton, NJ: Princeton University Press, 2004.

Gans, Herbert J. *People and Plans: Essays on Urban Problems and Solutions*. New York: Basic Books, 1968.

Garfinkel, Harold. *Studies in Ethnomethodology*. Englewood Cliffs, NJ: Prentice Hall, 1967.

Goffman, Erving. *The Presentation of Self in Everyday Life*. Garden City, NY: Doubleday, 1959.

Goffman, Erving. *Relations in Public: Microstudies of the Public Order*. New York: Basic Books, 1971.

Gonzalez, David. "In the South Bronx, the Grassroots Grows Up." *New York Times* (January 7, 1993): B1, B4.

Gumperz, John J. "The Speech Community." In *International Encyclopedia of the Social Sciences*, ed. D.L. Sills. New York: Crowell, Collier and MacMillan, 1968.

Gumperz, John J. "Ethnic Style in Political Rhetoric." In *Discourse Strategies*, ed. J. Gumperz. Cambridge: Cambridge University Press, 1982.

Hackman, Richard. *Groups That Work (and Those That Don't): Creating Conditions for Effective Teamwork*. San Francisco: Jossey-Bass, 1990.

Hymes, Dell. *Foundations in Sociolinguistics: An Ethnographic Approach*. Philadelphia: University of Pennsylvania, 1974.

Innes, Judith E. "Planning Theory's Emerging Paradigm: Communicative Action and Interactive Practice." *Journal of Planning Education and Research* 14 (1995): 183–189.

Innes, Judith E. "Planning Through Consensus Building: A New View of the Comprehensive Planning Ideal." *Journal of the American Planning Association* 62 (1996): 460–472.

Kochman, Robert. *Black and White Styles in Conflict*. Chicago: University of Chicago Press, 1981.

Lofland, John and Lyn H. Lofland. *Analyzing Social Settings: A Guide to Qualitative Observation and Analysis*. Boston: Wadsworth, 1995.

Mitchell-Kernan, Claudia. "On the Status of Black English for Native Speakers." In *Functions of Language in the Classroom*, eds. C. Cazden, V. John and D. Hymes. New York: Holt, Rinehart and Winston, 1972.

Osborne, David. *Reinventing Government: How the Entrepreneurial Spirit is Transforming the Public Sector*. Reading, MA: Addison-Wesley, 1993.

Peattie, Lisa R. "Reflections on Advocacy Planning." *Journal of the American Institute of Planners* 34 (1968): 80–88.

Putnam, Robert D. *Bowling Alone: The Collapse and Revival of American Community*. New York: Simon and Schuster, 2000.

Rein, Martin. "Social Planning: The Search for Legitimacy." *Journal of the American Institute of Planners* 35 (1969): 233–244.

Rohe, William M. and Lauren B. Gates. *Planning with Neighborhoods*. Chapel Hill, NC: University of North Carolina Press, 1985.

Sandercock, Leonie. "When Strangers Become Neighbors: Managing Cities of Difference." *Planning Theory & Practice* 1 (2000): 13–30.

Saville-Troike, Muriel and Jo Anne Kleifgen. "Scripts for Schools: Cross-cultural Communication in Elementary Classrooms." *Text* 6 (1986): 207–221.

Schön, Donald. "Some of What a Planner Knows: A Case Study of Knowing-in-Practice." *Journal of the American Planning Association* 48 (1982): 351–364.

Scott, James C. *Seeing Like a State: How Certain Schemes to Improve the Human Condition Have Failed*. New Haven: Yale University Press, 1998.

Searle, John. *Speech Acts*. London: Cambridge University Press, 1969.

Tauxe, Caroline S. "Marginalizing Public Participation in Local Planning: An Ethnographic Account." *Journal of the American Planning Association*. 61 (1995): 471–481.

Wolfgang, Aaron, editor. *Nonverbal Behavior: Applications and Cultural Implications*. New York: Academic, 1979.

CHAPTER 28

Community Organizing or Organizing Community?

Gender and the crafts of empowerment

Susan Stall and Randy Stoecker

Women's work and community organizing are both, to an extent, invisible labor (Daniels 1987). What people see is the flashy demonstration, not knowing the many hours of preparation entailed in building relationships and providing for participants' basic needs. Our analysis begins with the historical division of American culture into public and private spheres that split the "public" work done mostly by men in the formal economy and government from the "private" work done mostly by women in the community and home (Tilly and Scott 1978). The cult of domesticity in the mid-19th century attempted to idealize and confine women's activities to the domestic private sphere (Cott 1977). But African American, Latina, and Asian American women, treated as units of labor, were historically excluded from the dominant ideal of the family as a protected private haven (Glenn, Chang, and Forcey 1994). Instead, women of color and low-income women expanded the boundaries of mothering and the private sphere beyond the private household as they raised and nurtured children in extended family networks within communities struggling for survival (Stack 1974). Central to the institution of Black motherhood, for example, are women-centered networks of blood mothers and "other mothers"—"women who assist blood-mothers by sharing mothering responsibilities" (Collins 1991, 119).

The public and private spheres have influenced each other through routes such as the economic impact of women's unpaid domestic labor or the impact of economic policy changes on family quality of life but have been organized around different logics. The separation of spheres also led to two different community organizing styles. Community organizing typically begins in the expanded private sphere of the neighborhood. But because the neighborhood is not as isolated as the family, and its networks include secondary as well as primary relationships, it can also be a public sphere space. This may particularly be the case for the men in those neighborhoods, who are pressured by the separation of spheres to think of themselves as public sphere actors. Consequently, there is a public sphere approach and a private sphere approach to community organizing that parallels differences between the community experiences of men and women. The community organizing model we believe most exemplifies the public sphere approach has been most associated with Saul Alinsky. The community organizing model we believe best exemplifies the private sphere approach has been developed by a wide variety of women.

THE ALINSKY MODEL

The very term *community organizing* is inextricably linked with the late Saul Alinsky, whose community organizing career began in the late 1930s. While a graduate student at the University of Chicago, he took a job to develop a juvenile delinquency program in Chicago's "Back of the Yards" neighborhood—a slum of poor Poles, Lithuanians, and Slovaks downwind of the Chicago Stockyards. When he arrived, the Congress of Industrial Organizations (CIO) was organizing the male stockyard workers living there. Expanding the CIO model beyond workplace issues, Alinsky organized the BYNC from local predominantly male neighborhood groups, ethnic clubs, union locals, bowling leagues, and an American Legion Post. The success of BYNC in getting expanded city services and political power started Alinsky off on a long career of organizing poor urban communities around the country (Finks 1984; Reitzes and Reitzes 1987). Alinsky had little patience for the version of community organizing practiced by predominantly women social workers, saying, "They organize to get rid of four-legged rats and stop there; we organize to get rid of four-legged rats so we can get on to removing two-legged rats" (Alinsky 1971, 68). Alinsky also argued that a career as a community organizer had to come before all else, including family, and to enforce this he would keep his trainees up all hours of the night at meetings and discussions. Heather Booth, who went on to help found the Midwest Academy and Citizen Action, quit the Community Action Program of Alinsky's Industrial Areas Foundation (IAF), believing that the IAF was not sensitive to women's issues and provided them with inadequate training (Reitzes and Reitzes 1987).

Alinsky's approach has influenced an entire generation of organizers, producing powerful organizations and visible victories across the country: Back of the Yards and TWO in Chicago, SECO in Baltimore, FIGHT in Rochester, MACO in Detroit, ACORN in Little Rock, ETCO in Toledo, and COPS in San Antonio, among others. These organizations have in some cases saved entire communities from destruction and produced influential leaders who have gone on to change the face of the public sphere.

THE WOMEN-CENTERED MODEL

Unlike the Alinsky model, the women-centered model of community organizing cannot be attributed to a single person or movement. We trace the model to two main sources. First, bell hooks (1990) notes the historic importance for African Americans of "homeplace" as a site to recognize and resist

domination, hooks argues, Historically, African-American people believed that the construction of a homeplace, however fragile and tenuous (the slave hut, the wooden shack), had a radical political dimension, it was about the construction of a safe place where black people could affirm one another and by so doing heal many of the wounds inflicted by racist domination. Later, in the late 19th and early 20th centuries, African American women involved in the Black Women's Clubs organized day care centers, orphanages, and nursing homes. Others, such as Ida B. Wells, organized campaigns around such issues as lynching and rape (Giddings 1984). While engaging in individual and group actions to create "Black female spheres of influence within existing structures of oppression," Black women often find that they must simultaneously work for institutional transformation (Gilkes 1980; Collins 1991, 141).

Anglo women's "municipal housekeeping" activities of the 19th and early 20th centuries are the second source of current women-centered organizing efforts. Then public-spirited women, in attempting to overcome disapproval of their public role, explained that they were only protecting their homes and families by extending their activities from the home into the public arena. Women claimed the right to be guardians of the neighborhood, just as they were acknowledged to be guardians of the family (Haywoode 1991).

Since then, women have created numerous voluntary and benevolent associations to campaign for concrete reforms in local neighborhoods and broader reforms in municipal services, education, labor, housing, health care, and children's rights (Berg 1978; Tax 1980). The most famous of these were the settlement houses, founded primarily by college-educated white middle-class women who believed they should live in the neighborhood where they worked (Bryan and Davis 1990, 5). The most well-known settlement house organizer was Jane Addams, who with Ellen Gates Starr founded Hull House on Chicago's west side in 1889. They developed parks, playgrounds, community services, and neighborhood plans. They also participated in reform movements promoting labor legislation for women and children, care of delinquents, and women's suffrage. But community organizers often viewed them as engaging in charity work rather than adversarial social action (Brandwein 1987; Finks 1984), and clinical social workers saw them as violating the detached casework method that emphasized individual treatment over social reform and community development (Specht and Courtney 1994).

The women-centered model also carries a history of success different from the Alinsky model. The activism of women in the early settlement movement, the civil rights movement, and the consciousness-raising groups of the radical branch of the 1970s' women's movement allowed women to challenge private and public arrangements in ways that would forever affect their relationships, housework, parenting practices, and career paths. The consequent changes in women's health care and women's knowledge of their own bodies, in cultural practices around dating and relationships, and the relationship between work and family are still reverberating through society. Today, women of color and low-income/working-class women create and sustain numerous protest efforts and organizations to alter living conditions or policies that threaten their families and communities (Bookman and Morgen 1988; Gutierrez and Lewis 1992; Haywoode 1991; McCourt 1977; Naples 1992). These include, but are not limited to, tenant (Leavitt and Saegert 1990), low-income housing (Feldman and Stall 1994), welfare rights (Naples 1992), and environmental issues (Krauss 1997).

COMPARING THE MODELS

Human Nature and Conflict

The Alinsky model and the women-centered model have very different views of human nature and conflict.

Among all the tenets of the Alinsky model, the assumption of self-interest has the strongest continuing sway and is greatly influenced by the centrality of the public sphere

in the Alinsky model. Since Alinsky saw society as a compromise between competing self-interested individuals in the public sphere, conflict was inevitable, and a pluralist polity was the means by which compromise was reached. Because poor people are at an initial disadvantage in that polity, the organizer's job is to prepare citizens to engage in the level of public conflict necessary for them to be included in the compromise process. Reflecting the conflict orientation that is necessary for working in the masculine competitive public sphere, Alinsky contended that the only way to overcome the inertia that exists in most communities was to "rub raw the resentments of the people in the community" (1971, 116), relying on symbols and images that reinforced a "successful forceful masculinity."

The women-centered model begins with women's traditional roles in mothering, not inherently linked to biological sex but derived from a "socially constructed set of activities and relationships involved in nurturing and caring for people" (Glenn, Chang, and Forcey 1994). These activities and relationships become transformed by "community other mothers" in the Black community who build community institutions and fight for the welfare of their neighbors (Collins 1991). Building on Collins's work, Naples describes "activist mothering" as a broadened understanding of mothering practices "to comprise all actions, including social activism, that addressed the needs of their children and the community" (1992).

Rather than a morality of individual rights, women develop a collectivist orientation (Robnett 1996) and learn a morality of responsibility connected to relationships (Gilligan 1977). Their activism is often a response to the needs of their own children and of other children in the community (Gilkes 1980). Women-centered organizers view justice not as a compromise between self-interested individuals but as a practical reciprocity in the network of relationships that make up the community (Haywoode 1991; Stall 1991).

Power and Politics

For the Alinsky model, power and politics both occur in the public sphere. When power is zero-sum, the only way to get more is to take it from someone else—a necessity in a masculinized public sphere structured around competition and exploitation. Alinsky was adamant that real power could not be given but only taken. Thus, poor communities could gain power through public sphere action—picking a single elite target, isolating it from other elites, personalizing it, and polarizing it (Alinsky 1971).

In women-centered organizing, power begins in the private sphere of relationships is conceptualized as limitless and collective. "Co-active power" is based on human interdependence and the development of all within the group or the community through collaboration (Follett 1940; Hartsock 1974). The goal of a women-centered organizing process is "empowerment"—a developmental process that includes building skills through repetitive cycles of action and reflection that evoke new skills and understandings, and in turn provoke new and more effective actions (ECCO 1989; Kieffer 1984). Empowerment includes developing a more positive self-concept and self-confidence, a more critical worldview, and the cultivation of individual and collective skills and resources for social and political action (Weil 1986).

The Alinsky model sees community organizations as already in the public sphere and, consequently, already part of the political system. Alinsky believed that poor people could form their own interest group and access the polity just like any other interest group. They may have to act up to be recognized initially, but once recognized, their interests would be represented just like anyone else's. Because Alinsky did not question the masculine competitive structure of the public sphere and the self-interested personalities required of its participants, he did not see a need for dramatic structural adjustments in the political system.

The women-centered model approaches politics from a consciousness of the exclusionary qualities of the public-private sphere split. As a consequence, women have politicized the expanded private sphere as a means to combat exclusion (Kaplan 1982). Cynthia Hamilton (1991), a community organizer in South Central Los Angeles, described a primarily women-directed organizing campaign to stop the solid waste incinerator planned for their community in the late 1980s. These low-income women, primarily African American and with no prior political experience, were motivated by the health threat to their homes and children. They built a loose, but effective, organization, the Concerned Citizens of South Central Los Angeles, and were gradually joined by white, middle-class, and professional women from across the city. The activists began to recognize their shared gender oppression as they confronted the sarcasm and contempt of male political officials and industry representatives—who dismissed their human concerns as "irrational, uninformed, and disruptive" (Hamilton 1991, 44)—and restrictions on their organizing created by their family's needs. Eventually, they forced incinerator industry representatives to compromise and helped their families accept a new division of labor in the home to accommodate activists' increased public political participation.

Leadership Development

Leadership is another characteristic of these models that shows the influence of the public-private split. The Alinsky model maintains an explicit distinction between public sphere leaders, called "organizers," and private sphere community leaders. One goal of the Alinsky model is to develop those private sphere community leaders to occupy positions in formal organizations that can extend their leadership beyond the community into the public sphere. For Alinsky, the organizer is a paid professional consultant from outside the community whose job is to get people to adopt a delegitimizing frame (Gamson, Fireman, and Rytina 1982) that breaks the power structure's hold over them. The Alinsky model maintains a strict role separation between outside organizers and the indigenous leaders. Organizers have influence, but only through their relationships with indigenous leaders. Both the location of the organizer as outside of the local community and the elevation of rational, dispassionate role-playing contribute to the gendering of this role.

There is less separation between organizers and leaders in the women-centered model because women-centered organizers, rather than being outsiders, are more often rooted in local networks. They are closely linked to those with whom they work, and they act as facilitators of the empowerment process, premised on the belief that all have the capacity to be leaders/organizers. This is a conception of leadership as teaching (Payne 1989). They find they need to deal with women's sense of powerlessness and low self-esteem (Miller 1986) before involving them in sustained organizing efforts. Women-centered organizers develop "group centered" leadership (Payne 1989) that "embraces the participation of many as opposed to creating competition over the elevation of only a few" (ECCO 1989, 16). Analyses of women-centered organizing and leadership development efforts also underline the importance of "centerwomen," or "bridge leaders." These leaders use existing local networks to develop social groups and activities that create a sense of familial/community consciousness, connecting people with similar concerns and heightening awareness of shared issues (Robnett 1996). These leaders transform social networks into a political force and translate skills that women learn in their families and communities (e.g., interpersonal skills, planning and coordination, conflict mediation) into effective public sphere leadership.

The Organizing Process

Finally, these two models adopt organizing processes that reflect the influence of, and different conceptualizations of, the public–private split. Within the Alinsky model, the organizing process centers on identifying and confronting public issues to be addressed in the public sphere. Consequently, the organization needs to be public and traditionally masculine—big, tough, and confrontational.

Door knocking is the initial strategy for identifying issues. Those issues then become the means of recruitment to the organizing effort. The organization bills itself as the best, if not only, means of resolving those issues. The public activities of the mass march, public rally, explicit confrontation, and celebrated win are all part of building a strong organization that can publicly represent the community's interests.

In the Alinsky model, the organizer is not there just to win a few issues but to build an enduring formal organization that can continue to claim power and resources for the community—to represent the community in a competitive public sphere pluralist polity. These organizations typically have traditional decision-making structures that mirror the male-dominated public sphere structures they confront. The organizer is supposed to build the organization from the community's preexisting formalized organizational base of churches, service organizations, clubs, and so forth. This emphasis on building formal organization reflects the public sphere emphasis and the gendered assumptions of the Alinsky model.

The women-centered organizing model emphasizes creating an ideal private-sphere-like setting rather than a large public sphere organization. The process begins by creating a safe and nurturing space where women can identify and discuss issues affecting the private sphere (Gutierrez 1990). This model uses the small group to establish trust and build "informality, respect, [and] tolerance of spontaneity" (Hamilton 1991, 44). The civil rights organizer, Ella Baker, was dubious about the long-term value of mass meetings, lobbying, and demonstrations. Instead, she advocated organizing people in small groups so that they could understand their potential power and how best to use it, which had a powerful influence on the Student Nonviolent Coordinating Committee (Payne 1989). Gutierrez and Lewis affirm that "the small group provides the ideal environment for exploring the social and political aspects of 'personal' problems and for developing strategies for work toward social change" (1992, 126). Moreover, smaller group settings create and sustain the relationship building and sense of significance and solidarity so integral to community.

Because the women-centered model focuses less on immediate public sphere action, a continuing organization is not as central in initial organizing. In place of the focus on organization building are "modest struggles"—"small, fragmented, and sometimes contradictory efforts by people to change their lives" (Krauss 1983, 54). Engagement in modest resistance focused on the expanded private sphere allows women to immediately alter their community and gain a sense of control over their lives.

CONCLUSION: SEPARATE MODELS, LINKED ISSUES

This chapter represents an attempt to get behind the scenes of social movements—to look at the community organizing that provides the foundation for effective social movement work. We have elaborated two models of community organizing that have developed both from the gendered positions of their founders and their consequent experientially derived conceptualizations of the public and private spheres. Although we do not see the qualities or values of the Alinsky model or the women-centered model as inherently linked to biological sex, community organizing is shaped through the specificity of men's and women's action within particular historical circumstances and periods.

What are the implications of these two models for the future of community organizing? Within the field, women-centered organizing has transformed the traditional organizing agenda so that issues formerly considered "private"—violence against women (Park 1997; Wittner 1997), toxic waste disposal (Krauss 1997), and postpartum depression (Taylor 1996)—have, through women-centered organizing, been moved from the realm of private troubles to public issues, in many cases transforming the agendas, the constituents, and the strategies of traditional organizing. Community organizing is committed to democratic goals and is supportive of humane ends. With the greater

influx of women into the Alinsky model of community organizing and the popularization of feminist goals among men and women, there is evidence that the inclusion of sexuality, emotionality, and procreation in community organizing is slowly transforming its gendered logic and practice, the sexual division of labor among community organizers, and the issues that community organizations are willing to address (Stall 1986).

Still, the corporate and government sectors show no signs of becoming less competitive, and there are continuous conservative cries to preserve a private sphere protected from the brutalities of public life. In this context, the weaknesses of one model are the strengths of the other.

The strengths of the women-centered model are in building the relationships that can sustain a struggle over the long haul. The social role of motherhood is still important for women's activism. And while we have argued that the women-centered model can span the boundaries between the public and private spheres—making personal issues into public issues, we are concerned that the model cannot, by itself, transform the public sphere. Women-centered organizing can move private sphere issues such as health, housing, and sanitation into the public sphere. But their resolution is subject to the competitive processes of that sphere. Thus, the women-centered model, and community organizing in general, face a "paradox of empowerment"—the need to organize simultaneously at the personal and structural levels (Rappaport 1981).

But how do we combine the models? First, we need to understand whether there are times when one model is more viable than the other. Second, we need to learn whether certain circumstances might call for certain organizing models. Third, we need to investigate the existing examples and the future implications of women engaging in the Alinsky model of organizing and men engaging in women-centered organizing.

The gendered biases of social movement theory have led to neglect of not just women's work in social movements but of an entire substructure of action, based in informal groupings, predominantly of women, engaged in building the relationships necessary to sustain long-term struggles. We need to correct these biases to recognize social action that may not immediately appear as such, because it provides a foundation for the social movement action more typically studied.

REFERENCES

Alinsky, Saul. 1969. *Reveille for radicals*. New York: Vintage.

Alinsky, Saul. 1971. *Rules for radicals*. New York: Vintage.

Berg, Barbara J. 1978. *The remembered gate: Origins of American feminism: The women and the city 1800-1860*. New York: Oxford University Press.

Bookman, Ann, and Sandra Morgen. 1988. *Women and the politics of empowerment*. Philadelphia: Temple University Press

Brandwein, Ruth A. 1987. Women and community organization. In *The woman client*, edited by Dianne S. Burden and Naomi Gottlieb. New York: Tavistock.

Bryan, Mary Lunn McCree, and Allen E. Davis. 1990. *100 years at Hull-House*. Bloomington: Indiana University Press.

Collins, Patricia Hill. 1991. *Black feminist thought: Knowledge, consciousness, and the politics of empowerment*. New York: Routledge.

Cott, Nancy E 1977. *The bonds of womanhood: "Woman's sphere" in New England, 1780–1835*. New Haven, CT: Yale University Press.

Daniels, Arlene Kaplan. 1987. Invisible work. *Social Problems* 34: 403–15.

Education Center for Community Organizing (ECCO). 1989. *Women on the advance: Highlights of a national conference on women and organizing*. Stony Point, NY: ECCO.

Feldman, Roberta M., and Susan Stall. 1994. The politics of space appropriation: A case study of women's struggles for homeplace in Chicago public housing. Edited by Irwin Altman and Arza Churchman. Human Behavior and Environment Series, *Women and the Environment* 13: 167–99. New York: Plenum.

Finks, P. David. 1984. *The radical vision of Saul Alinsky*. New York: Paulist Press.

Follett, Mary Parker. 1940. *Dynamic administration*. New York: Harper & Row.

Gamson, William A., Brace Fireman, and Steven Rytina. 1982. *Encounters with Unjust Authority*. Homewood, IL: Dorsey.

Giddings, Paula. 1984. *Where and when I enter: The impact of Black women on race and sex in America*. New York: William Morrow.

Gilkes, Cheryl Townsend. 1980. Holding back the ocean with a broom: Black women and their community work. In *The Black woman*, edited by L. R. Rose. Beverly Hills, CA: Sage.

Gilligan, Carol. 1977. In a different voice: Women's conceptions of self and •morality. *Harvard Educational Review* 47(4): 481–517.

Glenn, Evelyn Nakano, Grace Chang, and Linda Rennie Forcey. 1994. *Mothering: Ideology, experience, and agency*. New York: Routledge.

Gutierrez, Lorraine M. 1990. Working with women of color: An empowerment perspective. *Social Work* 35: 149–154.

Gutierrez, Lorraine M., and Edith A. Lewis. 1992. A feminist perspective on organizing with women of color. In *Community organizing in a diverse society*, edited by Felix G. Rivera and John I. Erlich. Boston: Allyn & Bacon.

Hamilton, Cynthia. 1991. Women, home, and community. *Women of Power* 20 (Spring): 42–45.

Hartsock, Nancy. 1974. Political change: Two perspectives on power. *Quest: A Feminist Quarterly* 1(1): 10–25.

Haywoode, Terry L. 1991. Working class feminism: Creating a politics of community, connection, and concern. Ph.D. diss., The City University of New York, New York.

hooks, bell. 1990. *Yearning: Race, gender, and cultural politics*. Boston: South End.

Kaplan, Temma. 1982. Female consciousness and collective action: The case of Barcelona 1910–1913. *Signs: Journal of Women in Culture and Society* 7(3): 545–66.

Kieffer, Charles H. 1984. Citizen empowerment: A developmental perspective. In *Studies in Empowerment: Steps toward understanding action*. edited by Julian Rappaport, C. Swift, and R. Hess. New York: Haworth.

Krauss, Celene. 1983. The elusive process of citizen activism. *Social Policy* (Fall): 50–55.

Krauss, Celene. 1997. Challenging power: Toxic waste protests and the politicization of white, working-class women. In *Community activism and feminist politics*, edited by Nancy A. Naples. New York: Routledge.

Leavitt, Jacqueline, and Susan Saegert. 1990. *From abandonment to hope: Community-households in Harlem*. New York: Columbia University Press.

McCourt, Kathleen. 1977. *Working class women and grassroots politics*. Bloomington: Indiana University Press.

Miller, Jean Baker. 1986. *Toward a new psychology of women*. Boston: Beacon.

Naples, Nancy A. 1992. Activist mothering: Cross-generational continuity in the community work of women from low-income urban neighborhoods. *Gender & Society* 6: 441–63.

Park, Lisa Sun-Hee. 1997. Navigating the anti-immigrant wave: The Korean women's hotline and the politics of community. In *Community activism and feminist politics*, edited by Nancy A. Naples. New York: Routledge.

Payne, Charles. 1989. Ella Baker and models of social change. *Signs: Journal of Women in Culture and Society* 14(4): 885–99.

Rappaport, Julian. 1981. In praise of a paradox: A social policy of empowerment over prevention. *American Journal of Community Psychology* 9(1): 1–26.

Reitzes, Donald C., and Dietrich C. Reitzes. 1987. *The Alinsky legacy: Alive and kicking.* Greenwich, CT: JAI.

Robnett, Belinda. 1996. African-American women in the civil rights movement, 1954–1965: Gender, leadership, and micromobilization. *American Journal of Sociology* 101: 1661–93.

Sacks, Karen Brodkin. 1988. *Caring by the Hour.* Urbana: University of Illinois Press.

Specht, Harry, and Mark E. Courtney. 1994. *Unfaithful angels: How social work has abandoned its mission.* New York: Free Press.

Stack, Carol. 1974. *All our kin: Strategies for survival in a Black community.* New York: Harper & Row.

Stall, Susan. 1986. Women organizing to create safe shelter. *Neighborhood Works* 9(8): 10–13; 9(9): 10–11, 12.

Stall, Susan. 1991. "The women are just back of everything . . .": Power and politics revisited in small town America. Ph.D. diss., Iowa State University, Ames, Iowa.

Tax, Meredith. 1980. *The rising of the women: Feminist solidarity and class conflicts, 1880–1917.* New York: Monthly Review Press.

Taylor, Verta. 1996. *Rock-a-by baby: Feminism, self-help, and postpartum depression.* New York: Routledge.

Tilly, Louise A., and Joan W. Scott. 1978. *Women, work, and family.* New York: Hold, Rinehart & Winston.

Weil, Marie. 1986. Women, community, and organizing. In *Feminist visions for social work*, edited by Nan Van Den Bergh and Lynn B. Cooper. Silver Springs, MD: National Association of Social Workers.

Wittner, Judith. 1997. Reconceptualizing agency in domestic violence court. In *Community activism and feminist politics*, edited by Nancy A. Naples. New York: Routledge.

CHAPTER 29

How Does Community Matter for Community Organizing?

David Micah Greenberg

OVERVIEW

This theoretical chapter describes ways that community context can matter for community organizing and its outcomes. In doing so it seeks to reframe a particularly contentious debate in organizing and development practice—the relative efficacy of conflict vs. consensus modes of organizing. Proponents of consensus organizing hold that "traditional" models of organizing, those which emphasize protest and divergent interests, are not likely to succeed. Proponents of other organizing modes, sometimes implicating community development practices, see consensus organizing as the manipulation of existing networks without changing terms of power. Instead of viewing conflict or consensus-based strategies in a vacuum, I view these strategies as emerging in local political cultures where patterns of conflict or consensus are *themselves* key dimensions of political institutions. This is an argument that community "matters" in community organizing, in that organizing promotes a vision or frame of community itself. This vision finds confluence or resistance from existing political structures and inter-organizational patterns of interaction. While institutional resistance to a campaign's frames about community may make it more difficult for campaigns to succeed, this resistance also holds open the possibility for broad shifts in power and in inter-organizational dynamics.

WHY LOOK AT ORGANIZING SERIOUSLY—AND CRITICALLY?

Community organizing can make a difference in poor people's lives. It can develop indigenous leaders, shift power toward the disenfranchised and toward persons of color (Fainstein and Fainstein 1974), create social capital and community cohesion (Saegert 2001) and direct additional resources to distressed areas (Rubin 1992; Greenstone and Peterson 1973). However, any critical account of the role of organizing must also understand that it does not always accomplish its goals—or that it can produce different types of outcomes that may fall short of the transformative ambitions from which it stems. This fact, well understood by veterans of collective action, is often neglected both by writers on community organizing and by scholars of movement activity generally (Giugni 1998). While much writing on organizing focuses on its successes, many efforts stumble or are defeated (Marcuse 1999; Stone 2001). Some campaigns may build power for the organization without achieving any external goals. Others may achieve their immediate objectives but not affect broader social or political dynamics. Given the range of potential outcomes of community organizing, is there any framework that can help us understand what dynamics may lead to different types of successes and failures?

Within communities of practice around organizing, one attempt to explain the scale and significance of changes lies in assessments of the relative merits of conflict and consensus organizing. This debate is closely related to another highly-charged question, whether or not Community Development Corporations (CDCs) operate in a proper relationship to political action. Stoeker (1997, 2001) argues that CDCs operate within a flawed framework that emphasizes the manipulation of existing arrangements, as opposed to seeing the world in its truest terms: full of conflict and interests that relegate the disadvantaged to that status. In a later piece, Stoeker argues that CDCs who attempt to conduct community organizing will not be successful, even though *not* organizing will relegate them to irrelevance. Stoeker's positions about CDCs (and about organizing by CDCs) is situated in relationship to a belief that consensus organizing, a recently-developed offshoot of organizing practice, is less effective than other models articulated in the United States since the 1950s. Although purposive attempts to change urban neighborhoods and government through collective action at the grass roots are probably as old as cities and states themselves (Castells 1983), discourse about community organizing within the United States draws extensively on the institutional history of a practice developed from Saul Alinsky's work in the Chicago's Back of the Yards (see Alinsky, 1971). Alinsky emphasized contentious tactics and confrontation to provoke positive action toward communities by powerful actors. In recent years, a different approach to organizing emerged in reaction to organizing's tendency to emphasize conflict. For Michael Eichler, founder of the Consensus Organizing Institute, the confrontation model often results in failure because it refuses to create issues of mutual self-interest that can bring together broad constituencies:

> The organizer who sees the world in terms of absolutes is doomed. Most people, regardless of income, realize how complicated the world has become. Just ask any parent. We can no longer afford to oversimplify. Instead, we have

to admit how complicated and contradictory the world has become ... We need to teach people how to analyze the self-interest of potential partners and have the ideological flexibility to mix and match partners.

(1998)

Of special relevance to CDCs, Eichler directed a demonstration project for the Local Initiatives Support Corporation to test principles of consensus organizing. This program used a consensus-organizing model to bring together stakeholders (including neighborhood associations, service groups, banks, and elected officials) in the Monongahela Valley region, Phoenix, and other areas, so they could come together to form new CDCs. For proponents of consensus organizing—prominently, Ross Gittell and Avis Vidal (1998), whose book describes the LISC demonstration project—this organizing for CDC formation proves that more confrontational organizing is counterproductive.

Arguments around conflict and consensus organizing stem, at least in part, from diagnoses of community development as an industry, and may be seen as purposive attempts to alter discourse and therefore practice by community groups. However, as hypotheses to predict *outcomes* of organizing, I argue that they are theoretically incomplete, because *both* do not sufficiently account for dynamics of community context and structure. As analysts of community change processes, proponents of both conflict and consensus organizing privilege issues of framing and tactics over issues of community structure. That is, those who hold that mobilization (on either model) is more effective believe that people's collective capacity to analyze community structure is one of the most important factors that determines whether or not they will be able to create change. Both argue that seeing the world in terms of powerful conflicts, on the one hand, or seeing the world in potential allies on the other (and adopting the tactics that stem from either analysis) will result in more significant outcomes for change. I argue that this position is analogous to what Margaret Archer (1988) calls "upward conflationism"—the theoretical stance that practices on the part of individuals and groups from below create larger structural patterns.

Archer's argument is that there are three types of errors that social theorists sometimes make. The first is a "downward conflationism," with which she associates many Marxist writers. Downward conflationists write that structural forces, or those "above" the realm of individual and collective agency, help constitute the practices of those actors. The second is an "upward conflationism," held by microsociologists or rational choice proponents, who see larger cultural practices to be determined from the actions of individuals and groups from "below." The third error is a "medium conflationalism;" where writers argue that structure and agency constitute each other. Archer's argument is that each type of "conflationism" makes it harder to gather insights about the periods of change or stasis. Archer's argument is relevant to the consensus vs. conflict organizing debate, because it directs attention to the possibility that different organizing campaigns (*agentic* efforts) may interact with different neighborhoods (*structural* factors) in different ways, sometimes succeeding in creating change, and sometimes failing to create change or to reinforce them. But if agentic issues—framing and tactics—are only one side of the story about organizing and its potential impacts, how can we conceptualize neighborhood and community context in a way that might be more complete?

WHAT ASPECTS OF COMMUNITY STRUCTURE MIGHT MATTER FOR ORGANIZING?

Community organizing is based in place. Place is the resource from which organizers draw residents and organizations. Place is also a *target* for change, in that it seeks to sway its concrete outcomes and local institutions that a campaign attempts to sway. However, the role of varied community contexts as both resource and target for organizing is significantly under-theorized in the organizing literature. That is, while sensitive to the possibility of varied community needs in the very model of local, self-defined

empowerment, organizing practitioners often describe organizing practice as if it occurred in a vacuum of social or community space. For example, Delgado (1986) describes the ACORN model as avoiding inter-organizational work and seeking to create new power-building organizations through a universal process. In fact, in accounts of social movement activity more broadly, the role of varied context or local structure is often obscured. Even Castell's sympathetic, comparative account of urban movements sees the articulation of community as a stage in a mobilization process—and potentially a hindrance—in the development of class consciousness. This lack of appreciation of the *variety* of contexts is somewhat indicative of trends in the social movements literatures to see structure dichotomously, as political opportunities that are either "open" or "closed" (McAdam 1982), with the former facilitating movement-building and the latter shutting it down. Instead, I argue that political structure should be seen as a mediating variable with which movement interacts.

I argue that two aspects of community-level institutions should be taken seriously in our analysis of the context of organizing. The first aspect involves community organizational networks—the ways that local groups interact with each other. As writers on community structure have understood since analysis of inter-organizational networks in the 1970s (Lauman 1977), power within neighborhood systems is greatly influenced by the structure of relationships among local groups. Although organizing creates relationships among individuals, it also may change the balance of power among existing community groups, or change the *terms* of interaction among them—affecting local dynamics of cooperation or contention. The second critical aspect of neighborhood institutions involves rules, policies or practices on the part of place-based actors. While concrete "wins"—getting funds for a school program, getting the city to shut down an unwanted business—are significant accomplishments, we should also look carefully at the ways that organizing may redirect agencies to be increasingly open to political participation in a sustained way, as these are the changes most likely to benefit neighborhoods. In the case of organizing around housing or community development issues, these practices are mostly likely to be seen among agencies or policies that influence local development activities and outcomes.

These two structures—organizational networks and political institutions—are both relational, dynamic structures. As relational structures, they are possessed of different *terms* of interaction, or different political cultures. One way to understand the context for organizing is to identify a neighborhood's distinct, recognizable, political culture typified by qualities of practice, terms of exchange, and recognized discourses. These terms of interaction are significant to assess from an organizing perspective, as campaigns occur within—and sometimes attempt to change—these political cultures. Within these local cultures, conflict and consensus are not simply key terms in the debate around organizing practice. They are also embedded within local political cultures themselves.

WHAT ARE SOME RELEVANT DIMENSIONS OF COMMUNITY'S POLITICAL CULTURE?

Drawing on the democratic deliberation literature (Mouffe 2000; Benhabib 1996) and the literature on race and political action, I argue that there are two important dimensions of political culture to consider in understanding how organizing emerges in diverse neighborhoods. These dimensions involve (1) the presence of *conflict*, and (2) the articulation of racial and ethnic *difference* in community. The first dimension, conflict, is widely understood as fundamental to political activity. The model I espouse for understanding neighborhood context adds an additional dimension, by understanding that conflict in the US is often set in relationship to issues of racial and ethnic difference. Both local government and community organizations make issues of racial and ethnic difference an important part of their culture, or otherwise make its omission also salient for the ways they project authority and challenge. For example, Mollenkopf's (1994)

account of New York City during the Koch Administration identifies discourse around race as a critical component to maintaining governing coalitions. In their extensive account of the Community Action program, Greenstone and Peterson (1973) write that community groups' mobilization of African-Americans around issues of discrimination was an important part of the challenge they posed to urban political systems.

Along these lines, I argue that discourse about race and about conflict not only helps structure relationships between local government and residents, but also that these claims provide the basis for interaction among community organizations. This is because community organizations, many of whom formed in relationship to urban political challenges of the 1960s and 1970s, have their roots deeply touched by issues of race. In the forty years after Community Action, urban challenge, and local disruptions, questions of race remain an extremely important component to local political challenges and political structures. For this reason, both community organizations and political institutions are intensely aware both of issues of conflict, and issues of difference. That is, the ways that local groups interact with each other is informed by an understanding about the role of difference and the role of conflict in community life. I elaborate on both dimensions below.

Conflict

I define the presence of "conflict" in community culture as the *extent to which groups and government employ coercive means, contentious tactics, and tension*. This definition is consistent with the normative, theoretical literature on democratic deliberative theory (see Mouffe 2001), and also on social movement studies about the institutionalization of protest (Piven and Cloward 1977). Sometimes coercive means and punitive tactics are employed by political machines, and by groups seeking to challenge these machines. But even outside of "machine" political systems, issues of conflict are particularly salient. The salience of this dimension of political culture is illustrated by the difference between Giuliani and Bloomberg Administrations' approaches to governance in New York City.[1] The Giuliani Administration relied successfully on conflict-oriented, "hard-ball" approaches to governance and political action, seeking contentious, wedge issues (such as welfare reform and homeless rights) that mobilized the Mayor's white ethnic base. In contrast, the Bloomberg Administration's approach to governance has been marked by relatively conspicuous efforts at consensus-building around the same, potentially contentious policy issues. At the same time, a mayoral administration's strategy is not the only factor which defines a political culture, with many advocacy groups refusing to participate in consensus-building efforts.

Difference

I draw on language employed by democratic theorists (Benhabib 2001; Marion Young 2000) to describe representation of racial and ethnic difference as a second important dimension of local political culture, calling it *the extent to which communities articulate fundamental distinctions among constituencies*. The presence of "difference" as a variable in local political culture should not be confused with the ways that race *objectively* figures into local outcomes, but instead as a critical frame for community action that is either voiced or not voiced. Either explicitly, through inclusion, or implicitly, through de-emphasis, political cultures make representations about race-based patterns of political and economic exclusion impacting their neighborhoods. Communities for whom racial or ethnic difference is an important component of political culture may have many national or ethnic associations, or support diverse, multi-lingual outreach by organizations and government. In contrast, local cultures that de-emphasize difference may frame action in more general terms, without explicit reference to the racial, ethnic, or class composition of their constituencies, even when constituencies are primarily people of color.

These two dimensions of political culture are separable from each other, as illustrated by Figure 29.1 and elaborated in descriptive paragraphs below.

Diverse-Inclusive Neighborhoods

First, cultures I characterize being "diverse-inclusive" (low evocation of conflict, high evocation of difference) attempt to incorporate new groups into neighborhood and civic life without excessive conflict. These cultures attempt to accommodate difference through sensitivity to diversity through communication, negotiation, and deliberation over contentious tactics and separatist/nationalist claims (on the part of organizations), or punitive or coercive modes of incorporation (on the part of local government). Some hypothetical cases might include resource-rich, progressive suburbs with the political institutions to incorporate and provide in some way for new constituencies.

Consensus-Pluralist Neighborhoods

"Consensus-pluralist" local cultures (low evocation of conflict, low evocation of difference) emphasize attempts to build broad and inclusive agreement based on shared values. These cultures de-emphasize the potential that particular interests may supersede the ability of institutions to accommodate them. In such communities, coalitions may emphasize shared values, articulate a vision of "one community" acting in concert for self-betterment, build openness in communication among partners, and share information between state and public groups. Some hypothetical cases include places where New England, town-meeting type institutions prevail and have helped enforce deliberation and consensus-building.

Partisan-Advocate Neighborhoods

"Partisan-advocate" cultures (high evocation of conflict, low evocation of difference) understand the basis for inter-group interaction within neighborhoods or cities in terms of particularist agendas driven by personal history and organizational affiliation. In these cultures, ideology, race, class, or other social groupings suggest little to actors

	Low evocation of difference	High evocation of difference
Low evocation of conflict	Consensus-pluralist	Diverse-inclusive
High evocation of conflict	Partisan-advocate	Agonistic-pluralist

Figure 29.1 Two dimensions, and four types of community political cultures

about the need for change. These cultures are characterized by contentious tactics, but racial and ethnic difference is not a central frame through which political action is organized. Examples of these may include neighborhoods where community politics is dominated by a few, elite interests or associations that are not fully cohesive; or even ethnically-diverse neighborhoods where "machine" politics provides the basis for incorporation, rather than cultural associations.

Agonistic-Pluralist Neighborhoods

Communities that emphasize both difference and conflict I call "agonistic-pluralist," borrowing the term from writers about democratic deliberation (Mouffe 2000; Benhabib 2001). Bonnie Honig's articulation of "agonism" characterizes this culture well: "the inescapability of conflict and the ineradicability of resistance to the political and moral projects of ordering subjects, institutions, and values ... it is to give up on the dream of a place called home ... free of power, conflict, and struggle" (Benhabib 2001: 186). Such cultures stress tension and conflict as means toward political action, and frame this action within an explicit context of racial and ethnic difference. Progressive, contentious neighborhoods (New York's Lower East Side or Williamsburg; San Francisco's Mission District; Boston's Jamaica Plain) are examples of these types of communities.

HOW DOES ORGANIZING (OF DIFFERENT MODELS) INTERACT WITH LOCAL POLITICAL CULTURES?

Getting back to this chapter's original (but side-stepped) question, I argue *that in different neighborhood contexts, conflict organizing or consensus organizing might create different types of responses from local and state actors.* In practice, organizing groups take different approaches to collective action—some avoid conflict or seek it selectively, and some embrace it. Similarly, as campaigns are developed, leaders make decisions about whether to emphasize or de-emphasize these issues of racial and ethnic difference. Claims articulated in campaigns are important not only because they appeal to identities of groups and individuals in organizing campaigns, but also because patterns of interaction between residents, local groups, and the state form complementary (or competing) claims to those advanced by the organizing. Regardless of its particular source, claims about community structure and community change intrinsic within organizing, and the tactics that followed these orientations, significantly inform the ways that other groups responded to organizing, helping determine whether they remained bystanders, joined up with the cause, mobilized against it, or otherwise attempted to influence the campaign.

The stakes that successful organizing might have on local political institutions becomes clearer to organizers and activists as they interact with neighborhood groups, elected officials, and governmental agencies about broad and potentially issues within community life. By holding meetings with residents, pushing agendas with members of other community organizations, carrying out actions and demonstrations, and interacting with governmental agencies and elected officials, groups learn whether their efforts might be incorporated into existing community dynamics, or if they pose a more radical threat to political institutions. As leaders interact with staff and members of other groups, other organizations recognize the character of a group's claims toward race and toward conflict, how it relates to their own efforts, and whether it is complementary or dissonant with their own. That is, while the specific demands of campaigns can themselves be seen to be significant by other groups, equally important are the ways that these demands are viewed as an extension of broad claims about race and about conflict within community.

Where agreement forms, or where tensions stemming from divergent views about race and about conflict are quickly accommodated, collective action may build on previous successes, or continue general setbacks within that neighborhood. Where dissonance forms between groups about the orientation of organizing work, campaigns spark more friction within the community, and between residents and government. While this friction presents challenges for organizing, making it more difficult to "win," it also holds out the potential to reshape relationships among community groups and to change power dynamics between neighborhoods and city hall. These shifts in culture are also likely to be associated with shifts in local power structures—in the networks of organizations, or in the orientation of governmental institutions. Similarly, changes in the way that state actors frame their work is likely to be associated with changes in substance of their policies and their inclusivity of resident groups.

This dynamic is illustrated by (Figure 29.2).

As such, I argue that context "matters" for organizing outcomes, because participants in organizing themselves develop a collective understanding of place, and because contests over this representation influence what change becomes possible through organizing. This perspective is a critical augmentation to the debate on consensus organizing, as scene in different hypothetical scenarios. For example, what might be a radical orientation toward difference and conflict in one setting, proves to be accepted and easily-incorporated by another community—as in the case of a progressive, challenge-oriented neighborhood group acting in a neighborhood with institutions that are already oriented toward norms of racial justice; in such a case, organizing (when successful) may exist to reinforce against "external" political forces (such as gentrifiers, with a different political orientation and resource demands) and to *maintain* local institutions. In another situation even tentative evocations of challenge or racial and ethnic consciousness may be met with fierce resistance, enact dynamics of contention and challenge, and carry the potential to introduce new policies and discourses as a result. Similarly, one could be consensus-oriented in a dysfunctional, machine-dominated, conflictual community, and by winning campaigns introduce the potential for "a new way of doing business" where the consistent articulation of consensus-building principles still poses a radical threat to community dynamics.

WHAT ARE IMPORTANT CAVEATS?

In the model here, I talk about the implications of dissonance and confluence as *potential* outcomes, because success is likely dependent on factors other than the orientation of a group toward challenge or toward consensus. Although developing a specific orientation toward community—a frame for local action—is one way to attempt to capture "hearts and minds" of residents over the course of organizing (as the literature on social movement framing suggests), the power to *enact* community changes does not come through rhetorical appeal alone or through more passive appeal to identity. Instead, we should be open to other aspects

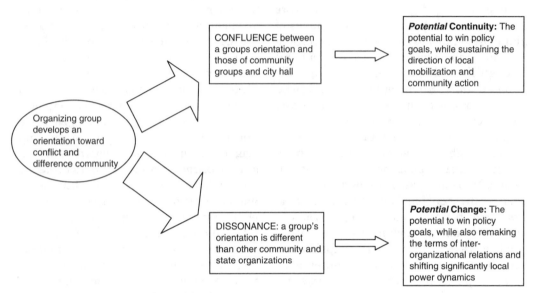

| Orientation toward conflict and difference | Results in dynamic path within organizing campaign | Forms a potential organizing outcome |

Figure 29.2 Theoretical model of organizing in context

of practice—ones that are more sensitive to the basic skills of organizational power-building, such as building relationships, developing leaders, and providing opportunities for collective decision-making. In essence, while my argument is that framing processes cannot be understood in a vacuum, it is also that framing processes *alone* do not change neighborhoods. In reductionist terms, how "angry" a handful of residents are, how sensitive they are to issues of race, how inclusive and cooperative they are, or how color-blind they imagine themselves to be, does not alone effect change. Instead, residents must learn to build effective organizations.

CONCLUSION

My overall goal in this chapter has been to move toward a more nuanced theoretical account of organizing outcomes. In my view, this account would both avoid the dichotomously-posed debates around consensus and challenge-based organizing. We should also be sensitive to exploring *ways* of contending—understanding that there is not just one form that struggle can take. We should also be sensitive the *specific context* in which these struggles occur—understanding that practices effective in one neighborhood might provoke a different response in others. We should also depict the phenomenon of organizing in a way that describes the role of *both* human agency and social structure. The model described above tries to illustrate the interaction between the two broad categories of agency and structure—at least as collective action and movement activity at the neighborhood level illuminates them.

NOTE

1. The author acted as an organizer and advocate during both Administrations.

REFERENCES

Alinsky, Saul. 1971. *Rules for Radicals: A Practical Primer for Realistic Radicals*. New York: Random House.

Archer, Margaret S. 1988. *Culture and Agency*. Cambridge: Cambridge University Press.

Benhabib, Seyla. 1996. *Democracy and Difference*. Princeton: Princeton University Press.

Castells, Manuel. 1983. *The City and the Grassroots*. Berkeley: University of California Press.

Delgado, Gary. 1986. *Organizing the Movement: The Roots and Growth of ACORN*. Philadelphia: Temple.

Eichler, Michael. 1998. *Organizing's Past, Present, and Future*. Shelterforce 101: September/October.

Fainstein, Norman, and Fainstein, Susan. 1974. *Urban Political Movements: The Search for Power by Minority Groups in American Cities*. Englewood Cliffs: Prentice Hall.

Gittell, Ross and Vidal, Avis. 1998. *Community Organizing: Building Social Capital as a Development Strategy*. Thousand Oaks: Sage.

Giugni, Marco. 1998. "Was it worth the effort? The outcomes and consequences of social movements." *Annual Review of Sociology* 24: 371.

Greenstone, J. David, and Peterson, Paul E. 1973. *Race and Authority in Urban Politics: Community Participation and the War on Poverty*. New York: Russell Sage Foundation.

Lauman, Edward O. *et al.* "Community-Elite Influence Structures: An Extension of a Network Approach." AJS 83: 3. 1977.

McAdam, Doug. 1982. *Political Process and the Development of the Black Insurgency, 1930–1970*. Chicago: University of Chicago Press.

Marcuse, Peter. 1999. "Housing Movements in the USA" in *Housing, Theory and Society*, vol 16, pp. 67–86, 1999.

Mollenkopf, J. 1994. *A Phoenix in the Ashes: The Rise and Fall of the Koch Coalition in New York*. Princeton, NJ: Princeton University Press.

Mouffe, Chantal. 2000. *The Democratic Paradox*. London: Verso Books.

Piven, Frances Fox, and Cloward, Richard A. 1977. *Poor People's Movements: Why They Succeed, How They Fail*. New York: Pantheon Books.

Rubin, H.J., and Rubin, I.S. 1992. *Community Organizing and Development*. Boston: Allyn and Bacon.

Saegert, Susan *et al.* 2001. *Social Capital and Poor Communities*. New York: Russell Sage Foundation.

Stoeker, Randy. 1997. "The Community Development Corporation Model of Urban Redevelopment: A Political Economy Critique and an Alternative." *Journal of Urban Affairs (19)*.

Stoeker, Randy. 2002. "Community Organizing and Community Development: Apples and Oranges? Chicken and Egg? Paper presented on COMM-ORG: The On-Line Conference on Community Organizing and Development. *http://comm-org.utoledo.edu/papers.htm*.

Stone, Clarence, *et al.* 2001. *Building Civic Capacity: The Politics of Reforming Urban Schools*. Lawrence, Kansas: University Press of Kansas.

Vidal, Avis C. 1996. "CDCs as Agents of Neighborhood Change: The State of the Art". In *Revitalizing Urban Neighborhoods*, edited by W. D. Keating, Kumholz, Norman, and Star, Philip. Lawrence, Kansas: University of Kansas Press.

Young, Iris Marion. 2000. *Inclusion and Democracy*. Oxford: Oxford University Press.

PART IV

Theoretical Conceptions and Debates

CHAPTER 30

Introduction to Part IV

James DeFilippis and Susan Saegert

This final section of the book addresses some of the key theoretical issues involved in community development. There are three sub-sections that make up this section, and they represent—aside from the questions around the basic structures and character of *community* (which is discussed in Chapter 1, and at length in Part III)—the three most fundamental sets of issues that community development practitioners and students must come to terms with. The point of this Part is not to provide definitive answers to the problems posed by these issues, but rather to enable more thoughtful and productive engagement with these problems. Solutions to the issues raised here are not to be found in either the abstract or a generalized template. Instead, working through these issues and problems is both context-specific and an ongoing and imperfect process.

The first sub-section returns to the concepts of housing and domestic property that were first addressed in Stone's chapter. Housing is a vital part of community development practice. Because community is the realm of social reproduction, and housing plays such a central role in reproduction, it is vital that we have a thorough understanding of housing as an abstract idea, and the policies that play such an important role in shaping the housing stock in American communities. Davis's Chapter 31 asks some very fundamental questions about the extent to which property is a unitary thing—or even if it is a *thing* at all. Instead, he argues that property is a set of six different interests that coalesce around the two basic interests of accommodation and accumulation. While he doesn't say so explicitly here, the implication

is the kinds of tenurial relations people can have vis-à-vis property are therefore not limited to owner and renter, and instead can encompass a range of different forms which can combine the different rights and interests of property in different ways. Pitcoff's Chapter 32 is less ambitious, but no less controversial. In it, he argues that the goal of making all Americans homeowners is one that fundamentally needs to be re-thought. His arguments have significant implications for the CDCs that build housing, and for the foundations and public sector agencies that support them.

The second sub-section addresses the basic issues of oppression in American society. The first chapter in this section (by Marion Young) is a broad, sweeping essay that analyzes oppression as a set of processes that occur in different types of social, political and economic relationships. It explicitly rejects the notion of a hierarchy of oppression (in which some forms of oppression are *more oppressive* than others), and instead argues that groups—and oppression is a process felt by groups rather than just individuals—are oppressed in different ways. The next two chapters examine oppression and difference in more particular ways—that is, through the lenses of race and gender in American cities. Given the importance of race and racism in structuring American cities, it is almost remarkable that the observations in Lawrence's chapter are so often over-looked by community development practitioners who are trying to improve the conditions of life in American cities. But it is precisely because Lawrence's call to address race and racism more seriously and comprehensively than is normally done is so rarely heard that his chapter is so vital to this book. Garber's Chapter 35 on gender and community starts from a slightly different position than Lawrence's and it asks the basic questions of what theories and practices of *community* mean for women in North America. Women are a definitive part of communities in the United States. And by this we mean two things. First, women play a disproportionate role in community organizing and community development work (something also discussed in Chapter 28 by Stall and Stoecker). Second, and related to that, if community is the realm in which social reproduction occurs, then it must be recognized that social reproduction has long been gendered, in the social division of labor, as "women's work." This, of course, is directly related to the disproportionate role women play in community work. But when the two halves come together it means that women simultaneously find their most open and accessible political space (compared to other forms of political engagement) in the arena of community involvement, but they can also be simultaneously "kept in their place" (so to speak) in that engagement. It is these issues that Garber works through and disentangles in her chapter.

Finally, the section ends with a set of chapters that ask perhaps the most fundamental questions of all, and they are: how much can we improve things at the community scale?; and are these the most productive forms of intervention we can make to try to transform and improve life in American communities? These questions were asked in Chapter 1's introduction, and will be touched upon again in Chapter 39's conclusion. But these three chapters provide a much more thorough analysis of the issues involved. The sub-section starts with Stoecker's famous essay that challenges the whole institutional framework of the CDC (Chapter 36). He argues that by internalizing the fundamentally antagonistic relations between community and capital, CDCs have forever compromised themselves and their ability to either improve conditions for the

communities they work in, and are part of, or mobilize that community to demand the kind of larger-scale changes needed to fundamentally improve lives for poor communities throughout the United States. Fraser *et al.*'s Chapter 37 takes a slightly different approach, and analyzes the limits of community interventions in the contemporary political economy. To Fraser and his colleagues, the issue isn't necessarily the institutional structure of the community organization, but rather the transformation of the larger political economy that we have witnessed since the 1980s and how that greatly constrains the ability of community-scale interventions to affect change. The section ends with the chapter from Kubisch *et al.* who are a bit more optimistic than either Stoecker or Fraser and his colleagues. They recognize the problems inherent in community building efforts (and community-focused interventions more generally), but also try to find ways beyond these limits. It is for this reason that we end the section on theories and debates with this chapter. For while we share the legitimate concerns of Stoecker and Fraser, *et al.*, and we have more than a little ambivalence about the potential and limits of community development, we also think it's important to find ways to analyze and practice community development that recognize and try to mitigate its limitations and contradictions.

The problem on the agenda for the next generation of community development is to move beyond critique and abstract debates about inherent limits to new theory and practice. The problems of historically reified ideologies around private property, historically hardened forms of oppression and exclusion, and the huge power and resource difference between local actors within communities in need of development and external larger, wealthier and more powerful actors do not argue for eschewing altogether the local scale. We have assembled the pieces of this Reader in hopes that it will facilitate real learning, discussion, and innovation in ways to address the current limits faced by disadvantaged communities at multiple scales.

CHAPTER 31

Domestic Property Interests as a Seedbed for Community Action [1]

John Emmeus Davis

"Do communities act?" Even as Charles Tilly (1974) posed this provocative question, he was never really in doubt that collective action on a territorial basis can and does occur. After all, American cities were just emerging from a period of political protest, popular mobilization, and social conflict as intense as any they had known, most of it organized on the basis of residential neighborhoods. "Of course communities act," answered Tilly, and embarked on a search for when and why.

We are engaged here in a similar quest, attempting to explain collective action in the place of residence. The Marxist theory of collective action argues that objective, relational interests may be the basis for group formation and inter-group conflict. The neo-Weberian theory of "housing classes" argues that such interests inhere not only in a group's relationship to productive property, but also in a group's relationship to "domestic property"—land and buildings that are used for housing.[2] Combining these theoretical strands, we are led to the proposition that the cleavages and conflicts of residential neighborhoods may be explained, in part, by the different and competing interests that people have in a neighborhood's land and buildings. A better understanding of the conditions for collective action on a territorial basis begins with a better understanding of the interests engendered by domestic property.[3]

There are two basic types of domestic property interests: accommodation and accumulation. People have an interest in the use value of domestic property, utilizing residential land and buildings for personal shelter, or they have an interest in the exchange value of domestic property, utilizing residential land and buildings for financial gain. Some people have an interest in both. Accommodation and accumulation are actually *clusters* of interests, each describing various benefits that people derive from their relationship to domestic property. Three use interests are preeminent: security, amenity, and autonomy. On the other side, three exchange interests are preeminent: equity, liquidity, and legacy. These half-dozen domestic property interests do not exhaust the field. Each could be subdivided again and again to yield an ever-longer list. These six denote the principal lines of demarcation most frequently found within the complex mosaic of competing property interests that give rise to many of the groups and much of the conflict arising within the place of residence.

EQUITY

Equity refers to the unencumbered value inherent in land and buildings. In a market economy, equity is the fair market value of real property minus any debt that encumbers that property. It is the value that exists free and clear once a mortgage, lien, or any other liability has been paid off. Part of this value is created by the dollars and labor of the individual owner, poured into the property over a period of time. Another part, often the larger part, is less a product of the owner's investment than a gratuitous windfall bestowed by the surrounding society. This "social increment" is a function of numerous factors, including the public's investment in services, facilities, and infrastructure, the region's growth, and the relative scarcity of land and housing. It is also a function of the general amenity of a parcel's setting. As Cox (1981: 434) has noted, "a variety of property-value studies ... find that such resources as school quality, public safety, quiet, and even views of Pacific sunsets are indeed reflected in house values." Whether created by the property's owner or by the surrounding society, equity accrues to individual parcels of property and belongs to whoever happens to be the property's owner. Equity is commonly defined as "the owner's interest."

Domestic property can be regarded as a kind of financial repository where a combination of personally created and publicly created wealth is embedded in residential land and buildings. Unlike savings in a local bank, however, the financial stake that a person has in domestic property is neither protected nor predictable. Equity in land and buildings is not a private, autonomous transaction between owner and owned, where a dollar in is always a dollar out. Equity, instead, is a relational advantage, contingent upon the decisions and behavior of many actors. Much of what gives value to domestic property is social, not individual.

Equity is also precarious, since many of the conditions that contribute to a property's value can also take it away, should circumstances change. Even the equity which an individual creates through his or her own investment can be wiped out by changes in the maintenance or amenity of proximate parcels of domestic property, by changes in the level of private or public investment in the surrounding neighborhood, or by changes in the regional economy.

Since equity may be harmed as well as enhanced by the actions of others, it is not only a precarious advantage, but often a contentious one as well. The financial benefit that one group of people expects to enjoy from domestic property can be threatened by a competing use that another group intends for proximate parcels of property. Equity is both a product of social relations, therefore, linking every property to those around it, and frequently a source of social conflict

as well, pitting one interest group against another.

LIQUIDITY

On the most basic level, liquidity is synonymous with "ease of sale," the facility with which equity can be converted into cash. Liquidity is more than marketability, however, because domestic property may also produce a stream of income without being sold. Residential land and buildings may generate income from monthly rents. They may be used for collateral, permitting the owner to raise cash for personal use or profitable investment. Equity may be unlocked from a parcel of property through a "reverse equity mortgage," creating an annuity for a homeowner who continues to inhabit the house. Domestic property may also function as a tax shelter, reducing the owner's tax liability on income derived from other sources.

Liquidity is clearly related to equity. Generally, the higher the equity, the greater a property's income potential; the lower the equity, the lower its income potential. Anything that affects the equity in a parcel of domestic property will usually affect the income that can be realized from that parcel. But liquidity also has a life of its own. There are factors that affect liquidity rather differently than they affect equity. Favorable tax breaks or governmental rent subsidies, for example, can generate a stream of income that is much higher than a neighborhood's severely depressed property values might otherwise allow. Conversely, a property with a high value may become unrentable because of high vacancy rates in the local rental market, the low amenity of the surrounding neighborhood, or the low status of the surrounding neighbors. Laws such as rent control, anti-conversion ordinances, and zoning may also limit the income that can be derived from rental property that is otherwise quite valuable.

Aside from the fact that equity and liquidity can vary independently, they should be treated as separate property interests for the simple reason that domestic property is regularly used in two very different ways. It can be used to accumulate wealth through appreciating property values (equity), a benefit usually realized upon the property's sale. Or it can be used to generate income (liquidity), a benefit usually realized throughout the property's tenure. The different uses reflect different ways that people exploit the financial potential of land and housing. They represent different benefits that people derive from domestic property.

LEGACY

Domestic property is an inheritable estate, often the single most valuable possession that is passed from one generation to another. Since inherited property may also be used for personal shelter by one's heirs, there is some reason to consider legacy as much of a "use interest" as an "exchange interest." Indeed, many homeowners who bequeath domestic property to their children do so in the hope that one of their children will actually occupy the dwelling.

Such a legacy of use, however, is not as common in the United States as it once might have been, or as common as it tends to be in other countries. More typical are those cases in which the bequeathed property is quickly sold and the proceeds divided among several heirs, or the property is immediately rented out, providing heirs with an annual income. It is the exchange value of domestic property, not its use value, which is often the greater interest of those who bequeath the property and, even more frequently, of those who receive the property.

Although closely related to equity and liquidity, there are three reasons to differentiate legacy from these other accumulative interests: there is the potential for one's heirs to inhabit the property, where its use value temporarily trumps its exchange value; the futurity of the interest casts the property's profitability in a different light; and some social factors, such as public policies governing taxes and estates, affect legacy differently from equity and liquidity. Legacy involves a person (or group) in a set of relationships and bestows an orientation toward action

that is different than the relational ties and action orientation engendered by equity or liquidity.

SECURITY

With security, we turn from interests of exchange to those of use. If exchange depends on domestic property being "worth something," use depends on the property being safely and predictably "with someone." It depends on someone having a secure hold over whatever housing he or she occupies. Even more basic than security of tenure, but closely related, is physical safety. Domestic property shelters one from the weather, shields one from the lawless and, if there is a garden, nourishes one as well.

Security as safety is a function, in part, of the condition, repair, and design of the property itself. In this respect, security and amenity (another use interest) go hand-in-hand. Security is also a function, however, of the social climate from which the occupants of domestic property seek shelter. Safety does not stop at a person's front door. A milieu in which assault or theft is common jeopardizes the physical safety of the occupants of even the most structurally sound dwelling. The security of domestic property and the security of the surrounding neighborhood are interrelated.

Equally dependent on this interrelationship of property and place is security of tenure. Although largely a function of the legal arrangements under which a property is owned, occupied, and used, the "right to stay put" is affected by other factors as well.[4] Cycles of private investment and disinvestment, for instance, not only raise or lower the exchange value of domestic property; they often exert displacement pressures on renters and homeowners alike. Abandonment and redlining on one side of the cycle, and gentrification, condominium conversions, and office building development on the other, can threaten whatever residential security a population may have.

Public investment—or disinvestment—can also jeopardize security. The sort of massive removal of thousands of low-income residents that occurred under urban renewal is less common today, but government-initiated displacement still occurs, directly or indirectly. As Hartman (1984: 303) has pointed out, "a great deal of ostensibly private-sector displacement is supported by or the indirect result of government policies, programs or actions." Low-interest loans for downtown redevelopment, tax policies that encourage luxury renovation of historic buildings, landlord-tenant laws that permit easy eviction or credit laws that permit easy foreclosure are only a few of the factors that may adversely affect residential security.

Security, like the other interests of domestic property, is a social product of the neighborhood and society in which a property is embedded. Security is a relational advantage, made precarious by its contingency upon many social factors. Furthermore, to the extent that a person's security can be undermined or threatened by other actors, near and far, as they avidly pursue their own economic or political interests, security is not only a precarious advantage, but frequently a contentious one as well.

AMENITY

Amenity refers to the quantity and quality of one's living space. At its most basic level, amenity is a matter of sound housing in good repair. It is what housing activists and public health officials have long sought to achieve via health, safety, and building codes. Amenity has many gradations, however, and quickly rises beyond basic health and safety. It includes a broad range of quantitative and qualitative variations in the size, design, decoration, and energy efficiency of a residential building, as well as variations in the acreage, topography and other physical attributes of residential land. All of these make a parcel of domestic property more or less comfortable, pleasant, and appealing. All are part of a property's amenity.

Amenity, like security has a large social component. The quality of one's personal living space is inseparable from the safety, health, beauty, and ambiance of the communal living space—that is, one's neighborhood. The availability of essential services and the proximity of jobs, stores, schools, and recreational facilities are also a part of neighborhood amenity.

Amenity encompasses, therefore, both the individual and the social, private space and public space. It is contingent, in both realms, upon a host of factors and actors, especially the political decisions of public officials in allocating facilities and services and the economic decisions of private investors in making loans, buying property, and developing commercial and residential buildings. Closer to home, amenity is contingent upon whatever one's neighbors are doing with *their* property and whatever is happening in the neighborhood as a whole. The quality of one's personal living space and the quality of the communal living space tend to rise or fall together.

AUTONOMY

Autonomy refers to both the degree of control that one is able to exercise over domestic property and the degree of individuation that such property impresses upon its occupants. Autonomy as *control* is essentially a matter of one's ability to use, shape, and develop his or her housing independently of the dictates of another. Autonomy as *individuation* refers to the contribution that domestic property makes to personal privacy, power, and identity. The homeplace functions for many persons as a "realm of personal control in a world where he or she generally feels impotent" (Rakoff, 1977: 101). It is a private, separate sphere, providing some insulation against the self-images imposed by the larger society. Domestic property may also function as a status symbol, raising or lowering personal esteem in the eyes of one's neighbors. As Logan (1978: 407) has pointed out, "a home is not just where you live; it is a location in a well-developed status ecology." Autonomy and identity are tightly intertwined.

On a more macro level, the autonomy of domestic property has been associated with the political independence of individuals and the "home rule" of local areas. The notion that personal control over domestic property provides a basis for an independent, self-governing citizenry is a recurrent theme of political theory. Especially in America there was early acceptance of the view that men of property possessed a moderation of desire, a freedom of thought, and an independence of political judgment lacking in those who owned no land. Only landowners were permitted to vote. Although the United States long ago extended the franchise, there is still a cultural tendency to associate autonomy in the private realm of domestic property with independence and participation in the public, political arena. Those who exercise greater control over their private space, by virtue of owning domestic property, are believed to participate more freely and fully in public affairs. Perin (1977: 56) has described this lingering ideological association between homeownership and citizenship in the starkest way: "Homeowners are full fledged citizens. Renters are not."

Of all the interests of domestic property, autonomy would seem the least social, the least relational. Yet the degree of privacy and control that one enjoys over domestic property is regularly affected by the surrounding social environment. The freedom to use and improve domestic property, for example, is dependent upon whatever land-use controls, building codes, rental guidelines, or anti-conversion ordinances happen to be in effect at the time. Use and improvement are contingent, as well, on contractual relations between the owners of property and the lenders who finance it. Most mortgage and development loans carry a stipulation of inspection and approval by the lender for any major changes that the owner may later propose for the mortgaged property.

The latitude that an owner has in using his or her property is also affected, to some degree, by neighborhood norms—the expectations that one's neighbors may have concerning the "proper" maintenance, design, improvement, and use of domestic property. As for non-owners, whatever privacy or control they possess will depend largely on the legal language of their lease, but the condi-

tions of their occupancy are also a social product of landlord–tenant law and housing quality standards governing rental property.

The control that one is able to exercise over a parcel of property is contingent, in short, upon numerous social factors. Autonomy is a relational advantage, a precarious product of the social environment in which a property is embedded. Furthermore, to the extent that part of its precariousness is due to the strategic activity of other groups pursuing *their* advantage, sometimes to the detriment of one's own, autonomy is also inherently contentious. An interest in autonomy not only draws one into relation with various policies, institutions, and norms that delimit one's privacy and control over domestic property, therefore. It also draws one into relations with various social groups who may threaten the autonomy that one already has.

DOMESTIC PROPERTY AS A "BUNDLE OF INTERESTS"

These six relational advantages of domestic property might be treated theoretically as housing preferences (or "values"), housing services (or "utilities") or, in the jargon of real estate law, as "sticks" in a property's "bundle of rights." For the purpose of explaining collective action, however, they are better seen as "interests." The attributes that make them "interests" are their material, objective, collective, and relational character, as well as the action orientation they bestow upon different domestic property positions.

To say that these advantages are *material* is to claim for equity, liquidity, legacy, security, amenity, and autonomy little more than that they originate in the tenures and functions of a physical entity—land and buildings used for shelter. They also affect the physical or economic well-being—i.e., the material condition—of those who have a personal stake in such property.

These six advantages are *objective* in the sense that one's position in relation to domestic property carries a probability of particular benefits, a susceptibility to particular costs, and a propensity to act in certain ways that inhere in the position itself, regardless of whether the incumbent of that position is aware of this state of affairs. Saunders (1984: 207) puts it well, when describing the "objective conditions" that distinguish homeowners from tenants:

> Owner-occupiers, for example, form a distinct sectoral interest not because as property owners they mainly *believe* that they have the same sort of stake in the capitalist system, nor because their lifestyle (e.g., suburbanism) leads them to *claim* a superior status to that of non-owners, but because the objective conditions of their material existence are such as to drive a wedge between their interests and life-chances and those of non-owners.

A group does not need to be aware of its property stake for someone else to gauge what the group's interests might be. It is not even necessary for people to want those interests or to defend them for an outside observer to assess the interests inherent in their property position or what relation those interests may have to social factors that threaten or enhance them. There will be times, in fact, when an outside observer can make a judgment of a person's (or a group's) interest that is more accurate than that which is made by the "interested" party. The six interests of domestic property are objective in a double sense, therefore. They inhere in one's objective relation to land and buildings used for shelter, and they can be objectively assessed by an uninterested observer.

To assert that domestic property interests are *collective* is not to embrace the dubious thesis that interests are structural properties of collectivities, having nothing to do with individual actors. Interests are collective only in the sense that people who share a common relation to domestic property are presumed to share a common set of interests. These common interests are a latent, relational bond, existing among similarly situated individuals, which *may* become the basis for solidarity and collective action among them.[5]

Equity, liquidity, legacy, security, amenity, and autonomy have also been described

as being *relational*. They each have a character that is social, locational, precarious, and sometimes contentious. They are "social" in the sense that all of these interests are contingent upon numerous factors in the environment surrounding any parcel of domestic property. Whatever private interest an individual may have in using domestic property is invariably defined, limited, threatened, or enhanced by market forces, public policies, and social conditions of the encapsulating social structure. These interests are "locational" in the sense that every parcel of domestic property is situated in—and connected to—a given locale. Some of the most important conditions affecting one's property interests are those that are associated with the parcels and actions of one's closest neighbors. Proximate parcels and proximate actors are linked together in a "community of fate." To have a stake in property is to have a stake in place as well.[6]

The relational character of domestic property interests is also "precarious" and "contentious." These interests are precarious because, in their contingency upon so many social and locational factors, they are susceptible to fluctuation, erosion, or loss. Their precariousness, in particular, is a consequence of many actors pursuing *their* advantage at the expense of one's own. People may find themselves antagonistically related, therefore, even if they neither recognize nor want such enmity, simply because of a different and conflicting stake in domestic property. Their interests are objectively contentious.[7]

To have an interest in a parcel of domestic property, within a specific territorial space, is to become enmeshed in a complex web of local and extra-local relations that both affect one's advantage, for better or worse, and orient one's behavior in a particular way. This *action orientation* reflects the propensity of people to act in pursuit or defense of their own property interests. These interests bestow not only a propensity to act, but a propensity to act with or against other people. There is a latent tendency for the incumbents of the same property position, sharing a common set of interests, to act *collectively* in defense (or enhancement) of those interests. Similarly, there is a latent tendency for the incumbents of different property positions, having antagonistic domestic property interests, to act *contentiously* in defense (or enhancement) of their respective interests. Whether this dual orientation actually leads to collective action and inter-group conflict will depend on many conditions of consciousness and organization. Even when people's interests are threatened, there is no certainty that they will act collectively or contentiously—or act at all. There is only a *possibility* that they will behave in this way, though a possibility made more probable by the interests that are theirs.

In the end, it is this probability of patterned and predictable behavior that provides the principal reason for treating the relational advantages of domestic property as a "bundle of interests," rather than preferences, utilities, or rights. To regard these advantages as property *interests*, within the Marxist meaning of that term, is to discover a means by which collective action and inter-group conflict *on a territorial basis* might be explained. These interests establish an essential theoretical connection between the property and polity of the place of residence: linking a locality's material base with the differentiation and political action of its indigenous groups; linking the spatial and the social. Interests of equity, liquidity, legacy, security, amenity, and autonomy provide a means of comprehending why the *territory* of a common locale can sometimes become a seedbed for collective action. They provide the raw materials for an explanation of group formation and inter-group conflict in the residential urban neighborhood.

NOTES

1. Excerpted from "Domestic Property as a Bundle of Interests," Chapter 4 of *Contested Ground: Collective Action and the Urban Neighborhood*. Ithaca, NY: Cornell University Press, 1991.
2. The analysis of housing classes most relevant to the present discussion is found in Saunders (1984) and Pratt (1982).
3. This builds upon Molotch (1976: 311) who argued that every locality should be seen "not merely as a demarcation of legal, political or topo-graphical features, but as a mosaic of competing land interests capable of strategic coalition and action."
4. A longer discussion of the "right to stay put" can be found in Hartman (1984), who coined the phrase.
5. At least ten property-based collectivities may be found in urban neighborhoods that have a diversity of types and tenures of housing: the homeless, public tenants, private tenants, social homeowners, household homeowners, acquisitive homeowners, landlords, financiers, developers, and speculators. These "domestic property interest groups" exist only in embryo. They are objectively constituted social formations that may or may not develop into consciously organized, politically active groups.
6. "Community of fate" was coined by Logan (1978), although I am using the term differently. My own use is closer to that of Blum and Kingston (1984: 175), who speak of homeowners sharing "an important economic fate with their neighbors." A similar idea is expressed by Qadeer (1981) who speaks of the "web of externalities" in which urban land is enmeshed.
7. Property interests that are different are not always antagonistic. Cooperation, rather than conflict, is occasionally possible across the political divide created by different property positions and property interests.

REFERENCES

Blum, Terry C. and Paul W. Kingston. 1984. "Home-ownership and Social Attachment." *Sociological Perspectives* 27 (April): 159–80.

Cox, Kevin R. 1981. "Capitalism and Conflict around the Communal Living Space." Pp. 431–55 in Michael Dear and Allen J. Scott (eds.), *Urbanization and Urban Planning in Capitalist Society*. New York: Methuen.

Hartman, Chester. 1984. "The Right to Stay Put." Pp. 302–18 in Charles Geisler and Frank Popper (eds.), *Land Reform, American Style*. Totowa, NJ: Rowman and Allanheld.

Logan, John R. 1978. "Growth, Politics, and the Stratification of Places." *American Journal of Sociology* 84(2): 404–15.

Molotch, Harvey. 1976. "The City as a Growth Machine." *American Journal of Sociology* 82 (September): 309–31.

Perin, Constance. 1977. *Everything in Its Place: Social Order and Land Use in America*. Princeton, NJ: Princeton University Press.

Pratt, Geraldine. 1982. "Class Analysis and Urban Domestic Property: A Critical Reexamination." *International Journal of Urban and Regional Research* 6(4): 481–501.

Qadeer, M.A. 1981. "The Nature of Urban Land." *American Journal of Economics and Sociology* 40(2): 165–82.

Rakoff, Robert. 1977. "Ideology in Everyday Life: The Meaning of the House." *Politics and Society* 7(1): 85–104.

Saunders, Peter. 1984. "Beyond Housing Classes: The Sociological Significance of Private Property Rights in Means of Consumption." *International Journal of Urban and Regional Research* 2 (June): 202–25.

Tilly, Charles. 1974. "Do Communities Act?" Pp. 209–40 in Marcie Pelly Effrat (ed.), *The Community: Approaches and Applications*. New York: Free Press.

CHAPTER 32

Has Homeownership Been Oversold?

Winton Pitcoff

Discussion about homeownership almost always seems to begin with some reference to owning one's own home being a part of "The American Dream." Homeownership has come to stand for wealth, stability and civic participation. As such, many view homeownership not merely as something for low-income families to aspire to, but as their ticket out of poverty.

Whatever the collective and individual benefits of homeownership—and they are still subject to debate—the costs are significant, especially for low-income households whose resources are limited.

One of the most telling statistics of the recent home-buying surge is the accompanying rise in the number of homeowners who are leveraged. Until the 1930s, homebuyers typically paid 40 percent down. In the 1970s and 1980s, 15 percent down payments were common. Today, loans with zero-down payments are readily available, with some mortgage companies even offering mortgages greater than the equity value of the house, providing cash to cover transaction and moving costs. Forty percent of first-time borrowers are putting down 10 percent or less; 16 percent of all borrowers put down 5 percent or less on their mortgages in 2000. Homeowners owe almost $5.7 trillion on mortgages, an increase of 50 percent in just the past four years, which is greater than the federal government or corporate sector debt.

SELLING HOMEOWNERSHIP

Tax laws have long supported homeownership, most notably through the deductibility of mortgage interest, property taxes and other costs. These deductions total about $100 billion each year, more than three times HUD's current annual budget to support affordable housing. Tax law also allows the exclusion of house price appreciation from capital gains tax and penalty-free withdrawal of money invested in IRAs for first-time homebuyers.

However, this largess is not evenly distributed. Since the Mortgage Interest Deduction and related benefits are available only to those with incomes high enough to itemize deductions, 63 percent of these deductions goes to those in the top one-fifth of the income distribution, and only 18 percent goes to those in the bottom fifth. Similarly, very few low-income households have IRAs to draw from.

Federal programs insure more than a million loans a year to help home buyers with fewer funds available for a down payment, low incomes, or poor credit histories, mostly through the Federal Housing Administration. The secondary mortgage market, primarily Fannie Mae and Freddie Mac, purchases more than half of the loans originated by mortgage lenders, and is required to do a certain amount of business each year that benefits low-income and other underserved markets. But as for-profit, publicly traded companies, these institutions must continually expand their markets. With the upper-income homebuyers market virtually saturated, they have turned their attention to traditionally underserved low-income and minority households.

Regulation of the banking industry, through fair lending laws, the Community

Reinvestment Act and the Home Mortgage Disclosure Act, was designed to encourage homeownership by reducing lending discrimination in traditionally underserved markets. Banks, in turn, have aggressively targeted low-income and minority neighborhoods with mortgage and other loan products. While such strategies may well be in response to the regulations, banks have also had to turn to new markets in order to remain profitable.

"Mortgages are always good business for banks," says Kathy Tullberg of the Massachusetts Community and Banking Council. "Many banks think that low-income homebuyers will eventually move into needing additional loans for cars or education, as well as other banking products, and that these homebuyers will come back to the same bank where they got their mortgage."

Some HUD programs originally designated for rental subsidies have been adapted for homeownership. For example, some Section 8 voucher holders can use their subsidies toward mortgage payments. HOME and Community Development Block Grants now allow funds to be used for grants or loans toward down payments and closing costs. Forty-nine percent of HUD's HOME program funds were used for rental housing in 1995; that number declined to 36 percent by 1997. Many municipalities and states also have programs that provide direct subsidies to first-time and low-income homebuyers.

HUD's national homeownership strategy works to educate the public about its benefits, certifies counseling agencies and includes a small number of direct subsidy programs. While much of the counseling has proven positive, some programs do little more than provide pamphlets, help potential homebuyers meet real estate agents, or assist with cleaning up credit records, leaving many people unprepared for the responsibility of homeownership.

"We need to come up with a better way to measure success in homebuyer counseling," says Tullberg. "Some say that success should be based on the number of new homebuyers, but it should be based on the appropriateness of the decision for the families."

THE ECONOMICS OF LOW-INCOME HOMEOWNERSHIP

As typically presented by homeownership advocates, the formula seems obvious—why pay rent when you could build equity? Paying a mortgage can be a form of forced savings. The median wealth of low-income homeowners is more than 12 times that of renters with similar incomes—66 percent of the wealth of all low-income homeowners is accounted for by home equity.

Buying a home with a fixed-rate mortgage also means that some monthly costs will remain the same, as opposed to rents, which usually rise on a regular basis. Many housing proponents argue that if a homeowner's wages rise over time, real housing costs as a percentage of income actually decline because the mortgage remains constant, while rent often increases at a rate greater than inflation and wages.

But the formula is not so simple. Transaction and maintenance costs can negate low mortgage payments in some areas. Payments may remain constant over the life of a 30-year mortgage, but insurance, taxes, utilities and other expenses will likely increase. Lower-income families are more likely to borrow against the equity in their home, often at high rates, diminishing any accumulated wealth. Some studies have found that, setting aside the growth in home equity, low-income homeowners actually save less than renters and have fewer funds available for home maintenance or to cushion against income loss. With most or all of their savings in their homes, low-income homeowners are vulnerable to housing market downturns.

And yet the number of low-income homeowners continues to grow. Loans to low-income homebuyers increased by 94 percent between 1993 and 1999. Mortgage volume in 2001 was higher than ever before, in no small part due to record low mortgage rates. More than $2 trillion was borrowed, 59 percent for refinancing. Subprime lending, which targets low-income and high-risk borrowers with high-interest loans, was expected to top $210 billion in 2002. One in five homeowners refinanced their mortgage debt in the past year. As much as 30 percent of them did so to pay down other—mostly credit card—debt. At the same time, a record number of homeowners have filed for bankruptcy protection.

"We can't just get overly obsessed with getting people into homeownership," says Nicolas Retsinas, director of Harvard University's Joint Center for Housing Studies. "We have to make sure they stay in homeownership." He notes that the biggest revolution in mortgage lending in the past seven years is an automated underwriting system that has expanded lending opportunities for low-income families, but it has yet to be tested in a slow economy.

Such tests appear to be coming. Defaults on loans in 2000 amounted to approximately one million households losing their homes to foreclosure, during the height of an unprecedented economic expansion. As the economy has softened, those numbers have worsened, with delinquencies and foreclosures on all loans rising steadily and reaching an all-time high in the second quarter of 2002. Foreclosures on FHA-backed loans to low-income households have risen the fastest, to a rate of nearly 3 percent, with an additional 12 percent behind in their payments in the second quarter of 2002.

Overall, homeownership has proven to be a good investment, consistently performing better than the "safer" bond market, although not as well as the more volatile stock market. But these gains are also making homeownership less affordable to low-income households. The median price for a single-family home rose nearly 45 percent during the 1990s, while the poorest 40 percent of Americans had a growth in their income of just 35 percent during that same time. In 2000 alone, tax-adjusted housing costs as a share of income were 8 percent higher than the year before, while real incomes increased only 2 percent. And while the average single-family home has appreciated every year since 1950, there have been many downturns in individual markets.

For those low-income homeowners who keep up with maintenance and mortgage payments, there is no conclusive research about how they fare in building equity. Eric Belsky, executive director of the Joint Center

for Housing Studies at Harvard University, says low-income households tend to purchase homes when the housing cycle is depressed and prices are lower, and as such are often at less risk of losing equity. As the share of loans to low-income households has increased in recent years, he says, more low-income buyers may be vulnerable now.

LIMITED CHOICES

Low-income homebuyers are limited by the available housing stock and by what they can reasonably afford. Between 1997 and 1999 about a half million new units, or 30 percent of new construction, were affordable to households earning 80 percent or less of Area Median Income. That gain was more than eclipsed by the number of homes that became unaffordable because of market conditions at the time. In addition, houses affordable to low-income buyers are often older, in need of costly repair and located in depressed, crime-ridden neighborhoods with few jobs.

In Baltimore, where there were more foreclosures than home sales in 2001, deteriorating housing stock is a major problem. Houses with major structural or mechanical problems masked by cosmetic repairs are often sold at inflated prices to low-income families, says Becky Sherblom, executive director, Maryland Center for Community Development. Many of those homes are later foreclosed on or abandoned. At the same time, local CDCs bought abandoned or deteriorating houses and rehabbed them to sell to low-income buyers. Such fix-up projects often cost more than $100,000 in communities where the homes could only be sold for $60,000, leaving the CDCs to fill the gap with CDBG or other subsidy money, Sherblom says.

"Homeownership policy is being treated as an economic development strategy and a wealth enhancement policy, but it's really gambling," says Anne Shlay, director, Center for Public Policy at Temple University. "Low-income people are being encouraged to buy older homes with an unclear shelf life that may or may not appreciate in value."

House Proud

To limit a discussion of homeownership to economics, however, is to miss the very emotional and social aspects of owning one's own home. "People tend not to look at their houses as investments but as a community resource, a place for them to live where their kids can grow up," says Bruce Dorpalen, director of ACORN's housing division. "They want to not have to worry about a landlord's rules. They want to paint their house how they want, and that's really important." In this context, owning is a status symbol, and renting carries a stigma.

"Renting is seen as inferior to owning, rather than simply another form of tenure," says Sheila Crowley, president of the National Low Income Housing Coalition.

Research on the effects of homeownership is relatively new, but as one would expect, most of it finds numerous benefits: adults are better citizens, healthier physically and mentally, and children achieve more and behave better. What is not clear, however, is whether homeownership stimulates these traits or if those most likely to own their homes are already predisposed toward such behavior because of income, wealth, education, age, stability or family composition.

Belsky says that civic engagement has more to do with the tax base and political clout of a community and can be found in communities of any combination of renters and homeowners. "Communities under stress usually get organized because they have a reason to, and renters definitely do get involved in their communities," he says.

Other studies find that homeownership can have negative social effects. For example, some homeowners may try to keep lower-income families or minorities out of their communities; others may fail to maintain their home, default on the mortgage and ultimately abandon the house.

Helping move people into homeownership could make sense as part of a broader plan to develop jobs and the economy, and improve neighborhoods and schools. But the idea that these improvements will organically follow an increase in homeownership rates is "silly," says Shlay. "Schools are in bad shape due to suburbanization and out-migration, not because of low homeownership rates."

A well-developed rental policy could be just as effective as part of a neighborhood economic development plan. "The owner-renter distinction is at best a false one," says Shlay. "Because tenure is correlated with so many other things, tenure could be an outcome, not a cause."

OTHER PLAYERS

CDCs and other community-based groups that work on housing issues have also become more focused on homeownership.

"Increasing homeownership is great, but it shouldn't come at the expense of other programs," says Carol Wayman, policy director for the National Congress for Community Economic Development. "It's not a silver-bullet cure for neighborhood revitalization. We need a balance of housing types that meets the needs of the community. CDCs need help making an intentional determination about what to do, rather than being driven by what money is available."

The money available is no small matter. For example, the Ford Foundation now focuses all of its housing-related grantmaking on homeownership, and no longer supports groups that exclusively focus on rental housing or housing advocacy.

"We've decided to focus on homeownership as a means of building assets," says George McCarthy, a Ford program officer. "Homeownership is the main means by which people have been able to gain wealth and it's the most viable option for housing low-income people, because the rental market doesn't work and is pushing them out. The challenge is how to make homeownership available for the lowest-income families."

Ford's strategy does not include limited-equity opportunities such as community land trusts or mutual housing. "It's too hard to move into market rate housing from those kinds of housing," McCarthy says. "You don't have enough opportunity to build assets, which is what low-income people need."

But just because homes usually appreciate doesn't mean everyone should own one, says Woody Widrow, project director of the Texas Individual Development Account Network.

"Homeownership may not be the best wealth-building strategy," says Widrow. "Being a renter and owning a business or saving money to send your kids to college may be a better strategy."

WHAT ABOUT RENTERS?

Thirty-three percent of the households in America are renters, and the American Housing Survey found that among householders age 25 or under, renters make up 81 percent. So if most people are renters for at least some part of their lives, what's happening to the rental housing market with homeownership in the spotlight?

"In the euphoria around homeownership, rental housing runs the risk of losing resources when it's already grossly underfunded relative to the need of renters," says Belsky. "Rental is an important housing option that has the potential to be affordable and stable and produce a lot of benefits."

Widrow notes that most renters who want to move into homeownership cite security of tenure, control of their living conditions and the chance to build equity. "What if we had a rental policy that could provide those things for renters?" he asks.

But such policy is not likely to come about as long as the public perceives rentals as public housing and subsidized units failed efforts to house the poor. "We have to move away from the perception that renters are losers," Widrow says. Until then, "people will opt to buy even though it may not be their best housing choice."

For millions of Americans, owning a home is a major step toward financial self-reliance, stability and having a stake in a community. It's hard to find fault in a policy that wants to make these opportunities available to everyone.

Where fault lies, however, is in perpetuating the myth that homeownership is risk-free and appropriate for everyone. With mortgage delinquencies and foreclosures at record levels, particularly among low-income households, millions of poor families might have been better off today had they not chosen to purchase a home. Instead, they have lost savings, are on their way to losing their homes and will soon be forced into a rental market that is tighter and less affordable than ever.

More face the same fate unless the strategy to promote homeownership includes a plan for ongoing support to help families stay in their homes, keep them well-maintained and realize the potential growth in wealth. Homeownership will never be right for everyone, and continual support for the rental market is needed as well. As constructed today, however, with limited research, obvious economic peril to a large population and potential for backlash that could have broad repercussions for the larger economy, the strategy of promoting homeownership for all seems dangerously short-sighted.

CHAPTER 33

Five Faces of Oppression

Iris Marion Young

I have proposed an enabling conception of justice. Justice should refer not only to distribution, but also to the institutional conditions necessary for the development and exercise of individual capacities and collective communication and cooperation. Under this conception of justice, injustice refers primarily to two forms of disabling constraints, oppression and domination. While these constraints include distributive patterns, they also involve matters which cannot easily be assimilated to the logic of distribution: decisionmaking procedures, division of labor, and culture.

For contemporary emancipatory social movements oppression is a central category of political discourse. Entering the political discourse in which oppression is a central category involves adopting a general mode of analyzing and evaluating social structures and practices which is incommensurate with the language of liberal individualism that dominates political discourse in the United States. A major political project for those of us who identify with at least one of these movements must thus be to persuade people that the discourse of oppression makes sense of much of our social experience. Yet we have no clear account of the meaning of oppression.

In an effort to offer such a definition I aim to systematize the meaning of the concept of oppression as used by such diverse political movements as women, Blacks, Chicanos, Puerto Ricans and other Spanish-speaking Americans, American Indians, Jews, lesbians, gay men, Arabs, Asians, old people, working class people, and the physically and mentally disabled, and to provide normative argument to clarify the wrongs the term names.

Obviously the above-named groups are not oppressed to the same extent or in the same ways. In the most general sense, all oppressed people suffer some inhibition of their ability to develop and exercise their capacities and express their needs, thoughts, and feelings. In that abstract sense all oppressed people face a common condition. Beyond that, in any more specific sense, it is not possible to define a single set of criteria that describe the condition of oppression of the above groups. Consequently, attempts by theorists and activists to discover a common description or the essential causes of the oppression of all these groups have frequently led to fruitless disputes about whose oppression is more fundamental.

The contexts in which members of these groups use the term oppression to describe the injustices of their situation suggest that oppression names in fact a family of concepts and conditions, which I divide into five categories: exploitation, marginalization, powerlessness, cultural imperialism, and violence. Each may entail or cause distributive injustices, but all involve issues of justice beyond distribution. One reason that many people would not use the term oppression to describe injustice in our society is that they do not understand the term in the same way as do new social movements. In its traditional usage, oppression means the exercise of tyranny by a ruling group. Thus many Americans would agree with radicals in applying the term oppression to the situation of Black South Africans under apartheid. Oppression also traditionally carries a strong connotation of conquest and colonial domination.

New left social movements of the 1960s and 1970s, however, shifted the meaning of the concept of oppression. In its new usage, oppression designates the disadvantage and injustice some people experience not because a tyrannical power coerces them, but because of the everyday practices of our society. Thus, oppression also refers to systemic constraints on groups that are not necessarily the result of the intentions of a tyrant. Oppression in this sense is structural and refers to the vast and deep injustices some folks suffer as a consequence of often unconscious assumptions and reactions of well-meaning people in ordinary interactions, media and cultural stereotypes, and structural features of bureaucratic hierarchies and market mechanisms—in short, the normal processes of everyday life. We cannot eliminate this structural oppression by getting rid of the rulers or making some new laws, because oppressions are systematically reproduced in major economic, political, and cultural institutions.

The concept of oppression has been current among radicals since the 1960s partly in reaction to Marxist attempts to reduce the injustices of racism and sexism, for example, to the effects of class domination or bourgeois ideology. From often heated discussions a consensus is emerging that many different groups must be said to be oppressed in our society, and that no single form of oppression can be assigned causal or moral primacy (see Gottlieb, 1987). The same discussion has also led to the recognition that group differences cut across individual lives in a multiplicity of ways that can entail privilege and oppression for the same person in different respects. Only a plural explication of the concept of oppression can adequately capture these insights.

Accordingly, I offer below an explication of five faces of oppression as a useful set of categories and distinctions which I believe is comprehensive, in the sense that it covers all the groups said by new left social movements to be oppressed and all the ways they are oppressed.

EXPLOITATION

The central function of Marx's theory of exploitation is to explain how class structure can exist in the absence of legally and normatively sanctioned class distinctions. In precapitalist societies domination is overt and accomplished through directly political means. In both slave society and feudal society the right to appropriate the product of the labor of others partly defines class privilege, and these societies legitimate class distinctions with ideologies of natural superiority and inferiority. Capitalist society, on the other hand, removes traditional juridically enforced class distinctions and promotes a belief in the legal freedom of persons. Workers freely contract with employers and receive a wage; no formal mechanisms of law or custom force them to work for that employer or any employer. Thus the mystery of capitalism arises: when everyone is formally free, how can there be class domination? Why do class distinctions persist between the wealthy, who own the means of production, and the mass of people, who work for them? The theory of exploitation answers this question.

Profit, the basis of capitalist power and wealth, is a mystery if we assume that in the market goods exchange at their values. The labor theory of value dispels this mystery. Every commodity's value is a function of the labor time necessary for its production. Labor power is the one commodity which in the process of being consumed produces new value. Profit comes from the difference between the value of the labor performed and the value of the capacity to labor which the capitalist purchases. Profit is possible only because the owner of capital appropriates any realized surplus value.

The injustice of capitalist society consists in the fact that some people exercise their capacities under the control, according to the purposes, and for the benefit of other people. Through private ownership of the means of production, and through markets that allocate labor and the ability to buy goods, capitalism systematically transfers the powers of some persons to others, thereby augmenting the power of the latter. Not only are powers transferred from workers to capitalists, but also the powers of workers diminish by more than the amount of transfer, because workers suffer material deprivation and a loss of control, and hence are deprived of important elements of self-respect. Justice, then, requires eliminating the institutional forms that enable and enforce this process of transference and replacing them with institutional forms that enable all to develop and use their capacities in a way that does not inhibit, but rather can enhance, similar development and use in others.

The central insight expressed in the concept of exploitation, then, is that this oppression occurs through a steady process of the transfer of the results of the labor of one social group to benefit another. Exploitation enacts a structural relation between social groups. Social rules about what work is, who does what for whom, how work is compensated, and the social process by which the results of work are appropriated operate to enact relations of power and inequality. These relations are produced and reproduced through a systematic process in which the energies of the have-nots are continuously expended to maintain and augment the power, status, and wealth of the haves.

The Marxist concept of class leaves important phenomena of sexual and racial oppression unexplained. Does this mean that sexual and racial oppression are non-exploitative, and that we should reserve wholly distinct categories for these oppressions? Or can the concept of exploitation be broadened to include other ways in which the labor and energy expenditure of one group benefits another, and reproduces a relation of domination between them?

Feminists have had little difficulty showing that women's oppression consists partly in a systematic and unreciprocated transfer of powers from women to men. Women's oppression consists not merely in an inequality of status, power, and wealth resulting from men's excluding them from privileged activities. The freedom, power, status, and self-realization of men are possible precisely because women work for them. Gender exploitation has two aspects, transfer of the fruits of material labor to men and transfer of nurturing and sexual energies to men.

Women provide men and children with emotional care and provide men with sexual satisfaction, and as a group receive relatively little of either from men (Brittan and Maynard, 1984, pp. 142–48). The gender socialization of women makes us tend to be more attentive to interactive dynamics than men, and makes women good at providing empathy and support for people's feelings and at smoothing over interactive tensions. Both men and women look to women as nurturers of their personal lives, and women frequently complain that when they look to men for emotional support they do not receive it (Easton, 1978). The norms of heterosexuality, moreover, are oriented around male pleasure, and consequently many women receive little satisfaction from their sexual interaction with men (Gottlieb, 1987).

In twentieth-century capitalist economies the workplaces that women have been entering in increasing numbers serve as another important site of gender exploitation. Alexander (1987) argues that typically feminine jobs involve gender-based tasks requiring sexual labor, nurturing, caring for others' bodies, or smoothing over workplace tensions. In these ways women's energies are expended in jobs that enhance the status of, please, or comfort others, usually men; and these gender-based labors of waitresses, clerical workers, nurses, and other caretakers often go unnoticed and under-compensated.

To summarize, women are exploited in the Marxist sense to the degree that they are wage workers. Some have argued that women's domestic labor also represents a form of capitalist class exploitation insofar as it is labor covered by the wages a family receives. As a group, however, women undergo specific forms of gender exploitation in which their energies and power are expended, often unnoticed and unacknowledged, usually to benefit men by releasing them for more important and creative work, enhancing their status or the environment around them, or providing them with sexual or emotional service.

Are there, then, racially specific forms of exploitation? There is no doubt that racialized groups in the United States, especially Blacks and Latinos, are oppressed through capitalist super-exploitation resulting from a segmented labor market that tends to reserve skilled, high-paying, unionized jobs for whites.

Is it possible to conceptualize a form of exploitation that is racially specific on analogy with the gender-specific forms just discussed? I suggest that the category of menial labor might supply a means for such conceptualization. In its derivation "menial" designates the labor of servants. Wherever there is racism, there is the assumption, more or less enforced, that members of the oppressed racial groups are or ought to be servants of those, or some of those, in the privileged group. In most white racist societies this means that many white people have dark- or yellow-skinned domestic servants, and in the United States today there remains significant racial structuring of private household service. But in the United States today much service labor has gone public: anyone who goes to a good hotel or a good restaurant can have servants. In our society there remains strong cultural pressure to fill servant jobs—bellhop, porter, chambermaid, busboy, and so on—with Black and Latino workers. These jobs entail a transfer of energies whereby the servers enhance the status of the served.

Menial labor usually refers not only to service, however, but also to any servile, unskilled, low-paying work lacking in autonomy, in which a person is subject to taking orders from many people. Menial work tends to be auxiliary work, instrumental to the work of others, where those others receive primary recognition for doing the job.

MARGINALIZATION

Increasingly in the United States racial oppression occurs in the form of marginalization rather than exploitation. Marginals are people the system of labor cannot or will not use. Not only in Third World capitalist countries, but also in most Western capitalist societies, there is a growing underclass of people permanently confined to lives of social marginality, most of whom are racially marked—Blacks or Indians in Latin America, and Blacks, East Indians, Eastern Europeans, or North Africans in Europe.

Marginalization is by no means the fate only of racially marked groups, however. In the United States a shamefully large proportion of the population is marginal: old people, and increasingly people who are not very old but get laid off from their jobs and cannot find new work; young people, especially Black or Latino, who cannot find first or second jobs; many single mothers and their children; other people involuntarily unemployed; many mentally and physically disabled people; American Indians, especially those on reservations.

Marginalization is perhaps the most dangerous form of oppression. A whole category of people is expelled from useful participation in social life and thus potentially subjected to severe material deprivation and even extermination. Advanced capitalist societies often recognize this deprivation and at least partially address it through welfare policies. Material deprivation, which can be addressed by redistributive social policies, is not, however, the extent of the harm caused by marginalization. Two categories of injustice beyond distribution are associated with marginality in advanced capitalist societies. First, the provision of welfare itself produces new injustice by depriving those dependent on it of rights and freedoms that others have. Second, even when material deprivation is somewhat mitigated by the welfare state, marginalization is unjust because it blocks the opportunity to exercise capacities in socially defined and recognized ways.

Liberalism has traditionally asserted the right of all rational autonomous agents to equal citizenship. Early bourgeois liberalism explicitly excluded from citizenship all those whose reason was questionable or not fully developed, and all those not independent (Pateman, 1988; Bowles and Gintis, 1986). Thus poor people, women, the mad and the feebleminded, and children were explicitly excluded from citizenship, and many of these were housed in institutions modeled on the modern prison: poorhouses, insane asylums, schools.

Today the exclusion of dependent persons from equal citizenship rights is only barely hidden beneath the surface. Because they depend on bureaucratic institutions for support or services, the old, the poor, and the mentally or physically disabled are subject to patronizing, punitive, demeaning, and arbitrary treatment by the policies and people associated with welfare bureaucracies. Being a dependent in our society implies being legitimately subject to the often arbitrary and invasive authority of social service providers and other public and private administrators, who enforce rules with which the marginal must comply, and otherwise exercise power over the conditions of their lives. In meeting needs of the marginalized, often with the aid of social scientific disciplines, welfare agencies also construct the needs themselves. Dependency in our society thus implies, as it has in all liberal societies, a sufficient warrant to suspend basic rights to privacy, respect, and individual choice.

Although dependency produces conditions of injustice in our society, dependency in itself need not be oppressive. One cannot imagine a society in which some people would not need to be dependent on others at least some of the time: children, sick people, women recovering from childbirth, old people who have become frail, depressed or otherwise emotionally needy persons, have the moral right to depend on others for subsistence and support.

An important contribution of feminist moral theory has been to question the deeply held assumption that moral agency and full citizenship require that a person be autonomous and independent. Feminists have exposed this assumption as inappropriately individualistic and derived from a specifically male experience of social relations, which values competition and solitary achievement (Gilligan, 1982). Female experience of social relations, arising both from women's typical domestic care responsibilities and from the kinds of paid work that many women do, tends to recognize dependence as a basic

human condition (Hartsock, 1983). Whereas on the autonomy model a just society would as much as possible give people the opportunity to be independent, the feminist model envisions justice as according respect and participation in decision making to those who are dependent as well as to those who are independent (Held, 1987). Dependency should not be a reason to be deprived of choice and respect, and much of the oppression many marginals experience would be lessened if a less individualistic model of rights prevailed.

POWERLESSNESS

As I have indicated, the Marxist idea of class is important because it helps reveal the structure of exploitation: that some people have their power and wealth because they profit from the labor of others. For this reason I reject the claim some make that a traditional class exploitation model fails to capture the structure of contemporary society. It remains the case that the labor of most people in the society augments the power of relatively few.

While it is false to claim that a division between capitalist and working classes no longer describes our society, it is also false to say that class relations have remained unaltered since the nineteenth century. An adequate conception of oppression cannot ignore the experience of social division reflected in the colloquial distinction between the "middle class" and the "working class," a division structured by the social division of labor between professionals and nonprofessionals. Professionals are privileged in relation to nonprofessionals, by virtue of their position in the division of labor and the status it carries. Nonprofessionals suffer a form of oppression in addition to exploitation, which I call powerlessness.

This powerless status is perhaps best described negatively: the powerless lack the authority, status, and sense of self that professionals tend to have. The oppression of powerlessness brings into question the division of labor basic to all industrial societies: the social division between those who plan and those who execute. The status privilege of professionals has three aspects, the lack of which produces oppression for nonprofessionals.

First, acquiring and practicing a profession has an expansive, progressive character. Being professional usually requires a college education and the acquisition of a specialized knowledge that entails working with symbols and concepts. Professionals experience progress first in acquiring the expertise, and then in the course of professional advancement and rise in status. The life of the nonprofessional by comparison is powerless in the sense that it lacks this orientation toward the progressive development of capacities and avenues for recognition.

Second, while many professionals have supervisors and cannot directly influence many decisions or the actions of many people, most nevertheless have considerable day-to-day work autonomy. Professionals usually have some authority over others, moreover—either over workers they supervise, or over auxiliaries, or over clients. Nonprofessionals, on the other hand, lack autonomy, and in both their working and their consumer/client lives often stand under the authority of professionals.

Professionals and nonprofessionals belong to different cultures in the United States. The two groups tend to live in segregated neighborhoods or even different towns, a process itself mediated by planners, zoning officials, and real estate people. The groups tend to have different tastes in food, decor, clothes, music, and vacations, and often different health and educational needs. Members of each group socialize for the most part with others in the same status group. While there is some inter-group mobility between generations, for the most part the children of professionals become professionals and the children of nonprofessionals do not.

Thus, third, the privileges of the professional extend beyond the workplace to a whole way of life. I call this way of life "respectability." To treat people with respect is to be prepared to listen to what they have to say or to do what they request because they have some authority, expertise, or influ-

ence. The norms of respectability in our society are associated specifically with professional culture. Professional dress, speech, tastes, demeanor, all connote respectability. The privilege of this professional respectability appears starkly in the dynamics of racism and sexism. In daily interchange women and men of color must prove their respectability. At first they are often not treated by strangers with respectful distance or deference. Once people discover that this woman or that Puerto Rican man is a college teacher or a business executive, however, they often behave more respectfully toward her or him. Working-class white men, on the other hand, are often treated with respect until their working-class status is revealed.

CULTURAL IMPERIALISM

Exploitation, marginalization, and powerlessness all refer to relations of power and oppression that occur by virtue of the social division of labor who works for whom, who does not work, and how the content of work defines one's institutional position relative to others. These kinds of oppression are a matter of concrete power in relation to others—of who benefits from whom, and who is dispensable.

Recent theorists of movements of group liberation, notably feminist and Black liberation theorists, have also given prominence to a rather different form of oppression, which following Lugones and Spelman (1983) I shall call cultural imperialism. Cultural imperialism involves the universalization of a dominant group's experience and culture, and its establishment as the norm. Often without noticing they do so, the dominant groups project their own experience as representative of humanity as such. Cultural products also express the dominant group's perspective on and interpretation of events and elements in the society.

An encounter with other groups, however, can challenge the dominant group's claim to universality. The difference of women from men, American Indians or Africans from Europeans, Jews from Christians, homosexuals from heterosexuals, workers from professionals, becomes reconstructed largely as deviance and inferiority. Since only the dominant group's cultural expressions receive wide dissemination, their cultural expressions become the normal, or the universal, and thereby the unremarkable, and others stereotyped as deviant.

As remarkable, deviant beings, the culturally imperialized are stamped with an essence. The stereotypes confine them to a nature which is often attached in some way to their bodies, and which thus cannot easily be denied. These stereotypes so permeate the society that they are not noticed as contestable. Just as everyone knows that the earth goes around the sun, so everyone knows that gay people are promiscuous, that Indians are alcoholics, and that women are good with children. White males, on the other hand, insofar as they escape group marking, can be individuals.

Those living under cultural imperialism find themselves defined from the outside, positioned, placed, by a network of dominant meanings they experience as arising from elsewhere, from those with whom they do not identify and who do not identify with them. Consequently, the dominant culture's stereotyped and inferiorized images of the group must be internalized by group members at least to the extent that they are forced to react to behavior of others influenced by those images. The culturally oppressed experience what W.E.B. Du Bois called "double consciousness" (Du Bois, 1969 [1903]). Double consciousness arises when the oppressed subject refuses to coincide with these devalued, objectified, stereotyped visions of herself or himself: While the subject desires recognition as human, capable of activity, full of hope and possibility, she receives from the dominant culture only the judgment that she is different, marked, or inferior.

The group defined by the dominant culture as deviant, as a stereotyped Other, is culturally different from the dominant group, because the status of Otherness creates specific experiences not shared by the dominant group, and because culturally oppressed groups also are often socially segregated and occupy specific positions in the social division of labor. Members of such groups express their specific group experiences and interpretations of the world to one another, developing and perpetuating their own culture. Double consciousness, then, occurs because one finds one's being defined by two cultures: a dominant and a subordinate culture. Because they can affirm and recognize one another as sharing similar experiences and perspectives on social life, people in culturally imperialized groups can often maintain a sense of positive subjectivity.

This, then, is the injustice of cultural imperialism: that the oppressed group's own experience and interpretation of social life find little expression that touches the dominant culture, while that same culture imposes on the oppressed group its experience and interpretation of social life.

VIOLENCE

Finally, many groups suffer the oppression of systematic violence. Members of some groups live with the knowledge that they must fear random, unprovoked attacks on their persons or property, which have no motive but to damage, humiliate, or destroy the person. In American society women, Blacks, Asians, Arabs, gay men, and lesbians live under such threats of violence, and in at least some regions Jews, Puerto Ricans, Chicanos, and other Spanish-speaking Americans must fear such violence as well. Physical violence against these groups is shockingly frequent. Rape Crisis Center networks estimate that more than one-third of all American women experience an attempted or successful sexual assault in their lifetimes. Violence against gay men and lesbians is not only common, but has been increasing. While the frequency of physical attack on members of these and other racially or sexually marked groups is very disturbing, I also include in this category less severe incidents of harassment, intimidation, or ridicule simply for the purpose of degrading, humiliating, or stigmatizing group members.

Given the frequency of such violence in our society, why are theories of justice usually silent about it? I think the reason is that theorists do not typically take such incidents of violence and harassment as matters of social injustice. No moral theorist would deny that such acts are very wrong. But unless all immoralities are injustices, they might wonder, why should such acts be interpreted as symptoms of social injustice?

What makes violence a phenomenon of social injustice, and not merely an individual moral wrong, is its systemic character, its existence as a social practice. Violence is systemic because it is directed at members of a group simply because they are members of that group. Any woman, for example, has a reason to fear rape. Regardless of what a Black man has done to escape the oppressions of marginality or powerlessness, he lives knowing he is subject to attack or harrassment. The oppression of violence consists not only in direct victimization, but in the daily knowledge shared by all members of oppressed groups that they are liable to violation, solely on account of their group identity. Just living under such a threat of attack on oneself or family or friends deprives the oppressed of freedom and dignity, and needlessly expends their energy.

Violence is a social practice. It is a social given that everyone knows happens and will happen again. It is always at the horizon of social imagination, even for those who do not perpetrate it. According to the prevailing social logic, some circumstances make such violence more "called for" than others. The idea of rape will occur to many men who pick up a hitch-hiking woman; the idea of hounding or teasing a gay man on their dorm floor will occur to many straight male college students. Often several persons inflict the violence together, especially in all-male groupings. Sometimes violators set out looking for people to beat up, rape, or taunt. This rule-bound, social, and often premeditated character makes violence against groups a social practice.

Group violence approaches legitimacy, moreover, in the sense that it is tolerated. Often third parties find it unsurprising because it happens frequently and lies as a constant possibility at the horizon of the social imagination. Even when they are caught, those who perpetrate acts of group-directed violence or harrassment often receive light or no punishment. To that extent society renders their acts acceptable.

An important aspect of random, systemic violence is its irrationality. Xenophobic violence differs from the violence of states or ruling-class repression. Repressive violence has a rational, albeit evil, motive: rulers use it as a coercive tool to maintain their power. Many accounts of racist, sexist, or homophobic violence attempt to explain its motivation as a desire to maintain group privilege or domination. I do not doubt that fear of violence often functions to keep oppressed groups subordinate, but I do not think xenophobic violence is rationally motivated in the way that, for example, violence against strikers is. On the contrary, the violation of rape, beating, killing, and harassment of women, people of color, gays, and other marked groups is motivated by fear or hatred of those groups. Sometimes the motive may be a simple will to power, to victimize those marked as vulnerable by the very social fact that they are subject to violence. If so, this motive is secondary in the sense that it depends on a social practice of group violence. Violence causing fear or hatred of the other at least partly involves insecurities on the part of the violators; its irrationality suggests that unconscious processes are at work. I offer a psychoanalytic account of the fear and hatred of some groups as bound up, with fears of identity loss. I think such unconscious fears account at least partly for the oppression I have here called violence. It may also partly account for cultural imperialism.

Cultural imperialism, moreover, itself intersects with violence. The culturally imperialized may reject the dominant meanings and attempt to assert their own subjectivity, or the fact of their cultural difference may put the lie to the dominant culture's implicit claim to universality. The dissonance generated by such a challenge, to the hegemonic cultural meanings can also be a source of irrational violence.

Violence is a form of injustice that a distributive understanding of justice seems ill equipped to capture. This may be why contemporary discussions of justice rarely mention it. I have argued that group-directed violence is institutionalized and systemic. To the degree that institutions and social practices encourage, tolerate, or enable the perpetration of violence against members of specific groups, those institutions and practices are unjust and should be reformed. Such reform may require the redistribution of resources or positions, but in large part can come only through a change in cultural images, stereotypes, and the mundane reproduction of relations of dominance and aversion in the gestures of everyday life.

APPLYING THE CRITERIA

I have arrived at the five faces of oppression—exploitation, marginalization, powerlessness, cultural imperialism, and violence—as the best way to avoid exclusions of some oppressed groups and reductions of one form of oppression to another. They function as criteria for determining whether individuals and groups are oppressed, rather than as a full theory of oppression. I believe that these criteria are objective. They provide a means of refuting some people's belief that their group is oppressed when it is not, as well as a means of persuading others that a group is oppressed when they doubt it. Each criterion can be operationalized; each can be applied through the assessment of observable behavior, status relationships, distributions, texts and other cultural artifacts. I have no illusions that such assessments can be value-neutral. But these criteria can nevertheless serve as means—of evaluating claims that a group is oppressed, or adjudicating disputes about whether or how a group is oppressed. One can compare the combinations of oppressions groups experience, or the intensity of those oppressions. Thus with these criteria one can plausibly claim that one group is more oppressed than another without reducing all oppressions to a single scale.

The presence of any of these five conditions is sufficient for calling a group oppressed. But different group oppressions exhibit different combinations of these forms, as do different individuals in the groups. Nearly all, if not all, groups said by contemporary social movements to be oppressed suffer cultural imperialism. The other oppressions they experience vary. Working-class people are exploited and powerless, for example, but if employed— and white—do not experience marginalization and violence. Gay men, on the other hand, experience severe cultural imperialism and violence. Similarly, Jews and Arabs as groups are victims of cultural imperialism and violence, though many members of these groups also suffer exploitation or powerlessness. Old people are oppressed by marginalization and cultural imperialism, and this is also true of disabled people. As a group women are subject to gender-based exploitation, powerlessness, cultural imperialism, and violence. Racism in the United States condemns many Blacks and Latinos to marginalization, and puts many more at risk; members of these groups often suffer all five forms of oppression.

Why are particular groups oppressed in the way they are? Are there any causal connections among the five forms of oppression? Causal or explanatory questions such as these are beyond the scope of this discussion. While I think general social theory has a place, causal explanation must always be particular and historical. Thus an explanatory account of why a particular group is oppressed in the ways that it is must trace the history and current structure of particular social relations.

REFERENCES

Alexander, David. 1987. Gendered Job Traits and Women's Occupations. Ph.D. dissertation, Department of Economics. University of Massachusetts.

Bowles, Samuel and Herbert Gintis. 1986. *Democracy and Capitalism*. New York: Basic Books.

Brittan, Arthur and Mary Maynard. 1984. *Sexism, Racism and Oppression*. Oxford: Blackwell.

Du Bois, W.E.B. 1969 [1903]. *The Souls of Black Folk*. New York: New American Library.

Easton, Barbara. 1978. Feminism and the Contemporary Family. *Socialist Review*. 39 (May/June): 11–36.

Gilligan, Carol. 1982. *In a Difference Voice*. Cambridge, MA: Harvard University Press.

Gottlieb, Roger. 1987. *History and Subjectivity*. Philadelphia: Temple University Press.

Hartsock, Nancy. 1983. *Money, Sex and Power*. New York: Longman.

Held, Virginia. 1987. A Non-Contractual Society. In Marsha Hanen and Kai Nielsen (eds.). *Science, Morality and Feminist Theory*. Calgary: University of Calgary Press.

Lugones, Maria and Elizabeth Spelman. 1983. Have We Got a Theory For You! Feminist Theory, Cultural Imperialism and the Demand for "the Woman's Voice." *Women's Studies International Forum*. 6: 573–581.

Pateman, Carole. 1988. *The Sexual Contract*. Stanford: Stanford University Press.

CHAPTER 34

Expanding Comprehensiveness

Structural racism and community building in the United States

Keith Lawrence

Since the settlement house movement of the early 1900s, government, philanthropic funders, not-for-profit local organizations and social scientists have shaped and sustained a wide variety of community revitalization initiatives across urban America. Over the years, these localized initiatives undeniably have improved the lives of many individuals and neighborhoods. Yet, on balance, they have done little to reduce the social and economic contrasts evident in many metropolitan areas.

Metropolitan disparities are particularly obvious when race is taken into account. Poverty occupies a predictable niche in larger cities and the poor are, disproportionately, individuals of color. Of these, African Americans are the most highly represented and politically visible racial group, but many other racial minority groups and subgroups bear a disproportionate share of the urban poverty burden.

But although this association between urban poverty and racial minority status has long been a constant, the preference among America's policy planners has been to approach urban poverty from vantage points that either subsume or ignore race. In contrast, this chapter examines the ways in which race and racism contribute to the persistence of urban problems, and their impact on the effectiveness of urban poverty initiatives over the years. The main theme is that past and present efforts to remedy urban disadvantage—that sphere called "community revitalization" and more recently, "community building"—have been severely undermined by racism embedded in the institutions, assumptions and practices of this field. More specifically, the assertion is that unchallenged assumptions about "progress" in these endeavors contribute to permanent racial hierarchies in educational attainment, employment, income, health, and other areas vital to inner-city well-being. Moreover, remedial measures that do not challenge economic, political, cultural and ideological norms that bear directly on the fates of these neighborhoods from a racial equality standpoint may hold little promise for generating locally sustainable change. With this outlook, a race-conscious framework for analyzing urban poverty and redefining the goals of community building is suggested. An argument is also made for the active advancement of racial equity as a planning principle and yardstick for evaluation by comprehensive community revitalization advocates.

In calling the field's attention to race, this discussion places its intellectual leaders at the center of something much larger than just urban neighborhood transformation. It assigns them a role in the ongoing challenge of American democracy itself: accession to its universalistic ideals despite its legacy of white privilege and nonwhite disadvantage. Community builders are asked to conceptualize what they do as democracy building, and not merely the repair of discrete neighborhoods and communities. Experience strongly suggests that the latter task will continue to be futile without attention to the former, and that both are unattainable within an unchanged context of racial inequality.

Several intellectual assumptions inform the discussion that follows. One is an equalitarian notion of the American social ideal. Another important assumption reflects the belief in the transformative potential of the social and cultural "space" outside formal politics and the economy in which people interact informally to define their cultures, identities and communities, and lead their private lives. The two biggest steps toward racial equality in the US—the civil rights revolution that swept away overt legal discrimination in the 1960s, and the abolition of slavery that preceded it a century before—were initiated by social movements within civil society. The democratic energy of local activists, reformers and protestors, was the timely and indispensable catalyst for the policy and attitudinal changes that ended those undemocratic regimes.

There has been ideological resistance to employing racial group equity as a central principle in designing urban anti-poverty strategies. Though racial minorities—especially blacks—made gains in the 1960s and 1970s that narrowed some opportunity gaps, the American tradition of disregard for the deeper historical legacy of race largely survived.

America's first neighborhood-based social welfare movement was partially a direct response to the chaos caused by massive European immigration into squalid big city slums at the turn of century. Progressives initiated the idea of neighborhood-based institutions as a vehicle for lifting recent immigrants into the urban mainstream, securing child labor laws, building up white labor unions and providing a range of other social services. Multipurpose neighborhood centers, or "settlements", were developed with charitable funding to serve as sites for service delivery and tools for knitting together the diverse local community. Segregationist norms meant that black urban poverty was relegated to the margins of this emerging movement.

The settlements promoted social integration, but explicitly excluded African Americans, whom most settlements simply refused to serve. (Halpern 1995: 38). Urban blacks were already being confined to their "own" ghettos early in the century via restrictive covenants, steering, threats and violence. Settlement leaders actively contributed to maintaining the color line where they could. "Racist realism" was the broad justification: whites did not like blacks and this social fact simply had to be acknowledged. Halpern (1995: 38–9) notes that the few attempts at African American settlements were short-lived. Lack of financial and technical support and difficulties in obtaining spaces for lease in racially changing neighborhoods, were formidable barriers.

After the Second World War, federal urban renewal and public housing schemes continued the tradition of insensitivity to race by *discounting* the significance of place to black and brown identity. The postwar period saw the beginnings of a massive migration of African Americans to the urban northeast and midwest from sharecropping and hopelessness in the rural south. As happened after the First World War, employment exclusion and other forms of discrimination continued to be serious problems for blacks despite their recent demonstrations of patriotism through military service. Federal urban renewal, public housing and highway construction programs exacerbated these difficulties by devastating black communities. In what really was slum clearance and coerced relocation, local real estate interests, planners and politicians conspired to destroy many central-city black communities, giving residents the dubious option of distant new public housing estates.

However, it is important to note that as the civil rights movement turned its focus to the North in the late 1950s, the dominance of planners, developers and consultants over community development was increasingly challenged from below. A wide variety of grassroots organizing efforts and nonviolent "direct actions"—rent strikes, sit-ins, boycotts, demonstrations—brought only modest tangible returns (Halpern 1995: 88) but helped to establish "community control" as the basic local development principle for the next two decades.

As described in O'Connor's chapter (Chapter 2, this volume), the War on Poverty of the 1960s tested the principle of federally led, community-based change. Both fell short of their own expectations for a complex of philosophical and practical reasons, including internal tensions between a desire to remain politically neutral and a desire to work actively to alleviate poverty and inequality (Halpern 1995: 100). However, they "signaled the end of the long era of acquiescence among inner-city neighborhoods to externally initiated reform" (ibid.) and encouraged the federal government to develop the concept of "community action" as the basis for its War on Poverty.

An important complement to community action was the Model Cities program of the new federal Department of Housing and Urban Development (HUD). Model Cities, according to Halpern (1995: 121), not only was to provide for a concerted, coherent social service effort but for construction of racially and economically integrated housing that would help keep upwardly mobile blacks and whites tied to central city neighborhoods. Reviews of Model Cities from the standpoint of race are mixed. One perspective holds that federal dominance of the program's early planning and implementation stages set back the push for community control of inner-city renewal, at the very time when these communities were savoring a degree of empowerment and demanding self-determination (ibid.). Another view contends that the program did provide unprecedented opportunity for local minority participation through its "block grant" provisions, even though this often proved to be a messy process (Thomas 1997). But in the final analysis, Model Cities failed to sustain the commitment of the federal government.

Ultimately, the War on Poverty was short-lived. Its demise lends credence to the argument that the federal and local governments initially underestimated the political impacts of enhanced participation in poor neighborhoods of color, and once these became clear, elites redefined local empowerment in ways that served the status quo.

The "new federalism" of the 1980s brought social welfare funding cuts and increasing devolution of responsibility for urban problems to the states. This contributed to a revival, in the 1990s, of antipoverty perspectives that were disconnected from social structure and history.

A major shift in the federal–state relationship in the 1980s, the continuing erosion of urban tax bases due to suburbanization, and massive urban job loss due to structural changes in the domestic economy, exacerbated central-city problems. As a result the community development sector became swamped by overlapping crises at the neighborhood level. Homelessness, service unavailability and inefficiency, deplorable housing or lack of it, inner-city isolation from job markets, drug dependency and related crime, and other problems, all grew larger in scope. Although there was an increase in the number and types of community-based organizations working in distressed areas, they were no match for the depth of devastation facing the inner city.

In response, since the mid-1980s, government, foundations and researchers have advanced a new generation of theories and strategies aimed at helping inner-city residents escape poverty. There have been welfare-to-work initiatives, poverty deconcentration or dispersal strategies, mobility strategies, self-sufficiency initiatives linked to public housing subsidies, and a variety of community-based initiatives—including federal Empowerment and Enterprise Zones—that emphasize both individual and community capacity-building.

Two important conceptual shifts accompanied these initiatives. First, the civil rights consciousness that infused community revitalization thought and practice in the mid-1960s and 1970s—that is, the sense that chronic minority group disadvantages were structural and institutional problems—began losing ground to the resurgent individualism of the "Reagan revival". "Empowerment", the most potent transformative idea to emerge in almost a century of anti-poverty effort (because, properly understood, it is the antidote to systemic disadvantage), rapidly became reinterpreted in this period as simply the enhanced personal capacity to make one's way in life (see Riger 1993).

"Comprehensiveness" effectively replaced empowerment, by the 1990s, as an organizing idea in community redevelopment. And, it was linked to the place-centered notion of "community building". Within this context, the comprehensive community initiative (CCI) emerged as a favored strategy (see Kubisch *et al.*, Chapter 38, this volume).

COMPREHENSIVE COMMUNITY INITIATIVES AND RACE

Interest in CCIs arose from several legitimate concerns, but racial equity was not one of them. In the largest sense it came from an awareness that providing pathways out of the inner city would not solve the poverty problem. Those individuals who could, would move up and out along those pathways, but a majority would remain stranded in their distressed neighborhoods. The realization was that, in the end, broken communities had to be fixed. And, the new climate of shrinking federal support for categorical programs made strategies emphasizing linkages across program areas all the more logical.

But the CCI scope did not encompass taking on fundamental racial barriers to local empowerment. Partially, this was because many community builders considered the racial equity issue almost moot, since CCIs already served mostly African American and Latino neighborhoods. As communities of color were the focus of their activities, there was an implicit assumption that CCIs would quietly accomplish racial equity goals sought through confrontation in the previous decades. Moreover, the urgency of quality of life problems, the seemingly unstoppable federal retreat from redistributive strategies, and the complexities of 1960s-style grassroots activism, all seemed to call for pragmatism rather than idealism on race and poverty. Indeed, one lesson of the previous generation of anti-poverty initiatives seemed to be that overemphasis on race might scare off irreplaceable private and philanthropic funders nervous about the appearance of ideological or political bias.

CCI pragmatism prevents them from dealing with race in ways that could enable them to achieve their social goals. In their outline of the theories of change guiding CCIs, Robert Chaskin and Prudence Brown (1996: 5) list six approaches, and only one— "enhancing political strength"—addresses the issue of community power and race. And few CCIs lead with a commitment to this particular strategy, though "most of them aim to accomplish it as part of the effort"

(p. 5). CCIs may be deterred from *confronting* race by the political and interethnic complications that would arise from a forthright treatment of race and power. Funders play a major role in how CCIs address race. Although the private foundations that sponsor these initiatives advocate empowerment and community control—principles that, taken seriously, could not disregard race and power, they generally lack the inclination, or institutional flexibility, to allow CCIs to follow explicitly race-conscious paths. The challenge for community building as a whole in the post-civil rights period has been to understand race as a problem of *context*, rather than just *process*. CCIs have been seeking ways to collaborate across racial and cultural lines without really taking on the responsibility of pushing for racial group empowerment. CCIs have not really explored how racial group *position* shapes community capacities in fundamental ways, and what is required to remove or counteract the society's racial hierarchy.

A RACE-CONSCIOUS FRAMEWORK FOR URBAN POVERTY AND COMMUNITY BUILDING

Contemporary approaches to urban poverty in the US, such as the CCI movement, reflect a historical legacy of social and ideological contradictions that severely constrain prospects for fundamental change. Three propositions are explored briefly. The first is that racial stratification has been a constant in American life despite a strong individualist creed, and the great leaps toward individual equality seen in recent US history. The second is that the ideological underpinnings of the American social contract relieve the body politic of collective responsibility for alleviating the racial group inequities caused by this stratification. And third, by operating *uncritically within* these ideological confines, the community building field helps perpetuate the disregard of systemic, societal solutions to inner city poverty.

As a first step, it is important to understand the nuances of American racism. Labels vary in the racism literature but three types of racism are frequently mentioned: individual, institutionalized, and structural.

Individual racism is the kind of overt anti-black prejudice, harassment and violence Americans associate with the periods of slavery and Jim Crow Reconstruction. This is, by far, the most widely understood meaning of racism in America. However, opinion studies today consistently find overwhelming majorities of white Americans expressing disapproval of such practices (see Bobo 1998). *Institutionalized racism* refers to the characteristics of formal political and economic structures that may cause them to generate racialized, but nevertheless widely legitimized public policy outcomes. Policy and administrative processes in public and private agencies and organizations may result in adverse outcomes for blacks and other minorities that cannot be traced to obvious racial biases in the policies or practices themselves, or to acts of individual racism by people in these institutions. Nevertheless these practices facilitate unequal outcomes for different racial groups.

More comprehensive is the idea of *structural racism*, which refers to all the enduring characteristics of American political, economic and civic life—tangible and psychological—that continually create, re-create and maintain white privilege. A structural definition allows us to see that individuals and institutions are parts of a dynamic process, greater that the sum of its parts, in which policies, institutions, individuals, attitudes and historical/social context interact to specify the boundaries of racial opportunity. Because race has played such a large role in the design of the fabric of American life racial boundaries of varying permeability and rigidity exist in most social political and economic settings. Legislative, attitudinal, demographic, and other major societal changes since emancipation have blurred many of these boundaries. What betray their existence, however, are persistent disparities in racial outcomes in employment, education, wealth accumulation health status, crime and punishment and other areas.

In a democracy, the postures of dominant public and private institutions and the official conduct of those who run them reflect a preponderance of the national will. What makes the seemingly benign cultures and practices of America's institutions produce racialized outcomes, are values, beliefs and ideas embedded in the "common sense" of individuals within those institutions, that implicitly endorse the superiority of white culture over others (see Dominelli 1992: 165).

LAISSEZ-FAIRE RACISM

What precisely are the "common sense" ideas that structure thinking and, ultimately, behaviors that foster racial inequity today? What is the nature of modern-day racist ideology? How does it relate to persistent minority disadvantage? Lawrence Bobo and colleagues offer the helpful notion of "laissez faire" racism (Bobo, Kleugel and Smith 1997).

Laissez-faire racism involves co-optation of the values and principles of the political economic system in the service of white privilege. Prior to the 1960s, this was not as necessary because discrimination in employment, voting, housing and other key areas was socially acceptable. Economic, social and legal realities in the contemporary period have encouraged manipulation of the "American Creed" (e.g. personal responsibility, fairness, merit-based achievement) to maintain *relative* white privilege. In this way, laissez-faire racism is indistinguishable from the "normal" influences on an individual's life chances in this society.

At the core of structural racism is a pervasive racial belief system held together by a set of assumptions relating to the characteristics of whites and non-whites as groups. This belief system includes a set negative stereotypes about people of color. Bobo and colleagues note that the 1990 General Social Survey found 56 percent of whites rated blacks as less intelligent, and 78 percent rating them as more likely prefer living off welfare than whites (Bobo, Kluegel and Smith, 1997, 3). Michael DelliCarpini (1998) cites findings that "significant percentages of whites still say that blacks are ... lazy (31 percent) lack discipline (60 percent), and are violent or aggressive (50 percent)."

The immense power of these negative

stereotypes is reinforced by continuous validation of white superiority in everyday life by prevailing institutional and cultural practices. Our mainstream culture steadily showcases mostly white images of virtue, beauty, self-discipline, intelligence, heroism, family, love, civility, compassion and artistic sophistication. It is important to recognize that racial minorities themselves internalize these stereotypes because they are so commonplace, durable and "normal." This reality, combined with minority under-involvement in institutional decision-making, perpetuate racialized core assumptions about whites and non-whites at the institutional level.

Racist political arrangements and the calculated exploitation of nonwhite labor gave structural racism its initial shape and character centuries ago. Today, a legacy of mirror image stereotyping of whites as non-whites, as much as any other factor, helps to preserve the racial hierarchy. Often, this racist conventional wisdom simply overpower formal institutional rules or policies intended to prevent discrimination, as exemplified the persistence of "racial profiling" by law enforcement personnel, despite the institutionalization of racial sensitivity or awareness training in most big-city police departments. One striking aspect of this issue is the lack of evidence that minority police officers in those departments are significantly less likely than white counterparts to engage in this practice.

NEW LOCALISM

For contemporary community revitalization practice, recent ideological trends have translated into yet another round of neighborhood-focused activity that attaches low priority to fundamental problems of structural inequity. Social science has contributed to this bias toward inadequate local and individual solutions. A recent literature review by Teitz and Chapple (1998: 38) identified six major hypotheses about inner-city poverty in recent decades, only one of which squarely emphasizes non-local causes. Briefly, the reviewers listed inadequate human capital, racial and gender discrimination in employment, spatial mismatch between workers and jobs, inadequate social capital, low levels of minority entrepreneurship and access to capital, and the unanticipated consequences of public policy.

Since the brief interruption of the War on Poverty, there has been a return to the non-governmental anti-poverty tradition. Interest in social and human capital, personal mobility, local entrepreneurship and other reductionist diagnoses has led to a new consensus perspective that might be called "new localism." New localism basically holds that distressed communities need to develop indigenous resources, as well as initiate the kinds of collaborative relationships with outside institutions that could bring external resources into the inner city. Essentially, it leaves prevailing economic and political paradigms unchallenged and approaches urban poverty as, first and foremost, a local- and individual-level problem. "People", "places" and local systems are priority points for intervention by civic actors who recognize local assets and opportunities for synergistic benefits through program coordination, potential public–private partnerships, and "leveraging" external resources. Local sustainability and individual economic self-sufficiency (and not structural change) are the new localism's primary goals.

In overemphasizing the catalytic roles of neighborhood, family and individuals in the revitalization process, this renewed interest in nongovernmental solutions has pushed the obligations of the larger society toward poor communities too far into the background. The danger of new localism is its implicit assumption that communities that have been systematically exploited and neglected for generations, and that have been isolated from lucrative job markets, public transportation networks and adequate educational and service systems, can nevertheless begin to revive themselves, essentially by their own efforts. Structural and institutional barriers that continue to block racial minority advancement can be overcome or made irrelevant, it is assumed, by denser collaborative networks —within neighborhoods and across institutional, functional and jurisdictional boundaries.

The challenge for new localism is, first, recognition that racialized values embedded in overarching social, political, economic and psychological structures play a critical role in limiting key collaborations and in sustaining the patterns of urban poverty we see. For instance, minority isolation in inner cities prevents formation of important "weak ties" to white opportunity networks (see Granovetter 1973).

Furthermore, since new localism implicitly derives from a partial theory of urban poverty (that is, one that does not give sufficient weight to historical and other contexts), it needs to be aware that prescriptions may be only partial. It needs to be skeptical of local remedies that do not outline how poor individuals and communities can themselves become agents for reforming societal norms and institutions, or that do not simultaneously leverage other resources to promote systemic and structural change.

FUTURE DIRECTIONS IN COMPREHENSIVE COMMUNITY BUILDING PRACTICE

The community revitalization enterprise is at a peculiar juncture in its history. The choice facing the field is continuation of what amounts to palliative work for the people and the. places victimized by structural racism, or alternatively, expansion of its mission to include race-conscious goals on multiple levels.

All the evidence suggests that continuing to do business as usual may be irrational— even immoral. A "comprehensiveness" that treats race as just another exogenous factor, thereby disregarding its foundational significance to the social distribution of opportunity and power in the US, flies in the face of all that is obvious about urban disadvantage. Moreover, there is a wealth of latent resources available to community builders for addressing issues of racial inequality.

One compelling reason why community building should take up a challenge that some see as better suited to the political sphere, is that impetus for racially progressive change must come from civil society.

History advises that we need not wait for transforming presidential and legislative leadership, or for the spontaneous emergence of a kinder, gentler version of the economic marketplace. Political and business elites have little incentive to initiate the reallocation of power, resources and privilege.

However, as community builders attempt to play a more leading role in this civic dimension, they must be mindful of the complexities and deep stratifications of American civil society. Indeed, race-based privilege in civil society complicates prospects for the kinds of grassroots, cross-racial coalition building that many see as the civic antidote to structural forces (for instance, see Wilson 1999).

CCIs enjoy significant comparative advantages over other would-be change agents in the civic sphere:

- CCIs, CDCs, and a range of other nonprofit advocacy and service organizations are firmly grounded in poor communities.
- Many community building organizations already play an intermediary role that links their clients to strategic institutions inside and outside the civic realm— that is, they possess invaluable "bridging" social capital, as they are usually embedded in rich resource networks in which they are respected.
- Community building organizations are among the few civic institutions that interact with and gain the trust of immigrants coming to the inner city today.

What is to be done? First, community building could assume an intellectual leadership role in integrating race and structure in ways that deepen the popular understanding of urban poverty. We can begin by sketching out a research agenda for proceeding in that direction.

Three areas of work seem to be called for. Influential voices in the field could:

- redefine comprehensiveness and community building from a structural racism perspective for funders, practitioners and other stakeholders;

- encourage research into how structural racism manifests itself at each level (individual, civic, and institutional) in the domains of greatest significance to distressed communities;
- encourage practitioners and funders to integrate a structural racism consciousness (as opposed to race-neutral, liberal assumptions) into the "theories of change" they use to plan and evaluate community building initiatives.

A genuinely comprehensive framework would recognize the existence of cognitive, cultural and other intangible mediating structures between the state and its social groups and individuals. It would explicitly challenge myths about concentrated black and brown poverty, e.g. that its incidence depends entirely upon the interplay of individual attributes and "natural" market forces. To be a legitimate strategy for change, notions of comprehensiveness must recognize all the barriers to equality associated with race—particularly how "whiteness" as social resource and "non-whiteness" as social liability, limit opportunity and empowerment.

To counteract the racial inequity so deeply ingrained in American life, community revitalization must deploy an alternative paradigm that is cognizant of the significance of white privilege at every level. It must develop and promote a perspective that is also cognizant of the historical, institutional and psychological dimensions to race in American life. It must draw as much attention to the systemic sources of poverty—institutional and ideological—as it does to people and place.

It should be stressed that a structural analysis does not imply that community-level cooperation and social capital are irrelevant or detrimental to building community. Rather, the question it poses is: cooperation and networks of trust in pursuit of *what* visions of community change? It suggests that an exclusive focus on functional cooperation is a serious self-limitation, given the heavy challenge posed by racial inequity.

To end structural racism, it seems that cooperation should seek more immediate social policy goals. Communitarian sens-

ibilities could be blended with realistic appraisals of where the color line exists in facets of our society that heavily determine individual life chances. "Power" coalitions need to be forged across unions, academic institutions, white and black churches, philanthropic organizations, trade and professional associations, political parties, progressive media and other civic institutions, to articulate and legitimize new social values. The call here is for leadership by the community revitalization field in constructing and socializing an ideological framework for such social change networks.

Another point that bears clarification is that attitudes and ideas relating to race—the public "common sense"—form an important and inseparable part of the institutional decision context. Comprehensiveness must also come to mean an interest in reshaping broad public perceptions of nonwhite poverty, and not just local and individual self-images.

Broadening the community rebuilding mission is important, but so is identifying the right audiences for the new message, and tailoring the communication for greatest effectiveness. Community builders need to reach a wider public and also to promote linkages across institutional and academic disciplinary boundaries. A broader array of civic organizations, social science researchers, professional organizations, labor unions, environmental groups and suburban allies across metropolitan regions, need to be pulled into the structural racism debate. For this to be feasible, the message must not just be redefined, but "packaged" in ways that make it readily comprehensible.

It might be worthwhile, for instance, for community builders to explore the institutional norms associated with the tenuous underclass-labor force connection, even as they pursue workforce development strategies. For example, collective bargaining, a labor market tool of great potential significance for today's growing "workfare" army, has been severely weakened by federal and state institutional treatments of labor unions. Recognition of employment issues like these bring the institutional and civic levels more into the picture and significantly expand the range of appropriate medium- and long-term employment outcomes for community practitioners. Policy level reform appears as a higher priority. Also, it may seem appropriate to challenge the normalcy of the racial unemployment gap on an industry-by-industry basis. Strategically, public education and institutionally focused employment advocacy campaigns might receive more emphasis, and as a consequence, grassroots organizing and lobbying might receive greater tactical emphasis.

Finally, researchers in community building could advance theory-based program planning and evaluation techniques currently being explored in some CCIs (see Fulbright-Anderson, Kubish and Connell 1998) by incorporating the structural racism analysis. Again, this work might be elaborated at various functional levels and community building domains. The theory-building should be grounded in historical, regional and other contextual information.

More specifically, the theoretical work could recommend sets of race-conscious outcomes that reformers might use as benchmarks in a given area of intervention. Practitioners desperately need these kinds of "precision tools" as they address issues of race and equity in their community programs.

REFERENCES

Bobo, L.D. (1998) Mapping Racial Attitudes at the Century's End: Has the Color Line Vanished or Merely Reconfigured? Paper prepared for the Aspen Roundtable Project on Race and Community Revitalization.

Bobo, L.J., Kluegel, J. and Smith, R.A. (1997) Laissez-faire Racism: The Crystallization of a Kinder, Gentler, Antiblack Ideology, in S. Tuch and J. Martin (eds), *Racial Attitudes in the 1990s: Continuity and Change* (Westport, CT: Praeger).

Chaskin, R. and Brown, P. (1996) Theories of Neighborhood Change, in R. Stone (ed.), *Core Issues in Comprehensive Community—Building Initiatives* (Chicago: The Chapin Hall Center for Children).

DelliCarpini, M.X. (1998) Race and Community Revitalization: Communications Theory and Practice. Paper prepared for the Aspen Roundtable Project on Race and Community Revitalization.

Dominelli, L. (1992) An Uncaring Profession? An Examination of Racism in Social Work, in P. Braham, A. Rattansi and R. Skellington (eds.), *Racism and Antiracism: Inequalities, Opportunities and Policies* (London: Sage Publications).

Fulbright-Anderson, K., Kubisch, A. and Connell, J. (eds) (1998) *New Approaches. to Evaluating Community Initiatives* (Washington, DC: Aspen Institute).

Granovetter, M. (1973) The Strength of Weak Ties, *American Journal of Sociology* 78, (May), 1360–80.

Halpern, R. (1995) *Rebuilding the Inner City: A History of Neighborhood Initiatives to Address Poverty in the United States* (New York: Columbia University Press).

Junn, J. (1998) Education, Race and Community Building. Paper prepared for the Aspen Roundtable Project on Race and Community Revitalization.

Kubisch, A.C., Brown, P., Chaskin, R., Hirota, J., Joseph, M., Richman, H. and Roberts, L.M. (1997) *Voices from the Field: Learning from the Early Work of Comprehensive Community Initiatives* (Washington, DC: The Aspen Institute).

O'Connor, A. (1999) Swimming against the Tide: A Brief History of Federal Policy in Poor Communities, in R. Ferguson and W. Dickens (eds), *Urban Problems and Community Development* (Washington, DC: The Brookings Institution).

Pincus, F.L. (1996) Discrimination Comes in Many Forms: Individual, Institutional, and Structural, *The American Behavioral Scientist* (Nov./Dec.).

Riger, S. (1993) What's Wrong with Empowerment, *American Journal of Community Psychology* 21:3.

Teitz, M.B. and Chapple, K. (1998) The Causes of Inner-City Poverty: Eight Hypotheses in Search of Reality, *Citiscape: A Journal of Policy Development and Research* 3:3.

Thomas, June Manning (1997) Model Cities Revisited: Issues of Race and Empowerment, in J. M. Thomas and M. Ritzdorf (eds.), *Urban Planning and the African American Community: In the Shadows* (Thousand Oaks, CA: Sage).

Wilson, William Julius (1999) *The Bridge over the Racial Divide* (Berkeley, CA: University of California Press).

CHAPTER 35

Defining Feminist Community

Place, choice, and the urban politics of difference

Judith Garber

THE "COMMUNITY PROBLEM"

Community poses a problem for feminism because too many political theories romanticize traditional community forms oriented toward place. Feminist critiques of this "community problem" have exposed the gender, class, and racial implications of various community concepts. As a result of this inquiry, local communities of place—the "family, neighborhood, school, and church web" (Friedman, 1989) prescribed in past and current communitarian theories—are counterposed against communities of choice—friendships and identity groups consistent with diversity and feminist ideals (Friedman, 1989, pp. 286–287; Young, 1990b, p. 172). I argue that this dualistic framework fails to capture the depth or range of women's community relationships, and it misses the feminist potential of democratic places. One possible escape from the limits of this dichotomy are communities of purpose, where shared situations foster local political action. Donning feminist analytical lenses requires us to keep a critical distance from traditional community notions, because there are real dangers in a blind devotion to place-based social and political forms. However, critiques of community must appreciate how women approach the challenge of creating space for democratic, diverse communities in the places they inhabit.

THE FLIGHT FROM COMMUNITY

Feminist distress about communities of place is directed at democratic theory and practice in which a community with settled, embedded values organizes political life. Most communitarians endorse smaller rather than larger governments and direct citizen participation over representative schemes. The most intellectually coherent and familiar strain of communitarian theory is civic republicanism. A crop of philosophers continues to voice the essential civic republican sentiment that politics and citizenship are predicated on "individual ... fulfillment in relationships with others in a society organized through public dialogue" (Bellah, Madsen, Sullivan, Swidler, & Tipton, 1985, p. 218).

Liberal feminists, like all liberals, worry that the natural rights of individual women are subsumed in strong-community schemes (Gutmann, 1985). Another danger is that women suffer under close-knit, authoritative, and homogeneous communities of place, whether real or imagined. Too often, such arrangements produce systematic exclusions and oppressions; not the least of which is patriarchy.

This second complaint about community is integral to feminist theory sharing a broadly deconstructionist perspective. Deconstruction of social and political life involves recognizing contingency, subjectivity, and dissonance. Thus, no unqualified concept such as *women* is valid, and a woman's interests can be defined only from her own experience of her social position (Nicholson, 1990). In this literature, there is also a pervasive argument for shifting political imperatives away from their traditional territorial and governmental referents toward group interests articulated from the standpoint of race, sex, and sexuality.

This line of argument is trenchant, particularly in its skepticism about the appropriateness of attempting to reach the "common understandings" (Phelan, 1989, p. 156) communitarianism requires. However, key feminist deconstructionist treatments of community suffer from a highly constricted conception of the central subject of their inquiry, taking as given what is actually at issue. Feminists much too readily would give up the ability to define community to the philosophers who have presented disappointing models of it. At the same time, they contest the ideological appropriation of community by White men. Current feminist theory tends to present women a stark choice between suffering bad political and social arrangements and rejecting local community altogether. Valuing such communities is not widely acknowledged to be a viable option.

The flight from defining place-based community is a contradiction. A prominent theme of deconstructionism is that politics cannot proceed when conflict is denied in favor of majority rule or consensus. Because this is a cautionary note well worth heeding, taking local community as given is particularly unsettling. It appears that as long as women cannot insert themselves into the dominant ideology, community is judged a fundamentally flawed idea rather than one that has worked badly and could be rescued if conflicts over community, citizenship, justice, and so on were brought to the fore.

This is a theoretical issue, but critics of communitarianism do not take care to understand how actual women regard community, overlooking a crucial fact: Women participate daily in "ongoing ideological conflict over the meaning of place" (Hummon, 1990, p. 28) in their struggles to make community their own. Local places often succeed at providing meaningful opportunities for women to express their multifaceted desires for relationships in a public sphere. These relationships are alive in the denser central-city settings where women, and above all poor women, increasingly find themselves. And urban research has demonstrated that there is a bond between community and city for many women. This implies that feminist political thought is not driven by an expansive enough view of community or a deep understanding of cities.

Cities are pervasively gendered, to the disadvantage of women at work, at home, and in public spaces. These findings about cities have not, however, been adequately applied to the sexual inequalities embedded in the institutional relationships of governance, citizenship, and community.

Thus we have two bodies of feminist knowledge at hand: political theory and urban analysis. Each incomplete, but they have obvious sympathies. Together, they can help determine whether cities (in theory and real life) must be cut loose from their traditional community moorings or if place-based community can be sufficiently redefined to meet feminist goals.

COMMUNITY AS FRATERNITY

Community is steeped in fraternal imagery and practices that are most damaging because they conjure up something that has always been largely mythical. Small towns and manicured suburbs can exact a high price from women and other outsider groups. Because interlopers may breach the consensual nature of public decision-making that is predicated on the sameness of the citizenry, they can justifiably be shunned or silenced. Strangers might so threaten the community's perceived identity and economic self-interest that certain people are denied entrance or driven out. Besides techniques to exclude subsidized and rental housing, people of color, group homes, or untraditional families, violence by neighbors and police is not unheard of.

More subtly, a set democratic process and preexisting norms aimed at fashioning political agreement are taken to be necessary for perpetuating the community. They are not themselves usually open for discussion or contestation. As in more intentional forms of exclusion, the requirements of the whole conspire against honoring basic objections to the community will, such as stating that there is unequal treatment of women or that genuine consensus is impossible or fictitious. Liberals have always insisted that the harmonious public sphere oppresses individuals. It more readily silences people as members of groups—as women, young or elderly people, gays and lesbians, people of color, or immigrants.

Finally, there has historically been a gendered division of political labor in local communities that gives the lie to certain classical justifications for communitarianism. Female local activism, although political leadership, has tended to mirror women's domestic concerns—housing, child care, welfare, safety, the environment. In a sense, these activities amount to "public housekeeping" (Morgen, 1988, pp. 111–113), in which women organize to take up the slack left by "city fathers" but with fewer of the political and economic resources conferred by the state, particularly for women who are not White and middle-class. It is thus doubtful whether communal democracy lives up to its advertised ability to bring the public and private spheres closer, create an engaged and empathetic citizenry, and promote social obligations.

DIFFERENCE AND THE MYTH OF COMMON UNDERSTANDINGS

Community need not be fraternal to be oppressive or exclusive, because women differ by race, class, immigration status, language, religion, sexuality, marital status, age, and physical ability. The desolate material conditions of so many urban women's lives concretely manifest these differences. Because women are not positioned equivalently with respect to structures of power and privilege, proclamations about the existence of a unified *feminist* civic sphere are suspect. In this context, the benefits of community cannot redound to all women, and what constitutes community or benefits will itself be deeply controversial.

Local communities that satisfy the primary conditions for feminist politics—diversity and equality—are therefore elusive. This realization evokes an uncomfortable question: Will feminist efforts to create political communities of place invariably founder on the shoals of a misplaced or even pernicious

desire for "shared final ends" (Young, 1990b, p. 238) in the civic sphere? One answer is provided by deconstructionism, which helps debunk the myth that anything in politics can be genuinely common across an entire jurisdiction.

But feminist deconstruction of cities and communities comes at the price of depriving us of the recourse to political understandings—admittedly grindingly difficult—built on conflict but that are true understandings nonetheless. Positing "difference" as the primary descriptive and normative window on local political life sets communities of choice or identity groups against communities of place.

COMMUNITIES AND CITIES

On the street and in the academy, city is interchangeable with community. Perhaps the most important effort within feminist theory to disengage them has been articulated by Iris Marion Young. Young (1990b) argues that justice is hindered by community and locality, but not necessarily by cities, conceived properly. "As an alternative to the ideal of community" proffered by civic republicanism she offers "an ideal of city life as a vision of social relations affirming group difference" (p. 227). The vast potential of cities to foster nonexclusive social differentiation, variety, eroticism, and publicity (pp. 13, 238–240) is what constitutes "city-ness" for her. It remains only "an unrealized social ideal" (Young, 1990b, p. 227), because cities have cultivated the worst characteristics of both communitarianism and liberal capitalism.

SIZE

As a general rule, the larger the city, the better chance that diverse identities will be honored instead of being merged into communal norms or forced underground. Like Jacobs (1961), Young believes that metropolises counteract the conformist pressures within smaller communities. Young, however, does not believe that city identity is a positive political value. Urban places, defined as spaces in which anything and anyone goes, would be ideal if the complicating factor of local governments and communities were eliminated. In their absence, the politics of difference could flourish; this major amendment to civic-oriented political theories is integral to her feminist vision. For these reasons Young (1990b, pp. 252–255) proposes restructuring cities into regional units capable of regulating diversity-maintaining mechanisms that municipalities and neighborhoods lack. Neighborhood assemblies would be represented regionally and "have autonomy over a certain range of decisions and activities . . . only if [they] do not" harm, inhibit, or dictate the conditions of individual agency (pp. 250–251).

But Young's overall picture of city life is flawed. We might reasonably conclude that smaller units that invariably resolve themselves into communities based on geographic, social, and/or cultural proximity are prerequisites to successful metropolises. Jacobs herself argued that cities must encompass three sizes of "neighborhood" units, each retaining certain powers of self-governance (p. 117). Particularly at the street scale, neighborhoods provide a measure of safety out of proportion to their size (p. 119), which is no mean achievement. Contrast this with Young (1990b, p. 237), for whom the most prominent attribute of the city is the cloak of anonymity it offers those who would stand out as nonmembers of the monolithic community, a place where neighbors who watch out for you would merely be nosy. Identity groups—based on attributes such as sex, race, or sexuality—could serve to bridge the gap between anonymity and social connectedness that virtually everyone needs for safety and sanity, especially in the big city. But the subtler conceptual distinctions between community and identity groups threaten to slide into semantics, in part because the neighbors hoped for by communitarians and feared by difference theorists are both caricatures.

POLITICAL ACTION

Both identity and anonymity are valued urban attributes, but they work at political cross purposes. Hence the political implications for cities of the distinction between an anti-communitarian pluralism and a community that requires pluralism are great. Just as marginalized residents of cities are unlikely to gather their political strength spontaneously, affirming group difference without striving for shared ground on at least some issues is the ultimate estrangement of political empowerment and action. It is unsurprising that Young (1990a) defines what remains of locality without political referents, envisioning cities as "vastly populated areas[s] with large-scale industry and places of mass assembly" (p. 317). Conjuring this sterile city helps illustrate that, politically, city and community are mutually dependent, and it feeds the suspicion that banishing effective community from the local scene out of deference to irreconcilable difference turns cities into branch plants of the central state. Community can make cities sites of political action, whereas decorative neighborhood assemblies underneath structures of "democratized regional planning" (p. 253) are unlikely to radicalize anybody.

PLACE AND CHOICE

Jacobs (1961) presaged certain primal fears about the communitarian ideal currently expressed by feminist critical theorists, but she did not shrink from community. She argued that:

> for all the innate extroversion of city neighborhoods, it fails to follow that city people can therefore get along magically without neighborhoods . . . Let us assume that city neighbors have nothing more fundamental in common with each other than that they share a fragment of geography. Even so, if they fail at managing that fragment decently, the fragment will fail . . . Neighborhoods in cities need not supply for their people an artificial town or village life, and to aim at this is both silly and destructive. But neighborhoods in cities do need to supply some means for civilized self-government.
>
> (p. 117)

Notably, Jacobs uses neighborhood with precisely the same level of generality and substantive implications that people normally connect with the term community but without the dichotomy between place and choice that is a pillar of the feminist "difference" critique of communitarianism. At base, this dichotomy is false and misleading.

First, communities are not merely containers holding people who share a unidimentional identity. In neighborhoods and localities, identity and place necessarily shape one another's character, because territorial communities are little more than the people who make them up, plus society's reaction to those people. The interaction between place and people is one reason why an impoverished African American community in rural Georgia is politically and culturally miles away from an impoverished African American community in urban St. Louis, why the initial gay politics of AIDS was radically different in New York and San Francisco, and also why places change.

The intersection between women's collective attention to place and their collective concern for a particular class, race, or ethnicity fuels their political strength. Although some women form coalitions across identity lines to secure joint benefits for the local place in which they live, one's sense of identity might well encompass people far beyond the neighborhood or city limits. Especially for those with few privileges, nationalist identity is a counterweight to the dominant culture. Grassroots work in the urban arena cultivates political efficacy and identity consciousness, and it forges links to larger social movements. Such "strateg[ies] of diverse but pragmatic affiliations" (Gilkes, 1988, p. 55) need not divert focus from the local community; instead, solidarity on several levels may actually make local action more attractive and significant. Where the fortunes of one's neighbors and friends are seen as being connected—if they are connected—the stakes of political action become very high. Viewed this way, the community problem is that there are too few of them.

Second, people gravitate to particular geographic locales in part for togetherness, so one's community of place and community of choice may coincide. Neighborhoods and districts are not formed randomly but are to some extent composed of self-selected residents who may be choosing a comfortable identity fit or diversity. City dwellers, especially, often experience community primarily via the general type of plurality that Young advocates. This is not to deny that great barriers to free selection of places exist, that some moves are involuntary, or that not everyone desires or engages in community. People often flee constricting communities of origin and of happenstance as soon as possible. But these people go to *places*. Therefore, it exacerbates the community problem to, in essence, reduce geographic communities to "dependent children, elderly and others whose lives and well-being are at great risk" (Friedman, 1989, p. 290), immobile and lacking alternatives. It "denies people their roots *in* communities" (Ackelsberg, 1988, p. 302).

Third, occupying the same space supplies people with shared experiences, is a de facto commonality, and may create political cooperation among unlike individuals. For instance, although gentrification exerts pressures on housing affordability and neighborhood stability felt by poor and near poor "incumbent" female heads of households, female gentrifiers are economically more "marginal" than men, and there is evidence that women simply place a greater value on urban amenities. Therefore, women may discover common political ground around place-based issues, such as the quality of schools and public transportation, and the safety of streets and parks (Rose & Villeneuve, 1988, pp. 51–57).

DESCRIPTIVE AND NORMATIVE FRAMEWORKS

In short, a place-based versus an identity-based conceptual framework community fails on descriptive and analytical grounds. In terms of simple description, the framework is too rigid to describe all the communities women inhabit and seek out. In terms of analysis, a dualistic approach to community begs the question of how places and interests interact, which is perhaps the central issue in urban politics.

The dichotomous conceptual framework falls short as a normative hierarchy—identity trumps place—because there is no convincing method of ranking community concepts on practical or moral grounds. None guarantees democracy and it is indeed taxing to imagine a strong normative theory of politics or of cities in which the distinction between abstract communities is a key principle. For instance, there is really no reliable method for distinguishing an inner-city neighborhood of poor mothers fighting a toxic waste dump from a suburban community of White middle-class mothers fighting the same thing, unless perhaps the dump will be sited in one of those two neighborhoods. In the latter case the harms and benefits of urban life must be more equitably dispersed than at present, which requires that communities of all sizes adhere to basic rules about not poisoning people. But this rule is not inherently related to place-based community, an issue with prominent spatial elements. Space should not be "objectified as a perpetrator of inequality" (Wilder, 1993, p. 407), because it cannot be judged independently of the exclusionary "institutional processes [that] operate in space" (p. 408). Although they surely interact, injustice and compensatory justice (Young, 1990b) are not dimensions of territorial organization.

FEMINIST COMMUNITY IN PRACTICE

Feminists are the last assiduous practitioners of the basic tenets of communitarian politics, an irony that has not escaped feminist theorists (Pateman, 1989, p. 220). The *idea*, not to be confused with any *ideal*, of community is a motivating force in far-flung urban places, kept alive by women for whom it is their only source of political empowerment.

Why do women gravitate so easily to communities of place, given the feminist criticisms? The answer is that, as an abstraction, local community is deeply problematic; in practice, it may actually serve women more often than we think. The benefits of creating some shared public life explain why, when the formal political community of the city betrays women, they create their own. Feminist political theory has, rightly, pointed out that shared public lives have profound limits. Even so, imperfect community appears to go farther toward meeting some women's needs than nothing at all.

Housing is the intersection of community, locality, and domesticity, and it best exemplifies women's interests in linking place and politics. Women's housing cooperatives demonstrate that the prospect of building community from the ground up, attracts "powerless" women to intensely political endeavors. Wekerle's (1988a) account of Canadian co-ops portrays models of community substantially like cities in their governing responsibilities but different from patriarchal communities in process and ultimate aims. Women joined the co-ops not only for affordable shelter but also to attain certain political ideals, mutual support, and, according to a resident, "to share responsibilities, rights, democracy" (p. 108). Tenants make decisions about allocating space between communal and private uses, budgets, service delivery, membership, policy making and enforcement, management, redistribution, and economic development, in an urban setting. Similar findings have been reported from New York City's housing projects (Saegert, 1988, pp. 34–35), and Chicago's single room occupancy (SRO) hotels (Hoch & Slayton, 1989).

In the "community aspects" of these housing arrangements, individual women discovered relatively safe places for themselves. And this happened while engaging in fundamentally urban tasks. Localities can ensure individual/group and community needs simultaneously if they do not aim for unity or support the oppression of some women by other women under the guise of community. The trick is figuring out how to balance these competing tendencies within local social groupings. Grand theories help us understand more about the oppression perpetuated by exclusion and political inattention to the differing positions of people who make up communities. A more grounded focus would acknowledge that it is a particularly awkward moment for feminists to dissociate the urban from the community. In the United States, a search for roads leading back to functional communities of place occupies residents of inner-city neighborhoods and, particularly, the women who are their backbone.

COMMUNITIES OF PURPOSE

Politics makes little sense if it is not conceived as a joint effort—it is inescapably a *community of purposes* and sometimes also of interests. Communitarianism remains antithetical to feminism, however, as long as theorists continue to think that communities are composed of the "people," who formulate and voice consensual values and ideas. Locally, as globally, conflicts over differences degenerate into violence and repudiate "the community" of interpersonally generated understanding.

On the other hand, focusing criticism on "the privileging of face-to face relations by theorists of community" (Young, 1990a, p. 313) somewhat misses the point of cities. Face-to-face relations are part of urban life, like it or not. They may not be happy relations, but neither are they anonymous. Caught between the rock of claustrophobic local communities and the hard place of the elusiveness of achieving invisibility through group identification, perhaps the best that can be hoped for is a wary truce; perhaps this is the basis for communities of purpose.

For the practical purposes of action and self-help, a commonality of places and situations permits differences to be recognized, not ignored or (falsely) overcome. Communities of purpose for mutual responsibility and cooperation are integral to feminism and democratic cities if political action is a goal.

Accepting that communities empower some women and materially improve their lives means accepting certain manifestations of the flawed communitarian vision. There is, however, a crucial difference between a hegemonic community and the matrix of communities that serve as the political and cultural anchors for many women (and men) who dwell in urban and suburban cities. In the first case, the republican notion of the public sphere threatens those who do not already have power. In the second case, a meaningful public sphere encourages alternate political discourses that dissent from the majority and conflict with the dominant community's procedural and substantive agreements. If the communities that "we" attempt are understood as prerequisite to conditions of equality and diversity, and not as mirrors of some preconceived notion of these terms, then collective action and communities of purposes located in places make good sense.

However, feminist theorists of communal life must think as deeply and in as much detail about democratic process and institutional design as do communitarians. Process sets the terms for participation by stating how differences and histories of oppression must be accorded validity in setting community values. No wonder feminists concerned with radical democracy as well as deconstruction discuss community compellingly, for democracy demands attention to political action by equals and how this might be achieved. Individuals identify with a community because its own identity and political direction derive from them. Collective action toward social change is unthinkable outside the context of relationships between people who believe their well-being is tied together, for politics is not a singular endeavor.

CONTESTING COMMUNITY

It is true that "American culture incorporates different, contrasting community ideologies" (Hummon, 1990, p. 169), but the ideological clash has not been robust enough to institutionalize in local state-sponsored political processes the voices of marginalized groups. Until community discourse acknowledges women's versions that have been excluded from defining the "official" community or relegated to housekeeping for city politics, feminists will avoid communitarian theories for advocating political and social organization inhospitable to the differences that define people.

However, abandoning place-based community is not the only possible feminist stance. First, advancing the variety of social and economic issues that affect women entails political alliances extending beyond the group, neighborhood, city, or nation. Broader exercises of citizenship are likely to occur only when organization and empowerment are first practiced on at least one level of community. Second, many of the problems that female city dwellers experience as women—homelessness, violence against and by children, sexual assault, lack of public transportation, economic ghettoization—are indeed locally located, if not entirely locally produced. The intimate connections between the daily lives of women and the life of the city suggest that political activity by coalitions of women aimed specifically at defining inclusive, "good" communities might result in localities that are less marginalizing, hierarchical, and dangerous. Thus, informal and formal local communities are potential sources of women's empowerment and political change.

Conceptual wrangling will not resolve the tensions around the continuing, but highly problematic, relevance of place-based community for many women. At the same time, abandoning the name community for fear of invoking unsavory political arrangements lurking beneath it will not relieve us of the two basic "problems" that people do have different relationships with community and that the idea of local community is, apparently, much less appealing to feminist theorists than to women in urban contexts. Even supposing it is possible, genuinely, to accommodate the demands of more women to be citizens of open and humane cities, it remains to be demonstrated which communities are the best vehicles for that transformation. The "community problem" awaits further examination.

REFERENCES

Ackelsberg, M. (1988). Communities, resistance, and women's activism: Some implications for a democratic polity. In A. Bookman and S. Morgen (Eds.), *Women and the politics of empowerment* (pp. 297–313). Philadelphia: Temple University Press.

Bellah, R. N., Madsen, R., Sullivan, W. M., Swidler, A., and Tipton, S. M. (1985). *Habits of the heart: Individualism and commitment in American life.* Berkeley: University of California Press.

Friedman, M. (1989). Feminism and modern friendship: Dislocating the community. *Ethics,* 99, 275–290.

Gilkes, C. T. (1988). Building in many places: Multiple commitments and ideologies in Black women's community work. In A. Bookman and S. Morgen (Eds.), *Women and the politics of empowerment* (pp. 53–76). Philadelphia: Temple University Press.

Gutmann, A. (1985). Communitarian critics of liberalism. *Philosophy and Public Affairs,* 14, 308–322.

Hoch, C., and Slayton, R. A. (1989). *New homeless and old: Community and the skid row hotel.* Philadelphia: Temple University Press.

Hummon, D. M. (1990). *Commonplaces: Community ideology and identity in American culture.* Albany: State University of New York Press.

Jacobs, J. (1961). *The death and life of great American cities.* New York: Random House.

Morgen, S. (1988). "It's the whole power of the city against us!": The development of political consciousness in a women's health care coalition. In A. Bookman and S. Morgen (Eds.), *Women and the politics of empowerment* (pp. 97–115). Philadelphia: Temple University Press.

Nicholson, L. J. (Ed.). (1990). *Feminism/postmodernism.* New York: Routledge.

Pateman, C. (1989). *The disorder of women: Democracy, feminism, and political theory.* Cambridge: Polity.

Phelan, S. (1989). *Identity politics: Lesbian feminism and the limits of community.* Philadelphia: Temple University Press.

Rose, D., and Villeneuve, P., with F. Colgan. (1988). Women workers and the inner city: Some implications of labor force restructuring in Montreal, 1971–81. In C. Andrew and B. Moore Milroy (Eds.), *Life spaces: Gender, household, and employment* (pp. 31–64). Vancouver: University of British Columbia Press.

Saegert, S. (1988). The androgenous city: From critique to practice. In W. Van Vliet (Ed.), *Women, housing, and community* (pp. 23–37). Aldershot, UK: Avebury.

Wekerle, G. (1988a). Canadian women's housing cooperatives: Case studies in physical and social innovation. In C. Andrew and B. Moore Milroy (Eds.), *Life spaces: Gender, household, and employment* (pp. 102–140). Vancouver: University of British Columbia Press.

Wilder, M. G. (1993). Institutional processes: Shaping place within disciplinary walls, a reply to Anne B. Shlay. *Journal of Urban Affairs,* 15, 405–411.

Young, I. M. (1990a). The ideal of the community and the politics of difference. In L. J. Nicholson (Ed.), *Feminism/postmodernism* (pp. 300–323). New York: Routledge.

Young, I. M. (1990b). *Justice and the politics of difference.* Princeton, NJ: Princeton University Press.

CHAPTER 36

The CDC Model of Urban Development

A critique and an alternative

Randy Stoecker

THE CDC DEBATE

For many years I have followed and worked with community development corporations (CDCs). I have become increasingly distressed, however, by their lack of impact and by our fading memory of why CDCs exist. This chapter analyzes the role of the CDC in the urban political economy, exploring what purposes it serves and what impacts it can have. It also proposes an alternative model of urban redevelopment that emphasizes community organizing, community-based planning, and high capacity multi-local CDCs.

Despite the growth of CDCs in the last thirty years, numerous analysts, including CDC advocates, cannot find evidence that CDCs have enough impact to reverse neighborhood decline (Rubin, 1994b; Berndt, 1977; Pierce & Steinbach, 1990) or that the development they produce would not have happened anyway (Marquez, 1993). CDCs do better than local housing authorities at providing housing, but it is "a drop in an ocean of need." (Twelvetrees, 1989, p. 155). Twelvetrees (1989) argues that if CDCs are to be rated according to three levels of success (staying in existence, achieving their major objectives, and achieving those objectives efficiently), then only the largest CDCs show success beyond the first level. CDCs are rarely credited with improvements in quality of life, community stability, resident health and happiness, and personal empowerment (Taub, 1990). Vidal (1992) notes that only 25% of CDCs say they have sparked major increases in community pride, and half say they have made some progress in strengthen-

ing community leadership. Keating, Rasey, & Krumholz (1990, p. 213) conclude that CDCs fail to achieve the broader goals of "political and economic independence and self-sufficiency."

Consequently, some wonder if CDCs are a case of social movement co-optation. Many neighborhood association members see CDCs as having lost their grassroots mentality. Consequently, critics charge, CDCs have become another developer following a free market approach to redevelopment (Lenz, 1988; Taub, 1990) rather than fighting for the social change necessary to support sustainable communities. Taub (1990, p. 2) states that "The CDC world is filled with tales of ruthless screening, fast evictions, and strict enforcement of behavioral standards." Lenz (1988, p. 25) decries the "terrible paradox of thriving organizations and dying communities."

CDC advocates respond passionately. Like other service providers, they see their work as at least a necessary Band-Aid. We should not expect high productivity from CDCs, they say, because they operate in weak markets, precisely why forprofit developers avoid those neighborhoods. Without CDCs, they argue, there would be no development in urban America's most deteriorated neighborhoods (Bratt, 1989; Vidal, 1992). Further, CDCs are more likely to meets the needs of the poor and even raise expectations that will lead to political pressure for social change (Rubin, 1995). Additionally, CDC adherents argue that the community organizing model (a more confrontational, conflict-oriented political approach to addressing poverty) is no longer appropriate because neighborhood structure has changed, the targets are hidden, and there are fewer local vital organizations.

Missing in this debate is a theoretical understanding of the CDC. How does the CDC interact with the contradictions of urban capitalism? What are the political-economic forces impinging on the CDC, potentially hindering effectiveness? To understand these questions, we must look at urban political economy and how the CDC model of urban redevelopment interacts with it.

THE CDC MODEL

The continuing critiques of CDCs across three decades suggest that more is at issue than imperfect practice. My argument is not that CDCs have been doing bad things, or operate with evil intent. As Lenz (1988, p. 25) notes, CDC practitioners "are good people with bad theory." Many CDC directors hold dearly to the goals of community empowerment and political activism. Some CDCs succeed at avoiding the problems discussed later (Rubin, 1997), but those exceptions only serve to emphasize that it is not the CDCs, but the model we hold up for CDCs to meet and the US political economy that are the problems.

From the beginning CDCs were to accomplish bottom-up, comprehensive redevelopment. The bottom-up approach is supposed to help the community determine how to conduct redevelopment and produce more homes and businesses owned by community members. They are also supposed to empower whole communities through comprehensive treatment of social and physical conditions, measuring success in terms of physical redevelopment and community regeneration, participation, and empowerment. As Kelly (1977, p. 18) says, this model is "socialistic-sounding" but "the socialistic aspect is more apparent than real." For the third part of the CDC model is an acceptance of free market philosophy.

The CDC model originally attempted to correct three market failures: (1) the inability of potential investors to see opportunities in the neighborhood, (2) profit maximization

that prevented socially conscious investing, (3) and social/legal restrictions on investment such as zoning laws. However, as government finances disappeared, CDCs had to give up even this moderate "directed capitalism" and "accommodate themselves to, rather than redirect, the course of the free market" (Marquez, 1993, p. 289). Their goal is not to transform society but to "extend the benefits of the American economic mainstream . . . to [those] that are left out" (Pierce & Steinbach, 1990, p. 33). At best, poor neighborhoods are seen as weak markets requiring reinvestment rather than as oppressed communities requiring mobilization, leading CDCs to work within the existing economic rules.

It is important to understand that this model can work only by assuming that capital and poor communities have complementary interests. As Berndt (1977, p. 126) noted, "CDCs have accepted the rationale of the corporation within capitalist society." CDCs have come to operate more and more like businesses, narrowing their activities to physical development. Many CDCs impose rules on tenants that are no different from any other landlord rather than empowering residents to govern themselves.

POLITICAL ECONOMY OF THE CDC MODEL

Understanding the problems with the CDC model requires understanding the relationship between capital and community. The relationship between capital and community is at least potentially contradictory (Feagin & Parker, 1990; Logan & Molotch, 1987). Community's tendency is to preserve neighborhood space as a use value for the service of community members, while capital's tendency is to convert neighborhood space into exchange values that can be speculated on for a profit. This sets up an antagonistic relationship. Capital's conversion of neighborhood space into exchange values drives up rents, destroys green space, eliminates neighborhood-based commerce, and disrupts neighboring patterns. Capital is less willing to invest in neighborhood redevelopment that maintains neighborhood spaces as use values because that would prevent speculation and limit profit accumulation. Either through destructive investment or disinvestment community suffers.

Further antagonistic relationships exist in the city between workers and employers, and between renters and rentiers. Most important to the dynamics of this struggle, however, are those who are neither clearly workers nor owners, renters nor rentiers. Those in the middle occupy contradictory locations between the haves and have-nots. The members of this vast middle are part owner, and part proletariat. They also control their own housing, but still pay rent in the form of a mortgage. As a consequence, they are pulled in two directions at once. The middle class is therefore culturally unpredictable and politically constrained.

It is this insecure and unpredictable middle location that CDCs occupy. CDCs manage capital like capitalists, but do not invest it for a profit. They manage projects but within the constraints set by their funders. They try to be community-oriented while their purse strings are held by outsiders. They are pressured by capital to produce exchange values in the form of capitalist business spaces and rental housing. They are pressured by communities to produce use values in the form of services, home ownership, and green spaces. This is more than a "double bottom-line." It is the internalization of the capital-community contradiction and it leads to trouble. The result is three problems besetting the CDC model: (1) the limits to comprehensiveness, (2) the myth of community control, and (3) the development of disorganization.

Limits to Comprehensiveness

CDC work requires expertise ranging from finance, insurance, and real estate to architecture to zoning laws, along with a vast amount of capital. The things that can make CDCs community-based (their smallness and neighborhood roots) inhibit access to the capital and expertise that comprehensiveness demands. The community-based ideology in the CDC model promotes amateurism and volunteerism, isolating CDCs from prominent capital actors and experts.

The ideology of the CDC as community-based also leads to a belief that the CDC is an alternative to government programs. Only about half of CDC operating budgets are provided through government sources (Goetz, 1993). The public sector is reluctant to commit funds to CDCs because of the lack of CDC productivity caused by inadequate funding. Also, because CDCs purport to be community controlled, public administrators rationalize that their funding should come from the community as well. The impossibility of that occurring is ignored. Government funding of CDCs may be most useful for maintaining social order. Enough money is provided to stave off social unrest, but not enough to threaten the unequal balance of power. Conservative government celebrates CDCs while providing just enough money to help them fail—suggesting that government and corporations are systematically hostile to empowering community development.

The consequence is victim blaming. Developers are believed to fail or succeed based on their skills, not their circumstances, so project failure is attributed to the CDC (and thus the community) doing a bad job. The reality, however, is that CDCs are grotesquely underfunded organizations working in disinvested communities requiring massive capital infusion. Self-help is unrealistic under such conditions and "may worsen problems in neighborhoods that require more, not fewer, resources ... An emphasis on self-help should not be used to divert attention from the context" (Checkoway, 1985, p. 482).

The role of the CDC has become that of a means to divert our attention from the context. The media celebrate a single small initiative in a sea of decay and the public sees small CDC accomplishments portrayed as big victories and comes to believe there is little need for their taxes or their donations. Then they blame CDCs and their associated communities when redevelopment fails. Of course, the way to get beyond the problem of smallness and the failure associated with it is to access massive resources. That, however, carries its own burden and leads to the next problem.

The Myth of Community Control

The assumption in the model that CDCs are independent community-based solutions to urban decay mystifies the reality of external control. The problem of maintaining community control is rooted in the fact that poor communities do not have enough community controlled capital and must woo outside capital whose tendency is to transform use values into exchange values. The role of funders in subverting social change efforts has been well established generally (Roelofs, 1987) and in regard to CDCs (Kelly, 1977). The Local Initiatives Support Corporation (LISC), the single most lauded funder of CDCs, is controlled by elites who often view redevelopment from an exchange value perspective rather than a use value perspective. Other large foundation supporters of CDCs are little different, evaluating CDCs for their economic acceptability rather than their ability to serve community needs. While CDCs may be able to use those funds without technically being co-opted, the funds still impose limitations because they embody the profit principle, especially after government funding plummeted in the 1980s and was replaced by comparatively minuscule private sector funding.

This sets up a secondary contradiction between affordability and control. Outside capital resists supporting redevelopment that maintains community control. Government, bowing to market ideology, follows similar rules. CDCs often must choose between acting quickly enough to take advantage of fleeting funding opportunities and practicing more cumbersome democracy (Twelvetrees, 1989). Thus, redevelopment that maintains community control is expensive and redevelopment that is affordable requires giving up control to outside funders.

In addition, as funding becomes more scarce, CDCs package more complex, time consuming, costly, and hard to manage projects. CDCs often have more complex organizational structures than comparable for-profits. This increasing complexity removes even more control from the community. Control devolves to staff, who often live outside the community and are more likely to emphasize the technical details of development over community empowerment (Rubin, 1994a). CDC boards, at most, provide broad guidance rather than direct decision-making.

Even if the board maintains informed control, it may not represent the community. The board of the first CDC—Bed-Stuy Restoration Corporation—was dominated by U.S. Senator Jacob Javits, Ethel Kennedy, the chairman of Mobil Oil, and the president of Citibank (Berndt, 1977). Businesses often play a stronger role in directing CDC policy than residents (Vidal, 1992). The fact that board membership is neither glamorous nor exciting also hinders resident participation. This lack of participation can lead to decisions that do not reflect the community and produce festering resentments (Heskin, 1991). Even CDC supporters agree that CDCs do not "necessarily aim for, nor result in, widespread participation by the affected tenants" (Bratt, 1989, p. 312).

Regardless of how much those within CDCs think of themselves as having common interests with the community, it is questionable that they do. Two-thirds of CDCs manage the housing they develop (Vidal, 1992). Consequently, CDCs are landlords and thus have an interest in maintaining the financial solvency of the organization, even if they are nicer about it than for-profit landlords. Renters, however, have an interest in maintaining the affordability of their housing. This creates a structural antagonism that divides the CDC from the community. Bratt (1989, pp. 234–235) implicitly distinguishes "community-based group" (apparently referring to CDCs) and "its constituency" as if the concepts refer to different things. Residents also miss the contradiction. When redevelopment fails, they blame each other rather than targeting the external causes.

Ultimately, the control-affordability contradiction has "created responsibility without control . . . [and] transformed political questions for the political community into technical questions more accessible to experts" (Heskin, 1991, p. 73). Under these conditions, the CDC model is in danger of creating weaker rather than stronger communities.

The Development of Disorganization

Market processes are unpredictable, unstable, unaccountable, and disorganizing. They allow the destruction of communities through speculative investment and disinvestment. When CDCs behave as market-oriented organizations, they become part of those disorganizing forces. CDCs are also pressured to support the capital side of the capital-community contradiction and put organizational profit ahead of community benefit (Twelvetrees, 1989; Berndt, 1977).

When the CDC fails, it contributes to neighborhood decline. When the CDC succeeds, it may also lead to neighborhood decline by disorganizing the community. Community development, when it emphasizes the physical over the social and remains limited to the possibilities dictated by capital, may actually increase turnover and displacement within a community (Taub, 1990).

Can CDCs develop community? Analysts have emphasized that CDCs do "projects," but the continuing influence of the comprehensive emphasis has led to talk about CDCs promoting community organizing. It is unclear, however, whether CDC advocates understand what community organizing is, would want to do it if they knew, or could do it if they wanted to. The CDC model "has confused the building of power with the building of structures" (Traynor, 1992, p. 9).

The classic community organizing model does not appear to fit the CDC definition that uses advocacy synonymously with organizing. Community organizers understand organizing as developing relationships so people can press their demands collectively and gain power through that process. Advocacy is an expert speaking for a constituency, rather than helping them speak for themselves. Some analysts question whether CDCs do any substantial organizing, seeing them as consciously apolitical (Keating, *et al.*, 1990). Giloth (1985, p. 39) sums up the problem by citing that "There is housing advocacy and development—but little squatting." In other words, working within the rules, CDCs accept what trickles down rather than help people mobilize to reclaim what has been taken away. Not only is organizing neglected, but the CDC tries to be the neighborhood voice (Vidal, 1992). This is dangerous because we have already seen that CDCs are not adequate representatives of neighborhood interests. The CDC may compete for public attention with organizing groups, dividing the community between CDC supporters and organizing group supporters (Stoecker, 1994, 1995). The CDC also may delegitimize the organizing group by making it appear more militant because CDCs are less threatening to power holders than community action organizations.

Even if the CDC understands community organizing as a true empowerment strategy, it is unlikely the CDC is the best vehicle for conducting community organizing. Constrained by their funding, CDCs cannot take the risks necessary to produce empowering community organizing. Additionally, organizing and even service efforts take a back seat to development when financial or political pressures bear down. Rooted in the capital-community contradiction, development and organizing can become contradictory missions (Stoecker, 1994, 1995).

The CDC model potentially increases internal community conflict, displacement, and disempowerment when it fails and when it succeeds. While CDCs try to work where government left off, they depend on government; while they try to be community controlled, they must respond to outside schedules and funds, and while they are effective because they are small, the problems are big (Twelvetrees, 1989). What is to be done? Many groups got into development because they believed they were not getting enough out of community organizing, but they found that doing development affected fewer people and made organizing more difficult (Bratt, 1989).

A NEW MODEL

It is too much to expect a CDC to be resistant enough to ward off market pressures attempting to co-opt its agenda, accountable enough to remain under community control, yet large enough to do the job that is needed in disinvested communities.

Given that CDCs are not good at maximizing community participation and supporting community organizing, the sensible solution is to do away with the mythology of the CDC as community based. Removing the community-based label removes the possibility of scapegoating the community when redevelopment fails; admits to the CDC's potential community disrupting qualities, allowing residents to better organize to protect themselves; and removes a competing voice from the neighborhood, allowing residents voices to be heard without the filter of a developer.

Thus, we must also clean up the confusing collage of organizational definitions, and all the labels only confuse the distinction between community organizing and development. Let's reserve CDC for those organizations that build buildings and community organizing group for those organizations that build community power. And let's be wary of those that refuse to admit their priorities.

If we shift from a development model to a community empowerment model, we can find a place for the CDC that does not so readily contradict community. This new model must emphasize human development and organizing as much as physical development, demand non-market solutions to the problems of poverty, be wary of public–private partnerships, subordinate development plans to an organizing agenda, and promote community, not CDC, control of physical space. These principles lead to two components of a new redevelopment model: a community-controlled organizing/planning process; and the high-capacity multi-local CDC.

Organize, Organize, Plan

Organizing by itself may work as well as the CDC approach in creating redevelopment. The Dudley Street Neighborhood Initiative (DSNI) (Medoff and Sklar, 1994) focused on organizing as the means to development, while partnering with others to do actual physical redevelopment. In Minneapolis, the Cedar Riverside neighborhood residents conducted organizing through their Project Area Committee, limiting their CDC to only implementing plans produced through the organizing process. In San Antonio, Communities Organized for Public Service (COPS) resisted pressure to become a CDC (in the words of their lead organizer, Ernesto Cortes, "for the obvious reasons") as they achieved control of much of San Antonios CDBG budget.

Community organizing is difficult, however. Capitalist disinvestment has so disrupted community networks that organizing focused on rebuilding neighborhood relationships may be necessary before the community can engage in more public struggle. Defending against, and recovering from, the forces that cause neighborhood decay requires education and planning as much as strategy and tactics.

The most important part of a community organizing model that empowers residents is the planning process, increasingly seen by CDCs as central to development, even if still neglected in practice. Community-based planning, if done correctly, accomplishes four purposes. First, it builds a sense of community, becoming an organizing process. Second, it educates residents on what resources and threats exist in their neighborhood. Third, it builds community power, allowing residents to determine what redevelopment they want and thus better defend themselves against speculators. Finally, it helps residents plan for the ideal, without regard to limitations imposed by elites.

Harking back to the original CDC model, the importance of planning being truly comprehensive cannot be emphasized enough. One of the negative consequences of all past ghetto revitalization programs has been that residents move out as soon as their personal circumstances improve enough, disrupting community networks and draining community resources. People need a sense of control over their community. Residents also need material reasons to stay, which means that their personal circumstances and surroundings must improve together. And that means redevelopment cannot be conducted by a small CDC doing a house here or a business there. It requires a massive influx of resources at once, and that is where the high-capacity CDC comes in.

The High-Capacity Multi-Local CDC

We must build CDCs with adequate capital capacity. When we remove the community-based mythology from the CDC, individual neighborhoods should neither need nor want their own CDC. Large CDCs have more capital capacity, more political capacity, and more collective talent to conduct physical redevelopment that can outpace community deterioration. Of course, CDCs with greater technical, economic, and political capacity also have greater capacity to overrun community needs. But there are a number of ways to counterbalance these potential troubles.

The most important means of countering the large CDC's power is, to develop strong community organizing groups with comprehensive and detailed redevelopment plans. These groups should have enough expertise in the details of redevelopment to construct development contracts that hold CDCs accountable.

Fight the Power

Is such a model—reemphasizing community organizing, expanding the capitalization of CDCs, and planning for redevelopment practical or possible? Who is going to pay for this new community-driven approach? A federal government in financial tatters, walled in corporations, foundations that trickle minuscule resources on massive problems? Our acceptance of these political realities as technical realities, however, contributes to the problem. Of course development cannot be done without substantial government dollars, hefty private sector participation, and enormous foundation support. But the money is there. Accessing it is a political, not a technical, problem, which requires mobilizing communities to demand action.

Is this proposal too radical and unrealistic? Can funders be convinced to give tens of millions of dollars for comprehensive redevelopment in a single neighborhood? Can they be convinced to give that money in support of neighborhood-based plans? Can support grow for market-resistant subsidies to community-owned and -controlled businesses that keep wealth in the neighborhood?

The obvious, quick answer is no. No seems to be the answer only because we have come so far down the CDC model path that we have forgotten that the real issue is power, not development. The ideals of a new model that emphasizes community empowerment are unlikely to be achieved in the short term, which makes it even more important that we begin to rethink a redevelopment model that promotes current national and corporate priorities and myths and undermines the potential of communities.

REFERENCES

Berndt, H. E. (1977). *New rulers in the ghetto: the community development corporation and urban poverty*. Westport, CT: Greenwood Press.

Bratt, R. (1989). *Rebuilding a low-income housing policy*. Philadelphia: Temple University Press.

Bratt, R. (1994). From housing development to neighborhood revitalization: the saga of a Boston CDC. Paper presented at the Urban Affairs Association annual meetings.

Checkoway, B. (1985). Neighborhood planning organizations: perspectives and choices. *Journal of Applied Behavioral Science*, 21, 471–486.

Cortes, E. (1995). Remarks as panelist, Special Session on "The Legacy of Saul Alinsky" at the American Sociological Association Annual meetings.

Feagin, J. R., and Parker, R. (1990). *Building American cities: the urban real estate game* (2nd edn.). Englewood Cliffs, NJ: Prentice-Hall.

Giloth, R. (1985) Organizing for neighborhood development. *Social Policy*, 15, 37–42.

Goetz, E.G. (1993). *Shelter burden: local politics and progressive housing policy*. Philadelphia: Temple University Press.

Heskin, A.D. (1991). *The struggle for community*. Boulder, CO: Westview Press.

Keating, W. D., Rasey, K. P., and Krumholz, N. (1990). Community development corporations in the United States: their role in housing and urban redevelopment. In W. van Vliet and J. van Weesep (Eds.), *Government and housing: developments in seven countries*, pp. 206–218. Newbury Park, CA: Sage Publications.

Kelly, R. M. (1977). *Community control of economic development: the boards of directors of community development corporations*. New York: Praeger.

Lenz, T. J. (1988). Neighborhood development: issues and models. *Social Policy*, Spring. 24–30.

Logan, J. R., and Molotch, H. L. (1987). *Urban fortunes: the political economy of place*. Berkeley: University of California Press.

Marquez, B. (1993). Mexican American community development corporations and the limits of directed capitalism. *Economic Development Quarterly*, 7, 287–295.

Medoff, P., and Sklar, H. (1994). *Streets of hope: the fall and rise of an urban neighborhood.* Boston: South End Press.

Pierce, N. R., and Steinbach, C. F. (1990). *Enterprising communities: community-based development in America, 1990,* Washington, D.C.: Council for Community-Based Development.

Roelofs, J. (1987). Foundations and social change organizations: the mask of pluralism. *Insurgent Sociologist,* 14, 31–72.

Rubin, H. (1994a). Surviving in the niche: community-based development organizations and their support environment. Paper presented at the Urban Affairs Association annual meetings.

Rubin, H. (1994b). There aren't going to be any bakeries here if there is no money to afford jellyrolls: the organic theory of community-based development. *Social Problems,* 41, 401–424.

Rubin, H. (1995). Renewing hope in the inner city: conversations with community-based development practitioners. *Administration and Society,* 27, 128–161.

Rubin, H. (1997). Being a conscience and a carpenter: interpretations of the community-based development model. *Journal of Community Practice,* forthcoming.

Stoecker, R. (1990). *Foundation philanthropy in Toledo: assessing the potential for Foundation support of community-based development.* Toldeo: University of Toledo, Urban Affairs Center Research Report.

Stoecker, R. (1993). *Neighborhood-based planning in Toledo: a comparative study.* Toledo: University of Toledo, Urban Affairs Center Research Report.

Stoecker, R. (1994). *Defending community: the struggle for alternative redevelopment in Cedar Riverside.* Philadelphia: Temple University Press.

Stoecker, R. (1995). Community organizing and community development in Cedar-Riverside and East Toledo. *Journal of Community Practice,* 2, 1–23.

Taub, R. H. (1990). *Nuance and meaning in community development: finding community and Development.* New York: New School of Social Research, Community Development Research Center, Graduate School of Management and Urban Policy.

Traynor, W. (1992). Community development:: does it need to change? *Neighborhood Works,* April–May, 9–10, 22–23.

Twelvetrees, A. (1989). *Organizing for neighbourhood development.* Brookfield, VT: Avebury.

Vidal, A. C. (1992). *Rebuilding communities: a national study of urban community development corporations.* New York: New School for Social Research, Community Development Research Center, Graduate School of Management and Urban Policy.

The Construction of the Local and the Limits of Contemporary Community Building in the United States

James Fraser, Jonathan Lepofsky, Edward Kick, and J. Patrick Williams

The recent trend toward the neoliberal restructuring of urban governance, including the devolution and outsourcing of public services to private enterprises, has made reliance on *the local* integral to social service provisions. This is especially true in cities where the relative shift in responsibilities for providing social services occurs via civil society in which citizens play a large part in the care and management of the city (Clarke and Gaile 1998). In this reworking of the relationship between the state and civil society, community building has arisen as the preferred strategy to fill the void left by the reduction of state services (Duffy and Hutchinson 1997; McKnight 1995; Sampson 1999). Community building is a much-supported but undercriticized paradigm, especially with respect to questions about the benefits that impoverished neighborhood residents actually acquire from these initiatives. We examine community building as a process that is related to other agendas, identifying how community building is larger than the community that it portends to build (even while localizing its own activities for the resident participants), and we challenge many taken-for-granted notions about the benefits of this form of anti-poverty work.

The current mass of community-building projects needs to be understood as a spatial practice that produces complex sets of effects other than poverty alleviation. Community-building initiatives occur in an increasingly globalized context, providing opportunities for stakeholders other than residents to promote certain productions of space and place. Also, urban restructuring and the development of inner-city neighborhoods are arenas where developers, realtors, lending institutions, and other private ventures extract profit and instigate a particular vision of the city. This chapter also points out how community building, uses scale in particular ways to reconfigure spatial relationships and processes and aims at certain constructions of what it means to be living in contemporary, urban places.

In the first part of the chapter, we outline community-building theory and problematize it as a solution to inner-city poverty. Next, we provide a brief outline of some of the impacts of globalization on cities thus contextualizing community building in relation to these larger social forces and pointing to the localization that occurs alongside forms of globalization. Finally, we present a brief case study of an initiative occurring in a southern city in the United States to highlight how community building operates. We conclude by pointing out how community building may be detrimental to impoverished neighborhood residents in an era of devolution, offering suggested ways in which community building could open up the rights to the city for poor residents and truly expand their participation in the future of U.S. urban areas.

BUILDING COMMUNITY AND FIGHTING POVERTY IN THE LOCAL SCALE

One of the central explanations of inner-city poverty is Wilson's (1987) argument that focuses on the deindustrialization of the U.S. economy, the shift of jobs and people from inner-city locales to the suburbs, and out-migration of middle-class families to the suburbs. Inner-city neighborhoods, according to Wilson, are characterized by a lack of institutions, role models, and resources necessary to maintain an adequate quality of life. Furthermore, he contends that concentrations of male joblessness, poverty, and female-headed households may lead to a shift in social and cultural norms in a community.

The community-building field has embraced a version of Wilson's (1987) perspective and has argued that strengthening community-level structural features is a function of community-level processes, a theme that permeates programmatic efforts. Structural features refer to educational, economic, religious, recreational, and nonprofit organizations with an emphasis on strong community-based political organizations. A hallmark of community-building initiatives is that they strive to address these structural aspects of neighborhoods in a holistic manner because they are conceptualized as interrelated. The community-level processes include building community capacity and social capital formation that are meant to effectively foster relationships within a neighborhood as well as at different scales.

The breakdown in institutional ties between residents and the limited development of effective neighborhood-based groups, it is assumed, can lead to decreased social control and increased social problems, ranging from crime to psychological distress. Community capacity has been put forth as a remedy for such situations. This construct includes sense of community, the level of commitment among community members, the ability to solve problems, and access to resources. These dimensions are engaged at the individual level (i.e., skill, knowledge, participation), organizational level (i.e., community-based institutions), and network level (i.e., relations between individuals and organizations inside and outside the neighborhood). It is hypothesized that when community capacity increases and is mobilized, then organized institutional structures emerge and positive neighborhood outcomes may be achieved. Outcomes include, among others, effective neighborhood governance

entities that have the capacity to plan, navigate the social terrain of the larger metropolitan area, and advocate for their residents (Chaskin 2001).

There is also particular emphasis on social capital in mobilizing community capacity and a growing consensus among urban analysts that inner-city neighborhoods suffer from a lack of social capital. Because target neighborhoods are conceived of as not having strong social infrastructures in place to support successful revitalization efforts, urban policy recommendations now call for developing social capital in these "worst-off" areas of cities.

Central to our present critique is the manner in which community building is viewed as inherently related to poverty alleviation, neighborhood improvement, and the pursuit of a hopeful vision of the city, rather than a set of practices that emerge from the complex set of institutional arrangements and that have allowed areas in cities to decline (Walsh 1997; Schorr 1999; Naparstek and Dooley 1997). In particular, we raise the concern that the basic foundations of the community-building field function to mitigate the responsibility of extra-neighborhood, public and private institutions whose (in)action has played a major role in the creation of devalorized neighborhoods. The field calls upon "local" neighborhood residents to change their social and spatial situation without providing full access to the processes that contribute to neighborhood change.

Although it can be argued that the focus of social capital development is to connect isolated actors into these more powerful social networks, we remain skeptical as to how social capital development does this in a meaningful way. Putnam (2000), draws a distinction between *bonding* and *bridging* social capital (a community's internal and external networks, respectively). But the primary focus of community building is bonding social capital, and it has proven difficult to direct programmatic efforts to developing bridging social capital (Purdue 2001). Undue emphasis on neighborhood-level networks not only serves to put the responsibility of alleviating poverty onto the shoulders of residents residing in a small geographic area but also removes these people and these places from their broader context.

It is not only a matter of needing to connect isolated actors with more powerful and broadly networked ones but rather effective community-building work must also aim to enable impoverished neighborhood residents to change the processes that lead to a status of isolation. This is a task that requires an appreciation of the shifting position of cities in an era of increased globalization, the practices that are occurring in these urban locales, and a critical examination of community building in relation to these. Community-building initiatives have multiple effects that are produced by the intersection of these activities with other forces that alter the urban landscape and that are not all aligned with the goal of improving the quality of life for residents in central city neighborhoods.

CITY RESTRUCTURING AND THE MOVE TO BE INCORPORATED INTO THE GLOBAL SCALE

Community building needs to be seen as part of dominant trends in U.S. urbanism. Cities have become important locales in a rapidly globalizing world in which they remain as the key locations at which processes of globalization occur, intersect, and get managed (Harvey 1989; Sassen 1994). Globalization relies upon the mobility of capital, information, and resources through networks and a cultural economy of symbols and status. It also maintains a particular relationship between space and place. Although the expansion of capital accumulation embeds and uses infrastructure in a city (such as office buildings and the labor working within them), ultimately the dominant mode of capital accumulation occurs through the ability for quick movement between different places and the impermanence of that infrastructure for capital.

A political economy of place has therefore emerged through which cities compete to draw capital to their locale. However, the scale of the global market does not encompass every site on the planet, and the global political economy relies on an uneven distribution of participants. The activities of places to maintain or change their status in this political economy, in turn, shape the geography of the global scale. This locally done work, therefore, reconstitutes the global scale itself. As the global scale gets reshaped, the local scale subsequently gets redefined in terms of just how local it really is. Finally, this scalar flexibility is in part made possible in the new relationships between the public and the private, the state and civil society, and how significant extra-state actors are in shaping the direction and management of city affairs.

Another part of the reproduction of urban space and place has been the ongoing struggle to define what cities mean and for whom cities exist. These struggles often occur via a growing ambition by city leaders hoping to have greater control over how their city fits in the global political economy. The renegotiation of scalar relations also affects how many people understand the relationship between place, identity, and social responsibility. Urban revitalization has heightened the struggle over the meaning of cities and has moved this contest in the direction of those who are best able to express their citizenship in the city. This, in turn, shapes the definition of who is a citizen of the city and to whom the city belongs.

In the United States, such a context has given rise to community building as a key strategy to transform impoverished neighborhoods. Because community-building claims to simultaneously improve neighborhoods as well as the quality of life for those who reside in these locales, it is necessary to understand the ways in which it attends to the needs of the poor while concomitantly enhancing cities' efforts to operate at the global scale. Typically, community-building efforts have been theorized and evaluated without attending to multiple scales. The focus is on the neighborhood, defined by its constructed boundaries, without heed to how these boundaries get constructed. Such conceptual "localism" marginalizes contexts, and assumes that processes shaping the urban arena freeze and stay fixed for the duration of community building projects.

The issues above raise the questions that guide our study: (1) What are the scalar politics that inform the construction of community building? (2) Who are the key stakeholders that affect and are affected by community-building initiatives?

The Case Study

The case study is located in Chattanooga, Tennessee, where a community building initiative has been in progress for several years. Our study is in four areas contiguous to the downtown business district: Bushtown, MLK, Highland Park, and the Historic Southside District where the newly formed Community Impact Fund (CIF) launched their Neighborhoods of Opportunity community-building initiative. The consortium of key stakeholder groups funding the effort included the city, the United Way, and three foundations in the area. The CIF board has governed the project since its inception. The primary activities of the initiative have been directed at building social capital and community capacity through organizing groups of residents to collectively act on specific issues related to neighborhood wellness, developing leadership through activities aimed at selecting and promoting local leaders, and promoting organizational developments. CIF staff has also worked with neighborhood leaders to provide feedback and support during the strategic planning process, and to facilitate their connection to the information, technical skills, and resources needed to accomplish their goals.

THE EMERGENCE AND SCALE OF COMMUNITY BUILDING IN CHATTANOOGA

During the 1980s, Chattanooga had a host of typical urban problems, including an impoverished downtown business district and increasingly isolated, rundown inner-city neighborhoods surrounding the downtown area. Chattanooga's turnaround and downtown revitalization have focused on the role of public–private ventures beginning with the lead role played by the Lyndhurst Foundation during the 1980s. The city and Lyndhurst sponsored "Vision 2000," a planning exercise that included input from more than 2,500 residents in the area and that spawned a $45 million aquarium. Chattanooga has been re-imagined as "a city with a future" (Galleta 2002). The downtown business district has shown remarkable material signs of improvement. Similarly, Chattanooga is now recognized around the country as a "green" city that is environmentally and socially progressive (Reidel 2001). Chattanooga's revitalization efforts have been represented by the local and national media as nothing less than a citizen-driven "urban renaissance." But what remains unclear is the process by which such a citizenry gets defined and empowered. In other words, who are the citizens in citizen-driven change, and how do these citizens use and contribute to altering the relationship between state and civil society, the public and the private, in the city?

Central to the efforts of Chattanooga leaders has been their ability to reclaim devalorized areas, "reincorporating" them into the city, and building a landscape that is appealing to certain sensibilities. These sensibilities essentially are those associated with middle-class consumption and the related process of capital investment (e.g., convention center facilities, baseball stadium, shopping districts, university expansion). It is in this context that community-building initiatives can be conceived of and employed as strategies to reclaim inner-city neighborhoods, arguably transforming these areas from predominantly spaces of use by inner-city residents into sites for capital accumulation.

For example, when the community-building initiative was in its design stages, the Historic Southside District developed a $50 million expansion of the convention center, $43 million business center, $12 million garage, and millions of additional dollars dedicated to other shops, businesses, and middle- to upper-income housing. Many of these projects have been funded by public–private ventures.

Simultaneously, the community-building

initiative has focused on developing neighborhood crime prevention strategies and mixed-income housing ventures. However, neighborhood leaders closely affiliated with the community-building project emphasized that residents have had no input in the business development in their area. They added that, no existing residents had purchased any of the new housing. The feelings many residents discussed ranged from hope that these projects would actually benefit existing low-income people to frustration that the only role they had in the redevelopment of their neighborhoods was to attend collectively to plan to purchase a few parcels of property that they would control. They also feared that many older people and others in poverty would not be able to remain in their neighborhoods. In this context, the meaning of community-building becomes suspect. At least in part, it appears to be a strategy to create consent and present an image of citizenship being accessible to even the most disenfranchised.

Inner-city areas have become crucial in the reconfiguration of "hope" in Chattanooga. The transformation of these places—more than the eradication of the poverty of the people in these places—has become a central project in the redevelopment of Chattanooga, and is necessary to maintain Chattanooga's position in the broader political economy of place. The city has learned to its chagrin that deteriorating neighborhoods in the central city are inimical to progress. Consequently, these neighborhoods represent the intersection of the political, economic, and cultural expressions of how Chattanooga is reconstituting itself as having "a future," and the residents of these neighborhoods—or those that are willing and able to manage these neighborhoods—become implicated in this future vision.

This means that community building and its related activities become place-based efforts, and with the development of place as a bounded, localized entity separate from the people who live there, the place is reduced to the parts that can contribute to a particular vision for the future of the city overall. Impoverished neighborhood residents can pursue their vision through community-building efforts, but this will usually not come to fruition unless it is in line with the vision that is being pursued to sustain participation in the wider political economy of place for the city.

This became evident to residents in the MLK area of Chattanooga. In the community-building initiative, the University of Tennessee-Chattanooga (UTC) paid $1 to the University of Chattanooga Foundation for a large parcel of land to expand its campus. Planned and implemented simultaneously with the community-building initiative, UTC's expansion occurred without significant resident input, and there were no planning sessions between the community-building initiative staff and UTC on this matter. Some residents were skeptical of the benefit UTC's presence would have on people in the neighborhood, while others suggested that MLK residents could either "play the game and get some wins" or "get steamrolled" because UTC was moving into MLK regardless.

In these situations in which there are multiple agendas between groups of residents and other stakeholders, impoverished neighborhood residents have an unequal voice; their ability to speak and be heard is often dependent upon the conduit of a community-building project through which they can speak essentially as impoverished neighborhood residents and only about their impoverished neighborhood (as opposed to issues on "urban development," widely defined). Other stakeholders in the city's redevelopment have far greater opportunity and flexibility in how they can perform their civic engagement toward the city. Community building *localizes* impoverished neighborhood residents through civic engagement into the scale of the neighborhood while those who operate at larger scales can benefit from the work that these localized citizens do.

For example, the community-building initiative is central to the city's claim that civic participation is an integral part of its improvements. And the material and symbolic "successes" in Chattanooga not only allow people to imagine the city as a space of hope but also allow federal agencies and private foundations to constitute themselves as successful. Chattanooga is one of the lead affiliates of the Neighborhood Reinvestment Corporation and it is touted as an example of the organization's success. Other cities import best practices from Chattanooga and emphasize community building as a key component. Localities are responsible for state and national agendas just as much as the opposite is the case. The scale at which community building operates, like other urban-restructuring strategies, is not fixed to the neighborhood level by any means, and the work that is done in neighborhoods has a constitutive effect on scales of stakeholders that the development literature has yet to address.

Moreover, given the devolution of responsibility to the scale of low-income residents acting civically to fulfill responsibilities that were once the domain of governmental organizations, it is paradoxical that such a large field of professionals, foundations, and governmental initiatives are dependent on convincing residents to participate in community building- type initiatives that provide them with few rights to offset their obligations.

This is further complicated by the reality that while residents in inner-city neighborhoods are being asked to shoulder responsibility through building community, others are altering the landscape of their neighborhoods as well as the definition of who has a right to the place being created. These simultaneous spatial practices problematize the very meaning of the *local*, and call into question the promise of building community as the primary activity that residents in impoverished neighborhoods ought to be engaged in.

If the local scale is conflated with practices that originate within geographical boundaries of a neighborhood, then what is the relationship between the construction of this scale and the ever-changing scale of the city? And to what extent does community building provide residents the opportunity take part in leading the decisions about the production of the place they call home? Moreover, how does community building constitute a mechanism for other stakeholders to realize their

ambitions? To answer these questions is to understand the key stakeholder groups that affect and are affected by community-building initiatives.

WHO HAS A STAKE IN COMMUNITY BUILDING?

Typically, community-building efforts are promoted by extra-neighborhood institutions with aspirations of having meaningful neighborhood impact (Chaskin and Garg 1997). In Chattanooga, a public–private venture, the CIF, was organized to address problems that inner-city areas posed for Chattanooga and its citizens. The defining feature of the comprehensive community-building initiative, according to its founders, has been a "resident-driven" commitment "to mobilizing local resources and supporting people in distressed neighborhoods to develop and implement long-term strategies for improving the quality of life in their communities" (Lyndhurst Foundation 1998, 1). The foundational concept was to spur residents to develop plans for their neighborhoods using the expertise of a host of experts who had taken part in similar efforts in other cities. Community building could have had a real impact on the knowledge made available to residents, but the resources were being "policed" by the CIF staff. The CIF staff determined meeting times, locations, key speakers, and activities of the community-building effort. Early on, many residents reported that the learning exchanges had become one-way information sessions whereby residents were directed toward developing plans from a list of predetermined options.

CIF controlled the direction and activities of the initiative with a hierarchical, bureaucratic structure codified in daily interactions between residents, CIF staff, the CIF board, and community development experts across the United States. Residents were expected to communicate with their neighborhood associations and resident leaders who, in turn, would communicate directly with CIF neighborhood coaches. More senior CIF staff had even less direct contact with residents and more contact with the CIF board members and other relevant organizations. Such contact was often in the form of closed door meetings, with no resident input.

This is not to suggest that residents and communities of residents fail to resist these types of practices. In fact, the CIF had to largely restructure their entire effort after residents compiled a list of complaints about the lack of opportunities for residents to steer CIF activities. But a key question that emerges from our case study of community building is: Why is the standard of resident participation so minimal? Resident involvement was relegated to the scale of the neighborhood, many times focusing resident energy on cleanups, surveillance, and meetings as opposed to the structuring of the relationship between a smaller piece of geography (the neighborhood) and the larger area in which it is embedded (the city). As a specific illustration, neighborhood residents had no seat at the table when the decision was made to court developers from around the country to create mixed-income housing in their neighborhoods. And there was an understanding expressed to us by virtually all stakeholders outside the neighborhoods that attracting capital investment into the city was paramount and that these neighborhoods had become important places in Chattanooga's collective future.

These neighborhoods have been re-charted into the map of Chattanooga by virtue of their importance as contiguous areas to the downtown business district. The dilemma is that community building has worked in tandem with the development goals of the city and private foundations/corporations rather than providing a strategic plan to ameliorate poverty.

One component of the CIF's agenda was the provision of affordable, quality housing, and this came to be understood as mixed-income housing. In reality, because there were plenty of low-income properties in these neighborhoods, mixed-income housing meant the development of middle-class housing stock, which ended up falling in the $70,000 to $200,000 range. Resident leaders were aware of the impacts this might have on their neighborhoods and many wondered

what community was being built and who was going to be a part of it.

Stakeholders, including the city, the university, some middle-income residents, and the range of public and private entities, have gained a considerable amount in the name of neighborhood revitalization and community building. All of these groups sit on interlocking boards of directorates (Fraser, Kick, and Williams 2002). Many of the funders own land in the downtown business district, and many have interests in the tourist industry and/or development companies. Moreover, community building minimized the spaces where poverty (i.e., people in poverty) can manifest, a common strategy central to re-imagining the city and shoring up a city's participation in the political economy of places. All of this may occur within the context of community building can also add to the representation of a city as a place of progressive politics and civic engagement. Finally, cities like Chattanooga have also become important to the community-building/development industry itself.

The story about Chattanooga and all other community-building efforts is not that they are either effective or not, because spatial practices always produce effects, but rather, it is exactly about exploring the full range of these effects and the different impacts on all stakeholders and opening up the meanings that are attributed to community building itself. As one resident leader in a very impoverished neighborhood said to us, "It's been a mixed bag."

CONCLUSION

This chapter has attempted to analyze community building as a spatial practice, that is, as a concerted set of activities that are directed at reformulating the spatial configuration and the construction of a place. Rather than view community building as a limited social intervention, we demonstrate the inherently spatial aspect of community building as a practice that is changing the cityscape. This particular spatial practice is often part of a larger set that predominantly aims to reshape the city through the global political economy of place. Community building is therefore not a local phenomenon but rather part of the construction of a certain global scale as well as constructed by relationships that coalesce at the global, regional, city, and neighborhood scales. A paradox, then, is maintained by community building. It localizes impoverished neighborhood residents while globalizing an impoverished neighborhood inasmuch as the neighborhood becomes a central hinge on which a city's ability to participate in the global political economy swings.

We offer this perspective of community building to highlight the ambivalence and paradoxes of these efforts and prompt changes in community building and the scholarship that analyzes it. Community-building theorists and practitioners must be cognizant of the spatial implications of their actions and must aim at empowerment strategies that are honest to the spatial needs of impoverished neighborhood residents. In an era of increased reliance on civil society in the governance of cities, neighborhood residents can play a significant role in managing their affairs. But this does not occur in isolation from what is happening in other neighborhoods, the city, the region, or even the globe. Rather, community-building practitioners must open up the meaning and experience of community building so that localized neighborhood residents are brought to the processes taking shape at larger scales. A much more nuanced understanding of the relationship between the local and the global is necessary. If community building is to work as an effective antipoverty tool in today's urban arena, it must attempt to build community through the spatial formations that contribute to neighborhood decline, and the community that is to be built must be able to transcend narrow definitions of the local place.

REFERENCES

Chaskin, Robert J. 2001. Building community capacity: A definitional framework and case studies from a comprehensive community initiative. *Urban Affairs Review* 36(3): 291–323.

Chaskin, Robert J., and Sunil Garg. 1997. The issue of governance in neighborhood-based initiatives. *Urban Affairs Review* 32(5): 631–61.

Clarke, Susan E., and Gary L. Gaile. 1998. *The work of cities*. Minneapolis: Univ. of Minnesota Press.

Duffy, Katherine, and Jo Hutchinson. 1997. Urban policy and the turn to community. *Town Planning Review* 68(3): 347–62.

Fraser, James, Edward Kick, and Patrick Williams. 2002. Neighborhood revitalization and the practice of evaluation in the U.S.: Developing a margin research perspective. *City and Community* 1(2): 222–43.

Galleta, Jan. 2002. Visionaries focused early on aquarium. *Chattanooga Times*, 28 April, 1–4.

Harvey, David. 1989. *The condition of postmodernity*. Oxford, UK: Blackwell.

Lyndhurst Foundation. 1998. *Fact sheet: Community impact fund*. Chattanooga, TN: Lyndhurst Foundation.

McKnight, John. 1995. *The careless society: Community and its counterfeits*. New York: Basic Books.

Naparstek, Arthur J., and Dennis Dooley. 1997. Countering urban disinvestment through community-building initiatives. *Social Work* 42(5): 506–14.

Purdue, Derrick. 2001. Neighbourhood governance: Leadership, trust and social capital. *Urban Studies* 38(12): 2211–24.

Putnam, Robert. 2000. *Bowling alone: The collapse and revival of the American community*. New York: Simon and Schuster.

Reidel, Jon. 2001. Chattanooga chugs ahead. *Albany Herald*, 30–31 December, 1–16.

Sampson, Robert J. 1999. What "community" supplies. In *Urban problems and community development*, edited by R. F. Ferguson and W. T. Dickens. Washington, DC: Brookings Institution.

Sassen, Saskia. 1994. *Cities in a world economy*. Thousand Oaks, CA: Pine Forge.

Schorr, Lisbeth B. 1999. Fighting poverty and building community: Learning from programs that work. *American Journal of Orthopsychiatry* 69(4): 420–23.

Walsh, Joan. 1997. *Stories of renewal: Community building and the future of urban America*. New York: Rockefeller Foundation.

Wilson, W. J. 1987. *The truly disadvantaged*. Chicago: Univ. of Chicago Press.

CHAPTER 38

Strengthening the Connections between Communities and External Resources

Anne C. Kubisch, Patricia Auspos, Prudence Brown, Robert Chaskin,
Karen Fulbright-Anderson, and Ralph Hamilton

The concentration of poor people—especially poor people of color—in urban pockets of poverty did not occur by chance in this country, or solely as the result of choices made by residents of those communities. The racial and economic isolation, poverty concentration, and political disempowerment that characterize America's poor communities are largely the result of identifiable policies and practices embedded in public and private systems and in our society's power structures—factors that would exist even without a community-change agenda. They contribute to the persistently poor social and economic outcomes experienced in the neighborhoods that are the targets of community-change efforts, and they reinforce segregation by race and class.

This suggests that community-building solutions must understand how these systems, rules, and structures affect poor neighborhoods, and then make them work better by tapping into the resources of outside institutions and influencing their actions. That observation raises serious questions, however: How well do community-change efforts incorporate historical and structural phenomena into the solutions they develop? Does the very nature of community-based change lead to a bias toward "local" issues and away from overarching, structural ones? Is it possible to integrate the work done by community members on their own behalf, within neighborhoods, with efforts to influence external players—or do the demands of working within communities preclude or limit such activities? Are the limitations imposed by external funding sources, sys-

tems, economic dynamics, and public policies so forbidding that neighborhood improvement is the best that we can hope for? Will the political and funding climate tolerate this type of work, which is more politically oriented than in the past? What range of institutions and alliances do we need to tackle these issues? This chapter argues that participants in community building need to reinvigorate their approach to community change so that it addresses the external relationships and structural factors operating outside communities. Our discussion focuses especially on the inherent issues and tensions of four key activities: *broadening the analysis of the problem, finding powerful allies, working with the public and private sectors, and re-examining the assumptions and biases embedded in the community-building approach.*

BROADENING THE ANALYSIS OF THE PROBLEM

The principle of community building has several philosophical underpinnings that emphasize the power of "place" and the assets of neighborhood residents. Looking back at the way community-based initiatives unfolded and the evidence of what they have and have not achieved, there is a fundamental tension focusing inward on internal community dynamics and capacities and addressing external structures which can enhance or constrain their success. On one hand, practitioners and funders believe in the power of poor people in poor communities to change their environment and take control of their own destinies. Yet in practice, by focusing on neighborhood residents' capacity for change, many community-building efforts have diminished, underestimated, or been unable to influence the power of external institutions, public policies, and private market dynamics. Forward-looking participants in community change are looking for a new way to frame their work that captures the critical importance of addressing external issues, even as they continue to expand and deepen capacity-building efforts within their communities. They agree, as one person said, that "framing the problem really matters. If it is framed as internal, that leads to one set of actions; but if it is framed differently, it may lead to a very different set of priorities entirely." Acknowledging the power of the policy environment, many conclude that an internal focus is a losing strategy for even the most exemplary practitioners. They argue for a new approach that links policy, politics, and place on a metropolitan level around the goal of expanding opportunities for poor people.

Essentially, this "localism" leaves prevailing economic and political paradigms unchallenged and approaches urban poverty as a problem for neighborhoods and their residents. Critics suggest that, instead of adding an additional set of approaches and strategies to an aging toolbox in need of innovation, CCIs seemed to displace an older consciousness about the structure of poverty, racism, and the alignments of power that maintain the status quo.

Practitioners, scholars, policymakers and residents can point to several issues that need to be re-infused into the analysis of the problem. Problems with economic development and housing policies are particularly resonant. For example: Public policies and investments promoted the movement of middle-class workers and jobs to the suburbs and left poor people of color isolated in inner-city neighborhoods. As the regional and national economies shifted from manufacturing to service and technology, employment opportunities became more mobile, the labor market split into high- and low-wage sectors, and residents of poor communities were left behind. Housing policies exacerbated the problem. Public housing, intended as a temporary support for people in economic crisis, became in many places permanent housing for the persistently poor due to processes for selecting tenants, a lack of adequate services, discriminatory site-selection policies, the construction of high-density developments, and isolation from surrounding communities. Today, exclusionary zoning practices often preclude subsidized housing in the suburbs or raise the cost of building suburban housing to prohibitive levels. Property tax policies discourage economic integration in the suburbs and make mixed-income communities hard to create or maintain in cities.

These and similar issues, fueled by powerful political forces that are extremely difficult to budge, shape the context within which CCIs operate. In the words of one African-American researcher,

> These things did not happen by chance. Those distressed neighborhoods exist because of policies, procedures, and programs that have been in place in powerful neighborhoods. The zoning laws, the building codes . . . an entire infrastructure was built in the first half of the 20th century to create the type of segregation that meant that the communities that white people grew up in could only exist because of the type of communities that I grew up in. Now, the problem with all of this is that you can't change the conditions in that neighborhood without restructuring the whole paradigm.

The challenge is not to give up the local-level work but to do a better job of balancing and aligning the two levels. To find that balance, leaders of change in poor neighborhoods need to do two things. First, they must identify the causes of the problems they are experiencing, in the broadest possible way. That means stopping for a moment to consider the historical, institutional, and structural origins of problems. If people begin and end their analysis within the community, they may miss important contextual factors that affect everything they do. The second step is to identify sources of power outside the neighborhood that can be tapped or influenced to help the community. Again, the challenge here is to cast the net wide, well beyond traditional philanthropies or public programs, to include various levels of government and various types of policies as well as the role of the private sector.

Armed with the results of those activities, participants in community-change efforts can develop strategies for addressing fundamental issues. Judging from the experiences of recent CCIs and other endeavors, those strategies are likely to include finding powerful allies, working with the public and private sectors in new ways, and reexamining the assumptions and biases that are embedded in community building.

FINDING POWERFUL ALLIES

Although CCIs and other community-building ventures should recognize the *need* to engage forces outside their communities, they don't have to lead engagement efforts themselves. CCIs do not have the capacity or the power base for that responsibility. The people interviewed for this book offered the following observations about what those "strategic alliances" might look like.

Alliances with national, state, and local policy groups that advocate for disadvantaged groups give community-change initiatives access to expertise and influence in the policy world

The challenge for CCIs and other community-based groups lies in knowing how to reach out and build those alliances. Policy groups vary in their focus and strategies; some address specific populations, such as children, the elderly, or people of color, while others focus on topics, such as housing or transportation. Some concentrate on lobbying for money, while others pursue systemic change through the legal system.

It is unlikely that there will ever be a policy organization equipped to take on the full range of issues encompassed by a comprehensive community-change agenda. Therefore, alliances need to form across many different vehicles for change. For example, one avenue of work might revolve around policies, such as the housing mortgage tax deduction, which are broad and "non-targeted" but benefit the upper and middle classes more than low-income people. Here, alliances with national housing advocacy groups make sense. Other work might focus on key moments in the legislative cycle, such as reauthorization of welfare or of the Community Reinvestment Act. Or, there might be policy trends that offer opportunities for advocacy. One policy organization, for instance, has picked up on the issue of regionalism.

Coalitions across neighborhoods can expand the base and, consequently, the influence of political constituents

In one good example, a community group joined with people in two other neighborhoods to establish a leadership institute that taught residents how to influence policy at the city and state levels. "It was important to team with other communities in order to lobby and advocate—for example, with the school board," a practitioner recalled. Other practitioners, cognizant of the suburbs' influence on state legislatures, are considering connections with allies outside their neighborhoods, such as rural districts that are similarly poor but have more voting power.

Alliances across neighborhoods can become more powerful by including connections to middle-class communities as well as other poor neighborhoods, practitioners note. "If you only organize poor communities then you will largely be limited to federal funds, and they tend to come with more strings attached," one person observed. His coalition paired people from rich and poor neighborhoods.

Activities that mobilize residents' political power and use it to influence policy discussions increase the pressure on political forces outside the community

The problems of poor neighborhoods are as much political as they are technical. That fact suggests the need for a new "politics" of community building—one with explicit strategies for exerting pressure on the people and institutions who do not naturally serve the interests of disadvantaged people.

Participating in the political arena can lead to examination of and (sometimes) conflict around fundamental ideological issues. As a former public official observed,

> If we want to have the honest conversation about how to do something for poor neighborhoods, we are actually engaging on the most controversial aspect of American poverty. We have to be clear about why those neighborhoods got into such a serious state of distress. And then we have to work our way from that explanation to what the strategies for change are that aren't just about trying to "fix those people" by telling them to pull up their socks and be responsible for themselves.

Many practitioners and even some funders now call for a more explicit political agenda, both to put pressure on the public and private sectors and out of a core commitment to reaching and activating residents.

The new emphasis on politics occurs at the most basic level of neighborhood work, on issues that directly affect children and families. It involves "pressure organizing, coalition building, and collaborative negotiation," in the words of one executive director. The political side of community building means mobilizing residents' political power around neighborhood concerns, for example, and activating voters. A CDC that targeted voter apathy claimed to have doubled the turnout in precincts where it worked and then turned its attention to holding the newly elected representatives accountable to the community. Others have mobilized parents to plan school reform and influence local school boards

The development of political consciousness does not necessarily entail large-scale movements or electoral activities. Efforts to build political connections encompass a range of organizing styles

Community organizing runs the gamut from "hell raising" to "relationship building." Observers suggest the need for both ends of the spectrum:

> I feel like we keep shifting back and forth between confrontation-style organizing and consensus-style organizing. On the ground, there needs to be a blend if we're smart. I think it's more about how to be proficient at both—being able to talk like equals to the corporate heads and the lieutenant governor as well as to be able to talk tough to them.

Some practitioners take a pragmatic approach; they will work with anyone, at any level of the political system, who can help them address local concerns. Others look for simple, practical ways to assert their power.

The ability to use information strategically is as important as policy acumen and an agenda for change

Knowledge about the nuances of power and policy making helps community stakeholders organize, understand, and prepare for policy changes. Current community-building efforts are beginning to track and share information about broad issues at the state and local levels, such as transportation and land use. Communities that lack capacity for gathering and analyzing such information are forming connections with universities and statewide organizations to expand their reach. In one community, for instance, university students have worked with residents to understand trends in gentrification and to help them find ways to address the problem. There are many other examples of this type of work. Practitioners also are beginning to think strategically about the information that decision makers get about their communities, and they are finding ways to shape the public dialogue. For example, when race-based assumptions began to drive discussions about welfare reform in a state legislature dominated by suburban interests, a community organization produced information that recast the discourse to recognize that white and suburban communities received as many or more benefits that black communities.

WORKING WITH THE PUBLIC SECTOR

Community-building efforts have come of age at a time when ideas about government responsibility for developing, testing, and replicating model programs are changing. People can no longer assume that the public sector will provide money for successful approaches. At the same time, many practitioners and funders suggest that initiatives have not been resourceful enough in pursuing public money. Public officials say that government wants to join with private and nonprofit supporters of communities, and that the timing is ripe. The challenge is to figure out how to make the relationship work effectively, in part because the relationship between community building initiatives and government is a tricky one—part collaboration, part supplication, and part a quest for reform. Experienced participants in publicly funded community building offer the following observations as guidance.

Community organizations need a better sense of the public funding streams that come into their neighborhoods

Very few community-level actors have a clear sense of the amount and types of government money that flows into their neighborhoods. Getting a full picture of funding streams is a first step in understanding where the opportunities for increases or changes are likely to be. But practitioners say it is very difficult to get the information, because each funding stream is organized and directed differently. Representatives of community organizations further suggest that government workers have little incentive to disclose the information, because it would give outsiders tools for negotiating and pressuring the system.

Nonetheless, financial experts have helped people in some communities put information into the hands of residents so they could hold the public sector accountable for investments. In one neighborhood, a CCI convened 20 residents for a year-long process of assessing organizational effectiveness, using a standard set of questions and a framework for analyzing responses. That process produced an informed watchdog group that could exert pressure when organizations outside the neighborhood, such as the community college or health department, failed to meet community needs. Using financial information to

enforce accountability is especially important in low-income communities that receive substantial government resources "on behalf of the community" without formal accountability requirements.

Engaging effectively with the public sector means looking beyond financing to broad policy issues that affect poor communities

Many public policies that have a significant impact on neighborhood circumstances seem distant to people who are working to change communities, but in fact community members can engage local policymaking institutions—including workforce investment boards, economic development authorities, business improvement districts, school boards, and transportation authorities—around a variety of issues.

Community groups might target specific agencies, such as a police department's "stop and frisk" policies, which affect communities of color much more than other neighborhoods. Or they might analyze a variety of public policies and practices that add up to a "report card" for the local government. Even extremely specific policies offer opportunities to exert community pressure. For example, when a city council considers granting a tax abatement to a company, community participants might negotiate to make livable wages or hiring agreements a precondition.

Local government should figure much more prominently in community-change initiatives

Former government officials have expressed surprise that CCIs had not developed better methods for working with local government. Local government not only is the source of much public money, it also has broader powers and responsibilities that affect communities. It is the maker, interpreter, or enforcer of rules governing how federal and state programs are implemented, from decentralization mandates to local purchasing policies to the blending of funding streams. Local government also is an information conduit between communities and outside entities.

Although the involvement of top city officials often boosts community change initiatives, it does not always translate into long-term change. Political rivalries, turnover in leadership, and bureaucracy can disrupt the community-building process

Mayors and other city officials have taken active roles in neighborhood revitalization, bringing resources, legitimacy, and visibility. But these political connections are not without risk. Constituencies can become alienated, newly elected officials frequently abandon their predecessors' projects, and deeply embedded bureaucratic interests may block action.

Moreover, the senior administrators who support community building are not the people charged with carrying out public policies on the ground. "We discovered that getting the policy right wasn't enough," recalled one public official. "So we set up a middle management training system to be able to sustain the initiatives on the execution side . . . If you focus just on the state capital then you miss the people who do the transactions."

WORKING WITH THE PRIVATE SECTOR

Distressed communities need the deep pockets of the private sector to help them achieve their ambitious goals for community change. But private-sector connections are an unmined resource for most community-change initiatives. Community change ventures that have used or considered private-sector resources offer the following observations.

The greatest challenge is to connect with mainstream capital markets in ways that do not disrupt the community

For several years, people have discussed the advantages of investing in inner-city neigh-borhoods. With their access to transportation, physical infrastructure, and historic appeal, poor inner-city neighborhoods can be attractive investment sites. Thus corporations that are unlikely to give money for nonprofit activities might find reasons for more intensive investments in poor communities. In the words of an experienced technical assistance provider, "The fate of regions and low-income communities is tied up with the new economy. At the community level, we need to find and reduce the hidden costs of doing business so that we can get businesses to harness their resources to the benefit of the community." Experience shows that there are risks with this strategy, however. As a former public official noted,

> I think many of us think that income diversification in a neighborhood is a good thing. But obviously the unacceptable price that you could end up paying is complete displacement of the population; the very people you want to heal are driven away. How do we accomplish [progress] in a way that doesn't hurt people?

In some areas, it is possible to tap into private-sector resources and still maintain community control over their use.

People who think creatively about funding community change can find support from unconventional sources

There are many sources of money that are not necessarily obvious to community groups and other local engines of community change. Some local organizations report success in obtaining private capital for community trust funds, construction, and home mortgages. Some use eminent domain authority to support affordable housing and economic development. Private companies may also divert a portion of the funds in their investment portfolios for social purposes. For example, insurance companies interested in investing some portion of their funds in safe securities have agreed to give up a few points on their earnings to help with endowments of historically black colleges.

There have been examples of credit union

groups encouraging mainstream credit unions to put some of their money into an investment pool and agreeing that a small proportion of the earnings will go to communities. Community-building initiatives can also tap people who have spent their careers in the corporate world for knowledge about funding streams, innovative financing tools, and hidden market opportunities.

It isn't easy to ensure corporate accountability to neighborhoods, but some communities report successes

Corporations receive many public subsidies and loans, and some grassroots groups have drawn corporations into community-building activities by holding them accountable for these privileges. Approaches include campaigns for: livable wages and benefits, community hiring goals and agreements, job training and retention services, improved local environmental standards, and retail services that meet community needs. But the battle is an uphill one. As one community planner reported,

> In the poorest neighborhood in my city there are more than 10,000 jobs. And there are almost 50,000 jobs within walking distance of the neighborhood. The problem is that the people who live in the neighborhood are not connected to those jobs.

Some people fear that the moment to push for greater corporate accountability peaked in the late 1990s when the labor market was tight. "That would have been the time to negotiate over the quality of jobs and the benefits and security that came with the jobs," one analyst said. "We let them keep the agenda focused on 'soft skills' rather than taking up questions like the composition of the work investment boards which are still all corporate."

Poor communities are losing out in the rapid transformations of the private sector

Corporations are going through many changes that have dramatic effects on low-wage workers and low-income communities. They are downsizing, increasing their num-

bers of contractors, cutting benefits, and moving overseas. Globalization, revolutions in information technology, and shifting demographics are all trends that are likely to benefit those with access to power and influence at the expense of the poor and politically weak. Thus it is vitally important for low-income communities and their supporters to understand how to reduce the negative consequences of globalization and maximize the positive ones.

RE-EXAMINING THE ASSUMPTIONS AND BIASES EMBEDDED IN THE COMMUNITY-BUILDING APPROACH

Although practitioners and funders of community building generally have deep experience with the historical, structural, and racial constraints imposed on poor people by mainstream society, most have limited their focus to the local neighborhood. They view it as both the starting point and the fundamental core of community change. Why? There are several possible explanations, all of which represent ongoing tensions in the community-building arena.

Some observers defend the core assumptions behind recent community-change efforts but say the political climate narrowed the range of possible strategies for change

The social justice and democracy movements of the 1960s and 1970s were powerful forces behind the proliferation of CDCs and other local change efforts of the time. In those years, political empowerment, grassroots participation, and institutional change emerged as important local capacity issues. But the civil rights consciousness that infused community revitalization theory and practice in the beginning—especially the sense that chronic disadvantages for minority groups were structural and institutional problems—lost ground to the resurgent individualism of the "Reagan revival" during the 1980s.

Some observers believe that the resulting funding climate constrained the activities of change agents. Foundations, too, retreated from "political" funding, and progressive values adopted a more communitarian outlook. When it came time to translate the assumptions into action, critics suggest, funders would not support fundamental social change or tackle the really tough political and structural issues of power, access, and race faced by poor communities. Some practitioners now wonder whether foundations can ever truly be in the vanguard of democratic social change since they are, after all, the direct by-products of corporate power and historical privilege.

Community-change efforts have promoted collaboration across racial and cultural lines but have not taken the lead in advocating for responses to the fact that all levels of the political economy sort Americans by race—institutionally, geographically, and psychologically

Many residents and frontline practitioners describe the problems of poor, inner-city communities in ways that reflect a structural analysis of racism. These observers highlight assumptions, practices, and institutional behaviors that consistently give poor people of color too few of society's benefits and too many of society's punishments. They recognize that entrenched white privilege and minority stereotyping in major institutions continually undermine individual and local community gains, as revealed by the policies and practices of public education, housing, employment, transportation, law enforcement, and other social institutions. They suggest that attention to race necessarily leads to a more externally oriented strategy for rectifying race-related disparities in urban outcomes, a strategy that addresses institutional and systemic issues. This knowledge does not carry over into the design of community-change ventures

Many observers believe that the focus on developing broad social relationships, networks, partnerships, and collaborations in communities failed to address issues of social justice, which are firmly rooted in policies and arrangements of power

Many participants in community change have operated under the assumption that the work of reinforcing social connections could rebuild the fabric of a community and lead to other broader positive changes. Their work generally focused on building trust and understanding among stakeholders, through collaboration and consensus. While that dimension of the work continues to be important, there is some concern that it underestimates the crucial work of "politicizing" communities so they can tackle tough political and policy issues.

Some analysts believe that the commitment to place-based approaches underestimated the dynamic nature of communities

Some critics say that community building treats people and communities as fixed and unchanging, while in reality communities are dynamic. Most Americans move frequently, and most jobs are located outside workers' neighborhoods. Instead, they suggest, community change efforts should enable residents to choose where they live so they can have better access to jobs. CCIs and other community-change efforts have engaged only sporadically and superficially in efforts to make policies, power structures, and other influences outside their neighborhoods work on behalf of poor communities. As this chapter suggests, however, opportunities do exist to overcome, shape, or exploit those elements.

Change can happen if people think broadly, act more politically and proactively than in the past, and form nontraditional alliances across sectors. Those obligations should therefore be on every current agenda for comprehensive community building.

CHAPTER 39

Conclusion

James DeFilippis and Susan Saegert

The community development industry/movement is now more than four decades into the period of growth and maturity that began with Bobby Kennedy's famous visit to Bedford-Stuyvesant in 1966. There remain, however, some basic unresolved issues and questions. In this concluding chapter we will briefly discuss long-standing challenges in community development, as well as describe some of the emerging tensions, contradictions and difficulties that we see as vital in terms of interpreting the future of community development. We first re-visit the tensions that have been evident in community development since its inception as a movement/industry, and then discuss those that have emerged over the course of its 40-year modern history. The point here is not to present a catalogue or laundry list of unresolved problems, because that would be neither intellectually stimulating nor practically useful. At the same time, we would be remiss if we let the book conclude without a recognition of the fundamental conundrums that remain and are emerging in the field. We do not offer a guide for how to respond to these issues, but hope that in the writing we will enable the kind of clear-eyed analysis and practice needed to mitigate the problems and embrace the opportunities.

UNRESOLVED ISSUES (PRESENT AT THE CREATION)

There are several problems inherent in community development as a framework for improving and changing society, and have been part of community development from the beginning.

Community development contains within itself a set of goals and aspirations that, on some irreducible level, are (at best) in tension with each other or (at worst) in direct contradiction with each other (for an early discussion of these tensions, see Sturdivant, 1971). The first of these is the rather well-known issue of the relationship between markets (efficiency) and equity. Communities most in need of development begin their efforts from a position of market failure. The efforts that energized significant victories for the community development movement such as the fight for the Community Reinvestment Act (CRA) staked their claims on notions of equity and fairness. But like CRA, solutions ultimately were required to contend with market forces and find ways to work with them. O'Connor traces this tension through much of the development of the movement. Since 1980, pretty much all efforts to resolve problems of social equity rely on market mechanisms. For example, the largest source of capital for the community development of housing has come for many years from tax credits for corporations for funds devoted to this purpose.

Reliance on market mechanisms to resolve equity issues often falter because the aims and goals of successful markets and equity are not the same. Communities in need of development are by definition failing in the market. The goals of community development are inherently redistributive. The organizing component of community development, as Stoecker points out, works to employ the power of political mobilization of disaffected peoples to force a redistribution of power and resources that would and could not occur through market forces. All theories of community development recognize that markets as they exist are not the ideal free markets of economic theory but instead products of the existing distribution of power and resources. Those with the most power and wealth write the rules. Community organizing aims to rewrite them. Unlike Stoecker, we see the contradiction between the goals of organizing and those of local production of goods and services as a tension that community development must live with because the residents of poor communities must both have the necessities of life and struggle to reposition themselves politically and economically. But that does not mean the contradiction has been or can be resolved. And as community development has become more market-based in the last 25 years, this inherent tension—which was there at the beginning—has only become re-emphasized and enhanced.

The first issue is closely related to the second one, which is the tension between doing development and/or service delivery and organizing. The best community development organizations, we would argue (in agreement with Greenberg) are able to do both. And we do not accept a rigid binary where it is one (development/service delivery) or the other (organize). But, having said that, there are real and meaningful tensions between organizing and development/service delivery. These tensions exist both in theory and in practice.

On the one hand, the success of community development (and certainly the budgets of community development corporations) have come from real estate development or service provision. But on the other hand, both of these require close cooperation with private sources of capital and operating expense funds, and with government. This money comes with strings attached, but it is necessary if organizations are to provide actual goods and services. These functions of community development conflict with community organizing goals to challenge existing power and resource dynamics and to change them so that previously neglected communities gain more. Stoecker lays out the conflicts between these two different functions and regards them as incompatible while Traynor presents development as one possible outcome of increasing the social connections and capacity to act collectively. Warren's discussion of the Texas IAF makes the case that by stressing the development of engaged citizenship that challenges the exclusion of marginalized groups from democratic participation, previously oppressed communities will participate in mainstream forms of development through provision of government services and private investment, as well as by developing community oriented services and programs with community residents. The Texas example may provide a clue for the next step in overcoming these tensions by shifting the scale of development and service provision beyond the local, and extending the scope of organizing to larger geographical scales. At the same time this approach relies on intense citizen engagement within local neighborhoods and institutions.

The problem of scale is in fact the third persistent problem for community development. By this we mean two related, but distinct, things. First, even the most successful community development organizations are relatively small—given the amount of decent affordable housing or adequate social services needed in most metropolitan areas. Even if the components of capacity-building highlighted in Glickman and Servon's chapter were enacted, and the problems and potential pitfalls discussed in Rohe, Bratt, and Biswas's chapter were avoided, there would still be the problem of the needs simply outstripping the ability of community organizations to meet those needs. The second problem with scale is that the multiple and shifting problems of localities are interconnected by the flow of capital, populations, political influence, and changing economic and institutional bases. The chapter by Fraser, *et al.* points this out nicely. Forty years ago, it made more sense to talk about at least national political economies. Today, that is not possible. And current events like the tidal wave of foreclosures in some communities throw into sharp relief the embeddedness of community crises in international financial markets (Apgar, 2005; Immergluck and Smith, 2006a, 2006b). Thus, and as we argued in Chapter 1, most of the problems evident in communities do not originate in those communities. Therefore the solutions cannot be found in efforts that focus solely on communities.

EMERGING ISSUES

The foreclosure crisis has revealed to the public what the financial sector has long known, and in fact innovatively and energetically created: a global finance system that constantly mutates in search of larger profits and new markets. When community development corporations first came on the scene, residential mortgage investment came primarily from locally or state-based banks. As Squires' chapter notes, the CRA was based on the simple idea that banks had an obligation to meet the credit needs of the communities in which their branches were located. Banking regulations limited the geographic scope of mortgage lenders. Apgar and Duda (2003) summarize the numerous changes in the mortgage industry which result in less than 30% of mortgages in 2003 being subject to the Act (p. 170), and the many ways in which changes in the CRA have failed to keep pace with financial sector innovations. Several of these changes have had major impacts on community development. These include the ever expanding consolidation of banks, emerging financial services that provide credit and other banking services through unregulated and not fully understood mechanisms, the securitization of debt, and the fragmentation of the various components of loan origination, servicing, and ownership. As local communities experience neighborhood, municipal and state-level impacts of foreclosure, it has been hard or impossible to identify which institutions had "any skin in the game."

The challenges for community development have been threefold. First, regulation of industries so that they have responsibilities to local communities has become increasingly difficult both because of weakened regulatory agencies and because the financial sector is constantly reforming in ways that make it hard to identify who should be held accountable. Second, the mutual interest between local residents and local banks in encouraging a viable local economy has eroded. Third, local bankers have often been major partners in local community development projects. Now there may be no such thing as a local bank or a local banker. Thus both the targets of community organizing and the partners for community development have become harder to identify and more difficult to affect when they are identified.

The issues of globalization and community development, however, are not limited to the changing character of capital, but also extend to the realm of labor. And immigration, which on some irreducible level is about globalizing labor markets, is the second key emerging issue that confronts community development theory and practice. The chapter by Cordero-Guzmán and Quiroz-Becerra usefully discusses the particular roles played by immigrant organizations, and the specific needs of immigrant communities in American cities. But the larger questions of how immigration is transforming the meanings of both community and development remain under-explored in the academic and policy literatures in the field. For instance, if the members of a Mexican-American Hometown Association (HTA) in Pilsen, Chicago, are pooling money to build a community center in their town of origin in rural Puebla, is that community development in Chicago? Or if a community development credit union (CDCU—of the kind described in the chapter by Benjamin, Sass Rubin and Zielenbach) in the south Bronx, New York, is seeing some of its larger loans go to building houses in the Cibao (in the Dominican Republic) for its members to retire to later in life, is that community development in the Bronx?

The fundamental issue, it seems to us, is the potentially radical separation of the notion of community from attachment to *a place*. In both of the examples, the development is what *the community* wants and needs. But in both, the community is trans-national. This does not at all de-legitimize the needs of the community but it does call for a re-examination of many of the basic assumptions of community development as interventions *in places*. This re-examination is particularly important for the foundations, religious congregations, and local governments that are so important as institutions in community development (as discussed in Chapters 14–16). These institutions, to varying degrees, see their role in the world in terms of specific places. This is perhaps most true for local governments, who are place-defined and play a vital role in the enabling or constraining what people have called the "community development industry" system (see Chapter 5, this volume).

While the scale of organization of capital and labor has been globalizing, the scale of government as it relates to community development has been shrinking. The growing importance of local governments in community development brings us to the third key issue in the community development to emerge in its 40-year history. This is the restructuring of the state in American society.

The past 30 years have witnessed fundamental restructurings of the American state. There are several components to this shift which are important for us here, but the most important are the two inter-related processes of devolution and fiscal retrenchment. First, devolution of responsibility for and, to a significant degree, control over, housing and other social services for low-income people and communities began under the Nixon administration and has continued largely uninterrupted in the 35 years since it began (see Bockmeyer, 2003; Eisinger, 1998; Goetz, 1995). What this has meant is that increasingly the federal government has been block-granting social service provision to the state, and to some degree, local level, and it is up to states and localities how to spend that money, in what ways, and with what priorities. This is evident in subsidized housing, in which states and localities control the allocation of Low Income Housing Tax Credits (LIHTC)—the single most important source of federal subsidies for new affordable housing construction, and a staple funding source for community-based organizations. It is also evident in welfare, in which Temporary Aid to Needy Families (TANF), the largest income assistance program for low-income families is a block grant which provides significant leeway to states and localities in terms of how that money is to be spent (that is, how much for subsidized childcare, how much for workforce development, etc.). And the pattern repeats itself for other forms of social services as well.

Second, and not unrelated to devolution, is an overall shrinking of state resources for low income people and communities. For instance, the US Department of Housing and Urban Development (HUD) shrank from 7% of the total federal budget in 1976 to 1% in 2005 (National Low Income Housing Coalition, 2004). Similarly, Community Development Block Grants (CDBGs), a staple in federal funding for development in low income communities declined by 48% in real dollars from 1977–2003 (ibid.). Other examples abound, particularly in the arena of housing, which has witnessed the 1983 elimination of the project-based Section 8 program, the passage in 1992 of the "HOPE VI" program, which subsidizes the demolition of public housing projects and the relocation of some of their residents, and the 1998 public housing reform which made it illegal for local housing authorities to build new public housing (except to replace units demolished under HOPE VI). To some extent this is not unrelated to the process of devolution, which both limits the growth of federal spending when economic downturns create increased demands for housing and social service assistance (by fixing the amount given to states for multiple years at a time, regardless of what the economic circumstances of those years might be), and encourages states and localities to move people off of public assistance (by limiting the amount of money, despite population growth and increased demands). Importantly, and as the CDBG example illustrates, block grants and the other forms of federal devolution have a tendency towards long-term decline in the amount of money allocated to them (Finegold, Wherry, and Schardin, 2004).

There are several consequences for community development of devolution and shrinking of federal resources for assisting low-income people and communities. One of these has been the increasing reliance on community-based, not-for-profit organizations to fill roles formerly played by government. Another involves increasing competition for local governmental resources as more and more functions of the state are devolved. The third consequence is the increasing inability of locally based organizations to confront national and international sources of inequity.

Confronting structural racism and gender bias at the local scale is indeed necessary in order to engage people in forging new relationships of greater equity and inclusion in everyday life. Local institutions such as schools and local businesses are the places where exclusion and differential treatment occur. Localities are defined and neighborhoods formed by the processes of residential segregation. But capital and population movement have sources in the national and global scale. Thus inequitable allocations of capital and changing forms of oppression all are enacted in local places. Yet the scale of government is increasingly inadequate to regulating these forces.

Related to both devolution and retrenchment, and largely as a result of fiscal pressures placed upon them, local governments and states are turning to the community-based not-for-profit sector to fill in the gaps created by state retrenchment. Accordingly, there has been a major shift in the provision of social services and the meeting of basic human needs in Western political economies. A whole host of human needs are increasingly being met by public–private partnerships and the not-for-profit sector. Thus, community organizations become implicated in these state transformations in important ways. First, they receive funding from the government (at the federal, state, and, most often, local levels) to provide services that used to be public sector services. This enables the community organizations to provide services (by transferring resources to them), but it also can impact *what kinds of services* they provide and to whom. It also means that their abilities to organize to demand better, more comprehensive, services from the government—on behalf of their communities—have become compromised because they themselves are the service providers. So not only are community groups left in a position of filling needs that are beyond their capacities, but they are also less able to effectively demand that the government meet those needs itself.

The shrinking allocation of government resources for low-income people and communities has been only the most extreme example of the declining role (and efficacy) of the government in performing its domestic functions. The pitiful federal response to Hurricane Katrina related to devolution of responsibilities to local levels without adequate provision of resources or coordination of levels of government, and to the decreased efficacy of federal agencies in performing core missions. Failures in protecting public health, occupational safety, food and drug safety, and environmental quality have similar roots. Thus cities and states increasingly must pick up these responsibilities, further depleting their resources and decreasing funds for community development.

Foreign governments have even stepped into the void left by the national government in providing for local disadvantaged communities is an extreme illustration of the global dimension of local development. For example, a housing development organization in New Orleans received two million dollars from the government of Qatar for its community rebuilding programs.[1] And the government of Venezuela has been providing low cost home heating oil to people in the Northeastern states to heat their homes in recent winters. International relief organizations such as Oxfam observed the confused and inadequate response of the U. S. government and U.S. based charities like the Red Cross and decided to offer the kinds of relief that they routinely provide in developing countries (Strom, 2006).

These changes have altered the terrain on which community development is practiced and understood. And they have often done so in ways that have reinforced tensions inherent in community development. But the story here is not uniformly ominous, and community development has demonstrated itself to be both a vital component in the improvement of urban and rural neighborhoods, and able to adapt to changing structural conditions. If we are able to make the kinds of communities we want—communities that support the ability of individuals and households to thrive—both emotionally and materially—then the organizations involved in community development certainly have a central role to play. We hope this book will play its part in that process by enabling community development theorists and practitioners to better understand the meanings and implications of their craft.

NOTE

1. Source: personal communication April 25, 2007 with Carey Shea, Associate Director at the Rockefeller Foundation, in charge of Rockefeller Foundation involvement in the Unified New Orleans Plan.

REFERENCES

Apgar, W.C. and Duda, M. (2003) The twenty-fifth anniversary of the Community Reinvestment Act: Past accomplishments and future regulatory challenges. *Federal Reserve Bank of New York Economic Policy Review, June*, 169–191.

Apgar, W.C. and Duda, M. (2005) *Collateral Damage: The Municipal Impact of Today's Mortgage Foreclosure Boom*. Minneapolis, Minnesota: Homeownership Preservation Foundation.

Bockmeyer, Janice (2003) Devolution and the Transformation of Community Housing Activism. *The Social Science Journal* 40: 175–188.

Eisinger, Peter (1998) City Politics in an Era of Federal Devolution. *Urban Affairs Review* 33(3): 308–325.

Finegold, K., L. Wherry and S. Schardin (2004) *Block Grants: Historical Overview and Lessons Learned*. Washington, DC: Urban Institute New Federalism Program.

Goetz, Ed (1995) Potential Effects of Federal Policy Devolution on Local Housing Expenditures. *Publius: The Journal of Federalism* 25(3): 99–116.

Immergluck, D. and Smith, G. (2006a) The Impact of Single-family Mortgage Foreclosures on Neighborhood Crime. *Housing Studies* 21: 851–866.

Immergluck, D. and Smith, G. (2006b) The External Costs of Foreclosures: The Impact of Single-family Mortgage Foreclosures on Property Values. *Housing Policy Debate* 17: 57–79.

National Low Income Housing Coalition (2004) *Changing Priorities: The Federal Government and Housing Assistance: 1976–2005*. Washington, DC: published by author.

Strom, Stephanie (2006) After Storm, Relief Groups Consider More Work in U.S. *New York Times*, Jan. 1, section 1, p. 14.

Sturdivant, Frederick (1971) Community Development Corporations: The Problem of Mixed Objectives. *Law and Contemporary Problems* 36: 35–50.

Yin, Jordan (1998) The Community Development Industry System: A Case Study of Politics and Institutions in Cleveland, 1967–1997. *Journal of Urban Affairs* 20(2): 137–157.

PERMISSIONS

and an alternative," *Journal of Urban Affairs*. Copyright © 1997 by Blackwell Publishing Ltd. and the Urban Affairs Association. Reprinted with permission.

Chapter 37: From James Fraser, Jonathan Leposfky, Edward Kick, and J. Patrick Williams, "The Construction of the Local and the Limits of Contemporary Community Building in the United States," *Urban Affairs Review*, 38(3): 417–445. Copyright © 2003 by Sage Publications. Reprinted by Permission of Sage Publications.

Chapter 38: From Anne C. Kubisch, Patricia Auspos, Prudence Brown, Robert Chaskin, Karen Fulbright-Anderson, and Ralph Hamilton, "Strengthening the Connections between Communities and External Resources," Chapter VI in *Voices from the Field II: Reflections on Comprehensive Community Change*, pp. 78–99. Washington, DC: The Aspen Institute. Copyright © 2002 by The Aspen Institute. Reprinted with permission from The Aspen Institute.

INDEX